D0845324

3 0700 10699 5201

DOUBLE
MINORITIES
OF SPAIN

DOUBLE
MINORITIES
OF SPAIN

A Bio-Bibliographic Guide
to Women Writers
of the Catalan, Galician,
and Basque Countries

EDITED BY
Kathleen McNerney
and
Cristina Enríquez de Salamanca

Modern Language Association of America
New York   1994

Library of Congress Cataloging-in-Publication Data

Double minorities of Spain : a bio-bibliographic guide to women
  writers of the Catalan, Galician, and Basque countries / edited by
  Kathleen McNerney and Cristina Enríquez de Salamanca.
      p.   cm.
   Includes bibliographical references.
   ISBN 0-87352-397-0 (cloth)
   1. Catalan language—Women authors—Bio-bibliography—
Dictionaries.   2. Gallegan literature—Women authors—Bio-
bibliography—Dictionaries.   3. Basque literature—Women authors—
Bio-bibliography—Dictionaries.   4. Women authors, Spanish—
Biography—Dictionaries.   I. McNerney, Kathleen.   II. Enríquez de
Salamanca, Cristina.
PC3904.D68   1994
809'.89287—dc20   94-27639

Published by The Modern Language Association of America
10 Astor Place, New York, New York 10003-6981

THIS WORK IS DEDICATED

TO THE MEMORY OF

Helena Valentí

AND

Montserrat Roig

WHO HEARD SO MUCH ABOUT IT

BUT DID NOT LIVE TO SEE THE FINAL PRODUCT

Table of Contents

Introduction

The purpose of this guide is to recover the work of writers doubly marginalized—by prejudice against their sex and against their choice of literary language. In association with forty contributors, we have compiled information about the lives of women who have written creative works in Catalan, Galician, and Basque; their works, including books, publications in periodicals, and unpublished manuscripts; translations of their works into English or Castilian; and secondary studies and criticism.

Double Minorities of Spain has its roots in the history of the Iberian peninsula. While social intolerance and gender oppression exist nearly everywhere, this area has been uniquely marked by its different political and cultural groups. Catalonia and the Basque country, despite their economic development, have long existed on the fringes of the central power based in Castile. Likewise, Spanish has traditionally meant the Castilian language, and Spanish literature has meant literature written in Castilian.

The phenomenon of a national Spanish literature, as it is currently recognized, was the product of nineteenth-century literary studies. Conforming to a vision of political and spiritual unity, critics outlined a paradigm of Spanishness that had a linguistic basis in the Spanish of Castile and a religious basis in Catholicism, both of which could be traced to the classical Latin tradition. For one critic, Marcelino Menéndez Pelayo, the concept "Spanish" included anything that bore any relation to Spain, Portugal, and Latin America (Zulueta 19). This mystical, ahistorical notion, oddly enough, came into being at the end of the Spanish colonial empire's disintegration, perhaps in an attempt to contain the decentralizing political process that gave rise to resurging nationalism in Catalonia, Galicia, and the Basque country. Furthermore, while many critics recognized the importance of the varied languages and literatures living side by side within the Iberian peninsula, the literary histories written in the nineteenth century—and even well into the twentieth—usually relegated these traditions to appendixes of Castilian or Spanish literature, under the heading "Regional Literature." With this caption mainstream critics hoped to limit the literary revival of Catalan, Galician, and Basque merely to picturesque expressions of local phenomena (Enríquez de Salamanca 20).

1

Contrary to orthodox Spanish literary history, the political and cultural activity of the middle classes in the Catalan, Galician, and Basque countries during the nineteenth century gave rise to a new flowering in each of the ethnic groups. This renaissance, known as *Rexurdimento* in Galician and *Renaixença* in Catalan, formed a major part of the regional nationalist movements in those areas that had historically enjoyed their own political structures or their own cultural and linguistic identities or both. The nationalist movements, which grew in tandem with the creation of the modern Spanish state during the nineteenth century, went through several phases, under the names of *provincialism, regionalism*, and *nationalism*, depending on the degree of political consciousness at the time. In each stage there was a progressive distancing of these communities from the central, Madrid-based government. This separating process, interrupted during the Franco era (1939–75), led to Spain's current division into seventeen *autonomías* (autonomous regions).

Thus, this work deals with the existence of a cultural plurality on the Iberian peninsula and specifically with non-Castilian tongues. In linguistic circles there seems to be a general agreement that Catalan, Galician, and Basque, the languages of the so-called *autonomías tradicionales*, are separate languages, whereas Bable, spoken in Asturias, and Leonés, spoken in León and Asturias, are dialectal forms of Castilian.

Basque, or *Euskera*, is the language of the *Euskaldunak* people, who live in the provinces constituting the Autonomous Community of the Basque Country—Gipuzkoa, Bizkaia, and Araba—as well as in parts of the Autonomous Community of Navarra and in the eastern part of the French department Pyrénées-Atlantiques.[1] Basque is the sole survivor of those languages spoken in southwestern Europe before the Roman conquests. It does not belong to the Indo-European family and its origins are unknown. Under Roman domination, the Basque sphere of influence was severely reduced, and during the Middle Ages it lost even more ground to competition from the Navarran tongue and Provençal.

The publication in 1545 of the first book in Basque, *Lingua Vasconum Primitiae* (Bordeaux), by Bernard d'Etchepare, is usually given as the beginning of the Basque literary tradition. In reality, however, there was a strong oral tradition, thanks to the village poets, or *bersolaris*. Spanish literary criticism notes the scarcity of Basque epics; only fragments from the fourteenth and fifteenth centuries remain of the *Cantar de la Batalla de Beotivar*. The best-known epics are the *Canto de Lelo*, transcribed by Wilhelm von Humboldt in 1801, and the *Canto de Altabiscar*, found in 1794 in an old manuscript in Gipuzkoa and transcribed by Garay de Monglave. Besides the songs, proverbs, and Basque legends, which have come down to us in nineteenth-century anthologies, the pastorals, performed in rural springtime settings that attracted inhabitants of the surrounding villages, are important Basque artistic contributions. They are a form of total theater, combining mime, music, poetry, sermons, and dance. Over one hundred different manuscripts have been preserved, dating largely from the seventeenth century.

Until the nineteenth-century literary renaissance, publications in Basque consisted mainly of religious and ascetic tracts. Although the Basques lost their *fueros* (local rights) as a consequence of the Carlist wars in the last few years of the nineteenth century, a group of Basque intellectuals set up annual competitions, prizes, literary reviews, and the floral games, a form of artistic fair to encourage the literary use of the Basque tongue. These activities were interrupted by the onset of the Spanish Civil War in 1936 and were not resumed until the 1960s.

Unlike Basque, Galician is a Romance language closely related to Portuguese. It is the official language of the Autonomous Community of Galicia, which covers the territory of the old kingdom of Galicia in the northwest Iberian peninsula. Literary historians divide Galician literature into two periods, the medieval and the modern. The former, known from the Galician-Portuguese lyrics, flourished from the end of the twelfth to the middle of the fifteenth or early sixteenth century and was characterized by the development of lyric poetry, which is preserved in the *cancioneiros* (songbooks) written in an already archaic language that maintained the early Galician-Portuguese linguistic unity. This language of convention, or koine, passed from one poet to another but had its roots in the educated courtly society. The three *cancioneiros* are the *Cancioneiro da Ajuda*, dating from the end of the thirteenth century or the beginning of the fourteenth, the *Cancioneiro da Biblioteca Nacional (Colocci-Brancuti)*, and the *Cancioneiro da Vaticana*. A fourth extant Galician-Portuguese work, the thirteenth-century *Cantigas de Santa María* of King Alfonso X (Alfonso the Wise), consists of narrative poems about miracles performed as a result of a plea to the Virgin Mary.

The compositions of the Galician-Portuguese troubadours are grouped into four main genres: *cantigas de amor, cantigas de amigo, cantigas de escarnio*, and *cantigas de maldizer*. In the *cantigas de amor*, an imitation of the Provençal *cançó*, the poet celebrates the beauty and desirability of his beloved. Three kinds of *cantigas de amor* have been identified: rustic scenes of country life, love stories, and depictions of courtly love. The *cantigas de amigo* often employ a woman's voice, but this may be a rhetorical ploy used by the troubadours and based on a long European and Arabic tradition of female love songs. Among the *cantigas d'escarnio e de maldizer*, similar to the Provençal *sirventés*, are songs that contain religious and moral reflections, political subject matter, parodies of almost every kind of *cantigas*, and, most often, accounts of minor events in the poet's own life.

3

The use of Galician in medieval prose is infrequent, largely because of the kingdom of Galicia's traditional lack of political autonomy and its dependence first on the Asturian-León monarchy and later on the Castilian crown. The use of Galician in official documents was suppressed as early as the middle of the thirteenth century, and literary historians speak of the period dating from Ferdinand and Isabella's reign to the nineteenth century as "the long silence." The Galician cultural revival was closely linked to the rural bourgeoisie's confrontation with the Spanish monarchy's centralizing policy and with the disastrous social and economic conditions in Galicia.

In this period of literary rebirth a woman, Rosalía de Castro, played a central role. In 1863 a collection of her poems, entitled *Cantares gallegos* (Galician songs), appeared in Vigo and was an immediate success. From that date onward, authors and publishers threw themselves into the task of writing and publishing in a language considered by most a mere dialect, incapable of anything more literary than folktales. Following the *Cantares gallegos*, the *Rexurdimento* burst into full flower with the publication in 1880 of Manuel Curros Enríquez's *Aires de miña terra* and Valentín Lamas Carvajal's *Saudades gallegas*.

The third language, Catalan, is currently spoken in the Autonomous Community of Catalonia (Barcelona, Girona, Tarragona, and Lleida), in the eastern strip of the Autonomous Community of Aragon (Huesca, Zaragoza, and Teruel), in the Valencia region, and in the Autonomous Community of the Baleares. It is also spoken in the French department Pyrénées-Orientales, or old Roussillon, in the principality of Andorra, and in the city of Alghero, on the western coast of Sardinia.

Literary historians divide the history of Catalan literature before the nineteenth century into two periods, the medieval and the decline. Initially, Provençal was employed for courtly and folk poetry, while Catalan was used for works in prose. Although the lays of the Catalan troubadours are in Provençal, they are included in the history of Catalan literature because of the cultural and political links that bound Provence and Catalonia together in a relationship similar to that experienced by the Castilian lyric poets who wrote in Galician-Portuguese during the same period. The works of twenty-four Catalan troubadours have been preserved, among whom Guillem de Berguedà (12th c.), Guillem de Cabestany (13th c.), and Cerverà de Girona (13th c.) are best known. Ausiàs March (1397–1459) began a new literary era, writing in true Catalan; his work continues to influence Catalan poets. In Catalan prose Ramon Llull (13th c.), the author of philosophical, didactic, and mystical works, stands out. Four important medieval historical chronicles—of Jaume I (13th c.), Bernat Desclot (13th c.), Ramon Muntaner (13th–14th c.), and Pere el Cerimoniós (14th c.)—have also survived.

In Catalonia, as in Italy, around the middle of the fourteenth century a great humanistic movement began, and medieval conceptions and beliefs were discarded. Many period works were translated from Catalan to Castilian and influenced fifteenth-century Castilian literature. There were two great humanists of the era: Bernat Metge (14th c.), who translated Boccaccio and Petrarch and whose *Lo somni* is viewed as the first humanistic work in Catalan literature, and Fray Antoni Canals (d. 1419), author of ascetic-mystical writings and translator of classical works, whose *Escala de contemplació* is seen as the earliest testimony of the Devotio Moderna in Catalonia. The great Catalan novel of chivalry, *Tirant lo Blanc*, by Joanot Martorell and Martí Joan de Galba, was composed in the 1460s and published in 1490 in Valencia.

Literary historians usually speak of the period between the sixteenth and eighteenth centuries as one of decadence in Catalan letters, though a revision of this concept is now under way. The decline began with the Trastamara dynasty's accession to the throne of Aragon in the late fifteenth century, and Catalan ceased to be the language of the court during Ferdinand and Isabella's reign. As a result of the War of the Spanish Succession (1701–14), which put the House of Bourbon on the throne, Philip V banned the use of Catalan in Valencia, Catalonia, and the Baleares. The revitalization of Catalan language, literature, and culture began with efforts of language students and grammarians in the early nineteenth century. The *Renaixença* was part of the development of Catalan political activity, a process that had parallels in Galicia and the Basque country during the same period.

By the beginning of the twentieth century, Catalans, Galicians, and Basques had started a course of progressive linguistic standardization that reached its peak during the years of the Second Spanish Republic (1931–36). Home rule was established and the languages enjoyed their own statutory guarantees. This condition was shattered by the Civil War (1936–39) and the victory of Franco's forces in 1939. Since 1975, however, the minority languages have achieved a legal and social status equal to that of Castilian. This new state of affairs allows, among other things, the compilation of works like this guide, a tool that may aid in building the concept of Hispanic literature on foundations of cultural and linguistic plurality.

With such an aim in mind, we have chosen the writers in this book on the basis of three criteria: linguistic, biological, and literary. First, authors must have written in Catalan, Galician, or Basque. Second, they must be women. Third, any type of original creative literature, including children's literature, is included. Writers of essays, history, or textbooks are omitted.

With regard to the first standard, a linguistic rather than a nationalistic criterion has been followed. Thus, we have included not Catalan, Galician, or Basque women but rather women who wrote in Catalan, Galician,

5

or Basque. No political principles are involved here; for while we question the concept of Spanishness, we are not concerned with the essence of what is Catalan, Galician, or Basque. We do not equate language and nationality. Given Spain's diverse political forms and the changes in the official use of languages other than Castilian, a strict linguistic criterion cannot be applied, since bilingualism in all its variations is a common phenomenon, often due to circumstances beyond the individual's control. On the other hand, sometimes other criteria prevail, such as for Federica Montseny. The only woman cabinet minister in Spanish history until the recent democracy, the anarchist Montseny wrote just one work in Catalan. However, excluding her from this guide would be a historical injustice to this remarkable political individual of the Second Spanish Republic.

Chronologically this volume begins with the anonymous poems of two medieval Catalan women and an entire subgenre of medieval songs contained in the anthology *Cançoneret de Ripoll*. Known as *Les Malmonjades*, these poems express a traditional resistance to convent life. The writer of this section, Montserrat Villas i Chalamanch, defends the female authorship of the genre and presents arguments against the theory of male authorship. The first individual contribution in Galician is a short poem by Isabel Castro y Andrade, which appeared in *La Araucana* (Madrid, 1589) and was dedicated to Alonso Ercilla. Basque literature, being a fundamentally oral tradition that was systematized only relatively recently, waited until the 1920s for the first samples of women's writing.

The guide contains 421 Catalan writers, 31 Galicians, and 20 Basques who have written creative works in any of the traditional genres—poetry, prose, or plays. Those writing in Catalan are indicated with a C next to their names; those writing in Galician with a G; those writing in Basque with a B. Within the genres there are naturally certain gray areas— memoirs, letters, and religious commentaries, particularly those commentaries written in the early literary periods or in periods when literary production was scanty, such as in eighteenth-century Catalonia. While the literary description for each of the authors deals preferentially with the literature created in the specific minority language, the bibliography includes her works in other languages.

As a listing of women writers, this work falls into the category of feminist literary criticism known as *her-story*. Scholars with this perspective attempt to reconstruct the past by incorporating the cultural contributions of women, who have traditionally been ignored in male-oriented literary history and criticism. This biological selection does not, however, involve any statement that *feminine* and *feminist* are equivalents, questions in an unresolved debate to which this study wishes to contribute.

A guide to women authors demands that we notice the intersection of gender and literary production, the problem of sex and language. The growing importance of this kind of analysis stems in part from the aware-ness that the linguistic behavior of women, as María Jesús Buxó Rey has pointed out, makes up what anthropologists call "un marcador de situación sexo-social" (a sociosexual situational marker), clarifying a woman's depen-dence in terms of her social role and status (15). Moreover, the silence to which Western culture has historically subjected the female voice makes any analysis of women's writing take on the nature of research into the enigmatic. As Ana Iriarte has shown, as early as the Greek myths heroines are engaged in weaving, narrating legends through their looms. In the *Iliad*, for example, Helen includes in her spindle work the various stages of the confrontation between the Achaeans and the Trojans. The art of weaving and the expression of symbolic language are used to recount leg-ends and are associated, in Greek tradition, with femininity and obscure language. For Ana Iriarte, "hablar enigmáticamente es tramar el conjunto de palabras que expresan un mensaje de forma velada, simbólica" (to speak enigmatically is to rework the message-bearing word-set in a veiled, sym-bolic form) (32).[2] The search for the subversive message characterizes some current feminist criticism: studies inspired by the palimpsestic character of women's texts and psychoanalytically related studies that register femi-ninity in the break with a phallocentric order of language.

In another sense, confirming the specific nature of a feminine lan-guage—the relation between a woman's body and her language—means confirming a specific identity for her. That is why those theoretical move-ments that postulate the registration of femininity in language coincide with the establishment of a sense of identity for cultural and political minorities, such as those dealt with in these pages. For these groups, the existence of a language makes up the clearest stamp of the identity of a people.

Thus, the language-gender relation grows in complexity when, as in the present situation, the minority tongues form a necessary part of the national identity. If masculinity and femininity occupy opposing spaces in Western thought, the public and the private respectively, in the specific case of minority languages the private feminine space has defined the survival of these vernaculars. For the nationalist Catalan, Galician, or Basque speaker, it is, or has been, the mother tongue. The private domestic space defines political community, in contrast to Castilian, the language of a superimposed public space. These differences do not necessarily imply hierarchical placement (i.e., Castilian would be the language for important matters, while Catalan, Galician, and Basque would be relegated to trivia); rather, they involve a politicization of things feminine and domestic. For cultural and political minorities, domestic affairs, on impact with public affairs, acquire connotations they do not bear in the "normal" order of things in modern societies. Domestic space becomes that of resistance.

Thus, changing the normal symbolic space of gender entails a set of consequences that must be considered when analyzing the texts of minority authors.

In the nationalist discourse, metaphors concerning gender have played an important part. The making feminine of things Galician, as well as equating the oppression of the Galician language with the oppression of women, are recurring themes explored in the literary criticism listed. The Catalan nationalistic doctrine is shot through with metaphors that legitimize the discourse by identifying the workings of nationalism with supposedly immutable natural processes. Woman, for example, hands down traditions and with them the nation's identity. The Catalan homeland is equated with the family as far as symbolic private space is concerned; national spirit or a national personality develops spontaneously. As Cristina Dupláa states, "En els textos nacionalistes . . . la figura femenina simbolitza la pàtria i és la peça central de la família pel fet de ser transmissora de la història/tradició a les noves generacions" (in nationalistic texts . . . the feminine figure symbolizes the homeland and is the centerpiece in the family for the mere fact of being the one who passes the tradition/history down to succeeding generations) (187). The position of woman in this discourse clearly contrasts with that of the *other*, to which the standard literary discourse tends to relegate things feminine.

Most of the women in this guide have been excluded from Spanish literary history, as well as from the official histories of Catalan, Galician, and Basque literature. Only Rosalía de Castro (1837–85) in Galician and Isabel de Villena (1430–90), Víctor Català (1869–1966), and Mercè Rodoreda (1908–83) in Catalan receive any mention in conventional works. Paradoxically, this book implicitly accepts the parameters that define what is usually called literature. A guide to women writers draws attention to new names, claiming for these women their rightful recognition as creators of culture and members of the literary canon.

However, to demand such a position for women means stirring up a wasp's nest at a time when literary criticism is already undergoing an identity crisis, when its most elementary concepts of author, history, and literature are being questioned. Currently a statement concerning the validity or invalidity of, for instance, the concept of author seems inescapable. If both the author and the subject—and by extension the subjective agency—are in question, the inspiration for publishing this work, that of trying to change the canon, has the rug pulled out from under it.

Roland Barthes's theory that literary authorship has given way to textual process ignores the existence of hierarchies in society and leads to a dead-end street when one tries to reclaim for Spanish literature the muted voices of its women writers. As Nancy K. Miller has pointed out, "the postmodernist decision that the Author is dead, and subjective agency along with him, does not necessarily work for women. Because the female subject has juridically been excluded from the polis, and hence decentered, disoriginated, deinstitutionalized, etc., her relation to integrity and textuality, desire and authority is structurally different" (106). Thus, if we accept the notion of the death of the author, we are accomplices in the suppression of women writers by male-dominated criticism. If we state that both history and the subject are ideological illusions, we are closing the gates on a feminist version of history and thus ensuring the predominance of the male-oriented version.

As Joan W. Scott indicates, however, the experience of her-story in other fields such as history shows that feminist claims for women writers are not sufficient to transform the basic disciplinary concepts of "literature" or "canon" so that the cultural authority of the female is taken into account. To shuffle women into the canon with no previous theoretical analysis of the parameters on which the canon is based may have no effect, since the literary establishment is more than capable of justifying the exclusion of women (as well as other groups of writers) and taking refuge in the well-known criteria of "literary quality." Clearly, simply demanding a place for women's names may result in the women writers' being classified as secondary and being studied exclusively by feminist critics.

What is needed, then, is both a criticism that acknowledges literature's role in forming thought patterns legitimizing the subordination of women and an analysis of literary works that makes sense of the organization and perception of literary consciousness. Given this goal, we aspire not merely to provide a guide to women writers but also to offer readers the tools for turning feminist research into literary fact and contributing in turn to the deconstruction of a patriarchal literary history that has been passed on to generations of citizens as a sign of national political identity.

Thus it will be necessary to explore the ways in which canons of the fringe literatures, like the Castilian literary canon, have been developed according to criteria that discriminate against both gender and social class. Within this schema masculine and feminine symbols are identified respectively with the positive and negative poles of literary efforts. In Castilian literature, the inclusion of Teresa de Jesús, Emilia Pardo Bazán, and Cecilia Böhl de Faber in the official canon is due partly to political motives. Their work has been interpreted as personifying the traditional view of Spain. The selection process excludes their most radical works and focuses on their more benign works. Even potentially subversive writings are interpreted in a way that downplays or ignores the subversive content and fits them into a mold of traditional literary forms and social thought. Some women writers have internalized the patriarchal values of their culture and uphold the status quo. Thus their masculine status is a function of their inclusion in the canon, to the extent that politics belongs to the symbolically masculine public sphere (Enríquez de Salamanca 12). It is hoped that this work will lead to further research in Catalan, Galician, and Basque literatures. For example, the identification of Rosalía de Castro with Galicia has political overtones. This did not, however, save her from total literary neglect until Azorín, in *Clásicos y modernos* (1913), brought her work back to the public eye. We might also wonder if Víctor Catalá's inclusion in the canon had anything to do with her depiction of the rural Catalan world, a useful theme for a nationalistic movement trying to construct a sense of Catalan political identity.

In addition, the material set forth in this guide is of particular interest from other points of view, such as that of the literary sociologist. Literature can be published in a wide range of formats—from serial magazines to special collectors' editions, clandestine works, limited editions, publicly or privately financed versions, and so on. The limited number of Spanish intellectual circles as well as the names of editors and writers of prologues allows us to trace the networks among which the writers moved. Publication history may also be useful in research that, following the lines of Jane Tompkins's *Sensational Designs*, attempts to clarify the mechanisms behind the construction of a literary classic.

The structure of this guide has its roots in earlier works by the two editors. Kathleen McNerney coordinated the entries dealing with Catalan, Galician, and Basque women writers for the volume *Women Writers of Spain: An Annotated Bio-Bibliographical Guide* (Galerstein and McNerney). Since 1984 Cristina Enríquez de Salamanca has been working on a catalog of Spanish women writers born between 1800 and 1936. These investigations made it clear that the basic bibliographic sources in existence do not cover in any depth women writers who published in Catalan, Galician, or Basque.[3]

The dual discrimination suffered by these writers multiplies the difficulties of locating and reading their work. To the general lack of information about literature created by women we may add the fact that bibliographic references are scarce and generally obsolete. The works themselves are scattered among myriad libraries and collections, often private. There is a dearth of biographical information, and often the writers themselves or their families are convinced of an absolute lack of literary interest in the women authors.

Given the recent trends in feminist criticism and the importance of studying unpublished material, we decided to include women whose theatrical works have survived and several writers who are not known to have published. References to the unpublished material are provided in the entries. The date of a work's composition is given parenthetically in the essay only if it differs from the date in the bibliography. All this material, which would be suppressed according to orthodox criteria, offers information of enormous interest for the study of certain topics, such as social censorship of women's writings.

Each article provides a brief biographical introduction to the writer in question. A general description of her works forms the core of the article, and a bibliographic section with up to four subsections follows. They include an alphabetical listing of books; an alphabetical listing of isolated publications in books, periodicals, and newspapers—of special interest for the study of nineteenth-century women writers; an alphabetical listing of works translated into Castilian or English, with the original title given in brackets; and critical studies listed alphabetically by author (this subsection is most often missing from the articles because of the dearth of such studies). For ten nineteenth-century writers, we also mention an interesting anthology of Catalan poetry gathered and translated into German under the direction of Johannes Fastenrath in 1890.[4] The length of each entry and the inclusion of the various subsections depend on the information available and do not reflect the quality of the writer's work.

The general formula "No biographical data available" indicates a lack of information, which affects both female authors of earlier times and, surprisingly, those of the present. The text also indicates authors whose specific works have not been located, even though their existence has been confirmed in other bibliographic sources. Thus we are presenting information about the actual bibliographic situation of the women writers and warning future researchers about the difficulties they will encounter. Evaluative comments in the listings reflect the opinion of the article's author.

Many writers listed here published solely in periodicals, and some individuals we know from only one poem or two or from a brief mention in a secondary source. Because of the difficulty of access to Spanish libraries and newspaper files, we provide as many references as possible to ease the task for those interested in further studies of specific authors.[5] In addition, a standard for inclusion based solely on the publication of books would have shown a complete lack of understanding of the problems these women faced when trying to publish their work and would have conflicted with the spirit that inspired the compilation of this guide. It is impossible to determine if someone is a "writer" by counting the number of her works. Other criteria are involved in judging literary achievement—value judgments, social effect, literary influence, and so on—which means that this label eludes easy definition. Furthermore, in the nineteenth century it was common to publish widely in the press as a means of entrée into the world of letters, but often the works were never collected into volumes.

The listing in this guide is alphabetical, combining authors in the three languages. Scholars working in literary criticism by periods will find the birthdate appendix helpful.

Given the precarious history of these languages, many differences have been found in the spelling of names, places, and titles. Whenever possible, homogeneous linguistic and orthographic criteria have been followed. In addition, the pioneering nature of this work makes it especially susceptible to errors of every kind. Therefore, it will be of great help to receive as many corrections as possible for incorporation into subsequent editions.

In compiling this guide, we have been able to count on the cooperation of people who, although outside the academic world, had personal relationships with writers or could provide access to their family members and acquaintances as well as to private archives and libraries. Thus a network of interconnections has been created, taking us from one person to another, leading to the work or the information we sought. Although the multiple perspectives have made our work both more complex and more complete, we have risked an unevenness in the text. We felt this was unavoidable given the nature of the material.

The completion of the entries would not have been possible without the generous efforts of the contributors, who have shown both personal interest and professional dedication in this project. We would like to extend special thanks to María Camino Noia Campos and Maite González Esnal, who coordinated the entries on Galician and Basque writers, respectively. We are also indebted to many others, among them Enric Bou, Anna Sánchez Rué, Montserrat Bayà, Fay D. Jacoby, Rita Gulstad, and Carole Frechon. Some of the writers themselves—Maria-Antònia Oliver, Isabel-Clara Simó, Angels Anglada, Sílvia Aymerich, and Renada-Laura Portet—helped us to locate other women writers. Michael Ugarte and Carlos Pedrós-Alió have been especially important, contributing their experience and invaluable knowledge of research techniques, computer skills, and support throughout these years. We are grateful for financial help from the Diputació de Barcelona, the Generalitat de Catalunya, West Virginia University, and the Program for Cultural Cooperation between Spain's Ministry of Culture and United States' Universities.

Kathleen McNerney
Cristina Enríquez de Salamanca

NOTES

[1] For the description of the Catalan, Galician, and Basque literatures, we rely on the following works: Díez Borque; Riquer, Comas, and Molas; Espalader; Tarrío Varela; Juaristi; Terry and Rafel.

²English translations of quoted material throughout the volume were done by Kathleen McNerney and the contributors.

³Those basic bibliographic sources are Serrano y Sanz and Criado y Domínguez. Another recent work is Simón Palmer.

⁴*Catalanische Troubadoure* includes poems by the female initiators of the Renaixença movement: Agnès Armengol, María de Bell-Lloch, Margarida Caimarí, Lluïsa Durán de León, Manuela Herreros de Bonet, Maria Josefa Massanés, Dolors Monserdà, Emília Palau González Quijano, Victòria Penya, and Agna de Valldaura.

⁵On occasion, the impossibility of consulting with the text for confirmation of volume, issue, or page numbers has resulted in the omission of that information.

WORKS CITED

Azorín, [José Martínez Ruiz]. *Clásicos y modernos*. Madrid: Renacimiento, 1913.

Barthes, Roland. "The Death of the Author." *Image, Music and Text*. Trans. Stephen Heath. New York: Hill, 1977. 142–48.

Buxó Rey, María Jesús. *Antropología de la mujer: Cognición, lengua e ideología cultural*. 1977. Madrid: Anthropos, 1988.

Criado y Domínguez, Juan P. *Literatas españolas del siglo XIX: Apuntes bibliográficos*. Madrid: Antonio Pérez Dubrull, 1889.

Díez Borque, José Maria. *Historia de las literaturas hispánicas no castellanas*. Madrid: Taurus, 1980.

Dupláa, Cristina. "Les dones i el pensament conservador català contemporani." *Més enllà del silenci: Les dones a la història de Catalunya*. Ed. Mary Nash. Barcelona: Generalitat de Catalunya, 1988. 173–89.

Enríquez de Salamanca, Cristina. "Gender and the Literary Canon: The Case of Nineteenth Century Spanish Women Writers." MA thesis. U of Minnesota, 1990.

Espadaler, Anton M. *Literatura catalana*. Madrid: Taurus, 1989.

Fastenrath, Johannes, ed. *Catalanische Troubadoure der Gegenwart. Verdeutscht und mit einer Uebersicht der catalanischen Literatur eingeleitet von Johannes Fastenrath*. Leipzig: Reissner, 1890.

Galerstein, Carolyn L., and Kathleen McNerney. *Women Writers of Spain: An Annotated Bio-Bibliographical Guide*. Bibliographies and Indexes in Women's Studies 2. Westport: Greenwood, 1986.

Iriarte, Ana. *Las redes del enigma: Voces femeninas en el pensamiento griego*. Madrid: Taurus, 1990.

Juaristi, Jon. *Literatura vasca*. Madrid: Taurus, 1987.

Miller, Nancy K. "Changing the Subject: Authorship, Writing and the Reader." *Feminist Studies–Critical Studies*. Ed. Teresa de Lauretis. Bloomington: Indiana UP, 1986. 102–20.

Riquer, Martí de, Antoni Comas, and Joaquim Molas. *Història de la literatura catalana*. 11 vols. Barcelona: Ariel, 1964–88.

Scott, Joan W. *Gender and the Politics of History*. New York: Columbia UP, 1988.

Serrano y Sanz, Manuel. *Apuntes para una biblioteca de escritoras españolas desde el año 1401 al 1833*. 4 vols. Madrid: Sucesores de Rivadeneyra, 1903–05. Biblioteca de Autores Españoles 268–71. Madrid: Atlas, 1975.

Simón Palmer, María del Carmen. "Escritoras españolas del siglo XIX. (I)." *Censo de escritores al servicio de los Austrias y otros estudios bibliográficos*. Madrid: CSIC, 1983. 99–119.

Tarrío Varela, Anxo. *Literatura gallega*. Madrid: Taurus, 1988.

Terry, Arthur, and Joaquim Rafel. *Introducción a la lengua y literatura catalanas*. Barcelona: Ariel, 1977.

Tompkins, Jane P. *Sensational Designs: The Cultural Work of American Fiction 1790–1860*. New York: Oxford UP, 1985.

Zulueta, Emilia de. *Historia de la crítica española contemporánea*. Madrid: Gredos, 1966.

Sources

LIBRARIES CONSULTED
Archiu del Monestir de Vallbona de les Monges, Vallbona de les Monges, Lleida.
Archivo Teatral Santos, Barcelona.
Biblioteca Bartomeu March, Palma de Mallorca.
Biblioteca Bergnes de las Casas, Barcelona.
Biblioteca de Catalunya, Barcelona.
Biblioteca de la Fundació Arús, Barcelona.
Biblioteca de l'Ateneu Barcelonès.
Biblioteca de la Universitat Autònoma de Barcelona, Bellaterra, Barcelona.
Biblioteca de l'Escola Universitària de Biblioteconomia i Documentació, Barcelona.
Biblioteca de l'Institut de Teatre Català, Barcelona.
Biblioteca de l'Institut Municipal de Història de Barcelona.
Biblioteca Gabriel Miró, Alacant.
Biblioteca Museo Víctor Balaguer, Vilanova i la Geltrú, Barcelona.
Biblioteca Nacional de Madrid.
Biblioteca Popular Carles Fages de Climent, Figueres, Girona.
Biblioteca Popular Francesca Bonnemaison de Verdaguer, Barcelona.
Biblioteca Pública de Girona.
Biblioteca Pública de Lleida.
Biblioteca Pública de Palma de Mallorca.
Biblioteca Pública de Tarragona.
Biblioteca Pública y Universitaria, Universidad Central de Barcelona.
Biblioteca Rosa Sensat, Barcelona.
Biblioteca Universitària de Valencia.

WORKS CITED AND CONSULTED: GENERAL
Annotated Bibliography, 1945–1982. Garland Reference Library of the Humanities 228. New York: Garland, 1984.
Bibliografía española. Revista general de la librería. Madrid: Ministerio de Educación y Ciencia, 1901– .

Blanco García, Francisco. *La literatura española en el siglo XIX.* 3rd ed. 3 vols. Madrid: Sáenz de Jubera Hermanos, 1909.

Catálogo general de la librería española 1931–1950. 4 vols. Madrid: Inst. Nacional del Libro Español, 1957–65.

Catálogo general de la librería española e hispanoamericana, años 1901–1930: Autores. 5 vols. Madrid: Inst. Nacional del Libro Español, 1923–51.

Cejador y Frauca, Julio. *Historia de la lengua y literatura castellana.* Vols. 6–10. Madrid: Tipología de Archivos, 1915–22.

Criado y Domínguez, Juan P. *Literatas españolas del siglo XIX: Apuntes bibliográficos.* Madrid: Antonio Pérez Dubrull, 1889.

Espadas, Elisabeth, et al. "Spain." *Women Writers in Translation: An Annotated Bibliography, 1945–1982.* Ed. Margery Resnick and Isabelle de Courtivron. New York: Garland, 1984. 211–26.

Galerstein, Carolyn L., and Kathleen McNerney. *Women Writers of Spain: An Annotated Bio-Bibliographical Guide.* Bibliographies and Indexes in Women's Studies 2. Westport: Greenwood, 1986.

Harner, James L. *On Compiling an Annotated Bibliography.* New York: MLA, 1985.

Hidalgo, Dionisio. *Diccionario general de bibliografía española.* Madrid: Varias Imprentas, 1862–81.

Instituto bibliográfico hispánico: Bibliografía española 1958. Madrid: Ministerio de Cultura, Dirección General del Libro y Bibliotecas, Secretaría General Técnica, 1959– .

Libro español. Madrid: Inst. Nacional del Libro Español, 1958– .

Libros españoles, 1972– . Catálogo ISBN. Madrid: Agencia Española del International Standard Book Number, 1973– .

Lliteratura asturiana y futuru. Uviéu: Serviciu Publicaciones, 1987.

Palau y Dulcet, Antonio, et al. *Manual del librero hispano-americano: Bibliografía general española e hispano-americana desde la invención de la imprenta hasta nuestros tiempos. . . .* 2nd ed., rev. and enl. 28 vols. Barcelona: Palau, 1948–77.

Quién es quién en las letras españolas. 3rd ed. Madrid: Inst. Nacional del Libro Español, Ministerio de Cultura, 1979.

Renza, Louis A. *"A White Heron" and the Question of Minor Literature.* Madison: U of Wisconsin P, 1984.

Saínz Rodríguez, Pedro. *Biblioteca bibliográfica hispánica.* 6 vols. Madrid: Fundación Universitaria Española Seminario "Menéndez Pelayo," 1975–87.

Serrano y Sanz, Manuel. *Apuntes para una biblioteca de escritoras españolas desde el año 1401 al 1833.* 4 vols. Madrid: Sucesores de Rivadeneyra, 1903–05. Rpt. Biblioteca de Autores Españoles 268–71. Madrid: Atlas, 1975.

Simón Díaz, José. *Bibliografía de la literatura hispánica*. 14 vols. to date. Madrid: CSIC, 1950– .

Williams, William Proctor, and Craig S. Abbott. *An Introduction to Bibliographical and Textual Studies*. 2nd ed. New York: MLA, 1989.

Woodbridge, Hensley C. *Guide to Reference Works for the Study of the Spanish Language and Literature and Spanish American Literature*. New York: MLA, 1987.

WORKS CITED AND CONSULTED: SPECIFIC SOURCES FOR CATALAN, GALICIAN, AND BASQUE WRITERS

Antologia da novíssima poesia català. Lisbon: Manuel de Seabra, 1974.

Antologia de la poesia reusenca. Reus, Tarragona: Secció de Literatura del Centre de Reus, 1957.

Antologia de poesia català contemporânia. Ed. S. Leonardos. Sao Paulo: Montfort, 1969.

Antologia poètica universitària. Barcelona: Els Llibres de l'Ossa Menor, 1950.

Badia i Margarit, Antoni. "Els poetes de les Illes i Montserrat." *Randa* 6 (1979): 152–73.

Bassa, Ramon, Jaume Bover, and Pere Carlos. *Llibres editats a Mallorca 1939–1972*. Palma de Mallorca: Mascaró-Pasarius, 1972.

Bilbao, J. *Eusko bibliografía*. 10 vols. San Sebastián: Auñamendi, 1970–80.

———. *Eusko bibliografía: Diccionario de bibliografía vasca . . . (1976–80)*. Bilbao: U del País Vasco, 1985– . Vol. 1.

Bover de Rosselló, Joaquim Maria. *Biblioteca de escritores baleares*. Palma: Gelabert, 1868.

Buenaventura, Ramon. *Las diosas blancas: Antología de la joven poesía española escrita por mujeres*. Madrid: Hiperión, 1985.

Cacheiro, Maximino. *Poetisas galegas do século XX*. Coruña: Gráfiga, 1987.

Cancionero amoroso: Poesías de autores valencianos contemporáneos. Valencia: Teodoro Llorente, 1883.

Carballo Calero, Ricardo. *Historia da literatura galega contemporánea*. Vigo: Galaxia, 1975.

———. *Historia de la literatura gallega*. Madrid: Nacional, 1975.

Charlon, Anne. *La condició de la dona en la narrativa femenina catalana (1900–1983)*. Barcelona: Edicions 62, 1990.

Les cinc branques: Poesia femenina catalana. Comp. and arranged by Esteve Albert, Roser Matheu, Octavi Saltor, Antoni Sala-Cornadó, and M. Assumpció Torras. Barcelona: Esteve Albert, 1975.

Ciplijauskaité, Biruté. *La novela femenina contemporánea (1970–1985)*. Barcelona: Anthropos, 1988.

Colet i Giralt, Josep, ed. *Selecció XXV: Prosa i poesia*. Barcelona: Dalmau, 1981.

Col.lecció els autors de l'ocell de paper. Barcelona: n.p., 1955–59.

Corominas, Joan. *Suplemento al diccionario crítico de los escritores catalanes.* Burgos: Arnaiz, 1849. Barcelona: Curial, 1973.

Costa i Via, Montserrat. *Estudi de l'obra d'Anna Rubiés.* Barcelona: Fundació Salvador Vives Casajuana, 1971.

Couceiro Freijomil, Antonio. *Diccionario bio-bibliográfico de escritores gallegos.* 3 vols. Santiago de Compostela: Gran Enciclopedia Gallega, for Editorial de los Bibliófilos Gallegos, 1951–54.

Curet, Francesc. *Història del teatre català.* Barcelona: Aedos, 1967.

Diccionari biogràfic. Barcelona: Albert, 1969.

Diccionario enciclopédico del país vasco. 7 vols. to date. San Sebastián: Haramburu, 1985– .

Díez Borque, José Maria. *Historia de las literaturas hispánicas no castellanas.* Madrid: Taurus, 1980.

Elias de Molins, Antonio. *Diccionario de artistas y escritores catalanes del siglo XIX: Apuntes y datos.* Barcelona: Fidel Gir, 1889.

Enciclopedia general ilustrada del país vasco. Cuerpo A: Diccionario enciclopédico vasco. 20 vols. to date. San Sebastián: Auñamendi, 1969– .

Espadaler, Anton M. *Literatura catalana.* Madrid: Taurus, 1989.

Fastenrath, Johannes, ed. *Catalanische Troubadoure der Gegenwart. Verdeutscht und mit einer Uebersicht der catalanischen Literatur eingeleitet von Johannes Fastenrath.* Leipzig: Reissner, 1890.

Fulls impermeables. Barcelona: Mall, 1983.

Gran enciclopèdia catalana. 24 vols. Barcelona: Edicions 62, 1969.

Gran enciclopedia de la región valenciana. Dir. Manuel Mas. 12 vols. Valencia: Gran Enciclopedia de la Región Valenciana, 1973–78.

Gran enciclopedia gallega. Dir. Ramón Otero Pedrayo. 30 vols. Gijón: Silverio Cañada, 1974–87.

Gran enciclopedia vasca. 14 vols. Bilbao: Gran Enciclopedia Vasca, 1980– .

Iborra, Josep. "La novel.la al país Valencià." *Arguments* 3 (1977): 63–103.

Janer Manila, Gabriel. *Els escriptors balears i la seva producció en català.* Palma de Mallorca: Conselleria d'Educació i Cultura de les Illes Balears, 1986.

Jocs Florals de Barcelona. Barcelona: La Renaxensa, 1859–1936.

Juaristi, Jon. *Literatura vasca.* Madrid: Taurus, 1987.

Lectura popular. Colecció d'escriptors catalans contemporanis. 30 vols. Barcelona: Ilustració Catalana, n.d. [1913–32].

Lecuona, Manuel. *Literatura oral vasca.* Tolosa: Kardaberaz, 1964.

Llibre de la Renaixença. Barcelona: La Renaixença, 1888.

Llibres en català 1982–1983–1984. Barcelona: Generalitat de Catalunya, Dept. de Cultura, 1986.

Lloberas, Pere, ed. *Antologia de poetes bisbalencs de la Renaixença.* La Bisbal, Girona: L'Aliança Bisbalenca, 1965.

Llombart, Constantí. *Los fills de la morta-viva: Apunts bio-bibliogràfichs pera la història del Renaiximent lliterari llemosí en Valencia*. Valencia: Pascual, 1879 (cover date 1883).

Llompart, Josep Maria. *La literatura moderna a les Balears*. Palma de Mallorca: Moll, 1964.

Manat d'homenatge a la reina Constança de Mallorca, la princesa Eleonor de Villena, Victòria Penya d'Amer, Víctor Català (Caterina Albert), Maria Antònia Salvà (Mallorca), Anzizu i Vila, Clarisa de Pedralbes, Sara Llorens de Serra, Pilar Pratdesaba de Surroca, Pinutxa Maffei de Ginesu (Alger), Palmira Jaquetti, Maria Perpinyà, Maria Verger, Maria Teresa Vernet. Barcelona: Esteve Albert, 1975.

March, Kathleen N. *Festa da palabra: An Anthology of Contemporary Galician Women Poets*. New York: Lang, 1989.

Massó i Torrents, Jaume. *Bibliografia dels antics poetes catalans*. Barcelona, 1914.

———. "Poetesses i dames intel.lectuals." *Homenatge a Antoni Rubió i Lluch*. Vol. 1. Barcelona: n.p., 1936. 405–17.

Massot i Muntaner, Jaume. *Els mallorquins i la llengua autòctona*. 2nd ed. Barcelona: Curial, 1985.

Matheu, Roser. *Quatre dones catalanes*. Barcelona: Fundació Salvador Vives Casajuana, 1973.

Michelena, Luis. *Historia de la literatura vasca*. Madrid: Minotauro, 1960.

Molas, Joaquim, and Josep Massot i Muntaner, gen. eds. *Diccionari de la literatura catalana*. Barcelona: Edicions 62, 1979.

Oliver, Miquel dels Sants. *La literatura en Mallorca 1840–1903*. Palma de Mallorca: n.p., 1964. Montserrat: L'Abadia, 1988.

Oller i Rabassa, Joan. *Memòria: Jocs Florals de Barcelona*. Barcelona: n.p., 1971.

Onaindia, Aita. *Mila euskal olerki eder*. Laréa-Amorbeita, Bizkaia: Karmeldar Idaztiak, 1954.

Pérez, Janet. *Contemporary Women Writers of Spain*. Boston: Hall, 1988.

Pérez Moragón, Francesc. *Publicacions valencianes (1939–1973)*. Valencia: Caixa d'Estalvis i Mont de Pietat, 1974.

Pi i Vendrell, Núria. *Bibliografia de la novel.la sentimental publicada en català entre 1924 i 1938*. Barcelona: Diputació de Barcelona, 1986.

Piquer i Jover, Josep Joan. *Abaciologi de Vallbona (1153–1977)*. Santes Creus, Girona: Fundació d'Història i Art Roger de Belfort, 1978.

Poetas baleares del s. XIX. Poesías de autores vivientes escritas en catalán. Premiadas la mayor parte en los Juegos Florales de Barcelona y publicadas con noticias biográficas y una traducción castellana. Palma: Pere Joseph Gelabert, 1873.

Pons, Damià. "Catàleg parcial dels narradors mallorquins del segle XIX." *Randa* 14 (1983): 71–91.

El pont: Vint i cinc novetats literàries. Barcelona: Arimany, S.A., 1956– .

Primera antologia 1965–1966–1967 del premi de poesia per a inèdits Mossèn Amadeu Oller. Barcelona: Joseph Maria Vidal Aunos, 1967.

Puig Torralva, J., and Francisco Marti Grijales. *Estudio histórico-crítico de los poetas valencianos de los siglos XVI, XVII y XVIII.* Valencia: Viuda de Ayoldi, 1883.

Lo rat-penat. Vol. 1. *Llibre d'or dels Jochs Florals.* 1895. Vol. 2. *Brots de llorer.* 1896. Vol. 3. *Flors d'enguany.* 1897. Vol. 4. *Capolls de rosa.* 1897. Valencia: Federico Domenech. [These books are the official organ of the Societat de Amadors de les Glòries Valencianes.]

Ribera Llopis, Juan M. *Literaturas catalana, gallega y vasca.* Madrid: Playor, 1982.

Rico García, Manuel, and Antonio Montero Pérez. *Ensayo biográfico-bibliográfico de escritores de Alicante y su provincia.* Alicante, 1888.

Riquer, Martí de, Antoni Comas, and Joaquim Molas. *Història de la literatura catalana.* 11 vols. Barcelona: Ariel, 1964–88.

Sarasola, Ibon. *Historia social de la literatura vasca.* Trans. Jesús Antonio Cid. Madrid: Akal, 1976.

Segura, Isabel, and Marta Selva. *Revistes de dones 1846–1935.* Barcelona: Edhasa, 1984.

Segura, Isabel, Helena Alvarado, Anna Murià, Carme Arnau, M. dels Angels Anglada, Geraldine C. Nichols, and M. Mercè Marçal. *Literatura de dones: Una visió del món.* Barcelona: LaSal, 1988.

Sis Poetas 83. Barcelona: Mall, 1983.

Simón Palmer, María del Carmen. "Escritoras españolas del siglo XIX. (I)." *Censo de escritores al servicio de los Austrias y otros estudios bibliográficos.* Madrid: CSIC, 1983. 99–119.

———. *Escritoras españolas del siglo XIX. Manual bio-bibliográfico.* Madrid: Castalia, 1991.

Tarrío Varela, Anxo. *Literatura gallega.* Madrid: Taurus, 1988.

Tayadella, Antònia. "La novel.la en català de 1862 a 1882. Catàleg." *Faig* 19 (Dec. 1982): 82–91.

———. "Novel.la i llengua al s. XIX: Història i conflicte." *L'Avenç* 27 (May 1980): 37–42.

Terry, Arthur, and Joaquim Rafel. *Introducción a la lengua y literatura catalanas.* Barcelona: Ariel, 1977.

Torrent i Tasis, Rafael. *Historia del periodismo catalán.* Barcelona: Noguera, 1965.

Torres Amat, Fèlix. *Memorias para ayudar a formar un diccionario crítico de los escritores catalanes y dar alguna idea de la antigua y moderna literatura catalana.* Barcelona, 1836. Barcelona: Curial, 1973.

Trias Mercant, Sebastià. *Història del pensament a Mallorca*. Vol. 1. Palma: Moll, 1985.

Los trovadors moderns: Col.lecció de poesías catalanas compostas per ingenis contemporáneos. Ed. Antoni de Bofarull. Barcelona: Salvador Manero, 1859.

Los trovadors nous: Col.lecció de poesías catalanas, escollidas de autors contemporáneos per Antoni de Bofarull. Barcelona: Salvador Manero, 1858.

Tubino, Francisco María. *Historia del renacimiento literario contemporáneo en Cataluña, Baleares y Valencia*. Madrid: Tello, 1880.

Unamuno, Miguel de. "La unificación del vascuence." *La Nación* [Buenos Aires] 16 Sept. 1920.

Vazquez i Estevez, Anna. *Catàleg de manuscrits de teatre en català de l'Institut del Teatre*. Barcelona: Generalitat de Catalunya, Dept. de Cultura i Mitjans de Comunicació, 1981.

Villasante, Luis. *Historia de la literatura vasca*. Burgos: Aranzazu, 1979.

Zubatsky, David S. "An Annotated Bibliography of Nineteenth-Century Catalan, Galician, and Spanish Author Bibliographies." *Hispania* 65 (1982): 212–24.

PERIODICALS AND NEWSPAPERS CITED AND CONSULTED

Academia bibliográfica Mariana de Lérida (Lérida, 1863–1956)

L'aiguadolç (Marina Alta, 1985–)

Albaida (Zaragoza, 1977–)

Album del Miño (Vigo, active 1858)

La alianza de los pueblos (?, active 1868)

Almanaque de Galicia (Lugo, active 1865–66)

Almanaque gallego (Buenos Aires, 1898–1927)

L'amic de les arts: Gaseta de Sitges (Sitges, 1926–76)

Andoriña (?, active 1985)

Arosa poética (Vilagarcía, active 1988)

La barretina: Semanari popular (Barcelona, 1868)

Boletín de la Real Academia de Buenas Letras de Barcelona (Barcelona, 1901–)

Boletín de la Sociedad Castellonense de Cultura (Castellón, 1920–)

Butlletí del Centre Català (Barcelona, 1882–88; published as *La veu del Centre Català* in 1888)

Cairell (Valencia, 1979–81)

Calendari català (Barcelona, 1865–1905)

Casa nostra (Lleida, 1980–)

El cascabel (Madrid, 1863–77?)

Catalana (Barcelona, 1918–21)

Catalan Review (Barcelona, 1986–)

Catalan Writing (Barcelona, 1988–)
Catecismo de niños y niñas (Santiago, 1904–21)
Catecismo de San Martín (Santiago, 1918–21; Bilbao, 1921–?)
Cavall fort (Barcelona, 1961–)
Coordenadas (Santiago, 1981–)
El correo catalán (Barcelona, 1876–1926; 1940–85)
El correo de la moda (Madrid, 1851–86)
El correo gallego (El Ferrol, 1878–1938; Santiago, 1938–)
Daina (Valencia, 1986–)
O diario (Porto, active 1985–86)
Diario de Pontevedra (Pontevedra, 1924–)
Diario español (Buenos Aires, 1881–?)
La dona catalana (Barcelona, 1925–38)
Dones en lluita (Barcelona, 1982)
Dorna (Santiago, 1981–)
Eco de Euterpe (Barcelona, 1859–1911)
Egan (San Sebastián, 1948–)
Encrucillada (Santiago, 1977–)
Escrita (Vigo, 1983–85)
L'espill (Valencia, 1979–)
La estafeta literaria (Madrid, 1944–78)
Estreno (Cincinnati, 1975–)
Euskerea (Donostia, 1919–35; Bilbao, 1937–)
Eusko deya (Paris, ?)
Faig (Manresa, 1975–)
Faro de Vigo (Vigo, 1870–)
Feminal (Barcelona, 1907–25)
Festa da palabra silenciada (Vigo, 1983–)
El figurín artístico (Barcelona, 1882–84?)
Flames noves (Barcelona, 1921–?)
La floresta (Barcelona, 1857)
Follas secas (Ourense, 1985–)
Lo Gay Saber (Barcelona, 1868–69; 1878–79; 1880–83)
Gazeta montanyesa (Vic, 1905–14)
Grial (Vigo, 1963–)
Hèlix (Vilafranca del Penedès, 1929–30)
El ideal gallego (Coruña, 1917–)
Identity Magazine (Cambridge, MA, active 1966)
La ilustración de la mujer (Barcelona, 1883–85)
La ilustración gallega y asturiana (Madrid/Oviedo, 1879–81)
La ilustración popular económica de Valencia (Valencia, 1869–89)
El imparcial (Madrid, 1842–?)
International Poetry Review (Greensboro, 1975–)

Joventut (Barcelona, 1900–06)
El liberal (Madrid/Barcelona, 1901–?)
The Literary Review (Madison, NJ, 1957–)
Lletres de canvi (Valencia, 1979–)
Llombriu (Valencia, active 1985)
La llumanera de Nova York (New York, 1874–81)
Luzes de Galizia (Coruña, 1985–)
Els marges (Barcelona, 1974–)
La marina (?, active 1961–66)
El matí (Barcelona, 1927–?)
Monographic Review / Revista monográfica (Odessa, TX, 1985–)
Mostra de narrativa reusenca (Reus, active 1980–84)
Mundo católico (Barcelona, 1935–43)
Museo balear de historia y literatura, ciencias y artes (Palma, 1875–77; 1884–88)
El museo universal (Madrid, 1857–69)
La naval (Coruña, 1985–87)
Nordés (Sada, 1975–)
Nós (Santiago, 1920–36)
A nosa terra (Coruña, 1916–36)
A nosa terra (Santiago de Compostela, 1977–80; Vigo, 1982–87)
Nostres faulelles (Valencia, 1961–65)
Las noticias (Barcelona, 1869–1939)
La novela nova (Barcelona, 1917–21)
Or y grana (Barcelona, 1906–07)
Poetry Canada (Kingston, ON, 1979–)
El pont (Barcelona, 1956–)
Las provincias. Diario de Valencia. Almanaque para . . . (Valencia, 1880–1917?)
Punt diari (Girona, 1979–)
Quaderns literaris (Barcelona, 1934–38)
La Rambla de Catalunya (Barcelona, 1930–32)
Lo rat penat: Calendari llemosí (Valencia, 1875–78; 1880–83)
Recull (Blanes, 1920–)
Reduccions (Vic, 1977–)
La región (Ourense, 1910–)
La renaixensa [also spelled *La renaixença*] (Barcelona, 1871–1905)
La revista (Barcelona, 1915–36)
Revista balear de literatura, ciencias y artes (Palma, 1872–74)
Revista da Federación de Asociacións Culturais Galegas (Santiago, active 1982)
Revista de Catalunya (Barcelona, 1924–)
Revista de Gerona (Girona, active 1877 and 1955–76)

Revista del Club de Vela Blanes (Blanes, 1978–)
Revista de poesía (Barcelona, 1925–27)
Revolatura (Barcelona, 1976–)
El Segre (Lleida, ?)
Sempre (Porto, active 1986)
Seneca Review (Geneva, NY, 1971–)
Serra d'or (Barcelona, 1959–)
Lo teatre catòlic (Barcelona, 1899–?)
Tintimán (Vigo, 1984–86)
Treboada (Barcelona, 1982–)
La veu de Catalunya (Barcelona, 1899–1937)
La veu del Centre Català (See *Butlletí del Centre Català*)
La veu de Montserrat (Vic, 1878–1901)
Vieiros (Mexico, 1959–68)
Vocablos (Valencia, active 1979–80)
La voz de Galicia (Coruña, 1882–?)
Webster Review (Webster Groves, MO, 1974–)
Yorick (Barcelona, 1965–?)

Contributors

Sílvia Aymerich Lemos is a teacher, translator, and poet. Her degree is in biology from the University of Barcelona. She has translated into Catalan works by Isaac Asimov, John Ruskin, and Bram Stoker. She has also worked for Catalan television and is active in the Catalan Writer's Association. Aymerich is the author of two books of poetry, *La meva Europa* and *Poemes de destemps i d'alba nua*, and a collection of stories, *Berlin Zoo*.

Lola Badia is professor of Catalan philology at the University of Barcelona and a member of the Schola Lullística. She has written numerous articles, including one on Víctor Català.

Imma Baldocchi i Puig is a librarian with a degree in Hispanic language and literature from the University of Barcelona.

Catherine G. Bellver is professor of Spanish at the University of Nevada, Las Vegas. She received her PhD from the University of California, Berkeley, in 1972 and has written articles on contemporary Spanish and Catalan women writers.

Emilie L. Bergmann is associate professor of Spanish at the University of California, Berkeley. She has written several articles on Spanish women writers, including "Flowers at the North Pole: Mercè Rodoreda and the Female Imagination in Exile" and "Reshaping the Canon: Intertextuality in Spanish Novels of Female Development."

Maryellen Bieder is professor of Spanish at Indiana University, Bloomington. She received her PhD from the University of Minnesota in 1972. She has written many articles on women writers, particularly of the nineteenth century, and several on Mercè Rodoreda.

Nancy L. Bundy is associate professor at Simpson College, Indianola, Iowa. She received her PhD from the University of Oklahoma in 1977.

Inés Calvo, a writer, has a degree in Hispanic philology from the University of Madrid.

Sandra Canepari is professor of Spanish at California State College, Chico. She has written several articles on Catalan literature.

Rosanna Cantavella is professor of Catalan literature at the University of Valencia. She coedited the new anthology of Isabel de Villena's *Vita Christi* for the collection Clàssiques Catalanes by LaSal.

Josefa Contijoch Pratdesaba is a poet and novelist. She has written film criticism and works as a translator for Zardoya Press of Barcelona. She has won several literary prizes for her work, including the Ciutat de Mallorca in 1990 for *La dona liquada*.

Ann Elliott is a lecturer in technical communications at the University of California, Berkeley. She has written several articles on, and translated work by, Pere Calders.

Elena Elorriaga received her degree in philology at the University of Barcelona and teaches at Boston University.

Cristina Enríquez de Salamanca is completing her doctorate at the University of Minnesota. Her dissertation, as well as published articles, focuses on Spanish women writers.

Albina Fransitorra Aleña contributed to several journals before the Civil War, such as *Nosaltres sols* and *L'almanac de les lletres*, and also worked for Catalunya Ràdio. She teaches Catalan for Omnium Cultural and the Diputació de Barcelona. She received a degree in philology from the University of Barcelona in 1983 and has written a biography of Carme Montoriol.

Manuel García Castellón received his PhD from the University of Georgia and teaches at New Orleans University.

Anna Gasol i Trullols is a librarian with the Biblioteca Rosa Sensat in Barcelona and a member of the Seminari de Bibliografia Infantil.

Maite González Esnal is a journalist, translator, and administrative assistant for the Basque Writers' Association. She has collaborated on the journals *El diario vasco, Ere*, and *Habe* and translated works by Mercè Rodoreda and Marguerite Yourcenar. She is the author of *Bertan Ikusia*.

Guillem-Jordi Graells is a playwright. He has written articles on Catalan literature and has translated dramatic works into Catalan.

Maria Luisa Guardiola-Ellis has a degree in Hispanic philology. An instructor at Swarthmore College and a doctoral candidate at the University of Pennsylvania, she has written articles on Marta Pessarrodona and other Catalan women writers.

Anna Gudayol i Torrell has a degree in Romance philology from the University of Barcelona and works as a librarian. She is preparing her doctorate on medieval literature.

Carme Junoy is a student at the North American Institute in Barcelona and a specialist in tourism and travel.

Kathleen March is professor of Spanish at the University of Maine, Orono. She received her PhD from the State University of New York, Buffalo. A founder of the Galician Studies Association, she has published a book and numerous articles on Galician literature.

Elisa Martí-López received her MA in Spanish literature from the University of Georgia and is now working on her doctorate at New York University.

Sheila McIntosh received a degree from the translation program at the University of Iowa. She has translated a novel by Isabel-Clara Simó.

Tara McNally received her BA in Spanish literature from Boston College. Her honors thesis was on Maria Vernet.

Kathleen McNerney is professor of Spanish at West Virginia University. She has written on Latin American and Spanish literature, focusing on Catalan women writers, and has translated poems and novels from Catalan.

Anna Montero i Bosch lives in Valencia and has written two books of poetry. She teaches French and translates literary texts from that language.

Candelas Newton is associate professor of Spanish at Wake Forest University. She has written several articles on Spanish poets and a book on Federico García Lorca.

Maria Camino Noia Campos is professor of Galician at the University of Santiago and also teaches at the Colexio Universitario of Vigo. Her doctorate was conferred by the University of Santiago in 1980. Coauthor of *Lingua galega* and coeditor of the women's magazine *Festa da palabra silenciada* (Vigo), she has also written several critical articles and translated literary works.

Maria Inmaculada Pausas is a librarian and teacher. Her degree is in philology.

Janet Pérez is professor of Spanish at Texas Tech University. She has published numerous books and articles and is the book review editor for *Hispania*. Her works on women writers include *Ana María Matute, Novelistas femeninas de la postguerra española*, and *Contemporary Women Writers of Spain*.

Núria Pi i Vendrell is a librarian and the author of a study of sentimental novels.

Isabel Robles Gómez is professor of Catalan Literature at the University of Valencia.

Anna Maria Sánchez Rué is a language teacher, nurse, and translator. She completed her MA in literature at the University of Virginia.

Mario Santana received his MA in Spanish literature from the University of Georgia. He is a doctoral student at Columbia University.

Marisa Siguán Boehmer is professor of German literature at the University of Barcelona. Her doctoral thesis examines the critical response of Catalan modernists to the works of Ibsen and Hauptmann. The author of several articles, she continues to explore the relations between German and Spanish literature.

Carmen Simón Palmer is a researcher at the Instituto de Filología del Consejo Superior de Investigaciones Científicas in Madrid. She has published a number of bibliographical studies.

Maria-Lourdes Soler i Marcet is a librarian in the Romance philology section at the University of Trier, Germany. A literary critic, she has published a number of articles on feminist themes in Catalonia, Germany, and the United States.

Sebastià Trias Mercant is professor of philosophy, rector of the Schola Lullística, and an editor of *Estudios lulianos* and *Antropológica*. He has done several studies of Margarida Baneta Mas i Pujol and has prepared a new selection of her works.

Montserrat Vilarrubla received a doctorate from the University of Madrid. She is assistant professor of Spanish at Illinois State University.

Montserrat Villas i Chalamanch teaches Catalan in an institute in Barcelona. She has published articles on linguistics as well as on the literature of the "Malmonjades," poems by nuns lamenting their status.

28

Bio-Bibliographic Listing

Note: Short citations in the bibliography sections are cross-references to works listed in the Sources section (pp. 15–24) or, occasionally, to books by the particular writers.

C Abanté i Vilalta, Antònia
(20th c.) Poet. No biographical information available.

A member of the group Poesia Viva, Antònia Abanté has published two books of poetry; some of her poems have been set to music. The common themes of *Poesia per al poble* (Poetry for the people) are everyday surroundings, country, and family.

BOOKS

Poesia per al poble. Pref. Josep Colet i Giralt. Illus. Alicia Tello. Barcelona: Poesia Viva, 1983.

Ressons de pàtria i família. Barcelona: n.p., 1979.

KATHLEEN MCNERNEY

C Abelló i Soler, Montserrat
(B. 1918, Tarragona– .) Translator and poet.

After a childhood spent in the south of Spain and in England, Montserrat Abelló studied in Barcelona and earned a degree in English. During the Spanish Civil War she took refuge first in France, then in Chile, where she married and had three children. An active feminist, Abelló has translated into Catalan Sylvia Plath's *Winter Trees* and Charlotte Perkins Gilman's novella *The Yellow Wallpaper*, which includes the epilogue by Elaine R. Hedges. These and other English and American women writers have influenced her poetry.

Vida diària: Paraules no dites (Daily life: Words unsaid), illustrated by her friend Roser Bru, contains Abelló's first book and previously unpublished works. *El blat del temps* (The wheat of time), which has a perceptive

preface by Maria Angels Anglada, is divided into three sections: the first
dedicated to "Tu," the second to "Jo," and the third to "Nosaltres." The
poems are short, usually featuring a single image and a consistent tone,
and this economy enhances unexpected concepts. Abelló often uses free
verse, and her poetry has a musical quality. Active in women's groups and
"tertulias" (social or intellectual gatherings), she is also involved in the
feminist publishing house LaSal.

BOOKS
El blat del temps. Pref. Maria Angels Anglada. Barcelona: Columna, 1986.
Foc a les mans. Pref. Maria Mercè Marçal. Barcelona: Columna, 1990.
Vida diària. Barcelona: Joaquim Horta, 1963.
Vida diària. Paraules no dites. Pref. Marta Pessarrodona. Illus. Roser Bru. Barcelona: LaSal, 1981.

TRANSLATIONS OF HER WORKS
"And inside Me a Voice Tells Me" [I dins meu una veu em diu] and "It Seems That Everything" [Sembla que ja està]. Trans. Montserrat Abelló. *Poetry Canada* 11.4 (1990): 20.
Poems, untitled. *Survivors*. Selected and trans. D. Sam Abrams. Barcelona: Inst. d'Estudis Nord-Americans, 1991. 45–55.

KATHLEEN MCNERNEY

C Abeyà Lafontana, Elisabet
(B. 1951, Barcelona– .) Translator and writer of children's literature.

Elisabet Abeyà received a degree in psychology from the University of
Barcelona and has taught Catalan to various age groups. She has translated several books, including Gandhi's *Nonviolence in Peace and War* and
the Bhagavad Gita, and has published books for children.

BOOKS
La bruixa que va perdre la granera i altres contes. Palma de Mallorca: Moll, 1985.
El nanet coloraina i més sorpreses. Palma de Mallorca: Moll, 1987.
Què seré quan sigui gran? Barcelona: La Galera, 1988.

KATHLEEN MCNERNEY

B Agirre Lasheras, María Dolores
(B. 1903, Regil, Gipuzkoa– .) Journalist, translator, and playwright.

Director of the Declamation School in San Sebastián, María Dolores Agirre
won the Azpeitia prize for her 1949 monologue "Aukeraren maukera,

azkenean okerra." Her article "Emakumeak, bear-beara" (Women are indispensable) encouraged women to cultivate the Basque language. Agirre translated Federico García Lorca's *Yerma* and Rabindranath Tagore's *Amal* into Basque.

WORKS IN BOOKS, PERIODICALS, NEWSPAPERS
"Aukeraren maukera, azkenean okerra" and "Emakumeak, bear-beara." *Egan* 5–6 (1950): 99–102.

MAITE GONZALEZ ESNAL

Alacseal, Virgili; *see* **Albert i Paradís, Caterina**

C Alba, Sermena
(19th c.) Playwright. No biographical information available.

The files of the Institut de Teatre Català in Barcelona contain the undated manuscript of a play, "Mirallets" (Mirrors), signed by Sermena Alba. There is no record, however, of its ever having been performed. The manuscript is bound with another play, dated 1871, which suggests that they belong to the same period. Set in Barcelona, "Mirallets" deals with the conflicts faced by a physician torn between the social duties imposed by his wealthy family and his own desire for altruistic action. The play includes debates on the ethics of using poor patients as guinea pigs for experimentation.

BOOKS
"Mirallets." Ms. 384. Institut de Teatre Català, Barcelona.

CRISTINA ENRIQUEZ DE SALAMANCA

C Albert i Paradís, Caterina
(B. 1869, L'Escala, Girona; d. 1966, L'Escala, Girona.) Known as Víctor Català and Virgili Alacseal. Poet, short story writer, novelist, playwright, and essayist.

The best-known and most widely read of nineteenth-century Catalan women writers, both in her own day and the present, Caterina Albert possessed extraordinary and unconventional talent for her generation. The daughter of a lawyer from a rural, landowning family, she received the convent and domestic schooling available to middle-class girls. Unsatisfied with her limited education, she devised her own rigorous program of reading and foreign language study at her home in a coastal town near Girona.

31

To develop her artistic talent, she took private lessons in painting and sculpture, skills that are reflected in the chiaroscuro effects and concrete imagery in her writing. Albert never married, managing her family property after her father's death and caring for family members. A private person who maintained a careful distance between her writing and her personal life, she was not, however, the recluse some critics have described. After 1904 she lived most of the year in her Barcelona apartment. Although Albert set most of her fiction in the rugged countryside, she knew the city well and kept abreast of the literature and theater of her time.

Following the pattern common among women writers of the period, Albert began by writing poetry, which she contributed, along with short stories, to the Barcelona literary magazine of the *Renaixença* movement, *Joventut*. In 1898 the Jocs Florals in Olot, Girona, awarded a prize to a dramatic monologue in verse, "La infanticida" (The girl who killed her baby), and the judges were surprised to learn that the author was a young woman, Caterina Albert. Her first publications appeared under the male pseudonym, Víctor Català, which she continued to use even after her identity became known in 1902. The name conveyed a combination of masculine strength (Víctor) and nationalism (Català), which in the public mind became inseparable from the author herself. These connotations, the label "naturalism" attached to her fiction, and her unmarried state led to the frequent characterization of Albert as a "masculine" writer.

When her first volume, *Quatre monòlegs* (Four monologues), appeared in print, she was thirty-two. Within a year she published twelve poems, *El cant dels mesos* (The song of the months), and the first of her collections of stories about country life, *Drames rurals* (Rural dramas). Her most famous work, the novel *Solitud* (Solitude), followed shortly, as did her second collection of rural stories, *Caires vius* (Sketches from life). Frequently termed sordid and crude, her fiction takes an implacable view of the human condition in a starkly drawn countryside. Portraying the individual's isolation in an unyielding natural or domestic environment, she traces the process of psychic disintegration or the struggle for survival. Elements of Romanticism, naturalistic detail, psychological realism, environmental determinism, *costumisme* (local color), and regional vocabulary and speech patterns are woven together in a cohesive and powerful literary expression.

In her "Pòrtic" (prologue) to *Caires vius* she stoutly defends the *ruralisme* of her fiction against charges of being outmoded, arguing that literary fashion has nothing to do with genius, which is "sempre iconoclasta i ultradogmàtic; trenca tots els motlles, capgira totes les teories i imposa noves lleis" (always iconoclastic and ultra-dogmatic; breaking all the molds, twisting all the theories and imposing new laws) (180). A decade

32

later, she wrote an innovative second novel, *Un film (3,000 metres)* (A film [3,000 meters]), that is set in Barcelona and utilizes the narrative structure and devices of film. Although she had probably written or begun the major portion of her fiction by 1907, with the exception of *Un film*, volumes of short fiction continued to appear, including *Contrallums* (Backlighting) in 1930 and *Vida mòlta* (Battered life), her third collection of rural dramas, in 1950. A new preface to *Ombrivoles* (Somber stories), "Les ulleres" (1948; Binoculars), dealt with her awareness of the change in literary tastes in the fifty years since she had begun publishing. In her last decades she saw the publication of her collected essays, *Mosaic*, and her unpublished short fiction, *Jubileu* (Jubilee). Her remaining dramatic works, *Teatre inèdit* (Unpublished plays), were published after her death.

Honored as president of the Jocs Florals in Barcelona in 1917, Albert received the distinction in 1923 of being the first woman elected to the Reial Acadèmia de Bones Lletres of Barcelona. But appreciation for her fiction faded in the face of a new generation of writers and a new literary aesthetic in the 1920s, and her second novel received harsh criticism. Because of her temperament, her family obligations, and her sex, Albert remained peripheral to the literary world. She did not participate in the organization of the women's movement or contribute to its journals. Independent and silent, she spent her final years in the family home in L'Escala.

Albert's fiction has appeared in multiple editions and translations. Her *Obres completes* (Complete works) contains virtually all her writing, including some correspondence. Montserrat Ciurana's thesis contributes additional letters. Despite the documentation, the biographies, and the availability of her works, Albert's writing has received limited scholarly attention, remaining largely mired in the debates over literary naturalism. Observing that in Albert's fiction "sovint, el seu lloc és el de la intel.ligencia i l'acció, al costat de la brutalitat o la força inexpressiva dels homes" (the woman's place is frequently that of intelligence and action, alongside the brutality or the inexpressive force of man), Helena Alvarado calls for "una nova revisió-interpretació" (a new revision-interpretation) of Caterina Albert (*La infanticida* 31, 35).

BOOKS

El cant dels mesos. Barcelona: n.p., 1901.
Contrallums. Barcelona: n.p., 1930.
Drames rurals. Caires vius. 1902; 1907. Barcelona: Edicions 62, 1982.
Un film. Barcelona: n.p., 1920.
La infanticida i altres textos. Col.lecció Clàssiques Catalanes 5. Barcelona: LaSal, 1984.

Jubileu: Novíssims contes inèdits. Ed. Josep Miracle. Barcelona: Selecta, 1951.
Mosaic. Barcelona: n.p., 1946.
Obres completes. Pref. Manuel de Montoliu. 1951. 2nd ed. Barcelona: Selecta, 1972.
Ombrívoles. 1904. 2nd ed. Barcelona: n.p., 1948.
Quatre monòlegs. Barcelona: n.p., 1901.
Solitud. 1905. Barcelona: Edicions 62, 1985.
Teatre inèdit: La infanticida, Verbagàlia, Les cartes, L'alcavota. Ed. Josep Miracle. Tàrrega: F. Camps Calmet, 1967.
Vida mòlta. Barcelona: Selecta, 1987.

WORKS IN BOOKS, PERIODICALS, NEWSPAPERS
El calvari d'en Mitus. La novela nova 1.3 (1917).
Giselda. La novela nova 1.18 (1917).
"Pòrtic." *Drames rurals. Caires vius.* Barcelona: Edicions 62, 1982. 177–91.

TRANSLATIONS OF HER WORKS
Soledad [Solitud]. Trans. Basilio Losada. Biblioteca de Cultura Catalana. Madrid: Alianza/Enciclopèdia Catalana, 1986.
Solitude [Solitud]. Trans. David Rosenthal. London: Readers International, 1992.

SECONDARY SOURCES
Alvarado i Esteve, Helena. "Caterina Albert/Víctor Català: Una autora motriu-matriu dins la literatura catalana de dones." Segura et al. 25–40.
———. "Víctor Català/Caterina Albert, o l'apassionament per l'escriptura." Albert, *La infanticida i altres textos* 7–35.
Badia, Lola. "*Solitud,* Novel.la." *Quaderns crema* 8 (Jan. 1984): 27–35.
Bloomquist, Gregory. "Notes per a una lectura de *Solitud.*" *Els marges* 3 (Jan. 1975): 104–07.
Capmany, Maria Aurèlia. "Epíleg: Els silencis de Caterina Albert." Albert, *Obres completes* 1851–68.
Castellanos, Jordi. "*Solitud,* novel.la modernista." *Els marges* 25 (May 1982): 45–70.
Ciurana, Montserrat. "Aportacions a l'estudi de V. Català: Unes cartes inèdites." Master's thesis. U of Barcelona, 1972.
Cortey, Maria Dolors. "Víctor Català." *Tres i molts.* Palma: Muntaner, 1977.
Garcés, Tomàs. "Conversa amb Víctor Català." *Revista de Catalunya* 3.26 (1926): 126–34. Albert, *Obres completes* 1746–55.
Miracle, Josep. *Caterina Albert i Paradís "Víctor Català."* Barcelona: Dopesa, 1978.
Möller-Soler, Maria-Lourdes. "Caterina Albert o la 'solitud' de una escritora." *Letras femeninas* 9 (1983): 11–21.
———. "El descenso liberador de Mila en *Solitud* de Caterina Albert." *Alba de Amèrica* 4.6–7 (1986): 79–91.
Oller i Rabassa, J. *Biografia de Víctor Català.* Barcelona: R. Dalmau, 1967.
Pérez, Janet. "Spanish Women Narrators of the Nineteenth Century: Establishing a Feminist Canon." *Letras peninsulares* 1.1 (1988): 34–50.
Porcel, Baltasar. "Víctor Català a contrallum." *Serra d'or* 7 (1965): 769–73.
Serrahima, Maurici. "Víctor Català (Caterina Albert)." *Dotze mestres.* Barcelona: Destino, 1973. 227–50.
Triadú, Joan. "Viatge de retorn: Víctor Català." *Serra d'or* 11 (1969): 643–45.

Vidal Alcover, Jaume. "Víctor Català, autenticitat i eficàcia." *Serra d'or* 11 (1969): 649–51.

Yates, Alan. "*Solitud* i els *Drames rurals.*" *Serra d'or* 11 (1969): 646–48.

MARYELLEN BIEDER

B Albizu, Balendiñe
(B. 1914, Zumaia, Gipuzkoa– .) Poet.

Balendiñe Albizu's groups of poems "Nere olerki txorta" (My handful of poems), "Nere bideetan" (My roads), and "Nere biotz dardarak" (My beating heart) were all written in Caracas, where she lived after fleeing Zumaia during the Spanish Civil War. Her work explores private themes, as the use of "my" in the titles indicates; love, motherhood, and homesickness are her main sources of inspiration. The style and rhyme of her poems are rooted in the Basque oral tradition.

WORKS IN BOOKS, PERIODICALS, NEWSPAPERS
"Nere olerki txorta," "Nere bideetan," and "Nere biotz dardarak." *Olerkiak.* Zarauz: Itxaropena, 1974.

MAITE GONZALEZ ESNAL

C Albó i Corrons, Núria
(B. 1930, La Garriga, Barcelona– .) Poet, novelist, and writer of children's literature.

Núria Albó has contributed to the Vic magazine *Inquietud* and actively participates in the cultural life of the Barcelona region. Her first collections of poems were *La mà pel front* (Head in hand), religious poetry in free verse, and *Díptic* (Diptych), a collaboration with Maria Angels Anglada. She then published three novels: *Fes-te repicar* (Get lost), *Agapi mou* (My love), and *Decencís* (Disenchantment). The last novel won the Vila d'Arenys prize in Barcelona in 1980, the same year her poetry collection *L'encenedor verd* (The green lighter) received the Caravel.la prize. In 1984 Albó published *Tranquil, Jordi, tranquil* (Be calm, Jordi, be calm), a novel that, like *Decencís* and *Fes-te repicar*, explores recent Catalan history. Albó has also written children's literature. *Mare, què puc fer?* (Mother, what can I do?) deals with the relation between a little girl and her environment and her various moods. *Cucut* (Cuckoo), winner of the 1981 La Xarxa prize for children's literature, is about the friendship between the protagonist and a cuckoo clock. *Mixet* describes a child's world, his family, school, friends, and his cat. *El fantasma Santiago* (Santiago the ghost), a puzzle story,

35

mixes history and fantasy; the drawings by Montserrat Tobella accentuate the ironic tale.

BOOKS

Agapi mou. 2nd ed. Barcelona: Pòrtic, 1984.
Cucut. Montserrat: L'Abadia, 1981.
Decencis. Barcelona: Magrana, 1980.
Díptic. With Maria Angels Anglada. Vic: Balmesiana, 1972.
L'encenedor verd. Barcelona: Vosgos, 1980.
El fantasma Santiago. Illus. Montserrat Tobella. 4th ed. Montserrat: L'Abadia, 1985.
Fes-te repicar. Barcelona: Destino, 1979.
Grills. Vic: Eumo, 1983.
La mà pel front. Barcelona: Pedreira, 1962.
Mare, què puc fer? Barcelona: La Galera, 1971.
Mixet. Montserrat: L'Abadia, 1985.
Tranquil, Jordi, tranquil. Barcelona: Pòrtic, 1984.

IMMA BALDOCCHI I PUIG

C Alcover Morell, Francisca
(B. ?; d. 1954, Mallorca.) Poet and journalist.

After Francisca Alcover's death in Majorca in 1954, following a long illness, her family entrusted Francisco Bonafé and Guillem Colom with revising her personal papers and selecting poems for publication. A year later they produced *Obra poética*, which contains poems dating from 1920 to 1954 and a prologue and epilogue by the editors. Although the collection includes poems written in Castilian, most are in Catalan. In his prologue Colom notes the influence of French poets and of Maria Antònia Salvà on Alcover's writing. However, religion inspired most of her work, which depicts the mysteries and dogmas of the Catholic church and celebrates local rituals. A more personal and lyrical note is found in the poems "Flores de Maria" and "Estampes Eucarístiques," which were influenced by the Catalan poet Jacint Verdaguer, and in poetry about her father's death. Alcover often establishes a personal dialogue with death and in some poems strives for spiritual perfection. In his epilogue about the poet, Bonafé tells us that "un alma había pasado por el mundo sin rozar la tierra" (a soul had passed through the world without touching the ground). Colom, too, insisted that Alcover was absorbed in "l'intim misteri del seu propi paisatge interior" (the intimate mystery of her own interior landscape) (*Obra* 200, 11). Alcover also wrote many articles for the local press on religious and patriotic topics and actively supported the national religious organization Acción Católica.

BOOKS
Obra poética. Ed. Francisco Bonafé and Guillem Colom. Sóller, Mallorca: n.p., 1955.

CRISTINA ENRIQUEZ DE SALAMANCA

C Aldrich i de Pagès, Trinitat
(B. 1863, Vullpellach, Girona; d. 1939, La Bisbal, Girona.) Poet.

A member of the lesser nobility, Trinitat Aldrich was orphaned at a young age, and her inherited income was greatly reduced by her brother's debts. She lived in one of the family homes most of her life. An interest in the humanities led her to amass an impressive library of six thousand books in several languages. A friend of important literary figures such as Jacint Verdaguer, Josep Pla, and Caterina Albert, Aldrich hosted private literary meetings (*tertulias*) in her home and directed the Jocs Florals of Girona in 1910. She advocated the right of women to participate in public life, but she also praised the poor, religious, working women of the countryside in contrast to the frivolous, high-society women of the city.

Aldrich's earliest poetry is in Castilian, but she later began to write in Catalan. Her respect for traditional values—patriotism, faith, and love—and her promotion of the Catalan language coincide with the values of the *Renaixença*. Believing that poetry is political, she associated people's emancipation with poetry and the refinement of the language. Religious themes predominate in her work, but the praise of nature and a spirit of of populism are also present. Children appear frequently in her poetry, and she meets adversity, such as the death of loved ones, with Christian resignation. Like many other nineteenth-century writers, Aldrich composed poems to celebrate family gatherings. Most of her work is lyrical, but she also wrote a few religious dramas, usually depicting the Virgin Mary intervening in human relations, which received prizes in the contests held by the Academia Mariana de Lérida in 1911 and 1927. A selection of her poems was included in Pere Lloberas's *Antologia de poetes bisbalencs de la Renaixença*, and in 1968 her nephew Jaume Vilahur edited a wide selection of her work.

BOOKS
De la terra al cel. Barcelona: Tipografía Católica, 1900.
Trinitat Aldrich: Su mundo y su obra. Ed. Jaume Vilahur. Pref. José Maria Pemán.
Barcelona: A. Núñez, 1968.

WORKS IN BOOKS, PERIODICALS, NEWSPAPERS
Poems, untitled. Lloberas 160–86.

MARISA SIGUAN BOEHMER

C Alemany i Grau, Cecília
(B. 1915, Barcelona– .) Poet.

The only information on Cecília Alemany has been found in the anthology of Catalan women's poetry *Les cinc branques*. In 1943 she professed the Order of San Benet and subsequently taught languages in the Benedictine Convent of Montserrat. According to *Les cinc branques*, some of her poems, which probably remain unpublished in the archives of the convent, are mystically inspired.

SECONDARY SOURCES
Les cinc branques 309.

CRISTINA ENRIQUEZ DE SALAMANCA

C Alibés i Riera, Maria Dolors
(B. 1941, Vidrà, Girona– .) Writer of children's literature.

With an interest in history and art, Maria Dolors Alibés writes imaginatively and in language that is simple, lively, and precise. Her works reveal a knowledge of the child's world. *Un botó ploraner* (A crying button) tells the adventures of a button, which, after many travels, becomes the first button factory in the world. The illustrations by Isidre Monés form an important part of the work. *Buscant un nom* (Looking for a name) is about an earth child and a boy from outer space. In *Màquines d'empaquetar fum i altres enginys* (Smoke-packaging machines and other clever inventions), boys and girls use their own inventions to try to solve the problems of today's world. *Tres trifulgues i una vaca* (Three difficult situations and a cow), in which a boy narrates his adventures with different animals, reflects the author's desire to bring children closer to the animal world. Alibés has also contributed sections to various textbooks for the teaching of Catalan.

BOOKS
Això són rates comptades. Barcelona: La Galera, 1986.
Un botó ploraner. Illus. Isidre Monés. Barcelona: La Galera, 1987.
Buscant un nom. 2nd ed. Barcelona: La Galera, 1982.
Joana, la bruixeta. Barcelona: Bruguera, 1980.
Màquines d'empaquetar fum i altres enginys. 6th ed. Barcelona: La Galera, 1987.
El planeta Mo. Barcelona: Cruïlla, 1988.
Si vols un androide, truca'm. Montserrat: L'Abadia, 1986.
Tres trifulgues i una vaca. Barcelona: La Galera, 1981.

IMMA BALDOCCHI I PUIG

Alícia; *see* **Tello Garcia, Alícia**

C Alonso i Bozzo, Cecília
(B. 1905, Barcelona; d. 1974, Barcelona.) Also known as Cecília
A. Mantua. Novelist and playwright.

Cecília Alonso used the name Mantua, an anagram of Manaut, the second
patronymic of her father, Gastó Alonso Manaut, who was also a dramatist.
She wrote comedies of manners and customs and enjoyed great popular
success, especially with *Ha passat una oreneta* (A swallow has passed), *La
Pepa maca* (Pretty Pepa), *La cançó de la florista* (The song of the florist),
and *La virreina* (The viceroy's wife; performed in 1965). This last work,
based on the life of the Viceroy Amat, won the Lluís Masriera prize offered
by F.E.S.T.A. (Foment de l'Espectacle Selecte i Teatre Associació). Alonso's
final important success was *Història d'un mirall* (The story of a mirror).
She also wrote unpretentious novels in Castilian for the general public.
After 1950, Alonso wrote scripts for Ràdio Barcelona in Castilian. In spite
of the simplicity of her themes, in the plays as well as in the novels,
Alonso's literary form is finely crafted.

BOOKS
El amor en silencio. Barcelona: Reguera, 1948.
Ave de paso. Barcelona: Hymsa, 1944.
Una aventura de Nochevieja. Madrid: Leex, 1947.
La cançó de la florista. Barcelona: Nereida, 1959.
Cayó una estrella. Barcelona: Bruguera, 1950.
La cinglerera de la mort: Drama en tres actes. Barcelona: Nereida, 1956.
Cupido sin memoria. Barcelona: Atlas, 1941.
La dama de Aragón. Barcelona: Bruguera, 1952.
Dos cartas de amor. Vigo: Cíes, 1951.
Ha passat una oreneta: Comèdia en tres actes. Barcelona: Bonavia, 1936.
Història d'un mirall. Barcelona: Millà, 1966.
El libro de la mujer. Barcelona: Albón, 1946.
Maria Corral (la pessebrista): Comèdia nadalenca en dos actes. Barcelona: Millà, 1961.
Una mujer de otro ambiente. Madrid: Pueyo, 1947.
Una mujer en mi vida. Vigo: Cíes, 1949.
Noche de Carnaval. Barcelona: Toray, 1948.
La novia del estudiante. Vigo: Cíes, 1949. Bilbao: Grijelmo, 1949.
Nuestro amor es imposible. Barcelona: Molino, 1944.
La Pepa maca: Novel.la. Barcelona: Millà, 1960.
La Pepa maca: Tragèdia en tres actes. Barcelona: n.p., 1955.
La princesa del Maharajá. Barcelona: Marco, 1952.
Una princesa en el camino. Barcelona: Bruguera, 1949.
Ráfaga de otoño. Barcelona: Reguera, 1948.
Un secreto entre los dos. Vigo: Cíes, 1950.

Sonata. El inquieto amor de Roberto Schumann. Evocación sentimental. Barcelona: Hymsa, 1942.
Sucedió en un taxi. Barcelona: Toray, 1949.
Su noche nupcial. Madrid: Leex, 1947.
. . . y llegó el amor. Barcelona: Amelles, 1946.

ALBINA FRANSITORRA ALENA

C Alzina i Camps, Margarida
(20th c.) Known as Guida. Poet. No biographical information available.

Anhels i petites rimes (Longings and little rhymes) are poems of love, solitude, and religious inspiration.

BOOKS
Anhels i petites rimes. Barcelona: n.p., 1983.
Bocins de silenci. Barcelona: Neoforma, 1984.

KATHLEEN MCNERNEY

G Amenedo, Cristina
(B. 1925, San Martín de Porto, Coruña– .) Poet.

Cristina Amenedo studied pedagogy, psychology, and music and taught in primary schools until she retired. She is an admirer of Juan Ramón Jiménez, Rabindranath Tagore, and Concepción Arenal. She writes in Castilian and Galician.

BOOKS
Con el tiempo y el silencio. Madrid: Torremozas, 1992.
Jerónimo Emiliani, un somasco divino. Coruña: n.p., 1985.
Mar aberto. Sada, Coruña: Castro, 1983.
La niña Saral. Coruña: n.p., 1979.
Silvo de vento mareiro. Sada, Coruña: Castro, 1988.

WORKS IN BOOKS, PERIODICALS, NEWSPAPERS
"Con el tiempo y el silencio." *Poesia Galicia 1991.* Ferrol: n.p., 1991. 9.

SECONDARY SOURCES
Precedo Lafuente, Jesús. "Nuevos poemas de Cristina Amenedo." *El ideal gallego* 24 May 1992: 13.
Quelen. "Cristina Amenedo . . . hasta Filipinas." *El ideal gallego* 28 Feb. 1991: 10.

MARIA CAMINO NOIA CAMPOS

C Amorós, Maria Lluïsa
(B. 1954, Reus, Tarragona– .) Writer of children's literature.

After studying philosophy and literature at the University of Tarragona, Maria Lluïsa Amorós worked in theater groups and in the Centre de Lectura de Reus; she also taught.

El misteri dels Farrioles (The Farrioles's mystery) is about a teenage girl who suddenly finds herself in great danger. In the midst of discovering her true parentage, she becomes involved with a young man who helps her unravel the mystery of a strange house. The dwelling seems abandoned but is run by a weird computer left behind years ago by the girl's unknown progenitor.

BOOKS
El misteri dels Farrioles. Barcelona: Cruïlla, 1987.
Poppis i Isolda. Barcelona: Cruïlla, 1986.

KATHLEEN MCNERNEY

C Amorós i Solà, Maria Eulàlia
(B. 1925, ?– .) Poet.

The only information on Maria Eulàlia Amorós i Solà has been found in *Les cinc branques*. Her poems appear in the *Antologia poètica universitària* (Anthology of university poetry) and in the *Antologia de la poesia reusenca* (Anthology of poetry from Reus).

WORKS IN BOOKS, PERIODICALS, NEWSPAPERS
". . . ," "Dual," and "En el silenci." *Antologia de la poesia reusenca* 13–15.
Poem, untitled. *Antologia poètica universitària* 9.
"Ve el dolor. . . ." *Les cinc branques* 204.

CRISTINA ENRIQUEZ DE SALAMANCA

C Andreu, Angels
(B. 1900?; d. ?) Poet and short story writer.

Angels Andreu contributed didactic stories about women's problems to the Barcelona magazine *Flames noves: Revista literària catalana*, which appeared in 1921 as the voice of the "joventuts literàries catalanes" 'literary Catalan youth.' First edited by Pere Pujol Casademont and then by Carles Sanahuja, it included a women's section called "Glosari femení" and published other Catalan women writers, such as Rosa Maria Arquimbau, Sara

Llorens de Serra, Maria Domènech de Canyellas, and Dolors Monserdà. *Flames noves* also announced Andreu's contribution to the magazine *Mujeres*, produced by the Conservatori de Bones Lletres de Barcelona and edited by Carles Sanahuja.

In 1927 Andreu published *Esplais d'un cor* (Voices from the heart), a collection of twenty-five poems. Most of these were devoted to women friends, but two were dedicated to Angel Guimerà and Jacint Verdaguer. Her poetry deals with common themes such as love, nature, and patriotic feelings. She generally uses long verses and prefers consonant rhymes.

BOOKS
Esplais d'un cor. Barcelona: Conservatori de Bones Lletres, 1927.

CRISTINA ENRIQUEZ DE SALAMANCA

C Andreu, Francisca de Paula
(B. 1889, Barcelona– .) Poet. No biographical information available.

According to *Les cinc branques*, Francisca de Paula Andreu's teachers were the Catalan poets Francesc Casas i Amigó and Jacint Verdaguer. Two poems from her unpublished collection "Recordances íntimes" (Intimate memories) were published in the magazine *Feminal*.

WORKS IN BOOKS, PERIODICALS, NEWSPAPERS
"A la Verge d'Avila" and "Llibres de la Verge." *Feminal* 73 (27 Apr. 1913).

SECONDARY SOURCES
Les cinc branques 309.

CRISTINA ENRIQUEZ DE SALAMANCA

C Andreu i Rubió, Montserrat
(B. 1929, Barcelona; d. 1974, Barcelona.) Poet.

The only information on Montserrat Andreu i Rubió appears in *Les cinc branques*. She studied at the Escuela Profesional de Asistentas Sociales and taught handicapped children. She received professional training in schools in France and Italy, particularly in Paul Haquet's Foyer de Vacances (France). Andreu won prizes in several Jocs Florals and the first prize in the Jocs Florals of Perpignan.

WORKS IN BOOKS, PERIODICALS, NEWSPAPERS
"Getsemaní." *Les cinc branques* 226.

CRISTINA ENRIQUEZ DE SALAMANCA

C Anfruns de Gelabert, Maria
(B. 1889, Cornellà de Llobregat, Barcelona; d. 1965, Cornellà de Llobregat, Barcelona.) Poet and playwright.

Maria Anfruns studied pedagogy and lace making. Her play *El retorn de la tia d'Amèrica* (The return of the American aunt), which was produced by the local religious women's organization Associació de Filles de Maria of the parish of Santa Maria de Cornellà, premiered successfully on 8 December 1933. It is a moralizing work in which painful and humble virtue is rewarded while pride and ostentation are punished. Anfruns wrote another didactic work, a Christmas play for children, *Florida de virtuts* (A flowering of virtues), which is accompanied by music. In her tragedies, a harmonic nature provides the background for the lives of humble people imbued with Christian submission. Christmas is represented as both a religious and a secular event.

Her poetry, two works published in a single volume by her husband, Angel Marsà, in 1960, is more abundant. In the prologue Marsà claims that these are her last two books, though the dates of the poems cover a long period and no previous books by her have been found. The first work, *Calaixet de blondes* (A little drawer of lace), is divided into chapters with titles related to embroidery and nature. Images from embroidery express themes of daily life; for example, everyday objects serve as companions and invokers of memories of the past. Her poetic vocabulary is at once simple and carefully chosen; she uses varied meters but tends toward long lines, especially the decasyllable with consonant rhyme. The second work, *Flaires de tardor* (Autumn fragrances), contains poems that reflect the serenity and melancholy of old age. Religious and patriotic feelings and a concern for the Catalan people, whose language and traditions Anfruns felt were losing ground, are cornerstones in this later work. Several poems alternate between past tragedies and triumphs; the deaths of two of her children are borne with religious resignation. The poem "L'amor florit," awarded the prize in the Jocs Florals of Hospitalet (Barcelona) in 1921, advises her young daughter to become a virtuous, home-loving, and patriotic woman.

BOOKS
Calaixet de blondes. Flaires de tardor. Prol. Angel Marsà. Barcelona: Bachs, 1960.
Fiesta en palacio. Barcelona: Bachs, 1965.
Florida de virtuts. El retorn de la tia d'Amèrica. Barcelona: Balcells, 1966.

MARISA SIGUAN BOEHMER

C   Anfruns i Badia, Montserrat
(B. 1958, Guardiola de Bergadà, Barcelona– .) Poet.

A resident of the Valencia area for many years, Montserrat Anfruns has participated in various performances and cultural activities as an actor and singer. She has published two books of poems: *Amb aquesta perfecta claredat* (With this perfect clarity) and *Entre les dents, fils d'aram i nicotina* (Between the teeth, threads of copper and nicotine). Her poetry revolves around the immediacy of the moment, emphasizing sensory impressions and images of childhood. Anfruns's work appears in the anthology *L'espai del vers jove* (The space for young verse).

BOOKS
Amb aquesta perfecta claredat. Valencia: Malvarrosa, 1988.
Entre les dents, fils d'aram i nicotina. València: La Forest d'Arana, 1988.

WORKS IN BOOKS, PERIODICALS, NEWSPAPERS
"Quan esclatarà," "Homenatge a Kavafis," "Epístola a Safo," and "Mancança de culpa." *L'espai del vers jove.* Mostra Poètica Jove 85. València: Conselleria de Cultura, Educació i Ciència de la Generalitat Valenciana, 1985. 71–75.

ISABEL ROBLES GOMEZ

C   Anglada d'Abadal, Maria Angels
(B. 1930, Vic, Barcelona– .) Novelist and poet.

After receiving a degree in classical languages from the University of Barcelona, Angels Anglada began teaching Latin and Greek in Figueres, Girona, in 1961. She has also offered courses in Catalan and has written essays on Catalan writers, including the poets Salvador Espriu and Josep Carner and the essayist Joan Fuster. A number of her articles have appeared in the magazines *Canigó, Hora nova, El pont, Reduccions*, and *El nou nou*.

Her first novel, *Les closes* (The enclosed fields), won the Josep Pla prize. A delicate, lyrical work, it reconstructs the life of Dolors Canal, a nineteenth-century woman who actually lived in the area of Figueres and became a local legend. Canal married the well-off Tomàs Moragues and was widowed only a few years later when he was murdered. Even though the crime was clearly committed by someone with political motivations, the innocent Canal was prosecuted. Anglada weaves together testimonies of various people, newspaper articles, letters, and other documents to create a family chronicle narrated by Canal's great-granddaughter. With the political intrigue of the 1860s as background, the novel depicts the lives of the rural landowning class of the area.

No em dic Laura (I'm not called Laura) contains three novellas. The

44

first, "També a tu, Cleanorides" (You too, Cleanorides), reveals the author's classical background and fascination with Greece; the story moves back and forth in time between the Greece of the colonels in the 1960s and a fifteenth-century Cretan village. "Flors per a Isabel" (Flowers for Isabel) returns to the Alt Empordà of *Les closes*, and its protagonists are members of the same family described in that novel. "No em dic Laura" takes place in the Vic of the author's childhood, during and after the Spanish Civil War.

The novel *Viola d'amore* relies on the world of music for its theme, structure, and characters, a trio whose voices form the narration. One trio member recalls the Moragues family of Anglada's first novel. A tense undercurrent of intrigue counterpoints the lyricism of the work. Anglada's second novel, *Sandàlies d'escuma* (Sandals of foam), won two prizes, the Lletra d'Or and the Crítica.

Anglada's collection of poems *Kyparíssia* evokes specific archeologic sites in Greece as well as mythological legends and heroes. The book also contains contemporary themes, including a celebration of the end of the Vietnam War and an elegy to Salvador Puig Antich, the Catalan political activist executed by the Franco government in 1974.

Angels Anglada has produced an anthology of poetry by classical Greek women, *Les germanes de Safo* (Sappho's sisters), which she researched and translated. Her preface to the volume is elegant and erudite. She has also collaborated with her husband, Jordi Geli, on a historical work, *Memòries d'un pagès del segle XVIII* (Memoirs of an eighteenth-century countryman).

BOOKS

L'agent del rei. Barcelona: Destino, 1991.
Artemisia. Barcelona: Columna, 1989.
El bosc de vidre. Barcelona: Destino, 1987.
Les closes. Barcelona: Destino, 1979.
Díptic. With Núria Albó. Vic: Balmesiana, 1972.
Les germanes de Safo. Barcelona: Edhasa, 1983.
Kyparíssia. Barcelona: Magrana, 1980.
Memòries d'un pagès del segle XVIII. With Jordi Geli. Barcelona: Curial, 1978.
El mirall de Narcís. Barcelona: Ausa, 1988.
No em dic Laura. Barcelona: Destino, 1985.
Sandàlies d'escuma. Barcelona: Destino, 1985.
Viola d'amore. Barcelona: Destino, 1983.

TRANSLATIONS OF HER WORKS

Los cercados [*Les closes*]. Barcelona: Destino, 1986.
El bosque de cristal [*El bosc de vidre*]. Barcelona: Destino, 1987.
"Tiryns" ["Tirynthos"], "Display Case" ["Vitrina"], and "Antigone" ["Antígona"]. *Survivors*. Selected and trans. D. Sam Abrams. Barcelona: Inst. d'Estudis Nord-Americans, 1991. 67–73.

KATHLEEN MCNERNEY

C   Anglada i Sarriera, Lola
(B. 1892/96, Barcelona; d. 1984, Barcelona.) Writer and illustrator of children's literature.

Lola Anglada is one of the best-known authors of Catalan children's literature. Her first book was *Contes del paradís* (Stories of paradise); *En Peret* (Peret) won her great acclaim. Her stories take place in settings familiar to Catalan children. As a disciple of the artist Joan Llaverias, Anglada illustrated all her works, some of which can be found in the Museum of Modern Art and the Museum of History in Barcelona. Her famous collection of dolls is located in Sitges, Barcelona, in a museum bearing her name.

BOOKS
Ametllonet. Illus. Lola Anglada. Col.lecció Follet 3. Barcelona: Políglota, 1933.
La Barcelona dels nostres avis. Illus. Lola Anglada. Barcelona: Fidel Rodríguez, 1949.
Clavelina i crisantem. Illus. Lola Anglada. Col.lecció Follet 1. Barcelona: Políglota, 1933.
Contes d'argent. Illus. Lola Anglada. Barcelona: Joan Sallent, 1934.
Contes del paradís. Pref. Millàs Raurel. Barcelona: Editorial Catalana, 1920.
Contes meravellosos. Barcelona: Fidel Rodríguez, 1947.
L'herba maleida. Barcelona: Políglota, 1933.
Margarida. Illus. Lola Anglada. Barcelona: n.p., 1928.
Martinet. Illus. Lola Anglada. Barcelona: Juventud, 1962.
La meva casa i el meu jardí. Illus. Lola Anglada. Barcelona: Obradors de Filògraf, 1958.
Les meves nines. Barcelona: Alta Fulla, 1983.
Monsenyor Langardaix. Illus. Lola Anglada. Barcelona: Alta Fulla, 1980.
Narcís. Illus. Lola Anglada. Barcelona: Políglota, 1930.
El parenostre. Barcelona: Pal.las, 1926.
En Peret. Illus. Lola Anglada. Sabadell: Joan Sallent, 1928.

TRANSLATIONS OF HER WORKS
Martin y Diana en el bosque [*Martinet*]. Trans. Aurora Díaz-Plaja. Barcelona: Juventud, 1963.

KATHLEEN MCNERNEY

C   Anonymous Catalan Medieval Woman Poet I
(2nd half of the 14th c.) Poet.

The Miscellaneous Medieval Poetical Manuscript 8 of the Biblioteca de Catalunya in Barcelona includes a love song written by a Catalan or Occitan woman. The poem, which begins "Axí cant és en muntanya deserta" (Like a song on a lone mountain), belongs to the highly rhetorical posttroubadouresque lyric tradition and was presented at an uncertain date in Toulouse's annual poetry competition. The poem was known in the fifteenth century by the poet Jordi de Sant Jordi, who included its lines 8 and 9 in his composition *Passio amoris secundum Ovidium.*

WORKS IN BOOKS, PERIODICALS, NEWSPAPERS
"Axí cant és en muntanya deserta." "Contribución al estudio de los poetas catalanes que concurrieron a las justas de Tolosa." *Boletin de la Sociedad Castellonense de Cultura* 24 (1950): 304–05.

SECONDARY SOURCES
Massó i Torrents, "Poetesses i dames intel.lectuals" 408–09.
Riquer, Martí de, and Lola Badia, eds. *Les poesies de Jordi de Sant Jordi.* Valencia: Tres i Quatre, 1984. 273.

LOLA BADIA

C Anonymous Catalan Medieval Woman Poet II
(2nd half of the 15th c.) Poet.

The Miscellaneous Medieval Poetical Manuscript 1744 of the Biblioteca de Catalunya in Barcelona contains a poem written by a woman who has lost her beloved, beginning "Ab lo cor trist envirollat d'esmay" (With a sad heart wrapped in grief). The text belongs to the posttroubadouresque lyric tradition and was also partially copied in another manuscript now in Florence.

WORKS IN BOOKS, PERIODICALS, NEWSPAPERS
"Ab lo cor trist envirollat d'esmay." "El plant amorós 'Ab lo cor trist . . .' (Assaig de restauració d'un text corrupte)." By Jaume Vidal Alcover. *Estudis de Llengua i Literatura Catalanes IV Miscel.lània Pere Bohigas.* Vol. 2. Montserrat: L'Abadia, 1982. 85–89.

SECONDARY SOURCES
Massó i Torrents, "Poetesses i dames intel.lectuals" 409–11.

LOLA BADIA

C Antonés i Grau, Eulàlia
(20th c.) Poet. No biographical information available.

Paraules (Words) is a songbook containing lyric poems by Eulàlia Antonés, which have been set to music. The themes include love, death, nature, and music itself; the rhythms are quite simple, often evoking folk songs. The book also includes one poem each by Joan Salvat-Papasseit, Carles Riba, and Salvador Espriu, also set to music.

BOOKS
Paraules. Barcelona: DIAULA, 1987.

KATHLEEN MCNERNEY

C   Anzizu i Güell, Mercè
(B. 1868, Barcelona; d. 1916, Barcelona.) Also known as Sor Eulària. Poet, biographer, and historian.

An orphan who had lost both her parents and her grandparents, Mercè Anzizu showed signs of a strong character early in life. The Reverend Jaume Collell relates in his introduction to her posthumous anthology *Poesies* that the adolescent spent her days between the church, where she was devoted to the mystical Franciscan tradition, and the palace of her famous cousin Eusebi Güell, the benefactor of Antoni Gaudí, where she found an enlightened atmosphere and a great interest in the arts. These places were the only sources of her self-taught education; she never attended school, nor did she follow any program of study.

Described as a beautiful woman, Mercè Anzizu attracted several suitors, but she rejected them all and confessed that men repelled her. A trip to Rome and Assisi and the blessing and laying on of hands by Pope Leo XII affected her deeply. Soon afterward she entered the Pedralbes monastery of the Santa Clara order in Barcelona, where she undertook all tasks, except that of prioress. She used all her personal wealth to completely restore the monastery. There she wrote *Vida de Sant Joseph Oriol* (Life of Saint Joseph Oriol); *Himne a Sant Joseph Oriol* (Hymn to Saint Joseph Oriol; later translated into Castilian) for his canonization; and *Novena*, also in his honor. *Santa Eularia de Barcelona* (Saint Eularia of Barcelona) examines the story of the patron saint of the city and the problem of historic verisimilitude and religious tradition. Anzizu published biographies of two fellow members, who had early vocations and had entered the convent against the will of their wealthy families. She organized and classified the monastery's files and published *Fulles històriques del real monestir de Santa Maria de Pedralbes* (Historical pages of the Royal Monastery Saint Mary of Pedralbes), a history of the monastery and a record of its documents in chronological order. Following the suggestions made by Pope Pius X on Gregorian chant, she harmonized and reformed her order's chants. She composed two chorus books, *Officia novissima* (1901) and *Psalterium e breviario romano*.

Anzizu published her first poems in the magazine *La veu de Montserrat* between 1886 and 1887. Her name is also mentioned in the magazine

Feminal. Two collections of poems were published posthumously: *Santa Clara de Assís* (Saint Clara of Assisi), in which she relates the background, influence, and life of the saint, the legend of her meeting with Saint Francis, and her religious faith and the idealized love between them, and the remarkable anthology *Poesies.* Collell asserts that Sor Eulària never claimed to be a poet and that her literary work flowed easily under the guidance of a quick inspiration. Her poetry, however, is rich in its variety of meters and strophes, alternating rhymes and rhythms. She uses a simple tone to describe the lives of the Holy Family and employs imagery from the mystical tradition. Her work includes such themes as love complaints, the prison of love, the anxiety to be with one's beloved, as well as poems dedicated to Saint John of the Cross and Ramon Llull and chants exalting her native country and language. She dedicated "Lo cant del sometent" (The song of the Militia) to the Virgin of Montserrat and also wrote a romance called "La conquista de Mallorca" (The conquest of Majorca). According to Collell, some of Anzizu's patriotic poems were censored and omitted from *Poesies* because of their stridency and references to well-known people. The book does not use the reformed Catalan orthography. Anzizu died of nervous exhaustion and heart trouble.

BOOKS
Apuntes biográficos de Sor Josefa Luisa Ferrer. Barcelona: Altés y Alabart, 1900.
Entre rosas y lirios: Apuntes biográficos de Sor Cecilia Boada y Gual. Barcelona: Altés y Alabart, 1914.
Fulles històriques del real monestir de Santa Maria de Pedralbes. Barcelona: Altés y Alabart, 1897.
Himne a Sant Joseph Oriol escrit ab motiu de sa canonisació. Music by Joseph Masvidal. Barcelona: Dotesio, n.d.
Notes hagiogràfiques del eminentíssim Senyor Dr. D. Salvador Caseñas y Pagès, Cardenal bisbe de Barcelona. Barcelona: Altés y Alabert, 1909.
Novena y gozos en honor de San José Oriol. 2nd ed. Barcelona: Altés y Alabart, 1910.
Poesies. Introd. Jaume Collell. Vic, Barcelona: Balmesiana, 1919.
Santa Clara de Assís: Llegendari Franciscà. Vic, Barcelona: Seràfica, 1928.
Santa Eularia de Barcelona, Verge y Martir: Vindicació de sa personalitat y breu tretzenari en llahor de la matexa Santa. Barcelona: Altés y Alabart, 1911.
Vida de Sant Joseph Oriol, escrita amb motiu de canonisació ab la novena del sant. Barcelona: Lluis Gili, 1909. 3rd ed. Barcelona: n.p., 1928.

WORKS IN BOOKS, PERIODICALS, NEWSPAPERS
"Nadala de la Verge." *Manat d'homenatge* 25–27.
"Poesies de Sor Eulària Anzizu i Vila." *La revista* 96 (Sept. 1919): 282–83.

TRANSLATIONS OF HER WORKS
Vida de San José Oriol [*Vida de Sant Joseph Oriol, escrita amb motiu de canonisació ab la novena del sant*]. Trans. J. Valls. Barcelona: Altés y Alabart, 1910.

MARISA SIGUAN BOEHMER

C   Aragay i Queralto, Martina
(B. 1920, Barcelona– .) Writer of children's literature.

Martina Aragay moved to Paris in 1947 and to Mendoza, Argentina, in 1970, where she teaches Catalan. She has traveled widely and returns to Catalonia often.

BOOKS
Ankh: Enigma al pais dels faraons. Montserrat: L'Abadia, 1981.
Karakóram. Montserrat: L'Abadia, 1986.
Rongo-Rongo. Montserrat: L'Abadia, 1983.

KATHLEEN MCNERNEY

C   Arderiu i Voltas, Clementina
(B. 1889, Barcelona; d. 1976, Barcelona.) Poet.

Clementina Arderiu studied music and languages, publishing her first book of poems in 1916, the year she married the poet Carles Riba. Her early poetry is full of joy and hope; she writes of giving birth and of love for her son and husband, at times comparing herself to a house or enclosure.

Before the Spanish Civil War Arderiu traveled through Europe; afterward she was exiled to France, crossing the border with her husband and the poet Antonio Machado. She returned to Catalonia in 1943 and contributed to the reconstruction of Catalan literary and artistic life.

Sempre i ara (Now and always) won the Joaquim Folguera prize in 1938, but war delayed publication, which followed in a semiclandestine way. The poems express Arderiu's everyday world and the new experience of war. Sadness and melancholy, anguish and fear show up vividly. She fights these feelings, seeking in solitude and peace the strength she needs. *Es a dir* (That is to say) won the Ossa Menor prize in 1958 and the Lletra d'Or prize in 1960. Although many of the poems describe nature, the sea, towns, and other places in Catalonia, these portrayals often mask a deeper search into the poet's own life and memory. Expressing a new sense of time gone by, Arderiu questions temporality in direct, urgent terms. In *L'esperança encara* (Hope still), written after her husband's death, she struggles against despair and loneliness. As the title suggests, she does find hope, mainly in the Christian faith and tradition.

There are four important collections of her work: *Poesies completes* (Complete poetry); *Antologia poètica* (Poetic anthology), a bilingual edition with translations in Castilian; *Obra poètica* (Poetic work), generally considered the definitive edition of her work; and *Contraclaror: Antologia poètica* (View against the light: Poetic anthology), which includes an insightful introduction by the poet Maria-Mercè Marcal.

50

BOOKS

L'alta llibertat. Barcelona: Editorial Catalana, 1920.
Antologia. Barcelona: La Rosa dels Vents, 1938.
Antologia poètica. Madrid: Rialp, 1961. 2nd enl. ed. Barcelona: Plaza & Janés, 1982.
Cançons i elegies. Barcelona: La Revista, 1916.
Cant i paraules. Barcelona: Lira, 1936.
Contraclaror: Antologia poètica. Introd. Maria-Mercè Marçal. Barcelona: LaSal, 1985.
Es a dir. Barcelona: Simpar, 1959.
L'esperança encara. Barcelona: Edicions 62, 1969.
Obra poètica. Barcelona: Edicions 62, 1973.
Poemes. Barcelona: Proa, 1936.
Poesies completes. Barcelona: Selecta, 1952.
Sempre i ara. Barcelona: Soc. Aliança d'Arts Gràfiques, 1946.

TRANSLATIONS OF HER WORKS

"El nombre" ["El nom"], "Canción de la hermosa confianza" ["Cançó de la bella confiança"], and "Muertes lejanos" ["Morts lluny"]. *Litoral femenino*. Ed. Lorenzo Saval and J. García Gallego. Granada: Litoral, 1986. 95–101.
"Song of Beautiful Trust" ["Cançó de la bella confiança"], "Dream or Freedom" ["Somni o llibertat"], "Presence of Death" ["Presència de la mort"], and "Now I Walk" ["Camino ara"]. *Survivors*. Selected and trans. D. Sam Abrams. Barcelona: Inst. d'Estudis Nord-Americans, 1991. 25–33.
"Song of Perfect Trust" ["Cançó de la bella confiança"] and "Distant Deaths" ["Morts lluny"]. Trans. Nathaniel Smith. *Webster Review* 12.1 (1987): 21–22.

SECONDARY SOURCES

Roig, Montserrat. "Clementina Arderiu o l'aventura de dona." *Retrats i personatges*. Barcelona: Barcanova, 1991. 35–51.

KATHLEEN MCNERNEY

Arenys, Teresa d'; *see* **Bertran i Rossell, Maria Teresa**

G Arias Castaño, Xela

(B. 1962, Sarriá, Lugo– .) Poet.

Xela Arias has lived in Vigo, Pontevedra, since she was twelve and currently works there for a publisher. Recognition of her poetry dates from 1980, when she began to publish in newspapers and magazines in Vigo. Arias was a finalist for the Losada Diéguez prize with her first book, *Denuncia do equilibrio* (Proclamation against equilibrium), and for the Esquío prize with her second, "Lilí sen pistolas" (unpublished; Lilí without pistols). Arias translated Jorge Amado's *O gato malhado* and Camilo Castelo Branco's *Amor de perdiçao* into Galician.

Her poetry reflects the struggles and the difficult daily life of a spiritual young woman who fights against solitude with poetic expression. It also portrays a ceaseless search for love. Arias depicts the city where she lives as an unfriendly industrial center offering a boring existence, and her tone is accented by melancholy and despair. Her desire to blend in socially and the impossibility of doing so are the contradictory impulses that impel her to write. She says that composing poetry helps her to study herself and to understand things. She explains:

A mi, amante de perdedores, sólo se me ocurre que escribir es una verdadera fuga hacia adelante, y digo *fuga* y digo *adelante* en un sentido musical y participativo. Porque me quedo con lo marginal, porque me interesa el tiempo en el que vivo, porque me quedo con lo marginal—esta es mi clase—con los vencidos, e intento un ritmo escrito para nuestras más íntimas conversaciones, los errores, los derroches, el amor, nuestras luchas: sólo estoy hurgando en la vida y localizando un ritmo, mi ritmo para ella. La poesía, total nada, debe ser un buen combinado de ideología y estética. Soy consciente de que mis poemas no son lineales, que hay que buscarse la vida si interesa, forzarse a entrar en ellos. Y yo lo quiero así, aquí, porque da también posibilidades a más lecturas, a variaciones rítmicas sin huir del tema. El medio, natural o urbano, me fascina. Tu y yo es lo mismo pero desgajado. Nosotros es grandísimo y nunca se parte. De esto no espero nada. Ser poeta es otra cosa más que escribir versos, y yo desprecio y me apenan los escribidores. Escribo en gallego porque estoy aquí y, desde luego, Galicia pertenece, todavía, a los derrotados. Soy irregular, mi vida tambien lo es, pero quizás consiga corregirme.

(Lecture)

(The only thing that occurs to me, lover of losers, is that writing is really a flight forward, and I say *flight* [fuga] and *forward* [adelante] in a musical and participatory sense. Because I'll take what's marginal, because I'm interested in the times I live in, because the marginal is my class—I write about the conquered. I strive for the rhythm of our intimate conversations, the mistakes, the defeats, love, our fights: I'm stirring up life and finding a rhythm, my rhythm. Poetry should be a good combination of ideology and aesthetics. I am aware that my poems are not linear, one has to look if one wants to, forcing oneself to enter in them. I want it that way, because that creates more possibilities of interpretation and rhythmic variations without changing the subject. Surroundings, urban or natural, fascinate me. *You* and *I* are the same, but disjointed. *We* is enormous and never comes apart. I don't expect anything out of this. To be a poet is not the same as writing verses, and I scorn and feel sorry for hacks. I write in Galician because I am here, and of course, Galicia still belongs to the defeated. I'm uneven, and life is, too, but perhaps I'll succeed in correcting myself.)

In a review of *Denuncia do equilibrio*, Kathleen March provides the following analysis:

The thematic allusions to fabrics and canvases, to spinning, weaving, tangling, sewing, and other women's activities are initially tied to the myth of Penelope, the wife who produced tapestries while she awaited her husband's return. The doing and undoing of this work represents a frustration accompanying the act of creation, an activity which never stabilizes in a final product. It is not difficult to see a comparison to the weaving of a literary text, particularly by female writers who, in order to do so, may have to leave their place of origin to tread city streets, metallically chaotic and alienating to them. Arias's poetic voice thus finds support in a classical female activity/condition: she suffers from feelings of fragmentation, but by not losing sight of her natural environment—that is, of nature—she begins to affirm her identity.

The fragmentary character of many verses, and on occasion of entire poems, creates a counterpart to the classical elements, for in *Denuncia do equilibrio* there is also a modern, avant-garde identity to be taken into account. Whether the technique resembles surrealism, as in certain, apparently chance juxtapositions of images, or whether it recalls cubist poetic structures such as those used by *creacionismo*, there is a unifying factor in the quest the "I" leads for love. It is a love expressed not only in terms of sensuality, but also as communication, intimate and collective. To the extent that love is achieved, so will the "I" survive.

. . . By the final poems, the voice has become "louder," more aggressive, as if accepting that there is no easy way out. In defiance, however, there is strength, and the ultimate triumph is the survival of the text, Arias's testimony to her own existence as a writer.   (272)

Arias has delved deeply into her creative resources and produced a book that merits critical attention.

53

BOOKS
Denuncia do equilibrio. Vigo: Xerais, 1986.
Tigres coma cabalos. Vigo: Xerais, 1990.

WORKS IN BOOKS, PERIODICALS, NEWSPAPERS
"Abandono xa a marcha da miña sombra" and "O vértigo enano." *Tintimán* 3 (1985): 53.
"Apátridas e outros poemas." *La voz de Galicia* 18 Oct. 1986: 6.
"Búsqueda situación límite" and "Avelaiñas." *Dorna* 8 (1985): 54–55.
"Centro de palla." *Luzes de Galizia* 2 Mar. 1986: 24.
"E di: Sabemos que fóra se perden." *Dorna* 7 (1984): 58.
"Eu cuestiono." *Dorna* 6 (1983): 22.
"O Galicia e nós." *O diario* 20 Jan. 1985: 5.
"Inmensamente os veleiros desfeitos." *Dorna* 10 (1986): 36.
Lecture. From an unpublished book presentation for *Denuncia do equilibrio.* Vigo, 1986.
"Nocturnidade." *Festa da palabra silenciada* 3 (1986): 40.
"Pérdida nos medidas." *Festa da palabra silenciada* 2 (1985): 51.
"Poem." *Festa da palabra silenciada* 4 (1987): 72.
"Poem." *Treboada* 5 June 1984: 20.
"Poems." *O diario* 18 May 1986: 9.
"Poems." *Faro de Vigo* 10 Jan. 1984: 8.
"Poems." *Faro de Vigo* 10 May 1984: 9.
"Poems." *Faro de Vigo* 5 June 1984: 6.
"Poems." *Faro de Vigo* 10 Aug. 1984: 7.
"Poems." *A nosa terra* 1982, 1984, and 1985. N. pag.
"Por anticipado recaída dun mal que impide o voo." *Faro de Vigo* 8 Mar. 1986, supp.: 4.
"Que lugar" and "Rostros pulcros." *Dorna* 11 (1987): 18–19.
"Revolta." *Sempre* 25 Apr. 1986: 7.
"Teño o cerebro cheo de fume." *Dorna* 5 (1983): 33.
"Versos novos." *Faro de Vigo* 24 June 1983: 6.
"Vin. . . ." *Dorna* 3 (1982): 26.

SECONDARY SOURCES
Alvarez Cáccamo, Alfonso. "*Denuncia do equilibrio* de Xela Arias." *Faro de Vigo* 23 Mar. 1986, "Libros" sec.
Blanco, Carmen. "Xela Arias, Ana Romaní, Pilar Cibreiro." *Literatura galega da muller.* Vigo: Xerais, 1991. 151–60.
March, Kathleen N. "Xela Arias, *Denuncia do equilibrio*, Vigo 1986." *World Literature Today* 61.2 (1987): 271–72.
Rivas, Manuel. "Xela Arias a escritora que convertiu os cabalos en tigres." *La voz de Galicia* 25 Mar. 1990.
Vázquez de Gey, Elisa. *Queimar as meigas.* Madrid: Torremozas, 1988.

MARIA CAMINO NOIA CAMPOS

C Aritzeta i Abad, Margarida
(B. 1953, Valls, Tarragona– .) Novelist.

With a degree in history and philology, Margarida Aritzeta contributed to a cultural program on the radio and worked at the Escola Universitària of Tarragona. Her fiction is imaginative and fanciful yet anchored partly in reality. Her first novel, *Quan la pedra es torna fang a les mans* (When stone turns to mud in our hands), won the Víctor Català prize. *Un febrer a la pell* (A February under the skin), winner of the Sant Jordi prize, is set against the infamous "golpazo" (coup d'état) of 23 February 1981. A man disappears, and the protagonist, realizing that this is not a "normal" disappearance, tries to figure out what happened by reconstructing the man's last days. Aritzeta offers a gallery of characters and events that form a puzzle for our times. The change of an ordinary working man into an individual capable of breaking with everything around him, including traditional sexual norms, gives rise to both comic and serious reflections. The mystery, maintained to the end, allows the reader to imagine the conclusion.

Vermell de cadmi (Cadmium red) is fantastic and realistic at the same time. It includes political cover-ups, deceptions, blunders, and manipulations of the press, as well as physical transformations of certain people into invisible beings who change gender and rapidly age. Using the devices of science fiction, the novel examines sexism and government control of people's lives by looking through the eyes of characters who have known both genders. *Grafèmia* (Grapheme), a science fiction work in the Orwellian tradition of criticizing politically motivated language, is about the destruction of writing. *Emboscades al gran nord* (Ambushes in the Great North) tells the plight of northern Canada's beleaguered Indians through the voice of Marina, a young Catalan visitor to the Montagnais tribe. *Temps de secada* (Dry season) is a collection of short stories—some realistic, others delightfully unreal, exaggerated, or absurd.

BOOKS
El cau del llop. Barcelona: Magrana, 1992.
Conte d'hivern. Valencia: Prometeo, 1980.
El darrer toro. Barcelona: Plaza & Janés, 1987.
Emboscades al gran nord. Barcelona: Edicions 62, 1985.
Un febrer a la pell. Barcelona: Edicions 62, 1983.
Grafèmia. Barcelona: Laia, 1981.
Quan la pedra es torna fang a les mans. Barcelona: Selecta, 1981.
Temps de secada. Valencia: Gregal, 1987.
Vermell de cadmi. Barcelona: Laia, 1984.
La vuelta al mundo del loro Gilberto. Barcelona: Teide, 1987.

KATHLEEN MCNERNEY

C Armangué, Josefa
(B. 1899, Barcelona– .) Autobiographer.

Josefa Armangué studied at the Sagrado Corazón religious school and married Santiago Rubió i Tudurí. Along with many members of the enlightened Catalan bourgeoisie, Armangué and her husband were forced to leave Spain for political reasons in 1935. Some of these exiles, including many women, wrote autobiographical accounts of their experiences in a war-torn Europe. Armangué's *Una família en exili: Memòries (1935–1965)* (A family in exile: Memories), a first-person account of her family's exodus, deals with different stages of their journey: the first stop in southern France, the years spent in the Auvergne, the experience of World War II, the family's move to Argentina, and their eventual return to Spain. In the first half of the work, the narrative alternates with fragments of dialogue. Spain is a recurring memory, and return was foremost in their thoughts:

> El present ens semblava que no comptava, que no tenia interès. Tots aquells dies i setmanes (i anys arribaren a ser) no eren més que un parèntesi que no comptaria. Per a nosaltres . . . allò no era vida, d'aquí la impressió que m'havien robat molts anys. Vaig sortir de Catalunya a trenta-vuit anys, i hi he tornat amb els cabells blancs. On ha passat la meva joventut?   (61)

> (The present seemed to us not to count at all, not to have any interest. All those days and weeks (and years they became) were no more than a parenthesis that was not to count. For us . . . that was not a life, thus the impression of having been robbed of many years. I had left Catalonia when I was thirty-eight, and I came back my head gray-haired. Where has my youth gone?)

Josefa Armangué's book of memories reads like a novel. Material hardships and hunger sharpened her sensitivity toward suffering people whom she never would have known had it not been for the Civil War.

Armangué described her return to Spain in the following way: "Espanya és un cavall de carreras travat. . . . Jo sentia un dinamisme que no havia sentit fàcilment a fora, però en canvi no veia els resultats d'aquest esforç. La gent no se n'adonaven, però estaven tristos" (Spain was a hobbled race horse. . . . I felt an energy that I had not felt easily when being abroad. However, I was not able to see the results of that effort. People were not aware of it, but they were gloomy)   (217).

BOOKS

Una família en exili: Memòries (1935–1965). Pref. Marià Manent. Barcelona: Curial, 1981.

CRISTINA ENRIQUEZ DE SALAMANCA

C Armengol i Altayó de Badia, Agnès
(B. 1852, Sabadell, Barcelona; d. 1934, Sabadell, Barcelona.)
Poet.

A member of the well-to-do bourgeoisie of Sabadell, Agnès Armengol received an education in several fields. As a student of literature in France, she became a disciple of the writer Gaston Cannet, a member of the French Academy. In her youth, Armengol contributed to cultural and literary journals of the *Renaixença*, won various prizes, and participated in nationalistic causes, trying especially to incorporate women in the movement. One of her principal interests was the purification of the Catalan language, which had still not been standardized, and she traveled to small towns in the provinces to research genuine Catalan words. After marrying an industrialist, Armengol continued her literary endeavors and cultivated interests in art and music, composing songs herself.

Her first two books of poetry, *Lays* (Lays) and *Ramell de semprevives* (Bouquet of evergreens), were dedicated to the memory of her mother and signed Agnès Armengol de Badia. She did not use her husband's name, de Badia, in later books. The poem *Redempció* (Redemption), set in the pre-Christian Roman Empire, is written almost entirely in hendecasyllables and decasyllables. A corrected version appeared in 1925 with a prologue by Josep Lleonart, who praises the simplicity and erudition of the author, as well as her search for the right word and the avoidance of repetition. *Rosari antic* (Antique rosary), with a prologue by the poet Anton Busquets i Punset, is dedicated to tradition and faith; a certain didacticism can be seen in some poems. Her unpublished book "Patriòtiques" was lost during the Spanish Civil War.

Armengol's poetry is perfect in form, executed with extraordinary skill, and never sentimental. The French influence is apparent in her work, and she occasionally uses gallicisms.

BOOKS
Els dies clars: Petits poemes. Pref. Anton Navarro. Sabadell, Barcelona: Biblioteca Sabadellenca, 1925.
Goigs a llaor de Nostra Dona de la Salut de Sabadell. Sabadell, Barcelona: Biblioteca Sabadellenca, 1927.
Lays. Sabadell, Barcelona, 1879.
Ramell de semprevives. Sabadell, Barcelona: Revista de Sabadell, 1891.
Redempció. Sabadell, Barcelona: Biblioteca Sabadellenca, 1912. 2nd ed. Prol. Josep Lleonart. Sabadell: Biblioteca Sabadellenca, 1925.
Rosari antic. Prol. Anton Busquets i Punset. Sabadell, Barcelona: Biblioteca Sabadellenca, 1926.
Sabadellenques. Sabadell, Barcelona: Biblioteca Sabadellenca, 1925.

WORKS IN BOOKS, PERIODICALS, NEWSPAPERS
"Poesies." *Lectura popular* 9: 353.

SECONDARY SOURCES
Tous Forrellad de Cirera, Pilar. *Agnès Armengol: Biografía.* Sabadell, Barcelona: Joan Sallent, 1957.

ALBINA FRANSITORRA ALENA

C Arnaiz Guillén, Maria Josep

(20th c.) Poet. No biographical information available.

BOOKS
De la lliçó de viure. Barcelona: El Tinter, 1982.

KATHLEEN MCNERNEY

C Arnavat, Maria Misericòrdia

(20th c.) Poet. No biographical information available.

In 1982, Maria Misericòrdia Arnavat published a collection of poems, *Diàlegs a una sola veu* (Dialogues in one voice). According to the author, the title came from her teaching experience, which was predisposed to one-sided conversations. The book is divided into three sections: "Diàlegs a una sola veu," "Corbes ovalades" (Ovaled curves), and "Paral.lelisme" (Parallelism). The first section deals with common poetic topoi, such as loneliness and the transience of life in contrast to the permanence of things. "Corbes ovalades" deals with the existence of another "space," unusual places, and strange structures. In "Paral.lelisme," a series of brief poems written in a concise language, the poet undertakes a spiritual journey. In the poem "Poesia descriptiva en monosíl.labs" (Descriptive poetry in monosyllables), Arnavat experiments with language, and "Punts de diagrama/del blanc al blau" (Diagram points/white to blue) completes a collection that, the author says, explores the everyday world.

BOOKS
Diàlegs a una sola veu. Reus, Tarragona: n.p., 1982.

CRISTINA ENRIQUEZ DE SALAMANCA

C Arnillas de Font, Maria Amparo

(Barcelona; active in 1880s.) Playwright.

Maria Amparo Arnillas wrote plays in both Catalan and Castilian during the Romantic movement; her plays in Catalan formed part of the *Renaixença. Pascual y los saboyanos* (1878; Pascual and the Savoyans) and a religious work, *San Dominguito del Val* (Little Saint Dominic of Val), are Castilian works. Her play in Catalan verse, *Lo patge de la comtessa* (The countess's page), reveals more breadth. This three-act drama premiered with great success, according to the published version, at the Teatre Romea on 26 March 1888. Charles V and the wars in the Low Countries form the background, and both are glorified. The plot involves a love story between a countess and a troubadour, the revelation that the protagonist is the son of a marquis, and the unmasking of an evildoer, themes popular in the theater of the day and rooted in the tradition of historical drama. The poetry is octosyllabic with alternating rhyme, and the archaic language is typical of its epoch and genre. Arnillas dedicated the work to Frederic Soler, known as Pitarra, who at the time was regarded as the innovator of Catalan theater. Josep Yxart, the best-known contemporary critic, indicated that this play was one of the most important and successful works of the era.

BOOKS

El Cristo de Mont Calvari: Comedia en tres actos y en verso. Barcelona: Bastinos, 1887. 2nd ed. Barcelona: Perelló y Vergas, 1915.

El ejemplo: Comedia en dos actos. Barcelona: Bastinos, 1886. 2nd ed. Barcelona: Bastinos, 1893.

El martir de Zaragoza: Drama en un acto. 5th ed. Barcelona: Librería Salesiana, 1941.

Pascual y los saboyanos: Comedia en un acto. 3rd ed. Barcelona: Bastinos, 1897. 4th ed. Barcelona: Bastinos, 1908.

Lo patge de la comtessa: Drame en tres actes y en vers. Barcelona: Luis Tasso y Serra, 1888.

San Dominguito del Val: Drama en un acto. Barcelona: Bastinos, 1888. 3rd ed. Barcelona: Bastinos, 1911.

MARISA SIGUAN BOEHMER

C Arquimbau, Rosa Maria

(B. 1910, Barcelona– .) Also known as Rosa de Sant Jordi.
Novelist, journalist, and playwright.

A well-known journalist and novelist during the 1930s, Rosa Maria Arquimbau went into exile after the Spanish Civil War, and her professional life suffered from the limited diffusion of Catalan literature after the war. She contributed to many leftist publications, and the documentary nature of her work is of great interest. Strong character analysis and a tendency toward escapism distinguish her novels and plays.

The protagonist of *Història d'una noia i vint braçalets* (The story of a girl and twenty bracelets) tells her story by linking her many bracelets with certain events in her life. The liberated protagonist of *Home i dona* (Man and woman), who is separated from her husband, reveals herself through a series of letters written to her best friend. In *Quaranta anys perduts* (Forty years lost), a young dressmaker working in a poor neighborhood suddenly becomes famous and decides what the aristocrats should wear. She passes easily from her proletarian origins to her new status. Arquimbau won the Joan de Santamaria prize for *L'inconvenient de dir-se Martines* (The inconvenience of being called Martines) and collaborated with Josep Maria Poblet on an unpublished play, "Estimat Mahomed," about the problem of Catalan emigration to the United States.

BOOKS
"L'amor i el dimoni." Ms. 82–1.406. Inst. de Teatre Català.
Es rifa un home. Barcelona: Bonavia, 1935.
Història d'una noia i vint braçalets. Barcelona: Llibreria Catalònia, 1934.
Home i dona. Barcelona: Quaderns Literaris, 1936.
L'inconvenient de dir-se Martines. Barcelona: Nereida, 1950.
La pau es un interval. Barcelona: Pòrtic, 1970.
Quaranta anys perduts. Barcelona: Club, 1971.

KATHLEEN MCNERNEY

Arritokieta; *see* **Azpeitia Gómez, Julene**

B   Artola, Rosario
   (B. 1889, ?; d. ?) Poet. No biographical information available.

Rosario Artola's poems, "Naigabea eta Atsegiya" (Joy and sorrow) and "Nere gitartxoari" (To my guitar), were collected in *Mila euskal olerki eder* (1954; One thousand beautiful Basque poems).

WORKS IN BOOKS, PERIODICALS, NEWSPAPERS
"Naigabea eta Atsegiya" and "Nere gitartxoari." Onaindia, *Mila euskal olerki eder* 358–59.

MAITE GONZALEZ ESNAL

C   Arumí i Bracons, Anna
   (B. 1952, Barcelona– .) Fiction writer.

Anna Arumí left her studies early and spent time in Paris and London. IIer jobs have varied greatly—from working in arts and crafts to training dogs. *La nina russa* (The Russian doll), her first book, was a finalist for the Sonrisa Vertical prize for erotic literature. The title refers to the wooden dolls that fit inside one another. In this collection of short stories and vignettes about sex, Arumí explores various preferences, obsessions, complexes, and fantasies from masculine and feminine points of view.

BOOKS
La nina russa. Illus. Perico Pastor. Barcelona: Tusquets, 1986.

KATHLEEN MCNERNEY

C   Avellaneda i Camins, Laura
(20th c.) Poet. No biographical information available.

Sense trascendència (Unimportant), a collection of poems written between 1952 and 1982, deals with religion and the family.

BOOKS
Sense trascendència. Barcelona: Ferrer, 1983.

KATHLEEN MCNERNEY

C   Aymerich i Lemos, Sílvia
(B. 1957, Barcelona– .) Translator, poet, and short story writer.

With training in several languages and literatures as well as a degree in biology from the University of Barcelona, Sílvia Aymerich brings a diversified background to her writing. She has translated into Catalan John Ruskin's *The Elements of Drawing*, Bram Stoker's *Dracula*, work by Isaac Asimov, and other titles. She has given a course on medical terms in English and worked in television as an interpreter of French. Currently she teaches a variety of courses in a school in the Maresme, near Barcelona.

Aymerich has traveled widely, and in her collection *La meva Europa* (My Europe) she devotes most of the poems to cities. She is especially attracted to those she identifies as marginal, such as Edinburgh, which she sees as defeated because of England's domination. On the other hand, she is critical of rich cities, such as Lucerne, which Aymerich accuses of false neutrality while admiring its beauty. *Poemes de destemps i d'alba nua* (Poems out of time and naked dawn) contains poems about love and a few about the act of writing. In the untitled first poem, she describes the difficult relationship between herself and words:

Si deixen d'encisar-me els   (If words ever stop fascinating
    mots   me,

els trec la closca	I'll knock their blocks off
... descobriré	... I'll discover
el gust intern,	their inner taste,
—insípid o groller—,	—insipid or crude—
el plany íntimament cobert,	the intimately hidden lament,
el tendre esclat	the tender blooming of their
del seu secret.	secret.)

The slim volume also contains illustrations by the author.

BOOKS
Berlin Zoo. Barcelona: Magrana, 1991.
La meva Europa. Barcelona: Mall, 1985.
Poemes de destemps i d'alba nua. Barcelona: Dalmau, 1981.

WORKS IN BOOKS, PERIODICALS, NEWSPAPERS
"Dualitat" and several untitled poems. Colet i Giralt 17–23.

KATHLEEN MCNERNEY

C Aznar Rovira, Maria Teresa

(B. 1955, Arenys de Mar, Barcelona– .) Poet. No biographical information available.

BOOKS
Poemes de pels i de silenci. Mataró, Barcelona: Agrupación Hispana de Escritores, 1981.

KATHLEEN MCNERNEY

B Azpeitia Gómez, Julene

(B. 1888, Zumaia, Gipuzkoa; d. ?) Known as Arritokieta. Short story writer.

Julene Azpeitia taught in several villages and wrote a weekly column called "En favor de los niños vascos" (In favor of Basque children) for the Bilbao newspaper *Euzkadi*. She published manuals on teaching reading and writing and in 1933 won the Kirikiño prize for the short story "Euli baten edestia" (A fly's song). In 1959–60 she won the Biarritz prize for the short story "Goizeko Izarra" (Morning star) and a second prize for the collection "Auntza Baratzan" (The goat in the garden). In 1961 Azpeitia received a prize from the Academia de la Lengua Vasca (Academy of the

Basque Language) for her collection of one hundred short stories, *Amandriaren altzoan* (On godmother's lap). Her short, fluid narratives have a marked *costumista* flavor, and the characters are deeply rooted in Basque rural life. Azpeitia describes the difficulties experienced by emigrants returning from America, disagreements and disputes between neighbors, and, in "Odolak odolari dei" (The call of blood) and "Martxela," the doubts of a young woman on whether to marry for love or money. In "Krabelin gorriak" (Red carnations) Azpeitia included rhyming poems following the Basque oral tradition, themes from folk literature, the farewell of a boy departing for military service and the letters he writes to his girlfriend, and religious songs for the female congregations of Mary. *Zuentzat* (As your own) is a collection of essays and stories for children.

BOOKS
Amandriaren altzoan. San Sebastián: Kuliska Sorta, 1961.
Zuentzat. San Sebastián: Soc. Guipuzcoana de Ediciones y Publicaciones, 1974.

WORKS IN BOOKS, PERIODICALS, NEWSPAPERS
"Auntza Baratzan." *Karmel.* N.p.: Padres Carmelitas, 1959–60.
"Odolak odolari dei," "Martxela," and "Krabelin gorriak." *Egan* (1969–70).

MAITE GONZALEZ ESNAL

C Balaguer Julià, Marta
(B. 1953, Barcelona– .) Writer of children's literature.

After receiving a degree in art history from the University of Barcelona, Marta Balaguer studied printmaking at the Escola d'Arts i Oficis of Barcelona and puppetry at the Institut de Teatre of Barcelona. Since 1978 she has been an illustrator, especially of books for children and young people. Balaguer has contributed to the magazine *Cavall fort*, presented puppet shows and Chinese shadow plays in the schools, taught art, and illustrated textbooks and popular stories. In 1980 she participated in the illustrators' exhibition at the Fair of Bologna and in 1982 in the Mostra d'Il.lustradors, an itinerant exhibit of Catalan illustrators. In 1985 Balaguer was awarded the Apel.les Mestres prize for her illustrations of David Cirici's story *Llibre de vòlics, laquidambres i altres espècies* (The book of *vòlics, laquidambres* and other species).

Balaguer has also written a series of books. The collection *Pau i Pepa* (Paul and Josie) offers young children their first images of the world around them. *Adeu, bon viatge!* (Goodbye, have a good trip!) and *En Baldovino s'enamora* (Baldovino falls in love) both feature animals as characters. *En Jaumet de les xanques* (Jamie on stilts) is a story about daily life in a village.

63

BOOKS

Adeu, bon viatge! Montserrat: L'Abadia, 1981.
En Baldovino s'enamora. Barcelona: Teide, 1987.
En Jaumet de les xanques. Montserrat: L'Abadia, 1982.
Pau i Pepa. Illus. Montserrat Ginestà. Montserrat: L'Abadia, 1984.

ANNA GASOL I TRULLOLS

C Ballester Figueras, Margarita
(B. 1942, Barcelona– .) Poet.

After earning a degree in history, Margarita Ballester studied psychology in Paris during the school year 1968–69. She currently teaches history in a Barcelona high school. Ballester has recently devoted her free time to writing poetry, and her first effort won the Rosa Leveroni prize in 1988. The collection, *L'infant i la mort* (The child and death), explores time and death. Often erudite, Ballester is inspired by the works of Emily Dickinson, Benedict de Spinoza, Franz Schubert, and Giacomo Leopardi. In her work, the poet gives herself up to the poetic act: "Les paraules saben més del que sé / per mi mateixa sense dir, / vénen de lluny i tenen la memòria impresa" (Words know more than I do / for myself without saying them, / they come from afar and have their memory imprinted) (*L'infant* 14). Ballester has also contributed to the poetry magazines *Reduccions* and *Negra & cendra.*

BOOKS

L'infant i la mort. Barcelona: Columna, 1989.

TRANSLATIONS OF HER WORKS

"Elegies to a Dead Poet" ["Elegies a un poeta mort"] and "They Are My Friends" ["Són els amics"]. *Survivors.* Selected and trans. D. Sam Abrams. Barcelona: Inst. d'Estudis Nord-Americans, 1991. 93–99.

KATHLEEN MCNERNEY

C Balzola, Asun
(20th c.) Writer of children's literature. No biographical information available.

BOOKS

La Christie i la caçadora de l'Indiana Jones. Barcelona: Cruïlla, 1987.
Santina el pastisser. Barcelona: Destino, 1986.

KATHLEEN MCNERNEY

Baneta, Sor; *see* Mas Pujol, Margalida

C Barbal i Farré, Maria
(B. 1949, Tremp, Lleida– .) Novelist and short story writer.

Maria Barbal left her hometown to study in Barcelona when she was fifteen, but her prose contains many words and expressions from her native Pyrenees. Her novel *Pedra de tartera* (Scree stone) is about a woman from a mountain village, but it shares many characteristics with Mercè Rodoreda's urban novel *La plaça del Diamant* (1962; The time of the doves), among them, the first-person narration by an ordinary working-class woman; the historical setting of the Republic (1931–36) and the Spanish Civil War (1936–39), in which the protagonist loses her husband; the rearing of children in difficult circumstances; and the simple, elegant flow of the narrative. Though not as rigorous as Rodoreda's work, the novel is lyrical and moving, and the understated tone accounts in great part for its popularity.

The stories in *La mort de Teresa* (The death of Teresa) are also set in the villages of the Pyrenees, where hard work and loneliness contrast with the beauty of mountain life. The characters are familiar types—shepherds, adolescents, old people, the crazy lady of the village, the glamorous city woman on vacation—but Barbal's style keeps them from becoming clichés.

BOOKS
Càmfora. Barcelona: Magrana, 1992.
Mel i metzines. Barcelona: Magrana, 1990.
La mort de Teresa. Barcelona: Empúries, 1986.
Pedra de tartera. Barcelona: Laia, 1985. 12th ed. Empúries, 1987.

KATHLEEN MCNERNEY

C Bardolet i Puig, Antònia
(B. 1877/79, Vic, Barcelona; d. 1956, Borredà, Girona.) Poet and fiction writer.

Because of her mother's death, Antònia Bardolet i Puig left school at a young age to take care of the family business. Bardolet published poems and fiction in Vic's magazine *Gazeta montanyesa* and short stories in the magazine *Feminal*. Some of her works won prizes in the Jocs Florals. She studied astronomy in the observatory of her friend Joseph Pratdesaba in Vic, and in 1910, the year of Halley's comet, she sent several notes about the Perseid meteor shower to the Astronomy Society of Barcelona. Bardolet spoke French and English and corresponded with experts in Esperanto all over Europe. She traveled extensively in France, England, Italy, and Belgium and lectured about these journeys.

Siluetes femenines (Feminine silhouettes) collects four short stories and one travel notebook. The first story, "Desilusió" (Disillusion), describes the feelings of a young girl facing her mother's death and her father's remarriage. The cowardice of the surrounding adults leaves the child in a situation in which the truth is never told and her sorrow is never resolved. "Resignació crudel" (Cruel resignation) shows how a man's infidelity causes his wife great pain and, ultimately, her death. The third story, "Justicia de Deu" (Justice of God), is set in the Catalan countryside and deals with the conflicts between a woman and her daughter-in-law, a theme treated by later women writers, such as Walda Pla in *Salt d'Euga* (1961; The mare's jump) and Maria Angels Anglada in *Les closes* (1979; The enclosed fields). In the last story, "Avaricia" (Greed), the female character personifies this vice and counterbalances the absurd generosity of her brother, the chaplain of a small town. The travel notebook, an account of Bardolet's trips through England, France, and Belgium, reveals her admiration for English women who fight for their rights.

Antònia Bardolet i Puig translated M. E. Henry Ruffin's *The Defender of Silence* into Catalan.

BOOKS
Siluetes femenines. Vic: Gazeta Montanyesa, 1913.

WORKS IN BOOKS, PERIODICALS, NEWSPAPERS
"Cor de mare." *Feminal* 58 (28 Jan. 1912).
"Justicia de Deu" and "Resignació crudel." *Lectura popular*, vol. 21.
"Reliquies d'àngel." *Feminal* 128 (Dec. 1917).
"Rondalla de la desobediencia castigagda." *Feminal* 113 (Aug. 1916).
"Rondalla de la veritat y la mentida." *Feminal* 89 (Aug. 1914).
"Rondalla del sabi endevinayre del pensament." *Feminal* 72 (30 Mar. 1913).

CRISTINA ENRIQUEZ DE SALAMANCA

Barnet, Maria Teresa; *see* **Vernet i Real, Maria Teresa**

C Barrera, Maria Rosa
(20th c., Barcelona.) Writer of children's literature. No biographical information available.

Tretzevents and *Cavall fort* have published some of her stories.

BOOKS
El capgirell. Montserrat: L'Abadia, 1985.
Just a l'alra part del món. Montserrat: L'Abadia, 1982.

KATHLEEN MCNERNEY

C Bartre, Llúcia

(B. 1881/91, Ille-sur-Têt, France; d. ?) Also known as Lucie Bartre. Playwright and poet.

According to *Les cinc branques* and the *Diccionari de la literatura catalana*, Llúcia Bartre, who was Mestra (Master) in Gai Saber de la Ginesta d'Or i del Felibridge (a writers' association founded in 1854 in Avignon, France), published four volumes of plays, which included comedies of manners, short farces, and sketches: *Primers pasos* (1931; First steps), *Retalls* (1933; Remnants), *Rialles* (1942; Laughter), and *Els set pecats capitals* (1948; The seven capital sins). The first three, however, have not been located in major libraries. *Les cinc branques* also mentions that Bartre published in French and that her plays were often staged by amateur companies.

Els set pecats capitals contains seven plays that, written in a friendly but ironic tone, portray the seven capital sins—pride, greed, lust, anger, gluttony, sloth, and envy. All the plays have a parallel structure in which the protagonist, who personifies one of the sins, is made fun of by the other characters. Bartre sets the dramas in rural Roussillon and praises the customs, values, and beauty of this part of France. She uses the Catalan spoken in the region and infuses the vocabulary with gallicisms. In "Les fades del Rosselló" (The fairies of Roussillon) the author constructs an allegory around nature: the Mediterranean Sea, the mountains, lakes, caves, woods, and vineyards are all symbolized by fairies. The text of the play includes ballet choreography to the song "Muntanyes Regalades" (Given mountains).

BOOKS
Els set pecats capitals. Perpignan, Fr.: Imprimerie du Midi, 1948.

WORKS IN BOOKS, PERIODICALS, NEWSPAPERS
"Lex xipoteres." *Les cinc branques* 80.

SECONDARY SOURCES
Molas and Massot i Muntaner 76.

CRISTINA ENRIQUEZ DE SALAMANCA

Bartre, Lucie; *see* **Bartre, Llúcia**

C Bassa de Llorens, Maria Gràcia

(B. 1883, Llofriu, Girona; d. 1961, Buenos Aires, Argentina.) Known as Gràcia B. de Llorens. Poet.

Maria Gràcia Bassa studied at the Escola d'Institutrius i Altres Carreres per la Dona in Barcelona. One of her teachers was the folklorist Rossend

Serra i Pagès, who fought to educate Catalan women and to make them missionaries of Catalanism. He later wrote a short biographical note about Bassa in her poetry collection in *Lectura popular*. Bassa joined the Centre Excursionista de Catalunya and along with other women writers, such as Sara Llorens, Adelaida Ferré i Gomis, Joana Vidal, and Maria Baldó, formed its folklore section. She did not, however, publish any folkloric work herself. She taught in rural schools and contributed poetry to the Barcelona magazine *Feminal* from 1907 to 1917.

Maria Gràcia Bassa married Joan Llorens i Carreres and then moved to Argentina, where she lived until her death. Some of her poetry appeared in South American journals, and in 1933 she published *Branca florida* (Flowery branch). Her major sources of inspiration are the Catalan countryside and a strong patriotism, although she rarely refers to specific places, traditions, or symbols of Catalonia. She also writes about maternity: "l'infant trem en ma entranya sotragada" (the child trembles in my shocked womb); "en contemplar la imatge de l'infant a contrallum, jo em sento el clam del llinatge" (looking at the child's image against the light, I feel deep down the voice of the lineage) (*Branca* 25, 39). In her poetry Bassa uses blank verse and a variety of stanzas and refers to Latin American poets, such as Rubén Darío and Delmira Agustini.

BOOKS
Branca florida. Barcelona: Llibreria Catalònia, 1933.
Esplays en la llunyania. Vol. 20 of *Lectura popular.*

WORKS IN BOOKS, PERIODICALS, NEWSPAPERS
"A ma germaneta Montserrat." *Feminal* 50 (28 May 1911).
"Angèlica." *Feminal* 11 (23 Feb. 1908).
"Anyoransa." *Feminal* 27 (27 June 1909).
"La dona catalana en l'Argentina." *Feminal* 64 (28 July 1912) and 94 (31 Jan. 1915).
"Entrada d'hivern." *Feminal* 126 (28 Oct. 1917).
"Penèlope." *Feminal* 127 (25 Nov. 1917).

CRISTINA ENRIQUEZ DE SALAMANCA

C Bassas i Biarnés, Elisabet
(B. 1956, Barcelona– .) Poet.

After practicing as a psychologist for three years, Elisabet Bassas returned to the University of Barcelona to study Catalan philology. She also attended the French School in Barcelona and began publishing poetry in the early 1980s, winning the Misión prize in Olot, Girona, in 1980.

Ombra oscil.lant (Oscillating shadow) is divided into four parts. The first and third, "Bressol d'ànsies" (Cradle of wishes) and "Desamor" (Lack of love), are dedicated to human relationships. The second, "Els mots, al besllum" (Conjectured words), focuses on poetry and words. In the book's brief introduction, the poet claims to identify most closely with the last section, "Per a la conquesta del goig" (To achieve joy), in which an optimistic tone prevails as she persists in the pursuit of happiness. This section is also the most visual, as the poet plays with mirages and contrasts light and darkness.

BOOKS
Ombra oscil.lant. Barcelona: Dalmau, 1981.

WORKS IN BOOKS, PERIODICALS, NEWSPAPERS
"Vigília," "Cambra entrefosca," and untitled poems. Colet i Giralt 25–31.

KATHLEEN MCNERNEY

C Bassas i Edo, Lliberta
(B. 1927, Barcelona— .) Journalist, poet, novelist, and short story writer.

Lliberta Bassas began writing poetry in Catalan when she was very young, but her first publications are novels written in Castilian: *Tierra parda* (Dark land), *El último hijo del sol* (The last son of the sun), and *Bosquejos* (Outlines). Her monograph "La mujer en la vida y la obra de don Juan Valera" (Women in the life and work of Juan Valera) received the Juan Valera prize in 1962, and the following year she won the Sant Martí prize.

Lliberta Bassas contributes to several journals. Her only book in Catalan, *Vi aigualit i altres historietes* (Watered-down wine and other stories), is a series of narratives, greatly varied in length, tone, and theme. "Aligues i pardals" (Eagles and sparrows), a story with a moral, portrays a girl who wants to marry up in society but instead becomes a maid; "Crepuscle" (Sunset) depicts an aging actor who feels she is a failure as a woman and as an actor; "Deslleialtat" (Disloyalty), told in epistolary form, is about plagiarism; and "200X," a science fiction tale, revolves around questions of courage or its appearance. In her most fanciful story, "Alfa-omega-alfa," Bassas uses the four basic elements—earth, fire, water, and air—to create a pure spirit, while examining traditional gender roles.

BOOKS
Bosquejos. Barcelona: Llesuy, 1959.
Kiwa. Barcelona: Llesuy, 1960.
Mi primer Sopena. Barcelona: Sopena, 1987.
Tierra parda. Barcelona: Rumbos, 1957.

El último hijo del sol. Barcelona: Llesuy, 1958.
Vi aigualit i altres historietes. Barcelona: Dalmau, 1978.

WORKS IN BOOKS, PERIODICALS, NEWSPAPERS
"Alfa-omega-alfa." Colet i Giralt 33–39.

KATHLEEN MCNERNEY

C   Bayona i Codina, Mercè
(B. 1903, ?; d. 1972, ?) Poet. No biographical information available.

BOOKS
Poesia. Girona: Palaverd, 1989.

KATHLEEN MCNERNEY

Bell-Lloch, Maria de; *see* **Maspons i Labrós, Maria del Pilar**

C   Bel Oleart, Joana
(B. 1965, Barcelona– .) Poet and short story writer. No biographical information available.

The short stories in *Parèntesi* (Parenthesis) have a common theme and style and form a collage of words. The title story won the 1986 Don.na prize.

BOOKS
Parèntesi. Barcelona: LaSal, 1987.
El risc de l'aigua i el silenci. Valencia: Eliseu Climent, 1990.

SHEILA MCINTOSH

Beltrán, Cecília; *see* **Solsona i Querol, Josefina**

C   Benet Roque, Amèlia
(B. 1914, Barcelona– .) Writer of children's literature.

In the late 1960s and early 1970s, when adequate educational books for children were lacking, Amèlia Benet Roque published a series of books in very simple language, about items that enter into a child's daily life—like vegetables, bread, and milk—whose origins might be especially difficult for city children to understand. She has also written stories with children as the protagonists. They include "Històries de l'Ivan" (Tales of Ivan); *Nit a la barca* (Night on a boat), about Christmas night; and *El carter robat* (The postman was robbed), about the pranks and capers of young people in groups.

BOOKS

El carter robat. Montserrat: L'Abadia, 1981.
Jo tinc un cavallet. Barcelona: Hymsa, 1980.
En Miquel a l'hivern. Barcelona: Juventud, 1980.
La Mireia a la tardor. Barcelona: Juventud, 1969.
Nit a la barca. Barcelona: La Galera, 1983.
Voleu saber com sóc? Barcelona: Hymsa, 1981.
En Xut és el meu gos. Barcelona: Hymsa, 1980.

ANNA GASOL I TRULLOLS

C Beneyto Cunyat, Maria
(B. 1925, València– .) Poet, novelist, short story writer, and literary critic.

Maria Beneyto spent her early childhood in Madrid, until the outbreak of the Spanish Civil War in 1936 sent her family back to Valencia. She has contributed book reviews and short stories to the Valencia journal *Levante* and has also published in Spanish and Venezuelan newspapers. Beneyto writes in Catalan and Castilian and has been awarded numerous literary prizes for her work.

In her first book of poetry, *Canción olvidada* (Forgotten song), Beneyto compares herself to a snail in whose shell all voices are echoed. Alert to the world around her, as well as to her private perceptions and experiences, she tries to find a meaning on which to base her own personal truth. She employs a variety of rhymes, verses, and stanzas to explore these outer and inner worlds. The panorama she sees is one of contradiction, and it persists throughout Beneyto's writings: passion and youth undermined by time, and happiness limited by reality.

Beneyto's early vacillations between immanence and transcendence are resolved in a full commitment to the here and now, the total "arraigo," present since her second book of poems, *Eva en el tiempo* (Eve-in-time). Her voice reveals a primitive attachment to nature and an awareness of its temporal and spatial limitations. In "La penitente" (The penitent), one of the most important poems in the book, the female protagonist decides to leave her corner—"Las menudas cosas femeninas del hogar" (the minute feminine things of the home)—in order to participate in the male-dominated center of society. In the end she finds herself rejected and condemned to continue her ceaseless questioning.

Beneyto attests to the pluralism of truth, calling herself a plural being in *Criatura múltiple* (Multiple being), her third book of poems. Man (and society) secludes woman within the "beautiful" confines of the home, but Beneyto asks for reintegration into a world where both sexes will form a union in which no one is excluded and the uniqueness of each is preserved.

In *Poemas de la ciudad* (City poems), Beneyto is nostalgic for a nature that has been diminished by an overly technological world. *Vida anterior* (Previous life) returns to the contradictory experiences already explored in *Canción olvidada*. Using childhood memories, Beneyto describes herself as a "mixed being," a receptacle of opposites: she is the suffering earth of urban Madrid, yearning for the freedom of the Valencian sea; she dreams of a fantasy world but is confronted with the misery of her milieu; her childhood games are set against the background of the Civil War; and the coming of spring appears simultaneously with the death of her father.

Many of these experiences are also explored in her prose works. In the six short stories in *La promesa* (The promise), the various protagonists are trapped in a mediocre existence from which an unexpected occurrence promises them a more fulfilling life. But reality constantly thwarts that promise and reminds them of the limitations of the world. In *Antigua patria* (Ancient fatherland) the protagonist finds her dream of escaping to an imaginary golden island frustrated by the outbreak of war. This autobiographical narrative—set approximately from the establishment of the second republic in 1931 to the outbreak of the Civil War in 1936—develops as a portrait gallery of various types: the radical worker, the socialist father, the Catholic mother, the liberal priest, and the romantic spinster, all seen through the eyes of Luz, the child protagonist who urges the reader to explore the "differences" in the surrounding world. As a projection of Beneyto herself, Luz becomes the voice where, like the snail shell, all other voices resound.

Beneyto's works in Catalan share the themes and preoccupations of her works in Castilian. The collection of short stories entitled *La gent que viu al món* (The people who inhabit the world) deals with the war, various kinds of relationships, women alone, and violence. "Massa depriment" (Too depressing) is a striking criticism of the upper-bourgeois ladies whose charitable acts are strictly for their own benefit. The heartless protagonist considers her children a nuisance and does not hesitate to express her disgruntlement to a woman who wants to have children. Beneyto's only novel in Catalan, *La dona forta* (The strong woman), depicts a mother-son relationship. Again, the woman lacks sensitivity and tenderness, especially toward her son, who becomes a weak person.

Beneyto's early books of poetry in Catalan are folkloric, patriotic, and religious, though the nature of the religious sentiment changes. The sea and Valencia are recurring topics, but some of the imagery is original and varied. Her last book of poems in Catalan, *Vidre ferit de sang* (Glass wounded with blood), contains strong, sometimes violent, images. The title poem begins with a shocking series of words: "Tacat de roja ràbia feridora / feréstega, / emmetzinat de tèbia agror humana / jeu, colpejat de mort, d'espessa / opaca ceguetat maligna" (Stained with wild wounding red rage, / poisoned with tepid human bitterness, / it lies, mortally wounded, by thick, / opaque, malignant blindness) (15). The poem recalls the force of some of Vicente Aleixandre's pieces. Another poem in the same collection, "L'home davant del got" (The man facing the wineglass), mixes drinking, sex, and violence in a powerful piece that includes "ràbia engabiada, / desesperada, impotent, l'empenta" (caged rage, / desperate, impotent, the shove) (20). The book also includes pieces about relationships and the ever-present sea.

BOOKS
El agua que rodea la isla. Caracas: Arbol de Fuego, 1974.
Altra veu. Valencia: Torre, 1952.
Antigua patria. Valencia: Prometeo, 1969.
Antología general. Caracas: Lírica Hispana, 1956.
Bibliografía breve del silencio. Alcoy: La Victoria, 1975.
Canción olvidada. Valencia: Tipografía Moderna, 1947.
Criatura múltiple. Valencia: Colección Murta de la Diputación Provincial de Valencia, 1964.
La dona forta. Valencia: Senent, 1967.
Eva en el tiempo. Valencia: Colección El Sobre Literario, 1952.
La gent que viu al món. Valencia: L'Estel, 1966.
Palabras para una mujer de otro tiempo. Bilbao: Gran Enciclopedia Vasca, 1972.
Poemas de la ciudad. Barcelona: Colección Fe de Vida de Joaquín Horta, 1956.
Poesía 1947–1964. Barcelona: Plaza & Janés, 1965.
La promesa. Alcoy: Inst. Alcoyano de Cultura A. Sempere, 1958.
Ratlles a l'aire. Valencia: Torre, 1956. 2nd ed. Barcelona: Foro, 1958.
El río viene crecido. Valencia: Diputación Provincial, 1960.
Tierra viva. Madrid: Adonais, 1956.
Vida anterior. Caracas: Lírica Hispana, 1962.
Vidre ferit de sang. Gandia: Ajuntament de Gandia, 1977.

CANDELAS NEWTON,
with remarks about Beneyto's work in Catalan by KATHLEEN MCNERNEY

C Bertrana i Salazar, Aurora
(B. 1899, Berga, Girona; d. 1974, Barcelona.) Novelist and journalist.

Aurora Bertrana began to manifest literary interests when she was very young, influenced, no doubt, by the personality of her father, the writer and painter Prudenci Bertrana, about whom she later wrote a biography, *Una vida* (A life). In Girona Bertrana began to study the cello, which she continued in Barcelona, where the entire family moved as a result of a lawsuit against her father in 1911. She played in a women's trio to help with family expenses. In 1923 she joined a small women's orchestra in a Swiss hotel during the summer season. Afterward she registered at the Institut Delacroze of Geneva to further her studies in rhythm and art and played in orchestras to finance her studies.

In 1924 she began contributing to the journal *La veu de Catalunya*, and from then on she never stopped writing for various Catalan and Swiss publications. Her work included chronicles and cultural and ethnological reports based on her travels to foreign countries (Switzerland, France, Polynesia, and Morocco). In 1926 Bertrana accompanied her husband, an engineer, to Tahiti; there she was named professor of music at the Normal School of Papeete. After her return to Barcelona in 1930, she gave lectures and wrote fiction based on her impressions of the customs, superstitions, and history of the South Pacific islands and on her personal experiences. Three works resulted: *Paradisos oceànics* (Oceanic paradises), a series of reports about the islands that she translated into Castilian as *Islas de ensueño* (Dream islands); *Peikea, princesa caníbal* (Peikea, cannibal princess), a tale in an exotic setting about the love of an indigenous princess for a French adventurer who abandons her; and *L'illa perduda* (The lost island).

In 1931 Bertrana tried to found a university for women workers. In spite of her apolitical stance, she presented herself as a candidate for deputy to the parliament in order to find support for this project. Representing the Republican Left of Catalonia, she lost by a few votes. In 1935 she traveled to Morocco, an experience recounted first in the newspaper *La publicitat* and later in her book *El Marroc sensual i fanàtic* (Sensual and fanatic Morocco). During the Spanish Civil War Bertrana finished *Edelweiss*, which she had begun ten years earlier while staying in Haute Savoie, where the novel takes place. *Ariatea*, a later novel, is also situated there. During the war, Bertrana and Carme Nicolau founded and edited the collection La Novel.la Femenina. Without affiliating herself with a party and always affirming her stance as a pacifist, Bertrana continued her activities in the literary and cultural life of the city. For a short time, out of economic necessity, she edited the women's weekly *Companya*, of Communist affiliation.

Bertrana went into exile in Geneva in 1938 and stayed until 1949, when she obtained permission to return to Spain. Despite financial hardship during those years, she continued to write in French and contributed to various Swiss magazines and newspapers; she also published a novel in French, *Fenua Tahiti*. After the Second World War, Bertrana went as a volunteer to Etobon (Haute Saône), a French town where German troops had shot all the men at one time during the occupation, leaving only widows and orphans. She wrote two novels on the basis of that experience, *Tres presoners* (Three prisoners) and *Entre dos silencis* (Between two silences), as well as a story, "Un pomell de violetes" (1959; A bouquet of violets). Some of her other works are *Oviri*, a collection of stories; the novels *Fracàs* (Failure) and *Vent de grop* (Tailwind); and *La ciutat dels joves* (The city of the young), a utopian novel set in a country where sex discrimination does not exist but people are forced to retire from civic life at the age of forty and are confined to residences outside town. In all her works, Bertrana advocates peace and understanding among people. Her two volumes of memoirs, *Memòries del 1935 fins al retorn a Catalunya* and *Memòries fins el 1935*, afford a view of Bertrana's complex personality and at the same time offer well-described and accurate information about the social and political history of the epoch in which she lived.

BOOKS

Ariatea. Barcelona: Alberti, 1960.
Camins de somni. Barcelona: Alberti, 1955.
La ciutat dels joves. Barcelona: EP, 1971.
Edelweiss. Barcelona: La Novel.la Femenina, 1937.
Entre dos silencis. Barcelona: Aymà, 1958.
Fenua Tahiti. Neuchâtel: Delachoux and Niestlé, 1943.
Fracàs. Madrid: Alfaguara, 1966.
L'illa perduda. Barcelona: Llibreria Catalònia, 1935.
El Marroc sensual i fanàtic. Barcelona: Mediterrània, 1936.
Memòries del 1935 fins al retorn a Catalunya. Barcelona: Pòrtic, 1975.
Memòries fins el 1935. Barcelona: Pòrtic, 1973.
La nimfa d'argila. Barcelona: Alberti, 1959.
Oviri. Barcelona: Selecta, 1965.
Paradisos oceànics. Barcelona: Proa, 1930. Introd. Maria-Aurèlia Capmany. Barcelona: LaSal, 1988.
Peikea, princesa caníbal i altres contes oceànics. Barcelona: Balaguer, 1934.
Tres presoners. Barcelona: Alberti, 1957.
Vent de grop. Madrid: Alfaguara, 1967.
Vértigo de horizontes. Barcelona: Torrell de Reus, 1952.
Una vida. Barcelona: Vergara, 1965.

TRANSLATIONS OF HER WORKS

La isla perdida [*L'illa perduda*]. Trans. Aurora Bertrana Salazar. Barcelona: Juventud, 1947.
Islas de ensueño [*Paradisos oceànics*]. Barcelona: Iberia, 1933.

SECONDARY SOURCES

Möller-Soler, Maria-Lourdes. "El impacto de la guerra civil en la vida y obra de tres autoras catalanas: Aurora Bertrana, Teresa Pàmies y Mercè Rodoreda." *Letras femeninas* 12.1–2 (1986): 33–44.

MARIA-LOURDES SOLER I MARCET

C Bertran i Rossell, Maria Teresa
(B. 1952, Arenys del Mar, Barcelona– .) Also known as Teresa d'Arenys. Poet.

Maria Teresa Bertran won the Amadeu Oller prize for her first collection of poetry, *Aor*, but she withheld it from public sale to group it with a more recent work, *Murmuris*. The pieces forming this dual presentation, *Aor/ Murmuris* (Aor/Murmurs), are mostly sonnets. *Aor* deals with solitude, night monsters, the search for identity, and, occasionally, love. Between writing these two compositions, Bertran published a volume called *Onada* (Wave). Inspired by the drowning death of a beloved person, this book often has the sea as the protagonist. Bertran won the Selva del Camp prize with "Versos de vi novell" (Verses of young wine) in 1977 but has not authorized its publication. Some of her poems have appeared in poetic anthologies in the Maresme area (1979 and 1984) and in the journal *Paraules* (1979).

BOOKS
Aor. Barcelona: Parròquia de Sant Medir, 1976.
Aor/Murmuris. Barcelona: Mall, 1986.
Onada. Vilassar, Barcelona: Quaderns de la Font del Cargol, 1980.

TRANSLATIONS OF HER WORKS
"Upon M. F. F.'s Feigned Death" ["A la fingida mort de M. F. F."], "Summer's End" ["Finals d'estiu"], "Lost Symbols" ["Símbols perduts"], "Mediterranean" ["Mediterrània"], and "Let's Stake Sun and Moon . . ." ["Juguem-nos a daus . . ."]. Trans. David Rosenthal. *International Poetry Review* 8.1 (1982): 85–95.

SECONDARY SOURCES
Alegret, Joan. "Lectura de *Murmuris* de Teresa d'Arenys." *Catalan Review* 5.1 (1991): 9–21.

KATHLEEN MCNERNEY

C Bes i Aubà, Maria Isabel
(B. 1957, Barcelona– .) Poet and short story writer.

Maria Isabel Bes i Aubà studied philology at the University of Barcelona and currently works at Ràdio Catalunya. *Afers* (Affairs) is a collection of poetry; *Afers de roba* (Affairs of clothing) brings together short stories previously published in *El llamp*.

BOOKS
Afers. Valencia: Tres i Quatre, 1986.
Afers de roba. Barcelona: El Llamp, 1988.

WORKS IN BOOKS, PERIODICALS, NEWSPAPERS
"El procés contra Isabel Cornell." *L'espill* 23–24 (1987): 83–94.

KATHLEEN MCNERNEY

C Bibiloni Pellicer, Mercè
(20th c.) Poet. No biographical information available.

Ramell de records (Bouquet of memories) is a collection of short pieces, many written in flowing prose rather than verse. They document the small details of daily life and the family. Some are religious.

BOOKS
Ramell de records. Pref. Sebastià Sánchez-Juan. Barcelona: n.p., 1978.

KATHLEEN MCNERNEY

C Boixadors, Jerònima de
(B. ?; d. 1562, Reial Monestir de Santa Maria, Vallbona de les Monges, Lleida.) Poet.

Jerònima de Boixadors, abbess of the Reial Monestir de Santa Maria, has been identified by the historian Josep Joan Piquer i Jover as the author or compiler of the work *Llibre de goigs i devocions de Vallbona* (Book of poems in praise of the Virgin and devotions of Vallbona). This anthology, preserved at the City History Institute of Barcelona, comprises fifty-one poems in praise of the Virgin and eight prayers. Piquer was able to date the work thanks to a sentence in one of the prayers in which the emperor and king of Spain places himself in the hands of God. As the historian points out in the preface to *Llibre*, this double mandate in Spain occurred only between the years 1556 and 1558, "dates de l'abdicació i mort de Carles I d'Espanya i emperador d'Alemany, mentre ell estava retirat a Yuste i regnara ja Felip II . . . aquests anys corresponen a Vallbona amb l'abadiat de Jerònima de Boixadors (1554–1562), autora molt probable d'aquesta i d'altres composicions que es troben en el llibre de referència" (dates of the abdication and death of Charles I, king of Spain and emperor of Germany, who had retired to Yuste, and of the ruling of Felipe II . . . these years correspond, in Vallbona, with the ruling of Jerònima de Boixadors [1554–1562], likely to be the author of this and other pieces found in the reference book) (6). Thirty-six of the poems are in Catalan and fifteen are in Castilian. They make numerous references to the monastery and its surroundings. The manuscript seems to have been written by different copiers, and the part attributed to the abbess Boixadors shows an elaborate

77

calligraphy, one that belongs to a person with a command of Castilian, Latin, and Catalan. The Boixadors family is one of the oldest among the Catalan nobility, and some of its members are outstanding men and women of letters.

BOOKS

Llibre de goigs i devocions de Vallbona atribuit a l'abadessa Jerònima de Boixadors (1554–1562). Pref. Josep Joan Piquer i Jover. Transcribed by Francina Solsona. Lleida: Vallbona de les Monges, 1986.

SECONDARY SOURCES

Piquer i Jover 194–96.

CRISTINA ENRIQUEZ DE SALAMANCA

C Bonaventura, Teresa

(20th c.) Short story writer. No biographical information available.

BOOKS

Conte dels instruments de la música. Montserrat: L'Abadia, 1986.

KATHLEEN MCNERNEY

C Bonet, Maria del Mar

(B. 1947, Mallorca– .) Folksinger, composer, and poet.

This popular composer and singer of folk music has published and illustrated some of her lyrics in *Secreta veu* (Secret voice). The title refers to a quotation from the poet Joan Vinyoli. The collection contains songs of love and sensuality, evocations of the islands and sea, and dances and cradle songs. Some of the pieces are dedicated to the poet Joan Oliver and the Chilean folksinger and composer Violeta Parra.

BOOKS

Secreta veu. Barcelona: Empúries, 1987.

KATHLEEN MCNERNEY

B Borda, Itxaro

(B. 1959, Bayonne, France– .) Novelist and playwright.

Itxaro Borda is a regular contributor to the Bayonne magazine *Maiatz*. She has published two novels: *Basilika* and *Udaran Betaurreko Beltzekin*

78

(Summer with sunglasses). *Infante zendu batendako pabana* (Pavane for a dead princess) is a historical play with reference to Maurice Ravel's *Pavane pour une infante défunte*.

BOOKS
Basilika. San Sebastián: Elkar, 1984.
Infante zendu batendako pabana. With Mark Legasse. Pref. Jokin Apalategi. Donostia (San Sebastián): Txertoa Argitaldaria, 1986.
Udaran Bataurreko Beltzekin. San Sebastián: Txertoa Agitaldaria, 1987.

MAITE GONZALEZ ESNAL

C Borja, Tecla
(B. 1435, València; d. 1459, València.) Poet.

Niece of Pope Calixtus III and sister of Pope Alexander VI, Tecla Borja was praised by poets in Italy and Valencia. Not only a singer and a poet, she was also a scholar. Only a brief text of hers has survived, a debate with the great poet Ausiàs March.

WORKS IN BOOKS, PERIODICALS, NEWSPAPERS
Debate. *Poesies*. By Ausiàs March. Ed. Pere Bohigas. Els Nostres Clàsics 5. Barcelona: Barcino, 1959. 133.

SECONDARY SOURCES
Massó i Torrents, "Poetesses i dames intel.lectuals" 411–14.

LOLA BADIA

C Bosch i Verdaguer, Magda
(B. 1944, Ripoll, Girona– .) Art critic and poet.

The spirals of *D'eròtica-Espirals* (On erotic spirals) refer to the poet's journey through the physical and mental convolutions of the passionate life. To support the main theme of "tu i jo," Magda Bosch often uses images from nature to heighten her sensual discourse, and she employs several types of rhyme, meter, and stanzas to express the varied qualities of the amorous relationship.

BOOKS
D'eròtica-Espirals. Pref. Marta Pessarrodona. Barcelona: Mall, 1982.

NANCY L. BUNDY

C   Brossa Jané, Marina

(Early 20th c.) Playwright. No biographical information available.

The library of the Theatre Museum of Barcelona holds the manuscript of the play "L'correu de la Senyoreta" (1911; The young lady's mail), first performed on 12 October 1911 in the Sala Imperi theater in Barcelona. This comedy in one act revolves around a misunderstanding among middle-class Catalan characters entangled in a simple love affair. The happy ending results in the formation of two couples. The play is written in a prenormalized Catalan.

BOOKS

"L'correu de la Senyoreta." Ms. 406–2. Institute Teatre Català, Barcelona.

MARISA SIGUAN BOEHMER

C   Buigas, Maria Rosa

(B. 1925, Barcelona– .) Poet, short story writer, and novelist.

Daughter of the writer and publisher Joaquim Buigas i Garriga, Maria Rosa Buigas wrote both prose and poetry. Her literary career began with two books of poems: *Dient coses . . . Les estacions de la vida* (Chatting . . . the seasons of life) and *El signe del matí* (Morning sign). Varied strophic structure and free verse characterize these works. Buigas uses alliteration, anaphora, acute rhyme, and monosyllabic words in her quest for musical sonority: "Música de campanes / que sempre sonareu / la vostra veu eterna / és signe d'adéu" (Bell music / you will always ring / your eternal voice / signals goodbye) (*El signe* 141). The predominant metaphors and comparisons, the many enumerations and descriptions are inspired by a pure and unaltered nature where birds, flowers, trees, the sun, the moon, the stars, and the seasons are manifestations of beauty and images of God. The two principal themes of Buigas's poetry, hope and love, are expressed through these symbols. For example, the rising sun represents hope and personal rebirth as well as the rebirth of humankind: "Entre la llum morent / i l'ombra que s'atansa / albiro una infantesa, / un SOL IXENT / d'un dia, resplendent / de joia i esperança" (Between dying sun / and approaching shadow / is a glimpse of childhood / a RISING SUN / a shining day / of joy and hope) (*El signe* 18). Buigas also evokes Catalan popular tradition. A large group of poems depicts an idyllic rural scene of "masies," "hostals," and "fadrines," a world distant from reality and close to the pastoral idealization characteristic of the Catalan bourgeoisie. *El signe del matí* also contains five poems in Castilian that, according to the author, "[h]an estat inspirats per una obra escrita pel meu pare, que s'intitula 'Proses selvà-tiques,' el contingut de la qual fou viscut per l'autor durant la seva estada a la pampa argentina, l'any 1906" (have been inspired by a work written by my father entitled *Proses selvàtiques*, whose accounts were experienced by its author during his stay in the Argentinian pampa) (205).

Maria Rosa Buigas's prose work comprises three short story collections, *Més lluny de l'estranger: Narracions i petites pinzellades de temes irònics d'ahir i d'avui* (Farther than from abroad: Narrations and brief sketches of ironic themes from yesterday and today), *De verdes i de madures* (Some green and some ripe), and *L'aranya roja i altres contes i narracions* (The red spider and other stories); three short stories included in *El signe del matí*; and one novel, *El cementeri dels elefants* (The elephant cemetery).

The short stories, as the subtitle of *Més lluny de l'estranger* indicates, are "petites pinzellades," brief, ironic sketches of local customs and manners. Buigas caricatures those members of the Catalan bourgeoisie who intend to be modern. Her emphasis on their vices and faults is closer to ridicule than to consistent social criticism. Marriages based on financial considerations, where the wife spends most of the day talking to friends on the phone or preparing for parties and where the husband seeks an affair with a young woman and trips to exotic places, are the anecdotal core of these stories. In addition to these is a different group of tales that deal with restlessness. In "L'aranya roja," "Avies d'avui" (Grandmothers of today), "Què farem dels vells?" (What will we do with the old people?), and "La velocitat" (Speed), Buigas is concerned with the brevity of time and its impact on the elderly, especially women. Nostalgia and the idealization of the past dominate these stories that, nevertheless, maintain their humorous tone.

In *El cementeri dels elefants*, Buigas portrays Eulàlia Arnau de Bismes, an elderly woman taken to a nursing home in Pedralbes, Barcelona, and abandoned by her son, who is busy with business and travels abroad. Eulàlia's loneliness is expressed by the acute contrast between her past and her present. Most of the novel's characters are women, and these residents of the nursing home represent the variety of bourgeois female loneliness: widows, lovers, and betrayed wives; forgotten mothers and women rejected by daughters-in-law who have no sense of family.

Maria Rosa Buigas's extremely fragmented style gives theatrical form to her short stories, which are organized in scenes where the narrator's voice is presented as a stage direction and the characters express themselves exclusively through direct dialogue. For structural purposes Buigas often adds popular songs and poems to the text. Her language intends to be representative of the characters and their social classes (brief Castilian sentences and words appear), and the narrator frequently uses popular refrains to end the stories.

BOOKS
L'aranya roja i altres contes i narracions. Barcelona: Maria Rosa Buigas, 1984.
El cementeri dels elefants. Barcelona: Maria Rosa Buigas, 1981.
Dient coses . . . Les estacions de la vida. Barcelona: Maria Rosa Buigas, 1968.
*Més lluny de l'estranger: Narracions i petites pinzellades de temes irònics d'ahir i
d'avui.* Barcelona: Aymà, 1976.
El signe del matí. Barcelona: Aymà, 1973.
De verdes i de madures. Barcelona: Maria Rosa Buigas, 1979.

ELISA MARTI-LOPEZ

C Burgos i Matheu, Zoraida
(B. 1933, Tortosa, Tarragona– .) Poet.

Zoraida Burgos won the Marius Torres prize with her book *D'amors d'enyors i d'altres coses* (Of loves, yearnings, and other things). This collection
of poetry is a collage of varying themes—fulfilled and unfulfilled love,
children, and politics. Sensuality and original imagery characterize the
sensitive piece "Gairebé havíen gastat l'amor pel costum" (We had almost
spent love by routine), in which she finds freshness in an old love, like
the spring blooms on an aging acacia. *Vespres* (Evenings) concentrates on
nature and the passage of time; *Reflexos* (Reflections) is her most philosophical work to date. "Penúltims blaus," her latest collection, may be published
in the near future. Closely identified with her local artistic scene, Burgos
has written poems to accompany shows of new artists.

BOOKS
D'amors d'enyors i d'altres coses. Lleida: n.p., 1971.
Reflexos. Tarragona: Inst. d'Estudis Tarraconenses, 1989.
Vespres. Tortosa, Tarragona: n.p., 1978.

KATHLEEN MCNERNEY

C Busquets, Cristina
(20th c.) Novelist. No biographical information available.

Cristina Busquets wrote several romance novels in Catalan and Castilian.
El jurament de Ferran (Ferran's pledge), in Catalan, was published serially
from 1925 to 1938 in the magazine *La dona catalana*; in 1935 the first of
several Castilian editions appeared. The action takes place in the area
between Pamplona and the French border during the First World War.
The protagonist, in order to honor a pledge made to a friend, finds himself
separated from the woman he loves. In the end the two lovers reunite,

and the misunderstanding that caused all their suffering is cleared up. Busquets's Castilian novels include *Fátima, El testamento* (The last will), and *El collar de Rosalinda* (Rosalinda's necklace). This last novel, a romance written in a moralizing tone, is set in Madrid and deals with an orphan girl, Rosalinda, who is taken in by relatives and endures their illtreatment and severity with humility and joy. Her guardians consider her a poor girl, but in the end they realize that there is no social difference between her and them and that she can marry her cousin.

BOOKS
El collar de Rosalinda. Barcelona: Casulleras, 1935. Sevilla: Sevillana, n.d. Barcelona: Diario de Barcelona, 1935.
Entre Rosas. Barcelona: Casulleras, 1932.
Fátima. Barcelona: Casulleras, 1932.
El jurament de Ferran. Barcelona: Bosch, 1935.
La novia del náufrago. Barcelona: Casulleras, 1932.
El testamento. Barcelona: Casulleras, 1932.

TRANSLATIONS OF HER WORKS
El juramento de Fernando [*El jurament de Ferran*]. Barcelona: Casulleras, 1935. Barcelona: Diario de Barcelona, 1936.

NURIA PI I VENDRELL

B Bustinza y Ozerin, Rosa
(B. 1899, Mañaria, Bizkaia; d. 1953, Mañaria, Bizkaia.) Also known as Mañariko and Mañariko Errose. Short story writer and poet.

Rosa Bustinza wrote mythological short stories under the title "Euskal Herriko ipuinak" for the magazines *Eusko Enda* (1939), *Jesusen Biotzaren Deia,* and *Anaitasuna.* Two love poems, "Abesti Zarra" and "Josu'ren Biotzari," and a lullaby, "Siaska Abestia," are included in the collection *Mila euskal olerki eder* (One thousand beautiful Basque poems).

WORKS IN BOOKS, PERIODICALS, NEWSPAPERS
"Abesti Zarra," "Josu'ren Biotzari," and "Siaska Abestia." Onaindia, *Mila euskal olerki eder* 756–58.

MAITE GONZALEZ ESNAL

C Cabanas-Duhalde, Josiana
(B. 1952, Perpignan, France– .) Short story writer.

In 1977 Josiana Cabanas began contributing stories and articles regularly to *L'almanac català del Rosselló* and to *Sant Joan i Barres*, publications of the Girup Rossellonès d'Estudis Catalans (GREC; Roussillon's Group of Catalan Studies). At that time, she also taught Catalan to a group of adult students.

Punts de creu (Cross-stitches), her third collection, presents the complexity of women's experiences in different environments and situations. Each story is independent of the others, yet all are built around characteristics common among women and reflect the emotions and feelings of everyday life. The psychological and physical descriptions seem like vivid pieces of embroidery out of which the writer, stitch by stitch, creates a whole work. Cabanas's stories are reminiscent of those of Renada-Laura Portet.

BOOKS

A través d'un vidre entelat, l'espera. Illus. Roger Cosme Esteve. Sant Esteve, France: Michel Fricker, 1985.
Punts de creu. Perpinyà, France: Trabucaire, 1986.
Senzilles històries de dones. Barcelona: GREC, 1983.

MONTSERRAT VILARRUBLA

C Cabré de Calderó, Maria
(20th c.) Poet. No biographical information available.

Maria Cabré's *Pinzellades* (Brush strokes) is a collection of poems praising the local countryside and reflecting on writing. The final poems speak of death and prayer. In keeping with the theme of brush strokes, the book contains drawings by various artists.

BOOKS

Espurnes. Reus, Tarragona: n.p., 1978.
Pinzellades. Introd. Maria Misericòrdia Arnavat. Reus, Tarragona: n.p., 1981.

KATHLEEN MCNERNEY

C Caimarí de Bauló, Margarida
(B. 1839, Bolivia; d. 1921, Palma de Mallorca.) Also Caymarí de Bauló, Margarita. Poet.

Raised in a Majorcan family who had moved to Latin America and later resettled on the island, Margarida Caimarí wrote in both Catalan and Castilian. She belonged to an early group of women writers who formed part of the Catalan *Renaixença*: Josefa Massanés, Victòria Penya, Maria de Bell-Lloch, Dolors Monserdà, Agnès Armengol, Agna de Valldaura, and Maria Manuela de los Herreros. Thus, her name often appeared in the

84

Barcelona journals *Lo Gay Saber* and *Calendari català* and the Majorcan publications *Museo balear* and *Revista balear*.

Caimarí was a close friend of the poet Manuela de los Herreros, to whom she dedicated poems and who probably exerted influence on her work. For example, Herreros's well-known poem "Lo so d'un infant" seems to have inspired Caimarí's "Lo so." Caimarí took part in the activities of the literary groups in Palma and in Barcelona. Her most characteristic themes are female friendship and motherly love, though her poetry often deals with *Renaixença* subjects as well, such as the beauty of the Catalan countryside and certain places that epitomize the Catalan nation.

WORKS IN BOOKS, PERIODICALS, NEWSPAPERS

"A Doña Lluisa Oliver Reus en la mort de sa filla." *Revista balear de literatura, ciencias y artes* 23 (1873).

"A mi hija." *Revista balear de literatura, ciencias y artes* 20 (1872): 311.

"A mi querida hermana del corazón Manuela de los Herreros Bonet." *Revista balear de literatura, ciencias y artes* 4 (1872): 56–72.

"A Miramar." *Calendari català* (1878): 81–83.

"Amor de mare." *Calendari català* (1882): 24.

"Anyorança." *Calendari català* (1869): 43.

"La caritat." *Lo Gay Saber* 10 (1868): 74.

"Catalunya." *Lo Gay Saber* 7 (1881): 71.

"En el álbum de la Srta Doña María Alomar." *Museo balear de historia y literatura, ciencias y artes* (May–Dec. 1884): 153.

"Es dos àngels." *Lo Gay Saber* 1 (1868): 1–2.

"Flores del alma." *Revista balear de literatura, ciencias y artes* 1 (1872): 9–10.

"Goitg i dolor." *Calendari català* (1870): 25–26.

"Lo meu desitg." *Lo Gay Saber* 13 (1880).

"Lo meu desitx." *Revista balear de literatura, ciencias y artes* 9 (1873).

"El so." *Lo Gay Saber* 20 (1881): 220.

"Lo so." *Lo Gay Saber* 35 (1869). 276.

"Veu de mare." *Lo Gay Saber* 5 (1878).

"Veu de mare." *Revista balear de literatura, ciencias y artes* 2 (1874).

SECONDARY SOURCES

Simón Palmer, *Escritoras españolas del siglo XIX* 149–50.

CRISTINA ENRIQUEZ DE SALAMANCA

C Canalias, Anna

(B. 1886, Magallón, Zaragoza; d. 1934, Molins de Rei, Barcelona.) Also Agna. Poet and translator.

Raised in a working-class family in Molins de Rei, where she spent her childhood, Anna Canalias became a teacher of working-class adults in the

Ateneo de Sants and at the Escola Mossén Cinto, both in Barcelona. She moved to Madrid to continue her studies, entering the Escuela Superior de Magisterio. After living in Osca, Segovia, and Tarragona, Canalias settled in Girona. Although all the bibliographical references mention three works, *Líriques* (Lyrics), *Nature*, and *Sonets erudits* (Scholarly sonnets), they are not available in major Catalan libraries.

A selection of her poetry appears in volume 14 of *Lectura popular*. These relatively short and undated poems are composed in a variety of meters, but the sonnet form predominates. Canalias's poetry is marked by conventions typical at the turn of the century: the exaltation of nature, mythology, floral motifs, and admonitory endings reminiscent of Bécquer. The search for love coincides with the search for an aesthetic ideal; the lover's attraction often rests on identification with an imagined poet. The collection also contains several poems intended as historical instruction, probably the result of Canalias's teaching activities: for example, "Orientales" (Orientals) is a legend inspired by Bernat Boades's *Llibre dels fets d'armes de Catalunya* (Book of wars of Catalonia). The volume also includes translations of Verlaine ("Green," "Plora dintre del meu cor" ["Il pleure dans mon coeur"], and "Cavitry" ["Çavitri"]).

Feminal published some of the poems in this collection between 1907 and 1913, as well as two articles describing education in ancient Greece and the religious ceremony of a Greek wedding. The article "Girona, ciutat migeval" (Girona, a medieval city), based on her years of residence in Girona, appeared in *Catalana*. Camilo Geis, in "Lo que encontré en el camino" (What I found on the road), characterizes Canalias as a woman of great literary knowledge, a translator of Goethe, Ronsard, Ravegnani, Carducci, D'Annunzio.

BOOKS
Poesies. Vol. 14 of *Lectura popular*.

WORKS IN BOOKS, PERIODICALS, NEWSPAPERS
"La ceremonia religiosa en el matrimonio griego" and "Díptichs." *Feminal* 76 (27 July 1913).
"La dançaire (del romancer popular recullit modernament pels grechs)." *Feminal* 101 (29 Aug. 1915).
"L'educació en la Grecia Antiga." *Feminal* 8 (24 Nov. 1907).
"Girona, ciutat migeval." *Catalana* 10 Aug. 1918.
"Poesies franciscanes: 'Els aucells germans,' 'Torneig místich,' and 'El roser franciscà.'" *Feminal* 96 (28 Mar. 1915).
"Siluetes cristianes: 'Dunsi Scott,' 'Sant Tomàs d'Aquí,' 'Sor Maria d'Agreda,' 'Regina Elisabeth d'Hungria.'" *Feminal* 108 (26 Mar. 1916).
"Sonets a Tórtola: 'València,' 'La maja,' 'La dança d'Anita,' 'La serp,' 'Dança arabe,' 'Dança de l'incens.'" *Feminal* 112 (26 Sept. 1916).
"Tyris (de Teòcrit)." *Feminal* 92 (29 Aug. 1914).

SECONDARY SOURCES
Geis, Camilo. "Lo que encontré en el camino: Anna Canalias." *Revista de Gerona* 17 (1961): 33.

CRISTINA ENRIQUEZ DE SALAMANCA

C   Canela i Garayoa, Mercè
(B. 1956, Sant Guim de Freixanet, Lleida– .) Writer of children's literature.

Currently a librarian for the European Common Market and a resident of Brussels, Mercè Canela grew up in Sant Guim, a village in La Segarra, Lleida, where she went to school until the age of fifteen. She then attended the University of Barcelona, where she received a degree in archaeology. Her first book, *De qui és el bosc?* (Whom does the forest belong to?), deals with such contemporary problems as environmental damage, social rebellion in teenagers, and interpersonal struggles. She won the Josep Maria Folch i Torres prize for children's literature for *L'escarabat verd* (The green beetle), a tale of a Carthaginian's adventures in the Mediterranean. In 1980 she received the *Serra d'or* prize for juvenile books for *La fantasia d'Antoni Gaudí* (The fantasy of Antoni Gaudí), in which she portrays the psychology and works of Gaudí through a dialogue between a man and his grandchildren as they walk through the streets of Barcelona. That same year her book *Uthinghami, el rei de la boira* (Uthinghami, king of the fog) was on the honor list for the C.C.E.I. (Comisión Católica Española de la Infancia) prize. An imaginary being is the protagonist of this fantasy-filled narrative. In 1982 she received the Esparver prize for *Lluna de tardor* (Autumn moon). This series of stories, also written with elements of fantasy, features a subtle perception of an imagined world, situations out of the characters' control, such as death or the overwhelming rapture of love, and sentiments that outlast time and memory. The following year she won the Guillem Gifre prize in Cologne for *Els set enigmes de l'iris* (The seven enigmas of the iris).

BOOKS
Ara torno. 2nd ed. Barcelona: Magrana, 1987.
Asperú, joglar embruixat. Barcelona: La Galera, 1982.
A una mà el sol i a l'altre la lluna. Barcelona: Argos Vergara, 1982.
De qui és el bosc? 1976. 4th ed. Barcelona: La Galera, 1982.
En Pere Trapella: Conte popular basc. 2nd ed. Barcelona: La Galera, 1986.
L'escarabat verd. 6th ed. Barcelona: La Galera, 1987.
La fantasia d'Antoni Gaudí. Barcelona: Blume, 1980.
Un gat dalt del teulat. Barcelona: La Galera, 1983.
Globus de lluna plena. Barcelona: Argos Vergara, 1983.

Lluna de tardor. Barcelona: Magrana, 1982.
Nicolasa braç de ferro. Barcelona: Argos Vergara, 1983.
L'oca d'or. Barcelona: La Galera, 1987.
L'ou de cristall. Barcelona: La Galera, 1987.
El planeta dels set sols. Terrassa: Xarxa de Biblioteques Soler i Palet, 1985.
Quan l'Eloi va ser música. Barcelona: La Galera, 1981.
El rastre de les bombolles. Barcelona: Magrana, 1990.
Els set enigmes de l'iris. 3rd ed. Barcelona: La Galera, 1986.
Uthinghami, el rei de la boira. 6th ed. Barcelona: La Galera, 1982.

TRANSLATIONS OF HER WORKS
El anillo del mercader [L'escarabat verd]. Barcelona: La Galera, 1977.
Asperú, juglar embrujado [Asperú, joglar embruixat]. Barcelona: La Galera, 1983.
¿De quién es el bosque? [De qui és el bosc?]. Barcelona: La Galera, 1976.
Eloy un día fue música [Quan l'Eloi va ser música]. Barcelona: La Galera, 1981.
En una mano el sol y en la otra la luna [A una mà el sol i a l'altre la lluna]. Barcelona: Argos Vergara, 1982.
Un gato en el tejado [Un gat dalt del teulat]. Barcelona: La Galera, 1983.
Globo de luna llena [Globus de lluna plena]. Barcelona: Argos Vergara, 1983.
El huevo de cristal [L'ou de cristall]. Barcelona: La Galera, 1987.
Nicolasa, muñeca de hierro [Nicolasa braç de ferro]. Barcelona: Teide, 1987.
La oca de oro [L'oca d'or]. Barcelona: La Galera, 1984.
Pedro pícaro [En Pere Trapella: Conte popular basc]. Barcelona: La Galera, 1983.
Los siete enigmas del iris [Els set enigmes de l'iris]. Barcelona: La Galera, 1984.
Uthinghami, el rey de la niebla [Uthingami, el rei de la boira]. Barcelona: La Galera, 1979.

IMMA BALDOCCHI I PUIG

C Canela i Garayoa, Montserrat
(B. 1959, Sant Guim de Freixanet, Lleida– .) Writer of children's literature.

After Montserrat Canela received her degree in history at the Universitat Autònoma de Barcelona, she taught briefly and then went to Cornell University to study English. Upon her return to Spain, she resumed teaching, but in 1984 she became director of the Arxiu Històric Comarcal de Cervera in Lleida, the historical archive of her native area, where she continues to work. She has contributed to various publications, notably *Cavall fort*, a magazine specializing in children's literature, and *El Segre*, a daily paper in the city of Lleida. She cofounded a local newspaper, *Casa nostra*, and is collaborating on a textbook that will include some of her original compositions as well as newly edited texts by others.

Her first book, *Les flors salvatges* (Wildflowers), won the Joaquim Ruyra prize for 1985; classified as juvenile literature, this novel interests an adult audience as well. It tells the adventures of young Sean, whose sympathies with the Irish cause turn into action during the Easter Rebellion of 1916. Hiding in Dublin after fleeing British soldiers, he participates in the spectacular escape of one of the movement's wounded members. He finds time to fall in love as well. Canela's writing style makes her work accessible to a large public.

BOOKS
Les flors salvatges. Barcelona: Laia, 1986.

KATHLEEN MCNERNEY

C   Cantalozella Mas, Assumpció
(B. 1943, Santa Coloma de Farners, Girona– .) Journalist and novelist.

A graduate of the Universitat Autònoma de Barcelona and the Escola Oficial d'Idiomes, Assumpció Cantalozella began her writing career as a journalist. Her novels—situated in the province and the city of Girona, where she has lived since 1972—center on women who have come of age in the twilight of the Franco regime and on their search for meaningful social, moral, and political values in a changing world.

Escubidú (Scooby-Do), set in the early sixties, is the story of a young woman's struggle to leave the small town where she was raised and to create an independent life in the city. Flashbacks of her early education and family life show the obstacles she faces in breaking with her past. In *Sauló* (Sandstone), three friends on a summer vacation in the late seventies test the boundaries of their chosen lifestyles. The lesbian relationship that evolves between two of them forces all three to reevaluate their life choices and to consider the price of independence. Cantalozella's characters share a willingness to break with established norms; they fear risks, but they take them. The author has been a political activist since her youth, and her intensely personal novels relate the political developments of the postwar years. Her effective use of dialogue establishes a distinctive voice for each character.

BOOKS
Escubidú. Barcelona: Pòrtic, 1982.
Sauló. Barcelona: Pòrtic, 1984.

SHEILA MCINTOSH

C Canyà i Martí, Llucieta
(B. 1898?, La Bisbal d'Empordà, Girona– .) Poet, playwright, and journalist.

Bibliographies indicate that Llucieta Canyà published two books of poetry, *Mare* (1929; Mother) and *Caixa de nuvia* (1933; Trousseau), but these works have been impossible to locate. Shortly before the outbreak of the Civil War, Canyà published a play, *L'estudiant de Girona* (The student of Girona). Set in Girona during the war against the French (1808–14), the play is inspired by Catalan patriotism and exalts the idea of liberty. The plot revolves around a typically Calderonian problem of honor in which the female protagonist is the victim of male pride.

L'etern femení (The eternal feminine), dedicated to Francesca Bonnemaison, was a great success and, with its moral rules and advice on childbearing and medical problems, became required reading for middle-class Catalan women. Although Canyà's ideology is conservative, Josep Maria de Sagarra defines her in his prologue as a feminist and makes such odd statements as the following: "el destí li ha concedit, com a màxima fortuna, aquell imprescindible esbojarrament d'ocell que han de tenir les noies per a ésser adorables" (she was gifted with that birdlike wildness girls must have to be adorable) (13). *L'etern masculí* (The eternal masculine) is a book of advice to men.

In the play *L'amor té cops amagats* (Love is full of surprises) Canyà develops themes from *L'etern femení*, such as mistaking illusion for love, the frailty of women's friendship, and the perils of coquetry. The comedy had its première in the Teatre Romea (Barcelona) on 5 April 1954. Canyà also contributed to the Barcelona magazine *La veu de Catalunya* and to the journal *El correo catalán*.

BOOKS
L'amor té cops amagats. Barcelona: Millà, 1954.
L'estudiant de Girona: Tres actes escrits en vers. Barcelona: El Nostre Teatre, 1936.
L'etern femení: Confessions, ideologies, orientacions. Prol. Josep Maria de Sagarra. Barcelona: Duran, 1934.
L'etern masculí: Orientacions, consells, esperances. Prol. Josep Maria de Sagarra. Barcelona: Contal, 1957. 2nd ed. Barcelona: Gràfiques Universitat, 1958. 4th ed. 1963.

CRISTINA ENRIQUEZ DE SALAMANCA

C Canyelles, Antonina
(B. 1942, Palma de Mallorca– .) Poet.

Antonina Canyelles won the 1979 Marian Agulló prize for her only book of poetry, *Quadern de conseqüències* (Notebook of consequences). She communicates her painful experience of living through short, acidic sentences. In her evocations of memory, she reveals a great tenderness toward children harmed by adults. Canyelles sees the world of adults as totally invented, one in which essences have been converted into simple decorative objects. From her perspective, death is a possible liberation. She often creates dialogues, using clichés ironically in her ferocious attack on hypocrisy. Her language avoids ornamentation, in an attempt to get to the bottom of things. Enumerations, wordplay, and repeated use of superlatives and diminutives give expressive force to her poems.

BOOKS
Quadern de conseqüències. Illus. Esperança Mestre. Palma: ACC, 1980.

SILVIA AYMERICH LEMOS

C Caparà i Busquets, Assumpció
(B. 1829, Terrassa, Barcelona; d. 1918, Terrassa, Barcelona.)
Poet.

A poet of the late Romantic period, Assumpció Caparà wrote in both Catalan and Castilian. Her work, dispersed through periodicals and single sheet publications, exalts traditional and religious values.

GUILLEM-JORDI GRAELLS

C Capdevila i Valls, Roser
(B. 1939, Barcelona– .) Writer and illustrator of children's literature.

With a degree from the Escola Massana in Barcelona, Roser Capdevila is best known as an illustrator of children's books, including La Galera's collection *Mirem* (Let's look), *Les tres bessones* (The triplets), and *Les memòries de la bruixa avorrida* (Memoirs of the bored witch). Among the stories she has written are *La cosidora* (The sewing machine), a tale of an old sewing machine that ends up in a museum and tries to transmit to children a sense of love for old objects; *Ep, no em deixeu sol* (Oh, don't leave me alone), about the activities of the sun; and *Una història de botons* (A story about buttons), an amusing story of a child who steals buttons to make a soccer team.

BOOKS
El be negre amb potes rosses. Barcelona: La Galera, 1987.
La cosidora. Barcelona: Destino, 1982.

91

Ep, no em deixeu sol. Barcelona: Destino, 1985.
Una història de botons. Barcelona: Argos Vergara, 1983.

IMMA BALDOCCHI I PUIG

C Capellades Ballester, Enriqueta
(B. 1919, Vilada, Barcelona– .) Playwright.

Daughter and granddaughter of teachers, Enriqueta Capellades has always been in touch with children. In 1976 she was awarded the Ciutat de Barcelona theater prize for her work "La criada Malabusques" (The servant Malabusques), entitled *Sis lladres del camí ral* (The robbers of the king's highway) in its edition for children. She currently lives in Castellterçol, Barcelona, where she is active in local drama productions.

BOOKS
El noi valent. Barcelona: La Galera, 1978.
Els pastorets del ferrer Magí. Barcelona: La Galera, 1982.
Sis lladres del camí ral. Barcelona: La Galera, 1976.

ANNA GASOL I TRULLOLS

C Capmany i Farnès, Maria Aurèlia
(B. 1918, Barcelona; d. 1991, Barcelona.) Novelist, playwright, and essayist.

Cultural Counselor for the city of Barcelona from 1983 to 1987, Maria Aurèlia Capmany was born into a family that cultivated both literature and Catalanism. She attended the Montessori school in the 1920s and continued at the Institut-Escola, finishing in 1937. Although her class at the university was the last to graduate under the Republic, her degree was not recognized and she had to take intensive courses after the war. To support herself, she worked as a glass cutter and engraver, learning the craft at the behest of her father, who believed everyone should have a skill. She earned a bachelor's degree in philosophy and worked on her doctorate for three years with Professor Pere Font i Puig. As a sporadic contributor to *Ariel* and a member of the group Miramar, she helped organize various cultural activities and lectured.

In 1951 Capmany was named director of the Women's College of the Institut Albèniz in Badalona, Barcelona. The following year she was awarded a scholarship by the Institut Français and went to the Sorbonne, where she took courses from Maurice Merleau-Ponty. In Paris she closely and critically followed such events and issues as the Sartre-Camus debate, the Cold War, Beckett's plays, the war in Indochina, the Algerian conflict, and the myth of Stalinism. She returned to Badalona to teach at the Institut Albèniz. During the 1960s she dedicated herself to literary translations from Italian and French, including works by Italo Calvino, Vasco Pratolini, Elio Vittorini, Luigi Pirandello, Marguerite Duras, and Georges Simenon. During the same decade, she directed the Joanot Martorell collection at Nova Terra press and cofounded the Escola d'Art Dramàtic Adrià Gual (EADAG). Capmany aided the director Ricard Salvat in the presentation of many plays and directed some on her own, including Georg Büchner's *Leonci i Lena* (*Leonce och Lena, ett lustspel*) in 1963 and Shakespeare's *The Merchant of Venice* in 1964. She was in Paris to attend the Festival of Catalan Letters during the uprising of May 1968. In 1972 she attended the Congress of Women Journalists in Washington. Beginning in 1970, she helped organize the summer school programs of the Catalan University in Prades and a series of conferences on Catalan literature throughout Catalonia. She directed the television program *Cita a mitja tarda* (1978–79; Midafternoon date) and wrote several scripts for radio and television.

Capmany's work is characterized by its dynamism as well as its variety; she excelled in fiction, drama, and the essay. As a journalist she contributed to several newspapers and magazines, including *Avui, Serra d'or,* and *Presència.* Capmany was one of the most notable literary figures of the postwar era; beginning during the difficult period of Francoist repression, she dedicated her life and her pen to supporting Catalan letters. Truthfulness characterizes her work, as she treats her themes with objectivity, distance, and a skilled narrative technique. Her early novels are psychological, featuring introspective characters preoccupied with their own microcosms. As she developed she included more extensive themes and her vision widened, but she never lost sight of small, individual problems, which she considered part of the history of the individual. In spite of her background in philosophy, her literature is more intuitive than dialectic. Her work is dominated by a healthy optimism and a vigorous humor, always stressing faith in each person's potential, especially women's; Capmany believes that women must be intelligent and lucid enough to know how to use their biological advantages. Time is also an important theme, almost becoming an obsession. Capmany can be considered a person of letters par excellence, both for her prolific production and for her true literary vocation.

Her first novel, *Necessitem morir* (We need to die; written in 1947 but withheld by the censors until 1952), has been characterized as Gothic and psychological by Capmany herself. It deals with a Frenchwoman, Georgina Desmoulins, who was raised in a Basque household. Her move at the age of forty to the Mediterranean shore represents the end of one life and the beginning of another. *El cel no és transparent* (The sky is not transparent; written in 1948 but rewritten and published in 1963 under the title *La pluja als vidres* [Rain against the windows]) depicts some personal tragedies with clear and precise language. *L'altra ciutat. Madame Adà. Estranys presoners d'Arenys a Sinera* (The other city. Madame Adà. Strange prisoners from Arenys to Sinera) presents three short pieces. The first is a novella in which the protagonist, Rosa, returns to her native Tarragona and finds that memories of the past constantly interfere with the present. "Madame Adà," a story later included in the collection *Coses i noses* (Things and obstacles), depicts the superficial, fleeting relationship between an ex-seminarian and an Italian-born Parisian fashion designer vacationing on the Catalan coast. In the third work Capmany describes her literary encounter with Salvador Espriu. The novel *Tana o la felicitat* (Tana, or happiness) depicts Tana's wedding day, which serves as the background for interweaving family relationships with the personal history of the protagonist; the figure of the groom remains marginal. *Betúlia* offers an image of the city of Badalona that differs from the one Badalonans have. Capmany outlines certain moments and historical situations, the past and the future of the town, which changes without a real transformation. The narrator, Niní, functions as the author's alter ego. *Com una mà* (Like a hand) is a collection of short stories, with widely varied themes and styles. *Ara* (Now), a novel about time, portrays a man who, in order to connect to the present, invents a past for himself. Capmany explores themes of hypocrisy and indeterminate time, where the past dominates the present. Her play *El desert dels dies* (The desert of days) is based on this novel. *Vés-te'n ianqui! o si voleu, traduït de l'americà* (Yankee, go home! or if you will, translated from the American; 1959; a second, longer version appeared in 1980) deals with an American millionaire whose son disappears in Albania. He hires a detective to find him, and the investigation in the small communist country simultaneously expands into an analysis of all kinds of economic, social, and political problems, on both a general and a personal level. In *El gust de la pols* (The taste of dust), a crime of passion is the pretext for Martí Gelabert, a lawyer, to criticize the traditional Catalan bourgeoisie. The author uses flashbacks in this complicated plot and incorporates personal ideas and reflections.

Un lloc entre els morts (1967; A place among the dead) is a well-documented biography of the poet and libertarian Jeroni Campdepadrós, who was born in 1789 (in 1976, Capmany wrote a theatrical version very different from the television adaptation by Terenci Moix). In *Feliçment, jo sóc una dona* (1969; Fortunately, I'm a woman), the protagonist, Carola Milà, narrates the story of her eventful life in the first half of the twentieth century. Sprinkled with historical events of the period, the novel introduces the reader to several levels of Barcelona society, as Milà recounts the ups and downs of her life—as the daughter of an unmarried woman, a clerk in a glove store, the lover of an anarchist who is murdered, the protégée of a charitable rich lady, and, finally, a maid and prostitute who marries a rich industrialist and enters Barcelona's high society. In *Vitrines d'Amsterdam* (Showcases of Amsterdam), the kidnapping of a rich businessman leads his brother to Amsterdam's neighborhoods of prostitution and introduces him to people who live on the margins of society. *Quim/Quima* (1971) begins with a prologue in the form of a letter to Virginia Woolf, in which Capmany confesses that she has taken the novel *Orlando* as her model. The history of Catalonia plays a major role in this tale of gender change, which begins in the year 1000 and goes up to the Spanish Civil War.

In *El jaqué de la democràcia* (Democracy jacket), Capmany uses a new narrative technique. The first part consists of fragments of an unfinished novel by a North American, which a young researcher wishes to study for his thesis. The reader is presented with an impressionistic vision of the political complications in the imaginary city of Salona, capital of Balvacària, which is not unlike Barcelona. In the second part, at the request of the researcher the writer assembles the fragments into a novel that falls somewhere between a detective story and science fiction. The novel describes the struggles of strong men against the forces of progress. *Coses i noses* collects short stories, most of them previously published. The novel *Lo color més blau* (The bluest color) takes its title from the poem "Oda a la patria" by Carles Aribau: "Adéu-siau, turons, per sempre adéu-siau / . . . per lo repós etern, per lo color més blau" (Goodbye, hills, goodbye forever / . . . for eternal rest, for the bluest color). Written in the form of letters between the daughter of a Communist who goes into exile in 1939 and the daughter of a middle-class liberal who stays in Barcelona under the Franco regime, this novel contrasts the vicissitudes of life in exile with the dispiriting certainties in postwar Spain.

Capmany is one of the few Catalan women authors who successfully dedicated themselves to theater work after the war; she was not only a playwright but also a director and an actor. She has produced numerous pieces for the stage as well as scripts for radio and television. Her profound themes concerning the individual and society are presented critically, ironically, and humorously. For her the theater is not just a pastime but an authentic diversion. In *Tu i l'hipòcrita* (You and the hypocrite) the protagonist tries to transcend the limitations of time and space through monologue. It is the autobiography of a middle-class man, a very common type in postwar Spanish society, who bases his existence on falseness and hypocrisy, attitudes born more out of passivity than of bad faith. Realizing that his present as well as his future are the result of his past, he dares not make plans for the future and even fears the apparent freedom to act in the present. "Dos quarts de cinc" (1963; Four-thirty) appeared on television and also at the Coliseu Theater. Time is again the main theme of this work, which is noted for its lyricism and the synthesis of its structure. Within a brief instant, just before separating, a couple oscillate between attraction and repulsion, love and hate, in a desperate attempt to stop the passage of time. *El desert dels dies* (The desert of days) deals with a man who invents a past to substitute for his real one and adapts the present to the false version. The theme of hypocrisy resurfaces, symbolizing a generation that has deliberately forgotten its past in order to live in the present.

Vent de garbí i una mica de por (Southwest wind and a little fear), an overtly political work, evokes three critical moments in the history of Catalonia: 1909, the Tragic Week; 1936, the beginning of the Civil War; and 1968, a period of turmoil boding an uncertain future. Set in the summer resort towns of Cadaqués, Sitges, and Caldetes, the action centers on the middle class's refusal to take any responsibility for social or political events. The tone is ironic; the dehumanized characters are caricatures of their class. *Dones, flors i pitança* (Women, flowers, and sustenance), "La cultura de la Coca-cola" (1969; Coca-Cola culture), and "Botxirel.lo" (1974) are cabaret pieces, which were performed at the Cova del Drac; *Tirant lo Blanc* (1980; Tirant lo Blanc) is an adaptation of the fifteenth-century novel by the Valencian Joanot Martorell. *Preguntes i respostes sobre la vida i la mort de Francesc Layret* (1971; Questions and answers about the life and death of Francesc Layret) is documentary theater of political action, influenced by Erwin Piscator and Peter Brook. It was written in memory of Francesc Layret, the advocate of workers in Catalonia, and was staged clandestinely in Terrassa on the fiftieth anniversary of his assassination. *L'ombra de l'escorpí* (The shadow of the scorpion), a historical-political play, takes place during the last hours of the battle of Muret in 1213 in Thermes, a fortress in Occitania and one of the most important Albigensian centers in the thirteenth century. The three major characters are Sabina de Thermes, a Cathar and sister of the count; the count's wife, who represents the eternal feminine; and Pere, a Barcelona lawyer caught between the two women. With perfect control of the dramatic action, the author presents a finale in which each protagonist must choose between fidelity and the desertion of the town.

In television and radio, Capmany produced *L'alt Rei en Jaume* (His highness King Jaume) in an eight-part series. *Història de Catalunya* (1977–78; History of Catalonia) appeared as a forty-five-chapter radio program and was later published with cassettes as *Temps passat: Notícia d'avui* (Time passes: Today's news). *Ca, barret!* (a play on the word *cabaret*; lit., Nonsense, chapeau!) contains a number of cabaret pieces put on at the Cova del Drac. Written in collaboration with Jaume Vidal i Alcover, these light, satiric works mix many literary genres together. In the late

1970s Capmany produced several television scripts: "Jaume I" (1977; Jaume the First); "Tereseta-que-baixava-les-escales" (1977; Teresa-who-came-down-the-stairs), an adaptation of a story by Salvador Espriu; "La nina" (1978; The doll), based on Henrik Ibsen's *The Doll House*; "Aquesta nit no vindrem a sopar" (1979; We won't be home for supper tonight); and "La nit catalana" (1979; The Catalan night).

Capmany also wrote essays on women, machismo, and the history of feminism. She insists on women's right to enjoy full equality with men, as long as the women possess comparable abilities and intellectual skills, and rigorously criticizes the hypocrisy of women who use the supposed weakness of their sex. Capmany also produced literary criticism and history, including studies on Manuel de Pedrolo and Salvador Espriu. Some autobiographical reflections are gathered in *Mala memòria* (Bad memory), the first volume of her memoirs, in which she prefers the spontaneity of anecdotes to an exhaustive, chronological narration.

In children's literature, she adapted classical works and wrote about Angela Davis in *Angela i els vuit mil policies* (Angela and the eight thousand policemen). Other works for children include *Anna, Bel i Carles* (Anna, Bel, and Carles), *Ni teu ni meu* (Neither mine nor yours), and *El malefici de la reina d'Hongria o les aventures dels tres patrons de nau* (1981; The curse of the queen of Hungary or the adventures of the three skippers). The last story takes place at the end of the eighteenth century, when Barcelona was recuperating from poverty and decadence and powerful nations were vying for supremacy in the Mediterranean. Based on a legend of three brothers, one of whom emerges victorious at the end without resorting to violence, the tale is told with historical accuracy. The short story "La mar galana i el mar astut" (The elegant sea and the astute sea) appears in *Joc d'asos* (Set of aces), a collection of stories that also contains work by Llorenç Villalonga, Mercè Rodoreda, Josep Pla, Salvador Espriu, and others.

BOOKS
Això era i no era. Barcelona: Planeta, 1989.
L'altra ciutat. Madame Adà. Estranys presoners d'Arenys a Sinera. Barcelona: Selecta, 1955.
L'alt Rei en Jaume. Barcelona: Aymà, 1977.
Angela i els vuit mil policies. Barcelona: Laia, 1981.
Anna, Bel i Carles. Barcelona: Lumen, 1971.
Antifèmina. With Colita. Madrid: Nacional, 1978.
Aquelles dames d'altres temps. Barcelona: Planeta, 1990.
Ara. Barcelona: Albertí, 1958. 2nd ed. Plaza & Janés, 1988.
Betúlia. Barcelona: Selecta, 1956.
Ca, barret! With Jaume Vidal i Alcover. Palma de Mallorca: Moll, 1984.
Cada cosa en el seu temps i lectura cada dia. Barcelona: Dopesa, 1975.
El cap de Sant Jordi. Barcelona: Planeta, 1988.

Carta abierta al macho ibérico. Madrid: Ediciones 99, 1973.
Cartes impertinents. Palma de Mallorca: Moll, 1971.
Cent pàgines triades per mi. Barcelona: La Campana, 1987.
Lo color més blau. Barcelona: Planeta, 1983.
El comportamiento amoroso de la mujer. Barcelona: Dopesa, 1972.
Com una mà. Palma de Mallorca: Moll, 1958.
Coses i noses. Barcelona: Magrana, 1980.
De profesión: Mujer. Barcelona: Plaza & Janés, 1971.
El desert dels dies. Barcelona: Occitània, 1966.
Dia sí, dia no. Barcelona: Llibres de Sinera, 1968.
Dies i hores de la Nova Cançó. Montserrat: L'Abadia, 1981.
Dietari de prudències. Barcelona: Hogar del Libro, 1982.
La dona a Catalunya: Consciència i situació. Barcelona: Edicions 62, 1966.
La dona: Dona, doneta, donota. Barcelona: Dopesa, 1975.
Dona, doneta, donota (comic book). With Avel.li Artís-Gener. Barcelona: Edhasa, 1979.
Dona i societat a la Catalunya actual. With Magda Oranich, Anna Balletbó, Maria Rosa Prats, and Isabel-Clara Simó. Barcelona: Edicions 62, 1978.
Dones, flors i pitança. Palma de Mallorca: Moll, 1968.
Feliçment, jo sóc una dona. Barcelona: Nova Terra, 1983.
El feminisme a Catalunya. Barcelona: Nova Terra, 1973.
El feminismo ibérico. Barcelona: Oikos-Tau, 1970.
El gust de la pols. Barcelona: Destino, 1962.
Històries de Barcelona. Barcelona: Barri Gòtic, 1963.
El jaqué de la democràcia. Barcelona: Nova Terra, 1972.
La joventut, una nova classe? Barcelona: Edicions 62, 1969.
El lector i la seva obra. Barcelona: Editex, 1956.
Un lloc entre els morts. Barcelona: Laia, 1982.
Mala memòria. Barcelona: Planeta, 1987.
El malefici de la reina d'Hongria o les aventures dels tres patrons de nau. Barcelona: Barcanova, 1981.
Maria Aurèlia Capmany en els seus millors escrits. Barcelona: Arimany, 1986.
Necessitem morir. Barcelona: Aymà, 1977.
Ni teu ni meu. Barcelona: La Galera, 1978.
Obra completa. Barcelona: Nova Terra, 1974.
L'ombra de l'escorpí. Valencia: Gorg, 1974.
Pedra de toc. Barcelona: Nova Terra, 1970.
Pedra de toc II. Barcelona: Nova Terra, 1974.
La pluja als vidres. Barcelona: Club, 1984.
Preguntes i respostes sobre la vida i la mort de Francesc Layret, advocat dels obrers de Catalunya. With Xavier Romeu. Barcelona: Magrana, 1976.
Quim/Quima. Barcelona: Laia, 1983.
La rialla del mirall. Barcelona: Empúries, 1989.
Salvador Espriu. Barcelona: Dopesa, 1972.
Subirachs o retrat de l'artista com a escultor adult. Barcelona: Pòrtic, 1975.
Tana o la felicitat. Palma de Mallorca: Moll, 1956.
Temps passat: Notícia d'avui. Barcelona: Vicens Vives, 1978.
Tirant lo Blanc. Valencia: Gorg, 1980.

Tu i l'hipòcrita. Palma de Mallorca: Moll, 1960.

Vent de garbí i una mica de por. Palma de Mallorca: Moll, 1965.

Vés-te'n ianqui! o, si voleu, traduït de l'americà. Barcelona: Laia, 1980.

Vitrines d'Amsterdam. Barcelona: Club, 1970.

WORKS IN BOOKS, PERIODICALS, NEWSPAPERS

"La mar galana i el mar astut." *Joc d'asos.* Ed. Alex Broch. Barcelona: Magrana, 1981. 85–95.

"Reixes a través." *Cita de narradors.* Barcelona: Selecta, 1958. 7–120.

TRANSLATIONS OF HER WORKS

La color más azul [Lo color més blau]. Trans. Carolina Rosés. Barcelona: Planeta, 1984.

"The Lady with the Umbrella" [from *Aquelles dames d'altres temps*]. Trans. Patricia Mathews. *Catalan Writing* 7 (1991): 30–35.

Un lugar entre los muertos [Un lloc entre els morts]. Barcelona: Nova Terra, 1970.

Ni tuyo ni mío [Ni teu ni meu]. Barcelona: La Galera, 1978.

Quim/Quima. Barcelona: Plaza & Janés, 1986.

"Tú y el hipòcrita" [from *Tu i l'hipòcrita*]. Trans. Teresa Valdivieso. *Estreno* 12.1 (1986): 11–32.

Vete yanqui [Ves-te'n ianqui!]. Barcelona: Laia, 1981.

"Viento del sur y un poco de miedo" [from *Vent de garbí i una mica de por*]. *Yorick* 10 Dec. 1965.

SECONDARY SOURCES

Arbonès, Jordi. *Teatre català de postguerra.* Barcelona: Pòrtic, 1973. 109–16.

Bartomeus, Antoni. *Els autors de teatre català: Testimoni d'una marginació.* Barcelona: Curial, 1976. 115–34.

Busquets i Grabulosa, Lluís. *Plomes catalanes contemporànies.* Barcelona: Mall, 1980. 115–24.

Ciplijauskaité, *La novela femenina contemporánea.*

Clemente, José Carlos. "A tumba abierta: Maria Aurèlia Capmany." *Diario de Barcelona* 4 Oct. 1970: 16–17.

Coca, Jordi. "Maria Aurèlia Capmany i Farnès: Una senyora entremaliada." *Serra d'or* Sept. 1981: 17–25.

Garcés, Tomàs. "Un lloc entre els morts." *Sobre Salvat-Papasseit i altres escrits.* Barcelona: Selecta, 1972.

Horta, Joaquim. *Maria Aurèlia Capmany (1918–1991).* Barcelona: Ajuntament, 1992.

Janer, Gabriel. "Conversa amb Maria Aurèlia Capmany." *Lluch* Sept. 1971: 13–14.

May, Barbara Dale. "The Power Dynamics of Women's Anger in Maria-Aurelia Capmany's *La color más azul.*" *Letras femeninas* 12.1–2 (1986): 103–13.

Misiego i Llagostera, Miquela. "Maria Aurèlia Capmany: Un feminisme diferent." *Actes del Segon Col.loqui d'Estudis Catalans a Nord-Amèrica.* Montserrat: L'Abadia, 1982. 389–403.

Möller-Soler, Maria-Lourdes. "La mujer de la pre- y postguerra civil española en las obras teatrales de Carme Montoriol y Maria Aurèlia Capmany." *Estreno* 12.1 (1986): 6–8.

Pedrolo, Manuel de. "Impressions-expressions sobre tres novel.les de la Maria-Aurèlia." Preface. Capmany, *Obra completa* 9–23.

Roda, Frederic. "Entrevista a Maria Aurèlia Capmany." *Serra d'or* June 1964: 34–35.

Roig, Montserrat. "Maria Aurèlia Capmany entre la polèmica i la fidelitat." *Serra d'or* June 1971: 33–35.

Sarsanedas, Jordi. "Llegeixo les novel.les de Maria Aurèlia Capmany." *Cita de narradors*. Barcelona: Selecta, 1958. 7–44.

Triadú, Joan. *La novela catalana de post-guerra*. Barcelona: Edicions 62, 1987.

Valdivieso, L. Teresa. "La poética dramática de Maria Aurèlia Capmany en *Vent de garbí i una mica de por*." *Estudis de llengua, literatura i cultura catalanes*. Montserrat: L'Abadia, 1979. 281–89.

———. "A propósito de la versión castellana de *Tu i l'hipòcrita*." *Estreno* 12.1 (1986): 9–10.

Vilanova, Antoni. "*Necessitem morir* de Maria Aurèlia Capmany." *Destino* 20 July 1957.

MARIA-LOURDES SOLER I MARCET

C Cardet i Güell, Dolors
(B. 1872, Mataró, Barcelona; d. ?, Barcelona?) Poet.

The only biographical information available is that Dolors Cardet i Güell was the daughter of Manuel Cardet i Viciana and Cristina Güell i Piferrer. She lived in Mataró and contributed to the Barcelona periodicals *Or y grana* in 1906 and 1907, *Feminal* in 1907, and *Lo teatre catòlic* in 1899 and 1900 and to the Mataró publications *Barró de la vior* in 1908, *La veu de la costa* in 1909, and *Diario de Mataró* in 1910, as well as to *Pàgina literària* in Badalona, Barcelona, in 1910.

In 1910 and 1917 she published two short collections of poems, *Dedicatoria: Poesías* and *Poesías*, respectively. Her poetry is inspired by religious sentiment, family feeling, and themes and motifs characteristic of the *Renaixença*.

BOOKS
Dedicatoria: Poesías. Mataró, Barcelona: L. Rosell, n.d. [1910].
Poesías. Mataró, Barcelona: Abadal, n.d. [1917].

WORKS IN BOOKS, PERIODICALS, NEWSPAPERS
"Adéu al Maig." *Feminal* 4 (28 July 1907).
"A Jesús." *Lo teatre catòlic* 5 Nov. 1899: 2.
"A la memoria de la inolvidable amiga Maria de la Assumpció Rissech." *Lo teatre catòlic* 15 Oct. 1899: 1.
"Jesús a l'Hort." *Lo teatre catòlic* 3 Apr. 1900: 5.

CARMEN SIMON PALMER

C Cardona i Bosch, Fina
(B. 1957, València– .) Poet.

Included in the so-called generation of the 1970s, Fina Cardona i Bosch published her first book, *Plouen pigues* (It's raining freckles), in 1978. Her poetry is distinguished by its intensity and condensation in generally short verses. She reflects on the past or on daily reality, capturing the fleetingness of a moment, the happiness or sadness of daily life, and the self within its circumstances. The language is generally simple, and the rhythm creates a characteristic musicality similar to that of popular song. The second book, *Pessigolles de palmera* (Tickled by palms), develops these techniques and employs stylized language, as the poet reflects on solitude and love.

BOOKS
Pessigolles de palmera. Pref. Maria del Mar Bonet. Barcelona: Mall, 1981.
Plouen pigues. Pref. Vicent Andrés Estellés. Valencia: Tres i Quatre, 1978.

WORKS IN BOOKS, PERIODICALS, NEWSPAPERS
"Nus mariner." *Lletres de canvi* 7 (Feb. 1982): 15–17.

ISABEL ROBLES GOMEZ

C Cardona i Codina, Maria
(B. 1923, Calella; d. 1972, Calella.) Poet.

Maria Cardona i Codina's *Una veu calellenca* (A voice from Calella) is a posthumous selection compiled at the behest of the City Council of that community. It contains a prologue by mayor Joan Llobet and a long introduction by Roser Matheu. Cardona i Codina won prizes at the Jocs Florals of Catalonia and Roussillon; her themes are family, nature, patriotism, and faith. She speaks of love but the book contains no personal love poems. Matheu writes that this collection is a small sample of her work. One of Cardona's most successful symbols is that of the sardana, which, she explains in "Sardana," we should take as a lesson: "si hem après la lliçó de la sardana / que ens ensenya de dur els braços oberts / i d'estrènyer ben fort la mà dels altres" (if we've learned the lesson of the sardana / which shows us to stretch out our arms / and tightly hold the hands of others). Cardona often uses the colors red and white, and her meters sometimes show the influence of popular songbooks. She attempted a more current style but remained quite traditional.

BOOKS
Una veu calellenca. Prol. Joan Llobet. Introd. Roser Matheu. Calella: Ajuntament, 1975.

KATHLEEN MCNERNEY

C Cardús i Malarriaga, Roser

(B. 1920, Barcelona; d. 1974, Barcelona.) Writer of short stories and children's literature.

Roser Cardús studied pharmacy in Barcelona, graduating in 1942. She married Antoni Solans Ferrer in 1945 and had five children. During her lifetime she published two books for children, *El príncep bandoler* (The Brigand Prince) and *La noia del rostre canviant i altres contes* (The girl with a changing face and other stories). Whereas the first book is written in a simple, direct style, the second shows more complexity in language and themes. But her early work, for which Roser Cardús claims the influence of Arthur Anderson, does not prepare the reader for her posthumous book, *Lepra d'or* (Golden leprosy). Published in homage to Cardús, it is a collection of seven short stories; the title comes from her introductory poem. Although the stories are set mostly in Catalonia and the characters have Catalan names, the themes are universal. A feeling of death is pervasive; as an out-of-place and out-of-time atmosphere prevails, the stories achieve an increasingly disturbing ambience. Roser Cardús describes subtle feelings but never falls into sentimentality. She effectively shows the ambivalent, changing moods of human beings—passion, cruelty, commiseration—in language and images that are carefully wrought. "Lelia i el temps" (Lelia and time) explains how a young man becomes a poet by experiencing the different effects of time on himself and on a beloved cousin, whose death at an early age makes her an adolescent forever. In "La subasta" (The auction), a failed painter is shown in a critical situation where his artistic self-esteem will be determined by the buyers. "Una catleia" (An orchid) tells how the gift of a flower can affect the destiny of a relationship. "Eleonora" describes the pathological passion of a painter toward a legendary statue. "L'abisme" (The abyss) and "Joc de nines" (Dolls' play) both present strong characters involved in relationships with weaker persons whom they protect. These involvements result in feelings of hate and even in death, when the stronger one, afflicted with guilt, assumes responsibility for the weaker one. "Viatge en tren" (A trip by train) portrays a failed poet whose writings since his youth have dealt with death. Confronted with the personality of his brother, a successful businessman, he commits suicide.

In 1982, the Barcelona magazine *El pont* published Cardús's science-fiction story, "La droga" (Drugs), which deals with some of the themes found in Anthony Burgess's *The Clockwork Orange*. This story was recently included in *Narracions de ciència ficció: Antologia* (Science fiction stories: An anthology). Some bibliographies attribute another book, *El temps ens ha fet així* (Time has changed us), to Roser Cardús, but this novel was written by Roser Grau. In 1938, during the Civil War, Cardús translated Virginia Woolf's *Flush* and Len Deighton's *Funerals in Berlin* into Catalan.

102

BOOKS
Lepra d'or. Barcelona: Miquel Arimany, 1976.
La noia del rostre canviant i altres contes. Barcelona: Miquel Arimany, 1960.
El príncep bandoler. Barcelona: Miquel Arimany, 1958.

WORKS IN BOOKS, PERIODICALS, NEWSPAPERS
"Darrera notícia." *El pont* 68 (1969): 8–13.
"La droga." *Narracions de ciència ficció: Antologia.* Ed. A. Munné-Jordà. Barcelona: Edicions 62, 1985. 23–30.

SECONDARY SOURCES
"Nota editorial." Editorial. *El pont* 68 (1969): 13.
Serra Estruch, J. "Els autors i les obres: *El príncep bandoler.*" *El pont* 14 (1959): 198–200.
Vilaginas, Carme. "Roser Cardús: *La noia del rostre canviant.*" *Serra d'or* Jan. (1961): 18.

CRISTINA ENRIQUEZ DE SALAMANCA

Carol, Montserrat; *see* **Crusells de Carol, Montserrat**

C   Carranza, Maite
(B. 1958, Barcelona– .) Writer of children's literature. No biographical information available.

BOOKS
Les cartes de la Còia. Barcelona: La Galera, 1988.
La insòlita campanya. Barcelona: Magrana, 1987.
Ostres tu, quin cacau! Barcelona: Magrana, 1986.
Prohibit de ploure els dissabtes. Barcelona, Magrana, 1988.
La revolta dels lactants. Barcelona: La Galera, 1987.

TRANSLATIONS OF HER WORKS
Las cartas de Quica [*Les cartes de la Còia*]. Barcelona: La Galera, 1988.
La rebelión de los lactantes [*La revolta dels lactants*]. Barcelona: La Galera, 1989.
¡Toma, castaña! [*Ostres tu, quin cacau!*]. Barcelona: Ediciones B, 1989.

KATHLEEN MCNERNEY

C   Carreras i Pau, Concepció
(B. 1894, Olot, Girona; d. 1961, Olot, Girona). Poet.

According to *Les cinc branques*, Concepció Carreras i Pau won prizes for her poetry in Olot and Lleida and published three books of poetry: *Elvira*

(1950), *Tribut al paisatge i fonts d'Olot* (1953; Tribute to Olot's landscape and fountains), and *De l'amor i la desamor* (1954; Of love and lack of love). These books have not been located.

WORKS IN BOOKS, PERIODICALS, NEWSPAPERS
"Renyines d'enamorats." *Les cinc branques* 90.

KATHLEEN MCNERNEY

C Cartañà Domenge de Sánchez de Ocaña, Elvira
(B. 1918, Barcelona– .) Poet.

Elvira Cartañà's collection of verse and prose poems *Al meu casal* (To my house) treats such themes as love, religion, death, and solitude. She avoids triteness through the repeated use of light and shadow in images often taken directly from nature. This impressionism and her sincere invitation "al meu casal" give an expansiveness to the quotidian but nevertheless important concerns of her poetry.

BOOKS
Al meu casal. Prol. Climent Forner. Illus. Manuel Sánchez Ocaña. Barcelona: n.p., 1985.
Clarianes. Barcelona: Torrell de Reus, 1980.
Terra blava. Barcelona: n.p., 1980.
Volada d'àngels. Barcelona: Altés, 1982.

NANCY L. BUNDY

C Casanova i Danés, Concepció
(B. 1906, Campdevanol, Girona– .) Translator and poet. No biographical information available.

Concepció Casanova i Danés has published one book of love poetry, *Poemes en el temps* (Poems in time).

BOOKS
Poemes en el temps. Barcelona: Altés, 1930.

WORKS IN BOOKS, PERIODICALS, NEWSPAPERS
"XXI—A J. Balcells." *Les cinc branques* 132.

NANCY L. BUNDY

C Casanovas i Berenguer, Caterina
(B. 1918, Fajardo, Puerto Rico– .) Known as Lina Casanovas.
Poet.

Lina Casanovas lived in Cuba and New York as a child and then moved to Badalona, Barcelona, with her father. The Spanish Civil War interrupted her pedagogical studies, and later she worked as a bilingual secretary. Because of her family background and her life abroad, she knows several languages—English, Italian, Castilian, and Catalan—and writes in the last two. Since 1953 she has lived in Argentona i Dosrius, Barcelona.

In 1966 she published her first collection of poetry, *A cavall d'un estel* (Riding on a star), and she is planning a second, "Retorn" (Coming back). The search for formalism and the use of language to avoid obscurity and to facilitate communication characterize her poetry. She says that the poet "no duu rellotge per treballar, fes com l'abella petit i forta / recull essències de bosc i d'horta" (does not wear a watch to work, does like the small and strong bee / that gathers essences from the forest and garden) (*A cavall* 35). Religious feeling, the basis of her poetry, is manifested in a wish for universal harmony, in generosity to others, and in the intuition of having become a divine instrument, which she lovingly accepts.

Nature is a source of imagery, with poems like "Pluja a montanya" (Rain in the mountain) and "Plugim" (Drizzle) celebrating a specific moment. Catalonia appears in "Dolça terra" (Sweet land) and "Sang catalana" (Catalan blood), which are linked to familial feelings.

Lina Casanovas has won awards in the Jocs Florals held outside Spain and is *Mestra* (Master) in Gay Saber.

BOOKS
A cavall d'un estel. Barcelona: n.p., 1966. 2nd ed. Argentona, Barcelona: n.p., 1986.

CRISTINA ENRIQUEZ DE SALAMANCA

C Castanyer i Figueres, Maria
(B. 1913, Girona– .) Poet and fiction writer.

Winner of prizes in various contests and Jocs Florals, among them the Flor Natural and the Viola de Plata in Perpignan in 1965, Maria Castanyer coedited the Girona journal *Presència* with Carme Alcalde. She formed a literary group during the dictatorship of Franco, which was attended by all the prestigious artists and writers in Catalonia; the sessions were conducted entirely in Catalan.

Her first book of poetry, *Cançons del color del temps* (Songs of the color of time), was published in 1948. *Retrobar-me en la terra* (Finding myself

105

again in the earth) is obsessed with death. Castanyer's poetry is distinguished by its intimate tone and clarity and its absence of rhetorical language. She often uses free verse. She has written one book in Castilian, *Muriendo en el silencio* (Dying in silence). Her novelette *La creu i la llum* (The cross and the light) was awarded first prize in the Oreig contest in 1984.

In 1947 Castanyer went to the United States and taught at Holy Names College and various other American universities, including the University of California at Berkeley and Brigham Young University. She returned to Catalonia in 1977 and settled in Blanes, Girona, where she contributed to several local papers and journals. Between 1977 and 1982 she translated the *Book of Mormon* into Catalan.

BOOKS
Cançons del color del temps. Prol. Josep Maria López Picó. Girona: Pla, 1948.
La creu i la llum. Blanes, Girona: n.p., 1984.
Muriendo en el silencio. Barcelona: Rumbos, 1954.
Retrobar-me en la terra. Prol. Tomás Roig i Llop. Barcelona: Rumbos, 1958.

WORKS IN BOOKS, PERIODICALS, NEWSPAPERS
"Cartes d'Amèrica." *Recull* 21 July 1974.
"Cartes d'Amèrica." *Recull* 21 Sept. 1976.
"Els deures, els mestres i els pares." *Punt diari* 9 Oct. 1984.
"La humanitat continua igual" and "Turisme si, gràcies! Turisme no, gràcies!" *Punt diari* 14 June 1984.
"Una nena de mirada trista." *Punt diari* 23 Aug. 1984.
"Nit màgica de Nadal" and "Ha nascut un noi." *Revista del Club de Vela Blanes* Dec. 1986.
"Revista del cor i altres coses." *Punt diari* 6 Nov. 1984.

ALBINA FRANSITORRA ALENA

C   Castellà i Vals, Teresa
(20th c.) Poet.

In 1952 a volume of poetry entitled *Veler de somnis* (Sailboat of dreams) by Teresa Castellà i Vals was published in Igualada, Barcelona. The prologue, by Tomàs Roig i Llop, states that she was the daughter of Gabriel Castellà i Raich, a learned man who worked in the City Archives of Igualada.

The book, which is dedicated to her father, is divided into three sections: "Religioses" (Religious), "Amoroses" (Love), and "Vària" (Various). The first section begins with a poem dedicated to the flag of Igualada.

This poem is typical of the genre produced since the *Renaixença* by the convergence of Catalan nationalistic sentiment and traditional Catholic verse. Other poems in this section, such as "A la Verge de la Pietat, Compatrona d'Igualada" (To the Virgin of piety, copatron of Igualada) and "A Sant Crist d'Igualada" (To Holy Christ of Igualada), are inspired by local devotional practices. The second section, "Amoroses," is the most extensive. Its opening poem, "Veler de somnis," won first prize (Flor Natural) in the Jocs Florals of Sant Just Desvern, Barcelona, in 1947. This section contains other award-winning compositions: "El romeu de l'amor" (Pilgrim of love) was honored at the Jocs Florals of El Prat de Llobregat, Barcelona; "L'inútil poema" (Useless poem) won first prize in the women's poetry at the Jocs Florals of the Parish Center of Santa Madrona, Barcelona, in 1947; and "La teva imminència" (Your imminence) was awarded a prize at the Literary Festival at the Center of Studies in Igualada. In this section, the poet's dialogue with her reluctant lover becomes the motive for poetic creation, and she constructs an image of the lover in which love—or its frustration—and poetry go together. The "Vària" section consists of a brief selection of poems in which memories of her deceased mother, the anniversary of a friend's death, and thoughts about her own death are treated in elegiac tones. "Aquarel.la" (Watercolor), the final poem, is written in Haiku form and evokes moments of quietude in nature.

BOOKS

Veler de somnis. Prol. Tomàs Roig i Llop. Igualada, Barcelona: n.p., 1952.

CRISTINA ENRIQUEZ DE SALAMANCA

C   Castellà Teixidor, Amanda

(20th c.) Poet. No biographical information available.

Amanda Castellà Teixidor's literary production seems to be limited to the book *L'abadessa: Simfonia mística: Poema líric* (The abbess: A mystic symphony: Lyric poem). In the grandiose plan of this long poem, she uses the format of medieval dialogue to present her religious and traditional messages. She returns to the ancient heroism of saints and legendary figures in an attempt to inspire patriotic and Christian values.

BOOKS

L'abadessa: Simfonia mística: Poema líric. Barcelona: n.p., 1952.

KATHLEEN MCNERNEY

C   Castellví i Gordon, Isabel Maria

(B. 1867, Madrid; d. 1949, Barcelona.) Poet, journalist, and short story writer.

Isabel Maria Castellví i Gordon, countess of Castellà and Carlet, came from a Catalan family living in Madrid. She married Salvador Armet y Picart and moved to Barcelona. Most of her work is written in Castilian. A highly educated person, she was fluent in several languages, traveled extensively, and was in touch with the foreign literary movements of her time. She became a professor in the national school of languages (Escuela Central de Idiomas) in Madrid, teaching etymology and phonetics.

Castellví began contributing to the journal *El liberal* (Madrid/Barcelona) in 1901 with an article about Lew Wallace's *Ben-Hur*. *El liberal* created the woman's section "Manos blancas" (White hands) for her. She brought the most prominent women writers to it: Emilia Pardo Bazán, Blanca de los Ríos, Sofia Casanovas, Concepción Jimeno de Flaquer, and La Baronesa de Wilson. Castellví devoted a few articles in this section to Alfred, Lord Tennyson, whose poetry she considered "esencialmente femenina y amorosa" (essentially feminine and loving) ("Mujeres de Tennyson"). Tennyson's Lady of Shalott inspired the poem "Como la dama de Shalott . . . Quisiera" (As the Lady Shalott . . . I would like) in Castellví's book of Castilian poetry, *Poema del cisne y la princesa* (Poem of the swan and the princess). This collection of sonnets explores modernist and Becquerian themes. "Al cisne. Señor de mis sueños" (Addressed to the swan. Lord of my reveries) contains rich, exploratory language that produces a shocking effect.

Castellví began writing in Catalan in 1907 and won first prize in the Jocs Florals of the Ateneu Obrer de San Martí de Provençals; the well-known Catalan writer Josep Carner won second prize. The same year she won second prize in the Jocs Florals of Monasteri de Sant Cugat del Vallès, Barcelona, for her poem "Tríptich ciutadà" (Triptych of the City). Her poem "Comiat" (Farewell) was included in the *Antologia de poetes catalans d'avui* (Anthology of Catalan Poets Today). She contributed poems and the short story "Sala de espera" to Barcelona's magazine *Feminal* from 1907 to 1911, and in 1916 she published an article about Palmira Ventós i Cullell (Felip Palma). In 1916, she also published *Urbanidad: Reglas de conducta* . . . (Urbanity: Rules of behavior . . .), a popular manual on behavior.

BOOKS

Gertrudis Gómez de Avellaneda. Gloria Hispano-Americana. Conferencia dada en el Centro de Cultura Hispano-Americana el día 27 de abril de 1913. Madrid: Establecimiento Tipográfico de El Liberal, 1914.

Poema del cisne y la princesa: Sonetos. Madrid: Hernando, 1911.
Urbanidad: Estudio de las reglas de conducta por la Excma. Señora Doña Isabel María del Carmen de Castellví y Gordon. Condesa de Castellà. Barcelona: Seix & Barral, 1916.

WORKS IN BOOKS, PERIODICALS, NEWSPAPERS
"Abril." *El liberal* 353 (1 Apr. 1902).
"Apunte. Aprendizas." *El liberal* 137 (20 Aug. 1901).
"Apunte. Nuestro inmortal." *El liberal* 424 (11 June 1902).
"Ben Hur." *El liberal* 33 (9 May 1901).
"El canto del cisne," "Comiat," "Nocturn del vianant," and "La retama." *Feminal* 53 (27 Aug. 1911).
"Comiat." *Antologia de poetes catalans d'avui.* Biblioteca Popular de L'Avenç 135. Barcelona, Llibreria L'Avenç, 1913. 35.
"Crónica. Agosto." *El liberal* 125 (8 Aug. 1901).
"Crónica. Agua." *El liberal* 167 (19 Sept. 1901).
"Crónica. Antifaces." *El liberal* 310 (10 Feb. 1902).
"Crónica. Charitas." *El liberal* 263 (25 Dec. 1901).
"Crónica. Desolación y heroismo." *El liberal* 146 (29 Aug. 1901).
"Crónica. En Enero." *El liberal* 297 (29 Jan. 1902).
"Crónica. Fuego." *El liberal* 326 (6 Mar. 1902).
"Crónica. In Pace." *El liberal* 210 (2 Nov. 1901).
"Crónica. Mayo." *El liberal* 388 (6 May 1902).
"Crónica. Noviembre." *El liberal* 224 (16 Nov. 1901).
"Crónica. Octubre." *El liberal* 187 (10 Oct. 1901).
"Crónica. Otoñal." *El liberal* 201 (24 Oct. 1901).
"Crónica. Sardanas." *El liberal* 131 (15 Aug. 1901).
"Crónica. Septiembre." *El liberal* 160 (12 Sept. 1901).
"Crónica. Tierra." *El liberal* 153 (5 Sept. 1901).
"Hogueras." *El liberal* 84 (23 June 1901).
"Instantáneas." *El liberal* 174 (26 Sept. 1901).
"Mujeres de Tennyson. Dora." *El liberal* 138 (22 Aug. 1901).
"Mujeres de Tennyson. Godiva." *El liberal* 181 (3 Oct. 1901).
"Mujeres de Tennyson. La dama de Shalott." *El liberal* 105 (18 July 1901).
"Mujeres de Tennyson. La Reina de Mayo." *El liberal* 89 (4 July 1902).
"Palmira Ventós i Cullell." *Feminal* 116 (26 Nov. 1916).
"Por Ben-Hur." *El liberal* 50 (26 May 1901).
"Por Verdi. Aida." *El liberal* 70 (16 June 1901).
"Retama." *El liberal* 62 (7 June 1901).
"Sala de espera." *Feminal* 4 (28 July 1907).
"Tríptich ciutadà" ("La seu," "El park," and "La rambla"). *Feminal* 6 (29 Sept. 1907).
"Visió." *Feminal* 57 (31 Dec. 1911).

SECONDARY SOURCES
Simón Palmer, *Escritoras españolas del siglo XIX* 174–75.

CRISTINA ENRIQUEZ DE SALAMANCA

G Castro, Luisa

(B. 1966, Foz, Lugo– .) Poet and short story writer.

A student of Hispanic philology at the University of Santiago, Luisa Castro collaborated on a 1986 television program about books in Galician. She won prizes for her short stories in 1979 and 1980. She began to contribute short stories to a newspaper in Lugo in 1982, where she won several awards. She also won the 1983 City of Ponferrada prize for her poetry in Castilian and published her first book of poetry in that language: *Odisea definitiva, libro póstumo* (Definitive odyssey, posthumous book). She won the Hiperión prize for poetry in 1986 for her book *Los versos del eunuco* (Poems of the eunuch). Since then she has contributed editorials to the newspaper *ABC*. Her Castilian poetry appears in three anthologies of poetry by women. She has published Galician poems in the magazines *Dorna, La naval,* and *Luzes de Galizia.*

Luisa Castro doesn't consider herself a member of any movement, and in *Odisea definitiva* she cultivates, in her own words, a kind of black poetry. Her poems feature more realism than lyrical expression in order to accumulate the images of a harsh, daily reality: "La luz eléctrica y / la primavera se reconocen en la mentira / insustituible de ser cada vez / más necesarias. / Y después las bombillas desnudas de las habitaciones de los / pobres / se soportan y se hablan" (Electric light and / spring recognize each other in lies / not substitutable for being more and more / necessary. / And afterward the naked light bulbs of the rooms of the / poor / put up with each other and talk) (30).

Los versos del eunuco is constructed from two visions, one surrealistic and the other impressionistic, which come together to reflect reality better, sometimes presenting strictly personal feelings and at other times distorting objective appearances. The eunuch represents multiple egos—the self that goes from the deepest intimacy to the objective representation of the other.

Castro's Galician poems create images of a miserable reality. *Baleas e baleas* (Whales, whales) continues the breaking away and demystifying tendencies of *Los versos del eunuco.* The poetic text depicts daily events in rough language. Castro alludes to human suffering and warns against the deception of pretty words, since rugged nature determines everything. Recurrent themes in the work include the solitude of the sailor, sexual obsessions, childhood games, the isolation of nuns, and domestic matters. The author rebels against poverty through the use of vulgar words and harsh expressions, creating an atmosphere of violence and repression.

BOOKS
Baleas e baleas. Ferrol: Caixa Galicia, 1988.
Los hábitos del artillero. Madrid: Visor, 1990.
Odisea definitiva, libro póstumo. Madrid: Arnao, 1984. 2nd ed. 1986.

El somier. Barcelona: Anagrama, 1990.
Los versos del eunuco. Madrid: Hiperión, 1986.

WORKS IN BOOKS, PERIODICALS, NEWSPAPERS
"Delenda" and "Soy tus pies y tus caderas." *Buenaventura* 236–37.
"E peor quedarse." *Luzes de Galizia* 7 (Summer 1987).
"Es sencillo." *Litoral femenino.* Ed. Lorenzo Saval and J. García Gallego. Granada:
  Litoral, 1986. 261–63.
"Estratexias de desastre." *La naval* 1 (Summer 1986).
"Merda para ti' meu amor," "Non o parece," and "Teño uns grandes ollos de centi-
  nela." *Luzes de Galizia* 4 (Fall–Winter 1986).
"Poetas: Luisa Castro Legazpi." *La voz de Galicia* 29 (Nov. 1986).

TRANSLATIONS OF HER WORKS
Ballenas [*Baleas e baleas*]. Madrid: Hiperión, 1992.

SECONDARY SOURCES
Blanco, Carmen. *Literatura galega da muller.* Vigo: Xerais, 1991. 160–72.
Castaño, Adolfo. "Los versos del eunuco, odio y malditismo." *Reseña de literatura,
  arte y espectáculos* 167 (Sept.-Oct. 1986).
Ferris, J. L. V. "Nuevas diosas." *La verdad* (Summer 1986).
Iglesias, Amalia. "Cuando el verso se transforma en cauce quebrado de palabras."
  El correo español–El pueblo vasco [Bilbao] 4 Sept. 1986.
Noia Campos, Camino. *Palabra de muller.* Vigo: Xerais, 1992. 26–29, 96–97.
Ugalde, Sharon Keefe. "Conversaciones y poemas." *La nueva poesía femenina es-
  pañola en castellano.* Madrid: Siglo XXI, 1991. 281–96.
Vázquez de Gey, Elisa. *Queimar as meigas.* Madrid: Torremozas, 1988. 217–21.

MARIA CAMINO NOIA CAMPOS

G Castro, Rosalía de
(B. 1837, Santiago de Compostela; d. 1885, Padrón, Coruña.)
Poet and novelist.

Rosalía de Castro was the daughter of an unmarried woman from a noble
family of rural origin, and the social norms of the time made her childhood
an unhappy one. From birth to the age of fifteen she was looked after by
an aunt on her father's side and then went to live with her mother, who
encouraged her education. She studied music in Santiago, Coruña, and
took part in the city's social life, getting to know the intellectuals of her
generation such as Eduardo Pondal and Aurelio Aguirre.
  In 1856, she moved to Madrid and the following year published a
collection of poems in Castilian, *La flor* (The flower). There she met Manuel
Murguía, another Galician intellectual and the author of *Historia de Galicia*. After their marriage in 1858, they worked in several Spanish cities.

111

They spent time in Vigo, where her book *Cantares gallegos* (Galician poems) was published, and in Santiago, Cáceres, Alicante, Murcia, and Lugo, where her novel in Castilian, *El caballero de las botas azules* (The gentleman with the blue boots), came out. In 1868, Murguía was named head of the Simancas Archives. During the eleven months spent in Simancas (1870–71) Castro wrote the poems in *Follas novas* (New pages), which was not published until 1880. On her frequent trips to Madrid she met the poet Gustavo Adolfo Bécquer, who was to influence her book *En las orillas del Sar* (On the banks of the Sar). After her return to Galicia, she lived in Coruña, Santiago, and, from 1872 onward, in Padrón. Several years during this last period of her life were spent with her four children; she was separated from her husband, who lived in Oviedo as director of the journal *La ilustración gallega y asturiana*. After a long and difficult lung ailment, Castro died on 15 July 1885.

Although Castro's earliest poems, the books *La flor* and *A mi madre* (To my mother), and her narrative prose were written in Castilian, her best poetic works, *Cantares gallegos* and *Follas novas*, were composed and published in her original language, Galician. *Cantares gallegos* was written during her stay in Castile. Remembering the fertility of her Galician homeland, Castro returned to her mother tongue; the poem "Adios, ríos; adios, fontes" (Good-bye, rivers; good-bye, fountains) was published in the magazine *El museo universal* in 1861. In the style of Antonio Trueba, the Biscayan poet and author of the *Libro de los cantares* (Book of songs) who breathed new life into Romantic poetry by finding inspiration in popular compositions, Castro used traditional Galician songs and devices such as repetition and parallelism. However, she went even further than Trueba, both in her richness of description and expression of feeling.

Follas novas consists of two parts: the first is in the popular, objective style of *Cantares*, but the second changes in theme and compositional form. The work is profoundly lyrical, born of harrowing intimacy with eternal problems: loneliness, death, spirituality, human coexistence, and, especially, the "saudade," a feeling of desolation due to the absence of something, physical or spiritual, which may even be near the person suffering from its absence. For Castro, the "saudade" was a radical feeling, of no definite cause, inherent and even necessary to the human being. Its disappearance leaves an even greater void, leading to a loss of interest in life, which can only be recovered through death, in union with God.

Social problems provide the theme for several poems in *Follas novas*. Sometimes angrily, sometimes melodiously, Castro attacks the injustice suffered by Galicia through poverty and neglect by the Castilian state administration. The poems in "Viudas de vivos" (Widows of the Living) deal with the consequences of male emigration: the unprotected homes and the fatherless children and women destroyed by loneliness and destitution. Castro's criticism is charged with deep personal feeling.

Castro writes from a female point of view, as a woman who is conscious of the world in which she lives and who is willing to take a stand. She is not interested in writing about the home full of flowers or the placidity of love and nature, because for her the world is not a pleasant place. Her strength stems from her inner life and her country. In her poetic work, Galicia and its tormented existence are the two major themes, in contrast to the abstractions that frequently inspire the Romantic poets. More sincere and realistic than the Romantics, Castro writes out of the need to communicate with herself and does not depend on conventional subjects. Not seeking literary glory, she wants only to speak of her feelings and of the misery of the peasants around her.

En las orillas del Sar, her last book, was published when Castro was already a well-known writer, and these Castilian poems, unlike her Galician ones, approach Romantic ideals. In Becquerian style, she asserts her claim to freedom and the glory of the poet. Full of Romantic vanity, she criticizes those who consider themselves "genios y sabios." The theme of glory is repeated in several poems in the book, but the poet ends by renouncing it in favor of silence and spiritual peace.

Castro is remarkably heterogeneous in choosing types of meter and combinations of verses, especially in *Follas novas* and *En las orillas del Sar*. Some poems are composed in the Romantic tradition, with "silvas" and blank hendecasyllables as in Heine or Bécquer; in others, the poet combines octosyllables with lines of ten, eleven, or fourteen syllables to achieve rhythmic variety and dissonance.

Castro's novels, all in Castilian, have been of much less interest than her poetry, not only to her own critics but to those later studying her work. She published five novels, three of them Romantic in construction and theme: *La hija del mar* (The daughter of the sea), *Flavio*, and *El primer loco* (The first madman). The other two were written in realistic style, with Romantic touches in "Ruinas" (1866; Ruins) and fantastic realism in *El caballero de las botas azules* (1867). The Romantic novels are full of clichés: exotic nature, impossible loves, suffering, misfortune, fatalism. In *El caballero de las botas azules* and *El primer loco*, a mixture of reality, dreams, and ideals evokes the style of E. T. A. Hoffmann (the German author most translated into Spanish), although the influence of Goethe, Byron, Chateaubriand, and lesser Romantic authors is also apparent.

Apart from her poetry and novels, Rosalía de Castro wrote articles for the press, among which "Las literatas: Carta a Eduarda," published in 1866, is noteworthy for dealing with the woman writer's social situation. In letter form, the author laments the criticism and ridicule that women

113

writers endure. They are not allowed to express their opinions or to hold "men's" ideas, their world being confined to home and children. Castro ironically concludes that women who write from the need to express themselves shouldn't make their activity public by publishing their work. In spite of its brevity and somewhat naïve ideas, the article reflects the attitude that conservative, nineteenth-century Galician society held toward women's writing.

BOOKS

A mi madre. Vigo: J. Compañel, 1863.

El caballero de las botas azules. Lugo: Soto Freire, 1867. *Obras completas.* Vol 4. Madrid, 1911.

Cantares gallegos. Vigo: J. Compañel, 1863. 2nd ed. 1872. *Obras completas.* Vol. 2. Madrid, 1909.

En las orillas del Sar. Pref. Manuel Murguía. Madrid, 1884. *Obras completas.* Vol. 1. Madrid, 1909.

Flavio. Madrid, 1861.

La flor. Madrid, 1857.

Follas novas. Madrid: La Propaganda Literaria de La Habana, 1880. *Obras completas.* Vol. 3. Madrid, 1909.

La hija del mar. Madrid, 1859.

Inéditos de Rosalía. Ed. Juan Naya Pérez. Santiago de Compostela: Patronato Rosalía Castro, 1953.

Obras completas. Pref. Victoriano García Martí. Madrid: Aguilar, 1944. 2nd ed. 1966. 3rd ed. 1972.

El primer loco. Madrid, 1881.

WORKS IN BOOKS, PERIODICALS, NEWSPAPERS

"Adios, ríos; adios, fontes." *El museo universal*, 1861.

"El cadiceño." *Almanaque de Galicia*, 1865.

"Conto gallego." *Almanaque gallego*, 1923.

"Costumbres gallegas." *Los lunes del imparcial* [*El imparcial*], 1881.

"Lieders." *Album del Miño*, 1858.

"Las literatas: Carta a Eduarda." *Almanaque de Galicia*, 1866.

"Nosa Señora da Barca." *El museo universal*, 1862.

"Padrón y las inundaciones." *La ilustración gallega y asturiana* [Oviedo], 1881.

"Ruinas." *El museo universal*, Feb.–Apr. 1866.

TRANSLATIONS OF HER WORKS

Beside the River Sar [*En las orillas del Sar*]. Trans. S. Griswold Morley. Berkeley: U of California P, 1937.

Poems of Rosalía de Castro. Trans. C. David Ley. Ed. and introd. J. Filgueira Valverde. Madrid: Ministry of Foreign Affairs, 1974.

Poems: Rosalía de Castro. Ed. and trans. Anna-Marie Aldaz, Barbara N. Gantt, and Anne C. Bromley. Albany: State U of New York P, 1991.

SECONDARY SOURCES

Actas do Congreso Internacional de Estudios sobre Rosalía de Castro e o Seu Tempo. Santiago de Compostela. 15–20 May 1985. 3 vols. Santiago: U de Santiago de Compostela, 1986.

Albert Robatto, Matilde. *Rosalía de Castro y la condición femenina.* Madrid: Partenón, 1981.

Alonso Montero, Xesús. *En torno a Rosalía.* Madrid: Júcar, 1985.

———. *Rosalía de Castro.* Madrid: Júcar, 1972. 5th ed. 1983.

———. "Rosalía de Castro: Compromiso, denuncia, desamparo y violencia." *Realismo y conciencia crítica en la literatura gallega.* Madrid: Ciencia Nueva, 1968: 57–85.

Alvilares Moure, José. *¿Proceso a la iglesia gallega? Testimonio de los escritores gallegos del siglo XIX.* Madrid: Marova, 1979.

Azorín [José Martínez Ruiz]. *Rosalía de Castro y otros motivos gallegos.* Lugo: Celta, 1973.

Balbontín, José A. *Tres poetas de España: Rosalía de Castro, Federico García Lorca y Antonio Machado.* México: n.p., 1957. 25–62.

Barja, César. *En torno al lirismo gallego del siglo XIX.* Northampton: Smith College; Paris: Champion, 1926.

———. *Libros y autores modernos.* Madrid: Rivadeneyra, 1925. Los Angeles: n.p., 1933.

Blanco, Carmen. "Las literatas." *Festa da palabra silenciada* 2 (1983).

Bouza Brey, Fermín. "La joven Rosalía en Compostela (1852–1856)." *Cuadernos de estudios gallegos* (1955): 201–58.

Briesemeister, Dietrich. *Die Dichtung der Rosalía de Castro.* Munich: n.p., 1959.

Caamaño Bournacell, José. *Rosalía de Castro en el llanto de su estirpe.* Madrid: Biosca, 1968.

Carballo Calero, Ricardo. *Aportaciones a la literatura gallega contemporánea.* Madrid: Gredos, 1955. 15–51.

———. *Contribución ao estudo das fontes literarias de Rosalía.* Lugo: Celta, 1959.

———. *Estudios Rosalianos: Aspectos de vida e da obra de Rosalía de Castro.* Vigo: Galaxia, 1979.

———. *Historia da literatura galega contemporánea.*

———. *Particularidades morfológicas del lenguaje de Rosalía de Castro.* Santiago: U de Santiago de Compostela, 1972.

———. "A poética de *Follas novas.*" *Nuevo hispanismo* 1 (1982): 27–38.

———. "Referencias a Rosalía en cartas de sus contemporáneos." *Cuadernos de estudios gallegos* 18 (1963): 303–13.

———. *Sete poetas galegos.* Pontevedra: n.p., 1955. 17–39.

Carnés, Luisa. *Rosalía de Castro: Raíz apasionada de Galicia.* México: Rex, 1945.

Cauces 11-12 (1937). Issue devoted to Castro.

Cela, Camilo José. "En torno a la morriña y otras vaguedades." *Nuevo hispanismo* 1 (Winter 1982): 11–26.

Cernuda, Luis. *Estudios de poesía española contemporánea.* Madrid: Guadarrama, 1957. 57–69.

Champourcín, Ernestina de. "Rosalía de Castro." *Hora de España* Feb. 1938.

Corona Marzol, Gonzalo. "Una lectura de Rosalía." *Revista de literatura* 44.87 (1982): 25–62.

Cossío, José María de. *Cincuenta años de poesía española (1850–1900)*. Vol 2. Madrid: Espasa-Calpe, 1960. 1051–65.

Costa Clavell, Xavier. *Rosalía de Castro*. Barcelona: Plaza & Janés, 1967.

Cultura gallega Mar.-Apr. 1937. Issue devoted to Castro.

Davies, Catherine. *Rosalía Castro no seu tempo*. Vigo: Galaxia, 1987.

———. "Rosalía de Castro: Criticism 1950–1980: The Need for a New Approach." *Bulletin of Hispanic Studies* 60.3 (1983): 211–20.

———. "Rosalía de Castro's Later Poetry and Anti-regionalism in Spain." *Modern Language Review* 79.3 (1984): 609–19.

———. "Rosalía's 'Camino blanco': The Way of Goodness." *Readings in Spanish and Portuguese Poetry for Geoffrey Connell*. Ed. Nicholas G. Round and D. Gareth Walters. Glasgow: U of Glasgow Dept. of Hispanic Studies, 1985. 16–28.

Del Barco, Pablo. "Caminando con las botas azules." *Cuadernos hispanoamericanos: Revista mensual de cultura hispánica* 426 (Nov. 1985): 57–61.

De Rosalía a Castelao: Galicia (1837–1950). Santiago: Museo de Pobo Galego, 1985.

Dias, Austin. "Rosalía de Castro: A Mother's Lament: Homage to Edgar C. Knowlton, Jr." *East Meets West*. Ed. Roger L. Hadlich and J. D. Ellsworth. Honolulu: U of Hawaii Dept. of European Languages and Literature, 1988. 32–39.

Díaz, Nidia A. *La protesta social en la obra de Rosalía de Castro*. Vigo: Galaxia, 1976.

Díaz-Plaja, Guillermo. *La poesía lírica española*. Barcelona: n.p., 1937. 338–40.

Diez Canedo, Enrique. "Una precursora." *La lectura* 2 (1909): 296.

D'Ors, Miguel. "Situación de Rosalía en la poesía de lengua castellana." *Revista de literatura* 46.92 (1984): 73–91.

Filgueira Valverde, José. *Con Rosalía Castro en su hogar*. Vigo: Patronato Rosalía Castro, 1974.

———. "Rosalía en el centenario de sus *Cantares Gallegos*." *Atlántida* 2 (1963).

Fiorentino, Luigi. *La protesta di Rosalía*. Milan: Mursia, 1979.

Galicia 17 July 1907. Issue devoted to Castro.

García, Constantino. "Descendentes do Lat. Solitas en Galego e en especial na obra Rosaliana." *Verba: Anuario galego de filoloxia* 12 (1985): 345–55.

García Martí, Victoriano. *Rosalía de Castro o el dolor de vivir*. Madrid: Aspas, 1944. Rpt. as Preface. *Obras completas*. By Rosalía de Castro. Madrid: Aguilar, 1944.

González Besada, Augusto. *Rosalía de Castro: Notas biográficas*. Madrid: Biblioteca Hispania, 1916.

González López, Emilio. "Rosalía de Castro o la angustia lírica." *Historia de la literatura española*. Vol 2. New York: Las Américas, 1965. 641–52.

González-Montes, Yara. "El mecanismo crítico-creador y el caso de Rosalía de Castro." *Actas del IX Congreso de la Asociación Internacional de Hispanistas*. Ed. Sebastian Neumeister. 2 vols. Frankfurt: Vervuert, 1989. 1: 57–64.

Graña, Bernadino. "Campanas, templos, sombras de Rosalía." *Grial* 9 (1965).

Grial 1-2 (1963). Issue devoted to Castro.

Havard, Robert G. " 'Saudades' as Structure in Rosalía de Castro's *En las orillas del Sar*." *Hispanic Journal* 5.1 (1983): 29–41.

Insula: Revista de letras y ciencias humanas 40.463 (1985). Issue devoted to Castro.

Jiménez, Juan Ramón. *El modernismo (Notas de un curso, 1953)*. Madrid: Aguilar, 1962.

———. "Rosalía de Castro." *Españoles en tres mundos*. Buenos Aires: Losada, 1942. 29–31.

Kirkpatrick, Susan. "Gertrudis Gómez de Avellaneda, Carolina Coronado y Rosalía de Castro: Estudios recientes." *Insula: Revista de letras y ciencias humanas* 44.516 (1989) 12–13.

Kulp, Kathleen K. *Manner and Mood in Rosalía de Castro: A Study of Themes and Style*. Madrid: n.p., 1968.

Landeira Irago, Ricardo. *La saudade en el Renacimiento y en la literatura gallega*. Vigo: Galaxia, 1970.

Lapesa, Rafael. "Bécquer, Rosalía y Machado." *Insula: Revista de letras y ciencias humanas* Apr. 1954: 100–01.

———. "Tres poetas ante la soledad: Bécquer, Rosalía y Machado." *Essays on Hispanic Literature in Honor of Edmund L. King*. Ed. Sylvia Molloy and Luis Fernández Cifuentes. London: Tamesis, 1983. 151–73.

Lázaro, Angel. *Rosalía de Castro: Estudio y antología*. Madrid: n.p., 1966.

Lorenzo, María Pilar. "Bécquer y Rosalía: Dos nihilistas románticos." *Revue romane* 17.1 (1982): 46–61.

Machado da Rosa, Alberto. "Rosalía de Castro, poeta incomprendido." *Revista hispánica moderna* 20 July 1954: 181–223.

Madariaga, Salvador de. *Mujeres españolas*. Madrid: Espasa-Calpe, 1972.

Martín, Elvira. *Tres mujeres gallegas del siglo XIX: Concepción Arenal, Rosalía Castro y Emilia Pardo Bazán*. Barcelona: Aedos, 1962. 87–154.

Mayoral, Marina. "*La hija del mar*: Biografía, confesión lírica y folletín." *Atti del IV Congresso sul Romanticismo Spagnolo e Ispanoamericano*. Ed. Ermanno Caldera. Genoa: Biblioteca di Letteratura, 1988: 80–89.

———. *La poesía de Rosalía de Castro*. Madrid: Gredos, 1974.

———. *Rosalía Castro*. Madrid: Fundación J. March/Cátedra, 1986.

———. *Rosalía Castro y sus sombras*. Madrid: Fundación Universitaria Española, 1976.

Mazei, Pillade. *Due anime dolenti: Bécquer e Rosalía*. Milan: n.p., 1936.

Miller, Martha LaFollette. "Aspects of Perspective in Rosalía de Castro's *En las orillas del Sar*." *Romance Quarterly* 29.3 (1982): 273–82.

———. "Parallels in Rosalía de Castro and Emily Dickinson." *Comparatist* 5 (May 1981): 3–9.

Mundo gallego 4 (Jan. 1959). Issue devoted to Castro.

Murguía, Manuel. "Rosalía de Castro." *Los precursores*. Coruña: Biblioteca Gallega, 1885. 129–51.

Nogales de Muñiz, Maria Antonia. *Irradiación de Rosalía de Castro: Palabra viva, tradicional y precursora*. Barcelona: n.p., 1966.

A nosa terra 1984. Issue devoted to Castro.

Odriozola, Antonio. *Rosalía de Castro: Guía bibliográfica*. Pontevedra: Museo de Pontevedra, 1981. Rpt. in *Nuevo hispanismo* 1 (1982): 259–83.

Otero Pedrayo, Ramón. *Romanticismo, saudade, sentimento da raza e da terra en Pastor Díaz, Rosalía de Castro e Pondal*. Santiago de Compostela: Nós, 1931.

Palley, Julian. "Rosalía de Castro: Two Mourning Dreams." *Hispanófila* 28.1 (1984): 21–27.

Pàmies, Teresa. *Rosalia no hi era*. Barcelona: Destino, 1982.
Pardo Bazán, Emilia. "La poesía regional gallega." *De mi tierra*. Coruña: Misericordia, 1888. 3–52. Vigo: Xerais, 1984. 11–94.
Pinna, Mario. "Motivi della lírica di Rosalia de Castro." *Quaderni ibero-americani* 21 (1957): 321–32.
Placer, Gumersindo. "El sacerdote en la vida y en la obra de Rosalía de Castro." *Grial* 23 (1969).
Posada Alonso, Caridad. "La representación y el espectáculo en *El caballero de las botas azules.*" *Investigaciones semióticas, II: Lo teatral y lo cotidiano*. Ed. Assn. Española de Semiótica. Oviedo: U de Oviedo, 1988. 335–51.
Poullain, Claude H. *Rosalía Castro de Murguía y su obra literaria*. Madrid: Nacional, 1974.
Prol Blas, José. *Estudio bibliográfico-crítico de las obras de Rosalía de Castro*. Santiago de Compostela: n.p., 1917.
Risco, Vicente. "Poesía gallega del siglo XIX." *Historia general de las literaturas hispánicas*. Ed. Guillermo Díaz-Plaja. Barcelona: n.p., 1956.
Rodríguez, Rodney T. " 'Yo voy soñando caminos' de Antonio Machado a la luz de un intertexto de Rosalia de Castro." *Explicación de textos literarios* 18.1 (1989-90): 35–41.
Rosalía. Santiago de Cuba: n.p., 1937.
Rosario Medina, Priscila. "El paisaje romántico en la novela *Flavio* de Rosalia de Castro." *Senara: Revista de filoloxia* 4 (1982): 231–38.
Rudat, Eva M. Kahiluoto. "La immortalidad y la tradición céltica en Rosalía Castro." *Studies in Honor of José Rubia Barcia*. Ed. Roberta Johnson and Paul C. Smith. Lincoln: U of Nebraska P, 1982. 151–74.
Santalla Murias, Alicia. *Rosalía de Castro: Vida poética y ambiente*. Buenos Aires: n.p., 1942.
Santos Sera, Luis. *Rosalía de Castro*. Madrid: Forma, 1977.
Seoane, Luis. "O pensamento político de Rosalía." *Galicia* 22 July 1939.
Siete ensayos sobre Rosalía. Vigo: Galaxia, 1952.
Stevens, Shelley. "Rosalía de Castro: Literary and Social Origins of the Galician Poetry." *DAI* 43.2 (1982): 464A.
Taibo García, Victoriano. *Rosalía de Castro, precursora da fala*. Coruña: Real Academia Gallega, 1972.
Tirrel, Marie Pierre. *La mística de la saudade: Estudio de la poesía de Rosalía de Castro*. Madrid: Jura, 1951.
Unamuno, Miguel de. *Andanzas y visiones españolas*. Madrid: Austral, 1955. 58–75.
———. *Por tierras de Portugal y España*. Madrid: Austral, 1955. 147–56.
Valera, José Luis. *La palabra y la llama*. Madrid: Prensa Española, 1967. 251–60.
———. *Poesía y restauración cultural de Galicia*. Madrid: Gredos, 1958. 145–211.
Vales Faílde, Javier. *Rosalía de Castro*. Madrid: n.p., 1906.
Vázquez Gil, Bernardo. "O humor en Rosalía Castro." *Senara: Revista de filoloxia* 3 (1981): 159–75.
Viana, Antonio Manuel Couto. "Um cantar de Rosalía de Castro num romance de Eça de Queiroz." *Coloquio/Letras* 89 (Jan. 1986): 21–26.
Zabala, Iris. "Estrategias textuales y entonación en Rosalía de Castro." *Filologia* 20.2 (1985): 191–205.

MARIA CAMINO NOIA CAMPOS

G Castro y Andrade, Isabel
(B. 1520?, Puentedeume; d. 1582?, Puentedeume.) Also known as Condesa de Altamira. Poet.

Isabel Castro was the granddaughter of Don Fernando de Andrade, a soldier in the military campaign that resulted in the Spanish domination of Naples (1503). Only two of her works are extant: "Competencia entre la rosa y el sol," a sonnet in Castilian, and a poem in Galician dedicated to Alonso Ercilla, which appears in *La Araucana*. Pérez de Guzmán claims to have seen manuscripts of her poetry in both Galician and Castilian in the Biblioteca Nacional, but these works have apparently been lost (Couceiro, 259–60).

WORKS IN BOOKS, PERIODICALS, NEWSPAPERS
"Competencia entre la rosa y el sol." *Antología de poetisas líricas.* 2 vols. Madrid: Real Acad. Española, 1915. 1: 50.
Poem, untitled. *La Araucana.* By Alonso Ercilla. 1597. Introd. Arturo Soto. Mexico: UNAM, 1962. 7–8.

SECONDARY SOURCES
Carré Aldao, Eugenio. "Una poetisa gallega del siglo XVI." *Boletín de la Real Academia Gallega* 10.110, 111, and 112 (1916).
Couceiro Freijomil 1: 259–60.
Pérez de Guzmán, Juan. *Cancionero de la rosa.* Madrid: Austral, 1992. 137–41.

KATHLEEN MCNERNEY

Català, Víctor; *see* Albert i Paradís, Caterina

Caymarí de Bauló, Margarita; *see* Caimarí de Bauló, Margarida

Celina; *see* Coll Domènech, Isabel

C Chordà i Requesens, Mari
(B. 1942, Amposta, Tarragona– .) Poet and filmmaker.

Alternating her time between Amposta and Barcelona, Mari Chordà has worked at LaSal, the feminist publishing house that she helped create. She studied education and fine arts and earned her living by teaching art and by painting for ten years. She has written and directed two shorts and one medium-length film, but the difficulty in obtaining backing for

119

this expensive medium caused her to turn to writing. Encouraged by the first Jornades Catalancs de la Dona in May of 1976, she published a collection of her poems, . . . *I moltes altres coses* (. . . And many other things), without signing her name, since she felt any woman could have written it. The book was reissued in 1981 with a prologue and drawings by the author. Many of the poems feature a feminist awakening and encounters with other feminists, a new sense of solidarity and sisterhood, and a rejection of the old notions of love that have trapped and deceived women in the past. *Quadern del cos i de l'aigua* (Notebook of the body and water) is a book of feminine erotic poetry celebrating the sensuality of newly found freedom. It is a bilingual edition with facing-page translations in Castilian and illustrations by Montse Clavé. Perhaps the strongest poem in the collection is its closing piece, "Blues del somni" (Dream blues), in which the fantasy of having three days to do nothing but eat, sleep, and make love is accompanied by the delightful, whimsical drawings.

BOOKS

. . . *I moltes altres coses*. Barcelona: LaSal, 1976.
Quadern del cos i de l'aigua. Illus. Montse Clavé. Barcelona: LaSal, 1978.

KATHLEEN MCNERNEY

G Cibreiro Santalla, Pilar

(B. 1952, Vilaboa, Ferrol– .) Poet and short story writer.

Born in Galicia, Pilar Cibreiro spent a few years in London and then moved to Madrid, where she currently lives. She contributed poems in Castilian to the collection *Las diosas blancas* (The white goddesses) in 1985. In the same year she published *El cinturón traído de Cuba y otros cuentos de invierno* (The belt brought from Cuba and other winter stories), a book of stories in Castilian about a small Galician town. The tales relate the childhood memories of the author as well as anecdotes of other inhabitants of the village.

O vasalo da armadura de prata (The silver-armored vassal) is a collection of Galician poems that had previously appeared in the literary magazine *Dorna*. They are intimate poems of love, death, and desires. The poet's sentiments and emotions are reflected in the opposing worlds of the village and the city. The village represents childhood, nature, and community life, whereas the city denotes the wild spirit of youth, frustrated possibilities, and loneliness, but also the freedom of anonymity. Feeling alienated in either place, the author explores the mentality of exile, clinging to the memory of love and peace in a faraway landscape.

BOOKS
El cinturón traído de Cuba y otros cuentos de invierno. Madrid: Alfaguara, 1985.
O vasalo da armadura de prata. Barcelona: Sotelo Branco, 1987.

WORKS IN BOOKS, PERIODICALS, NEWSPAPERS
"Un home e unha muher na praia do portiño." *Dorna* 8 (May 1985).
"Lumbrigar azul e lixeiro." *Dorna* 11 (Jan. 1987).
Poems, untitled. Buenaventura 85–93.

SECONDARY SOURCES
Couceiro, Mario. "Primeira saída de Pilar Cibreiro á poesía galega." *La voz de Galicia* 27 Aug. 1987.

MARIA CAMINO NOIA CAMPOS

C Cistaré, Eulàlia
(B. 1947, Barcelona– .) Known as Lali Cistaré. Journalist and short story writer.

Eulàlia Cistaré spent her childhood in Terrassa, Barcelona, in the vicinity of the textile industry in the Vallès region. She lost her father at the age of six months. When she was fourteen her family moved to Madrid, but they soon returned to Barcelona. She started working at an early age, as secretary and editor of the newspaper *Tele/Exprés*, and took evening art classes at the Massana School in Barcelona and English classes at the Berlitz Academy. She later worked for the Direcció General de Mitjans de Comunicació de la Generalitat and obtained a degree in Catalan philology. At present, she is the head of promotion for publications for the Department de la Presidència de la Generalitat de Catalunya.

In 1980, Cistaré's collection of short stories *La burra espatllada* (The broken-down donkey) was a finalist for the important Víctor Català prize. Featuring interior monologues by mainly female protagonists, the book focuses on vital experiences in the lives of middle- or lower-class women: the mutual sexual discovery of two teenagers living in a threatening religious environment; a marriage crisis precipitated by a disappointing encounter with friends from one's youth; a woman's confrontation with old age, her husband's physical decline, and the end of affection. The quick, narrative pace slows down only in the careful description of small, everyday details, and the strong feminist stance makes this an engaging volume in spite of its pessimistic view of life. Cistaré alternates narrative realism and the use of nonhuman protagonists, such as a doll in "Estranya relació" (Strange relation) or a little bird in "Qué bé que ens ho passàvem Irene!" (What fun we used to have, Irene!). "Por" (Fear), a story in which fantasy turns into actual experience, recalls the techniques of some Latin American fiction.

The author does not avoid harsh realities and even cruelty, which is intensified in her latest collection, *Ja no queden oliveres* (There are no olive trees left). The title story describes how a homosexual relationship can lead to the same alienating experience as a heterosexual one. Aging, seen from the perspective of elderly people in conflict with their families, plays an important role in this book, as do such themes as an unrequited love that leads to self-destruction in "Li deien 'El Pigat' " (They called him 'Freckles'), voyeurism in "La Casta Susana" (Chaste Susana), and the seduction of a maid by her master in "La Maria i don José" (Maria and José).

BOOKS
La burra espatllada. Pref. Manuel Ibáñez Escofet. Barcelona: Selecta, 1980.
Ja no queden oliveres. Barcelona: Edicions 62, 1988.

CRISTINA ENRIQUEZ DE SALAMANCA

Civera, Beatriu; *see* **Martínez Civera, Empar Beatriu**

C   Clavell d'Aranyó, Mercè
(B. 1899, Mataró, Barcelona; d. ?) Poet. No biographical information available.

Plujes de sentiments (Downpours of sentiments) contains poems about friendship, poetry, love, nature, and family. *Poesies de la llar* (Poems of the hearth) is a collection of family and Christmas poems.

BOOKS
Plujes de sentiments. Prols. Josep Maria Gironella, Isidre Julià Avellaneda, Baldiro Cruells, and Ramon Torrella. Illus. Jaume and Jordi Arenas i Clavell. Mataró, Barcelona: n.p., 1974.
Poesies de la llar. Mataró, Barcelona: n.p., 1966.

NANCY L. BUNDY and KATHLEEN MCNERNEY

C   Cobeña i Guàrdia, Judith
(20th c.) Poet. No biographical information available.

Arrosegant l'amor (Dragging love) is a collection of love poems with an inquisitive, exploratory nature. Judith Cobeña defines love at different moments as desire, tenderness, solitude, shivers, and dejection.

BOOKS

Arrosegant l'amor. Pref. Joan Margarit. San Feliu de Llobregat, Barcelona: Ajuntament, 1983.

KATHLEEN MCNERNEY

C Codina i Mir, Maria Teresa
(B. 1927, Barcelona– .) Writer of children's literature.

With degrees in classical languages and education, Maria Teresa Codina started the school Talitha in Barcelona in 1956, which inaugurated the Moviment de Renovació Pedagògica (Movement for Pedagogical Renovation). In 1973 she began directing her efforts to the poorer peripheral districts of Barcelona and through the neighborhood association helped create the Institut de Batxillerat de Can Tunis, where she met the Gypsy collective of that sector. Hired by the city of Barcelona, she worked on the development of broad-based education in Can Tunis, winning the Ramon Llull d'Experiències prize in the field of education in 1979. From that point on she concentrated on education for marginal groups through work she developed for the city of Barcelona and the Generalitat de Catalunya. She is currently head of the Programa d'Educació en la Diversitat for Barcelona. She has collaborated on various summer school programs and published articles in numerous specialized journals of education. She adapted popular folktales for children at a time when there was a lack of children's literature in Catalan. She has also been involved in writing textbooks; in 1984 she coauthored *Visquem plegats i bé* (Let's live together in harmony), a book that advocates mutual respect and cooperation for personal and social progress.

BOOKS

Visquem plegats i bé. With Clementina Roig i Planas and Montserrat Castanys i Jarque. Barcelona: Ajuntament, 1984.

ANNA GASOL I TRULLOLS

C Coll Domènech, Isabel
(20th c.) Also known as Celina. Poet.

Isabel Coll Domènech is a member of the group Poesia Viva.

BOOKS

Primera volada. Lloret de Mar, Girona: n.p., 1979.

KATHLEEN MCNERNEY

C Coll Hevia, Concepció

(B. 1925, Palma de Mallorca– .) Poet. No biographical information available.

BOOKS

La font enterrada. Barcelona: Sirocco, 1979.

KATHLEEN MCNERNEY

C Company Gonzàlez, Mercè

(B. 1947, Barcelona– .) Writer of children's literature.

Mercè Company refuses to follow the happy-ending syndrome of many writers of children's literature and insists on showing reality and truth, even when they are unpleasant. Her stories vary widely, but she tends to denounce social injustice, especially as it affects children. She addresses such problems as poverty, alcoholism, the effects of divorce on children, and peer pressure that leads to drug use, street crime, and dropping out of school. Her stories are finely crafted and display a sense of humor, tenderness, and fantasy, in spite of the often serious subject matter. *La imbècil* (The imbecile) is a collection of four stories set in the poorer neighborhoods of Barcelona; the title story is an account of the difficult relationship between a retarded girl and her depressed mother. Company won the City of Olot prize in 1982 and the Enric Valor of Valencia prize in 1983. She has been widely translated into several European languages.

BOOKS

Al fons del mar. Barcelona: Timun Mas, 1989.
L'arbre dels records. Barcelona: Timun Mas, 1989.
L'avís. Barcelona: Timun Mas, 1989.
El barri de la lluna. Barcelona: Empúries, 1989.
La cangur busca feina. Barcelona: Planeta, 1988.
Una casa als afores. Barcelona: Cruïlla, 1989.
La casa d'en Gatus. Barcelona: La Galera, 1984.
El cervell perdut. Barcelona: Empúries, 1987.
Charlot. Barcelona: Hymsa, 1984.
La dama del medalló. Barcelona: Timun Mas, 1989.
Les dents del lleó. Barcelona: Argos Vergara, 1984.
El descobriment de la colla petita. Barcelona: Planeta, 1989.
El diari d'un fantasma. Barcelona: Timun Mas, 1988.
Dràcula. Barcelona: Timun Mas, 1986.
En Gil i el paraigua màgic. Montserrat: L'Abadia, 1982.
L'espelma màgica. Barcelona: Timun Mas, 1989.
Estimades abelles. Barcelona: Timun Mas, 1988.
Fer-ne quaranta. Barcelona: Destino, 1987.
La festa de benvinguda. Barcelona: Planeta, 1988.

Una gàbia al menjador. Barcelona: Teide, 1986.
Les gallines pintores. Barcelona: Timun Mas, 1989.
La gata que desafinava. Barcelona: Timun Mas, 1989.
El germà gran. Barcelona: La Galera, 1985.
La història de l'Ernest. Barcelona: Cruïlla, 1985.
La imbècil. Barcelona: Empúries, 1986.
El jardí de l'espai. Barcelona: Angulo, 1989.
La llegenda de Fra Garbí. Montserrat: L'Abadia, 1984.
La llum està malalta. Barcelona: Timun Mas, 1988.
El mag. Barcelona: Timun Mas, 1989.
El millor reportatge. Barcelona: Laia, 1984.
Missió especial Hipotenusa. Barcelona: Timun Mas, 1982.
El món de les coses perdudes. Montserrat: L'Abadia, 1986.
Les nines de porcellana. Barcelona: Timun Mas, 1989.
La nit. Barcelona: Argos Vergara, 1984.
Nit de monstres. Barcelona: Timun Mas, 1988.
On és l'oncle Ramon. Barcelona: Timun Mas, 1982.
Ovelles de colorins. Barcelona: Timun Mas, 1989.
Les peripècies d'en Quico Pelacanyes. Barcelona: Destino, 1983.
La presència. Barcelona: Timun Mas, 1989.
La reina calba. Barcelona: Cruïlla, 1983.
Sota el llum d'un fanalet. Barcelona: Edebé, 1988.
Les tres bessones i en Ton i la Guida. Barcelona: Arín, 1988.
Les vambes màgiques. Barcelona: Timun Mas, 1989.
Les velletes del museu. Barcelona: Hymsa, 1986.
Volem una escola més gran. Barcelona: Planeta, 1989.

TRANSLATIONS OF HER WORKS
El aviso [*L'avís*]. Barcelona: Timun Mas, 1989.
La casa de Gatus [*La casa d'en Gatus*]. Barcelona: La Galera, 1984.
El cerebro perdido [*El cervell perdut*]. Barcelona: Paidós, 1989.
Charlot [*Charlot*]. Barcelona: Hymsa, 1984.
Cría hijos ["Cria fills"]. Barcelona: Destino, 1989.
Cumplir los cuarenta [*Fer-ne quaranta*]. Barcelona: Destino, 1987.
La dama del medallón [*La dama del medalló*]. Barcelona: Timun Mas, 1989.
El diario fantasma [*El diari d'un fantasma*]. Barcelona: Timun Mas, 1988.
Los dientes del león [*Les dents del lleó*]. Barcelona: Argos Vergara, 1984.
¿Dónde está el tío Ramón? [*On és l'oncle Ramon*]. Barcelona: Timun Mas, 1982.
Drácula [*Dràcula*]. Barcelona: Timun Mas, 1984.
El hermano mayor [*El germà gran*]. Barcelona: La Galera, 1985.
La historia de Ernesto [*La història de l'Ernest*]. Barcelona: Fundación Santa María, 1986.
La imbécil [*La imbècil*]. Barcelona: Lóguez, 1987.
Una jaula en el comedor [*Una gàbia al menjador*]. Barcelona: Teide, 1986.
El mago [*El mag*]. Barcelona: Timun Mas, 1989.
Misión especial Hipotenusa [*Missió especial Hipotenusa*]. Barcelona: Timun Mas, 1982.
Las muñecas de porcelana [*Les nines de porcellana*]. Barcelona: Timun Mas, 1989.

La noche [*La nit*]. Barcelona: Argos Vergara, 1984.
Perdidos en la cueva ["Perduts a la cova"]. Barcelona: Timun Mas, 1983.
Las peripecias de Don Paco Pelacañas [*Les peripècies d'en Quico Pelacanyes*]. Barcelona: Destino, 1983.
La presencia [*La presència*]. Barcelona: Timun Mas, 1989.
La reina calva [*La reina calba*]. Barcelona: Fundación Santa María, 1988.

KATHLEEN MCNERNEY

C   Conca i Martínez, Maria
(B. 1948, Beneixama, València– .) Writer of children's literature.

Maria Conca teaches at a university preparatory school in Valencia and specializes in language pedagogy. Her children's story *En l'olivera dels cimals alts* (In the olive groves at the summits) won the Enric Valor prize in 1982.

BOOKS
En l'olivera dels cimals alts. Valencia: Federació d'Entitats Culturals del País Valencià, 1983.
Escola i llengua al País Valencià. Valencia: Tres i Quatre, 1976.
Paremiologia. Valencia: Universitat de Valencia, 1986.
Els refranys catalans. Valencia: Tres i Quatre, 1989.
Els xiquets i xiquetes escriptors. Valencia: Federació d'Entitats Culturals del País Valencià, 1979.

ANNA MONTERO I BOSCH

Condesa de Altamira; *see* Castro y Andrade, Isabel

C   Congost i Caubet, Maria Dolors
(B. 1952, Olot, Girona– .) Poet.

Maria Dolors Congost moved to Barcelona to study medicine after she finished her preparatory studies. Her only published work, "Més paraules, encara" (Still more words), appears in a collection by four poets called *Poems ara* (Poems now). Several poems are addressed to an unborn child or spoken in the voice of that child. Her poetry shows a social conscience and at times a certain alienation from others. The volume is nicely illustrated by one of the other contributors, Joan Giné-Masdeu.

WORKS IN BOOKS, PERIODICALS, NEWSPAPERS
"Més paraules, encara." *Poemes ara*. With Joan Giné Masdeu, Josep Maria Figueras i Artigas, and Emília Oliveras i Planas. Illus. Joan Giné-Masdeu. Barcelona: Altés, 1971.

KATHLEEN MCNERNEY

Constança de Mallorca; *see* **Mallorca, Reina de**

C Contijoch Pratdesaba, Josefa
(B. 1940, Manlleu, Barcelona– .) Poet, novelist, and translator.

Born into a well-to-do family, Josefa Contijoch was immersed in the world of books, for her father ran a printshop and a bookstore in her hometown. She studied commerce, French, and English at the school of the Carmelite Sisters of Charity in Manlleu. She married in 1971 and moved to Barcelona, where she now works as a translator for a press agency.

Contijoch began writing poetry in Castilian during her teenage years and confesses to being most influenced by English and American writers, especially William Faulkner, James Joyce, and T. S. Eliot. In 1964, she published her first book, *De la soledad primera* (Out of the first loneliness), a collection of twenty-four poems, each beginning with verses from the Old and New Testaments. In this work she elaborates on personal suffering, loneliness, and her perplexity with life itself. Viewed from a distance, life is seen as a series of events that impose themselves on her. The author communicates her wish to share her suffering with fellow writers, relatives, or imaginary companions. An essential concern is the passage of time. Contijoch's poetry reflects an ambivalence toward life's cadences and the pain of growth, which is accompanied by the loss of innocence. She seeks a solution in religion in "Acerca del Sermón de la Montaña" (About the Sermon on the Mount) and assumes a puzzled attitude in this quest for an inner identity.

Aquello que he visto (That which I have seen) develops the anguished tone of her earlier work, using the "ubi sunt" theme. The dialogue between a divine figure and a human being is established, in which the latter requests wisdom. The use of English and French vocabulary and the reference to foreign countries reveals the poet's contact with other cultures. "Tombstone Blues" (Manlleu, 1967), a collection of six poems in a photocopied edition, derives its title from a Bob Dylan song. The cryptic language, the careful crafting of images, and the use of an intentionally nonlyrical vocabulary recall Spanish surrealistic trends.

At the age of twenty-seven Josefa Contijoch took a nationalist stand and began writing in Catalan. In 1981 she won the Miquel Martí Pol prize for Catalan poetry, awarded by Comisiones Obreras, for "Quadern de vacances (Una lectura de *El segon sexe*)" (Vacation notebook: A reading of *The Second Sex*), a prize she shared with Eduard Borràs and Jordi Dauder. Her first example of Catalan feminist poetry, this militant work has nine verses in which the poet alternates a personal voice in search of liberation with quotations from misogynist texts. This summary of antifeminist opinions in Western culture is juxtaposed with historic figures who have epitomized the female essence: Sappho, Teresa of Avila, and Dante's Beatrice. The poem concludes with the proposal to recover female sensuality and revalue the female body, giving priority to sensuality rather than to the procreative function.

In 1972 Josefa Contijoch won the Marisa Picó poetry prize for her unpublished "La corda de l'harpa i el coll de l'artista" (The harp-string and the artist's neck) and, in 1980, was runner-up to the first City of Tarragona poetry prize for "Orient-Express," also unpublished. In 1984 she revised these two works under the title of the first, "La corda de l'harpa i el coll de l'artista." Divided into three sections, "Dels records," "De l'amor," and "De l'anècdota," it contains themes from her earlier poetry—time, bewilderment about life and death—while showing considerable personal and stylistic maturity. Her poetry revolves around three fundamental worries: the struggle with life's realities, the past as an ever-present memory, and mortality. These themes are conveyed by images of the basic elements—water, fire, air, and earth—and by her own feelings. Time and memory give rise to fiery images. An objective poetry that aims for the absence of passion, Contijoch's work lies at the boundary between disillusion and the difficult acceptance of reality, the wish to find solid support for existence and the lucid perception of the futility of this very aim.

"Fosca es la nit" (Dark is the night) revises earlier work and includes some new poems. Compiled in 1986, this work is the author's favorite, and the title itself suggests the almost mystical cast of the collection; in the inner search, clairvoyance becomes darkness. An elegiac tone predominates in poems dealing with life and death.

Potala, Josefa Contijoch's first novel, takes its title from the name of a monastery in Lhasa, Tibet. Winner of the Ramon Llull prize for the Catalan novel in 1985 and of the Sant Joan prize in 1984, it is an adventure story describing the female protagonist's quest for a hard-to-find "narrative style." This unusual work presents an ironic answer to the nationalistic demand for a "Catalan novel." The heroine travels through her literary influences, which are portrayed allegorically. The light tone and sense of humor do not hide the fact that this book is a profound reflection on culture and the search for knowledge, and a criticism of conventional literary products. Her second novel, *No em dic Raquel* (I'm not Raquel), was a finalist for the Ramon Llull prize in 1988.

BOOKS

Aquello que he visto. Madrid: Alorca, 1965.
De la soledad primera. Barcelona: Trimer, 1964.
La dona liquada. Barcelona: Columna, 1990.
No em dic Raquel. Barcelona: Laia, 1989.
Potala. Barcelona: Laia, 1986.

WORKS IN BOOKS, PERIODICALS, NEWSPAPERS
"Canción de los veintitrés años," "Antevisión impersonal de mi muerte," "Visión de la libertad," "Morir no tiene mérito," "Mi reino es de este mundo," "Nocturno," "Tres crónicas," "Emigración," "Sometimes I Feel like a Motherless Child," and "Tombstone Blues." *Poesia femenina española (1950–1960)*. Ed. Carmen Conde. Madrid: Bruguera, 1971. 141–61.
"Quadern de vacances (Una lectura de *El segon sexe*)." *Dones en lluita* 2 (Feb. 1982): 42–43.

CRISTINA ENRIQUEZ DE SALAMANCA

C Corderas, Núria
(20th c.) Poet. No biographical information available.

Together with Amado Martínez and Jaume Duran, Núria Corderas published the collection *L'espill de la veritat* (The mirror of truth). In the prologue by the authors, Corderas's section is described as "el silenci de la Núria" (Núria's silence), because its theme is the difficulty of communication. In her prose poems, which touch on the importance of keeping spiritually alive, Corderas uses a doll as a metaphor for the little person inside who tries to come out in the daylight. The author's goal is selflessness, and her models parents and grandparents.

BOOKS
L'espill de la veritat. With Amado Martínez and Jaume Duran. Caldes de Montbui, Barcelona: n.p., 1983.

KATHLEEN MCNERNEY

C Cornet i Planells, Montserrat
(B. 1934, Barcelona– .) Novelist.

Montserrat Cornet studied at the Dames Negres, a convent school, and became a free-lance insurance agent. She has published articles and interviews in several technical journals in both Castilian and Catalan. Her first literary work, *Entre dos estius: Fragments de la vida d'una dona* (Between two summers: Fragments of a woman's life), placed third in the Premi Sant Jordi in 1980 and sixth in the Premi Ramon Llull in 1981. Written in the form of a journal, the book describes the struggles of a woman who separates from her husband after a long marriage. The author gives an introspective account of the woman's solitude, desolation, bitterness, low self-esteem, and economic hardship. As time goes by, the protagonist awakens to a new life, a new sensuality, and a new identity. She realizes that love for her children helps her to survive and love for her father encourages her when difficulties arise.

Fill, què hi fas a Polònia (Son, what are you doing in Poland), which is both narrative and diary, is her account of a trip to Poland to attend her grandchildren's baptism.

BOOKS

Entre dos estius: Fragments de la vida d'una dona. Pref. Teresa Pàmies. Barcelona: Pòrtic, 1984.
Fill, què hi fas a Polònia. Barcelona: Elfos, 1987.
Rusinyol, que vas a França. Barcelona: Romanya/Valls, 1987.

TRANSLATIONS OF HER WORKS

Entre dos veranos [Entre dos estius: Fragments de la vida d'una dona]. Barcelona: El Fos, 1988.
Hijo, por qué estás en Polonia [Fill, què hi fas a Polònia]. Barcelona: El Fos, 1988.

MONTSERRAT VILARRUBLA

G Corral, Clara
(B. 1847, Ourense; d. 1908, Coruña.) Poet.

Clara Corral published a number of poems in magazines and newspapers, most of which have been lost. *A Herminia* (To Herminia) is a book of poems about the countryside. Corral evokes the Galician landscape and portrays highly sentimental people. Her use of popular themes follows the style of the *Cantares gallegos* of Rosalía de Castro.

BOOKS

A Herminia. Pontevedra: n.p., 1891.

WORKS IN BOOKS, PERIODICALS, NEWSPAPERS

"A nada de canto el dixo," "Lonxe vai miña alegría," and "Com si a Virgen baixase." *La ilustración gallega y asturiana* [Oviedo] 30 (Oct. 1879).

SECONDARY SOURCES

Carballo Calero, *Historia da literatura galega contemporánea.*
Couceiro Freijomil, vol. 1.
Gran enciclopedia gallega, vol. 7.

MARIA CAMINO NOIA CAMPOS

C Correig i Blanchar, Montserrat
(B. 1945, Reus, Tarragona– .) Folklorist.

With studies in pedagogy at the Escola Normal de Tarragona and a BA in Romance languages from the University of Barcelona, Montserrat Correig has taught in schools in Barcelona and Reus, Tarragona. Since 1971 she has given courses and seminars for the Associació de Mestres Rosa

Sensat; since 1972 she has been a member of its Grup de Llengua Escrita, and from 1982 to 1984 she served as coordinator for the association's language consulting services. From 1976 to 1984 she was professor of education in Catalan for the Escola Universitària de Formació del Professorat d'Educació General Bàsica at the Autonomous University of Barcelona. In 1981, she worked with the department of education of the Generalitat in editing the official programs for primary education.

Correig has participated in conferences on the modernization of education, written articles for the magazine *Guix*, and edited textbooks. Her research on phonetics and phonology was published as *Fonologia aplicada: Primers passos en l'aprenentatge de la llengua escrita* (Applied phonology: First steps in learning written language). Correig collaborated on *Una capseta blanca que s'obre i no es tanca* (A little white box that opens but never shuts), a study of folklore that is addressed to parents and teachers of children in kindergarten and the first years of primary education.

BOOKS

Una capseta blanca que s'obre i no es tanca. With Laura Cugat and Maria Dolors Rius i Benito. Barcelona: Graó, 1984.

Fonologia aplicada: Primers passos en l'aprenentatge de la llengua escrita. Barcelona: Edicions 62, 1990.

ANNA GASOL I TRULLOLS

C Cortés Wyghlen, Guadalupe
(19th c.) Novelist. No biographical information available.

The popular weekly *La barretina* published Guadalupe Cortés's novel *Las joyas de la Roser* (Roser's jewels) as a serial during 1868. The publication of the magazine ceased, however, as a result of the 1868 Revolution and does not seem to have been resumed. An unconfirmed report in *La barretina* states that Llibreria d'Eubal Puig intended to publish the novel the same year, but it is not known if the work was ever completed.

The novel is dedicated to Serafí Pitarra and inspired by his play of the same name. The story portrays the daughter of well-to-do peasant gentry, who loses her parents in the war with the French and is taken in by a poor family. With the Bruc episode of the War of Independence (1808–14) providing the background, this novel includes realistic details of rural and daily life and features many traits of the serial novel (the abandoned daughter, incest, hidden treasure, and so on) and of the comedy of manners. The novel also provides an interesting psychological analysis of the characters and explores the female protagonist's transition to sexual maturity and male and female emotions within a relationship. An episode in which incest is insinuated between a brother and sister offers occasion for a close examination of female feelings of love. The work also describes numerous aspects of child-raising, the child's separation from the mother, and the beginning of independent life. The story contains moralizing digressions, such as the discussion of the advantages of breast-feeding, which do not interrupt the narrative pace.

WORKS IN BOOKS, PERIODICALS, NEWSPAPERS
Las joyas de la Roser: Novela catalana. La barretina: Semanari popular 1–42 (4 Jan.–9 Oct. 1868).

CRISTINA ENRIQUEZ DE SALAMANCA

C   Cortey, Maria Dolors
(B. 1927, Barcelona– .) Folklorist, novelist, and translator.

Though Maria Dolors Cortey was born in Barcelona, her family is from Girona and she lives in Majorca. She is well-known for her compilations of folktales and legends, in both Castilian and Catalan. *En gris i rosa* (In gray and pink) evokes childhood memories of Girona. *Dol sense negre* (Mourning without black) won her the Ciutat d'Olot prize. She was also awarded the medal of honor at the Jocs Florals of Thuir for her biography of three women writers, *Tres i molts* (Three and many), in which she studies the Marquise de Sévigné, Marguerite de Valois, and Víctor Català. *L'hereu Frigola* (The heir Frigola) is a short novel that won the Rosa d'Or de Cassà de la Selva prize in Girona. *Memòries d'en Nitus Resmés, gat de teulada* (Memoires of Just Nitus, roof cat) is a collection of children's stories. Cortey has written a number of essays and contributed to various newspapers. She has several unpublished works as well.

BOOKS
Contes d'arreu del món. Barcelona: Juan Granica, 1988.
Dol sense negre. Olot: Aubert, 1976.
En gris i rosa. Barcelona: Club, 1972.
L'hereu Frigola. Girona: Duch, 1979.
Llegendes de les nostres terres. Montserrat: L'Abadia, 1976.
Memòries d'en Nitus Resmés, gat de teulada. Olot: Aubert, 1979.
Les nostres llegendes. Olot: Aubert, 1981.
Tres i molts. Palma: Muntaner, 1977.

KATHLEEN MCNERNEY

C   Costa Mayans, Neus
(B. 1963, Sant Francesc Xavier, Formentera, Eivissa– .) Poet.

Impressions (Impressions), winner of the Baladre prize in 1980, is a collection of poems that reflects the delicate and sensitive temperament of the author. Featuring themes of love, the passage of time, and poetic inspiration, the book contains many images of her native islands.

BOOKS
Impressions. Eivissa: Inst. d'Estudis Eivissencs, 1981.

KATHLEEN MCNERNEY

C Coves Mora, Maite
(B. 1957, Elx, Alacant– .) Poet.

A professor of Catalan language, Maite Coves was a finalist in the 1981 L'Illa de Benidorm poetry prize. Her works, which appear in three anthologies, utilize popular forms and rhythms and are intended to recapture childhood. Her subjects are people whose experiences are rooted in the land and in their own consciousness. Time and memory, seen through the senses and materialized in accounts of daily life and nature, play an important role.

WORKS IN BOOKS, PERIODICALS, NEWPAPERS
"Aquells estius," "Absència," "Mentida," "La mar l'estimava," "Toc, toc, toc," and "Les dones del camí selves." *Entranyes per a l'augur (Antologia de jove poesia catalana al Baix Vinalopó—1980).* Elx, Alacant: Universitat Nacional d'Educació a Distància, 1980. 47–56.
"Coves de Valltorta," "Nueta, nueta," "Riure!," "Caminava sintàcticament pels corredors dels seus records," and "Lluna, lluneta." *Brossa nova: Poetes valencians dels 80.* Ed. J. Pérez Montaner, M. Granell, and A. Viana. València: Associació Cultural Universitària de Filologia, 1981. 57–65.
"Tardor," "Cau una gota de temps," "Del silenci," "Tot el temps de ma vida," "Un dia de sol," "Cendra i estels," "L'ús reiterat de paraules," and "S'escolen clams de nacre." *L'espai del vers jove. Mostra poètica jove 85.* València: Conselleria de Cultura, Educació i Ciència de la Generalitat Valenciana, 1985. 153–60.

ISABEL ROBLES GOMEZ

C Crusells de Carol, Montserrat
(B. 1929, Esparreguera, Barcelona–) Known as Montserrat Carol. Poet.

Montserrat Crusells studied pedagogy and philosophy. Her published work is limited to a single volume of poetry, *Bon dia, terra. Bon dia, mar* (Hello, Earth. Hello, Sea), for which her childhood in a small rural town provides much of the imagery. Nature pervades the work, though thematically Crusells moves from poetry about children to travel poems and lyrics praising her favorite musicians and writers. Her short, simple poems are written with clarity and surprising images: "La meva casa / fou com un vaixell / anclat al camp. / El mar el va llançar / amb fúria de les aigües / i ell, / perdut, / malalt, / cercà repós en una vall molt plana" (My house / was like a ship / anchored to the countryside. / The sea tossed it / out of its waters with fury, / and, / lost / and sick, / it looked for rest in a smooth valley) ("El mas" [The farm]). Crusells wrote another book of poetry in her youth, which was never published, and is currently preparing a third.

BOOKS

Bon dia, terra. Bon dia, mar. Barcelona: Ambito Literario, 1980.

KATHLEEN MCNERNEY

C Cruzate i Lanzaco, Amàlia
(B. 1915, Barcelona– .) Poet.

Amàlia Cruzate studied pedagogy at the Escoles Franceses. She married Francesc-Xavier Sabarté i Solà, who was active in the theater, and they traveled widely. Cruzate published her first book late in life, after becoming active in the group Poesia Viva. *Primaveres de tardor* (Autumn springs) and *Carpeta de núvols* (Folder of clouds) both begin with a prologue by the director of Poesia Viva, Josep Colet i Giralt, and are illustrated with drawings by Alícia Tello, also a member of the group. The first book is divided into five parts with interconnecting titles: "La mirada" (The gaze), "De la mirada al pensament" (From gaze to thought), "Del pensament al sentiment" (From thought to feeling), "Del sentiment a la fe" (From feeling to faith), and "De la fe a la pàtria" (From faith to fatherland). The second book is dedicated to Marta Ferrusola de Pujol, the first lady of Catalonia, and contains a poem addressed to her husband, Jordi Pujol. The imagery derives from nature, specifically daylight and darkness, clouds and sun, fog and thunder. The last section is patriotic and includes poems dedicated to such figures as Josep Carner, Angel Guimerà, Mercè Rodoreda, Salvador Espriu, and Miquel Martí i Pol, who also contributed a foreword.

BOOKS

Carpeta de núvols. Prol. Josep Colet i Giralt. Illus. Alícia Tello. Barcelona: Poesia Viva, 1984.
Dolls d'aigua. Barcelona: Poesia Viva, 1986.
Primaveres de tardor. Prol. Josep Colet i Giralt. Illus. Alícia Tello. Barcelona: Poesia Viva, 1983.

KATHLEEN MCNERNEY

C Cugueró i Conchello, Maria Candelària
(B. 1925, Barcelona– .) Translator and writer of children's literature.

After completing her studies at the University of Barcelona, Maria Candelària Cugueró worked in the business world and then turned to translation and library work at the Biblioteques de la Generalitat de Catalunya. Her only publication in Catalan is a book for young people, *Me'n vaig cap al sud* (I'm heading south).

BOOKS
Me'n vaig cap al sud. Montserrat: L'Abadia, 1985.

KATHLEEN MCNERNEY

C Dalí Domènech, Anna Maria
(B. 1905, Figueres, Girona– .) Prose writer.

Sister of artist Salvador Dalí and friend of his friends, especially of the poet García Lorca, Anna Maria Dalí wrote a book that blends travelogue, memoir, and fiction: *Tot l'any a Cadaqués* (All year at Cadaqués). The story relates the events of an entire year spent by the narrator in the coastal town, formerly a fishing village, in contrast with the few weeks seen by the swarm of summer tourists, whose perception of the charming locale is limited. The book follows the tradition of Josep Pla, who wrote many volumes of prose on specific Catalan places, including Cadaqués. *Tot l'any a Cadaqués*, with its fictionalized characters, is addressed especially to young people. *Des de Cadaqués* (From Cadaqués) adheres more strictly to the memoir form.

BOOKS
Des de Cadaqués. Barcelona: Montblanc-Martín, 1982.
Tot l'any a Cadaqués. Pref. Manuel Brunet. Barcelona: Joventut, 1951.

KATHLEEN MCNERNEY

G Dato Muruáis, Filomena
(B. ?, Ourense; d. 1926, Sada Coruña.) Poet.

As a young woman Filomena Dato Muruáis began participating in the Galician literary movement developed by Rosalía de Castro and the writers of the *Rexurdimento*. She contributed to the newspaper *El heraldo gallego*, winning many literary prizes for her work in both Castilian and Galician. She published four books of poems in Castilian: *Penumbras* (Shadows), *Romances y cantares* (Ballads and songs), *La letanía lauretana en verso*

(The Lauretian litany in verse), and *Fe* (Faith). The last two books have religious themes.

Follatos (Pages), her only book of poetry in Galician, begins with a long feminist poem, "Defensa das mulleres," which won a prize. Written in a combative tone, the verses lack lyricism and, with a few exceptions, can be considered versified prose. The work contains descriptive, narrative, and popular poems, and even a heroic ode, "A Galicia."

BOOKS

Fe. Coruña, 1911.
Follatos. Ourense: A. Otero, 1891.
La letanía lauretana en verso. Ourense, 1887.
Penumbras. Madrid, 1880.
Romances y cantares. Ourense, 1885.

SECONDARY SOURCES

Cacheiro, *Poetisas galegas do século XX.*
Carballo Calero, *Historia da literatura galega contemporánea.*
Couceiro Freijomil, *Diccionario bio-bibliográfico de escritores gallegos,* vol. 1.
Gran enciclopedia gallega, vol 8.

MARIA CAMINO NOIA CAMPOS

C Denis de Rusinyol, Lluïsa

(B. 1867, Barcelona; d. 1946, Barcelona.) Also Rusiñol. Poet, playwright, and short story writer.

A woman of great and diverse talents, Lluïsa Denis married the modernist painter and writer Santiago Rusiñol. Denis dedicated herself to literature and published *Versos per a cançons* (Poems for songs), a collection of poems she wrote and set to music. She also wrote several plays. The one-act tragedy *Una venjança com n'hi ha poques* (1911; An outstanding revenge) is a part of her generation's efforts at dramatic innovation influenced by Ibsen and other foreign playwrights. The drama, which has little action, depicts the celebration of an intimate supper. The plot development consists of progressively disclosing the personal tragedy of the protagonist, a prostitute. She unmasks herself as well as her protector as a prelude to her suicide, the tragic "revenge" of the victim. Denis's second play, *Els caçadors furtius* (The poachers), is a comedy in one act and two scenes in which a didactic-moralizing intention prevails: placing confidence in thieves brings out their good side. Their victim gives them resources, thereby making an honest life possible and rehabilitating them. Figures dear to modernists, such as the sad clown and the troupe of impoverished actors, lend a melancholy tone to the play. "Trompetes i timbals" (Trumpets and kettledrums), also a comedy, was first performed in 1911 in Barcelona.

Lluïsa Denis dedicated *Contes d'amor* (Love tales) to her grandchildren, to be read as they approached "aquella edat en què ens distreu més el que ens fa plorar que el que ens fa riure" (that age in which crying entertains us more than laughing) (*Contes d'amor*, dedication). Each tale is accompanied by a song composed by the author. Stories of great loves that end tragically, they are set in a variety of contexts: the historic or legendary; the magical, complete with apparitions of fairies; the religious, such as the monk in love; the folkloric, such as the hopelessly enamored humpback. All the characters victimized by love are treated with wistful tenderness.

In her last years Denis also painted, but without much commercial success. During her only exhibition, held at the Sala Pares in Barcelona, one picture was sold.

As a single parent, Denis lived with her daughter Maria during most of the early years of her marriage. In old age she cared for her sick husband, one of the unquestioned geniuses of Catalan modernism.

BOOKS
Els caçadors furtius. Barcelona: A. López, 1931.
Contes d'amor. Barcelona: S. Bonavía, 1924.
Una venjança com n'hi ha poques. Barcelona: A. López, 1931.
Versos per a cançons. Barcelona: n.p., n.d.

MARISA SIGUAN BOEHMER

C Devesa Rosell, Mercedes
(B. 1st decade 20th c., Olot, Lleida–?) Poet and novelist.

The daughter of a distinguished sculptor and the wife of Josep Maria de Sagarra, Mercedes Devesa lived in Paris for a long time. In 1931, she was runner-up for the Flor Natural in the Jochs Florals of Barcelona for a collection entitled "Muntanyenques" ("Mountain songs"). In her 1952 novel in Castilian, *Las adelfas* (Oleanders), she explores the sentimental conflicts in a family of nouveaux riches, showing, at times cruelly, the basest feelings of high society.

The entry in *Les cinc branques* mentions another unpublished novel.

BOOKS
Las adelfas. Barcelona: Juventud, 1952.

WORKS IN BOOKS, PERIODICALS, NEWSPAPERS
"Muntanyenques." *Jochs Florals de Barcelona: Any LXXIII de Llur Restauració*.
Barcelona: Estampa La Renaxensa, 1931. 49–54.

SECONDARY SOURCES
Les cinc branques 310.

CRISTINA ENRIQUEZ DE SALAMANCA

C Díaz Plaja, Aurora

(B. 1913, Barcelona– .) Journalist, translator, and writer of children's literature.

Aurora Díaz Plaja studied library science at the Escola de Bibliotecàries of Barcelona but then concentrated on journalism. Outstanding among her publications, which include various adaptations of works by such classical authors as Ramon Llull and William Shakespeare, are biographies of Gandhi and Albert Schweitzer. *Ahïmsa: La no-violència de Gandhi* (The non-violence of Gandhi) and *El doctor Schweitzer* (Dr. Schweitzer) stemmed from her profound admiration for the two men and were written for boys and girls. In *Vides paral.leles o contes de debó* (Parallel lives or true stories) she presents biographical sketches of twenty-two personalities who have worked on behalf of children.

Aurora Díaz Plaja has promoted children's books for libraries and been a critic for the press, radio, and television. She is a regular contributor to *Quaderns d'orientació familiar*, *Rodamon*, and *Serra d'or*, journals published in Barcelona. Her professional activity as a librarian has resulted in a series of works on the economics of library management, notably *La biblioteca a l'escola* (The Library in the School), winner of the 1969 Antoni Balmanya prize. In 1982 she published *Guia de lectura: Una eina de treball per als mestres entorn dels llibres infantils publicats en català* (Reader's guide: A tool for teachers of children's books published in Catalan), a bibliographical guide to children's literature, not including textbooks or comics.

Díaz Plaja has also written several stories for children, among them *Entre joc i joc . . . un llibre!* (Between games . . . a book!), where she tries to familiarize children with the world of books and libraries; *El foc de Sant Joan* (The bonfire of Saint John) and *El joc del foc follet* (1971; The jack-o'-lantern game), both dealing with fire and the festival of Saint John; and *La ruta del sol* (The route of the sun).

BOOKS

Ahïmsa: La no-violència de Gandhi. Barcelona: La Llar del Llibre, 1987.
La biblioteca a l'escola. Barcelona: Nova Terra, 1970.
Com es forma i funciona una biblioteca. Barcelona: Barcino, 1960.
El doctor Schweitzer. Barcelona: Juventud, 1968.
Entre joc i joc . . . un llibre! Barcelona: Juventud, 1968.
Les entremaliadures de Till Olibaspills. Barcelona: La Galera, 1979.
El foc de Sant Joan. Barcelona: La Galera, 1959.
Guia de lectura: Una eina de treball per als mestres entorn dels llibres infantils publicats en català. Barcelona: CEAC, 1982.
Les guies de lectura: Conferències al curs de pràctiques 1937–1938 a l'escola. Barcelona: Escola de Bibliotecàries de la Generalitat de Catalunya, 1938.
El joc del foc follet. Barcelona: Hymsa, 1984.
El llibre de les besties. Montserrat: L'Abadia, 1981.

La ruta del sol. Barcelona: La Galera, 1971.
El somni d'una nit d'estiu de William Shakespeare. Barcelona: La Galera, 1983.
Vides paral.leles o contes de debò. Montserrat: L'Abadia, 1980.

IMMA BALDOCCHI I PUIG

C Dodas i Noguer, Anna
(B. 1963, Folgueroles, Barcelona; d. 1986, Montpellier, France.)
Composer and poet.

Anna Dodas earned a degree in Catalan philology and began her doctorate in that field, while continuing her studies in music. Already the winner of several local prizes for her poetry, she was awarded the Amadeu Oller prize for *Paisatge amb hivern* (Winterscape). This brief collection with drawings and original musical scores features scenes from her native Vic to evoke feelings of solitude, love, abandonment, and hope. She constantly compares mountains to the seascape and urban scenes she came to know after she moved to Barcelona to complete her studies. On her way to a summer vacation with another young woman, this promising poet was brutally murdered near the city of Montpellier, France.

BOOKS
Paisatge amb hivern. Barcelona: Mall, 1986.

KATHLEEN MCNERNEY

C Domènech i Escaté de Canyellas, Maria
(B. 1877, Alcover, Tarragona; d. 1952, Barcelona.) Also Cañellas and known as Josep Miralles. Novelist, poet, and sociologist.

Maria Domènech wrote her novels in Catalan but used Castilian for her sociological essays and for her short stories published after the Spanish Civil War. Her use of Castilian reflects the political division that occurred as a result of Castilian immigration into Catalonia. Like Federica Montseny, she chose Castilian because it was the language of the working classes.

Domènech spent her first years in Tarragona, where she studied music and painting. There she began publishing in periodicals under the pseudonym Josep Miralles. She married and in 1910 moved to Barcelona, where she founded a union for women, the Federación Sindical de Obreras. She was actively involved in the social issues of her time and lectured about the need for women to obtain an education and financial independence through such institutions as the *ateneos* in Madrid and Barcelona and the Fomento del Trabajo Nacional in Madrid. She wrote the sociological studies

139

El profesionalismo y los sindicatos (1912; Professionalism and the labor unions) and *Constitución y finalidad de la Federación Sindical de Obreras* (Establishment and purposes of the Women Workers' Labor Union) and contributed to many Barcelona magazines, including *Feminal* and *Flames noves*. Soon after the publication of her first novel, *Neus* (Neus), she achieved recognition as a novelist.

Domènech's fiction deals with social problems and women's questions from a progressive, feminist position. Naturalistic ideas develop an increasing presence in her novels; whereas in the early works the protagonists fight for spiritual improvement, in her last novel heredity determines fate. Domènech shows female neuroticism as an illness resulting from an effort to survive in a hostile world, and her novels demonstrate her awareness of the new schools of psychological thought in Europe. Her descriptions of female "madwomen" are similar to those of English women writers of the period but are unique among her Catalan contemporaries. She was also alert to the changes that Catalan industrialization was producing in society.

Neus was written to show "que l'amor, la candidesa, la bondat, totes les belles qualitats de les ànimes pures, son freqüentment altres tants apetitosos esquers . . . en els quals l'enemic fa pressa sense dany per sa part" (how love, goodness, innocence, every quality of pure souls, are often tempting baits . . . which the enemies grasp at no risk) (*Neus* 7). It is the Bildungsroman of a sensitive young rural woman whose initial confrontation with her stepmother marks the beginning of a long, hard spiritual path. When Neus leaves home and moves to the city, she faces a dangerous, hypocritical world. Her work as a cleaning lady in a middle-class Barcelona home provokes in her feelings of hate and resentment. Domènech portrays the superficiality, selfishness, and laziness of middle-class families, whose women are engaged in empty socializing and whose men practice a dreary professional life. Characters are described in a somewhat schematic way, and the novel, which sometimes recalls the atmosphere of modern detective fiction, ends in the fight between good and evil. The author avoids sentimentality and has the protagonist understand evil as the inability of human beings to overcome their moral defects. Neus is rescued from moral infamy by the love and spiritual direction of her "señorito." She becomes a teacher and relates to him as an equal. The novel illustrates Domènech's ideas about the regenerating capacity of education and the importance of women's financial independence.

Contrallum (A view against the light) is a short novel published in the Catalan collection La Novela Nova, which presented works by such authors as Víctor Català and Narcís Oller. Set in a Catalan rural area, the story relates the struggle of a young man, Machado, to become an independent, productive person against the will of an overprotective family. His parents' idea of forcing him to live as a "señor" makes him feel like an outsider to society. Believing that his family really loves him and feeling guilty for not returning their love, Machado is unable to rebel and ultimately commits suicide. The author describes inner, subtle emotions in a realistic way and elucidates Machado's "España que bosteza" (Yawning Spain). She shows the psychological effects of parental power on children and how love is often confused with the need to control.

Gripaus d'or (Golden toads) is a satire of the newly rich Catalan classes who care for nothing but money and adopt any behavior to obtain it. Domènech's criticism is aimed at a social success based on lies and economic speculation rather than on hard work. As in her other novels, Domènech presents a sympathetic couple who represent purity in a corrupt world, but she does not stress their importance to the action. Situations are shown that could happen today as well, such as a character's embrace of Catalanism in order to obtain influence, an episode presented humorously. The author uses the final encounter between the daughter of the house and a former servant engaged in an opportunistic love affair to show how people who act like "gripaus" end up finding enemies like themselves. The novel has an open ending, and the author avoids a moralistic tone.

Herències (Heredity) is the last and most important novel of Domènech. With a strong naturalistic influence, the story relates the dramatic lives of two children from different classes whose families force them to marry for social and economic advancement. Isabel, the neurotic female protagonist, belongs to a noble family whose fortunes have dwindled, and her mother cannot change her feudal way of thinking in the face of changing times. Ramonet, the son of an alcoholic woman and a man from a lower class, amasses a fortune through usury and aims to become a noble. His father scorns him for being the weak offspring of an alcoholic. For Domènech, people like him are "tota una nisaga de miserables que amb aparièncla de defugir arcaics prejudicis anulen tota energia que no sigui en llur profit" (a race of ne'er-do-wells who, under the appearance of rejecting old prejudices, annul any energy not favoring them) (*Herències* 26). Isabel and Ramonet represent two incompatible breeds; their accumulation of past "herències" dooms their baby, and the child's death precipitates his mother's insanity.

The Civil War ended Domènech's career as a novelist and her work as a syndicalist. In 1946, she published a Castilian collection of short stories, *Confidencias* (Confidences), in which female protagonists describe their difficulties to a narrator/confidant. The same year she published *Al rodar del temps* (As time passes), a collection of Catalan poetry. Lectura Popular produced a selection of her writings, *Vers i prosa* (Poems and prose).

BOOKS
Al rodar del temps. Barcelona: NAGSA, 1946.
Confidencias. Barcelona: NAGSA, 1946.

Constitución y finalidad de la Federación Sindical de Obreras. Barcelona: Caridad, 1912.

Contrallum. La Novela Nova 25. N.p.: n.p., 1917.

El. Barcelona: Publicaciones Mundial, n.d. *La novela femenina* 1.18.

Gripaus d'or. La Novel.la d'Ara. Barcelona: n.p., 1919.

Herències. Barcelona: Soc. Catalana d'Edicions, 1925.

Memoria de los trabajos hechos en Suiza. N.p.: n.p., n.d.

Neus. Barcelona: Joventut, 1914.

El profesionalismo y los sindicatos. Barcelona: Ramón Tobella, n.d.

Vers y prosa. Lectura Popular, vol. 7.

WORKS IN BOOKS, PERIODICALS, NEWSPAPERS

"La beleta." *Feminal* 126 (28 Oct. 1917).

"Crisantems." *Feminal* 68 (24 Nov. 1912).

"De cultura femenina." *Feminal* 108 (26 Mar. 1916).

"De Tarragona." *Feminal* 16 (26 July 1908).

"La dona en l'obra social y cultural de Catalunya." *Feminal* 60 (21 Mar. 1912).

"Esclat." *Feminal* 6 (29 Sept. 1912).

"Mireya." *Feminal* 98 (30 May 1915).

"La moxa." *Feminal* 118 (25 Feb. 1917).

"La Santa Ma (Llegenda del Cister de Santas Creus)." *Feminal* 120 (29 Apr. 1917).

"Violes." *Feminal* 27 (27 June 1909).

SECONDARY SOURCES

"Gripaus d'Or. Novel.la d'ara, de Maria Domènech de Cañellas." *La revista* May 1919: 116.

CRISTINA ENRIQUEZ DE SALAMANCA

Dracs, Ofèlia

Pseudonym of a writers' collective, mostly men.

Flourishing in the 1980s, these writers contributed a story or two each to several collections, grouped according to type, that is, detective, erotic, and so on.

KATHLEEN MCNERNEY

C   Duran Armengol, Maria Teresa

(B. 1949, Barcelona– .) Writer and illustrator of books for children.

Maria Teresa Duran has taught drawing, done translations, and worked for Radio Catalunya. Her stories have appeared in *Cavall fort* since 1971.

BOOKS
Ara em toca a mi? With Miquel Martinez. Barcelona: La Galera, 1986.
El cavall del clot de l'infern. Barcelona: Magrana, 1986.
Joanot de Rocacorba 1431–1482. Barcelona: La Galera, 1983.
Mana qui mana. Barcelona: La Galera, 1981.

KATHLEEN MCNERNEY

C Durán de León, Lluïsa
(B. 1845, Barcelona; d. ?) Poet.

Lluïsa Durán wrote in both Catalan and Castilian. Her only known bio-graphical data come from Constantí Llombart's *Los fills de la morta-viva* (The sons of the living death), an early dictionary of Valencian writers who participated in the *Renaixença*. At the age of six Durán entered San Carlos de la Belle de May, a private girls' school in Marseilles, France, where she studied Italian, Latin, and French. She moved to Valencia with her family and became involved in the city's literary and artistic circles. Her first poetic composition was introduced in a literary contest held by the Ateneu Científic Lliterari in Valencia to honor Cervantes. Durán then published articles and poems in several periodicals: *Boletín revista del ateneo de Valencia* (Valencia), *El cascabel* (Madrid), *El último figurín* (Madrid), *Paris charmant artistique* (Paris), and *El correo de la moda.*

Her Castilian poetry is prosaic and descriptive, and her inspiration ranges from traditional romantic and familial themes to her devotion to friends and relatives. Although José María de Cossío considers Durán a follower of Bécquer, this influence is difficult to trace.

In the first *Jocs Florals* of Valencia (1879) Durán won a prize for "Lo castell d'En Perelló" (Perelló's castle), a poem of medieval inspiration. She published Catalan poetry in the periodicals *La renaixença, Lo rat penat, Calendari català,* and *La llumanera.* Her work contains the motifs, rhymes, and topics established by the Catalan *Renaixença.* She also wrote in Italian and French and was in contact with such eminent musicians as Anton Rubinstein and Franz Liszt. The Biblioteca Museo Balaguer, in Vilanova i la Geltrú, Barcelona, has in its collection some of her correspondence with Víctor Balaguer.

WORKS IN BOOKS, PERIODICALS, NEWSPAPERS
"A las niñas valencianas." *Lo rat penat* 1880: 80–82.
"Album de paz." *El correo de la moda* 26 (1876): 99.
"Amants records." *Lo rat penat* 1881: 66–68.
"A mi querida amiga María Eulalia de la Mesa." *El correo de la moda* 27 (1877): 323.
"Anyoransa." *La renaixença* Year 9, 2.1 (31 Mar. 1879): 44.
"Armònia crepuscular." *Lo rat penat* 1882: 65.

"El avaro." *El correo de la moda* 26 (1876): 168.
"La campana funeral." *El correo de la moda* 28 (1878): 107.
"Lo castell d'En Perelló." Llombart 601–06.
"Cielo estrellado." *El correo de la moda* 26 (1876): 150.
"Después de leída la tragedia (Safo) de Víctor Balaguer." *El correo de la moda* 27 (1877): 214.
"En el bosque." *El correo de la moda* 27 (1877): 23.
"En la catedral." *El correo de la moda* 27 (1877): 234–35.
"Fantasía crepuscular." *El correo de la moda* 28 (1878): 131.
"Flores y espinas." *El correo de la moda* 26 (1876): 175.
"La hermana de la Caridad." *El correo de la moda* 25 (1875): 75.
"Máximas a mi hijo." *El correo de la moda* 26 (1876): 250–51.
"Meditación." *El correo de la moda* 27 (1877): 323.
"Melodía." *El correo de la moda* 27 (1877): 115.
"La nina de dol." *Lo rat penat* 1883: 88–91.
"Otoño." *El correo de la moda* 25 (1875): 340.
"El poeta Bécquer." *El correo de la moda* 25 (1875): 282–83.
"Recuerdos del día de difuntos." *El correo de la moda* 26 (1876): 331.
"Vale más creer." *El correo de la moda* 28 (1878): 267.

TRANSLATIONS OF HER WORKS
"Das Schloss En Perello's" ["Lo castell d'En Perelló"]. Fastenrath 149–50.

SECONDARY SOURCES
Cossío, José María de. *Cincuenta años de poesía española (1850–1900)*. 2 vols. Madrid: Espasa-Calpe, 1960. 1: 444–45.
Llombart, *Los fills de la morta-viva.*
Simón Palmer, *Escritoras españolas del siglo XIX* 244–46.

CRISTINA ENRIQUEZ DE SALAMANCA,
with Castilian bibliographical information by CARMEN SIMON PALMER

B Eleizegi Maiz, Katalina
(B. 1889; d. 1963.) Playwright.

Katalina Eleizegi's first work, *Garbiñe*, is a three-act play set in the thirteenth century and contains some thematic parallels with Pérez Galdós's *Marianela*. *Garbiñe* won the Ayuntamiento de San Sebastián prize in 1916. In 1918 Eleizegi won the same prize for another play, *Loreti*, a historical tragedy based on the battles between the Cantabrians and the Romans in the first century BC. In 1934 she wrote a two-act play, *Yatsu*, on the conquest of Navarre. She left an unpublished play on Catalina de Erauso.

BOOKS
Garbiñe. Tolosa: López de Mendizábal, 1917.
Loreti. N.p.: Loiola, 1918.

MAITE GONZALEZ ESNAL

Elies, Martina d'; *see* **Valero i González d'Elies, Mercè**

C Ensenyat, Xesca
(B. 1952, Pollença, Mallorca– .) Poet and novelist.

Xesca Ensenyat studied medicine in Barcelona and then returned to Majorca, although she maintains many contacts in Barcelona and travels frequently to the city. She contributes articles on culture to various periodicals and edits her own magazine, *L'espira* (Spiral), which contains much of her work, including poetry and novels published serially.

She has written two novels: *Amagatall de guipur* (A hiding place of fine lace) and *Villa Coppola*. The two works share a style of densely packed prose, a fine irony, and a sense of humor. In *Amagatall de guipur*, which won the City of Manacor prize, Ensenyat varies narrative techniques and quotes several well-known poets, mostly Catalan, in epigraphs to the book's chapters. Her sustained but varying imagery holds together a rather loose story. Her sentences tend to be long and involved, mixing straightforward narrative with sharp social criticism: "reixes de ferro forjat en alguna llunyana república democràtica" (wrought-iron bars from some faraway democratic republic) (11). *Villa Coppola*'s fanciful story, told by a sarcastic female narrator, is about the people who come and go from the villa, their interrelationships, foibles, and problems. Her observations are sometimes delightful: "Vaig viure l'aventura de cercar un mot dels que fèiem servir en el nostre estimat subdialecte bantú per a cada una de les peces dels motors de benzina que ja existien, i fins i tot n'anomenàrem algunes abans d'inventar-se per alhora crear l'originalitat lingüística de fer aparèixer primer el mot que l'objecte que designa, fenomen que demostra que la vida és conseqüència de l'art, enlloc de ser a l'inrevés, com n'hi ha que creuen" (I lived the adventure of looking for one of the words we use in our beloved Bantu subdialect for each and every one of the parts to the benzine motor that existed, and we even named some before they got invented, to create at the same time the linguistic originality of making the word appear previous to the object it is to designate, a phenomenon that demonstrates that life is a consequence of art, and not the other way around, like some people think) (32–33).

Ensenyat's prose is rich with allusions to art and literature and with references to other basic human needs, such as food and drink and bodily functions: " . . . i qui la va informar sobre la regla amb un muntatge tan literari que a Munda li semblava que la regla era una cosa que servia per anar a l'òpera" (. . . and who informed her about periods within such a literary spectacle that Munda thought the period was something you used to go to the opera with) (*Villa* 166).

BOOKS
Amagatall de guipur. Mallorca: Mascaró Pasarius, 1976.
Ciutat d'horabaixa. Palma: Cors, 1969.
Villa Coppola. Barcelona: Magrana, 1985.

KATHLEEN MCNERNEY

B   Erramuzpe, Patxika
(20th c.) Poet. No biographical information available.

Patxika Erramuzpe published two poems: "Maita beti bizia" (Always love life), in praise of life and nature from the perspective of loneliness, and "Otxagabia," concerning a happy moment.

WORKS IN BOOKS, PERIODICALS, NEWSPAPERS
"Maita beti bizia" and "Otxagabia." *Colección Euskera.* N.p.: Soc. Guipuzcoana de Ediciones y Publicationes, 1964–69.

MAITE GONZALEZ ESNAL

Escardot, L.; *see* **Karr i d'Alfonsetti de Lasarte, Carme**

C   Escobedo i Abraham, Joana
(B. 1942, Barcelona– .) Novelist.

With a degree in arts and letters from the University of Barcelona and a diploma from the Escola de Bibliologia, Joana Escobedo is curator of the reserve section of special collections of the Biblioteca de Catalunya. In the novel *Silenci endins* (Silence within), which explores the protagonist's insomnia and the duality of reality and dream, the author shows the effects of years of repression, of a formal and rigid education, and of the intellectual atmosphere of the 1960s. *Amic, amat* (Friend, lover) examines the relationship of a couple and their personal identity crises.

As a member of the collective Ofèlia Dracs, Escobedo collaborated on the collection *Lovecraft, Lovecraft.* She has undertaken various erudite studies, published in specialized journals, and edited the catalog *Santiago Rusiñol (1861–1931).* She is also the author of grammatical texts on the teaching of Catalan and a contributor to the newspapers and reviews *Avui, Serra d'or,* and *L'Avenç.*

BOOKS

Amic, amat. Barcelona: Edicions 62, 1986.
Santiago Rusiñol (1861–1931): Catèleg de l'exposició organitzada en motiu del cinquentenari de la seva mort. Barcelona: Biblioteca de Catalunya, 1981.
Silenci endins. Barcelona: Edicions 62, 1982.

IMMA BALDOCCHI I PUIG

C Esplugues, Margarita
(B. 1738, Artà, Mallorca; d.?) Poet.

Two encyclopedic works of the nineteenth century mention Margarita Esplugues as the author of *Cánticos al Todopoderoso*. Joaquim Maria Bover de Rosselló's description is as follows:

> Virgen terciaria de San Francisco de Asís, y muy instruída en gramática, retórica, filosofía y sagrada teología, de cuyas ciencias escribió algunos tratados. Compuso unos *Cánticos al Todopoderoso* y murió . . . como aparece en las crónicas manuscritas de donde hemos sacado este artículo. De ella habla la obra *Monumenta seraphica* p. 284. El padre Oliver en sus Anales Mss de la Provincia de Mallorca trae alguna de sus poesías en idioma mallorquín.
>
> (*Biblioteca* 259)

> (Tertiary virgin of Saint Francis of Assisi and very well read in grammar, rhetoric, philosophy and sacred theology on which she wrote several papers. She composed the *Cánticos al Todopoderoso* [Canticles to the Almighty] and died . . . according to the manuscripts from which this article has been obtained. She is mentioned in *Monumenta seraphica* p. 284. Father Oliver includes some of her poetry, written in the Majorcan language, in his Annals of the Province of Majorca.)

Bover's information comes from a manuscript known as "Monumenta seraphica," by Antonio Oliver, a Majorcan Franciscan priest (1711–87). This manuscript is described by Manuel de Castro y Castro and by Andrés Caimari.

The second reference to Esplugues is found in Manuel Serrano y Sanz's *Apuntes*, which provides no further information.

SECONDARY SOURCES
Bover de Rosselló, *Biblioteca de escritores baleares*.
Caimari, Andrés. "El venerable P. Fr. Rafael Serra, observant (1536–1620). El

rostro homenatge en les festes centenaries que Inca sa patria li dedica." *Bolletí de la Societat arqueològica luliana* 18 (1921): 169–98.

Castro y Castro, Manuel de. *Manuscritos franciscanos de la Biblioteca Nacional de Madrid.* Madrid: Servicio de Publicaciones del Ministerio de Educación y Ciencia, 1973. 636–38.

Serrano y Sanz 1: 401.

CRISTINA ENRIQUEZ DE SALAMANCA and KATHLEEN MCNERNEY

C Esteva de Vicens, Maria
(20th c., Mallorca.) Poet. No biographical information available.

BOOKS
Cant a Mallorca. Palma: n.p., 1935.
Errada de compte. Palma: Politècnica, 1934.
Mallorca: Quadret líric. Palma: Politècnica, 1935.
Qui barata el cap se grata. Palma: Politècnica, 1935.

KATHLEEN MCNERNEY

G Estévez Villaverde, Emilia
(B. 1921, Ponteareas, Pontevedra– .) Poet and writer of children's literature.

Emilia Estévez's work as a dressmaker does not keep her from writing poetry, most of it in Galician. *Airiños do meu lugar* (Breezes from home) was very popular; *Monterreal* has a translation in Castilian; *Santiago en la leyenda* (The legend of Santiago) is a book of Castilian verses. In her stories for children Estévez portrays passive, docile girls in contrast to active, naughty boys. She has also written several historical tourist guides.

BOOKS
Airiños do meu lugar. Madrid: n.p., 1963.
Aventura y primavera. Pontevedra: n.p., 1985.
Bayona la Real y su parador. Pontevedra: n.p., 1984.
Felipito y sus travesuras. Madrid: n.p., 1979.
La historia del Apostol. Santiago: n.p., 1972.
Monterreal. Pontevedra: Paredes, 1965.
El nacimiento de los Reyes Magos. Pontevedra: n.p., 1981.
Ponteareas y el Condado en la historia. Pontevedra: n.p., 1980.
Santiago en la leyenda. Pontevedra: Puenteareas, 1972.
Vigo, Bayona y sus rutas. Pontevedra: Paredes, 1976.

TRANSLATIONS OF HER WORKS
A la sombra de Monterreal [*Monterreal*]. Pontevedra: n.p., 1966.
Bayona la Real and Its Parador [*Bayona la Real y su parador*]. Pontevedra: n.p., 1987.

SECONDARY SOURCES
Blanco, Carmen. *Literatura galega da muller*. Vigo: Xerais, 1991. 205–06.
Gran enciclopedia gallega, vol. 11.

MARIA CAMINO NOIA CAMPOS

C Estrada, Lola
(B. 1928, Sallent, Barcelona– .) Poet.

According to *Les cinc branques*, Lola Estrada has written and sometimes published verses in Catalan, Castilian, French, English, and Italian and has also published one book of poems, *Intimes*, with a prologue by Aurora Bertrana. *Intimes* is not available in major libraries in Catalonia.

WORKS IN BOOKS, PERIODICALS, NEWSPAPERS
"Trepig." *Les cinc branques* 220.

NANCY L. BUNDY

C Fabra Carbó, Francesca
(20th c.) Poet. No biographical information available.

BOOKS
Engrunes del meu jo. Barcelona: n.p., 1980.

KATHLEEN MCNERNEY

C Fàbregas, Marta
(B. 1920?, Barcelona– .) Playwright, children's literature writer, and translator.

Marta Fàbregas wrote in both Catalan and Castilian. According to a brief biography in Antoni Bernal's introduction to *Un pas en fals*, (A wrong step) her first years were spent in Argentina and she debuted as an actor in the Casal Català of Buenos Aires. She worked with professional theater companies and later managed her own, which performed in several countries in South America for seven years.

Fàbregas began her work as a dramatist with *Sólo tú* (Only you), which had its premiere in the Teatro Barcelona. Subsequent plays included *El joven Bredford* (The young Bredford), *A l'aztar de la vida* (The fate of life), *Doble condena* (Double condemnation), *No hay quien pueda contigo* (You are impossible), and *Lo que no vence el tiempo* (What time does not conquer). Most of these works, though, have been impossible to locate in major libraries in Catalonia.

In 1954 Fàbregas received an honorable mention for her work *Fill meu* (My son) in the FESTA contest. The same year she won the Teatro Juvenil Cadete prize for her comedy *Lección de amor* (Lesson of love), which had its premiere in the Teatro Barcelona. The play was successful and was put on by many theater companies in Catalonia. In 1958, she received the FESTA Prize for *Un pas en fals*. Both works deal somewhat sentimentally with family conflicts; the families belong to the middle class and exhibit moral values characteristic of the Spanish postwar period. The action develops in an easy rhythm, perhaps because the author's work as an actor helped her to master theatrical techniques. She uses contemporary language and draws secondary characters, such as the grandfather and the maid in *Un pas en fals*, in a humorous, refreshing way.

Fàbregas wrote a series of books for a young adult collection in Castilian about famous women, including Isabella I, Joan of Arc, Mary Stuart, Lucrezia Borgia, Marie Antoinette, Marie Curie, and Maria Taglioni. She has also translated and adapted books by Louisa May Alcott, Alphonse Daudet, James Fenimore Cooper, H. Rider Haggard, Victoria Segur, Henryk Sienkiewicz, Jean Webster, and J. R. Wyss.

BOOKS

Doble condena: Comedia en tres actos. N.p.: n.p., n.d.
Lección de amor. Barcelona: Nereida, 1959.
Lucrecia Borgia. Barcelona: Mateu, n.d.
Maria Antonieta. Barcelona: Mateu, n.d.
Maria Taglioni (Vida de una danzarina). Barcelona: Mateu, 1958.
Un pas en fals: Comèdia en tres actes. Introd. Antoni Bernal. Barcelona: Nereida, 1958.

CRISTINA ENRIQUEZ DE SALAMANCA

C Fàbregas Valentí, Elvira

(20th c.) Memoirist. No biographical information available.

Adéu, Putxet (Good-bye, Putxet) is a novelized and nostalgic account of a Barcelona neighborhood in rapid transition.

BOOKS

Adéu, Putxet. Barcelona: n.p., 1981.

KATHLEEN MCNERNEY

C Fabregat i Armengol, Rosa
(B. 1933, Cervera, Lleida– .) Poet and novelist.

After finishing her doctorate in pharmacology at the University of Barcelona, Rosa Fabregat worked in a research laboratory in Illertissen, Bavaria, and then directed a pharmacological laboratory in Barcelona. She is now the pharmacist of Llorenç del Penedès, Tarragona.

She began her literary career with poetry, which, like a modern troubadour, she recited herself in cultural centers and public squares, offering 111 such recitals between 1978 and 1983. Her verse has been collected in three volumes: *Estelles* (Splinters), *El cabdell de les bruixes* (The witches' tangle), and *Temps del cos* (The time of the body).

In addition to poems and stories published in various newspapers and magazines, she has published a collection of short stories, *La dona del balcó* (The woman on the balcony), and four novels, all influenced by her studies and profession. In the autobiographical *Laberints de seda* (Silk labyrinths), the author describes the gradual liberation of the protagonist through her studies and, afterward, her work in a laboratory in a foreign country. As she becomes involved in the maze of multinational companies, she confronts the inevitable: sex discrimination, fierce competition, and the oppression and manipulation suffered by the working masses. Once the system that fosters these conditions becomes clear to her, she decides to leave her managerial career and become the pharmacist in a small town.

El turó de les forques (Pitchfork hill) is a complex novel. Its form—fiction, interpolated stories, and personal journal—and its themes—reality, dreams, utopia—are united by a symbolism that, along with the rich, lyrical prose, rounds out the originality of the plot. Three emigrations take place over three generations; the grandfather goes to America and the daughter and son-in-law to Africa; one of the granddaughters moves to a European country and the other undergoes a cosmic emigration, taken by a being from another galaxy.

Embrió humà ultracongelat núm. F-77 (Ultrafrozen human embryo no. F-77) and its sequel, *Pel camí de l'arbre de la vida* (On the road to the tree of life), raise current, provocative questions about frozen embryos, test-tube babies, implantations in utero, and "mothers-for-hire," as well as deal with all the emotional and familial implications that genetic manipulation entails.

In *La capellana* (The priestess) the author situates the action in the future, when women will be allowed to practice as Catholic priests. The protagonist, the priest in a small town, unwillingly gets involved in a police intrigue.

BOOKS
Balda de la vida. Lleida: Pagès, 1991.
El cabdell de les bruixes. Valencia: Huguet Pascual, 1979.

La capellana. Barcelona: Elfos, 1988.
La dona del balcó. Valencia: Prometeo, 1981.
Embrió humà ultracongelat núm. F-77. Barcelona: Pòrtic, 1984.
Estelles. Barcelona: LaSal, 1978.
Laberints de seda. Barcelona: Pòrtic, 1981.
Pel camí de l'arbre de la vida. Barcelona: Pòrtic, 1985.
Temps del cos. Valencia: Huguet Pascual, 1980.
Tramada. Tarragona: Inst. d'Estudis Tarraconensis, 1980.
El turó de les forques. Barcelona: Pòrtic, 1983.

TRANSLATIONS OF HER WORKS
La capellana [*La capellana*]. Barcelona: Elfos, 1988.
Embrión humano ultracongelado núm F-77 [*Embrió humà ultracongelat núm. F-77*]. Barcelona: Plaza & Janés, 1985.

SECONDARY SOURCES
Möller-Soler, Maria-Lourdes. "El turó de les forques, per Rosa Fàbregat." *Serra d'or* 25 July 1984: 75–76.

MARIA-LOURDES SOLER I MARCET

G   Fariña y Cobián, Herminia
(B. 1904, Santiago de Compostela, Coruña; d. 1966, Santiago de Compostela, Coruña.) Poet and playwright.

Herminia Fariña began writing poetry at the age of thirteen and published her first book of poems, *Cadencias* (Cadences), in Castilian at eighteen. By age twenty she was engaged in intense literary activity, writing poems and articles. She also had two dramatic pieces performed in the 1920s: "Margarita a malfadada" (Margarita the bewitched), which has a musical background, and "O soldado froita" (The fruit soldier), a comedy.

In 1924 she published her second book of poems, *Seara* (A plot of arable land), in Galician. The poems are modernist in their meter and style but romantic in sentiment and dominated by sadness, as the Galician literary historian Ricardo Carballo has pointed out. Fariña often uses popular and rural themes. After her marriage she moved to Buenos Aires and continued writing. *Bajo el cielo porteño* (Under the skies of Buenos Aires) is a book of stories, and *Hosanna* contains poetry. She also republished *Cadencias* in Argentina and contributed to South American periodicals.

In 1944 Fariña made the following declaration to the magazine *La estafeta literaria:* "Soy aldeana: amiga de los astros y de los vientos, de los pinos y del mar; casi toda mi labor literaria es labriega, con dulzores de gaita y sosiego de corredoira" (I'm a country person: a friend of stars, wind, pine trees, and sea; almost all my literary work is rural, with sweet sounds of the 'gaita' and serenity of the 'corredoira').

BOOKS
Bajo el cielo porteño. Buenos Aires: n.p., 1930.
Cadencias. Pontevedra: n.p., 1922.
Hosanna. Buenos Aires: n.p., 1931.
Pétalos líricos. Mondariz: n.p., 1926.
¡Por España y para España! Vigo: Faro de Vigo, 1937.
Seara. Pontevedra: Celestino Peón, 1924.

WORKS IN BOOKS, PERIODICALS, NEWSPAPERS
Interview. *La estafeta literaria* 15 Dec. 1944.
"O retorno do gando." *A nosa terra* 211 (1 Apr. 1925).

SECONDARY SOURCES
Carballo Calero 609–10.
Couceiro Freijomil, *Diccionario bio-bibliográfico de escritores*, vol. 2.
Gran enciclopedia gallega, vol. 11.

MARIA CAMINO NOIA CAMPOS

C Farrès i Artigas, Josefina and Francesca
(19th c., Gracia, Barcelona.) Poets.

As the daughters of a notary, the Farrès sisters took part in the family literary salon, known as the Centre de la Baixineria, which combined reminiscences of Vallfogona with influences from the most conservative sectors of the *Renaixença*. They each left a large body of unpublished work, including Josefina Farrès's historical poem "Margarida de Ridaura" (1886; Margaret of Ridaura) and Francesca Farrès's poems "La creu del monestir" (The cross of the monastery) and "La torre de Sant Geroni" (The tower of Saint Jerome).

GUILLEM-JORDI GRAELLS

C Fernandez i Sempere, Susi
(B. 1961, Santa Pola, Alacant– .) Poet.

Susi Fernandez has worked in the Office for Language Teaching in Alicante. Two long poems appeared in the anthology *Entranyes per a l'augur* (Entrails for the augur). In this first sample of her work, she presents in a direct, experiential way a desire for happiness and inner freedom that recalls the past and rejects solitude.

WORKS IN BOOKS, PERIODICALS, NEWSPAPERS
"El llarg camí" and "Adéu soledat." *Entranyes per a l'augur: Antologia de jove poesia catalana al Baix Vinalopó.* Pref. Josep M. Llompart. Elx: U d'Educació a Distància, 1980. 63–71.

ISABEL ROBLES GOMEZ

C Ferran i Mora, Eulàlia
(20th c., Aretxabaleta, Gipuzkoa.) Poet.

Born in the Basque country of Catalan parents, Eulàlia Ferran spent her youth in Durango, Bizkaia. Her first book of poetry, *Pensament endins* (Inside thoughts), deals with domestic themes and talks about members of her family. In "Pobres criatures" (Poor creatures) she asks God to help her forgive humanity for its evil, but most of the poems have a lighter tone. In one love poem, "Ho vaig donar tot" (I gave it all), she claims to have given everything for love but that it was never enough.

In her second book, *Dos pobles, un cor* (Two peoples, one heart), the two peoples of the title are Catalonia and the Basque country. With a quotation from Ramon Vinyes, Ferran dedicates the book to her two countries, which share some of the same problems. Facing-page translations in Basque are by Xabier Kintana. The first poem is dedicated to the tree of Gernika, and several others create nostalgic pictures of her two regions.

BOOKS
Dos pobles, un cor. Pref. Josep Colet i Giralt. Illus. Ramon Zumalabe. Barcelona: Romargraf, 1979.
Pensament endins. Barcelona: Claret, 1976.

KATHLEEN MCNERNEY

C Ferré i Gomis, Adelaida
(B. 1881?, Barcelona; d. 1955.) Folklorist.

Adelaida Ferré studied in Barcelona at the Escola Normal, the Conservatori, the Escola d'Institutrius, Arts i Oficis i Belles Arts, the Institut de Cultura i Biblioteca Popular per la Dona, and the Institut de les Arts del Llibre. She was a distinguished teacher in several fields: artistic drawing and engraving at the Escuela Municipal de Arte in the eighth district of Barcelona, modeling and engraving at the Escuela Municipal de Ciegos, sewing and lace making at the Escuela Municipal de Oficios para la Mujer, and art history at the Escuela Profesional de la Diputación. She won many prizes for her artistic work.

A pupil of Rossend Serra i Pagès at the Escola d'Institutrius, she and other writers such as Sara Llorens and Gràcia Bassa formed part of a group of women who devoted themselves to studying folklore. She contributed articles to *La veu comarcal* (Ripoll, Lleida) and to the Barcelona periodicals *Art jove, Catalana*, and *La veu de Catalunya* and lectured at various institutions in Barcelona. Lectura Popular published a selection of her works under the title *De folklore* (About folklore). Included are "Les puntes de la litúrgia" (Liturgical lace), "A propòsit d'una pràctica curativa"

(About a curative practice), "Coteig de les rondalles d'en Perrault amb les Catalanes" (Perrault's and Catalan tales), "Le petit Poucet" (Little Poucet), and an excerpt from "El símbol a Barcelona" (The symbol in Barcelona).

BOOKS
De folklore. Vol. 28 of *Lectura popular.*

SECONDARY SOURCES
Serra i Pagès, Rossend. "La Porquerola (Rondalla Cerdana)." *Feminal* 39 (26 June 1910).

CRISTINA ENRIQUEZ DE SALAMANCA

C Ferrer Royo, Consol
(20th c.) Playwright. No biographical information available.

The files of the Institut de Teatre Català in Barcelona contain the manuscripts of two plays by Consol Ferrer Royo, which may never have been staged. "El glatir de la terra" (The yearning of the earth) deals with the conflict between rural and urban life, presented as opposite and incompatible ideals, in a family of farmers in the Baix Ebre (Tarragona) area. The protagonist, representing a new generation, idealizes rural life, in contrast to his parents, who regard it with bitterness. "Asfixia, una nota llírica," (1974; Asfixia, A lyrical note) describes the problem of literary creation in a commercial world and points out the meanness in dealings between writers and publishers.

Consol Ferrer Royo has also written a children's story, *Daurat a l'illa de la quietut* (Gilded on the isle of tranquillity), which deals with the young people's rebellion against the ways of life set by previous generations.

BOOKS
"Asfixia, una nota llírica." Ts. 36–642. Institut de Teatre, Barcelona.
Daurat a l'illa de la quietut. Tortosa: Balaguer, 1976.
"El glatir de la terra." Ts. 8–110. Institut de Teatre, Barcelona.

CRISTINA ENRIQUEZ DE SALAMANCA

C Florera Serra, Núria
(20th c.) Poet. No biographical information available.

BOOKS
Núria, cloenda d'un poema. Mataró, Barcelona: Agrupación Hispana de Escritores, 1981.

KATHLEEN MCNERNEY

C Fontanet López, Encarna
(20th c.) Poet. No biographical information available.

BOOKS
Un solc de lluna i set fulles seques. Barcelona: Pozanco, 1981.

KATHLEEN MCNERNEY

C Font de Cabestany, Maria
(20th c.) Poet. No biographical information available.

BOOKS
La mort del camp i d'altres poemes. Torelló, Barcelona: n.p., 1981.

KATHLEEN MCNERNEY

C Font i Codina, Mercè
(B. 1867, Vic, Barcelona; d. 1894 or 1900, Vic, Barcelona.) Poet.

At her untimely death, Mercè Font was considered the best woman poet in Vic. She was active in literary groups, particularly L'Esbart (The Group), and published poems in the Vic periodical *La veu de Montserrat.* She also participated in literary competitions, winning a secondary award for her poem "A Maria Inmaculada" (To Mary Immaculate) in the contest held by the Marian Academy in Lleida in 1887. Her poem "El cloquer de Ripoll" (The Ripoll belfry) appears in *Les cinc branques.* Her work reflects religious inspiration.

WORKS IN BOOKS, PERIODICALS, NEWSPAPERS
"El cloquer de Ripoll." *Les cinc branques* 48.

MARISA SIGUAN BOEHMER

C Forner, Maria
(19th c.) Poet. No biographical information available.

Maria Forner is cited by Juan P. Criado y Domínguez as a "poetisa, autora de varias composiciones en catalán" (poetess, author of several compositions in Catalan). Her only extant work is "Lo mort" (The dead).

WORKS IN BOOKS, PERIODICALS, NEWSPAPERS
"Lo mort." *La renaixença* 1 May 1872.

SECONDARY SOURCES
Criado y Domínguez 101.

CRISTINA ENRIQUEZ DE SALAMANCA

C Forteza, Margarita

(B. ?, Mallorca?; d. 20th c.) Poet. No biographical information available.

The public library in Palma has two booklets without a publisher's name or a publication date: *Sombras de amor* (Love shadows) and *Una vídua cerca novio: Diàlegs en vers* (Widow seeking boyfriend: Verse dialogues). The first, in Castilian, is a collection of four poems: "Soledad" (Solitude), "La moza flamenca" (The flamencan girl), "Adoración" (Adoration), and "Sombras de amor." The second, in Catalan and Castilian, concerns an unattractive widow who wants to remarry.

BOOKS
Sombras de amor. N.p.: n.p., n.d. Biblioteca Pública de Palma de Mallorca.
Una vídua cerca novio: Diàlegs en vers. N.p.: n.p., n.d. Biblioteca Pública de Palma de Mallorca.

CRISTINA ENRIQUEZ DE SALAMANCA

C Fullana, Maria

(B. 1958, València– .) Poet.

One of the most notable voices in new poetry from Valencia is Maria Fullana, who also teaches Catalan. Her first book, *Cants mimètics* (Mimetic verses), won the Manuel Rodríguez Martínez prize of Alcoy. She later won the 1988 Senyoriu d'Ausiàs March prize for an unpublished work. Her poems have appeared in the poetry magazines *Tac carbònica, La figuera,* and *Bavel.* She published her book of poems *I escadussers* (And what is left over) in 1987. Maria Fullana has developed a personalized poetry with rich imagery, frequently rooted in dreams, and mixes literary, cultural, and film references with tender memories of her own childhood and cultural history.

BOOKS
Blues. Valencia: Gregal, 1989.
Cants mimètics. Alcoi: Premi Manuel Rodríguez, 1986.
Contes feiners. Valencia: Tres i Quatre, 1990.
Icara. Valencia: Alfama, 1990.
I escadussers. Valencia: La Canyada, 1987.
Joc de dames. Barcelona: L'Eixample, 1992.

SECONDARY SOURCES
Pérez Montaner, Jaume. "La narrativa de Maria Fullana. Notes a *Joc de dames.*" *Caràcters* 1 (15 Oct. 1992): 5–7.

ISABEL ROBLES GOMEZ

C Furnó i Monsech, Maria Emília
(B. 1878, Barcelona; d. 1944, Barcelona.) Poet.

Maria Emília Furnó founded the School for Women in Barcelona between 1910 and 1920 and wrote *Nocions d'urbanitat* (Notions of manners) on the basis of this experience. In the book, she expresses somewhat conservative ideas about the limits and aims of women's education.

Between 1928 and 1933, she published eight books of poetry. In *Amor de cel: Poesies* (Heavenly love: Poems) many poems are inspired by devotion to Mary and by religious mysteries or festivities, particularly Christmas. Some poems are set to music, possibly for use in the school where she was headmistress. The introduction to *Apunts del natural* (Notes on natural things) includes a critical opinion by Lluís Bertran i Pijoan, which also appeared in the journal *La dona catalana* (The Catalan woman). The poems are inspired by a variety of themes, especially those relating to Barcelona, its Ramblas, and its women. The book also contains the lyrics to a sardana, "La festa major," and several poems of traditional Catalan sentiments. In his critical introduction to *Visions*, Manuel de Montoliu says of Furnó: "és tota naturalista, això és, s'emmotlla amb la més sorprenent agilitat i espontaneïtat als més diversos espectacles que l'atzar de la vida li posa davant dels seus sentits" (she is completely naturalistic, that is, she shapes herself with the most surprising agility and spontaneity to the different spectacles that chance puts before her senses) (7).

BOOKS
Amor de cel: Poesies. Barcelona: Rafael Casulleras, 1929.
Apunts del natural. Introd. Lluís Bertran i Pijoan. Barcelona: Rafael Casulleras, 1930.
Nocions d'urbanitat: Comportament que deuen observar les nenes. . . . Barcelona: Llibreria L'Avenç, 1919. 2nd ed. corrected and expanded. Barcelona: Rafael Casulleras, 1930.
Visions. Introd. Manuel de Montoliu. Barcelona: Rafael Casulleras, 1933.

WORKS IN BOOKS, PERIODICALS, NEWSPAPERS
"A guisa de pròleg," "Alegria," "Cançoneta," "De l'infantesa," "Festa," "Roses nadalenques," and "***." *Nadal 1954*. Ed. Enrich Pérez i Capdevila. Barcelona: Gràfiques Flos, n.d. [1954]. 22–31.

CRISTINA ENRIQUEZ DE SALAMANCA

C Fuster, Felícia
(B. 1921, Barcelona– .) Poet and translator.

Felícia Fuster studied painting, drawing, and engraving on glass before moving to Paris in 1950. She has remained in France, now residing in a small town where she continues various artistic projects in an atmosphere of tranquillity. She has translated Marguerite Yourcenar's works into Catalan. In Fuster's first book of poetry, *Una cançó per a ningú i trenta diàlegs inútils* (A song for nobody and thirty useless dialogues), the poet Maria-Mercè Marçal points out in her prologue, "Tard, però no pas a deshora" (Late, but well timed), that it is Fuster who should be writing prologues for her—a reference to Fuster's late entry into the world of poetry. Marçal is enthusiastic and finds Fuster's poetry "magnètic o màgic, que . . . pugui atrapar-nos amb tanta força que no es deixi abandonar fins al final" (magnetic or magic that . . . can trap us so forcefully that we can't leave it until the end). It is a poetry of love and abandonment, of one-person dialogues, with a sometimes striking imagery of solitude: "sense / trobar mai cap repòs / ni en les sales d'espera / on el temps es fa vell / i s'embruta" (without finding any rest / even in the waiting rooms / where time gets old / and dirty) (21). The speaker offers the absent one "amb el silenci tens / el jardí càlid dels meus braços" (with the tense silence / the warm garden / of my arms) (54).

Fuster's third book of poetry, *I encara* (And still), won the Vicent Andrés Estellés prize in the October 1987 literary contest in Valencia. The volume is divided into three sections: "I si" (And If), "I què dieu" (And What Do You Say), and "I més" (And More). The use of the conjunction "i" at the beginning of many poems and at the end of some at once follows an informal speech pattern in Catalan and creates a continuum, while the poet addresses themes of time, death, and inspiration. Fuster handles masterfully the classical Renaissance juxtapositions of opposites, particularly light and dark, but also movement and stillness, speed and slowness, life and death; in a surprising image, she finds that the abyss is a cradle. Some poems have multiple narrators, and some are addressed to the plural "vosaltres." Several poems speak of the anguish of not having the strength to survive in an alienating world; others sound a joyful note of empowerment.

BOOKS

Aquelles cordes del vent. Barcelona: Proa, 1987.
Una cançó per a ningú i trenta diàlegs inútils. Introd. Maria-Mercè Marçal. Barcelona: Proa, 1984.
I encara. Valencia: Eliseu Climent, 1987.

TRANSLATIONS OF HER WORKS

"And If" ["I si"], poems 5, 6, 10, and 11; "And What Do You Say" ["I què dieu"], poems 4 and 6; and "And More" ["I més"], poem 8 from *I encara*. Trans. Kathleen McNerney. *Catalan Review* 3.2 (Dec. 1989): 230–51.
"Dark" ["Fosca"] and "Who" ["Qui"]. *Survivors*. Selected and trans. D. Sam Abrams. Barcelona: Inst. d'Estudis Nord-Americans, 1991. 57–65.

KATHLEEN MCNERNEY

C Galícia i Gorritz, Montserrat
(B. 1947, Cornellà, Barcelona– .) Writer of children's literature.

In addition to receiving a teaching degree, Montserrat Galícia obtained degrees in geography and history. She has contributed a story to the juvenile magazine *Cavall fort*.

Her novel *P.H. 1A Copèrnic* (P.H. 1A Copernicus) is the first of a planned trilogy. This science fiction story describes a journey in space after the year 2000. The mission of the explorers is to find a more habitable planet than Earth, which is ravaged by war and pollution. A team from the spaceship Terra II indeed finds a planet, Copernicus, so similar to a primitive Earth that its crew begins detailed studies and maps. When they discover that the planet is inhabited, they must come to grips with conflicts among the Copernicans and at the same time try to reestablish contact with their ship. The novel allows its author to criticize Earth's society and, without idealizing the Copernicans, make observations about the possibility of a better world.

BOOKS
P.H. 1A Copèrnic. Barcelona: Laia, 1984.

WORKS IN BOOKS, PERIODICALS, NEWSPAPERS
"Compri tomàquets." *Cavall fort* 593–94 (Apr. 1987): 26.

KATHLEEN MCNERNEY

C García Bravo, Magdalena
(B. 1862, Valencia; d. 1891, Valencia.) Poet.

Magdalena García Bravo wrote in both Castilian and Catalan. A short biography of her is included in Constantí Llombart's Valencian dictionary, *Los fills de la morta viva*. García Bravo was the sister of the Valencian poet Enrich García Bravo and was educated in the Colegi de la Mare de Deu del Pilar in Valencia. She was barely into her teens when she began publishing poems, written in Castilian, in journals of Valencia (*La ilustració popular económica; El cosmopólita; La antorcha*) and of other provinces (*El correo de la moda; La lealtad española*, of Madrid; and *El riojano*, of Logroño).

García Bravo was one of the first Valencian women to begin writing in Catalan. Her poems also appeared in the Valencian almanac *Lo rat penat* and in the journal *Las provincias*. She won second prize at the Jocs Florals de Lo Rat-Penat in 1880 and first prize in 1886 at the Certamen de la Juventud Católica de Tortosa for a poem devoted to the Blessed Virgin. In 1882 she received second prize in the Jocs Florals de Lo Rat-Penat for "Cant de amor" (Love song). She later won awards in the literary

160

contests of the Academia Bibliográfica Mariana de Lérida in 1885 and 1890.

José María Cossío mentions her name in his *Cincuenta años de poesía española (1850–1900)* and, although he considers her a "romántica rezagada" (backward Romantic), he values some of her "versos que tienen todo este halago" (charming poetry). Her parents published a posthumous collection of her poetry, *Poesías de la Señorita Magdalena García Bravo* (Poems), in homage to their daughter. This short work contains Castilian and Catalan poetry and poems awarded literary prizes. The majority of the Castilian poems have religious themes in which devotion to the Virgin is predominant. A delicate sense of nature characterizes her poetry, which shows the influence of Carolina Coronado and Gustavo Adolfo Bécquer, and dazzling images and a strong sense of rhythm prevail. The theme of the book is the search for an ideal that is superior to earthly values and can save her soul from human disappointments; but some poems, such as "La loma" (The hillock), show a delicious capacity for joy born of deep feeling for her native land. The landscape is drawn with the vividness and clarity of bright enamel.

In 1892, Teodoro Llorente wrote an obituary for García Bravo in *Las provincias. Diario de Valencia. Almanaque para 1892.*

BOOKS

Poesías de la Señorita Magdalena García Bravo. Valencia: José Canales Romà, 1894.

WORKS IN BOOKS, PERIODICALS, NEWSPAPERS

"Al ángel de mi guarda." *La ilustración popular económica de Valencia* 314 (1878): 50.

"A la Virgen Divina en sus dolores." *La ilustración popular económica de Valencia* 419 (1881): 454–55.

"A la Virgen María en su Concepción Purísima." *La ilustración popular económica de Valencia* 437 (1881): 441–42.

"Al Niño Dios." *La ilustración popular económica de Valencia* 446 (1882): 1.

"A María." *La ilustración popular económica de Valencia* 401 (1880): 441–42.

"A mi hermana Josefina al regreso de un viage." *La ilustración popular económica de Valencia* 452 (1882): 111.

"A mi querida hermana Hilaria en su profesión religiosa." *La ilustración popular económica de Valencia* 392 (1880): 297–98.

"A mi querida hermana María en su entrada en el claustro." *La ilustración popular económica de Valencia* 354 (1879): 210–11.

"A mi querido papá. En sus días. Soneto." *La ilustración popular económica de Valencia* 350 (1879): 195.

"Las cadenas de Marsella. Romance inédito." *Las provincias. Diario de Valencia. Almanaque para el año 1892.* Valencia: Domenech, 1893. 115–16.

"Cant d'amor." *La ilustración popular económica de Valencia* 468 (1882): 354–55.

"Cant de amor." Llombart 634–37.

"Cant de amor." *Lo rat-penat. Brots de llorer.* Valencia: Domenech, 1896. 2: 111–15.

"Cant d'amor. Poesía premiada en los Jochs Florals de Valencia." *La renaixença* (1882): 270–72.

"Carta a mi hermano Enrique." *La ilustración popular económica de Valencia* 391 (1880): 283.

"Cecilia." *La ilustración popular económica de Valencia* 427 (1881): 280.

"Crepúsculo." *Las provincias. Diario de Valencia. Almanaque para 1889.* Valencia: Domenech, 1890. 231.

"Dempres dels Jochs Florals." *Lo rat penat* (1883): 156–57.

"Dos bodas." *La ilustración popular económica de Valencia* 464 (1882): 301.

"L'estiuet de San Martí." *Lo rat penat* (1882): 63–64.

"Una flor." *La ilustración popular económica de Valencia* 462 (1882): 263–64.

"Flor de primavera es lo meu cor." *Lo rat penat* (1881): 51–53.

"La fuente de la gota." *Las provincias. Diario de Valencia. Almanaque para el año 1892.* Valencia: Domenech, 1893. 223–24.

"Hasta en el sueño. A mi madre." *La ilustración popular económica de Valencia* 365 (1879): 258.

"Jesús." *La ilustración popular económica de Valencia* 338 (1879): 146–47.

"La mariposa y la flor." *La ilustración popular económica de Valencia* 321 (1878): 78.

"Un nuevo templo. En la inauguración de la nueva iglesia del Monasterio de la Zaidia. Valencia." *La ilustración popular económica de Valencia* 372 (1879): 282–83.

"Pobre flor." *La ilustración popular económica de Valencia* 352 (1879): 202.

"El poder de la pintura. A mi distinguido amigo el inspirado pintor D. Carlos Giner." *Las provincias. Diario de Valencia. Almanaque para el año 1884.* Valencia: Domenech, 1885. 235.

"Primavera y otoño." *Las provincias. Diario de Valencia. Almanaque para el año 1887.* Valencia: Domenech, 1888. 97.

"El Rei en Jaume." *Les cinc branques* 44.

"Lo Rey en Jaume." *Lo Rat-Penat. Flors d'enguany.* Valencia: Domenech, 1897. 3: 125.

"Un sueño. A María Inmaculada." *La ilustración popular económica de Valencia* 272 (1877): 170–71.

"Suspiros a la Divina Madre." *Academia bibliográfica Mariana de Lérida.* 1885. 49–52.

"Yo te amo, Virgen María." *Academia bibliográfica Mariana de Lérida.* 1890. 71–74.

SECONDARY SOURCES

Cossío, José María. *Cincuenta años de poesía española (1850–1900).* 2 vols. Madrid: Espasa-Calpe, 1960. 2: 916–17.

Llombart 632–38.

[Llorente, Teodoro]. "Necrología." *Las provincias. Diario de Valencia. Almanaque para 1892. Año decimotercero.* Valencia: Domenech, 1891. 341–42.

Simón Palmer, *Escritoras españolas del siglo XIX* 293.

CRISTINA ENRIQUEZ DE SALAMANCA

C Garcia i Cornellà, Dolors
(B. 1956, Girona– .) Fiction writer.

A psychologist, Dolors Garcia i Cornellà has practiced her profession, especially with children, in schools in Girona, Figueres, and Llançà. The title story of her book, *Albert* (Albert), clearly shows her mastery of and dedication to her work. This chilling narrative is told through the voice of a mentally ill child at the beginning of his adolescence; his cruel pranks early in the story become pathological and self-destructive. Since the point of view is the child's, the reader is left at times in a gray area, not sure how much to attribute to the boy's dark imagination and how much to the reality of his situation. The style successfully captures both the age of the narrator and the troubled workings of his mind. A second story included in this slim volume, "La mística" (The mystic), relates the fascination of one widow for another, while it addresses the relationship between a mother and her grown daughter. The book won the Just Maria Casero Prize in 1985. Garcia i Cornellà contributes sporadically to various regional publications.

BOOKS
Albert. Girona: El Pont de Pedra, 1986.
Canya plàstica. Girona: Cruïlla, 1988.

KATHLEEN MCNERNEY

C Garcia i Tudela, Maria Rosa
(B. 1956, Barcelona– .) Poet and fiction writer.

Maria Rosa Garcia's fiction deals with female adolescence and relationships among family, friends, and lovers; and her stories often have surprise endings. She also writes about her love for literature and the necessity to write. She has contributed short stories and, occasionally, poetry to various publications.

BOOKS
Un cel esquitxat d'estrelles. Barcelona: Dalmau, 1979.

WORKS IN BOOKS, PERIODICALS, NEWSPAPERS
"Els meus amants," "Homenatge," "S'ha rendit un delinqüent," and "Picardies." Colet i Giralt 57–63.

KATHLEEN MCNERNEY

C   Gardella Quer, Maria Angels

(B. 1958, Figueres, Girona– .) Writer of children's literature. No biographical information available.

BOOKS
Un armariet, un cofre i un diari. Barcelona: La Galera, 1981.
La gasolinera. Barcelona: Pirene, 1989.
El geni del viol. Barcelona: La Galera, 1982.
En Gilbert i les línies. Barcelona: La Galera, 1983.
La llegenda de Guillem Tell. Barcelona: La Galera, 1984.
El vaixell de l'ampolla. Barcelona: La Galera, 1985.

TRANSLATIONS OF HER WORKS
Un arcón, un cofre, y un diario [Un armariet, un cofre i un diari]. Barcelona: La Galera, 1981.

KATHLEEN MCNERNEY

C   Garriga de Cervelló, Maria Concepció

(20th c.) Poet. No biographical information available.

A traditionalist poet, Concepció Garriga published the volume *Recull de poesies d'ara i d'antany* (A collection of poems from now and the past).

BOOKS
Recull de poesies d'ara i d'antany. Barcelona: n.p., 1972.

GUILLEM-JORDI GRAELLS

C   Garriga i Martin, Maria dels Angels

(B. 1898, Sant Vicenç de Calders, Tarragona; d. 1967, Saifores, Barcelona.) Writer of children's literature.

Maria Garriga studied in the 1920s at the advanced Normal School of the Mancomunitat and worked as a teacher in a special pedagogical center. After the Civil War she was sent to a little village, Saifores, whose inhabitants are reflected in some of her works.

Garriga wrote short stories for children's periodicals, such as *Cavall fort* and *Tretzevents*, both of Barcelona, as well as the first books after 1939 for teaching Catalan to children. In 1966, she was a finalist for the Folch i Torres prize for her novel *Un rètol per a Curtó* (A road sign for Curtó), which describes the effort of a group of children to improve their village so that it merits a road sign with a proper name. The characters are simple but well delineated. In the novel, as in her short stories, she tries to show the importance of ordinary work in reaching one's goals.

BOOKS
Anem a buscar un cos. Barcelona: La Galera, 1965.
Dijous a vila. Barcelona: La Galera, 1965.
L'entremaliada del ramat. Barcelona: La Galera, 1965.
Una excursió . . . accidentada. Barcelona: La Galera, 1966.
El gran viatge de Gota blava i Gota verda. Barcelona: La Galera, 1964.
Un rètol per a Curtó. Barcelona: La Galera, 1967.
Tula, la tortuga. Barcelona: La Galera, 1964.

ANNA GUDAYOL I TORRELL

C Gasol i Llorach, Francesca
(20th c.) Also Francesca Gasol i Llorens. Novelist. No biographical information available.

BOOKS
L'engany. Montblanc: Requesens, 1982.

KATHLEEN MCNERNEY

C Gay, Simona
(B. 1898, Ille-sur-Têt, France; d. 1969, Ille-sur-Têt, France.) Also known as Simona Pons. Poet.

The daughter of Simón Pons, a doctor in Ille-sur-Têt, and of Antoinette Trainier, Simona Gay received her primary education in Ille-sur-Têt and at the Benedictine nuns' school of the Holy Sacrament in Port Bou. Her parents forbade her to go to Perpignan for painting lessons, but she taught herself watercolors and also took violin lessons in Ille-sur-Têt. At the age of nineteen she married León Gay and moved to Paris, where her husband served as a judge. There she studied Latin and read both English and French authors, including Shelley, Proudhon, and Mallarmé as well as such Catalan authors as Ramon Llull and Bernat Metge. Gay wrote poems in French and also compiled her own glossaries of expressions of the mountain folk and the people of the Costa Brava. With the onset of the Second World War she moved back to the family home in Ille-sur-Têt, where the strain of farm chores broke her health.

Possibly through her brother, Josep Sebastià Pons, Gay established relationships with the Catalan poets of the postsymbolist era: Tomàs

Garcés, Marià Manent, and Carles Riba. Garcés, with whom she maintained a close friendship, wrote the prologue to her first book and dedicated a posthumous article to her in the magazine *Serra d'or*. Carles Riba also dedicated a posthumous article to her in *Revista de Catalunya*, and Marià Manent wrote the prologue to her last book, *La gerra al sol: Poemes* (A jar in the sun: Poems).

As part of the *Renaixença*, Gay devoted herself to Catalan linguistic enrichment in the Roussillon area. Her poetry also reflects the strong influence of the literary currents inspired by Oriental poetry in the first third of the century. Her first two books were published in Catalan in Paris and include her own French translations. Since she lived in Roussillon and published in Paris, she was practically unknown in Catalonia either as a poet or as the sister of Josep Sebastià Pons.

The poetry of Simona Gay was composed over thirty years and appears in three books: *Aigües vives* (Lively waters), *Lluita amb l'àngel* (Battle with the angel), and *La gerra al sol*. Her work demonstrates thematic and technical continuity, generally avoiding personal emotions, aesthetic effects, and complex images. Gay seeks and finds another reality in the loving contemplation of the world of nature, and in this search can be found the heart of her poetry: "Música igual per l'oïda / el dolç corrent m'ha adormida, / tot deixant-me el cor obert / per altre viure més cert" (The same music for the ear / the sweet current sleeps me here, / but open leaves my heart's soft curtain / for another life more certain) (*La gerra al sol* 56).

The core of her poetry is not a psychological or philosophical exploration or a flight from reality but the perception of the balance in nature. She observes that this harmony leads to productive activity which, muted and efficient, causes a tireless making and remaking, the continuity of the natural cycles. Thus she says, "De la soca de vinya aprenc la paciència / quan espera la vida i sols s'en veu l'absència" (From the stem of the vine learn patience / when you wait for life but only see its absence) (*Lluita amb l'àngel* 124). Her poems seek the infinite charm of nature in specific evanescent moments, when the countryside is in a state of suspension and all its protagonists, the river, the grass, the oak, and the squirrel, participate in this state: "Acord callat / amb ritme enlairat / d'aquella branca . . . / Un esquirol salta la tanca / una castanya cau / i assenyala la pau" (Unspoken covenant / of the raised rhythm / of that branch . . . / A squirrel leaps the fence / a chestnut falls / and signals peace) (*La gerra al sol* 18).

The countryside of her native Ille-sur-Têt turns into an interior landscape, "mon pais de gràcies esquives" (my land of hidden delights) (*La gerra al sol* 51). The rhythm of the bells marks human time, in juxtaposition with the unbreakable flow of natural time: "Tota la vall escolta / quan l'hora vol sonar / la fressora ribera / va lligant temps segú / que la campana trenca / amb el seu cristal nu" (The whole valley listens / when time desires to ring / the river banks / link certain time / which church bell breaks / with its naked crystal) (*Lluita amb l'àngel* 108). Despite her lack of traditional religious sentiment, in her last poems she achieves dialogue with the infinite as she tries to penetrate the mystery of the sacred mount.

Aigües vives is divided into two parts. In the first section Gay deals with relationships, love, children, and friendship, and experiments with forms and traditional atmospheric effects. The second set of poems refers to specific places in her homeland. Loneliness is a prime element in the characterization of the landscape and of the poet's material. In *Lluita amb l'àngel*, the dark night of the poet is portrayed in the title poem. The poems of *La gerra al sol* are stylistically and thematically simpler and feature great chromatic interest and a painter's point of view, such as in "Al molí" (To the mill), "La gerra al sol," and "Casa vella" (Old house). The poems to her brother, who died in 1962, add an elegiac note to her work.

A prize-winner in the Jocs Florals in Girona, Gay contributed to magazines in Perpignan and kept an unpublished diary, which is a study of local Roussillon folklore.

BOOKS
Aigües vives. Eaux vives. Poemes catalanes avec la traduction française en regard. Introd. Tomàs Garcés. Paris: Occitane, 1932.

La gerra al sol: Poemes. Introd. Marià Manent. Col.lecció Tramuntana. Autors i Temes de les Contrades Pirinenques. Vol 10. Barcelona: Barcino, 1965.

Lluita amb l'àngel. Lutte amb l'ange. Poemes catalanes avec la traduction française en regard. Paris: Noël, 1938.

WORKS IN BOOKS, PERIODICALS, NEWSPAPERS
"Aigües vives," "Melangia," and "Sant Miquel de Llotes." *La revista* Jan.–June 1931: 57–58.

"El gorg estelat." *La revista* July–Dec. 1933: 46–50.

"Poble perdut." *Manat d'homenatge* 31–32.

SECONDARY SOURCES
Garcés, Tomàs. "Els tres llibres de Simona Gay." *Serra d'or* July 1970: 61–62.

Ribas, Carles. "Lluita amb l'àngel, per Simona Gay." *Revista de Catalunya* 94 (Dec. 1939): 109–12.

CRISTINA ENRIQUEZ DE SALAMANCA

B Genua, Enkarni
(20th c.) Novelist. No biographical information available.

Enkarni Genua's novels are *Erreka Mari*, about a mythological character; *Zezena Plazan* (The bull in the ring); *Hondarrezko gaztelua* (Sandiest);

Txori txiki polit bat (A pretty little bird); and *Altzor bat patrikan* (A treasure in your pocket).

BOOKS

Altzor bat patrikan. San Sebastián: Erein, 1988.
Erreka Mari. San Sebastián: Erein, 1979.
Hondarrezko gaztelua. San Sebastián: Erein, 1986.
Txori txiki polit bat. San Sebastián: Erein, 1986.
Zezena Plazan. San Sebastián: Erein, 1981.

MAITE GONZALEZ ESNAL

C   Gili i Güell, Antònia

(B. 1856, Vilafranca del Penedès, Barcelona; d. 1909, Vilafranca del Penedès, Barcelona.) Poet.

Antònia Gili earned a degree in education but, because of poor health, never practiced her profession. She lived an isolated life, reading and writing religious lyrics. Enthusiastic about the *Renaixença*, she wrote simple verses that show her awareness of Catalan history and traditions. She published short pieces in the Vic periodical *La veu de Montserrat*, which was edited by Jaume Collell, the archdeacon at Vic's cathedral. She also contributed to Catholic periodicals such as *Revista popular, Almanach dels amichs del Papa, Almanach de les Conferencies de Sant Vicenç de Paul*, and *Corona poética de Nuestra Señora de Ripoll*.

Gili achieved her first literary success in 1887, receiving the second Prize of Faith with her poem "A Maria en sa purificació" (To Mary in her purification) at the literary contest organized by the Joventud Catòlica in Barcelona. Such well-known poets as Jacint Verdaguer, Jaume Collell, Francesc Casas i Amigó, and Francesc Pelai Briz participated in the competition. Gili won prizes again in 1888, 1889, 1890, 1892, and 1894 and in other contests organized by the Marian Academy in 1896, 1897, and 1902.

A selection of her poems in *Lectura popular* deals with daily life, popular scenes, and miracles and episodes from the Bible. (The same volume includes works by Angel Guimerà, Enric Tintorer, and Antoni Maria Alcover.) In *Lo miracler de Barcelona* (The miracles of Barcelona) her poems relate the life and miracles of Barcelona's native saint, Josep Oriol, in various meters and a cultivated popular language. A volume on Marian poetry, *Maria: Recull de poesia mariana* (Mary: Collection of Marian poetry), was published posthumously, without having been definitively corrected by her. Scenes from the life of Mary and Jesus and subjects from the Bible are treated in simple strophes, with decasyllables alternating with alexandrines, reflecting Gili's effort to compose in classical forms. She is more successful when she uses short meters in the popular tradition.

BOOKS

Maria: Recull de poesia mariana. Barcelona: Llibreria Catòlica, 1910.

Lo miracler de Barcelona: Ramet poètich al Beato Josep Oriol. Barcelona: Tipografia Catòlica, 1899. 2nd ed. Barcelona: La Hormiga de Oro, 1933.

Poesies. Vol. 12 of *Lectura popular.*

WORKS IN BOOKS, PERIODICALS, NEWSPAPERS

"A la gloriosa Madona de Ripoll." *Corona poètica a Nuestra Señora Santa Maria de Ripoll.* Ripoll: n.p., n.d.

"Goigs en llahor de la Verge de Mont Toro." *Academia Bibliográfica Mariana.* Lérida: Tipografia Mariana, 1902.

MARISA SIGUAN BOEHMER

C Ginestà, Marina

(20th c.) Novelist. No biographical information available.

Marina Ginestà's only known novel, *Els antípodes* (The antipodes), takes place in the Caribbean. It is a love story between two exiles from Catalonia, set between the defeat of the Republic and the beginning of the Second World War. The pain of exile, always accompanied by some hope of return, is lessened by the characters' mutual understanding. The background is of Caribbean politics, influenced by North American domination and the legacy of Hispanic civilization and colonization.

BOOKS

Els antípodes. Barcelona: Dopesa, 1976.

KATHLEEN MCNERNEY

C Ginesta, Montserrat

(B. 1952, Selva, Barcelona– .) Illustrator and writer of children's stories.

Montserrat Ginesta studied at the Escola d'Arts i Oficis Artístics de Barcelona and has contributed to the children's magazines *Cavall fort* and *Tretzevents* as well as to the fashion magazine *Hogar y moda.* She participated in the First Salon of Comics and Illustration of Barcelona and in the exhibition of illustrations organized by the Generalitat de Catalunya. Illustrator of textbooks, folktales, and the series *Pau i Pepa* (Paul and Pepa) by Marta Balaguer, she has received illustration prizes for her stories *El barret d'en Jan* (Jan's hat) and *Bombolleta* (Little Bubble). She writes for very young children, who rely more on illustration than on text.

Double Minorities of Spain

BOOKS
Adelaida pastissera. Barcelona: Argos Vergara, 1983.
L'arbre dels cent vestits. Barcelona: Juventud, 1978.
El barret d'en Jan. Barcelona: Juventud, 1977.
Bombolleta. Barcelona: Juventud, 1983.
Els bonics colors del sol. Barcelona: Juventud, 1978.
La capsa verda. Barcelona: Destino, 1982.
La geganta i el Nap-Buf. Barcelona: La Galera, 1986.
Missenyora tigressa. Barcelona: Teide, 1985.

ANNA GASOL I TRULLOLS

Ginesu, Pinutxa; *see* **Maffei Ginesu, Pinutxa**

C Giralt, Maria Angela
(18th c.) Poet. No biographical information available.

Félix Torres Amat's dictionary of Catalan writers lists the following works by Maria Angela Giralt: "Rosari de la Reyna dels Angels Maria Santissima, junt ab les estacions de la via crucis y ab algunes lletras devotas que solen cantarse en las Santas missions a fi de que . . . etc. Barcelona, per Maria Angela Giralt, viuda, 1733" (Rosary of Most Holy Mary, Queen of the Angels, along with the Stations of the Cross and with some devout lyrics usually sung in the Holy Missions so that . . . etc. Barcelona, by Maria Angela Giralt, widow, 1733).

SECONDARY SOURCES
Torres Amat 713.

CRISTINA ENRIQUEZ DE SALAMANCA

C Girona Serra, Marina
(20th c.) Poet. No biographical information available.

Marina Girona's only collection of poetry, *Records i anhels* (Memories and Yearnings), contains about sixty poems. Throughout the work, she alternates lyrical and metaphysical pieces. The lyrical poems often deal with Catalonia—its people, geography, customs, and life-style. There are also some love poems. Her subjects are the home, family, society, loss (as of a lover who emigrates), and the growth of knowledge and strength.

Girona's metaphysical poems are brief, melodic renditions of Hermes Trismegistus for the New Age. Using traditional rhyme and meter, she expresses optimism about humanity's journey to a higher plane of existence. Girona also wrote a play in Castilian, *La llamada* (The call).

BOOKS
La llamada. Madrid: Escelier, 1968.
Records i anhels. Bilbao: Gran Enciclopedia Vasca, 1978.

SANDRA CANEPARI

C Gisbert, Mireia
(20th c.) Writer of children's literature. No biographical information available.

BOOKS
L'aventura d'un estel. Barcelona: n.p., 1977.
En Bernat d'alpac. Barcelona: Teide, 1984.
Martin quiere leer. Barcelona: Teide, 1984.

KATHLEEN MCNERNEY

C Gispert, Maria
(B. 1st decade 20th c., Sant Vicenç de Castellet, Barcelona– .) Poet and prose writer.

According to the index in *Les cinc branques*, Maria Gispert lives in Venezuela and has won several prizes for poetry and prose.

SECONDARY SOURCES
Les cinc branques 311.

CRISTINA ENRIQUEZ DE SALAMANCA

C Goberna, Maria Regina
(20th c.) Fiction writer.

A nun at Montserrat, Regina Goberna has written *El pare sant Benet* (The priest Saint Benedict), a novelized biography of the saint and founder of her order. Told from the saint's point of view and written for young people, the book was published on the fifteenth centenary of his birth. Goberna's *El cor de Catalunya* (The heart of Catalonia) insists on a positive and optimistic view of life while it recounts events in Catalan history and describes figures of historical or literary importance for adolescents. She uses classics of Catalan literature in her work, which has sociopolitical tones.

BOOKS
El cor de Catalunya. Montserrat: L'Abadia, 1984.
El pare sant Benet. Montserrat: L'Abadia, 1980.

KATHLEEN MCNERNEY

G Goldar, Xosefa

(B. 1953, A Estrada, Pontevedra– .) Poet and short story writer.

The daughter of a carpenter, Xosefa Goldar started to write short stories and poems in notebooks and textbooks. She studied Spanish philology at the University of Santiago, graduating in 1976. During her university years she devoted much of her time to reading her favorite authors: Francisco de Quevedo, Miguel de Unamuno, and Federico García Lorca in Castilian, Rosalía de Castro and Xosé Luís Méndez Ferrín in Galician. In 1977 she presented her doctoral thesis, "Onomasiología y folclore de seis animales reptantes en gallego" (Onomatology and folklore of six reptant animals in Galician). Since 1979 she has been teaching Spanish literature in a secondary school in Vigo, Pontevedra. She is married and has three children.

Goldar began to write stories for journals and in 1980 won second prize in a short story competition in *Vocablos*. In 1987 she published the collection *No fío do tempo* (Along the thread of time). Its fifteen stories vary in structure and theme but are united by two fundamental elements: a rich poetic prose and the absence of a narrative line. The stories are built around human anecdotes, interiorized by the protagonists themselves: the wounded man, the wife trying to flee the monotony of domestic life, the woman who unhappily finds herself pregnant. The precise vocabulary of the stories gives the text an intense literary quality and enhances the narrative techniques: the interior monologue, the cinematographic language with rapid shots of the human figure, the use of flashbacks. Called "scene stories" by the author, they portray defenseless beings heading inescapably toward tragedy. The book's vision is of the world's imminent destruction. For the author, optimism is nothing more than deceit instinctively used for self-preservation.

BOOKS
No fío do tempo. Vigo: Xerais, 1987.

WORKS IN BOOKS, PERIODICALS, NEWSPAPERS
"Un alento de morte." *Nordés* 3 (1981).
"Interior." *Vocablos* Dec. 1979.

"A maleta." *Nordés* 6 (1982).
"Outro." *Nordés* 8 (1982).
"Sin sentidos." *Vocablos* May 1980.

SECONDARY SOURCES
Goldar, Xosefa. *"No fío do tempo*, a narrativa enferma." *A nosa terra* 7 May 1987.
Méndez Ferrín, Xosé Luís. "Chucameles aos marraos." *Faro del lunes* 18 May 1987.
Vilela, Xosé Luís. "Novas criacións par a fuxir dos tópicos." *La voz de Galicia* 23 Apr. 1987.

MARIA CAMINO NOIA CAMPOS

C Gonzàlez i Cubertor, Assumpta
(B. 1917, Borriana, Castelló de la Plana– .) Playwright and poet.

Assumpta Gonzàlez has lived in Barcelona nearly all her life and in the neighborhood of Sants for many years. Author of a number of popular light comedies, she has also written plays for children. In 1952 she founded the Escola d'Art Dramàtic de l'Orfeó de Sants and directed it until 1958. In 1959 she started a similar school, La Rosa d'Or, for the Centre Catòlic of Sants and led it until 1968.

Written for mass audiences, her plays are simple and direct, with lively dialogue and a variety of themes. Among the most traditional is the Christmas drama *Quan aparegui l'estrella o El somni del rabadà* (When the star appears or the shepherd's dream). Her first play, *Dos embolics i una recomanació* (Two mix-ups and a recommendation), is a comedy of errors about a wealthy man's son and daughter who disguise themselves out of fear of gold diggers. *De més verdes en maduren* (Greener ones get ripe), which also deals with mistaken identities and misunderstandings, tells of an older woman who falls in love without bearing the brunt of cruel jokes; *La mare . . . Quina nit!* (My mother . . . What a night!), however, includes typical mother-in-law jokes. One of Gonzàlez's most interesting plays, *El preu d'una veritat* (The price of a truth), examines human feelings and sentiments. It is the story of two half sisters: one has a generous heart but serious identity problems; the other is capable of cruelty but learns a difficult lesson in the end.

Gonzàlez has won prizes for her plays for children, and she has also written two volumes of poetry. *Records que parlen: Poemes* (Memories that speak: Poems) includes love poems, from the points of view of both men and women; poetry addressed to children, the seasons, nature, and God; and a series of Christmas poems.

BOOKS
Arribaré a les set . . . Mort! Barcelona: Millà, 1972.
El crit del cel. Barcelona: Millà, 1973.

De més verdes en maduren. Barcelona: Millà, 1970.
Dos embolics i una recomanació. Barcelona: Millà, 1961.
Engrunes del cor. Barcelona: Morera, 1973.
Especialitat en homes. Barcelona: Millà, 1979.
La mare . . . Quina nit! Barcelona: Millà, 1983.
Les masies de la pau i Així juguen els infants. Barcelona: Millà, 1972.
El món a fer punyetes! Barcelona: Millà, 1984.
Necessito una infermera. Barcelona: Millà, 1976.
Nina i els altres. Barcelona: Millà, 1986.
El passadís de la mort. Barcelona: Millà, 1978.
La Pepeta no és morta! Barcelona: Millà, 1980.
Un polític supersticiós. Barcelona: Millà, 1981.
El preu d'una veritat. Barcelona: Millà, 1971.
Quan aparegui l'estrella o El somni del rabadà. Barcelona: Millà, 1976.
La rateta es vol casar. Barcelona: Millà, 1962.
Records que parlen: Poemes. Barcelona: D. Cochs, 1984.
Tots en tenim una. Barcelona: Millà, 1983.
El venedor de "coca." Barcelona: Millà, 1989.

KATHLEEN MCNERNEY

Gonzalez Maluquer, Concepció; *see* Maluquer i Gonzalez, Concepció

C   Grau de Llinàs, Roser
(B. 1926/28, ?– .) Fiction writer.

Born into a family of intellectuals, Roser Grau studied psychology, among other subjects. She spent her teens in Lyons, France, during the German occupation. When she returned to Catalonia, she came into contact with the Barcelona literary circles and, in particular, with Maurici Serrahima. In 1951, she was runner-up for the Joanot Martorell prize awarded by Editorial Aymà.

Grau found it hard to adapt to her native environment: "Amb els d'ací es parlava de revistes, de balls, de colònies d'estiueig, d'amistats i es criticava amb mesquinesa, implacablement" (People from here speak only of magazines, dances, summer camps, friends, and they criticize cruelly and implacably) ("Portada," *El temps*). Perhaps this difficulty led her to write *El temps ens ha fet així . . .* (Time has made us like this . . .), a short novel set in Barcelona that criticizes the superficial and irresponsible behavior of the young members of the upper class. Grau shows how the female protagonist's sentimentality makes her incapable of resisting male manipulation. This novel and the short story *Fascinació* (Fascination) belong to an especially precarious period for Catalan literature and should be classified among the semiclandestine attempts to continue the Catalan narrative tradition on the peninsula.

BOOKS
Fascinació. Col.lecció Els Autors de l'Ocell de Paper 16. Barcelona: Editex, 1957.
El temps ens ha fet així. . . . Pref. Joan Grases. Col.lecció Lletres 5. Barcelona: Club de Divulgació Literària, 1953.

WORKS IN BOOKS, PERIODICALS, NEWSPAPERS
"Un miratge." *El pont* 65 (1969): 17–23.

CRISTINA ENRIQUEZ DE SALAMANCA

C Grau i Puig, Roser
(B. 1911, Sant Andreu de la Barca, Barcelona– .) Poet.

According to *Les cinc branques*, Roser Grau i Puig entered the religious order of Sant Bernat and lives in Montserrat. She has written many poems.

SECONDARY SOURCES
Les cinc branques 311.

CRISTINA ENRIQUEZ DE SALAMANCA

C Grau Tarrafeta, Florència
(20th c.) Writer of children's literature. No biographical information available.

BOOKS
La bruixeta sense escombra. Barcelona: La Galera, 1981.
Els fills del pagès. Barcelona: La Galera, 1980.

KATHLEEN MCNERNEY

C Guasch i Darné, Maria Carme
(B. 1928, Figueres, Girona– .) Poet and novelist.

A professor of literature, Maria Carme Guasch has written two books of sonnets. *Vint-i-cinc sonets i un dia* (Twenty-five sonnets and one day) features love as the predominant theme and contains many allusions to other writers, mostly Catalan poets. Using a traditional form and conventional themes, Guasch surprises the reader with original images. Poem 7 begins with "Feliçment, jo sóc una dona," a quotation from a book by noted feminist and former minister of culture Maria-Aurèlia Capmany. In the poem the speaker wishes for the attributes of rain, stone, fog, and other elements of nature; then, for fresh insights, she asks for the word and the look of a child.

Amat i amic (Beloved and friend) takes its title from Ramon Llull's *Libre d'amich e amat* and constitutes an elegy; the love poems manifest loneliness and mourning. Every poem begins with a quotation from a poet and is usually dedicated to an individual. The poets quoted are all Catalan except Pablo Neruda. Guasch's only novel could be called a poem as well. Pensive in tone, *Trena de cendra* (Plait of ash) is divided into three parts, the second being a flashback. This somewhat autobiographical work expresses considerable self-criticism and praise of the loved one.

BOOKS

Amat i amic. Barcelona: Edicions 62, 1985.
Situacions insulars. Barcelona: Selecta, 1989.
Trena de cendra. Barcelona: Pòrtic, 1984.
Vint-i-cinc sonets i un dia. Olot: Aubert, 1978.

KATHLEEN MCNERNEY

Guida; *see* Alzina i Camps, Margarida

C   Guilló Fontanills, Magdalena
(B. 1946, Barcelona– .) Novelist.

Magdalena Guilló earned her degree in mathematics at the University of Barcelona and briefly taught at the Escola d'Arquitectura. She moved to Salamanca, where she still resides. The novel *En una vall florida al peu de les espases* (In a florid valley at the foot of the swords) won her the Josep Pla prize in 1977. It is the fascinating, hallucinatory account of the fictional Diego de Arjona, ex-Falangist and ex-minister of Franco, during the last eighteen days of the dictator's life. Postwar misery and Franco's deathbed deliriums alternate with Arjona's visions of democracy, while confused memories haunt the former minister as he tries to look ahead. In his dreams he sees the División Azul, the Spanish troops in the Second World War, defeated by Ivan the Terrible; the "Golden Age" of Franco; the ghost of José Antonio Primo de Rivera, founder of the Spanish Fascist Party, who does not want his body to go to El Escorial; an attempt to convert Hitler to Catholicism. Arjona makes a valiant effort to take responsibility for his past and look to the future, rejecting the pretenses he used to uphold. The novel ends with the headlines of Franco's death.

BOOKS
En una vall florida al peu de les espases. Barcelona: Destino, 1978.

KATHLEEN MCNERNEY

G Heinze, Ursula

(B. 1941, Cologne, Germany– .) Novelist and writer of children's literature.

Ursula Heinze studied Germanic philology in her native city, where she was also involved in a theater group and studied piano and singing. She taught English and German in secondary schools and began writing poetry and stories for German newspapers when she finished her studies. She met Ramón Lorenzo, a Galician poet and professor, married him, and moved to Santiago de Compostela in 1968. In 1973, her husband accepted a teaching position at the University of Valladolid, and Heinze became a lecturer in German there until 1977, when they returned to Santiago de Compostela, where they currently reside. They have collaborated on the translation of two German novels into Castilian: Heinrich Böll's *Und sagte kein einziges Wort* (*Y no dijo una sola palabra*) and Uwe Johnson's *Mutmassungen über Jakob* (*Conjeturas sobre Jacob*). Years later, Heinze translated children's stories by Mira Lobe and Elisabeth Heck from German into Galician.

Since her early work in German, Heinze's own literary creations have been in Galician. *O soño perdido de Elvira M* (The lost dream of Elvira M) is her first novel in Galician. Dealing with sociological themes, the work is narrated almost entirely in the second person, and its female protagonist addresses various interlocutors. *Remuiños en coiro* (Naked whirlwinds) is a collection of stories with different themes taken from the lives of actual women and men. In *Arredor da muller en dezaoito mundos* (On women in eighteen worlds), the author interviews eighteen women who tell of their personal lives and relations with men. The following works are children's stories: *O buzón dos nenos* (The children's box); *Sempre Cristina* (Always Cristina); and *A casa abandonada* (The abandoned house), which won the Merlín prize of 1986.

In both her children's stories and her adult literature, Heinze uses the real world as the point of departure. Two techniques characterize her style: improvised endings and the appearance of mystery. Her work is critical of current society, especially of institutions related to children, family, and school. She analyzes the customs, hopes, disillusions, and imaginations of people through the circumstances of their daily lives, which provoke the various conflicts they suffer.

Heinze appeals to the reader through irony, satire, and humor and describes human behavior that is at times absurd, yet realistic and contemporary. Some of her texts deal with young people's refusal to conform and their apathy about the future, which sometimes leads to rebellion against adults. In her stories for children, her objective is to entertain future readers and show them a good time by letting their fancies roam. She also denounces the marginalization of children in a world that undervalues their problems and desires.

Outstanding throughout the work of this Galician by adoption is the linguistic perfection with which she writes. Her language is carefully crafted and at the same time lexically rich, especially in the use of adjectives.

BOOKS
Anaiansi. Vigo: Iroindo, 1988.
Arredor da muller en dezaoito mundos. Vigo: Xerais, 1985.
O buzón dos nenos. Madrid: Fundación Santa María, 1985.
A casa abandonada. Vigo: Xerais, 1987.
Mulleres, crónica. Vigo: Xerais, 1991.
A nena de ouro. Vigo: Xerais, 1991.
Remuiños en coiro. Vigo: Xerais, 1984.
Sempre Cristina. Vigo: Xerais, 1986.
O soño perdido de Elvira M. Vigo: Xerais, 1982.
Xente coma min. Barcelona: Sotelo Blanco, 1989.

WORKS IN BOOKS, PERIODICALS, NEWSPAPERS
"A equivocación." *Dorna* 5 (1983).
"O mar." *Dorna* 8 (1985).
"Relata refero." *Dorna* 11 (1987).
"Os tres da Ponte." *La voz de Galicia* 27 Nov. 1987.
"Xelado de limón." *Dorna* 9 (1986).

SECONDARY SOURCES
Blanco, Carmen. "Ursula Heinze." *Literatura galega da muller*. Vigo: Xerais, 1991. 217–20.
Casares, Carlos. "O soño encontrado de Ursula Heinze." *La voz de Galicia* 15 Mar. 1984.
Noia, Camino. "Ursula Heinze, xente coma nós." *La voz de Galicia* 12 Nov. 1989.
Salgado, Xosé Manuel. "O mundo infantil de Ursula Heinze." *El correo gallego* 29 Dec. 1985.
———. "Ursula Heinze: De novo en Europa." *El correo gallego* 24 Feb. 1985.

MARIA CAMINO NOIA CAMPOS

G Herrera Garrido, Francisca

(B. 1869, Coruña, Coruña; d. 1950, Coruña, Coruña.) Poet, novelist, and essayist.

Born into a well-to-do family, Francisca Herrera lived in Coruña until she was forty-six, spending her summers in a small seaside village. Her residence there was instrumental in her writing career and she did most of her writing in Galicia. After the death of her mother, with whom she stayed since she was the only unmarried member of her family, she went to Madrid, where her two sisters lived. She continued her summer stays in Galicia and maintained her relationships with other Galician writers. Particularly important was her friendship with the family of Rosalía de Castro, whose poetry provided constant reading for Herrera. She resided in Madrid until 1936, when she returned to Coruña. She was surprised there by the Civil War, and she and her sisters became penniless as a result, having left all their belongings in Madrid. They survived thanks to the generosity of friends and relatives, but Herrera lived in poverty for the rest of her life.

Herrera started writing poems and stories when she was very young, but she did not begin to publish until she was forty-four years old. Her first three publications are collections of poetry: *Sorrisas e bágoas* (Smiles and tears); *Almas de muller . . . / Volallas n'a luz!* (Souls of woman . . . / Moths in the light), which contains a prologue by Manuel Murguía, the husband of Rosalía de Castro; and *Frores do noso paxareco* (Flowers of our garden). From approximately 1916 to 1930, she worked diligently for the newspaper of Coruña, *La voz de Galicia*, contributing articles on poetry, current commentaries, and creative work. Her best work in Galician is the lyrical novel *Néveda*. Other works written in Galician include the novels *A y-alma de Mingos* (Mingo's soul) and *Martes de antroido* (Shrove Tuesday) and the story "A neta da naipeira" (The fortune-teller's granddaughter). Her three novels in Castilian are *Pepiña*; *Réproba* (Damned), which originally appeared in serial form; and *Familia de lobos* (Family of wolves).

Herrera's productive years were between 1913 and 1930; afterward she sporadically wrote poems, translated religious texts, and began one story, which remains unpublished. She contributed editorials and creative work to various magazines until the Civil War, after which she stopped writing. During the war she wrote a poem in praise of General Franco. Herrera was elected a member of the Real Academia Gallega on 4 March 1945, but the endless bureaucratic paperwork outlasted the aging poet, and she died in 1950 without taking her seat in the academy.

Sociologically, it is of great interest that a woman of Herrera's class wrote in Galician for a Castilian-speaking audience: during that period only the upper classes could read, and they spoke Castilian. Herrera's Galician novels are thematically and stylistically similar: in all three works a rural atmosphere prevails, and most of the characters are country people. *Néveda* and *Martes de antroido* both alternate descriptions of urban settings and landscapes. *A y-alma de Mingos* takes place entirely in the country.

Herrera's stories always revolve around the Galician woman, who is represented as a maternal woman though not necessarily a mother. For Herrera, maternal instinct and duties inform all women regardless of their situations. These women are always portrayed as innocent victims, passive in their sentimental relationships, whether maternal, filial, or amorous. The plots typically pit a love relationship against the impossible obstacles introduced by malicious persons. The action is presented by an omniscient narrator—Herrera—who depicts the women as angelic beings suffering all kinds of injustices in silence. These works are not autobiographical; Herrera takes stories from life but re-creates them by her idealization of woman, who then becomes an alter ego, expressing the author's own social and moral beliefs. Herrera judges and directs her protagonists and comments on them to the reader, to whom she boldly offers advice.

Most of Herrera's poetry is collected in three volumes, but there are various poems in Castilian and Galician dispersed in periodicals, some of which have been lost. Her work is dominated by long, narrative poems, but she also wrote short, lyrical compositions. The vividness and passion in the majority of her works reveal a sensitive and compassionate soul that understands the sufferings of others.

Love for her deceased mother united with religious belief dominates most of the poems. As in the fiction, the theme of the woman-mother is recurrent. Herrera believed that all women are born mothers and their love is always unselfish. In all her work, she is observant of both nature and society, and some of her poems show a deep knowledge of her surroundings. Her ethnographic poems provide a vast repertory of customs and legends of Galicia, especially on death, work in the countryside, and superstitions. Her narrative poems, some of which are more than five hundred lines long, feature poor, abandoned girls who finally find comfort and welcome in maternal or religious love—a solution that Herrera possibly never found in her own life. Nature in its great variety and the social organization of Galician communities frame these poems.

Herrera uses a variety of meters in her poetry. The dominant form is the octosyllabic ballad, but, like Rosalia de Castro, she also employs the long hendecasyllables characteristic of Spanish Romanticism and popular songs. For its inspiration and treatment, Herrera's work must be classified as an archaic form of Romanticism, traditionalist and Christian. Her poetry lacks stylistic discipline, and, propelled by emotive sincerity, she sometimes creates prosaic texts using whatever words come to mind. But among the deficient pieces are some that work because of their fresh rhythms.

In her essays, Herrera appears extremely sentimental. She follows her own exuberant emotionalism and does not strive for objectivity, composing her texts of lyrical effusions and intimate thoughts. One of her most interesting essays is "A muller galega" (The Galician woman), which shows reactionary thinking with respect to the emancipation of women. She does not understand why women want to participate in political life by voting, since for her a woman's role is that of mother, caretaker of home and family. Herrera uses Galician women, especially country women, as models and encourages them to fight to defend their traditional position, which has been imposed by nature and divine design. Her principles as a conservative Catholic fuse with her concept of the woman-mother to create an antiprogressive discourse in which she denies women the same rights as men, even regarding education.

BOOKS
Almas de muller . . . / Volallas n'a luz! Prol. Manuel Murguía. Coruña: Roel, 1915.
Familia de lobos. Madrid: n.p., 1928. 2nd ed. 1942.
Frores do noso paxareco. Coruña: El Noroeste, 1919.
Martes de antroido. Coruña: Lar, 1925.
Néveda. Coruña: Roel, 1920. 2nd ed. Ed. and introd. María Camino Noia Campos.
    Vigo: Xerais, 1981.
Pepiña. Madrid: Marinada, 1922.
Réproba. Madrid: n.p., 1926.
Sorrisas e bágoas. Madrid: Imprenta Científica y Artística de alrededor del Mundo,
    1913.
A y-alma de Mingos. Ferrol: Céltiga, 1922.

WORKS IN BOOKS, PERIODICALS, NEWSPAPERS
"Camiño da Groria?" *Catecismo de niños y niñas* 115 (1917).
"Cantigas . . . ?" *A nosa terra* 167 (25 July 1922).
"Consellos d'unha madriña amante." *Catecismo de niños y niñas* 110 (1917).
"D'onde vai Xoaniño?" and "Sé xeneroso." *Catecismo de niños y niñas* 107 (1916).
"A Farruquiño, Porta d-a Enciña." *A nosa terra* 202 (1 July 1924).
"Follas murchas." *A nosa terra* 239 (25 July 1929).
"Lembranza d'unha invitada agasallosa." *A nosa terra* 215 (25 July 1925).
"Mi Dios" and "A nuestra Señora del sagrado corazón." *Catecismo de San Martín*
    119 (1919).
"A muller galega." *Nós* 6 (1921).
"A neta da naipeira." *Nós* 20 (1925).
"A nosa nai Galiza." *Nós* 91 (1931).
Prologue. *Cantares gallegos de Rosalía Castro.* Madrid: Paez, 1925.
"A riqueza d'un probe." *Catecismo de niños y niñas* 117 (1917).
"Rosalía Castro." *Diario español* (25 Oct. 1925).
"Al sagrado corazón de Jesús." *Catecismo de San Martín* 113 (1919).
"Sant Yago e Galicia." *A nosa terra* 203 (25 July 1924).

SECONDARY SOURCES
Barja, César. *En torno al lirismo gallego del siglo XIX.* Northampton: Smith College;
    Paris: Champion, 1926.

Blanco, Carmen. "O antisufraxismo e a condición feminina en 'A muller galega' de Francisca Herrera." *Grial* 92 (1986).

Calo, Xesús. "Unha romántica fora do seu tempo." *La voz de Galicia* 14 May 1987.

Carballo Calero, Ricardo. "De *Néveda* ao Coram." *Da fala e da escrita*. Ourense: Galiza, 1983.

———. *Historia da literatura galega contemporánea.*

Durán, J. A. "F. Herrera Garrido, colaboradora de *La voz de Galicia.*" *La voz de Galicia* 14 May 1987.

Fernández del Riego, F. *Historia da literatura galega.* Vigo: Galaxia, 1978.

Festa da palabra silenciada 3 (1986). Special issue devoted to Francisca Herrera.

Filgueira Valverde, J. "F. Herrera no arquivo do museo." *La voz de Galicia* 16 May 1987.

———. "Un inédito de F. Herrera Garrido." *La voz de Galicia* 17 May 1987.

———. "Unha primicia inédita na obra de F. Herrera." *Faro de Vigo* 17 May 1987.

———. "Uns versos inéditos de F. Herrera." *El correo gallego* 17 May 1987.

Fraguas Fraguas, A. "F. Herrera y Garrido." *El progreso* 13 May 1987. *Outeiro* 24 May 1987.

García Negro, P. "F. Herrera: Continuadora de Rosalía?" *El progreso* 13 May 1987.

J. B. "A muller galega de F. Herrera Garrido." *El correo gallego* 17 May 1987.

López Dobao, X. A. "O día das letras." *El correo gallego* 17 May 1987.

Noia Campos, Camino. "F. Herrera, unha escritora autodidacta e conservadora." *El progreso* 13 May 1987.

———. "F. Herrera, unha muller no día das letras." *Encrucillada* 52 (Mar.-Apr. 1987).

———. "Herrera Garrido, Francisca." *Gran enciclopedia gallega*, vol. 17.

———. Introduction. *Antoloxía da obra galega: Francisca Herrera Garrido (1869–1950).* Ed. Camino Noia Campos. Santiago: Xunta de Galicia, 1989.

———. "A palabra silenciada de F. Herrera." *Dorna* 12 (1987).

Ossian, Abente. "Semblante de F. Herrera Garrido." *El progreso* 13 May 1987. *Outeiro* 24 May 1987.

Quintáns Suárez, M. F. "Herrera Garrido, a historia dun infundio." *El correo gallego* 17 May 1987.

Review of *Néveda*. *Nós* 1 (1920).

Ríos Panisse, Maria Carme. "*Néveda* primeiro acerto lingüístico e estilístico na novela galega." *Grial* 90 (1985).

Vázquez, Efrén. "Francisca Herrera Garrido." *La voz de Galicia* 11 Mar. 1987.

MARIA CAMINO NOIA CAMPOS

C Herreros i Solà de Bonet, Maria Manuela de los

(B. 1845, Palma de Mallorca; d. 1911, Palma de Mallorca.) Poet.

On her mother's side, Maria Manuela de los Herreros i Solà de Bonet came from an old Majorcan family. She was educated in local schools and also learned drawing and painting. She studied French, English, and Italian and knew some German, possibly through her paternal grandmother who had a German surname. She married the lawyer Enric Bonet i Ferrer in

1873, had many children, and was widowed in 1889. In 1903, she took charge of administering the Majorcan possessions of an Austrian archduke, known locally as Luis Salvador. Herreros died in 1911; a few months later the City Hall named her Honorary Daughter of the City.

Herreros took part in many social activities and benefits for the Workers' Society of Saint Joseph, the Society for the Protection of Children, the Council for the Abolition of White Slavery, and the Council for Public Teaching. A popular writer, she achieved fame on the island and in literary circles of Barcelona and can be considered the Majorcan representative of the group of women writers who took part early in the *Renaixença*: Josefa Massanés, Victòria Penya, Dolors Monserdà, Agnès Armengol, Maria de Bell-Lloch, and Agna de Valladura. Herreros published poems in *Museo balear* and *Revista balear*, journals through which Mateo Obrador, who had dedicated a piece to commemorate her marriage, influenced the Majorcan cultural groups.

Like many nineteenth-century women writers, Herreros published in various periodicals but never collected her poems in one book. Recently, there has been a thorough compilation of her poetry, *Manuela de los Herreros: Obra litèraria dispersa* (Manuela de los Herreros: Scattered literary works), which also contains a short drama and some articles in both Catalan and Castilian. Her works have aroused interest because she describes local customs and uses popular stanzas. The original texts of her poems constitute a linguistic document of nineteenth-century Majorca.

In spite of her social position, Herreros reveals a peculiar affinity with the spirit of popular poetry. She provides a detailed observation of the local practices and people, in both rural and urban environments, and a rich lexicon. The description of characters, such as the Majorcan maid, the shepherd, the charcoal vendor, and the farmer, is unsentimental and at times prosaic. She distinguishes her native land from the rest of Catalonia and with great patriotic feeling proclaims the linguistic differences between Majorcan and Catalan. She said "[q]u'aquestas llenguas . . . son germanas . . . més son germanas casadas / que viuen emb son marid / y cada una á cà seua / visquent en es seu estil" (that these languages . . . are sisters . . . but married sisters / who live with their husbands / each one in her own home / living with her own style) (*Obra* 211).

Herreros participated in the linguistic debate between the defenders of archaic Catalan and the defenders of the current language. The first group, characterized by poets who wrote in a florid style, was satirized in her well-known poem "Parl perque m'entengan" (I speak to be understood). She told those who wanted to resuscitate archaic Catalan, "Perque á Castilla no escriuen / aixi com parlava el Cid?" (Why don't they write in Castile / the way the Cid spoke?) (*Obra* 209).

Her descriptive poetry, which she herself called "contar y cantar" (telling and singing) (*Obra* 40), is full of humor and irony; she criticizes the customs and the hypocrisy of Majorcan society and answers wittily to antifeminist critiques. Religious sentiment, expressed in a traditional way, is regarded as a source of psychological support in the present and hope for peace in the afterlife. "Amor de s'ànima" (Love of the soul) deals with a spiritual vision of love but indicates that female friendship on earth has a more passionate feeling. The poems of her last period—"Notas y harmonies del mar" (Notes and harmonies of the sea), "La vida. Poema agre.dols" (Life. Bittersweet poem), and "Realidat" (Reality)—display a more personal tone and elaborate on thoughts about the proximity of death.

Herreros prefers assonant rhyme and uses repetition, contrast, and popular sayings. The influence of familiar Castilian poetry is reflected in her "Seguidillas." Some of her poems are like children's songs, as they emphasize the sound effect of words, regardless of their possible meaning. In "Lo so d'un infant" (The sleep of a child), the vision of children's dreams is developed with rhythm and charm. This poem is included in several anthologies, most recently Sanchis Guarner's *Els poetes romàntics de Mallorca* (The Romantic poets of Majorca).

Herreros published in Barcelona journals such as *Lo Gay Saber* and *Calendari català*. In 1869 her poem "Amor a la llengua" (Love of the language) was read by Josep Lluis Pons i Gallarza at a celebration of the public literature section of the Ateneo Balear. The Catalan newspaper *La llumanera de Nova York* published her "Mallorca" in its issue devoted to Catalan women (May 1879).

BOOKS

Manuela de los Herreros: Obra litèraria dispersa. Palma de Mallorca: Caja de Ahorros y Monte de Piedad de las Baleares, 1978.

WORKS IN BOOKS, PERIODICALS

"A Doña María Pons de Pons." *Museo balear de historia y literatura, ciencias y artes* 10 (31 May 1875): 312–13.

"Amor a la llengua de mos avis." *Lo Gay Saber* 27 (1869): 211–12.

"Amor de s'ànima." *Calendari català* (1879): 31–32.

"Amor de s'ànima." *Lo Gay Saber* 20 (1880): 230.

"A n'es meu nin." *Museo balear de historia y literatura, ciencias y artes* 11 (15 June 1875): 347–50.

"A un ulls." *Lo Gay Saber* 23 (1869): 180–81.

"Un bon poll." *Museo balear de historia y literatura, ciencias y artes* 12 (30 June 1875): 378–79.

"Es pages enamorat." *Lo Gay Saber* 7 (1868): 50.

"Glosas." *Calendari català* (1869): 65–66.

"Mallorca." *La llumanera de Nova York* May 1879.

"No ho prengueu per verbàs." *Lo Gay Saber* 18 (1868): 139.

"Recorts." *Lo Gay Saber* 11 (1868): 83.

"Sa criada mallorquina." *Lo Gay Saber* 20 (1880): 258–61.

"Sa moda." *Lo Gay Saber* 24 (1880): 277–79.

"Ses matances." *Els poetes romàntics de Mallorca.* Ed. M. Sanchis Guarner. Palma: Moll, 1950. 233–38.

"So d'un infant." *Calendari català* (1874): 19–22.

"Lo so d'un infant." *Els poetes romàntics de Mallorca.* Ed. M. Sanchis Guarner. Palma: Moll, 1950. 228–32.

"Lo so d'un infant" and "Recorts." *Poetes balears setgle XIX.* Palma: Pere Joseph Gelabért, 1873. 612, 620.

"Un tresor d'amor." *Calendari català* (1868): 91–92.

"Veu des cor ó La Margalida." *Museo balear de historia y literatura, ciencias y artes* 2nd ser. 3.6 (31 May 1886): 229–34.

TRANSLATIONS OF HER WORKS
"Mallorca" ["Mallorca"]. Fastenrath 193–95.

SECONDARY SOURCES
Massot i Muntaner, Josep 54.

Simón Palmer, *Escritoras españolas del siglo XIX* 351–52.

Tous y Maroto, José María. *Doña Manuela de los Herreros. Hija ilustre de Mallorca. Notas biográficas leídas en la sala de sesiones del Excmo Ayuntamiento de Palma el 31 de diciembre de 1911.* Palma: J. Tous, 1912.

CRISTINA ENRIQUEZ DE SALAMANCA

C Ibars i Ibars, Maria
(B. 1892, Benissa, València; d. 1965, Benissa, València.) Poet and novelist.

In Castilian, Maria Ibars wrote *Como una garra* (Like a claw) and *Graciamar* (1963). In Catalan, she published the collection *Poemes de Penyamar* (Poems from Penyamar), various poems in the weekly *La marina* between 1961 and 1966, and the novels *Vides planes* (Flat lives) and *L'últim serf* (The last serf). Her most important poetic work can be found in *Poemes de Penyamar*, which includes "Pluja" (Rain), previously published under the title "Tristors" (Sadness).

According to Joan Fuster, Maria Ibars falls within the group of writers known as representatives of "paisatgisme sentimental" (sentimental landscape). Following the tradition of Teodor Llorente, they exalt the land and its way of life. In the case of Maria Ibars, the region is La Marina, especially the area around Dènia, which inspired her romantic, populist verses.

In *Vides planes* the daily life of the people and the central theme of love and death develop in relation to the landscape, which is dominated by the mountain of Montgó. The author deals with feelings and human relationships, recording them in an almost anthropological way and showing how they are influenced by the presence of the mountain. The book is a literary account of customs, celebrations, songs, children's games, and collective work in the fields, as well as of the changes leading to progressive commercialization. *L'últim serf* similarly deals with the people of Dènia. Categorized as a "social novel," it re-creates the world of workers in the raisin industry at the turn of the century. The atmosphere at the warehouse, the source of livelihood and wages, produces characteristics in the protagonists that nourish their dreams and cause their humiliation. In time these men and women develop an awareness of their condition and their power. Between the workers and the owner is the last serf, an intermediary, who, though sensitive to the suffering of the people, is still absolutely loyal to his master and submissive to feudal authority.

BOOKS
Como una garra. Valencia: Guerri, 1961.
Graciamar. Valencia: Unicrom, 1963.
Poemes de Penyamar. Pref. Carles Salvador. Valencia: n.p., 1949.
L'últim serf: A l'ombra del Montgó. Valencia: Sicània, 1965.
Vides planes. Valencia: Sicània, 1962.

WORKS IN BOOKS, PERIODICALS, NEWSPAPERS
"Camp d'ús." *Nostres faulelles* 4 (1961): 9–28 and 5 (1961): 31–54.
"La descalumniada." *Nostres faulelles* 2 (1961): 5–23.
"La fe dels altres." *Nostres faulelles* 14 (1965): 48–54.
"Flor de nisperer." *Nostres faulelles* 8 (1962): 5–25 and 9 (1962): 27–50.
"La presa." *Nostres faulelles* 17 (1966): 7–15.

SECONDARY SOURCES
"Dossier: Homenatge a Maria Ibars." *L'aiguadolç* 16–17 (Summer 1991). Entire issue devoted to Ibars.
Fuster, Joan. *Antologia de la poesia valenciana (1900–1950).* Valencia: Tres i Quatre, 1980. 52.
Llopis, Tomás. "A propòsit de *L'últim serf*, una novel.la 'social' de Maria Ibars." *L'aiguadolç* 4 (Summer 1987): 79–82.
Prats, Antoni. "Aproximació a l'obra poètica de Maria Ibars." *L'aiguadolç* 1 (Fall 1985): 57–64.
———. "Pròleg." Prologue to a facsimile edition of *Poemes de Penyamar.* Dènia: Ajuntament, 1992.

ISABEL ROBLES GOMEZ

C   Igual, Maria Pilar
(20th c.) Poet. No biographical information available.

BOOKS
La intimitat d'una dona. Barcelona: Rovrich, 1986.

KATHLEEN MCNERNEY

C Illa, Helena
(20th c.) Poet. No biographical information available.

El bell sol de l'hivern (The beautiful winter sun) is dedicated to Vincent Van Gogh. The poems reveal a social and ecological awareness. Several describe city life and especially how it has changed and continues to change. A few poems in Castilian are included.

BOOKS
El bell sol de l'hivern. Pref. Jordi Torio i Riera. Barcelona: n.p., 1982.

KATHLEEN MCNERNEY

B Irastorza Garmendia, Tere
(B. 1961, Zaldibia, Gipuzkoa– .) Poet.

Tere Irastorza is the author of several poetry books: *Gabeziak* (Lackings), *Hostoak, Gaia eta Gau aldaketak* (Leaves, themes, and changes in the night), *Alkoholaren Poemak* (Alcohol poems), *Derrotaren fabulak* (Fables of defeat), and *Osinberdeko kanthoria* (The green fountain song). In 1980 she obtained the Crítica Literaria de España prize and the Resurrección María de Azkue de Vizcaya prize for Basque poetry.

BOOKS
Alkoholaren Poemak. Pamplona: Pamiela, 1984.
Derrotaren fabulak. Pamplona: Pamiela, 1986.
Gabeziak. Pamplona: Pamiela, 1980.
Hostoak, Gaia eta Gau aldaketak. Bilbao: Caja de Ahorros de Vizcaya, 1983.
Osinberdeko kanthoria. Pamplona: Pamiela, 1986.

MAITE GONZALEZ ESNAL

B Iriondo, Lourdes
(20th c.) Writer of children's literature. No biographical information available.

Lourdes Iriondo wrote *Hego Haizearen Ipuinak* (South wind stories) and *Sendagille maltzurra* (The cunning doctor). Iriondo composed *Buruntza Azpian* for children's theatre. *Lotara joateko ipuinak* (Bedtime stories) was written in collaboration with others.

BOOKS
Buruntza Azpian. San Sebastián: Erein, 1975.
Hego Haizearen Ipuinak. San Sebastián: Erein, 1973.

Lotara joateko ipuinak. With A. Lertxundi and E. González. San Sebastián: Erein, 1973.
Sendagille maltzurra. San Sebastián: Erein, 1973.

MAITE GONZALEZ ESNAL

C   Jaén Calero, Maria José
(B. 1962, Sevilla– .) Novelist.

Maria José Jaén moved to Barcelona to pursue her studies in Catalan philology. Her first novel, *Amorrada al piló* (With her mouth to the stick), forms a part of the neoporn trend and is one of its most popular examples. The protagonist is host of a nighttime radio show whose purpose is to keep people aroused. The cover of the book promises to do the same for its readers, but some will find it male-oriented in spite of the seemingly liberated female protagonist. *Sauna* continues in the same titillating vein but is better developed; the plot revolves around an amorous triangle and its inevitable jealousies and misunderstandings. Both novels have been made into films with the same titles.

BOOKS
Amorrada al piló. Barcelona: Columna, 1986.
Color verd, esperança d'ase. Barcelona: Columna, 1987.
Sauna. Barcelona: Columna, 1988.

TRANSLATIONS OF HER WORKS
El escote [*Amorrada al piló*]. Barcelona: Seix Barral, 1986.
Sauna. Barcelona: Seix Barral, 1988.

KATHLEEN MCNERNEY

C   Janer, Maria de la Pau
(B. 1966, Palma de Mallorca– .) Journalist and novelist.

Maria de la Pau Janer studies philology and regularly contributes to the journals *Baleares, Lluc,* and *Palau Reial.* She has also worked in radio and television. *Els ulls d'ahir* (The eyes of yesterday) was a finalist for the Ciutat de Palma Prize in 1987. In an unusual literary technique, the narrator recounts the protagonist's love story to the protagonist, evoking details of memory for her, especially a pair of mysterious, reappearing eyes.

BOOKS
L'hora dels eclipsis. Valencia: Eliseu Climent, 1989.
Els ulls d'ahir. Valencia: Eliseu Climent, 1988.

KATHLEEN MCNERNEY

C   Jaquetti i Isant, Palmíra
(B. 1895, Barcelona; d. 1963, Vilafranca del Penedès, Barcelona.)
Poet, musician, and folklorist.

According to her biographer, Roser Matheu, Palmíra Jaquetti came from a poor family. Her grandfather had migrated from Italy to Catalonia. Her father, a manual worker with intellectual and artistic interests, cared about giving his daughter a good education. She studied in Barcelona, graduating in Hispanic literature, and finished musical studies at the City School and at the Conservatorio in Barcelona. While working as a teacher in Vilafranca, Barcelona, Jacquetti began collecting popular songs and won a prize in a contest of the Catalan Choral Society. She was commissioned by this society to collect popular songs of the Empordà area, to be included in the *Cançoner Popular de Catalunya.*

In 1927 Jaquetti married a Frenchman and had to change her citizenship. That circumstance, together with an unhappy marriage and a serious illness, disrupted her professional life. The Civil War stopped her work as a folklorist and left her feeling isolated. She died in a car accident in 1963.

Apart from her musical work, Jaquetti published only one book during her lifetime, *L'estel dins la llar* (A star in the home), which is divided into two parts. The first, without a title, contains seventeen poems. In five of them, "Bugada" (Washing), "Setmana" (Week), "Cançó del cosir" (Sewing song), "Tinc la roba per planxar" (I have clothes to iron), and "Faig ganxet al pendís de la tarde" (I crochet at sunset), the poet evokes daily female activities, searching for her inner voices and the images for her simple tasks. The language is concise and clear, and the influence of her musical studies is strong. The author's playful style with words reminds one of children's songs, and the tone is happy and bright. This treatment of female endeavors is unusual even among women poets of her time and achieves a charming effect.

The second part of the book, "Joguines" (Toys), is inspired mostly by children's songs. Some of the poems show the poet's search for her inner identity through poetic activity, such as in "El cor per fanal" (The heart as a lamp), or through love, as in "Si em pregunten el nom" (If they ask my name). Although Jaquetti was interested in Catalan folklore, her poetry lacks any patriotic sentiment.

Jaquetti's unpublished prizewinning collections include "Muntanya de joia" (Mountain of joy), "Oració" (Prayer), "Elegies," "Elegies II," "Claror" (1956; Brightness), "Ofrena" (1959; Offering), "Amor" (1961; Love), and "El poblet" (1962; The village). "Elegies II" received first prize in the Jocs Florals of Costa Rica in 1955 and of Alghero in 1961 and was also honored in the Jocs Florals of Madrid and Mendoza in 1958.

BOOKS
L'estel dins la llar. Barcelona: Oasi, 1938.
Mis canciones: Poesía y música de Palmira Jaquetti. N.p.: Favencia, 1943.

SECONDARY SOURCES
Cardona, Oswald. "Record de Palmira Jaquetti." *Serra d'or* (1964): 156.
Matheu, Roser. *Quatre dones catalanes.* Barcelona: Fundació Salvador Vives Casajuana, 1973. 169–92.

CRISTINA ENRIQUEZ DE SALAMANCA

C Jardí, Berta
(B. 1956, Barcelona– .) Fiction writer.

Berta Jardí has worked as a promoter and organizer of concerts for most of her career; *Carnaval* (Carnival) is her first book. This playful but not superficial collection of short stories is fanciful, imaginative, and sometimes brutal. "L'abric" (The coat) is part nightmare, part science fiction: an overcoat emanating a certain glow attracts a passerby, who inevitably pursues it and puts it on, only to find it eating into him. When he finally escapes, he sees the same incident repeated with other individuals. In "Relacions de veïnatge" (Relations among neighbors), stereotyped behavior prevails over role reversals in an unusual love triangle. "Havia de passar-li al pobre Quim" (It had to happen to poor Quim) and "Transposició i fuga de dues imatges" (Transposition and flight of two images) are both similar to the fiction of Gabriel García Márquez; in the first, a characteristically hard-luck person is cut in two by a beam of light; in the second, mental images get their owners mixed up, with chaotic results. "L'entrevista" (The interview) and "Li agradaven les flors" (She liked flowers) feature more common themes: the fear of being interviewed on live radio and suddenly having nothing to say; the eternal wait for the date who never comes. One of the most hallucinatory stories is "Vitamines per a peixos" (Vitamins for fish), in which an unfortunate person goes to perform the simple, if unusual, errand of buying vitamins for his fish and finds himself unwillingly adopting a huge black pig. "Carnaval" is at once charming in its descriptions and frightening, as the unicorn repeats its yearly ritual battle against the Mardi Gras costume.

BOOKS
Carnaval. Barcelona: Magrana, 1986.

KATHLEEN MCNERNEY

C Jaume i Carbó, Quima
(B. 1934, Cadaqués, Girona; d. 1993, Barcelona.) Poet.

With a degree in Catalan philology, Quima Jaume i Carbó taught literature and language. The maturity with which she entered the literary world accounts for her freedom in the treatment of her subject—love—according to the poet Marta Pessarrodona in her preface to Jaume's collection *El temps passa a Cadaqués* (Time Passes in Cadaqués). Pessarrodona also sees the influence of Rosa Leveroni, whom they both knew. Jaume's visual imagery of Cadaqués is sometimes striking and often specific. She was active in literary and feminist groups in Barcelona.

BOOKS
Pels camins remolosos de la mar. Barcelona: Proa, 1990.
El temps passa a Cadaqués. Pref. Marta Pessarrodona. Barcelona: Columna, 1986.

KATHLEEN MCNERNEY

Jonqueres d'Oriols, Remei; pseudonym for **Carles Reig i Morell**

C Jordà i Puigmoltó, Milagros
(B. 1823, Alcoi, Alacant; d. 1886, Orihuela, Alacant.) Poet.

According to Manuel Rico García and Antonio Montero Pérez, Milagros Jordà was born in a well-to-do family from Alcoy and educated in the Convento de las Salesas in Orihuela, Alicante. A very religious person, she gave money to the Church and was involved in many charitable activities. In 1886 she published a collection of Marian poetry, *Album poético*. She also contributed poems and folktales to local journals. Her last years were spent in the convent of the Salesas.

BOOKS
Album poético dedicado a la Purísima Concepción de la Fuente Roja, amadísima patrona de Alcoy con motivo de la restauración de su santuario. Alcoy: Francisco Company, 1886.

SECONDARY SOURCES
Rico García and Montero Pérez, *Ensayo biográfico-bibliográfico de escritores de Alicante y su provincia.*

CRISTINA ENRIQUEZ DE SALAMANCA

191

C Jové, Helena
(20th c.) Poet. No biographical information available.

BOOKS
Poemes de Calonge. Barcelona: n.p., 1974.

KATHLEEN MCNERNEY

C Julió, Montserrat
(B. 1929, Mataró, Barcelona– .) Translator, screenwriter, and novelist.

At the age of ten, Montserrat Julió went into exile with her family, first in France and then in Chile, where she made contact with other exiled Catalan writers. Julió studied dramatic arts in Santiago and acted in several Chilean theater companies for ten years. She returned to Barcelona to work with the Agrupació Dramàtica, as director and actor. Julió moved to Madrid, where she continued in theater and began to work in films as well. She has also done theatrical translations, television screenplays, and a study of the history of the Liceu theater of Barcelona.

In her novel *Memòries d'un futur bàrbar* (Memories of a barbarous future), Julió imagines a world without children. She experiments with controlled language and produces an almost Orwellian ending. Julió pursues her theater work in both Madrid and Barcelona.

BOOKS
Memòries d'un futur bàrbar. Barcelona: Edicions 62, 1975.

KATHLEEN MCNERNEY

C Kampistraus, Ana
(20th c.) Playwright. No biographical information available.

The files of the Institut de Teatre Català in Barcelona contain the manuscript of a farce, "El Batip Benpurgat -o- La forsa imnòtica de la faba màgica: Espatotxada paròdica una mica americana i bon tros poca solta en un acte i en prosa" (The well-purged batip or the hymnotic strength of the magic bean: A lively parody, somewhat American, rather naughty, in one act and in prose). The handwritten manuscript, almost illegible, is signed by Ana Kampistraus. There is no record of the play ever having been staged.

BOOKS

"El Batip Benpurgat -o- La forsa imnòtica de la faba màgica: Espatotxada paròdica una mica americana i bon tros poca solta en un acte i en prosa." Ms. 981. Institut de Teatre Català, Barcelona.

CRISTINA ENRIQUEZ DE SALAMANCA

C Karr i d'Alfonsetti de Lasarte, Carme
(B. 1865, Barcelona; d. 1943, Barcelona.) Known as L. Escardot and Xènia. Short story writer, playwright, composer, and essayist.

Carme Karr made broad contributions to the literary, social, and educational life of Spanish women. As a major figure in the middle-class women's movement in the first decades of the twentieth century, she led the second wave of feminism in Catalonia away from exclusive concern with the domestic sphere and into social and political issues. Dolors Monserdà i Vidal de Macià, the leading figure in the earlier and more conservative generation of the women's movement, called Karr the first Catalan feminist.

Karr first gained public acclaim for her simple and original Catalan songs, written under the pen name L. Escardot, which she retained in her early prose works. Her first prose sketches and short stories appeared in *Joventut*, the magazine of the cultural *Renaixença*. In 1906 she published two collections of prose pieces, *Bolves, quadrets* (Specks of dust, sketches) and *Clixés, estudis en prosa* (Photographic negatives, studies in prose), using both her pen name and her own name. Both collections focus on the socially marginal—children, women, and the poor—and on the emptiness of social values. *Bolves* combines country vignettes and city sketches, contrasting dream and reality in both, while *Clixés* builds on the visual metaphor of the title and closes with an afterword to the reader.

In 1907 the illustrated cultural magazine *La ilustració catalana* named Karr editor of its new monthly women's supplement, *Feminal*, which broke with the more traditional feminism of the earlier *Or y grana*. Karr edited the magazine for the next ten years, writing a regular column called "Consideracions" (Considerations) while she contributed to other cultural and literary publications. In 1910 she gave a series of lectures at the Ateneo de Barcelona and published them under the title *Cultura femenina, estudi i orientacions* (Women's culture, a study and future prospects). As an advocate of education for women, she maintained the traditional bourgeois values of home and religion while working for cultural and educational parity. To further her goals, in 1913 she established a residential center, named La Llar (The Home), for the continuing education of women teachers and students and served as its director. In 1921 she helped found and direct

193

the middle-class feminist organization *Acció Feminina*, which defended the moral, social, and political interests of women.

On the literary front, Karr received a silver cup at the 1912 Jocs Florals in Barcelona for her novella *De la vida d'en Joan Franch* (The life of Joan Franch). This story of power, powerlessness, and charity contrasts the lives of a rich but childless lawyer, an abandoned and pregnant wife, and a poor woman with small children. Published with it is a second novel about charity, *L'esquitx* (A slip of a girl), in which a dying servant-girl's adoration of her mistress's dead daughter moves the rich woman to treat her as a daughter.

Karr saw her one-act play, *Els idols* (Idols), staged at the Teatre Romea in Barcelona on 10 May 1911. The play treats the theme of marital infidelity in a conversation between a mother and daughter, and the daughter learns that women's "idols" have feet of clay. Karr also wrote two other plays, *Caritat* (Charity) and "Raig de sol" (Sunbeam). In her later years, Karr wrote children's stories: *Cuentos a mis nietos* (Stories for my grandchildren), in Castilian, and *Garba de contes* (A sheaf of stories), in Catalan. Tales of virtue rewarded, these stories rework familiar legends and myths from various cultural traditions. Her last publication was a children's book, *El libro de Puli* (Puli's book), designed for families and for school libraries in Franco's Spain.

Karr was the niece of the popular nineteenth-century French novelist Alphonse Karr. She married the writer and journalist Josep M. de Lasarte i de Janer, and they had three children: Joan, Paulina, and Carme.

BOOKS

Bolves, quadrets. Biblioteca Popular de L'Avenç 53. Barcelona: Llibrería L'Avenç, 1906.

Caritat. Barcelona, 1918.

Clixés, estudis en prosa. Barcelona: Joventut, 1906.

Cuentos a mis nietos. Burgos: Hijos de Santiago Rodríguez, 1932.

Cultura femenina, estudi i orientacions. Barcelona: Llibrería L'Avenç, 1910.

De la vida d'en Joan Franch. L'esquitx. Barcelona: Ilustració Catalana, 1912. Rpt. in *Lectura popular* 3 (1913?): 545–74.

Garba de contes. Gerona: Dalmau Carles Plá, 1935.

Els idols, quadre en un acte i en prosa. Biblioteca de Tots Colors. Barcelona: B. Baxarias, 1911. Rpt. in *La novela nova* 1.30 (1917).

El libro de Puli. Barcelona: Edicions Ars, 1942.

WORKS IN BOOKS, PERIODICALS, NEWSPAPERS

"La nostra finalitat." *Feminal* 1.1 (1907).

SECONDARY SOURCES

Capmany, Maria Aurèlia. *El feminisme a Catalunya.* Barcelona: Nova Terra, 1973. 68–85.

Fagoaga, Concha. *La voz y el voto de las mujeres: El sufragismo en España, 1877–1931*. Barcelona: Icaria, 1985. 155–57 passim.
La novela femenina. 1.22 (1914). Entire issue devoted to Karr.

MARYELLEN BIEDER

G Kruckenberg Sanjurjo, María del Carmen
(B. 1926, Vigo, Pontevedra– .) Poet.

María del Carmen Kruckenberg began writing verses at the age of fourteen and loved reading poetry, especially by Antonio Machado, Rilke, Baudelaire, and Rosalía de Castro. She took part in all the poetic activities that were celebrated in Vigo and worked with her fellow poets and painters on various journals in the postwar period (1945–49).

After her marriage in 1949, Kruckenberg left for Italy and, a short time later, went to Buenos Aires, where she lived until 1953. During this period her only daughter was born and Kruckenberg was divorced. In Buenos Aires, Montevideo, and Sao Paulo she met many important writers. Upon her return to Spain, she stayed in Madrid for a few months and became acquainted with Gerardo Diego and Vicente Aleixandre. In 1954 she spent nine months in the United States, moving in the circles of exiled Spanish intellectuals. Kruckenberg has been living in Vigo since 1955.

To date, she has published fifteen generally short books: ten in Castilian and five in Galician. Her first work, *Las palabras olvidadas* (Forgotten words), is actually a folder with three poems devoted to peace.

Kruckenberg deals with a wide range of themes in her poetry. She constantly defends peace and attacks injustice ("enterremos las armas" [let's bury the arms], *Las palabras*). In *Memorias de mi sueño* (Memories of my dream), she accuses men of cowardice and fear in their incapacity to fight evil, and, at the same time, she advocates a pacifying and redeeming love. Other subjects are the fleeting quality of life, the exploration of one's surroundings, and resignation in the face of difficulty or loneliness—themes around which her autobiography revolves. The writer Alvaro Cunqueiro, referring to her *Cantares de mi silencio* (Songs of my silence), called it "un breviario de las más íntimas soledades en los que muchas veces aflora una angustia que la autora no disimula, la acepta como material esencial de la vida. Se nos habla desde la soledad y la nostalgia y esto en definitiva lo ha sido siempre la más alta poesía" (a breviary of the most intimate loneliness, in which there often arises an anguish which the author does not hide, accepting it as essential material for life. She speaks to us through loneliness and nostalgia, and this has always been the very highest poetry).

BOOKS

Canaval de ouro. Vigo: Galaxia, 1962.
Cantares de mi silencio. Vigo: n.p., 1980.
Cantigas de amigo a R. González Sierra do Pampillón. Vigo: n.p., 1972.
Cantigas do vento. Vigo: Colección Alba, 1956.
Cantigas para un tempo esquencido. Sada: Castro, 1986.
Farol del aire. Vigo: Noroeste, 1958.
Memorias de mi sueño. Vigo: n.p., 1964.
Las palabras olvidadas. Buenos Aires: n.p., 1953. Vigo: n.p., 1956.
Los parajes inmóviles. Vigo: Noroeste, 1957.
Rumor de tiempo. Vigo: Noroeste, 1957.
A sombra ergueita. Vigo: Castrelos, 1976.
Tauromaquia en línea y verso. Vigo and Madrid: Abril, 1964.
Veinte poemas rescatados del olvido y una elegía a Chuca Pereda. Vigo: n.p., 1983.

SECONDARY SOURCES

Alonso Montero, Xesús. "Kruckenberg Sanjurjo, Maria del Carmen." *Gran enciclopedia gallega*, vol. 18.
Cunqueiro, Alvaro. *Faro de Vigo* 5 July 1980.
Fernández del Riego, F. *Antoloxía da poesía galega: Do post-modernismo aos novos.* Vigo: Galaxia, 1980.
González Alegre, Ramón. *Antología de la poesía gallega contemporánea.* Madrid: Rialp, 1959.
Méndez Ferrín, X. Luis. *De Pondal a Novoneyra.* Vigo: Xerais, 1984. 246–48.
Noia Campos, Camino. *Palabra de muller.* Vigo: Xerais, 1992. 30–33, 98–99.
Vázquez de Gey, Elisa. *Queimar as meigas.* Madrid: Torremozas, 1988. 80–87.

MARIA CAMINO NOIA CAMPOS

C Lafontana i Prunera, Maite
(B. 1948, Barcelona– .) Poet and short story writer.

Maite Lafontana's *Indrets d'argila* (Places of clay) is divided into three sections. "Indret de dubte" (Place of doubt) and "Indret de soledat" (Place of solitude) are filled with images of darkness, silence, fear, and psychic suffering. "Indret d'endreça" (Place of arrangement) shows self-doubt but also the beginning of a healing process. The author, who sees death as a liberation from pain, finds in solitude the most reliable approach to life. She prefers to isolate herself and to avoid sharing her disillusions. With others one risks being misunderstood, while in solitude, one can resort to dreams without incurring any danger. Lafontana's stories in *Selecció XXV: Prosa i poesia* (ed. Colet i Giralt) reveal a tender melancholy and feature her principal themes: love, death, and life's difficulties, which are clear from the first terrible moment of birth.

BOOKS
Indrets d'argila. Barcelona: Dalmau, 1980.

WORKS IN BOOKS, PERIODICALS, NEWSPAPERS
Stories, untitled. Colet i Giralt 81–87.

SILVIA AYMERICH LEMOS

B Landa Etxebeste, Mariasun
(B. 1949, Orereta, Gipuzkoa– .) Journalist and writer of children's literature.

After contributing to several magazines, Mariasun Landa Etxebeste concentrated on children's literature. Her first work, *Amets Uhinak* (Dream waves), was published in 1981 and the second, *Kaskarintxo*, in 1982. That year she obtained the Lizardi prize for *Txan fantasmaren etengabeko istorioa* (Ghost Txan's never-ending story). In 1984 she received the third prize of the Certamen Ciudad de San Sebastián for her short story "Nire eskua zurean" (My hand in yours). The same year she published *Elisabete lehoi domatzailea* (Elizabeth, lion tamer), *Partxela*, and *Joxepi dendaria* (Joxepi, the storekeeper) and, in 1985, *Izar berdea* (The green star). She shows a concern for children in all her stories but avoids being dogmatic. She likes to indulge in fantasy and treats the child's world as if it were a world apart, with its own life conflicts and its special relation to adults.

BOOKS
Amets Uhinak. San Sebastián: Elkar, 1981.
Elisabete lehoi domatzailea. San Sebastián: Elkar, 1984.
Izar berdea. San Sebastián: Elkar, 1985.
Joxepi dendaria. San Sebastián: Elkar, 1984.
Kaskarintxo. 1982.
Partxela. San Sebastián: Elkar, 1984.
Txan fantasmaren etengabeko istorioa. San Sebastián: Erein, 1984.
Txan fantasmatxoa. San Sebastián: Euskal Liburu eta Kantuan Argi, 1984.

TRANSLATIONS OF HER WORKS
La botiga de la Pepa [*Joxepi dendaria*]. Trans. Angel Serra. Barcelona: La Galera, 1984.
Chan, el fantasma [*Txan fantasmatxoa*]. Barcelona: La Galera, 1984.
A estrela verde [*Izar berdea*]. Vigo: Galaxia, 1985.
L'estrella verda [*Izar berdea*]. Barcelona: La Galera, 1985.
A tenda da Pepa [*Joxepi dendaria*]. Vigo: Galaxia, 1984.
La tienda de la Pepa [*Joxepi dendaria*]. Barcelona: La Galera, 1984.
Txan el fantasma [*Txan fantasmatxoa*]. Trans. Francesc Boada. Barcelona: La Galera, 1984.

MAITE GONZALEZ ESNAL

C   Lanuza i Hurtado, Empar de
(B. 1950, València– .) Writer of children's literature.

Empar de Lanuza specializes in teaching children with language, reading, and writing disabilities. She has worked for the Secretariat de l'Ensenyament de l'Idioma de Valencia, where she prepared Catalan language courses. Because of her profession, she understands the need to develop children's interest in reading and, as a result, has written stories that feature things that form part of their world. Among her works are *Bon viatge, Pitblanc!* (Good travels, Pitblanc!); *La cuca Quica* (Quica the bug); *El savi rei boig i altres contes* (The crazy wise king and other tales), a collection of short stories that won the Josep M. Folch i Torres award in 1978 and the C.C.E.I. (Comisión Católica Española de la Infancia) prize in 1980; and *El fil invisible i dos contes més* (The invisible thread and two other stories). The last two collections contain stories in the fabulist style. In the *Llibre d'anar anant* (Book of going along) Lanuza compiles songs, games, stories, poems, and riddles from the Valencia region and presents them in story form. *De qui serà?* (Whose is it?), *Història de mans* (A story of hands), and *Els números accidentats* (Unlucky numbers) are didactic works intended to initiate children into the world of reading.

BOOKS
Abecedari de diumenge. Valencia: Diputació de Valencia, 1988.
Aventura d'una desventura. Valencia: Gregal, 1985.
Bon viatge, Pitblanc! 3rd ed. Barcelona: La Galera, 1982.
Criatures minúscules. Valencia: Direcció General de Cultura de la Generalitat Valenciana, 1986.
La cuca Quica. Barcelona: La Galera, 1986.
De qui serà? Valencia: Federació d'Entitats Culturals del País Valencià, 1983.
L'escletxa assassina. Barcelona: Gregal, 1987.
La família feroç. Barcelona: Aliorna, 1988.
El fil invisible i dos contes més. Valencia: Federació d'Entitats Culturals del País Valencià, 1985.
Història de mans. Valencia: Federació d'Entitats Culturals del País Valencià, 1982.
L'home de Penyagolosa. Barcelona: Gregal, 1986.
El llarg viatge dels habitants de Bíbila-Bíbila. Barcelona: Teide, 1987.
Llibre d'anar anant. Illus. Manuel Boix. Valencia: Eliseu Climent, 1982.
Mitja dotzena. Valencia: Eliseu Climent, 1984.
Els números accidentats. Valencia: Federació d'Entitats Culturals del País Valencià, 1983.
Reis i no reis. Barcelona: Magrana, 1987.
El savi rei boig i altres contes. 5th ed. Barcelona: La Galera, 1984.

TRANSLATIONS OF HER WORKS
Buen viaje, Petiblanco [*Bon viatge, Pitblanc!*]. Barcelona: La Galera, 1979.
La grieta asesina [*L'escletxa assassina*]. Barcelona: Gregal, 1988.

El largo viaje de los habitantes de Bibilis-Bibilis [*El llarg viatge dels habitants de Bibila-Bibila*]. Barcelona: Teide, 1987.
La luciérnaga Luci [*La cuca Quica*]. Barcelona: La Galera, 1986.
El sabio rey loco [*El savi rei boig*]. Barcelona: La Galera, 1979.

IMMA BALDOCCHI I PUIG

B Lasa, Amaia
(B. 1948, ?– .) Poet.

Amaia Lasa's *Poema bilduma* (Collected poems) and *Nere Paradisuetan* (In my paradises) exhibit a tone of protest. She claims to rebel against all doctrines and to deny all gods. Eroticism, absent until now from Basque women's literature, is present in her poems.

BOOKS
Nere Paradisuetan. San Sebastián: Vascas, 1979.
Poema bilduma. Bilbao: Etor, 1971; San Sebastián: Erein, 1971.

MAITE GONZALEZ ESNAL

B Lazkano, Maite
(20th c.) Novelist. No biographical information available.

Maite Lazkano learned Basque in adulthood. Her two books, *Gartzelako ateak* (The jail doors) and *Damurik gabe* (Without repentance), have a simple syntax and are designed for people who are learning Basque.

BOOKS
Damurik gabe. San Sebastián: Elkar, 1981.
Gartzelako ateak. San Sebastián: Elkar, 1981.

MAITE GONZALEZ ESNAL

G Ledo Andión, Margarita
(B. 1951, Castro de Rei, Lugo– .) Journalist, poet, and fiction writer.

Margarita Ledo Andión obtained a degree in journalism from the Universitat Autònoma de Barcelona in 1981 and completed her doctoral thesis, "Foto-Xoc e xornalismo da crise" (Photo-shock and crisis journalism) at the Escuela Oficial de Periodismo of Barcelona, where she now works. A militant nationalist in the most radical party of the 1970s, she was forced into exile in Portugal, where she lectured in the Galician language at the Facultad de Letras of Oporto from 1974 to 1976. Ledo wrote for the periodical *El ideal gallego* and edited *A nosa terra* (Santiago de Compostela) between 1977 and 1980. She has written frequently for Galician periodicals, including *Escrita*, the organ for the Association of Writers in the Galician Language, and *Festa da palabra silenciada* (Vigo), a journal coordinated and produced by women. She has also contributed to numerous Castilian periodicals.

As a journalist, Ledo has published the following works: *Prensa e galeguismo: Da prensa galega do XIX ao primeiro periódico nacionalista* (Press and Galicianism: Galician press from the nineteenth century to the first nationalist newspaper) and "Do proceso de connotación na fotografía de prensa" (About the connotation process in photojournalism). Her first published creative works are two books of poems: *Parolar cun eu, cun intre, cun inseuto* (Talking with an I, with a moment, with an insect) and *O corvo érguese cedo* (Raven, get up early). Her poetry aims to break with the intimacy and ruralism characteristic of Galician poetry prior to the Civil War. She writes about the personal dilemma in which one's own beliefs and the dialectic materialism of Marxism coexist and conflict at the same time. To convey this struggle between the individual and the collective, Ledo departs from the traditional forms of expression and even from the conventional relation between the signified and the signifier, with the result that her creative work is difficult to understand.

In 1983 Margarita Ledo published a book of stories, *Mama-Fé* (Mommy Faith), and, in 1985, a novel, *Trasalba ou Violeta e o militar morto* (Trasalba or Violet and the dead soldier). Although she still writes poetry, which appears in Galician newspapers and journals, she has not published any more books of poems. In both verse and prose, Ledo uses the same techniques and themes: artifice as the resistance of a suppressed language and the mixture of different codes, particularly the montage of events in which characters from different historical and cultural periods appear. These come together in the mind of the observer-protagonist and, by extension, the mind of the reader. The uniting of reader and protagonist is achieved through references to a common memory, that is, to the intertext.

Margarita Ledo's fiction contains cultural references to the Galician world as well as to the cultures of other countries. The literary discourse relies on sequences that form a continuum, with analogical games and other actions in the text. The story "Dona Inés e o xusticieiro" (Dona Inés and the judge) in *Mama-Fé* provides a good example. Two subplots alternate with the main story, establishing connections with it, such as the appearance of a "sapocuncho" (tortoise) in an elevator, with no narrative function other than to act as a parallel to the character of the housekeeper, or the "orchesta solare" (sun orchestra) that plays Mozart's *Magic Flute*, a work with numerous Masonic symbols. The novel *Trasalba ou Violeta* . . . , which also contains the difficult techniques of fragmentary literature, uses a robot as the unifying figure throughout the complicated narrative. This contradictory character, who sometimes acts as narrator, represents a hero of the twenties, one of the most splendid periods in Galician culture, in opposition to the hero of "la etapa liberal rectilíneo y agónico, en pos de la causa justa" (the straight, agonizing liberal stage, seeking just causes), as the author indicates in the prologue. This character turns out to be a stereotype used by the author to characterize an era in Galician history, portrayed through a series of still shots, as in the cinema, but without a script.

BOOKS
O corvo érguese cedo. Monforte de Lemos, Lugo: Xistral, 1973.
Foto-Xoc e xornalismo en crise. Sada, Coruña: Castro, 1988.
Linguas mortas. Barcelona: Sotelo Blanco, 1990.
Mama-Fé. Vigo: Xerais, 1983.
Parolar cun eu, cun intre, cun inseuto. Monforte de Lemos, Lugo: Xistral, 1970.
Porta blindada. Vigo: Xerais, 1991.
Prensa e galeguismo: Da prensa galega do XIX ao primeiro periódico nacionalista.
   Vinte anos da Nosa terra (1916–1936). Sada, Coruña: Castro, 1982.
Trasalba ou Violeta e o militar morto. Vigo: Xerais, 1985.

WORKS IN BOOKS, PERIODICALS, NEWSPAPERS
"Arc en terre." *La voz de Galicia* 13 May 1983.
"Cántolle ao home. . . ." *La voz de Galicia* 9 Mar. 1985.
"Desprendín cos silencios. . . ." *La voz de Galicia* 9 Mar. 1985.
"O día no que un home se viu desvestido." *La región* 14 Sept. 1985.
"Do proceso de connotación na fotografía de prensa." *I seminario galego de arte/comunicación.* Sada, Coruña: Castro, 1983.
"A escaleira." *La voz de Galicia* 9 Mar. 1985.
"Lentos." *Coordenadas* May 1981.
"Linguas mortas," "Guaraní," "Peyote," and "Licor café." *Follas secas* 1 May 1985.
"O momento que nos une co último 'round' " (interview). With A. Avendaño. *Faro de Vigo* 24 May 1984.
"Rematado a man." *Traballos premiados no 8° concurso de narracións curtas M. F. Figueiredo.* Sada, Coruña: Castro, 1983.
"Renda no muro." *Contos eróticos/Elas.* Vigo: Xerais, 1990. 40–48.
"A Santiña, tómese—bebido—varias veces ao día." *Follas secas* 2 Aug. 1985.
"Variacións Golberg." *Revista da Federación de Asociacións Culturais Galegas* 17 May 1982.
"Xana." *Dorna* 1 May 1981.

SECONDARY SOURCES
Blanco, Carmen. "Sobre o comportamento literario da muller. O caso de M. Ledo." *Grial* 88 (1985). Rpt. in *Literatura galega da muller.* Vigo: Xerais, 1991. 275–93.
Cacheiro, *Poetisas galegas do século XX.*

Casares, Carlos. "Os contos de M. Ledo." *La voz de Galicia* 1985, "Suplemento de Cultura" sec.

Fernández del Riego, F. *Poesía galega do dezanove a hoxe.* Vigo: Galaxia, 1975.

García, X. Lois. *Escolma da poesía galega 1976–84.* Barcelona: Sotelo Blanco, 1984.

Moreno, Maria Victoria. *Os novísimos da poesía galega.* Madrid: Akal, 1973.

Noia Campos, C. "Linguas mortas frente á realidade." *La voz de Galicia* 11 Sept. 1989.

———. "Tendències narratives." *El país* 30 Nov. 1986, "Quadern" sec.

Outeiriño, M. "Barcelona, Lisboa, París, Trasalba." *Faro de Vigo* 19 June 1986, "Artes e Letras" sec.

Pallarés, Pilar. "*Trasalba ou Violeta e o militar morto* de M. Ledo." *Luzes de Galizia* 2 (Mar. 1986).

Tarrío, A. "Dez anos de narrativa." *Grial* 89 (1985).

Vaincova, Julia (Méndez Ferrín). "Dúas importantes novedades literarias." *Espiral* 17 (1986).

Vázquez de Gey, Elisa. *Queimar as meigas.* Madrid: Torremozas, 1988. 162–67.

MARIA CAMINO NOIA CAMPOS

C Leveroni i Valls, Rosa

(B. 1910, Barcelona; d. 1985, Barcelona.) Poet, short story writer, and translator.

Best known as a poet, Rosa Leveroni expresses the excitement, pain, and joy of love in a thoughtful and circumspect tone. Her work, which strives for formal, classical perfection, shows the influence of *Noucentisme* (a cultural movement at the turn of the century) and of several Catalan poets whose work she studied. She uses elements of nature, in her stories as well as her lyrics, to explain her inner self and sometimes employs traditional imagery to describe her feelings and experiences. She worked as a librarian at the University of Barcelona until 1939 and is known for her research on the poet Ausiàs March. Carles Riba and Salvador Espriu encouraged her to write, and both praised her as an excellent poet in introductions to her books. She also contributed to the journals *Ariel* and *Poesia* and translated T. S. Eliot, but she stopped producing creative work around 1952. There are two collections of her poems: *Poesia* (Poetry) and *Presència i record* (Presence and memory). She won a prize in the Jocs Florals of 1956 celebrated in Cambridge, England. Her stories, many of them previously unpublished, were gathered and edited by LaSal in the collection *Contes*, which includes a perceptive introduction by the novelist Helena Valentí; most deal with love relationships and seem like prose extensions of her lyrical images.

BOOKS
Contes. Introd. Helena Valentí. Barcelona: LaSal, 1985.
Epigrames i cançons. Prol. Carles Riba. Barcelona: Gili, 1938.
Poesia. Prol. Maria-Aurèlia Capmany. Barcelona: Edicions 62, 1981.
Presència i record. Prol. Salvador Espriu. Barcelona: Ossa Menor, 1952.

TRANSLATIONS OF HER WORKS
"Absence, VII" ["Absència, VII"]. Trans. Lynette McGrath and Nathaniel B. Smith. *Webster Review* 12.2 (1987): 22.
"Testament" and "Five Desolate Poems" ["Cinc Poemes Desolats"]. *Survivors*. Selected and trans. D. Sam Abrams. Barcelona: Inst. d'Estudis Nord-Americans, 1991. 35–43.

SECONDARY SOURCES
Marçal, Maria Mercè. "Rosa Leveroni en el llindar." *Literatura de dones: Una visió del món*. Barcelona: LaSal, 1988. 97–120.

KATHLEEN MCNERNEY

C Lewi, Elvira Augusta
(B. 1910, Barcelona– .) Journalist and fiction writer.

Elvira Lewi received her early education at a German school in Barcelona and went on to study music and art. Her novel *Un poeta i dues dones* (A poet and two women) is the story of a young German poet who uses his art to exact tremendous sacrifices from the women in his life. His elderly mother and two sisters live in poverty because he refuses to look for work; he deserts his fiancée for a glamorous opera singer who abandons her career to marry him. After his mother's death, her memory becomes his muse, and his wife must confront his newfound conviction that passion is a hindrance rather than an inspiration to art.

The short stories composing "Els habitants del pis 200" (The occupants of apartment 200) also deal with men's attitudes toward women and with the nature of art, but they show a more mature style and greater originality. Fantasy intersects with reality, as death, love, and art are explored in the lives of characters who are firmly rooted in society and its norms.

BOOKS
Un poeta i dues dones. Badalona: Proa, 1935.

WORKS IN BOOKS, PERIODICALS, NEWSPAPERS
"Els habitants del pis 200." *Quaderns literaris* 107 (1935): 5–67.

SHEILA MCINTOSH

C Lienas i Massot, Gemma
(B. 1951, Barcelona– .) Writer of children's stories and fiction.

A graduate in philosophy and letters, Gemma Lienas i Massot began working in a psychology counseling office and then as a language teacher of Catalan and Castilian. Later she entered the publishing world in the field of textbooks and juvenile literature. The year 1985 marks her entrance as a writer with the novel *Cul de sac* (Dead-end), which deals with human relationships. In 1987 she was awarded three literary prizes: the Francesc Puig i Llensa given by the magazine *Recull de Blanes* for her story *El gust del cafè* (The taste of coffee); the Ramon Muntaner prize for juvenile literature in Girona for *Dos cavalls* (Two horses), a novel about social marginalization; and the Andrómina prize in Valencia for the novel *Vol nocturn* (Night flight), the chronicle of a phobia.

BOOKS
Així és la vida, Carlota. Barcelona: Empúries, 1989.
Cul de sac. Barcelona: Empúries, 1987.
Dos cavalls. Barcelona: Empúries, 1987.
El gust del cafè. Barcelona: Pòrtic, 1989.
La lluna en un cove. Barcelona: Cruïlla, 1987.
Vol nocturn. Valencia: Eliseu Climent, 1987.

TRANSLATIONS OF HER WORKS
Callejón sin salida [*Cul de sac*]. Barcelona: Aliorna, 1987.
Querer la luna [*La lluna en un cove*]. Barcelona: Fundación Santa María, 1989.

ANNA GASOL I TRULLOLS

C Linyan, Mercè
(B. 20th c., Canals, València– .) Novelist.

Mercè Linyan has contributed to the journal *El pont* and written a novel, *L'Eros de Piccadilly Circus* (The Eros of Piccadilly Circus), whose title reflects the author's long period of residence in England. *L'Eros* presents the spontaneous confession of a lost girl, Mary, and of her alienation as a sensitive person in a big city. Grimly realistic, the novel depicts the chaotic, crude life of down-and-outers. The author claims to know the characters of whom she speaks.

BOOKS
L'Eros de Piccadilly Circus. Barcelona: Club, 1971.

KATHLEEN MCNERNEY

C Lisson Quiros, Assumpció
(B. 1933, Barcelona– .) Writer of children's literature.

Assumpció Lisson worked in the Costa i Llobera school of Barcelona. A librarian, she coordinates with Maria Eulàlia Valeri the Seminar on Children's Bibliography of the Associació de Mestres Rosa Sensat, which publishes the selective bibliography of new children's literature, entitled *Quins llibres han de llegir els nens?* (Which books should children read?). Lisson has collaborated in the editing of textbooks and has published articles on reading and school libraries for various magazines and newspapers, including *Mainada-Express, Avui,* and *Perspectiva escolar.* She has taught summer courses in the Escola d'Estiu de Rosa Sensat and in other summer schools around Spain and has participated in seminars and conferences on juvenile literature, reading, and school libraries.

Lisson has copublished with Maria Eulàlia Valeri collections of games, riddles, and songs, as well as stories for young children. She is an adviser to various Catalan publishing houses that specialize in juvenile literature.

BOOKS
Aquest fa les sopes. Barcelona: La Galera, 1971.
Cargol treu banya. Barcelona: La Galera, 1971.
La casa de les mones. Barcelona: La Galera, 1971.
La lluna, la pruna. Barcelona: La Galera, 1971.
Olles, olles de vi blanc. With Maria Eulàlia Valeri. Barcelona: La Galera, 1975.
Quins llibres han de llegin els nens? With Maria Eulàlia Valeri. Barcelona: Rosa Sensat, 1977.
Rotllo, rotllo. Barcelona: La Galera, 1971.

ANNA GASOL I TRULLOLS

B Lizundia, Eustaquia
(B. 1899, Izurza, Bizkaia– .) Prose writer.

Eustaquia Lizundia wrote fifteen short works in epistolary form. They deal with *costumista* (local color) themes and have a religious and moral message.

MAITE GONZALEZ ESNAL

C Llach i Tersol de Sospedra, Concepció
(20th c.) Playwright. No biographical information available.

Concepció Llach was an actor who dedicated herself to various aspects of the theater, but her only literary work is *La petita Maria Teresa* (Little

Maria Teresa). This play calls to mind a collage of scenes and situations from classical theater: love letters written by the lover's friend, as in *Cyrano de Bergerac*; the simpleton at the opera, as in *Martín Fierro*; the intuitive grandmother, as in *La casa de Bernarda Alba*; there is even a reference to *The Taming of the Shrew*.

BOOKS

La petita Maria Teresa. Barcelona: Millà, 1961.

KATHLEEN MCNERNEY

C   Llauradó, Anna
(B. 1959, Barcelona– .) Journalist, short story writer, and scriptwriter. No biographical information available.

BOOKS

Plaers. Barcelona: Columna, 1989.
Profecia. Barcelona: Area Contemporànea, 1989.

KATHLEEN MCNERNEY

C   Lleal Galceràn, Coloma
(B. 1944, Ceuta– .) Poet.

Coloma Lleal Galceràn teaches philology at the University of Barcelona. She lives in Badalona, Barcelona, and has two children. She has contributed numerous poems to anthologies and literary magazines and has also written various articles on language teaching. *Dels dels sons* (From the sounds), whose unusual title is explained in the prologue by Joan Argenté, is divided into four sections: "Preludi" contains poems of sexual and intellectual liberation and one poem on pedagogy, which is dedicated to her students. "Suite" comprises poems dedicated to specific individuals she admires, mostly poets, but also a delightful one to the "lady crooners"— Sarah Vaughn, Billie Holiday, and Ella Fitzgerald. "Cadència" features love poems, but the themes are abstract and the poet is preoccupied with her solitude: "Si fos saxofon / amarg i sol / no ho fóra tant / com ara . . ." (If I were a saxophone, bitter and alone, I still wouldn't be so as much as I am now . . .) (48). The final section, "Final," is dedicated to Joan Argenté.

BOOKS

Dels dels sons. Introd. Joan Argenté. Badalona: Ajuntament, 1987.
Poemes. Paris: Foc Nou, 1967.

WORKS IN BOOKS, PERIODICALS, NEWSPAPERS

Poems, untitled. *Antologia da novíssima poesia catalã*.

Poems, untitled. *Antologia de poesia catalã contemporânia*. 128–31.

Poems, untitled. *Gespa-Price: Festival de poesia de primavera*. Bellaterra: UAB, 1975. 66.

Poems, untitled. *Homenatge a Vicent Andrés Estellés*. Tarragona: Universitat de Tarragona, 1983.

Poems, untitled. *Poesia catalana de la guerra d'Espanya i de la resistència*. Ed. S. Cartwright. Paris: n.p., 1969.

Poems, untitled. *Poetes per la Pau*. Badalona: n.p., 1986.

KATHLEEN MCNERNEY

Llorens, Gràcia B. de; *see* Bassa de Llorens, Maria Gràcia

C Llorens i Carreres de Serra, Sara
(B. 1881, Buenos Aires, Argentina; d. 1954, Perpignan, France.) Also Llorens i Carreras. Folklorist and writer of children's literature and fiction.

Sara Llorens i Carreres de Serra was born in Argentina but her family soon moved to Catalonia. She studied in Barcelona at the Normal School, the School of Fine Arts, and a school for women tutors. In this last institution she was a student of Rossend Serra i Pagès, a Catalan folklorist who campaigned to educate Catalan women so they would become promoters of nationalistic ideas. This self-appointed trainer of Catalan women wrote the introduction to one of Llorens's books, and she, in turn, gathered together his writings and wrote a prologue for the collection after his death. Sara Llorens became a member of Barcelona's Excursionist Center, where she was acquainted with other women writers such as Maria Gràcia Bassa, Adelaida Ferré i Gomis, Joana Vidal, Mercè Ventosa, and Manuela Fina. She also lectured in Barcelona in 1911 on folklore in the Canary Islands.

Llorens married Manuel Serra i Moret in 1908 in Trenque Lanquen, Argentina, and shortly afterward they moved to her estate house in Pineda (El Maresme, Barcelona), where she performed social work in collaboration with her husband. She had fragile health and required medical treatment abroad for long periods, so she traveled extensively. In 1902 she began collecting popular songs of Pineda and continued working for many years in collaboration with musicians and experts in folklore. Her work *El cançoner de Pineda* (Popular songs from Pineda) was finally published in 1931. It contains 238 songs and 210 tunes and was the first part of a more extensive collection of folklore from El Maresme that was never published.

Monòlegs per infants (Monologues for children), which won the prose prize in the Jocs Florals in Santa Coloma de Farnés, Girona, in 1904, was later published with great success. These monologues were written to be performed by children four to thirteen years old. The author says in the introduction that, because she wanted to write the book as if it had been written by a child, she had to forget the knowledge she had as an adult. The majority of the monologues show the opposition between a child's and an adult's point of view, as in "Com me dec dir" (What should I call myself), where the protagonist wonders whether Joan is his real name or one of the nicknames used by his family. Other monologues have a poetic or musical quality, and some reflect the feelings of adolescents beginning their working responsibilities.

Llorens contributed short stories to Barcelona's magazine *Feminal* from 1907 to 1911. In 1954 she published a personal diary *El llibre del cor* (Book of the heart), an excerpt of which was included in *Manat d'homenatge a la Reina de Mallorca.* . . .

BOOKS

El cançoner de Pineda. Vol. 1 of *Folklore de la Maresma.* Barcelona: Joaquim Horta, 1931.
Monòlegs per infants. Barcelona: Joaquim Horta, 1918.
Petit aplech d'exemples morals. Introd. Rossend Serra i Pagès. Barcelona: Fidel Giró, 1906.

WORKS IN BOOKS, PERIODICALS, NEWSPAPERS

"La Felicitat y la Bellesa." *Feminal* 58 (27 Aug. 1911).
El llibre del cor (excerpt). *Manat d'homenatge* 33–36.
"Maternal." *Feminal* 18 (27 Sept. 1908).
"Una muller." *Feminal* 27 (27 June 1909).
"Nota biogràfica." *Alguns escrits del professor Rossend Serra y Pagès. Coleccionats y publicats a honor del Mestre per les seves dexebles en ocasió del cinquantenari del seu professorat (1875–1925).* Barcelona: Miquel-Rius, 1926. vii–xxxi.
"Proses." *Lectura popular* 16: 313–36. Introd. Rosend Serra i Pagès.

CRISTINA ENRIQUEZ DE SALAMANCA

C Llúria i de Margola, Maria de
(B. 1630/32, Barcelona?; d. 1701, Vallbona de les Monges, Lleida.) Abbess of Vallbona. Religious writer.

Maria de Llúria came from an aristocratic family. Evidence situates the Llúria territorial possessions in western Catalonia during the seventeenth century. It is assumed that she was born in Barcelona, the city of her mother, Isabel de Margola i de Genovart, wife of Joan Roger de Llúria i de Sacirera. Llúria entered the Vallbona monastery at the age of ten or twelve, was made a novice in 1646, and took the habit in 1648. She devoted her life to her religious vocation and to the service of the convent, gradually moving up from subtreasurer to abbess, a position she held for two months and four days in 1701. Llúria was noted for her efficient administration of convent funds and for her sociability.

Although she was not a writer in the vocational sense, her *Llibre de dona Maria de Llúria* includes a smaller book called *Directori espiritual* (Spiritual guide), which deserves literary recognition. The *Llibre* was a diary in which the nuns wrote down details of their lives and convent duties. Maria de Llúria's contains the family coat of arms, the most significant events in her religious life, her duties, some "Añades de Psalteris" (Psaltery glosses), and her *Directori espiritual*, which occupies pages 11 to 58. In this book of reflections and prayers, she expresses her worries and spiritual regrets, thoughts on her vocation, and the passion she feels for God. The main themes are her vows of chastity, obedience, and poverty, as well as humility, peace of spirit, and love. The treatment of these subjects adheres to the orthodox Catholic teachings of the time, and her sincerity and intensity shine through these intimate passages. Her texts are simple and clear, expressed in language devoid of rhetorical figures and written in an eastern variant of Catalan that is full of Castilianisms.

BOOKS
Directori espiritual: Llibre de dona Maria de Llúria. L'Abadessa Maria de Llúria, Mestra d'Espirit. Ed. Josep-Joan Piquer i Jover. Barcelona: Balmesiana (Biblioteca Balmes), 1983.

ELISA MARTI-LOPEZ

C   López i García, Núria
(B. 1962, Vilassar, Barcelona– .) Poet.

Winner of a number of prizes and honorable mentions, Núria López i García is the secretary of the Young Writers' Association of Catalonia. Her degree is in psychology.

WORKS IN BOOKS, PERIODICALS, NEWSPAPERS
Poems, untitled. *Inflable.* Barcelona: El Llamp, 1988.

KATHLEEN MCNERNEY

C Lorente, Angels
(20th c.) Writer of children's literature. No biographical information available.

Cap pelat (Bare head), Angels Lorente's only known publication in Catalan, is the delightful story of a little girl who finds joy in her differentness from others. The drawings by Elsa Plaza are as charming as the text.

BOOKS
Cap pelat. Illus. Elsa Plaza. Barcelona: LaSal, 1980.

KATHLEEN MCNERNEY

C Maffei Ginesu, Pinutxa
(B. 1914, Alghero, Italy; d. 1961, Alghero, Italy.) Also Ginesu, Pinutxa. Poet. No biographical information available.

Manat d'homenatge a la reina Constança de Mallorca . . . contains Pinutxa Maffei Ginesu's poem "Fontana pinta" and a short note saying that she published a few collections of poems and was awarded prizes in the Joc Florals of Paris in 1954. According to *Les cinc branques*, Maffei Ginesu wrote two volumes of poetry, *L'arbre* (The tree) and *L'aigua* (Water), which are not available in major Catalan libraries.

WORKS IN BOOKS, PERIODICALS, NEWSPAPERS
"Fontana pinta." *Manat d'homenatge* 47–48 and *Les cinc branques* 156.

NANCY L. BUNDY and CRISTINA ENRIQUEZ DE SALAMANCA

C Magraner, Margarita
(B. 1935, Mallorca– .) Poet.

The Joan March Library of Palma de Mallorca has one of the 250 copies of Margarita Magraner's *Poemes en quatre temps* (Poems in four seasons). The title refers to the seasons of the year and to the sections into which the collection is divided. Time and nature's cycles are points of reference that the poet uses to construct an investigation of love and philosophy. This temporal division symbolizes the fragmentation reflected in her poetry. She establishes communication with an individual interlocutor on the basis of a dynamic concept of love: "Amor, què hi ha dins tu que no sia un moviment sempre interromput / i renovat?" (Love, what is there in you that's not a constant movement, interrupted / and renovated?) (27). The poet suggests the static image of expectant desire: "Quin goig més venturós, el de

210

l'espera / No té por qui espera l'alba" (Expecting is a fortunate joy / No one who expects dawn is afraid) (28).

BOOKS
Poemes en quatre temps. Palma: La Font de les Tortugues, 1958.

CRISTINA ENRIQUEZ DE SALAMANCA

C Malgrau i Plana, Fina
(B. 1953, Banyoles, Girona– .) Writer of children's stories.

Fina Malgrau teaches at the Gavina School in Valencia and specializes in language pedagogy. Her work features female protagonists. *El país de la Nomemòria* (Nonmemory country) deals with the adventures of a girl in search of her lost memory.

BOOKS
Gegants. Barcelona: Barcanova, 1983.
El país de la Nomemòria. Barcelona: Aliorna, 1988.
Sona de lletres. Valencia: Gregal, 1984.
Xino-xano. Valencia: Gregal, 1986.

ANNA MONTERO I BOSCH

C Mallarach Berga, Mercè
(B. 1924, Olot, Girona– .) Poet and contributor to newspapers and radio.

According to *Les cinc branques*, Biblioteca Olotina published in Olot in 1966 an untitled volume of poetry by Mercè Mallarach Berga; it is not available in major libraries in Catalonia.

WORKS IN BOOKS, PERIODICALS, NEWSPAPERS
"Esqueix." *Les cinc branques* 197.

NANCY L. BUNDY

C Mallorca, Reina de
(1st half of the 14th c.) Poet.

The Miscellaneous Medieval Poetical Manuscript 8 of the Biblioteca de Catalunya in Barcelona contains a gentle love song attributed to a "Reina de Mallorca" that begins "Ez yeu am tal qu'es bo e bel" (I love one who is good and lovely). The same text is included after the first *giornata* in the Catalan translation of Boccaccio's *Decameron* of 1429; that love song, belonging to the troubadour genre *descort*, laments the absence of the beloved, the husband gone to France. The mysterious queen of Majorca has been identified as either Constança d'Aragó (1313–46), sister of King Pere el Ceremoniós d'Aragó, or Violant de Vilaragut, both of whom were wives of King Jaume III of Majorca, who died in 1349.

WORKS IN BOOKS, PERIODICALS, NEWSPAPERS
"Ez yeu am tal qu'es bo e bel." Miscellaneous Medieval Poetical Manuscript 8. Biblioteca de Catalunya, Barcelona. The poem also appears in Irénée Cluzel's "Princes et troubadours de la maison royale de Barcelone-Aragón," *Boletín de la Real Academia de Buenas Letras de Barcelona* 27 (1957–58): 371–73.

TRANSLATIONS OF HER WORKS
"I love one who is good and lovely" ["Ez yeu am tal qu'es bo e bel"]. Trans. Kathleen McNerney. *Catalan Review* 5.2 (1991): 163–67.

SECONDARY SOURCES
Massó i Torrents, "Poetesses i dames intel.lectuals" 406–07.
Pagès, Amédée. "Les poésies lyriques de la traduction catalane du Décaméron." *Annales du Midi* 46 (1934): 201–17.
Riquer et al. 1: 519–20.

LOLA BADIA

C Malmonjades, Les
(Songs of the unwilling nuns; 14th c.) Poets.

Malmonjades is the name literary critics have given to a tradition of poems written by women who live in convents against their wills and lament the fact that they cannot enjoy love. This tradition goes back to the Latin Middle Ages and appears in the early poetry of various Romance languages. One of the several examples in Catalan is the refrain and a verse from the beautiful anonymous dance of the mid-fourteenth century, which opens the anthology "Cançoneret de Ripoll," a manuscript of the period kept at the Archive of the Crown of Aragon, in Barcelona. According to Jaume Massó i Torrents (*Malmonjades. Repertori*), the author is a woman, but Martí de Riquer believes it could have been a man. Although some of the *malmonjades* may have been written by goliards, the fact that Charlemagne prohibited nuns from writing poetry in 789 indicates that their practice of describing their troubles and desires in poems was so widespread that the emperor felt impelled to forbid it.

On the other hand, Georges Duby believes that because of the establishment of the prebourgeois society in the twelfth century, women were losing their active roles in love relationships to men. Traces of this "matriarchal" culture are found in various literary forms in Europe prior to the twelfth century: the mozarabic *khardjes*, the Galician-Portuguese *cantigas*

212

de amigo, the Catalan *cançons de donzella*, the French *chansons de femme*, and the Castilian, Germanic, Celtic, and Occitan *cançons de muller*. Even if some of these poems could have been written by men, it would be a case of twelfth-century male poets adopting a lyrical tradition of poems written much earlier by women. In these poems, the young woman addresses her mother or sisters, her girlfriends, inanimate objects of nature, or even herself—but never a man. The poems speak clearly of the anxieties, griefs, fears, doubts, hopes, dreams, sensations, passions, loves, and sufferings in the soul of the woman. This poetry constitutes an outpouring of female sentiment and psychology. Thus, the *malmonjades* should indeed be considered a poetic tradition created by women, in which they manifest their pains and their longings; for even if the authors of the surviving examples are unknown, what is certain is that the poems were gathered from popular tradition and rewritten. People had for centuries transmitted poetry by nuns who complained of their situations.

WORKS IN BOOKS, PERIODICALS, NEWSPAPERS

"Cançoneret de Ripoll." Ms. 129 of Ripoll. Archive of the Crown of Aragon, Barcelona.

Malmonjades (selections). "Observaciones sobre la poesía popular con muestras de romances catalanes inéditos." By Manuel Milà i Fontanals. *Obras completas.* Vol. 6. Barcelona: Verdaguer, 1895.

Malmonjades (selections). *Repertori de l'antiga literatura catalana.* By Jaume Massó i Torrents. Barcelona: Alpha, 1932.

Romancerillo catalan. Barcelona: Verdaguer, 1882.

TRANSLATIONS OF THEIR WORKS

"Alas! If I Had Married" ["Lassa, mays m'agra valgut"]. *An Anthology of Medieval Lyrics.* Ed. Angel Flores. Trans. William Davis. New York: Modern Library, 1962.

SECONDARY SOURCES

Duby, Georges. *Le chevalier, la femme et le prêtre: Le mariage dans la France féodale.* Paris: Hachette, 1981.

———. *Tiempo de catedrales.* Barcelona: Argot, 1983.

———. *Los tres órdenes o lo imaginario del feudalismo.* Madrid: Petral, 1980.

Lapa, M. Rodrígues. *Liçoes de literatura portuguesa.* Coimbra: Coimbra Editora, 1977.

Riquer et al. 2: 16–17.

Rubió i Balaguer, Jordi. "Del manuscrit 129 de Ripoll del segle XIV." *Revista de bibliografia catalana* 8 (1905): 285–378. Rpt. Barcelona: L'Avenç, 1911.

MONTSERRAT VILLAS I CHALAMANCH

C Maluquer i Gonzalez, Concepció
(B. 1918, Salas, Lleida– .) Poet and novelist.

Though she was born in the Pyrenees, Concepció Maluquer i Gonzalez has lived most of her life in Barcelona and makes the city a theme of some of her works. She won the Premi Ciutat de Barcelona prize for her long poem *La creu dels vents* (The crossroads of the winds), a dialogue between the city and the four cardinal winds. Another long poem, *La ciutat i les hores*, (The city and the hours), a finalist for the same prize, presents the twenty-four hours of the day personified by twenty-four female characters. Some of Maluquer's poetry is included in the anthology *Lleida, vuit poetes* (Eight poets of Lleida). Later works, notably the novels *Parèntesi* (Parenthesis) and *Què s'ha fet d'en Pere Cots?* (What happened to Pere Cots?), depict upper-class individuals bored by the monotony of their lives. Her novels contain rich observations of phenomena that affect the life of contemporary Catalans: tourism and immigration.

BOOKS
Aigua tèrbola. Andorra: Alfaguara, 1967.
La ciutat i les hores. Barcelona: Moderna, 1960.
La creu dels vents. Barcelona: Moderna, 1959.
Dues coses. Barcelona: Arimany, 1960.
Gent del nord. Barcelona: Club, 1971.
Gent del sud. Barcelona: Club, 1964.
Parèntesi. Barcelona: Alberti, 1962.
Què s'ha fet d'en Pere Cots? Andorra: Alfaguara, 1966.

WORKS IN BOOKS, PERIODICALS, NEWSPAPERS
Poems, untitled. *Lleida, vuit poetes.* Barcelona: Ariel, 1968.

KATHLEEN MCNERNEY

Mañariko; *see* **Bustinza y Ozerin, Rosa**

C   Manent Rodon, Montserrat
(B. 1940, Mataró, Barcelona– .) Poet.

Montserrat Manent has worked in photography since she was fifteen, recently concentrating on artistic and documentary photography. She has also written various pieces since her teen years: plays, stories, and, above all, poetry. Some of her poetry is included in journals and collections.

Her first book, *Descoberta de temps* (Time uncovered), constitutes for its author "poemes de la meva Espera i, encara que potser no ho sembli, poemes d'esperança" (poems of my Wait and, even though it may not seem so, poems of hope) (7). Indeed she does not always appear so hopeful. "I estic ací, amb sol i estabornida / perquè no sóc capaç d'estimar-me" (I'm here, with sun, and stunned / because I'm not capable of loving myself) (18). Some of the poems are tender love poems; others are about writing,

214

or creating, a poem. She begins a short piece with a variation on Ausiàs March's "Amor, Amor, un àbit m'é tallat" (Love, Love, I made myself clothing), a work often imitated by the Castilian Golden Age poets: "He teixit un vestit de desig / i me l'he posat" (I wove a dress of desire and put it on) (71). Some of Manent's work shows keen social criticism, as in "Seguritat social," where she must humble herself before bureaucrats, speak Castilian, and "encara donaré les gràcies" (still be grateful), and in the poem "Una dona vella m'ha demanat que li comprés un panet tou perquè tenia gana i no tenia dents" (An old lady asked me for soft bread because she was hungry but had no teeth).

Uri retains the sensibility of Manent's earlier book but reveals a richer, more suggestive creativity. The poet uses color to create a magic space but also features images of fear and uncertainty. She sees a cyclic dimension in stone, vegetation, blood, and the moon. The purifying final poem, "Un altre càntic" (Another song), is a metaphor of light and strength, of the positive, and displays an innovative style of poetry.

BOOKS
Descoberta de temps. Mallorca: Palma, 1982.
Uri. Prol. Vicent Andrés Estellés. Valencia: Eliseu Climent, 1987.

KATHLEEN MCNERNEY

Mantua, Cecília A.; *see* **Alonso i Bozzo, Cecília**

C Manzana, Sílvia
(B. 20th c., Girona– .) Novelist. No biographical information available.

BOOKS
Oasi. Girona: Pont de Pedra, 1989.
Tendra és la nit. Girona: Pont de Pedra, 1988.

KATHLEEN MCNERNEY

C Marçal i Serra, Maria-Mercè
(B. 1952, Ivars d'Urgell, Lleida– .) Poet.

Maria-Mercè Marçal studied philology at the University of Barcelona and now teaches Catalan and literature at the Institut Rubió i Ors in Barcelona. She helped found the Llibres del Mall, a publishing house, in 1973, and in 1976 she won the Carles Riba prize for her book of poetry *Cau de llunes*

215

(Lair of the moons). She has published poetry in various journals, and some of her lyrics have been sung by Marina Rosell, Ramon Muntaner, Maria del Mar Bonet, and other representatives of the Nova Cançó. She has also participated in juries of poetry prizes and has written critical articles on other poets, including Felícia Fuster, Clementina Arderiu, and Rosa Leveroni. The epigraph from *Cau de llunes* indicates her sociopolitical orientation: "A l'atzar agraeixo tres dons: haver nascut dona / de classe baixa i nació oprimida / i el tèrbol atzur de ser tres voltes rebel" (I thank chance for three gifts: having been born a woman / of the lower class and an oppressed nation / and the turbid blue of being three times a rebel). The poems in the book are divided into four thematic parts. The first and last sections, in different styles, are love poems, and in the last the poet uses traditional forms to create musical poetry. The second section is inspired by her sociopolitical attitude, and the third by her feminist commitment.

In *Bruixa de dol* (Witch in mourning), a collection of poems and songs written between 1977 and 1979, the author finds her own voice while reviving some Catalan literary traditions. Images of witches, fairies, and other marginal beings pervade this sensual, feminist poetry. In *Sal oberta* (Open salt) she continues speaking in her own voice, from her own experience as a woman. *Terra de mai* (Neverland) is a collection of fifteen sestinas, in which the poet successfully uses the medieval form for modern preoccupations and imagery. Her language and rhythm flow gracefully in this six-line, six-stanza pattern with its closing tercet.

La germana, l'estrangera (The sister, the stranger) contains *Terra de mai* and two new sections, "Sang presa" (Imprisoned Blood) and "En el desig cicatritzat i en l'ombra" (In the scarred desire and in the shadow). As Marçal explains in her prologue, "Sang presa" is a thematic continuation of *Terra de mai*, and "En el desig cicatritzat i en l'ombra" reflects parts of *Sal oberta*. This last section of the book is dedicated to the poet's daughter, Heura, and has a fresh and honest look at motherhood. Marçal's imagery is striking and sometimes violent, such as her comparison of the newborn to a hand bitten off by a shark, now moving independently of her commands, or to a chicken with its head cut off. Fear is also a constant theme; for example, she has qualms about following old traditions too closely or limiting the freedom of her offspring too strictly. The last section is dominated by poems about a love that no longer exists, about forgetting—or trying to forget—old habits and sorrows, and about replacing dreams with harsh reality. Marçal begins one poem, "El teu desig engendrà el meu desig" (Your desire engendered my desire), and concludes it by turning the tables: "i el meu desig es menja el teu desig" (and my desire devours your desire) (91).

BOOKS
Bruixa de dol. Barcelona: Mall, 1979.
Cau de llunes. Barcelona: Aymà, 1977.

216

La germana, l'estrangera. Barcelona: Mall, 1985.
Llengua abolida (1973–1988). Valencia: Eliseu Climent, 1989.
Sal oberta. Barcelona: Mall, 1982.
Terra de mai. Valencia: El Cingle, 1982.

TRANSLATIONS OF HER WORKS
"Motto" ["Divisa"], "On a Painting by Frida Kahlo" ["Sobre una pintura de Frida Kahlo"], and untitled poems. *Survivors.* Selected. and trans. D. Sam Abrams. Barcelona: Inst. d'Estudis Nord-Americans, 1991. 101–13.
"Witch in Mourning" (selections from *Bruixa de dol*). Trans. Kathleen McNerney. *Catalan Review* 1.2 (1986): 180–81.
"Witch in Mourning" (selections from *Bruixa de dol*). Trans. Kathleen McNerney. *Seneca Review* 16.1 (1986): 45–48.

KATHLEEN MCNERNEY

C Maresma Matas, Assumpció
(B. 1956, Arenys de Mar– .) Journalist and novelist.

Assumpció Maresma Matas won the Avui prize for journalism in 1986 and has worked on publicity for the Barcelona Film Festival. *El complot dels anells* (The conspiracy of the rings) is a novel based on a film of the same name directed by Francesc Bellmunt and written by Ferran Torrent and Bellmunt. A spy story about Catalan politics and the 1992 Olympic Games, its protagonists are an American journalist, a Catalan activist, and a wishy-washy politician, who form an amorous triangle.

BOOKS
El complot dels anells. Barcelona: Magrana, 1988.

KATHLEEN MCNERNEY

C Margarit i Tayà, Remei
(B. 1935, Sitges, Barcelona– .) Folksinger and poet.

De la soledat i el desig (From solitude and desire) is a collection of Remei Margarit's songs and poems about love. The book features an opening epigraph by Pedro Salinas and a closing one by Miguel Hernández.

BOOKS
De la soledat i el desig. Introd. Isidre Molas. Barcelona: Edicions 62, 1988.

KATHLEEN MCNERNEY

C   Margenat, Assumpta
(B. 1953, Santa Eulàlia de Ronçana, Barcelona– .) Novelist.

Assumpta Margenat's *Escapa't a Andorra* (Escape to Andorra) is a detective novel with a female protagonist.

BOOKS
Escapa't a Andorra. Barcelona: Magrana, 1989.

TRANSLATIONS OF HER WORKS
Wild Card [Escapa't a Andorra]. Trans. Sheila McIntosh. Seattle: Women in Translation, 1992.

KATHLEEN MCNERNEY

G   Mariño Carou, María
(B. 1918, Noia, Coruña; d. 1967, Parada do Caurel, Lugo.) Poet.

After spending her childhood in the seaside village of Noia, María Mariño left for Santiago and then Coruña. During the Civil War she stayed in Algorta, in the Basque country, where she had been visiting her sister when war broke out. When the war ended in 1939, Mariño returned to Galicia with her parents and married a primary school teacher. She accompanied him on his continuous transfers around Galicia and the Basque country. In 1947, the couple settled in the school of Parada do Caurel, in the mountains of Lugo, where she was to spend the last years of her life and whose landscape was to form part of her poetic identity. Mariño started writing at the age of thirty-nine, ten years after arriving in the solitary spot. In Caurel, she met the poet Uxío Novoneyra, who became a close friend and whose poetry served as a model for her. Novoneyra, who grew to be an enthusiastic admirer of Mariño's poetry, encouraged the publication of her works, and, in 1963, her first book, *Palabra no tempo* (Word in time), appeared. When she died after a long illness, she left another book, *Verba que comenza* (Beginning word).

Palabra no tempo presents Mariño's experiences in relation to the Galician rural landscape, from the Lugo mountainside to the Coruña rivers. It is a landscape in chiaroscuro that includes elements from her private life: bells, bridges, houses. Nature masks the lyrical "I" as the author identifies herself with it. Her transitory "I," when faced with the afterlife, asks about her own identity and the reality of life in close fusion with the cosmos: "Son a chuvia, son a neve, son o vento da xeada. / Son alba daquel vivir, / hoxe noite daquel sentir" (I'm rain, snow, freezing wind. / I'm the dawn of life, / today the night of feeling). The poet apostrophizes death, whom she calls "friend," and asks where it is taking "uno por uno a cada ser" (every being, one by one) (54).

218

One of the outstanding features of Mariño's poetry is the wordplay in which she distorts the language for sound effects: alliteration, anaphoras, reduplication, and so on. In *Verba que comenza*, nature once more masks the poetic self. It appears even more clearly in the loneliness shown by the author, tormented by the idea of dying. In the poems written shortly before her death, María Mariño holds on to nature in the wish to blend in with its elements and thus remain there forever. Today and yesterday, like the seasons, are used to question her own reality.

In Uxío Novoneyra's opinion, "María Mariño es el primer poeta místico de Galicia, una mística sin dogma actual con todo el agonismo del hombre de hoy y todo el patetismo que da la inminencia de la propia muerte fundamentalmente cuando ésta es prematura" (María Mariño is Galicia's first mystical poet, a mysticism without dogma, belonging to today like all the agony of the man of today and all the pathos that the imminence of one's own death can bring, especially when it is premature).

BOOKS
Palabra no tempo. Lugo: Celta, 1963.
Verba que comenza. Noia, Coruña: Concello, 1990.

WORKS IN BOOKS, PERIODICALS, NEWSPAPERS
"Eu non sei quen manda hoxe que fixo de min," "Sempre verba do chan máis fondo," and "Néboa longa en día rabelo vertía no sol." *Dorna* May 1982.

SECONDARY SOURCES
Blanco, Carmen. "A figura e a obra de María Mariño Carou." *Literatura galega da muller*. Vigo: Xerais, 1991. 231–74.
———. "A figura literaria de María Mariño Carou." *Boletín galego de literatura* 2 (Nov. 1989): 41–57.
Cacheiro, *Poetisas galegas do século XX*.
Equipo Reseña. *La cultura española durante el franquismo*. Bilbao: Mensajero, 1977.
Fernández del Riego, F. *Historia da literatura galega*. Vigo: Galaxia, 1971. 278.
Fole, Anxel. "Memoria de María Mariño." *El progreso* May 1967.
Novoneyra, Uxío. "Maria Mariño Carou, noiesa do Courel, dinamiteira da fala." *A nosa terra* 17 May 1982: 189–90.

MARIA CAMINO NOIA CAMPOS

C Martí, Ferranda
(B. 1962, Catarroja, València– .) Poet.

With degrees in geography and history, Ferranda Martí is on the editing staff of the magazine *Afers*. As a poet she has had her work published in *Reduccions* of Vic and *Daina* of Valencia.

WORKS IN BOOKS, PERIODICALS, NEWSPAPERS
Poems, untitled. *Daina* 4 (Jan. 1988): 93–95.
Poems, untitled. *Reduccions* 33 (Mar. 1987): 28–29.

ISABEL ROBLES GOMEZ

C Martínez Civera, Empar Beatriu

(B. 1914, València– .) Also known as Beatriu Civera. Novelist
and biographer.

Empar Beatriu Civera worked for the newspaper *La voz valenciana* during
the Spanish Civil War. Afterward, encouraged by a group of intellectuals
who were her friends, she adopted Catalan as her literary language and
worked to fill the void that existed in postwar Valencian narrative. Civera
has published biographies of the musician Joan B. Cavanilles, the scholar
Gregori Mayans i Ciscar, and the painter Vicent López. She has also written three novels and two collections of short stories. One of these novels,
"La crida indefugible" (The inevitable cry), which obtained the Joan Senet
prize of Valencia in 1969, remains unpublished.

Entre el cel i la terra (Between sky and earth), a realistic novel, portrays
the lives of women from the Valencian bourgeoisie who do charity work
and, with their false religiosity, contribute to the further marginalization
of women from the dispossessed social groups. Penetrating the processes
of human degradation, Civera denounces this double marginalization
based on class and gender. Civera also reflects on the existential poverty
of those women of the upper classes, who are no more than an appendix
to their husbands and who lead unsatisfied lives. *Una dona com una altra*
(A woman like any other) again contrasts the classes; but here Civera
adopts a plot from the romantic novel and recounts the material and sentimental experiences of the protagonist, a modest director of a high-fashion
dressmaker's establishment, who seeks the love of an aristocrat. The book
is written in the style of early nineteenth-century works; in the prologue
to *Vides alienes* (Alien lives), Vicenç Riera Llorca says that it seems to be
"desfigurada per influències literàries de les quals no havia sabut encara
alliberar-se" (disfigured by literary influences it has not yet figured out
how to free itself from) (7). But always evident in Civera's writing are
her skill and care in the use of language, often culled from its Valencian
variations.

In *Vides alienes*, a collection of short stories, the author creates realistic
characters who are marginalized by society—nonconformists and people
desiring change. They include an ex-con, a teacher of modest origins, a
woman who sacrifices marriage for the material welfare of her family,
students and workers wanting justice and freedom, a mature woman who

wants to live her own life, and a journalist who refuses to renounce his ideals. With these stories, which were preceded by many others published in *Nostres faulelles*, Beatriu Civera won the Víctor Català prize for 1974, the first important Catalan prize awarded to a Valencian author since Ernest Martínez Ferrando received the Joan Creixells in 1935.

Confidencial (Confidential) reiterates previously mentioned themes: marginalization, rebellion, the search for authenticity, and lack of communication. Indeed, in this collection six of the eight stories feature a woman as the main character. These women speak of jealousy and insecurity, of frustration in love, of the transformation of ingenuousness and purity into hatred as a result of social prejudice, of rebellion against their husbands' egocentrism, and of women's emancipation. This concentration of women's voices led Jaume Pérez Montaner to say in the prologue that Beatriu Civera is "l'escriptora que, potser intuïtivament va encetar entre nosaltres el tema de la dona" (the writer who, perhaps intuitively, first introduced the theme of the woman among us) (16).

BOOKS
Confidencial. Prol. Jaume Pérez Montaner. Valencia: Gregal, 1986.
Una dona com una altra. Prol. Manuel Sanchis Guarner. Valencia: Sicània, 1961.
Entre el cel i la terra. Prol. Antoni Igual. Valencia: Sicània, 1956.
Vides alienes. Prol. Vicenç Riera Llorca. Barcelona: Selecta, 1975.

WORKS IN BOOKS, PERIODICALS, NEWSPAPERS
"L'encís de cel.luloide." *Nostres faulelles* 1 (1961): 17–32.
"Fantasies." *Nostres faulelles* 4 (1961): 29–41.
"Un pobre home." *El pont* 18 (1960): 45–52.
"El rossinyol i el teuladi." *Nostres faulelles* 3 (1961): 23–35.
"El secret del secreter." *Lletres de canvi* 3 (May 1980): 19–25.
"El senyor Octavi." *Nostres faulelles* 13 (1964): 17–28.
"Simonet el revolucionari." *Nostres faulelles* 12 (1964): 33–42.
"Tan sols una mentida." *Nostres faulelles* 6 (1961): 7–17.

ISABEL ROBLES GOMEZ

C Martínez i Pastor, Esther
(20th c.) Poet. No biographical information available.

Esther Martínez y Pastor is a member of the group Poesia Viva.

BOOKS
Sol de capvespre. Barcelona: Poesia Viva, 1982.
La virtut original. Barcelona: Poesia Viva, 1986.

KATHLEEN MCNERNEY

C Martínez i Vendrell, Maria

(B. 1940, Barcelona– .) Writer of children's literature and educational material.

With a degree in psychology and education from the University of Barcelona, Maria Martínez i Vendrell works with teachers outside of the school. She is concerned particularly with the effect of the first year of school on a child's life and has contributed preschool material to the collection *Pensament i llenguatge* (Thought and language). In 1986 she undertook an interview project with Angeleta Ferrer, the daughter of Rosa Sensat; the result of these conversations is the book *Angeleta Ferrer: Maria Martínez*.

Martínez's stories for small children deal with a child's daily problems, such as fear of the dark, jealousy over a new baby in the house, and dread of going to the doctor. Written in a calm tone, the works minimize the drama of disturbing situations. Some of the stories are illustrated by Carme Solé. In 1983 Martínez won the Apel.les Mestres prize for the book *Jo les volia* (I wanted them), which tells about the death of a woman from the point of view of her seven-year-old daughter.

BOOKS

Angeleta Ferrer: Maria Martínez. Barcelona: Laia/Ayuntamiento de Barcelona, 1986.
Bon dia escola: Fitxes de treball. With Carme Solé i Vendrell. 3 vols. *Pensament i llenguatge.* Barcelona: Casals, 1986–87.
Els conflicts de l'Anna. Barcelona: Destino, 1988.
Jo les volia. Barcelona: Destinó, 1984.
La nit. Barcelona: Destino, 1986.
Plorar i riure. Barcelona: Destino, 1986.
Quin mal! Barcelona: Destino, 1986.
Un de més. Barcelona: Destino, 1986.
El vermell inoportú. Barcelona: Destino, 1986

ANNA GASOL I TRULLOLS

C Martín i Martorell, Maria

(20th c.) Poet. No biographical information available.

BOOKS
A vegades. Palma: n.p., 1982.

KATHLEEN MCNERNEY

C Mas, Hermínia

(B. 1960, Caserres, Barcelona– .) Poet.

With a degree in Catalan philology, Hermínia Mas teaches Catalan to adults in Barcelona and Berga. Her only available work is "Retalls de foc"

(Bits of fire), published in *Sis Poetes 83* (Six poets of 1983). For the most part it features poems about love, both past and present. The title poem is a technically difficult sonnet of strangely juxtaposed images.

WORKS IN BOOKS, PERIODICALS, NEWSPAPERS
"Retalls de foc." *Sis Poetes 83*. Col.lecció Impermeable. Barcelona: Mall, 1983. 25–37.

KATHLEEN MCNERNEY

C Masdeu i Abril, Josefina
(B. 1958, Reus, Tarragona– .) Short story writer. No biographical information available.

Josefina Masdeu i Abril's narratives have appeared in successive volumes of the *Mostra de narrativa reusenca* (Narrative writing in Reus).

WORKS IN BOOKS, PERIODICALS, NEWSPAPERS
Short stories, untitled. *Mostra de narrativa reusenca* 1 (1980); 3 (1982); and 4 (1984).

GUILLEM-JORDI GRAELLS

C Masip i Biosca, Magdalena
(B. 1897, Barcelona; d. 1972, Puigcerdà.) Poet.

Magdalena Masip i Biosca married Tomàs Torrent Orri, from Olot, and the couple moved to Puigcerdà, where she opened a notions shop. Both of her collections of poetry were published posthumously. *Retrunys interns* (Inner rumblings) was gathered by an anonymous group of people who also wrote the prologue. Something of an ecologist *avant la lettre*, Masip focuses on nature, and a few poems are religious. Her style is clear and straightforward. *Des de Cerdanya* (From Cerdanya) shows her love for her adopted home in the Pyrenees; it begins with a poem for each month and closes with several Christmas poems written over the years.

BOOKS
Des de Cerdanya. Prol. Esteve Albert and Bertranorida. Forewords by Francesc Cabana and Rafael M. Bofill. Illus. Marisol Punsola i Ginesta. Puigcerdà, Lleida: Inst. d'Estudis Ceretans, 1985.
Retrunys interns. Olot, Girona: Aubert, 1976.

KATHLEEN MCNERNEY

223

C Masllorens, Martha
(B. 1949, Barcelona– .) Poet.

Martha Masllorens's second volume of poetry, *Sirena de sofre* (Sulphur mermaid), is dedicated to Miquel Martí i Pol, and the four sections bear dedications to and citations of other Catalan poets. The first section, opening with lines by Martí i Pol, speaks of solitude and remembrances of past happiness. The second, quoting Feliu Formosa, is inspired by music; specific pieces by Mozart, Debussy, Mahler, Vivaldi, Albinoni, Tchaikovsky, and Holst suggest themes and cadences of the poems. Salvador Espriu's patriotism and nostalgia for the land informs the third section. The fourth begins with a line by Maria-Mercè Marçal and contains the title poem, which ends "Et saps embarassada, / Sirena, d'idees, / que no saps com pair" (You know you're pregnant / with ideas, Mermaid, / that you don't know how to give birth to).

BOOKS
El llarg estiu. Bibliophile edition, 1983.
Sirena de sofre. Prol. Ramon Folch. Barcelona: Laertes, 1984.

KATHLEEN MCNERNEY

C Masoliver, Liberata
(B. 1911, Sabadell, Barcelona– .) Novelist.

Author of a remarkable number of novels in Castilian, many of them based on the Spanish Civil War, Liberata Masoliver produced only one work in Catalan, *La bruixa* (The witch). According to the information given by the author, she wrote the book, financing the edition herself, as a homage to the illustrator Gloria Serra, who was terminally ill and wanted to see the book published before her death. In Carolyn L. Galerstein and Kathleen McNerney's *Women Writers of Spain*, *La bruixa* is described as "a modern fairy tale for children written in Catalan verse." Two children are carried off by the witch Pirulina and have many adventures with her until they return to their parents.

BOOKS
La bruixa. Illus. Gloria Serra. Barcelona: Jaimes Libros, 1961.

SECONDARY SOURCES
Galerstein and McNerney, *Women Writers of Spain* 200.

CRISTINA ENRIQUEZ DE SALAMANCA

C Masó Maristany, Angels
(20th c.) Journalist and novelist. No biographical information available.

BOOKS
La muerte de papá Noel. Barcelona: Planeta, 1986.

KATHLEEN MCNERNEY

C Maspons i Labrós, Maria del Pilar
(B. 1841, Barcelona; d. 1907, Barcelona.) Known as Maria de Bell-Lloch. Poet, folklorist, and novelist.

Because of her family background and her social position, Maria del Pilar Maspons was part of Barcelona's literary *Renaixença* and one of its most productive contributors. Sister of the well-known folklorist Francesc Maspons, she married the writer Francesc Pelai Briz, editor of the periodical *Lo Gay Saber* and juror of the Jocs Florals of Barcelona. Her poems are written in a simple language, full of references to themes and places beloved by *Renaixença* writers. She won prizes in many poetry contests, including the 1875 Joc Florals and the 1880 Academia Bibliográfica Mariana of Lleida. She gathered and wrote down many popular legends and published collections of them, such as *Elisabeth de Mur* (1880), *Llegendas catalanas* (Catalan legends), and *Montseny*.

Vigatans i botiflers (The boys from Vic) is a historical novel set during the eighteenth-century War of Succession in Catalonia. The title refers to the nicknames given to the supporters of the German and French candidates to the Spanish crown, and through the adventures of two heroines the novel relates the loss of Catalan autonomy. The author demonstrates her knowledge of local life and the environment and her love for the traditions and customs of the rural property owners and farmers. Maspons also contributed to the Catalan periodicals *La renaixença, Lo Gay Saber, La il.lustració catalana, La veu de Montserrat,* and *La veu de Catalunya.*

BOOKS
Elisabeth de Mur. Barcelona: Novel.la Catalana, 1924.
Llegendas catalanas. Barcelona: Tipografia Espanyola, 1881.
Montseny. Barcelona: Biblioteca de la Tomasa, 1890.
Salabrugas: Poesias catalanas. Barcelona: La Renaixença, 1874.
Vigatans i botiflers. Barcelona: Joan Roca, 1878. 2nd ed. Barcelona: Curial, 1986.

CRISTINA ENRIQUEZ DE SALAMANCA

C   Mas Pujol, Margalida Baneta

(B. 1649, Valldemossa, Mallorca; d. 1700, Valldemossa, Mallorca.) Known as Sor Anna Maria del Santissim Sagrament. Diarist and religious writer.

Margalida Mas Pujol was the daughter of a well-to-do, well-known rural family in Majorca, according to Dr. Gabriel Mesquida. Her paternal grandfather, the rector of the village, and the hermits in Valldemossa, sparked Margalida's interest in rigorous asceticism. The founding of the Dominican monastery of Santa Catalina in Palma between 1650 and 1659 aroused a religious vocation in many Majorcan girls. "Fonch occasió," according to Mesquida, "que Margalida . . . volia ésser religiosa del nou convent" (It was the occasion that . . . caused Margalida to become a nun in the new convent) (9: 68). However, she had to wait until 1677 before the nuns would accept her.

The first years in the convent for Sister Anna Maria went by monotonously, but when Mesquida was appointed father confessor, her life in the monastery changed completely. In 1678 she was named head novice and in the same year began her commentary on the *Libre d'amic e amat* (Book of friend and loved one), by Ramon Llull, using Joan Bonllaví's 1521 edition of Llull's *Blanquerna*. This edition was flawed and its version of the *Libre d'amic e amat* included a number of apocryphal verses. Sister Anna's *L'exposició de los cantichs del . . . B. Ramon Llull* (Exposition of the canticles of Ramon Llull), which contains a general introduction and a commentary on the first ninety-four verses, was begun in 1687 and was completed in 1691.

Considered linguistically, Sister Anna's work reflects three main characteristics: a style typical of the time when Castilianisms were freely mixed with the purest forms of Majorcan Catalan; a conservative attitude regarding the spelling of words of Latin appearance; and the use of dialect and colloquial forms and a hesitation over spelling and grammar. The literary style is "natural, sencillo, apacible y algunas veces declina en humilde" (natural, simple, even-tempered and at times humble), according to P. Antoni Reynés in his introduction to Sister Anna's *Exposición de los cánticos de Amor* (1: 46). Sister Anna's writings in *L'exposició* provide personal impressions about the love of God and a subjective interpretation of the *Libre d'amic e amat*, often drawing on biblical quotations from the nuns' prayerbook. The book is an intimate diary of her spirituality.

Tomás and Joaquim Carreras Artau said with respect to the *Libre d'amic e amat* that the historian of philosophy has the responsibility of correcting "l'arbitrarietat de les exposicions" (the arbitrariness of expositions) (1: 588), such as those of Sister Anna. But the nun from Valldemossa did not intend to write a philosophical commentary or theological exegesis, something that, she affirmed, "dexaré per les escoles" (I'll leave to the acolytes) (*Càntics i cobles* 84). She considered Llull's book a collection of brief examples and parables, which, because they included such high science, needed an explication to be understood. Consequently, Sister Anna worked out a semantics that, based on spiritual experience, permitted her to see through Llullian theory to contemplation and charity.

The core of the theory, according to Sister Anna, is the question "Què cosa es Déu?" (What is God?). The answer constitutes the art of knowledge that formulates "l'escola i l'art de contemplació que ofereix l'oració" (the school and the art of contemplation offered by prayer). Sister Anna makes the first argument and lesson brief, because there is so much material to cover. For her, prayer, which consists of "pensar i considerar si podem obrar tots en el servei del Senyor" (thinking and considering if we can all work in God's service), must be long. Therefore, by its nature it includes duties and responsibilities. In this sense devotion is "un cuydado que tenia lo Amich de estar molt prompta per cumplir totas las suas obligacions" (the care which the Friend must take to be prompt in fulfilling all his obligations). This concept of devotion distances Sister Anna from the radical quietism of the time and places her closer to the Spanish mystical tradition. While prayer supposes a heightened understanding of divine contemplation, union with God means giving less attention to other people. However, for Sister Anna, the religious life is a two-way street: devotion to God and to the people around her. In a kind of sociological mysticism, she desires welfare and peace for everyone, to make of "la terra un paradís . . . un cel" (the earth a paradise . . . a heaven) (*Càntics i cobles* 19, 142, 133, 123, 129).

Between 1693 and 1700, Sister Anna wrote letters on spiritual themes and problems of conscience to P. Josep Andreu, a Carthusian from Valldemossa. Unfortunately, they have been lost.

BOOKS
Càntics i cobles. Ed. Sebastià Trias Mercant. Mallorca: Moll, 1988.
Exposició de los cantichs del D. Illm y Martir de Christo el B. Ramon Llull. Original ms. in the Archive of the Bishopric of Majorca. (Incomplete copies exist in the library of the Col.legi de la Sapiència and the public library of Majorca.)
Exposición de los cánticos de Amor compuestos por . . . el B. Raymundo Lulio . . . dada . . . por la Ven. Madre Sor Ana Maria. . . . 2 vols. Selected and ed. Protectors de la Causa Pia Lul.liana. Introd. P. Antoni Reynés. Mallorca: Oficina de Ignacio Frau Impresor del Rey, 1760.

SECONDARY SOURCES
Carreras Artau, Tomás, and Joaquim Carreras Artau. *Historia de la filosofia española*. 2 vols. Madrid: Real Academia de Ciencias Exactas, 1939–43.
Guasp, Bartomeu. "Notas sobre Sor Ana." *La cartuja de Jesús Nazareno y los*

ermitaños mallorquines, 1646–1835. Palma: Politècnica, 1948. 56–57, 68, 98–101.

Mesquida, Gabriel. "Vida de Sor Anna Maria del Santissim Sagrament escrita pel Dr. . . . de l'any 1690 al 92." Ed. Jaume Garau. *Boletin Sociedad Arqueológica Luliana* 9 (1901–02): 56, 68, 126, 137, 153, 229, 281, 356 and 10 (1903): 37, 112, 152, 171.

Rogent, Elies, and Estanislau Duran. "Anna Maria del Santissim Sagrament: Llibre de càntichs expositats del Beato Ramon Llull." *Bibliografia de les impressions Lul.lianes.* Barcelona: Inst. d'Estudis Catalans, 1927. 348–51.

Trias Mercant. "La mística quietista: Sor Anna Maria del Santissim Sagrament i Fra Pere Fullana." Trias Mercant 172–81.

———. "Un nuevo manuscrito del P. Raymundo Pasqual." *Estudios Lulianos* 78: 77–84.

Vallespir, Lorenzo. *Vida de Sor Aina Maria del Santissimo Sacramento.* Mallorca: n.p., 1741.

SEBASTIA TRIAS MERCANT

C Massana i Mola, Maria
(20th c.) Fiction writer. No biographical information available.

BOOKS
Un amor diferent. Mataró, Barcelona: n.p., 1982.

KATHLEEN MCNERNEY

C Massanés i Dalmau, Maria Josefa
(B. 1811, Tarragona; d. 1887, Barcelona.) Poet.

Josefa Massanés is a writer who stands out because of her dual commitment to art and politics. On the one hand, she devoted herself to the renewal of Catalan culture and letters, and, on the other hand, she became the intellectual leader among Catalan women writers of the second half of the century. Massanés and the writers Victòria Penya, Agnès Armengol, Dolors Monserdà, Agna de Valldaura, Manuela Herreros, Margarida Caimarí, and Maria de Bell-Lloch formed a group of Catalan women intellectuals who were among the earliest to grasp the banners of the *Renaixença* and whose studies contributed to the rebirth of Catalan literature. In pursuit of this task they found both a social and an ideological justification for their work.

Born during the War of Independence, Massanés lost her mother at the age of four and was entrusted to the care of her paternal grandparents. Her father, José Massanés Mestres, a soldier and an architect, collaborated on defense plans, public works, and pioneering projects for city planning, which were precursors of modern urban renewal and, in particular, of Ildefonso Cerdà's work in Barcelona. But because of the political upheaval of the time and the continual setbacks he suffered as a liberal officer in a conservative corps, José Massanés emigrated to France. The ensuing financial hardships for his family in Spain meant that his daughter had to take in sewing, work for which women were traditionally exploited during Catalan industrialization. The details of Josefa Massanés's life during this period sometimes appear in her poetry.

Massanés received a sound basic education that she further developed on her own. From her personal papers, we know that she was fluent in both French and Italian. She also studied Latin, and her biblical poems reveal more than a passing acquaintance with the Bible. A woman of great intellectual acuity, she was highly disciplined in her work. These facts are reflected in the carefully produced edition of her works in Castilian and in the bibliographical references accompanying her poems. At thirty-two years of age, she married Fernando González de Ortega, a military man. Because of his many transfers, they lived in Madrid as well as in various places in Catalonia before finally settling down in Barcelona. Their marriage was childless, but they subsequently adopted nieces and nephews.

Beginning in 1837 Josefa Massanés became involved in literary projects that led to her participation in numerous social and literary circles and also to the publication of her poems in Barcelona magazines such as *El vapor, La guardia nacional,* and *La religión.* She exemplified Catalan Romanticism, which resembled French Romanticism and included the works of Pau Piferrer, Víctor Balaguer, Joan Cortada, Josep Coll i Vehí, and Manuel de Cabanyes. Carolina Coronado describes Massanés as the first among Spanish women poets.

Massanés's Castilian poetry is published in two volumes: *Poesías* (Poetry) and *Flores marchitas* (Wilted flowers). These gained literary renown for her within and outside Catalonia, although her fame had begun earlier with "El beso maternal" (The maternal kiss), a poem included in books officially approved for little girls and a work translated into English. Her Castilian poetry is a blend of the brilliant and the prosaic. She moves from a sentimental tone to an exaltation of "masculine" images such as violence, warlike symbols, and even morbidly cruel expressions. Motherhood also plays a major role, especially in "Cantos bíblicos" (Bible songs), one of the most original and attractive examples of her poetry.

From the 1850s onward Massanés wrote in Catalan. Her name appears, with that of Isabel de Villamartín, in the first two collections of

Catalan poetry, *Los trovadors nous* (New troubadors) and *Los trovadors moderns* (The modern troubadors). In 1862 Massanés was crowned queen of the Jocs Florals in Barcelona, and in 1864 she received a prize for her poem "Creure es viure" (To believe is to live). Some of her Catalan poetry was collected in *Respirall. Col.lecció de poesies catalanes titulada 'Darreras guspires'* (Sigh. Collection of Catalan poetry called 'Last sparks'), which is also included in the anthology *Rimas* (Rhymes). A planned collection, "Cuadros de costums catalanas," never reached publication, but *Poesies de Maria Josefa Massanés* (The poetry of Maria Josefa Massanés), edited by Francesc Matheu, was published posthumously.

Josefa Massanés managed to reconcile two facets of her personality, the woman of letters and the Catalan matron. As the former, she participated in numerous enterprises in Catalan society and wrote occasional poetry, generally at the behest of institutions. Her patriotic spirit combines a fierce nationalism with uncompromising Spanish loyalty. Her Catalan pride surfaces early, and the poem "Catalunya," which opens her first book, *Poesías*, is a long descriptive composition about her homeland. She interweaves her life as a woman of letters with her role as a Catalan matron through her sincere belief in the ideals of the *Renaixença*. Her Catalan poetry reflects the unshakable faith typical of a woman of her class, whose serenity is challenged by secular social movements that threaten the religious foundation of society. Her work also reflects a longing for a past seemingly free of religious doubts. In "Les dones catalanes" (Catalan women) she upholds the myth created by the Catalan bourgeoisie that woman is the vehicle for transmitting Catalan language and culture. "La roja barretina catalana" (The red Catalan cap), written on the return of Catalan volunteers from the African War in 1860, made the author a national celebrity and the "barretina," the red cloth cap worn by the peasants, a symbol of Catalonia. A more personal tone is used in "Mon darrer viatge" (My last voyage), a Machado-like premonition of death: "Tinch de fer un llarg viatge / a ignotes regions estenses, / mes no sé quan de partir / serà lo temps y hora certa / ni com ni per hont s'hi va, / ni'l pervindre que n'hi espera" (I must take a long trip / to vast unknown lands / but I do not know the time / the exact moment of departure / nor how nor where to go / nor what awaits me there) (*Poesies* 148).

Massanés spent the last years of her life in isolation. Her close friend Dolors Monserdà successfully lobbied to include her in the Gallery of Illustrious Catalans in the Barcelona City Hall.

BOOKS

Flores marchitas. Nueva colección de poesías. Barcelona: A. Brusi, 1851.

Importancia de la perfecció dels brodats. Barcelona: La Renaixença, 1881.

María Josepa Massanés. Antología poética. Ed. Ricardo Navas Ruiz. Madrid: Castalia, 1991.

Poesías. Barcelona: J. Rubió, 1841.
Poesies de Maria Josefa Massanés. Ed. Francesc Matheu. Prol. Dolors Monserdà. Barcelona: Ilustració Catalana, 1908.
Respirall. Col.lecció de poesies catalanes titulada 'Darreras Guspires.' Barcelona: Estampa Peninsular, 1879.
Rimas. Barcelona: Joan Roca y Bros, 1879.

WORKS IN BOOKS, PERIODICALS, NEWSPAPERS
"Agrahiment." *Calendari català* (1882): 33–34.
"¿Ahont van?" *Calendari català* (1878): 124–27.
"A la Reina del Cel." *Academia bibliográfica Mariana de Lérida.* 1878. 107–10.
"A la Reyna del Cel." *Calendari català* (1880): 107–08.
"Allí dalt." *Calendari català* (1877): 117–19.
"Als emigrants que la cobdicia porta á la America del sur." *La renaixença* Year 10, 1.5 (15 Mar. 1880): 225–26.
"Als meus estimats fillets adoptius. La flor del cel." *Los trovadors nous* 62–68.
"Amor," "Ana ruega al Señor le conceda un hijo," and "La mujer." *Antología poética de escritoras del siglo XIX.* Ed. Susan Kirkpatrick. Madrid: Castalia, 1992. 185–96.
"Los àngels de la terra. Coneguts baix lo nom humil de Germanas de la Caritat." *Calendari català* (1875): 84–86.
"Los annals del poble. Imitació del poeta polaco Makiewiez." *Calendari català* (1867): 86–88.
"Castas espinas." *Calendari català* (1868): 117–18.
"La comarca ampurdanesa." *Calendari català* (1869): 86–87.
"Consideracions sobre la instrucció de la dona." *Lo Gay Saber* 14 (1879): 77–91.
"Consideracions sobre la instrucció de la dona." *Lo Gay Saber* 15 (1879): 188–91.
"Lo consol en la adversitat." *Lo Gay Saber* 24 (1879): 317.
"Les dones catalanas" and "La creu del terme." *Los trovadors moderns* 289–305.
"La flor del cel. Fragment." *Calendari català* (1865): 101–03.
"La patria. Poesia original de'n Ventura Ruiz." *Lo Gay Saber* 12 (1880): 141–44.
"Lo postrer consol." *Lo rat penat* 1880: 17–22.
"Lo postrer consol." *Los trovadors nous* 412–17.
"Quadro de costums catalanas. La batuda de las olivas en lo Ampurda." *Lo Gay Saber* 1 (1879): 4.

TRANSLATIONS OF HER WORKS
"Keusche Dornen" ["Castas espinas"] and "Die rothe catalanische Mutze" ["La roja barretina catalana"]. Fastenrath 252–56.

SECONDARY SOURCES
Coronado, Carolina. "Galería de poetisas." *La discusión* 1 May 1857.
Gras i Elias, Francisco. "Na Maria Josefa Massanés de González." *Siluetes d'escriptors catalans.* Second Series. Barcelona: L'Avenç, 1909. 17–33.
Mané i Flaquer, Juan. "*Flores marchitas*, nueva colección de poesias de Doña Josefa Massanés de González." *Diari de Barcelona.* Vol 1. 1851. 625–29.
Monserdà de Macià, Dolors. *Biografia de Na Mª Josepa Massanés i Dalmau en l'acte de col.locar en la Galeria de Catalans Il.lustres de la Casa de la Ciutat*

el retrat d'aquella celebrada poetessa i llegida per D. F. Puig i Alfonso, regidor de Barcelona en Sessió pública celebrada el dia 26 de juny de l'any 1915. Barcelona: P. de la Caritat, n.d.

Navas Ruiz, Ricardo. "Discurso feminista y voz femenina: Las *Poesías* de María Josepa Massanés." *Escritoras románticas españolas.* Ed. Marina Mayoral. Madrid: Fundación Banco Exterior, 1990. 177–95.

———. Introducción. *María Josepa Massanés. Antología poética.* Ed. Navas Ruiz. Madrid: Castalia, 1991. 7–63.

Quadrado, José Maria. "Poesías de Doña Josefa Massanés." *Almacén de frutos literarios.* Vol 1. Palma de Mallorca, 1841. 133–39.

Simón Palmer, *Escritoras españolas del siglo XIX* 427–31.

Vilarrubias, Felio A. *Noticia de una colección de papeles de José Massanés y Mestres (1777–1857) y Josefa Massanés de González (1811–1887) existentes en la sección de manuscritos.* Barcelona: Diputación Provincial de Barcelona, 1966.

CRISTINA ENRIQUEZ DE SALAMANCA

C Massip, Laura
(B. 1920?, Barcelona– .) Novelist.

From a landowning family in the Priorat, Tarragona, Laura Massip became a teacher and moved to Barcelona. Her novel *El cercle* (The circle), winner of the fiction contest Immortal Ciutat de Girona in 1972, is set in the Priorat, a rural mountainous area, at the turn of the century. The dramatic life of a woman teacher, investigated and told by a colleague-narrator after her death, allows the author to describe the difficulties and misery of a small town's residents. The narrative time is marked by the changing seasons. The mountains symbolize the "cercle" that encloses the protagonist's life, while the river Siurana represents escape to a place where her personality can develop. The protagonist has to decide between a stable, secure marriage, and a relationship with a cosmopolitan painter who offers an exciting life. The town's inhabitants, who are malevolent toward the protagonist, form a presence as enclosing as the mountains. The author describes the tensions among the women vying for dominance in the family, a theme that has been used by other women writers, including Antònia Bardolet, in *Siluetes femenines*, Walda Pla, in *Salt d'euga*, and Maria Angels Anglada, in *Les closes*. Massip presents a detailed portrait of the landscapes, customs, and beliefs in the Priorat; the tone becomes elegiac at times.

BOOKS
El cercle. Barcelona: Club, 1973.

CRISTINA ENRIQUEZ DE SALAMANCA

C Massot i Planas, Mercè
(B. 1894, Palma de Mallorca– .) Poet and journalist.

According to *Les cinc branques* Mercè Massot i Planas published two volumes of poetry, *Violetes* (Violets) and *Semprevives* (Everlasting flowers), which are not available in major libraries in Catalonia.

BOOKS
Semprevives. Palma: Alcover, 1959.
Violetes. Palma: Moll, 1945.

WORKS IN BOOKS, PERIODICALS, NEWSPAPERS
"Finestra tancada." *Les cinc branques* 89.

NANCY L. BUNDY

C Mata i Garriga, Marta
(B. 1926, Barcelona– .) Writer of educational materials and children's literature.

The daughter of Angels Garriga, Marta Mata has been an active educator throughout her life. She attended primary school at the Institut-Escola del Parc de la Ciutadella of Barcelona, where she remained until the end of the Civil War. After a long illness interrupted her studies in biology, she took a degree in education and obtained a position on the teaching staff of the Talitha school, working primarily in the library. During this period she also took care of her ailing mother in the small village of Saifores, in the Baix Penedès, where the Mata family had their home. In 1955 Mata and a group of teachers concerned with the state of education created the Escola de Mestres Rosa Sensat in Barcelona. Outstanding among their organizations is the Escola d'Estiu, which in its early years had the teachers Pau Vila, Artur Martorell, and Alexandre Gala on its advisory board. Since 1980 Rosa Sensat has been an association of teachers, and Mata, although still on the board of directors, is no longer involved professionally. In 1972 she helped set up the Escola Normal de la Universitat Autònoma de Barcelona, where she gave a few classes.

   Within the general field of education Mata has paid particular attention to the teaching of reading and writing. She was coauthor and coordinator of the program *Lletra per lletra* (Letter for letter) and of the book *Quadres de fonologia catalana per a l'ensenyament de la llengua i l'escriptura* (Catalan phonology notebooks for teaching and writing). She has also contributed to and edited collections of children's books for various Catalan publishers. In 1976, along with Assumpció Lisson and Maria Aurèlia Valeri, she organized the Seminari de Bibliografia Infantil, which produced

Quins llibres han de llegir els nens? (What books should children read?), a selective bibliography of new juvenile books. Attentive to the problems of immigrant children, especially in the Barcelona area during the Franco regime, Mata published *L'escola per a l'immigrant* (Schooling for the immigrant).

In addition to preparing essays on education for journals and newspapers, Marta Mata has appeared in numerous round-table discussions and seminars and given courses and conferences on school and education. In 1977 she entered politics to represent educational issues, running for deputy in the parliament of Madrid and of Catalonia. In 1986 she was named director of education for the city of Barcelona.

Her story *El país de les cent paraules* (The land of a hundred words) was adapted for the theater by Núria Tubau. Mata has also done her own adaptations of various popular tales.

BOOKS

L'escola per a l'immigrant. Barcelona: Estela, 1966.
El país de les cent paraules. Barcelona: La Galera, 1981.
Pensem en la nova educació. With Maria Josep Udina. Barcelona: Rosa Sensat, 1984.
Quadres de fonologia catalana per a l'ensenyament de la llengua i l'escriptura. With Josep Maria Cormand. Barcelona: Bibliograf, 1976.

ANNA GASOL I TRULLOLS

C Matheu i Sadó, Maria del Roser
(B. 1892, Barcelona; d. 1987, Barcelona.) Poet, bibliographer, biographer, and editor.

Roser Matheu was the daughter of Francesc Matheu, a figure of the *Renaixença* who organized the Jocs Florals and edited *La ilustració catalana* (Barcelona) and *Lectura popular*, a collection that published the work of many Catalan writers. Her mother, Joaquina Sadó, came from the upper Catalan bourgeoisie and was known as a poet, although she never published any of her work. Roser Matheu studied in Barcelona, completing her education in music, drawing, painting, and crafts. Her intellectual growth took place in one of the best environments possible; she witnessed conflicts between the different political factions and observed the literary dimensions of Catalan nationalism. This experience is reflected in her poetry. The biography she wrote about her father stemmed from the need to clarify certain events for which Francesc Matheu was attacked and to preserve the memory of someone who devoted his life to the rebirth of Catalan literature.

According to the biographical note in her last book, *Roser Matheu. Poesies. Miscel.lània poètica* (Miscellaneous poems), Roser Matheu started writing poetry as a child and won her first prize in the Felip Palma contest celebrated in 1905 in the home of her brother-in-law, the editor Jaume Massó i Torrents. In the same year Matheu wrote for a French teenagers' magazine under the pseudonym Rosier de Catalogne. In 1912 she won a medal in the Festa de Joventut, which was organized by *La ilustració catalana* and celebrated in the Palau de la Música. Throughout her life, she won numerous prizes in the Jocs Florals and other competitions: the Englantina in the Jocs Florals of Sarrià, 1923; the Flor Natural in Barcelona, 1932; the Flor Natural in Girona, 1933; the Souci, in Toulouse; special mention in Lourdes; and a diploma in Perpignan. In 1921, she married Antoni Gallardo i Garriga, an engineer, archaeologist, and composer. She was widowed in 1942 with two children.

Apart from her creative work, Matheu undertook the immensely valuable bibliographical task of preserving and disseminating the work of Catalan women writers. She wrote a detailed biography of Dolors Monserdà, which has been the basis of all later studies of the author. *Quatre dones catalanes* (Four Catalan women), runner-up for the Concepció Alemany i Vall prize, brings together her biographies of Monserdà, the writer Palmíra Jaquetti, the botanist Maria Garriga, and Francesca Bonnemaison, founder of the Institut d'Estudis per a la Dona. Together with Esteve Albert, Octavi Saltor, Antoni Sala-Cornadó, and Maria Assumpció Torras, Matheu edited *Les cinc branques: Poesia femenina catalana* (The five branches: Catalan women's poetry), a bibliographic index and anthology of two hundred Catalan poets, from the anonymous medieval writers to those born in the 1950s. Matheu also wrote the prologue for a volume of poetry by Maria Cardona i Codina, *Una veu Calellenca* (A voice from Calella), and edited the complete works of Dolors Monserdà.

The publication of Roser Matheu's poetic works began in 1933 with the edition of *La carena* (The mountain ridge) and ended in 1982 with *Miscel.lània poètica*. In between she wrote *Cançons de setembre* (September songs), *Poemes a la filla* (Poems to my daughter), and *Poema de la fam* (Poem of hunger). Her work tends toward formal perfection; she uses a great variety of verse forms but generally avoids free verse, and she searches more for precise expression of feeling than for images or brilliant effects. From her first poems, she reveals herself as a poet of technical and personal maturity, whose verses reflect dark spiritual zones. *Poema de la fam* is her most intense work. Her central themes are time; a view of life as something that takes place between two transcendental events, birth and death, over which the human will has no control; a Christian faith that does not avoid the existential questions; an acute and ever-present perception of pain, which modifies all events and feelings; undefined but inevitable desire, which is always unsatisfied; and a vision of humanity torn by its antagonistic tendencies.

In the prologue to *La carena*, Father Miquel d'Esplugues, who professes a feminist faith based on the Christian ideal, declares that "la dona en literatura . . . ha estat subjecta a un mutisme torturant" (the literary woman has been subject to a torturous muteness). In this extensive collection of poems, the few that are dated cover the period 1924 to 1933. One of Matheu's themes is the search for happiness, often denied by society. In beautiful sonnets inspired by Rosalía de Castro, pain is personified as a divine being with whom the author maintains a personal relationship. The poet talks to this divinity in a sometimes guilty tone and expresses the contradictory impulses of the body as it fights with the spirit. In other works, such as "L'abeurador" (The waterer), she is inspired by King David's songs; in "El molí vell" (The old mill) divine action is silently felt upon the passive soul. Other poems feature the conflict between civilization and nature, to which the tortured mind rushes in search of rest. Themes from traditional Catalan poetry appear in "Vespral" (Dusk), "Nocturn," and "D'una muntanya" (Of a mountain). Her most personal moments are found in "Sonets del dolor" (Sonnets of pain) and the "Estances del desig" (Abodes of desire), where she expresses tension between unceasing desire and its inevitable limits. An overflowing expression of love in the Romantic style, a yearning for a love beyond death, characterizes one untitled poem.

Cançons de setembre is a collection of poems dating from 1924 to 1935. "Temple" shows an unshakable faith in a divine omnipresence; but faith presents no obstacle for wanting life's pleasures here and now, in "Plany de setembre" (September complaint), or for considering the mediocrity of existence, in "Humans" (Humans). The poems "L'amada diu" (The beloved says) and "Diu l'amat" (The lover says) reflect the fight between flesh and spirit, between human and divine love. This collection features destructive images of desire (in "Cançó aspra" [Bitter song]), of sexuality (in "Cançó del faune" [Faun's song]), and of existence (in "La petite suite del temps" [The little suite of time]).

In the prologue to *Poema de la fam*, Matheu states that the work was inspired by the Civil War, during which she suffered not only from hunger but from the death of her father. The tone and themes of the collection parallel the coarse realism of the Spanish novel in the postwar era, and she focuses on the emotions and on the personal changes caused by this distress. The poet identifies herself with a dog rummaging in the garbage for food and is excited by the sight of a mere onion. Faith is shaken when one is faced with this kind of misery and the fear of losing one's children, and memories are the only means of escape.

One of the most interesting facets of Roser Matheu's work is her treatment of motherhood, which begins in *La carena* and develops in *Poemes a la filla*. Her poetry is unique in the context of Catalan women's poetry. The maternal sentiment that inspired much *Renaixença* poetry was generally expressed in abstract terms or concentrated on the pain of losing a child. Matheu departs from this tradition and analyzes the relationship that develops during successive stages of a child's growth. She explores her pregnancy, in "La fugida" (The flight); the transformation undergone through the child's development, in "Despertar" (The awakening); the affirmation of motherhood as a permanent female creative force within a destructive culture, in "Els estels" (The stars); the mother's effort to protect the child from fear and pain, in "Serenitat" (Serenity); bewilderment when faced with the inevitable independence of the child, in "Un dia" (One Day); and, in "Regne" (Kingdom), the boundaries to which "the kingdom of women" stretches, where her own daughter is headed in spite of her mother's wishes.

Miscel.lània poètica contains an unsigned biographical note and a list of her unpublished works. When Matheu died in Barcelona in 1987, her death passed completely unnoticed.

BOOKS

Cançons de setembre. La Revista ser. 138. Barcelona: La Revista, 1936.
La carena. Prol. Miquel d'Esplugues. La Revista ser. 119. Barcelona: La Revista, 1933.
Les cinc branques: Poesia femenina catalana. Comp. and arranged by Esteve Albert, Roser Matheu, Octavi Saltor, Antoni Sala-Cornadó, and M. Assumpció Torras. Barcelona: Esteve Albert, 1975.
Les nadales de Mossèn Muntanyola. Monografies de Vila Seca-Salou. Miscel.lània Mossèn Muntanyola Extret 2. Vila Seca-Salou: n.p., 1974.
El nimbe florit. Lecture in homage to Maria Ponsà. Barcelona: Juvenil, 1956.
Notes biogràfiques d'Antoni Gallardo i Garriga. Barcelona: n.p., 1962.
Poema de la fam. Barcelona: Barcino, 1952.
Poemes a la filla. Barcelona: Torrell de Reus, 1949.
Poesies. Vol. 26 of *Lectura popular.*
Quatre dones catalanes. Fundació Salvador Vives Casajuana ser. 18. Barcelona: Fundació Salvador Vives Casajuana, 1973.
Roser Matheu. Poesies. Miscel.lània poètica. Barcelona: Fundació Salvador Vives Casajuana, 1982.
Vida i obra de Francesc Matheu. Fundació Salvador Vives Casajuana ser. 9. Barcelona: Fundació Salvador Vives Casajuana, 1971.

WORKS IN BOOKS, PERIODICALS, NEWSPAPERS
Prologue. *Una veu Calellenca.* By Maria Cardona i Codina. Calella: Ajuntement, 1975.
"Qui va ésser la senyora Monserdà?" *Miscel.lània Barcinonensia* 8.23 (1969): 43–74.

CRISTINA ENRIQUEZ DE SALAMANCA

C   Mathieu Valette, Renée
(B. 1928, Arles, France– .) Also Renada. Translator and writer of children's literature.

Officially a French citizen, Renée Mathieu Valette identified first with the Occitan culture and then with her adopted Catalan culture. She moved to Barcelona when she married in 1955 and studied Catalan culture and language and library science. She has written for and edited various publications in Catalan.

    Quatre sota un pi (Four under a pine tree), inspired by a trip to Menorca, is a collection of stories and essays that has been used as a textbook in schools. Attracted to literature for young children, Mathieu published *El fugitiu de Queragut* (The fugitive of Queragut), which won the Folch i Torres prize in 1975. Most of her work involves the translation and adaptation of stories for youngsters, ranging from La Fontaine's fables to modern French and German stories and tales. Mathieu has also worked as a secretary, an interpreter, and a teacher of Catalan and French. She has published a biography of General Josep Moragues and has contributed to other textbooks.

BOOKS
A la cort del rei Benet. Barcelona: La Galera, 1980.
L'ase que es va beure la lluna. Barcelona: La Galera, 1986.
Les bèsties i la pesta. Barcelona: La Galera, 1984.
Els dos muls. Barcelona: La Galera, 1985.
El fugitiu de Queragut. Barcelona: La Galera, 1976.
Homenatge al General Moragues. Barcelona: Generalitat, 1986.
Quatre sota un pi. Barcelona: Teide, 1971.
El ratolí, el gat i el gall. Barcelona: La Galera, 1987.
Sons i cançons. Barcelona: Joventut, 1988.
Els tres desigs. Barcelona: La Galera, 1980.

TRANSLATIONS OF HER WORKS
Los animales y la peste [*Les bèsties i la pesta*]. Barcelona: La Galera, 1984. Hyspamerica Ediciones Argentinas, 1985.
El asno que se bebió la luna [*L'ase que es va beure la lluna*]. Barcelona: La Galera, 1986.
Los dos mulos [*Els dos muls*]. Barcelona: La Galera, 1985.
En la corte del rei Bals [*A la cort del rei Benet*]. Barcelona: La Galera, 1980.

El fugitivo en el castillo [*El fugitiu de Queragut*]. Barcelona: La Galera, 1976.
El ratín, el gato y el gallo [*El ratolí, el gat i el gall*]. Barcelona: La Galera, 1987.
Los tres deseos [*Els tres desigs*]. Barcelona: La Galera, 1980.

KATHLEEN MCNERNEY

C Maureso i Moragues, Joana
(B. 1902, Soler, France– .) Poet and short story writer.

According to *Les cinc branques* Joana Maureso i Moragues published one book of poems, *Es Perpinyà* (The Perpignan), which is not available in major libraries in Catalonia.

WORKS IN BOOKS, PERIODICALS, NEWSPAPERS
"Ball de Ramellet," "Un passeig a Cabestany," and "Nostra Senyora de la Reial." *Les cinc branques* 116–18.

NANCY L. BUNDY

G Mayoral Díaz, Marina
(B. 1942, Mondoñedo, Lugo– .) Literary critic and fiction writer.

A teacher of literature at the Universidad Complutense of Madrid and a specialist on the work of Rosalía de Castro, Marina Mayoral has written novels and short stories in Castilian that feature themes of personal liberty in the postwar era. She incorporates the legends and customs of Galicia into many of them. Her first novel in Castilian, *Cándida, otra vez* (Cándida, again), appeared in 1979 and won second prize in the Ambito Literario of Barcelona. In 1980 she won two more prizes, the Ramón Sijé for *Plantar un árbol* (To plant a tree) and the Premio de Novela e Historia Corta de Madrid for *Al otro lado* (On the other side). The novel *La única libertad* (The only freedom) appeared in 1982; *Contra muerte y amor* (Against death and love) appeared in 1985 and was published in Galician in 1987.

Mayoral's first work written in Galician, *Unha arbore, un adeus* (A tree, a goodbye), is a collection of connected stories in which she plants a series of trees, while relating to a friend the part of her past evoked by each tree. The philosophical thought in each planting is presented in a lyrical context, sensitively but not sentimentally. *O reloxio da torre* (The tower clock), the story of a family, is told through the monologues of Leo and Amelia, a twin brother and sister who have an extremely close relationship, which at times manifests tinges of incest on Leo's part. Amelia's love for another man provokes conflict between the siblings and is the plot around which the story evolves. The impressions, complaints, and memories of

239

Leo and Amelia alternate in the narrative and relate their lives to those of family and friends. By the end of the story it is clear that—through parallel accounts, experiences, and images—the present coincides with the past. Marina Mayoral's stories employ a key element in women's narrative: a reencounter with former experience as a means of analyzing current reality. The meaning of life is sought through the examination of attitudes and feelings of the past and their re-creation in the present.

BOOKS

Al otro lado. Introd. Antonio Valencia. Madrid: Magisterio Español, 1980.
Unha arbore, un adeus. Vigo: Galaxia, 1988.
Cándida, otra vez. Barcelona: Ambito Literario, 1979.
Chamábase Luís. Vigo: Xerais, 1989.
Contra muerte y amor. Madrid: Cátedra, 1985.
Morir en tus brazos y otros cuentos. Alicante: Aguaclara, 1989.
Plantar un árbol. Orihuela: Ministerio de Cultura, 1981.
La poesía de Rosalía Castro. Madrid: Gredos, 1974.
O reloxio da torre. Vigo: Galaxia, 1988.
Rosalía Castro. Madrid: Fundación J. March–Cátedra, 1986.
Rosalía de Castro y sus sombras. Madrid: Fundación Universitaria Española, 1976.
La única libertad. Madrid: Cátedra, 1982.

WORKS IN BOOKS, PERIODICALS, NEWSPAPERS

"Contra muerte y amor" (excerpt). *Litoral femenino.* Ed. Lorenzo Saval and J. García Gallego. Granada: Litoral, 1986. 310–13.

TRANSLATIONS OF HER WORKS

Unha árbore, un adeus [Plantar un árbol]. Vigo: Galaxia, 1988.
Contra morte e amor [Contra muerte y amor]. Vigo: Xerais, 1987.
El reloj de la torre [O reloxio da torre]. Madrid: Mondadori, 1991.

SECONDARY SOURCES

Alborg, Concha. "Marina Mayoral's Narrative: Old Families and New Faces out of Galicia." *Women Writers of Contemporary Spain: Exiles in the Homeland.* Ed. Joan L. Brown. Newark: U of Delaware P, 1991. 179–97.
Blanco, Carmen. "A Galicia Mindoniense de M. Mayoral." *Literatura galega da muller.* Vigo: Xerais, 1991. 347–63.
Cantarella, J. "Entrevista con Marina Mayoral." *La voz de Galicia* 8 Aug. 1991.
Cerezales, Manuel. "Relevo generacional, *El reloj de la torre* de M. Mayoral." *El sol* 26 Apr. 1991.
García Rey, José Manuel. "Marina Mayoral: La sociedad que se cuestiona en medio de una dudosa realidad." *Cuadernos hispanoamericanos* 394 (Apr. 1983): 214–21.
Gullón, Germán. "La (cambiante) representación de la mujer en la narrativa española contemporánea: *Chamábase Luis* de M. Mayoral." *Letras femeninas.* Forthcoming.
———. "El novelista como fabulador de la realidad: Mayoral, Merino, Guelbenzu."

Nuevos y novísimos. Ed. Ricardo Landeira and Luis T. González del Valle. Boulder: Soc. of Spanish-American Studies, 1987. 59–70.

Noia Campos, Camino. "Claves de la narrativa de M. Mayoral." *Letras femeninas* 19 (1993): 35–44.

Zatlin, Phyllis. "Detective Fiction and the Novels of Mayoral." *Monographic Review / Revista Monográfica* 3.1–2 (1987): 279–87.

MARIA CAMINO NOIA CAMPOS

C Menero Ciutat, Maria Teresa
(B. 1945, Barcelona– .) Playwright.

Maria Teresa Menero's "La revolta de les aixetes" (The revolt of the faucets) was presented in Barcelona in 1979 by the theater company Teatre Gent. The protagonist is a man who rediscovers his childlike imagination and becomes marginalized for not working. The same acting group presented "Merde" (Shit) in 1978 in Sitges. *Juguemos, bobos, juguemos: Juguem, tanoques* (Let's play, fools), originally known as "Després de Godot" (After Godot), is about a jaded couple with nothing to wait or wish for. It evokes Ionesco as well as Beckett and won the Casandra prize in 1986. It is a bilingual work, written in Catalan and translated into Castilian by the author.

BOOKS

Juguemos, bobos, juguemos: Juguem, tanoques. Madrid: La Avispa, 1986.

KATHLEEN MCNERNEY

C Mestre i Ferrando, Cassandra
(20th c.) Writer of memoirs. No biographical information available.

Arreu la sorra (Sand everywhere) is an account of Cassandra Mestre's exile and life in a concentration camp as a result of the Civil War.

BOOKS

Arreu la sorra. Barcelona: El Llamp, 1986.

KATHLEEN MCNERNEY

C Milans, Mary de
(B. 1890, Barcelona; d. ?) Poet, short story writer, and songwriter.

Mary de Milans's three short stories in "Gent que passa" (Passersby) and her collection of songs remain unpublished. Her poetry, including *Mosaic de lletanies* (1960; Mosaic of litanies), has been published in private editions. *Recull d'hores* (Collection of hours) is a book of religious poems illustrated with museum reproductions from the eleventh, twelfth, and thirteen centuries. The *Visions mediterrànies* (Mediterranean visions) volumes consist of occasional poems on nature and the family.

BOOKS
Cantates místiques. N.p.: n.p., 1961.
Recull d'hores. Barcelona: Salvà, 1962.
Visions mediterrànies. Mallorca. Barcelona: n.p., 1968.
Visions mediterrànies. La Maresma. Barcelona: n.p., 1966.

WORKS IN BOOKS, PERIODICALS, NEWSPAPERS
"Badall Rioler," "Bon dia!" and "Nocturn Imperial." *Les cinc branques* 76–77.

NANCY L. BUNDY and KATHLEEN MCNERNEY

B Minaberri, Marixan
(B. 1926, Banka, Navarra– .) Writer of children's literature.

Marixan Minaberri edits the periodical *Sud-Ouest*. All her works in Basque are for children. Many popular Basque songs are based on her stories and poems. She has published the following works: *Mari Gorri* (Mary the Red); *Itxulingo anderea* (The Lady from Itxulin); *Xoria Kantari* (The singing bird); and *Haur Antzerki* (Children's theater), which won the Euskaltzaindia and Caja de Ahorros Vizcaína Toribio Alzaga prizes in 1982.

BOOKS
Haur Antzerki. N.p.: Euskaltzaindia and Caja de Ahorros Vizcaya, 1983.
Itxulingo anderea. 1963.
Mari Gorri. Hendaya: Gure Herria, 1961.
Xoria Kantari. Hendaya: Ikas, 1971.

MAITE GONZALEZ ESNAL

C Mínguez i Negre de Panadès, Núria
(B. 1927?, Barcelona– .) Novelist.

Núria Mínguez i Negre, a pharmacologist who has lived in various cities and in the countryside, returned to Barcelona to reside permanently. While her fiction does not fit exactly the classic style of detective novels, there is always some suspense and usually a few crimes to be solved. *Les forces del mal* (The forces of evil), in spite of its title, sees the triumph of nature's good forces over seemingly overwhelming evils. *El món és una mentida*

(The world is a lie) is a lighthearted adventure story, complete with terrorists and princes, hidden diamonds, and penniless Italian aristocrats. *Una casa a les Tres Torres* (A house in Tres Torres), winner of the Ciutat de Palma prize, tells the stories of various residents of an apartment house, focusing on a girl who is injured in an accident in the building's elevator. *El crim d'una nit d'estiu* (A summer night's crime) portrays a wealthy but ill Civil War exile returning home to find himself the victim of an assassination plot. *Amanda, Amanda*, winner of the Pous i Pagès prize, is the first-person narrative of an adolescent girl. Her father, fearing her first adventure with a boy, sends her to visit an aunt in a convent, where the reader gets a surprising view of cloistered life. *Una dona ha de morir* (A woman has to die) is a collection of five tales of suspense. Mínguez's style is clear, straightforward, and abundant with dialogue, and her plots are well-constructed if not always convincing.

BOOKS
Amanda, Amanda. Barcelona: Club, 1987.
Una casa a les Tres Torres. Barcelona: Club, 1974.
El crim d'una nit d'estiu. Barcelona: Llar del Llibre, 1981.
Una dona ha de morir. Barcelona: Llar del Llibre, 1987.
Les forces del mal. Barcelona: Llibreria Catalònia, 1970.
El món és una mentida. Barcelona: Club, 1972.

KATHLEEN MCNERNEY

B Mintegi Lakarra, Laura
(B. 1955, Estella, Navarra– .) Journalist and fiction writer.

Laura Mintegi contributes to several newspapers and weekly magazines. *Ilusioaren ordaina* (Illusions' dues) is a collection of seven short pieces, one of which, "Satorzuloa" (The mole's burrow), has been translated into Castilian and English. Her novel *Bai ... baina ez* (Yes ... but no) won the Resurrección María de Azkue prize in 1985.

BOOKS
Bai ... baina ez. Madrid: Susa, 1986.
Ilusioaren ordaina. Donostia: Erein, 1983.

TRANSLATIONS OF HER WORKS
Hole Mole ["Satorzuloa"]. Reno: U of Nevada P, 1987.
"La topera" ["Satorzuloa"]. *Antología de la narrativa vasca actual*. Ed. Jesús M. Lasagabaster. Barcelona: Mall, 1986. 117–31.

MAITE GONZALEZ ESNAL

C Miquel i Diego, Carme

(B. 1945, La Nucia, València– .) Writer of children's literature.

Carme Miquel's stories reflect a rural usage of language because of her frequent stays in the area of La Marina Alta. Some of her works are adaptations of traditional popular stories.

BOOKS

Açò diu que era. Valencia: Organització del Concurs Joanot Martorell, 1971.
Barrets barata rialles. Valencia: Gregal, 1984.
Escola i llengua al País Valencià. Valencia: Tres i Quatre, 1976.
Estimem la nostra llengua. Valencia: Institució Alfons el Magnànim, 1981.
Un estiu a la Marina Alta. Valencia: Organització del Concurs Joanot Martorell, 1970.
Guia didàctica del Xarq Al-Andalus. With Josep Piera. Valencia: Conselleria de Cultura de la Generalitat de Valencia, 1987.
Holdria, holdrio. Valencia: Conselleria de Cultura de la Generalitat de Valencia, 1986.
Marieta. Barcelona: La Galera, 1974.
Mirotxa. Valencia: Institució Alfons el Magnànim, 1981.
Pavotet. Valencia: Gregal, 1984.
La rabosa. Barcelona: La Galera, 1975.
Sucret. Valencia: Gregal, 1984.
Vola, Topi. Valencia: Institució Alfons el Magnànim, 1979.

ANNA MONTERO I BOSCH

Miralles, Josep; *see* Domènech i Escaté de Canyellas, Maria

C Mirallets i Piu, Rosa

(19th c.) Playwright. No biographical information available.

Rosa Mirallets i Piu wrote plays in Catalan and Castilian. According to a reference given in her only surviving work, *La gata moixa: Pessa'b un acte en català del d'ara y en vers* (False modesty: One-act play in current Catalan in verse), she premiered her Castilian play *Igualdad en categorías* (Equality of categories) in 1865 in Barcelona's Teatro Jardí de Varietat. She was also preparing four Catalan works: *La Pepa de Cal Barber* (The girl of Chez Barber), *Roda'l món y torna'l born* (Everything comes back), *Més val un boix conegut . . .* (Better a known madman . . .), and *Bufa y fé ampollas* (It's a piece of cake).

La gata moixa was inspired by Enric Pérez Escrich's *La mosquita muerta*, as the author states in her introduction. The play shows how a young woman in love disguises herself as a naïve little girl in order to protect her relationship from the manipulations of a greedy tutor, who wants her to remain single so he can benefit from her wealth. The text is very difficult to read because of the prenormalized Catalan spelling.

BOOKS

La gata moixa: Pessa'b un acte en català del d'ara y en vers. Escrita en catalan del d'ara y en vers per Doña Rosa Mirallets y Piu. Extreta de la que'en castella's titula La mosquita muerta. Barcelona: D. Manuel Sauri, 1865.

CRISTINA ENRIQUEZ DE SALAMANCA

C Monserdà i Vidal de Macià, Dolors

(B. 1845, Barcelona; d. 1919, Sarrià, Barcelona.) Poet, playwright, short story writer, novelist, journalist, and essayist.

Surrounded by the books of her bookbinder father and book-loving mother, Dolors Monserdà grew up reading and listening to the discussions of her father's writer friends. Her early essays treat such contemporary social issues as slavery, education for women, imprisonment of children, and workers' conditions. In her fiction she merges these social concerns with a moralistic framework, as in "El ocio y el trabajo" (1863; Idleness and work), a story Roser Matheu claims was published in *La bordadora* but which has not been located ("Qui va ésser" 53, n12).

In 1871 Monserdà married a successful Barcelona jewelry designer, Eusebio Macià, who died in 1899. They had four children; two daughters survived to adulthood. Like most women writers of her generation, Monserdà was a poet who wrote in a sentimental vein. She voiced a woman's emotions and experiences in *La plegaria de una madre* (A mother's prayer) and *Ma corona* (My crown), a volume dedicated to her youngest daughter, who died in 1877.

In 1870 (according to Roser Matheu, who corrected Monserdà's own recollected date of 1875 ["Qui va ésser" 53]), on a visit to the monastery of Montserrat Monserdà pledged to write in her native Catalan language. Her first play, in Castilian, is *Sembrad y cogeréis* (Sow and ye shall reap), a verse play in three acts staged at the Teatre Romea on 5 January 1874. Two years later a two-act play in Catalan, *Teresa o un jorn de prova* (Teresa or put to the test), also appeared at the Teatre Romea. Aware of her husband's displeasure at her public success, Monserdà ceased writing plays. Her reputation as a poet grew, and in 1878 the Jocs Florals in Barcelona awarded her a prize for her verse legend *La comtessa Mahalta* (Countess Mahalta), a work cited by Matheu but not located ("Qui va ésser" 55). Twenty years later the same Jocs Florals honored her as their first woman president. Over her long career, Monserdà's writings garnered some fifty prizes from cities throughout Catalonia and southern France.

Poems selected from her collection *Poesies* (Poems) were translated into several languages.

At the end of the century Monserdà turned to the novel, writing about economic and moral crises in the middle-class Barcelona family in *La Montserrat* (A girl named Montserrat), *La família Asparó* (The Asparó family), *La fabricanta* (The female factory owner), *La Quitèria* (The orphan girl), and *Maria-Glòria*. *La fabricanta* was illustrated by her brother, Enric, and *Maria-Glòria* was dedicated to her granddaughter. *La família Asparó* contains a long interior monologue by the male protagonist, which brings Monserdà's skill with the dramatic monologue into the novel form. She looks closely at financial problems of daily life, detailing the economic reality of seamstresses, craftswomen, and middle-class women. Through her female protagonists Monserdà. portrays the problems of women in contemporary urban society: spinsterhood, orphanhood, poverty, limited education, low-paying work, and double moral standards. The short stories in her two-volume collection, *Del món* (On the world), treat similar themes in the lives of women of all ages; several stories feature a first-person female narrator. The title of another novella synthesizes Monserdà's call for moral reform in social and marital relations: *No sempre la culpa és d'ella* (It's not always her fault). Over the decades many of these works have enjoyed new editions, such as a recent selection of stories from *Del món*, and have been translated into Castilian.

A frequent contributor to literary and cultural magazines, in both Castilian and Catalan, Monserdà published pieces in *La veu de Catalunya* and *Lo Gay Saber* and wrote the "Revista de Barcelona" (The Barcelona scene) column for *La ilustración de la mujer*. A leading figure in the first generation of the Catalan women's movement at the end of the nineteenth century, she advocated moral and economic reform supported by the church rather than by social or political change. She played a prominent role in charitable organizations to benefit workers, especially women, such as the Patronato de las Obreras de la Aguja (Society for Seamstresses). As a writer, she worked with the major Barcelona women's magazines: as contributor to *La llar*, in 1871, and *El figurín artístico*, from 1882 to 1884; as director of *Moda y labors*, a supplement of the *Diari català*, in 1880; and as codirector of *La ilustración de la mujer*, from 1883 to 1885. She also wrote for a later generation of women's magazines, *Or y grana* and *Feminal*. When Barcelona honored Josefa Massanés, Monserdà wrote a biography of the much-admired poet, her predecessor in the world of Catalan letters. Monserdà's lectures and essays on women's issues include *El feminisme a Catalunya* (Feminism in Catalonia) and *Estudi feminista* (Study in feminism). Reaffirming her belief in women's education, she contributed the essay "La maestra rural catalana" (The woman schoolteacher in rural Catalonia) to Faustina Sáez de Melgar's volume *Las mujeres españolas, americanas, y lusitanas, pintadas por si mismas* (Spanish, American, and

Portuguese Women, Drawn by Themselves). Monserdà's kind of feminism espoused the moral reform of the middle class and the improvement of the working class through education, the work ethic, and better working conditions. Maria-Aurèlia Capmany characterizes her as "la conciència social de la dreta" (the social conscience of the right) (33).

BOOKS

Amor mana, comèdia en tres actes. Monserdà, *La Quitèria*, 2nd ed., 223–73.

Biografia de Na Maria Josepa Massanès i Dalmau. Barcelona: Ajuntament Constitucional, 1915.

Buscant una ànima, novel.la de costums barcelonines. 1919. 3rd ed. Barcelona: Políglota, 1929.

Del món. Selections and introd. Isabel Segura. Barcelona: LaSal, 1983.

Del món, quadres en prosa. 2 vols. 1907–08. Barcelona: Políglota, 1930.

Estudi feminista, orientacions per la dona catalana. 1909. 2nd ed. Barcelona: n.p., 1910.

La fabricanta, novel.la de costums barcelonines, 1860–1875. Illus. Enric Monserdà i Vidal. 1904. 4th ed. Barcelona: Selecta, 1972.

La família Asparó, novel.la de costums del nostre temps. 1900. 3rd ed. Mataró: Minerva, 1929.

El feminisme a Catalunya. Barcelona: Francesc Puig, 1907.

La influència de l'home en el camp de les obres femenines. Barcelona: Bloud y Gay, 1919.

Ma corona. Barcelona: n.p., 1877.

Maria Glòria, novel.la de costums barcelonines. 1917. 2nd ed. Barcelona: Políglota, 1928.

La Montserrat, novel.la de costums del nostre temps. Barcelona: La Renaixensa, 1893.

No sempre la culpa és d'ella. Per lluir. Els rellogats. La novela nova 1.11 (1917).

Una orientació sobre'l problema dels captayres. Barcelona: n.p., 1906.

La plegaria de una madre. Barcelona, 1863.

Poesies. 1911. 2nd ed. Barcelona: Antonio López, 1912.

Poesies catalanes. Barcelona: La Renaixensa, 1888.

La Quitèria. 1906. 2nd ed. Barcelona: Políglota, 1928.

Els rellogats, els captaires, els vells. La novela nova 2.63 (1918).

Sembrad y cogeréis, comedia en tres actos y en verso. Barcelona: n.p., 1874.

Tasques socials: Recull d'articles, notes rurals i conferències. Barcelona: n.p., 1916.

Teresa o un jorn de prova, comèdia en dos actes. Barcelona: n.p., 1876.

WORKS IN BOOKS, PERIODICALS, NEWSPAPERS

"A la temprana muerte de mi querido hijo." *Eco de Euterpe* 1867.

"La belleza del alma." *Eco de Euterpe* 12 Aug. 1863.

"La calamitat de lo barato." *La renaixença* 15 Dec. 1895.

"Carta oberta a la redacció del setmanari *Or y grana*." *Or y grana* 1 (6 Oct. 1906): 3–4.

"La contribución de la sangre." *La alianza de los pueblos* 7 Dec. 1868.

"Gabriela." *El figurin artístico* 15 Aug.-15 Nov. 1882.

"La instrucción de la mujer." *La ilustración de la mujer* 2.30 (1884): 42–43.

"La maestra rural catalana." *Las mujeres españolas, americanas, y lusitanas, pinta-das por si mismas.* Ed. Faustina Sáez de Melgar. Barcelona: Juan Pons, n.d. [1881]. 562–88.
"El restablecimiento del divorcio en Francia." *La ilustración de la mujer* 2.26 (1884): 10–11.

TRANSLATIONS OF HER WORKS
Montserrat, novela de costumbres [*La Montserrat, novel.la de costums del nostre temps*]. Barcelona: Librería Catòlica, 1912.

SECONDARY SOURCES
Capmany, Maria Aurèlia. "La petita burgesia il.lustrada." *El feminisme a Catalunya.* Barcelona: Nova Terra, 1973. 49–63.
Castellà, Condesa de. "El feminismo de doña Dolores Monserdà." *Raza española* 1.4–5 (1919): 18–22.
"Dolores Monserdà de Macià." *La voz de la mujer* June 1897.
Duch i Plana, Montserrat. "La Lliga Patriòtica de Dames. Un projecte del feminisme nacional conservador." *Quaderns d'alliberament* 6 (1981).
"Escriptores catalanes: Dolors Monserdà de Macià." *Feminal* 120 (29 Apr. 1917).
"Galería de mujeres notables: Dolores Monserdà de Macià." *La ilustración de la mujer* 2.30 (1884): 42–43.
Matheu, Roser. "L'obra literària i social de la senyora Monserdà." Matheu, *Quatre dones catalanes* 7–110.
———. "Qui va ésser la senyora Monserdà." *Miscel.lanea barcinonensia: Revista de investigación y alta cultura* 8.23 (1969): 43–74.
McDonogh, Gary W. "Monserdà's Barcelona: Women and the City at the Turn of the Century." *Ideas '92* 7 (Fall 1990): 53–61.
Pérez, Janet. "Spanish Women Narrators of the Nineteenth Century: Establishing a Feminist Canon." *Letras peninsulares* 1.1 (1988): 34–50.
Pujol de Collado, Josefina. "Galería de mujeres ilustres: Dolores Monserdà de Macià." *El album de la mujer* 1889.
Segura, Isabel. Introduction to *Del món.* By Monserdà. 7–33.
Segura, Isabel, and Marta Selva. *Revistes de dones (1846–1935).* Barcelona: Edhasa, 1984. 27–31 *passim.*

MARYELLEN BIEDER

Montclar, Elisenda de; *see* **Nicolau i Masó, Maria del Carme**

C Montells i Vilar, Maria Angels
(B. 1917, Blanes, Girona– .) Playwright and poet.

Although none of Maria Angels Montells's work has been published, her dramatic writings have appeared on stage. Montells has dedicated herself to various aspects of the theater, including acting, and has also contributed periodically to *Reculls.* A teacher, she writes mainly for young people.

Some of her work is available, in manuscript form, at the municipal library of Blanes.

BOOKS
"Dèu entre nosaltres: Poema nadalenc." 1973. Ms. Municipal Library, Blanes.
"La princesa ensopida." 1979. Ms. Municipal Library, Blanes.
"La Ramoneta que escombrava l'escaleta." 1974. Ms. Municipal Library, Blanes.
"El regal de la Mariona." 1979. Ms. Municipal Library, Blanes.

KATHLEEN MCNERNEY

C Montero i Bosch, Anna
(B. 1954, Logroño– .) Poet and translator.

Anna Montero's *Polsim de lluna* (Moon dust) won the Ciutat de Xirivella poetry prize in 1981. In these poems, the speaker reflects on friendship and love. An intimate journey full of doubts and contradictions begins with a hopeful waking, introduced by night and sea. The journey evolves through absence, love's yearning, and solitude, arriving definitively at the world of dreams. The dreams of the beginning now show a stronger, more conscious poetic self that accepts its own contradictions. The lyrical intention has themes enclosed upon themselves, insistently expressed with a rich and sensual imagery emphasizing seascapes, with winds and stars, moons and evenings. Montero's careful use of language leads to a fluid and precise verse, especially toward the end of the volume.

Montero teaches French and translates literary texts from that language, including works by Charles Baudelaire and Jean-Charles Huchet.

BOOKS
Arbres de l'exili. Valencia: Gregal, 1988.
Polsim de lluna. Valencia: Victor Orenga, 1983.

WORKS IN BOOKS, PERIODICALS, NEWSPAPERS
Poems. *Camp de mines. Poesia catalana del País Valencià 1980–1990.* Ed. Francesc Calafat. Valencia: Guerra, 1991. 167–71.
Poems. *L'espai del vers jove.* Valencia: Conselleria de Cultura, Educació i Ciència de la Generalitat Valenciana, 1985. 258–64.

ISABEL ROBLES GOMEZ

C Montoriol i Puig, Carme
(B. 1893, Barcelona; d. 1966, Barcelona.) Translator and playwright.

Carme Montoriol was born to an Empordan family in 1893 in Barcelona, where she spent most of her life. She studied linguistics with Pompeu

Fabra at the University of Barcelona and, under the direction of Professor Vidiella and Frank Marshall, entered the world of music. Initially she excelled as a concert pianist and played at the Palau de la Música in Barcelona. However, her first recognition by the Catalan cultural world came with her complete translation of Shakespeare's sonnets in 1928, which was highly praised for its fidelity to the English form. Her translations into Catalan include other Shakespearean works—*Cymbeline, Twelfth Night*, and *As You Like It*—and the novel *Daphne Adeane*, by the Englishman Maurice Baring.

During the period she was translating, Montoriol also wrote for the theater. Her works created a stir because she confronted her contemporaries with themes they considered daring. For example, *L'abisme* (The abyss), a play in three acts, portrays a woman, Maria, in conflict with her own daughter over a man they both desire. Presenting more than a simple triangle, the play is structured around a dialectic that opposes personal fulfillment and faithfulness in love. The characters struggle between self-realization and obligations to family. Thus, in Montoriol's first work, when Maria has to choose between her love for Ramon and her love for her daughter, her duty as a mother demands that she renounce Ramon.

In 1935 Montoriol premièred *L'huracà* (The hurricane), whose protagonist, Joana, is torn by her son's Oedipal love. Montoriol analyses the dialectic of passion more at the level of her individual characters than through the social framework. It is significant that in her only novel, *Teresa o la vida amorosa d'una dona* (Teresa or a woman's love life), she deals with problems similar to those in the two plays. The novel features a woman who, after leaving her husband because of his continual infidelity, must face loneliness and the difficulties of independence. When she manages to acquire the inner resources needed for a happy life and finds a new love, the demands of fidelity to her husband and children prevent her from attaining personal fulfillment. The novel's melodramatic tone, evoking Victorian sensibilities, accentuates the fundamental conflict of characters who, struggling to affirm their own identities, are dragged by passionate love in contrary directions.

Avarícia (Avarice), first staged in 1936, focuses on the study of this vice in its main character, Mr. Marial. The play lacks the dramatic force of Montoriol's previous works; here, the maternal conflict is replaced by a blind fatherliness that is dominated by the desire for material security. Montoriol's theatrical work ended with "Tempestat esvaïda" (1936; Vanished storm), an operetta with music by Joaquim Serra. Montoriol also published a collection of short stories, *Diumenge de juliol* (Sunday in July). The ten stories, written between 1921 and 1935, present a wide thematic range but concentrate on socially unacceptable characters and criticize hypocrisy and social intransigence.

Not only a major force in the cultural life of Catalonia in the 1930s, Montoriol was also a significant social and political figure as well. She was president of the Lyceu Club and played an important role as speaker. Her literary commitment was interrupted by the outbreak of the Civil War, which caused her to devote herself fully to the intellectual world on the side of the Republic. In 1937 two of her articles, "La novel.la de guerra" and "L'escriptor i el moment actual," appeared in the collective work *Escriptors de la revolució*, published by the Catalan Writer's Union. During the war she concentrated her activities on the Council of Culture within the Commissary of Propaganda. After a brief period of exile in Lyons, Carme Montoriol returned to Barcelona in 1940 for family reasons and led a life apart from the impoverished postwar cultural world. The People's Library of Carles Fages de Climent in Figueres contains most of her personal papers, thanks to the generous bequest of her sister, Lina.

BOOKS
L'abisme. Barcelona: Millà, 1930.
L'abisme. L'huracà. Introd. Albina Fransitorra. Barcelona: LaSal, 1983.
Avarícia. Barcelona: Millà, 1936.
Diumenge de juliol. Barcelona: Rosa dels Vents, 1936.
L'huracà. Barcelona: Millà, 1935.
Teresa o la vida amorosa d'una dona. Barcelona: Llibreria Catalònia, 1932.

WORKS IN BOOKS, PERIODICALS, NEWSPAPERS
"La novel.la de guerra" and "L'escriptor i el moment actual." *Escriptors de la revolució.* Barcelona: Grup Sindical d'Escriptors Catalans, 1937.

SECONDARY SOURCES
Anglada, Maria dels Angels. "Carme Montoriol." *Literatura de dones: Una visió del món.* Barcelona: LaSal, 1988. 55–79.
Möller-Soler, Maria Lourdes. "La mujer de la pre- y postguerra civil española en las obras teatrales de Carme Montoriol y Maria Aurèlia Capmany." *Estreno* 12.1 (1986): 6–8.

MARIO SANTANA

C   Montseny i Mañé, Federica
(B. 1905, Madrid; d. 1994, Toulouse, Fr.) Journalist and novelist.

Daughter of Juan Montseny and Teresa Mañé, two intellectual leaders of the Spanish anarchist movement better known by their pseudonyms Federico Urales and Soledad Gustavo, Federica Montseny continued the intellectual work and militant activities of her parents. After returning from exile in Great Britain, Federico Urales started the magazine *La revista blanca* in Madrid. Along with such magazines as *El luchador* and *El mundo al día*, it became one of the most important vehicles for the theorization and popularization of anarchism. *Revista blanca* was published in two eras, the second one—from 1923 to 1936—with Federica Montseny's participation. The family's publishing house edited two serial novels, *La novela ideal*, appearing weekly, and *La novela libre*, appearing monthly. In these serials, love stories predominate, but the underlying theme is the struggle against the alienating capitalist ideology. The contribution of Federica Montseny to these serials was important.

In 1936, following the military revolt against the Spanish Republic, Montseny went to Madrid as a member of the anarchist organization C.N.T. (Confederación Nacional del Trabajo) and late that year became minister of health during the government of Largo Caballero. The first woman in Spain's history to form part of the cabinet, she advocated women's control of their bodies and signed Spain's first abortion rights law. Her political activity ended in 1937 with the confrontation between anarchists and Communists. In 1939 she went into exile with her family in France. After numerous problems under the Nazi occupation and the Second World War, she finally settled in Toulouse. There she managed the local anarchist organization with her husband Germinal Esgleas, who was in charge of propaganda and edited the magazine *Espoir*. After the consolidation of the Franco regime, the French authorities prohibited its publication. Her only work in Catalan, in addition to some journalistic pieces, is a novelized autobiography, *Cent dies de la vida d'una dona* (One hundred days in one woman's life). First published serially in Castilian as *El éxodo* in Toulouse in 1949–50, the book is a fictional account of her exile in France.

BOOKS
Cent dies de la vida d'una dona. Barcelona: Galba, 1977.
El gran desastre. Toulouse: n.p., 1949.
Jaque a Franco. Toulouse: n.p., 1950.

SECONDARY SOURCES
Pons, A. *Converses amb Federica Montseny.* Barcelona: Laia, 1977.

MARISA SIGUAN BOEHMER

C Morell, Sussi
(B. 1951, Barcelona– .) Journalist and novelist.

Ara que ja no és amb mi (Now that she's not with me) is a study of the erotic psychology of its male narrator, a middle-aged professor with a history of clandestine political activity in the Franco years and continuing activism after the dictator's death. Following an intense love affair with an adolescent girl, he wavers between love and hate.

BOOKS
Ara que ja no és amb mi. Palma: Moll, 1988.

KATHLEEN MCNERNEY

C Morera i Font, Glòria
(B. 1939, Barcelona– .) Poet. No biographical information available.

BOOKS
Atibes. Palafrugell: Dasa, 1981.
Phileo. Santa Coloma de Farners: Columba, 1982.

KATHLEEN MCNERNEY

C Morlius i Balanzo, Remei
(B. 1845/55, Barcelona; d. c. 1930, Barcelona.) Journalist and poet.

Remei Morlius began publishing articles and poems in Castilian in the periodicals *La enciclopedia médico-farmacéutica* (The medical-pharmaceutical encyclopedia), *El monitor de la salud* (The health adviser), *La nation* (The country), and *El diario mercantil* (The commercial daily). She also published a study under the strange title *Toxicología psíquica, la avaricia, la envidia, la ira, la lujuria, la pereza, la soberbia y la gula* (Psychic toxicology, avarice, envy, ire, lewdness, laziness, arrogance, and gluttony).

Her poetry is conspicuously religious, and her Catalan work won numerous prizes in poetry contests. She also published a collection of poems in Castilian under the title *Un libro* (A book). When she began writing in Catalan and joined the *Renaixença*, she added Catalan traditions, legends, histories, and patriotic elements to her frequently tortured religious work. In the twenty-eighth volume of *Lectura popular*, a selection of her poems was published along with work by Francesc Cambó, Manuel Folch i Torres, Adrià Gual, Frederic Pujulà, and Alfons Maseras. In these works she employs a great variety of meters and subjects. "El rosari de la vella" (The old woman's rosary) relates the complaints of a hated old woman who searches for relief in prayer; "La núvia blanca" (The white bride) is the lament of an unhappily married young woman whose wedding dress is in fact a shroud. In "El cavaller de les roses" (The cavalier of the roses)

Morlius recounts the legend of Saint George as well as scenes from the life of Jesus and tales of the wandering Jew.

Morlius won prizes in several competitions held by the Marian Academy in Lleida. Her poems range from praise of the Virgin Mary and descriptions of her miraculous acts and advantageous influences to themes about the rivalries between Catalonia and Castile, which, in "La Virgin de Pirene" (Virgin of Pyrenees), are settled by Mary.

BOOKS

Un libro. Barcelona: Renaixença, 1878.

Toxicología psíquica, la avaricia, la envidia, la ira, la lujuria, la pereza, la soberbia, y la gula. Barcelona: J. Miret, 1878.

WORKS IN BOOKS, PERIODICALS, NEWSPAPERS

"Cant a la Verge de la Almudena," "La Virgen del Pirene," and "Virolai a la Verge de la Sacristia." *Academia bibliográfica Mariana de Lérida* 1925.

"Oda a la Inmaculada." *Academia bibliográfica Mariana de Lérida* 1930.

"Poesies." *Lectura popular*, vol. 28.

"La Verge dels nins," "A María en la pérdida y hallazgo de su Hijo Divino," and "La llantia de la Verge." *Academia bibliográfica Mariana de Lérida* 1923.

MARISA SIGUAN BOEHMER

G Morris, Anne Marie

(B. 1916, Evanston, Illinois– .) Poet.

In 1959, Anne Marie Morris was teaching Spanish and was completely unaware of the existence of the Galician language, until she discovered its poetry through medieval lyrical songs and the works of Rosalía de Castro, Ramón del Valle Inclán, and Manuel Curros. She read these works with such enthusiasm that she learned several poems by heart and ended up by assimilating sentences and words of this language. She discovered its meaning through the unconsciousness of sleep. One night, while Galician poetry was going through her mind, she went out into the garden and composed a poem in Galician: "Marmurio / movimento de prata / o vento errante zoa no luar / voz fuxitiva / nun río perdido / chorando / camiño do mar" (Murmur / movement of silver / the wandering wind hums in the place / fugitive voice / in a lost river / weeping / toward the sea) (*Voz fuxitiva* 19). Little by little, other poems took shape almost unconsciously, says the author: "Casi de forma inconsciente . . . No sé como fue . . . Fue sin querer. No lo podría explicar. Quizás la lengua inglesa no tiene las palabras para expresar lo que yo siento dentro de mi" (I don't know how . . . I couldn't help it. I couldn't explain it. Perhaps the English language doesn't have the words to express what I feel inside) (*Voz fuxitiva*, prol.).

Morris attended Galician classes at the University of California at Los Angeles in order to learn the language that has become her poetic vehicle. In 1964 she published the book of poems *Voz fuxitiva* (Fugitive voice), which contains all her work from the preceding five years. She also wrote three literary articles in Castilian for the journal *Grial*. Morris's poetry is full of deep intimacy; it reveals an aching spirit, a lonely dreamer who finds its only company in nature. Her lamenting spirit wanders through nocturnal landscapes, crossing the boundary between dreams and reality. The trees cry, the winds groan, and the stars appear like spectral lights. Nature is sad and thus in tune with the poet's pain, which is meaningful only in her private world, where she is shut off from the realities and stimuli of daily life. Morris uses few motifs in her poems: the search for lost love, a bodiless, intangible love, and the desire for liberation from an old, unreal passion. The obsessive reiteration of these motifs is her main stylistic feature. In her poetry, one can clearly see the tragic world of Rosalía de Castro, whom Morris admits to worshipping.

BOOKS
Voz fuxitiva. Prol. Ernesto Guerra da Cal. Vigo: Galaxia, 1964.

WORKS IN BOOKS, PERIODICALS, NEWSPAPERS
"Análisis de 'En los ecos del órgano.' " *Grial* 6 (1964).
"Lo fatal de Rubén Darío" *Grial* 14 (1966).
"Rosalía de Castro en inglés." *Grial* 12 (1966).

SECONDARY SOURCES
Cacheiro, *Poetisas galegas do século XX*.
Martín Gaite, C., and A. Ruíz Tarazona. *Ocho siglos de poesía gallega*. Madrid: Alianza, 1972.

MARIA CAMINO NOIA CAMPOS

C Mortes, Antònia
(20th c.) Poet. No biographical information available.

BOOKS
L'esclat de la poesia. Barcelona: n.p., 1980.

KATHLEEN MCNERNEY

B Mújica, Robustiana
(B. 1888, Deba, Gipuzkoa; d. ?) Also known as Tene. Poet and playwright.

Robustiana Mújica contributed poems to the collection "Idazki eta olerki" (Writings and poems). Watson Kirkconnell included some translations from her unpublished collection "Udazken-ala" in *European Elegies*. Her rhyme and meter follow the poetic oral tradition, and her themes are religious or inspired by love for children. Mújica also wrote for the theater and in 1935 published *Gabon*, a play for children. *Joan Joxe* is a three-act monologue for children.

BOOKS
Gabon. Tolosa: n.p., 1935.
Gogo Oñazeak. Tolosa: López de Mendizábal, 1934.
Joan Joxe. N.p.: n.p., 1936.

WORKS IN BOOKS, PERIODICALS, NEWSPAPERS
"Idazki eta olerki." *Miren Itziari Idazkiak eta Olerkiak.* Zornotza, Vizcaya: n.p., 1923.

TRANSLATIONS OF HER WORKS
Poem, untitled. *European Elegies.* Ed. Watson Kirkconnell. Ottawa: Graphic, 1928. 46.

MAITE GONZALEZ ESNAL

C Mulet, Maria
(B. 1930, València– .) Novelist and poet.

Maria Mulet served as director of the Escuela de Orientación Marítima in Cullera, Valencia. Most of her work is in Castilian, but she wrote a few poems in Catalan.

BOOKS
Amor, la misma palabra. Valencia: Prometeo, 1969.
Nada al cor. Valencia: n.p., 1973.

KATHLEEN MCNERNEY

C Mulet i Salvà, Margalida
(1st third of the 20th c., Mallorca.) Religious writer. No biographical information available.

Cansons de la Beata Catalina Thomàs. Inspiradas per na Margalida Mulet Salvà (Songs of the Blessed Catalina Thomàs. Inspired by Margalida Mulet Salvà) is a collection of popular songs based on the hagiographic traditions in the life of the nun, Margalida Mulet i Salvà, who was affiliated with the monastery of Valldemosa in Majorca. Included are typical episodes of saints' lives, such as demoniac temptations, physical and spiritual abuse by relatives, and the saints' own expressions of scorn for the world.

BOOKS
Cansons de la Beata Catalina Thomàs. Inspiradas per na Margalida Mulet Salvà. Palma de Mallorca: Imp. de la Empresa Soler, 1931.

CRISTINA ENRIQUEZ DE SALAMANCA

C Mur, Mireia
(B. 1960, Barcelona– .) Poet and translator.

Mireia Mur collaborated in the creation of the publishing house Llibres del Mall, which specializes in poetry. With a degree in Catalan philology from the University of Barcelona, she taught Catalan and has been active in the theater as well as in publishing. Her work as a translator is varied: she collaborated on translations into Castilian of Salvador Espriu's prose and poetry, and she translated various works from French and English into Catalan, including compositions by Sylvia Plath and HD. *A despit del rei* (In spite of the king), her first book of poetry, is as irreverent as the title suggests. The volume contains powerful images, some of which constitute entire poems, such as number IV—"—Tant de temps, tant de temps!, d'estimar-te, / i només ara entenc / per què el corb fa set cercles / abans d'acarnissar-se / damunt de qualsevol despulla" (—So much time, so much time loving you / and only now do I understand / why the crow circles seven times / before devouring / any remains)—or the poem that closes the book: "Roja la lluna / amb dents de llet que es claven. / La nit s'atura" (Red the moon / with milky teeth that thrust. / Night stops).

BOOKS
A despit del rei. Barcelona: Mall, 1982.

KATHLEEN MCNERNEY

C Murià i Romaní, Anna
(B. 1904, Barcelona– .) Journalist, translator, and novelist.

Anna Murià studied in Barcelona at the Institut de Cultura i Biblioteca Popular de la Dona. She took part in the campaign for women's suffrage in the Estatut Català in 1931, together with other writers such as Rosa Maria Arquimbau and Aurora Bertrana. As secretary for the Club Femení i d'Esports she published several reports of its activities. In 1932 Murià,

257

Arquimbau, and Carme Montoriol organized the Front Unic Femení Esquerrista, a group of women who supported nationalism and opposed social inequality. In 1938 Murià was elected member of the Comité Central of the Estat Català party and, during the war, formed part of the secretarial branch of the Institució de les Lletres Catalanes and of the Grup Sindical d'Escriptors Catalans. After the war, she went into exile in France (Perpignan, Toulouse, Roissy-en-Brie) together with other writers, including Mercè Rodoreda and Agustí Bartra, whom she married. The couple then lived in several countries in Latin America and settled in Mexico, where they remained until their return to Catalonia in 1970.

In the prewar period Anna Murià contributed to Barcelona journals and periodicals. She had a regular column in *Dona catalana*, "La vostra bellesa," and wrote articles on Catalan women such as Francesca Bonnemaison de Verdaguer, founder of the Institut de Cultura i Biblioteca Popular de la Dona; Carme Montoriol i Puig; Víctor Català; and Pilar Padrosa, a practicing lawyer. She wrote for the sports news weekly *La Rambla de Catalunya* in 1931 and 1932, usually appearing in the section "Ciutadania femenina" with reports on the Club Femení i d'Esports, working women, and feminist issues. She also contributed to the journal *Companya* and the Barcelona newspapers *La nau* and *Diari de Catalunya*, acting as editor of the latter during the last months of the war.

In this first period of her career, Murià published two novels, *Joana Mas* and *La peixera* (The fish tank), both of which she later rejected for being of poor quality. *Joana Mas*, which deals with female introspection, portrays a woman in the process of being transformed, both physically and mentally, from a provincial teenager to an exuberant married woman. The underlying feminist theme of self-fulfillment through the body contrasts with the protagonist's total dependence on her husband. She undergoes all the experiences of married life, situations that may be clichés but are realistic. Her return to her starting point as a pregnant widow, seen as a quest for "real life," suggests that the author has seen the earlier process as a mere prologue. In *La peixera*, the protagonist, Gaspar, uses the memoir style to describe the lives of several coworkers in a sinister office he calls the fish tank. Employing a narrative technique that is more successful than in her first novel, the author depicts Gaspar's struggle to avoid being suffocated by life's dullness. This book, published in 1938 by an author noted for her civic ideals, can also be regarded as the story of one person's rebellion against authority.

During her years in exile, Murià translated several English and French works into Castilian, including Ronald Magowan's *Black Ace of Death*, William Glasser's *Person and Ego: Mental Health or Mental Illness?*, Mary Higgins Clark's *Where Are the Children?*, Lawrence M. Brammar's *Therapeutical Psychology*, and J. M. Synge's play *Rider into the Sea*. After her return to Catalonia, she contributed articles to *Serra d'or* and short stories and tales for children to *Cavall fort* and *Tretzevents*. She adapted some of Chekhov's tales into a theater piece titled "El fantasma de contrabaix" (The double-bass ghost), which was staged in various parts of Catalonia in 1980 and 1981. Her translation of a series of poems by Georg Seferis appeared in a bilingual Greek-Catalan version in the journal *Faig* in October 1977. In 1975 she published *L'obra de Bartra: Assaig d'aproximació* (The work of Bartra: An attempt at approximation), an examination of the elements in Bartra's poetry, which provides a practical guide for those studying her husband's work.

The publishing house LaSal in Barcelona has published the correspondence between Anna Murià and Mercè Rodoreda between 1939 and 1956. *Cartes a l'Anna Murià 1939–1956* includes one letter by Murià to Rodoreda. LaSal also brought out Murià's latest novel, which took her forty years to write: *Aquest serà el principi* (This will be the beginning). Sketchily told and somewhat difficult to follow, the story portrays a group of people caught up in the madness of war. The central idea of the work is stated by the author in the prologue: "Tenim tants principis. . . . Potser la Vida és un infinit repetir de principis" (We have so many beginnings. . . . Perhaps life is an infinite repetition of beginnings) (10).

Anna Murià has won various literary awards, including the prize for Catalan prose in the 1930 Jocs Florals in Roussillon and several prizes for fiction in Jocs Florals while she was in exile.

BOOKS

A Becerola fan ballades. Barcelona: La Galera, 1978.
Aquest serà el principi. Clàssiques Catalanes 10–11. Barcelona: LaSal, 1986.
Crònica de la vida d'Agustí Bartra. Barcelona: Martínez Roca, 1967. 2nd ed. Andorra: Serra Airosa, 1983.
Joana Mas. Barcelona: Llibreria Catalònia, 1933.
El llibre d'Eli. Barcelona: Selecta, 1982.
El meravellós viatge de Nico Huehuetl a través de Mèxic. Barcelona: La Galera, 1974. 4th ed. 1985.
L'obra de Bartra. Barcelona: Vosgos, 1975. 2nd ed. Barcelona: Pòrtic, 1992.
El país de les fonts. Barcelona: Ausiàs March, 1978.
La peixera. Barcelona: Edicions Populars Literàries, 1938.
Pinya de contes. Montserrat: L'Abadia, 1980.
Res no és veritat, Alícia. Barcelona: Picazo, 1984.
Via de l'Est. México: Lletres, 1946.

WORKS IN BOOKS, PERIODICALS, NEWSPAPERS

"Els banys a l'hivern." *La Rambla de Catalunya* 15 Feb. 1932.
"Correspondència d'el cultiu de la bellesa d'Anna Murià (Anna-Maria)." *La dona catalana* 254 (15 Aug. 1930).
"Els deures de la dona. Ja no és hora de parlar de drets." *La Rambla de Catalunya* 11 Jan. 1932.

"La dona que treballa. El servei domèstic." *La Rambla de Catalunya* 23 May 1930.

"La dona que treballa. Les oficinistes." *La Rambla de Catalunya* 27 June 1930.

"Les dones de Catalunya: Carme Montoriol Puig, la Víctor Català de nostra generació." *La dona catalana* 260 (26 Sept. 1930).

"Les dones de Catalunya: Caterina Albert." *La dona catalana* 262 (10 Oct. 1930).

"Les dones de Catalunya: Pilar Padrosa." *La dona catalana* 261 (3 Oct. 1930).

"L'esport femení considerat seriosament." *La Rambla de Catalunya* 11 Apr. 1932.

"L'estel." *La dona catalana* 253 (8 Aug. 1930).

"¡Força! (Dels 'Apunts' . . .)." *La dona catalana* 257 (5 Sept. 1930).

"Francesca Bonnemaison, vídua de Verdaguer." *La dona catalana* 256 (29 Aug. 1930).

" 'Genet Cap a la Mar,' per J. M. Synge, traducció d'Anna Murià." *El pont* 12 (1958): 15–30.

"La gràcia femenina al servei dels desvalguts." *La Rambla de Catalunya* 4 Jan. 1932.

"Una història vulgar." *La Rambla de Catalunya* 18 Apr. 1932.

"La nostra joventut: Maria Teresa Gibert." *La dona catalana* 268 (21 Nov. 1930).

"La nostra joventut: Soletat Kühnel." *La dona catalana* 267 (14 Nov. 1930).

"Pel carrer." *La dona catalana* 255 (22 Aug. 1930).

"Senyores i Senyoretes." *La Rambla de Catalunya* 7 Mar. 1932.

"To Mercè Rodoreda." 30 May 1940. *Cartes a l'Anna Murià 1939–1956.* Barcelona: LaSal, 1985. 48–52.

"Vacil.lacions per un mot. La terra erma." *Serra d'or* 309 (15 June 1985): 37–38.

"Les venedores dels mercats." *La Rambla de Catalunya* 21 Mar. 1932.

"El vianant de les esteles." *El pont* 46 (1970): 7–13.

"La vostra bellesa." *La dona catalana* 258 (12 Sept. 1930).

SECONDARY SOURCES

McNerney, Kathleen. "Catalanes exiliados en México: Anna Murià y Agustí Bartra." *El exilio de las Españas de 1939 en las Américas: ¿Adónde fue la canción?* Ed. José María Calderón Naharro. Barcelona: Anthropos, 1991. 285–91.

———. "Pens and Needles: Survival Techniques of Mercè Rodoreda and Anna Murià." *Actes del sisè col.loqui d'estudis catalans a Nord-Amèrica.* Ed. Curt Wittlin et al. Montserrat: L'Abadia, 1992: 279–86.

JOSEFA CONTIJOCH PRATDESABA, with bibliographical material by
CRISTINA ENRIQUEZ DE SALAMANCA

C Mussons i Artigas, Montserrat

(B. 1914, Barcelona– .) Writer of children's stories.

Montserrat Mussons i Artigas worked as a librarian in the Biblioteca de Catalunya until 1982. In 1964 she won the Folch i Torres prize for children's literature. Her work is somewhat didactic, with well-presented messages. In *Silenci al bosc* (Silence in the forest), a domineering lark tries to get all the other birds to sing the same song, but the result is silence. The lark learns to live and let live and comes to realize that there is beauty in diversity. Excerpts of her stories have appeared in the school readers *El finestró* and *Estornell*.

BOOKS
En picacuques el pollet atrevit. Andorra: Maià, 1985.
Piu Piu. Barcelona: La Galera, 1967.
Silenci al bosc. Barcelona: La Galera, 1968.
Tres narracions per a infants. Barcelona: La Galera, 1968.

WORKS IN BOOKS, PERIODICALS, NEWSPAPERS
Stories (excerpts). *Estornell.* Barcelona: Barcanova, 1987.
Stories (excerpts). *El finestró.* Barcelona: Santillana, 1980.

KATHLEEN MCNERNEY

C Nadal i Baixeras, Maria dels Angels de
(20th c., Barcelona.) Novelist.

Daughter of the well-known politician and journalist Joaquim Maria de Nadal i Ferrer (1883–1972), who published a number of chronicles of Barcelona life, Angels Nadal continues her father's somewhat "costumbrista" (local color) approach in her novel *Darrera els vidres* (Behind the panes). It is an account of life in the Eixample neighborhood, where she grew up. Because of her father's position and popularity, Nadal knew many of Barcelona's prominent citizens, and they appear in her book. Nadal married Lluís Portabella and lived for a time in Sevilla and Girona before returning to Barcelona.

BOOKS
Darrera els vidres. Barcelona: n.p., 1983.

KATHLEEN MCNERNEY

C Nicolau i Masó, Maria del Carme
(B. 1901, ?; d. ?) Also known as Elisenda de Montclar. Novelist, poet, journalist, and translator.

Maria Nicolau published the magazine *La dona catalana* (The Catalan woman) from 1925 to 1938. It was addressed to female readers, and she was its main contributor, writing the editorials, several poems and short stories, and articles relating to women and to children's literature. She also conducted interviews and wrote four novels for the magazine's romance series, which was published under the name Biblioteca de la Dona Catalana. Her first novel, *Cau roig* (Red Lair), was very successful after being presented to

261

the public through Ràdio Barcelona. Beginning in 1937 Nicolau and Aurora Bertrana edited the collection La Novel.la Femenina, which was published by Edicions Mediterrània and issued novels by well-known female writers, such as Víctor Català and Carmen de Burgos. After 1940 Nicolau worked as a scriptwriter for the popular program "Consultorio de la Señora Francis" on Ràdio Barcelona. She also wrote some cookbooks, including *La mujer en su intimidad* (Women at home). She translated several novels into Catalan: *Quo vadis Domine?*, by Henryk Sienkiewicz, *La Dame*, by Guy des Cars, and *La Communauté Bretonne en France*, by Yann Foueré.

BOOKS
August Martí. N.p.: n.p., 1937.
Cau roig. N.p.: n.p., 1935.
Cuina catalana. Barcelona: Arimany, 1977.
Els herois neixen. N.p.: n.p., 1938.
La mujer en su intimidad. Colección Nuestro Hogar 3. Barcelona: Arimany, n.d.
Una pobra noia. Biblioteca de la Dona Catalana. Barcelona: Bosch, n.d.

KATHLEEN MCNERNEY, with material provided by NURIA PI I VENDRELL

C Noguera Algué, Montserrat
(20th c.) Poet. No biographical information available.

BOOKS
Esperances. Barcelona: Casals, 1983.

KATHLEEN MCNERNEY

C Novell i Picó, Maria
(B. 1914, Figueres, Girona; d. 1969, Barcelona.) Writer of children's literature.

Maria Novell i Picó left her hometown for Barcelona, where she studied the humanities and librarianship at the university and worked afterward as a teacher. She soon began to contribute to the children's periodicals *El sigronet, El noi català*, and, especially, *Cavall fort*.

In 1966 she won the Folch i Torres prize for children's literature with the historical novel *Les presoneres de Tabriz* (The women prisoners of Tabriz). Nearly all her works can be considered as an attempt to show history to children in an interesting way. Her protagonists are young people who live in historic periods. In *Les presoneres de Tabriz*, Xeixa and Pere are teenagers who travel with the Crusaders and participate in their conquests and battles in the Mediterranean Sea. In the novelized biography

Jaume el conqueridor (James the conqueror), the little prince James becomes king and conqueror of Catalonia and Aragon. Her short stories, which first appeared in *Cavall fort*, were compiled in *Viatge per la història de Catalunya* (Journey through the history of Catalonia). At a time in which speaking about Catalan identity was forbidden, Novell i Picó taught through her stories the important events of Catalan history and portrayed the common life of previous centuries. She also wrote short plays, such as *Tres vegades era un rei . . .* (Thrice upon a time there was a king . . .), *En Perot joglar* (Little Peter Minstrel), and *Les orenetes* (The swallows), and the text for a children's comic book, "De Balaguer a Kum-ram" (From Balaguer to Kum-ram)—all with a historical background. Her vivid dialogues, simple descriptions, sense of humor, and narrative sensibility make history enjoyable for her public.

BOOKS
En Perot joglar. Barcelona: Taber, 1968.
Jaume el conqueridor. Barcelona: Aymà, 1972.
Les orenetes. Barcelona: La Galera, 1967.
Les presoneres de Tabriz. Barcelona: La Galera, 1967.
Tres vegades era un rei. . . . Barcelona: La Galera, 1969.
Viatge per la història de Catalunya. Barcelona: La Galera, 1975.

WORKS IN BOOKS, PERIODICALS, NEWSPAPERS
"El barret de cascavells." *Cavall fort* 131 (Sept. 1968): 18–19.
"De Balaguer a Kum-ram." *Cavall fort* 160 (Nov. 1969)–178 (July 1970).
"El llogarret." *Cavall fort* 106 (Oct. 1967): 6–7.
"El rei presumit." *Cavall fort* 114 (Feb. 1967): 6–7.

ANNA GUDAYOL I TORRELL

C Nyffenegger i Gerber, Beatrice
(B. 1940, Murten, Switzerland– .) Poet, short story writer, and translator.

Beatrice Nyffenegger studied nursing in Berne but has lived in Manresa, Barcelona, since 1963. She has published two books of verse, *Uriel, jo i la meva mare* (Uriel, my mother, and myself) and *Darrera les paraules* (Behind the words), as well as a collection of stories, *El pont de colors* (The bridge of colors). Nyffenegger has also translated the Grimm brothers' stories into Catalan; the first volume was published in 1986.

BOOKS
Darrera les paraules. Manresa: Nyffenegger, 1984.
El pont de colors. Montserrat: L'Abadia, 1986.
Uriel, jo i la meva mare. Manresa: Nyffenegger, 1983.

MARIA-LOURDES SOLER I MARCET

C Obrador Torres, Margarida
(20th c.) Poet. No biographical information available.

BOOKS
Somnis, colors i silencis. Palma: n.p., 1981.

KATHLEEN MCNERNEY

C O'Callaghan i Duch, Elena
(B. 1955, Barcelona– .) Writer of children's literature.

Elena O'Callaghan is a teacher who has contributed to various periodicals for children.

BOOKS
Bestieses i animalades. Barcelona: Cruïlla, 1987.
El petit roure. Barcelona: Cruïlla, 1987.

KATHLEEN MCNERNEY

C Oleart i Font de Bel, Maria
(B. 1929, Barcelona– .) Poet and short story writer.

Maria Oleart has been active in various cultural organizations, such as the Associació d'Escriptors en Llengua Catalana and the Institut de Projecció Exterior de la Cultura Catalana. Her poetry collections *La mort i altres coses* (Death and other things) and *Enllà* (Further) deal with the trauma of death as a sudden breaking off of communication between people. She can accept it, however, and finds courage, because her father has already made the journey: "On tu has anat, jo puc anar-hi" (Where you have gone, I can go too) (*Enllà* 21).

M'empasso pols quan beso la terra (When I kiss the ground I swallow dirt) deals with her disillusioned view of life, old wounds that abcess because they were never cured, and her unending wait for death. For Oleart, life wears her out: "Descrostonar la terra m'ha romat les ungles" (Peeling the earth has worn down my fingernails) (21). The dream that always threatens to disappoint is in the end the only certainty, since clinging to life brings bitterness, a belief reflected in the title of the collection. She therefore opts for the dream, "Cada dia començo a somniar" (Each day I begin to dream) (73).

Oleart has contributed short stories to various periodicals, such as *Avui, Tretzevents,* and *Alella,* a local publication of her town. These narratives constitute an escape from reality through imagination, which makes everything possible. She retains the details of everyday life in order to give verisimilitude to dreams. Her characters run the risk of not being believed and even of being taken for mad. When death appears in her short stories, it is treated with a distance. In the stories in which animals appear, usually cold-blooded lizards or distant and independent cats, a tenderness found in her poetry is evident. *Les onades* (The waves) tells the story of Triu, a girl who gets "waves" in her stomach after eating too much chocolate. She goes to a doctor, who takes X rays and finds fish, algae, and starfish. She then takes up yoga at a herb store, where a witch tells her to dig a hole in the ground and try to root herself. Triu ignores this advice and one day wakes up to find everything back to normal; she decides never again to have X rays taken, so they won't find anything strange. Oleart has won various prizes: the Víctor Català at the Jocs Florals in Lausanne in 1976, the Medalla d'Honor at the Ginesta d'Or in Perpignan in 1976, and the Flor Natural in the Jocs Florals in Munich in 1977.

BOOKS
Contes estrafets. Barcelona: LaSal, 1988.
Enllà. Prol. Anton Sala Cornadó. Barcelona: Oleart, 1974.
M'empasso pols quan beso la terra. Palma: Moll, 1983.
La mort i altres coses. Barcelona: Torell de Reus, 1965.
Les onades. Barcelona: Magrana, 1987.
Versos a Anaïs. Barcelona: Columna, 1989.

TRANSLATIONS OF HER WORKS
"I Am Sure There Are Red Women" ["Estic segura que hi ha dones vermelles"], "I Will Tell You About" ["T'explicare"], and "Moon Born from the Moon" ["Lluna nada de la lluna"]. Trans. Montserrat Abelló. *Poetry Canada* 11.4 (1990): 23.

SILVIA AYMERICH LEMOS

C Olesti, Isabel
(B. 1957, Reus, Tarragona– .) Short story writer.

Desfici (Restlessness), Isabel Olesti's first collection of stories, earned her the Octubre prize. Varied and witty, the stories range from computer nightmares to the lyrical death of a stubborn, traditional old man.

BOOKS
Desfici. Valencia: Eliseu Climent, 1988.

KATHLEEN MCNERNEY

C   Oliu Carol, Maria Dolors
(20th c.) Poet. No biographical information available.

Una dent de lleó (A lion's tooth) has varied themes but emphasizes nature and poetry itself. Each section of the book begins with a quotation from Pierre Seghers.

BOOKS
Una dent de lleó. Barcelona: n.p., 1979.
Hac. Barcelona: n.p., 1981.

KATHLEEN MCNERNEY

C   Oliveras i Planas, Emília
(B. 1948, Barcelona– .) Poet.

Though born in Barcelona, Emília Oliveras finds much inspiration for her poetry in the mountains and addresses a long piece to the Canigou range in France. Her subjects include the passage of time, in "Un gra de sorra en el temps" (A grain of sand in time) and "Naufragi en el temps" (Shipwreck in time), and a moving elegy for a Mexican friend who died on a visit to Catalonia. Perhaps her most successful piece is "Càntic del vell pescador" (Song of the old fisherman), in which the tired old-timer asks his lifetime companions, the sea birds, to keep him company in his old age, as they so often did when he went to sea. The volume in which Oliveras's work appears is a collection of four poets, handsomely illustrated by one of them, Joan Giné-Masdeu.

WORKS IN BOOKS, PERIODICALS, NEWSPAPERS
"Des del balcó de la falconera la història es fa" and "De portes en dintre la branca té un nou rebrot." *Poemes ara.* Illus. Joan Giné-Masdeu. Barcelona: Altés, 1971. 81–113.

KATHLEEN MCNERNEY

C   Oliver i Cabrer, Maria-Antònia
(B. 1946, Manacor, Mallorca– .) Novelist, translator, journalist, and scriptwriter.

Maria-Antònia Oliver is best known for her imaginative style and literary fantasies, which reflect some of the magical heritage of her native island. Her translations into Catalan of French and English literature include works by Virginia Woolf, whose impact on Oliver's own writing is significant. In addition to long and short fiction, Oliver has also written travelogues, criticism, and screenplays. She is married to writer Jaume Fuster.

Oliver's first novel, *Cròniques d'un mig estiu* (Chronicles of a half summer), portrays adolescent rites of passage to adulthood from the perspective of an innocent village boy. His sexual awakening, loss of innocence, and physical suffering are symbolically mirrored in the transformation of his native region, a sleepy, rural area of Majorca that has been radically changed by the tourist invasion and threatened with environmental chaos by indiscriminate commercial developers. *Cròniques de la molt anomenada ciutat de Montcarrà* (Chronicles of the oft-named city of Montcarrà) also deals with the theme of Majorca's destruction, this time in the form of a family chronicle. Although the chronology is linear, narrative segments are fragmented in order to present simultaneous accounts of three generations of related families. Part of the proletarian class, these families send some members to America, and the emigrants' adventures in the New World are incorporated into the plot. *Rondalles* (Majorcan folktales), popular sayings, and songs are woven into the narrative, with the resulting fantastical elements (fairies, giants, and mythical creatures from the *rondalles*) becoming the agents of destruction in a somewhat apocalyptic finale. As in the previous novel, the intent is to indict the false progress of the tourist boom by means of the symbolic disappearance of the homeland.

Coordenades espai-temps per guardar-hi les ensaïmades (Space-time coordinates to keep the pastries), a novella inspired by a dream of the author, describes a return to her childhood in Manacor. It is also included in the collection *Figues d'un altre paner* (Figs from a different basket), which has an important prologue by the author explaining the development of some of her fiction. Several stories provide the seeds for later novels and screenplays. *El vaixell d'iràs i no tornaràs* (The ship that never returns) blends elements from folk and fairy tales with philosophical reflections and feminist motifs. Magical and mythical adventures are introduced into a timeless, symbolic society, where problems are eventually solved by a resolute woman. The unquestioned actions of the conformist majority are satirized in this fantasy, which becomes a study of adolescent passage to womanhood as well as of matriarchal tutelage.

Punt d'arròs (Knit-purl) begins with a quotation from Virginia Woolf. A variation on the theme of the quest for identity, this story stresses the woman's need for solitude in order to find her true self. The title alludes to a major structuring image, in which knitting symbolizes the repetitive routines of a woman's daily domestic chores. *Vegetal i Muller qui cerca espill* (Vegetal and Women who look in mirrors) comprises two screenplays. In the prologue Oliver explains her view of the relations between the screenplay and the novel. *Vegetal* portrays a middle-aged widow whose life had been totally dominated by her paternalistic husband. Treated as a hothouse flower and forced to vegetate, she turns into a potted plant and cannot cope with the sudden existential freedom forced upon her by widowhood. *Muller qui cerca espill* similarly addresses women's limited options, presenting a lackluster engagement and dull, conventional marriage in counterpoint with the bride's imaginary conception of herself as a triumphant screen star. When everyday reality effectively ends her dreams, she smashes her mirror.

Crineres de foc (Manes of fire), which weaves together two stories—the protagonist's maturation and the growth of a nearby town—recalls Oliver's earlier concern with the social and environmental consequences of economic development. Combining science fiction, fantasy, and psychological themes within an epic framework, this novel also addresses the quest for identity in the individual woman and in social groups. *Estudi en lila* (Study in lilac) is an experiment with the detective, or crime, novel currently popular in Spain as a vehicle for feminist issues. Oliver focuses on the investigation of a rape and its aftermath. The three major characters—the detective and two dissimilar victims—are all female. Oliver's characteristic contrapuntal structure appears again as the detective interrelates the reaction of the two victims as they struggle with their feelings of shame, helplessness, fear and guilt, outrage, and desire for revenge. The novel has been serialized for the radio by the author. *Antipodes* (Antipodes), a sequel to *Estudi en lila*, takes the detective, Lònia Guiu, to Australia, where she uncovers a ring of female slavers with connections in Majorca. *Triptics* (Triptychs), a collection of stories, includes "Fils trencats," an early sketch for *Estudi en lila*. Oliver has delved into the realm of children's literature with *Margalida, perla fina* (Margalida, fine pearl) and *El pacaticu* (The pacaticu).

BOOKS
Antipodes. Barcelona: Magrana, 1988.
Coordenades espai-temps per guardar-hi les ensaïmades. Barcelona: Pòrtic, 1975.
Crineres de foc. Barcelona: Laia, 1985.
Cròniques de la molt anomenada ciutat de Montcarrà. Barcelona: Edicions 62, 1972.
Cròniques d'un mig estiu. Barcelona: Club, 1970.
Estudi en lila. Barcelona: Magrana, 1985.
Figues d'un altre paner. Palma: Moll, 1979.
Les illes. With Toni Catany. Montserrat: L'Abadia, 1975.
Joana E. Barcelona: Edicions 62, 1992.
Margalida, perla fina. Montserrat: L'Abadia, 1985.
El pacaticu. Montserrat: L'Abadia, 1988.
Punt d'arròs. Barcelona: Galba, 1979.
Triptics. Barcelona: Edicions 62, 1989.
El vaixell d'iràs i no tornaràs. Barcelona: Laia, 1976.
Vegetal i Muller qui cerca espill. Barcelona: La Llar del Llibre, 1982. Available on video. Dir. Mercè Vilaret.

TRANSLATIONS OF HER WORKS
Antipodes. Trans. Kathleen McNerney. Seattle: Seal, 1989.
Estudio en lila [*Estudi en lila*]. Barcelona: Vidorama, 1989.

Study in Lilac [*Estudi en lila*]. Trans. Kathleen McNerney. Seattle: Seal, 1987.
"Vegetal" (acts 3 and 4), trans. Nathaniel Smith, and "Broken Threads" ["Fils trencats"], trans. John Dagenias. *On Our Own Behalf*. Ed. Kathleen McNerney. Lincoln: U of Nebraska P, 1988. 107–53.
"Where Are You, Monica?" ["On ets, Monica?"]. Trans. Kathleen McNerney. *A Woman's Eye*. Ed. Sara Paretsky. New York: Delacorte, 1991. 370–99.

SECONDARY SOURCES
Hart, Patricia. "The Mystery as Midwife." *Armchair Detective* (Summer 1992): 330–34.
McNerney, Kathleen. "Catalan Crazies: The Madwomen in Maria-Antònia Oliver's Attic." *Catalan Review* 3.1 (1989): 137–44.
———. "Contrasts in 'La Ciutat Condal': Visions of Barcelona in the Novel." *Ideas '92* 7 (Fall 1990): 103–08.
———. "Crossing Parallel Lines: Maria-Antònia Oliver's Fiction." *Romance Languages Annual*. Ed. Ben Lawton and Anthony Tamburri. West Lafayette: Purdue Research Foundation, 1990. 536–39.
———. "Funciones bipolares en la obra de Maria-Antònia Oliver." *Actas del X Congreso de la Asociación Internacional de Hispanistas*. 3 vols. Barcelona: Promociones y Publicaciones Universitarias, 1992. 3: 97–103.
Pérez, Janet. "Metamorphosis as a Protest Device in Catalan Feminist Writing: Rodoreda and Oliver." *Catalan Review* 2.2 (1987): 181–98.
———. "Plant Imagery, Subversion, and Feminine Dependency: Josefina Aldecoa, Carmen Martín Gaite, and Maria-Antònia Oliver." *In the Feminine Mode*. Ed. Noël Valis and Carol Maier. Lewisburg: Bucknell UP, 1990: 78–100.

JANET PEREZ

C Ollé i Romeu, Maria Angels
(B. 1937, Sant Sadurní d'Anoia, Barcelona– .) Writer of books for children.

Maria Angels Ollé has written many instructional books for very young children, usually with the collaboration of illustrators.

BOOKS
Adéu. Barcelona: Magrana, 1981.
Ahir. Barcelona: La Galera, 1973.
A l'escola. Barcelona: La Galera, 1971.
L'amic. Barcelona: La Galera, 1980.
Els anys. Barcelona: La Galera, 1980.
L'aprenent. Barcelona: La Galera, 1979.
Ara no plou. Barcelona: La Galera, 1971.
L'ascensor. Barcelona: La Galera, 1979.
Les avellanes. Barcelona: La Galera, 1980.
El barret del rus. Barcelona: La Galera, 1989.

El berenar. Barcelona: La Galera, 1980.
Els bessons. Barcelona: La Galera, 1980.
Brillant. Barcelona: La Galera, 1964.
La capsa. Barcelona: La Galera, 1979.
La carta. Barcelona: La Galera, 1972.
El cercle. Barcelona: La Galera, 1979.
El conte. Barcelona: La Galera, 1980.
Conte contat. Barcelona: Onda, 1982.
El conte de la lluna callada. Barcelona: La Galera, 1972.
El cotxe. Barcelona: La Galera, 1979.
Una cullereta a l'escola. Barcelona: La Galera, 1963.
Del cel cauen cireres. Barcelona: La Galera, 1972.
Dos gossos llustrosos. Barcelona: Onda, 1987.
Es. Barcelona: La Galera, 1989.
Les estacions. Barcelona: La Galera, 1980.
La família Massatard. Barcelona: La Galera, 1980.
La fotografia. Barcelona: La Galera, 1979.
Les fulles. Barcelona: La Galera, 1980.
Les galetes. Barcelona: La Galera, 1979.
El gat i el gos. Barcelona: La Galera, 1972.
El gat i el lloro. Barcelona: Nova Terra, 1966.
Els gegants. Barcelona: La Galera, 1979.
Gronxa-gronxa. Barcelona: La Galera, 1989.
Guia del mestre. Barcelona: Onda, 1982.
Les hores del dia. Barcelona: La Galera, 1980.
El joc del parxís. Barcelona: Onda, 1984.
El llibre. Barcelona: La Galera, 1980.
El lloro. Barcelona: La Galera, 1980.
Les mans. Barcelona: La Galera, 1979.
La mare. Barcelona: La Galera, 1981.
Mel i mató. Barcelona: La Galera, 1973.
El meló. Barcelona: La Galera, 1980.
El mesos de l'any. Barcelona: La Galera, 1980.
El meu dietari. Barcelona: Onda, 1988.
Miau, miau. Barcelona: La Galera, 1971.
El mitjà. Barcelona: La Galera, 1980.
La mona. Barcelona: La Galera, 1979.
La moto. Barcelona: La Galera, 1989.
Els naps. Barcelona: Onda, 1987.
El nap viatger. Barcelona: Onda, 1987.
El nen té tos. Barcelona: La Galera, 1971.
Neva neu. Barcelona: La Galera, 1972.
La nina. Barcelona: La Galera, 1979.
Pa i peix. Barcelona: La Galera, 1973.
Els panellets. Barcelona: La Galera, 1980.
Les parts del dia. Barcelona: La Galera, 1980.

Però no ho diguis a ningú. Barcelona: Magrana, 1981.
El piano de cua. Barcelona: La Galera, 1989.
El pobre pagès. Barcelona: La Galera, 1980.
El príncep. Barcelona: La Galera, 1980.
El quadrat. Barcelona: La Galera, 1979.
Quan era petita. Barcelona: La Galera, 1980.
La Quica. Barcelona: La Galera, 1972.
Qui vol patinar? Barcelona: La Galera, 1989.
Ratlles. Barcelona: La Galera, 1979.
El rei, la reina i el ratolí. Barcelona: La Galera, 1972.
Ric rac, ruc. Barcelona: La Galera, 1971.
Les sabates. Barcelona: La Galera, 1979.
Samir. Barcelona: Onda, 1988.
La set. Barcelona: La Galera, 1980.
La son. Barcelona: La Galera, 1989.
La sopa. Barcelona: La Galera, 1971.
El submarí groc. Barcelona: Onda, 1988.
Tinc por. Barcelona: Magrana, 1981.
Els tres savis. Barcelona: La Galera, 1980.
El triangle. Barcelona: La Galera, 1979.
L'ullera de llarga vista. Barcelona: La Galera, 1986.
L'urbà. Barcelona: La Galera, 1979.

TRANSLATIONS OF HER WORKS
El aprendiz [L'aprenent]. Barcelona: La Galera, 1987.
Las avellanas [Les avellanes]. Barcelona: La Galera, 1986.
El catalejo [L'ullera de llarga vista]. Barcelona: La Galera, 1986.
Dos perros lustrosos [Dos gossos llustrosos]. Barcelona: Onda, 1986.
Los dulces [Els panellets]. Barcelona: La Galera, 1987.
El guardia urbano [L'urbà]. Barcelona: La Galera, 1986.
Las hojas [Les fulles]. Barcelona: La Galera, 1987.
La muñeca [La nina]. Barcelona: La Galera, 1986.
Príncipe [El príncep]. Barcelona: La Galera, 1987.
Samir. Barcelona: Onda, 1988.
El submarino amarillo [El submarí groc]. Barcelona: Onda, 1988.
Los tres sabios [Els tres savis]. Barcelona: La Galera, 1986.
El triángulo [El triangle]. Barcelona: La Galera, 1987.

KATHLEEN MCNERNEY

C   Oller i Giralt, Carme
(B. 1943, Badalona, Barcelona– .) Poet.

Carme Oller studied to become a business assistant and also took drawing courses at the Escola d'Arts Aplicades i Oficis Artístics de Llotja. She was a member of the Estrop group and in 1965 and 1967 took part in the

Mossèn Amadeu Oller contest for unpublished poets. The anthology of these awards from 1965, 1966, and 1967 includes two of her poems: "Introducció al Zenc" (Introduction to zinc) and "Verd Zenc (Fragment)" (Green zinc). Her contribution to *Quatre poetes* (Four poets) includes a protest poem criticizing American intervention in Vietnam and arms sellers all over the world.

WORKS IN BOOKS, PERIODICALS, NEWSPAPERS
"Badalona," "Pacificament," "Amic-I," "Mai," "Prega," "Com una agulla," and "Diré." *Quatre poetes*. Barcelona: Barcelonesa, 1968. 35–45.
"Introducció al Zenc" and "Verd Zenc (Fragment)." *Primera Antologia 1965– 1966–1967* 48–49.

CRISTINA ENRIQUEZ DE SALAMANCA

C   Oller i Torres, Maria Montserrat
(B. 1933, Terrassa, Barcelona– .) Novelist and writer of children's literature.

Montserrat Oller i Torres started her career writing for adults but soon began concentrating on juvenile literature. She adapts themes of Catalan history to novels for young age groups. She has also published stories in the children's magazines *Cavall fort* and *Tretzevents*. Her only work for adults is the novel *Llaurer i mirar enrera* (Plow and look back).

BOOKS
L'Almogàver ferit. Terrassa: Diario, 1984.
El capità Toni. Barcelona: La Galera, 1980.
Contalles de Terrassa. Terrassa: Omnium Cultural, 1976.
Llaurer i mirar enrera. Terrassa: Joan Morran, 1972.
Els raptors misteriosos. Montserrat: L'Abadia, 1987.

ANNA GASOL I TRULLOLS

C   Orberà i Carrión, Maria
(B. 1829, València; d. ?) Writer of educational books and poet.

A primary school teacher, Maria Orberà was placed in charge of the Escuela Pràctica de la Normal de Maestros of Valencia in 1866. She wrote pedagogical books, such as *La joven bien educada* (The well-mannered girl) and *Nociones de historia de España* (Notions of the history of Spain), which were rewritten as a single text in 1882. She contributed to various periodicals, including *La estrella* (Madrid), *Los niños* (Madrid), *Diario de Almería* (Almería), and *El eco de la religión*.

Constantí Llombart included Maria Orberà in his dictionary of Valencian writers, *Los fills de la morta-viva*. According to Llombart, two of her compositions in Catalan, a sonnet and an ode, appeared in the *Album* that the Valencian poets dedicated to Saint Vincent Ferrer on the fourth centenary of his canonization in 1855. The sonnet is also included in Llombart (556–57). An honorary member of the Valencian society Lo Rat Penat, Orberà is thought to have contributed poetry to the collection *Corona poética*, which was published to commemorate the centenary of the Virgen de los Desamparados. No copies of this work have been found.

BOOKS
La joven bien educada. Valencia: Mariano y Sanz, 1875.
Nociones de historia de España. Prol. Aureliano Fernández Guerra. Valencia: Mariano y Sanz, 1878.

WORKS IN BOOKS, PERIODICALS, NEWSPAPERS
"Oda" and "Sonet." *Album.* Valencia: n.p., 1855.

SECONDARY SOURCES
Llombart 533–57.

CRISTINA ENRIQUEZ DE SALAMANCA

C Orfila i Cirach, Dolors
(20th c.) Short story writer. No biographical information available.

In a style reminiscent of fairy tales, the stories in Dolors Orfila i Cirach's *Petits contes cruels i breus narracions* (Cruel little stories and short narrations) contain some cruel motifs. Most of the protagonists are youngsters, as lucid and unfortunate as they are brutal and mean-spirited. "La nina" (The doll) features a little girl fascinated by a doll; "L'estel" (The kite) is about a girl who wants freedom either flying or living at the bottom of the sea; "No volem prodigis" (We don't want prodigies) tells of a girl who feels especially qualified for love because she has six arms, but her peers consider her a monster and reject her. One of the most interesting of the "breus narracions" is "Clixé de dona" (The common woman), in which an older woman reveals the scandalous secrets of her youth, only to have the evidence destroyed by her survivors. The last story ends with the line "L'amor pot fer miracles" (Love can work miracles), an idea not realized in most of the stories in the collection. The book is illustrated with simple drawings by the author.

BOOKS

Petits contes cruels i breus narracions. Manresa: Bausili, 1981.

KATHLEEN MCNERNEY

C   Ormeu, Elisabet d'
(20th c.) Playwright. No biographical information available.

The Institut de Teatre in Barcelona holds an autographed manuscript, belonging to the Romea files and signed by Elisabet d'Ormeu, entitled "Els tres reis d'Orient (The three kings of the Orient)." It is a comedy for children divided into three acts. There is no record of it having been staged.

BOOKS

"Els tres reis d'Orient. Comèdia per a infants dividida en tres actes i set quadros." Romea Archives, ms. 119–2. Institut de Teatre, Barcelona.

CRISTINA ENRIQUEZ DE SALAMANCA

C   Orriols i Monset, Maria Dolors
(B. 1919, Vic, Barcelona– .) Novelist and short story writer.

Maria Dolors Orriols married when she was sixteen and moved to Barcelona. In spite of a period of censorship that was particularly difficult for women, Orriols had a strong desire to write. Her narrative style is straightforward, well-constructed, and varied, and her meaning is clear and easy to grasp. No two of her books or characters are alike, and the realism and immediacy of her works engross the reader.

Cavalcades, a book of delightful short stories that won the Concepción Rabell prize in the 1949 Jocs Florals in Montevideo, is unified by a single protagonist—a horse—but maintains a lively variety in style and plot. *Retorn a la vall* (Back to the valley) is her first novel; *Reflexos* (Reflections) is a group of tales that won a prize in the Jocs Florals in London. *Cop de porta* (Beat on the door) realistically portrays the personality, femininity, and dignity of Claudia Ginès and her strong will and courage in the politically repressive society of the 1940s. The novel is set in the author's hometown and may be somewhat autobiographical. *Contradansa* (Contredanse) is a well-written and original novel about the realistic-fantastic world of Jeromi and Joana, an elderly couple who meet in a nursing home after forty years without seeing each other. *Petjades sota l'aigua* (Tracks beneath

274

the water) takes place in Les Guillaries at the time the swamp of Sau was being constructed; the protagonist is the valley itself and what it represents—beauty, verdancy, and life. Once the powerful flow of water covers the valley, only tracks or footsteps will remain to represent what has been lost. It is a moving and dramatic ecological prediction, rich in detail and deep in feeling.

Orriols's last novel, *Molts dies i una sola nit: Una altra sonata a Kreutzer* (Many days and just one night: Another sonata to Kreutzer), draws on her lifelong interest in music. In an original way she shows how most young people in her country currently live. Everything in this period is changing, particularly for women, and the transition has consequences for men as well; after centuries in power they see their traditional image diminishing in strength, and many cannot find their place in a puzzling evolution.

BOOKS
Cavalcades. Barcelona: Aymà, 1949; Eumo, 1986.
Contradansa. Barcelona: Pòrtic, 1982.
Cop de porta. Barcelona: Pòrtic, 1980.
Molts dies i una sola nit: Una altra sonata a Kreutzer. Barcelona: La Llar del Llibre, 1985.
Petjades sota l'aigua. Valencia: Eumo, 1984.
Reflexos. Barcelona: Juris, 1951.
Retorn a la vall. Barcelona: Juris, 1950.
El riu i els inconscients. Barcelona: Columna, 1990.

CARME JUNOY

C Padró i Canals, Maria Rosa
(20th c.) Translator and poet. No biographical information available.

BOOKS
A la vora de la mar nostra. Tarragona: n.p., 1981.

KATHLEEN MCNERNEY

C Palau de Vall-Llosera, Encarnación
(19th c.) Poet. No biographical information available.

Encarnación Palau de Vall-Llosera is cited by Juan P. Criado y Domínguez as a Valencian poet, but her name does not appear in Constantí Llombart's *Los fills de la morta-viva.*

WORKS IN BOOKS, PERIODICALS, NEWSPAPERS
"A la decana de las escriptoras espanyolas, la eminentísima poetisa catalana Na Maria Josepha Massanés de González." *Lo rat penat* (1880): 38–39.

SECONDARY SOURCES
Criado y Domínguez, *Literatas españolas del siglo XIX.*

CRISTINA ENRIQUEZ DE SALAMANCA

C Palau i González Quijano de Prats, Emília
(B. ?, Mayagüez, Puerto Rico; d. 1883, Barcelona.) Poet.

Emília Palau wrote in both Castilian and Catalan. Her brother, the poet Melcior de Palau, used the pseudonym El Cantor de Mayagüez. Emília Palau's only known biographical data is that, after being widowed, she joined the religious order Hijas de María Reparadora and spent her last years in its convent in Barcelona. From 1873 to 1882 she won prizes in five poetry contests held by the Academia Bibliográfica Mariana de Lérida. In the first poem, "A Maria," she frankly complains of being looked down on by the world: "Y el món . . . de mi sempre se'n burla y del meu plant se'n riu . . ." (And the world makes fun of me and my laments . . .). In the ballad "Lo nin perdut" (The lost child), the author uses two strongly symbolic elements of Catalan culture: La Moreneta, the black Virgin of Montserrat, and the eighteenth-century War of Succession, when the Catalans lost their traditional rights. The other three prizewinning poems were "A la regina del cel y terra" (To the queen of heaven and earth), "Notas del cor" (Notes from the heart), and, in Castilian, "Mater" (Mother).

Her poem "Ma casa" was included in *Llibre de la Renaixença* and in *Catalanische Troubadoure*. The poem describes mystic love, in which Palau compares her love for her deceased husband with her love for God: "L'aymador que allí m'espera no me'l pendrá, no, la mort . . ." (The lover who there waits for me will not be taken away by death . . .). Later women poets, Palmíra Jaquetti, Simona Gay, and Mercè Vila, used the house as a symbol in their poetry as well.

Palau was a friend of Victòria Penya, to whom she addresses the poem "A ma inspirada amiga y llorejada poetisa Na Victòria Penya d'Amer" (To my inspired friend and prizewinning poet Victòria Penya d'Amer). It is a song to women's friendship and a homage to Penya for her leadership as a poet.

WORKS IN BOOKS, PERIODICALS, NEWSPAPERS
"A la regina del cel y terra." *Academia bibliográfica Mariana de Lérida* 14 (1874).
"A ma inspirada amiga y llorejada poetisa Na Victòria Penya d'Amer." *La renaixença* (1875) 190.

"A Maria." *Academia bibliográfica Mariana de Lérida* 14 (1873).
"Ma casa." *Llibre de la Renaixença.*
"Mater." *Academia bibliográfica Mariana de Lérida* 7 (1882).
"Lo nin perdut." *Academia bibliográfica Mariana de Lérida* 13 (1876).
"Lo nin perdut." *La llumanera de Nova York* 49.4 (1879).
"Notas del cor." *Academia bibliográfica Mariana de Lérida* 11 (1875).

TRANSLATIONS OF HER WORKS
"Mein Haus" ["Ma casa"]. Fastenrath 291–92.

CRISTINA ENRIQUEZ DE SALAMANCA

C   Palau i Vergés, Montserrat
(B. 1958, Tarragona– .) Poet and novelist.

A professor of literature at the University of Tarragona, Montserrat Palau i Vergés is associated with the most avant-garde and modern writers of the region and contributes to various journals, including *La gent del llamp, Arsenal,* and *El fenici de Reus.* She has published *Just a Dream* and *Mithos* as well as the novels *Gramont's Chinese Theatre* and *Suspiria,* which show strong influences from the English-speaking world of film, comics, and rock.

BOOKS
Gramont's Chinese Theatre. Reus: Felice, 1986.
Just a Dream. Barcelona: Foc Nou, 1978.
Mithos. With Josep Bargalló. Illus. Xavier Izquierdo. Torredembarra: Carpetes Babilonia, 1982.
Suspiria. Tarragona: Almedo, 1988.

GUILLEM-JORDI GRAELLS

C   Paler i Trullol, Enriqueta
(B. 1842, Figueres, Girona; d. 1927, Figueres, Girona.) Poet.

As the daughter of a Latin professor, Enriqueta Paler i Trullol grew up in an atmosphere favorable to letters; nevertheless she hid her own work for a long time. Her poems appeared in *La veu de Montserrat* and in magazines in Barcelona, Figueres, Vic, Mataró, Lérida, Girona, and Perpignan, France. A selection of her poetry was published in *Lectura popular,* along with works by Joan Maragall, Josep Aladern, and Conrat Roure. The editor of the volume is critical of Paler, characterizing her lyrics, as he does those of other women poets of her time, as having little personality, an almost simplistic religious sentiment, and "un gran entusiasme per tot lo bell, noble i gran" (a great enthusiam for everything that is beautiful, noble, and high). Without explaining what is reproachable about the latter, he goes on to say that these sentiments resulted from women's social condition during that period.

Paler does, in fact, deal with conventional themes, as did many of her contemporaries, both male and female. Her themes are often religious, dedicated to virgins or saints or important church personalities such as Torres i Bages, the bishop of Vic and one of the principal detractors of modernism. Her laments about solitude and grief for the loss of loved ones—her father, sister, mother, and finally the brother with whom she lived—are tempered by religious resignation, submission to a benefactor or higher will, and hope for a better life to come. A conservative social ideology shows in her poetry: for example, in "A la classe obrera" (To the working class), Paler rails against social agitators who fill the hearts of working people with hate; instead, she recommends love and honesty as appropriate goals for workers. However, she also agrees with some of her Catalan contemporaries, who were influenced by the German philosopher Karl Krause, and, in the ironic "La Espanya feliç" (Fortunate Spain), criticizes her country's farcical opulence during disastrous economic times. In "Mon d'avuy" (Today's world), Paler sees the lack of religion as the world's greatest problem. In "Les arenas" (The bullrings), she criticizes bullfighting and makes it clear that the custom is a non-Catalan one. Also in *Poesies*, she writes about the heroism of the people of the South African provinces Orange and Transvaal, presenting them as a model for Catalonians. Paler's verse forms are limited; decasyllables and heptasyllables predominate in varying combinations of stanzas. Her poem "Desolació" (Desolation) appears in the *Llibre de la Renaixença*, along with poems by such well-known poets as Angel Guimerà, Jacint Verdaguer, and Miquel Costa i Llobera.

WORKS IN BOOKS, PERIODICALS, NEWSPAPERS
"Desolació." *Llibre de la Renaixença.*
Poems. *Poesies. Lectura popular*, vol. 15.

MARISA SIGUAN BOEHMER

C   Pallach i Estela, Maria
(B. 1939, Tarragona– .) Poet.

Maria Pallach trained as a librarian at the Escola de la Diputació in Barcelona. Her poem "Normalitat" (Normalcy) appears in *Primera antologia*, a collection of poems awarded the Mossèn Amadeu Oller poetry prize. Pallach says in "Normalitat": "Jo me creia que tot això / que fa la vida d'una dona / no tenia importància per a ningú / . . . Es com el pa, que, perque en mengem cada dia / ens sembla que no té importància" (I thought all those things / that make up a woman's life / weren't of importance to anyone / . . . It's like bread, that, since we eat it every day / we take it for granted).

WORKS IN BOOKS, PERIODICALS, NEWSPAPERS
"Normalitat." *Primera antología 1965–1966–1967.*

CRISTINA ENRIQUEZ DE SALAMANCA

G Pallarés, Pilar
(B. 1957, Culleredo, Coruña– .) Poet.

Like many Galicians, Pilar Pallarés began to write in Castilian but later turned to her native language. Her poetry has a profound tone, from the intimate and existential to the nationalistic and accusatory. A teacher of Galician language and literature, she is firmly committed to the advancement of Galician culture and to her own role in the creation of a modern Galician literature; she cites Pablo Neruda, who sought to be a voice for Latin America, as her model. The combination of interlocutors in the poems *Entre lusco e fusco* (Dusk) and *Sétima soidade* (Seventh solitude) creates a sense of wandering in her verse: the *I* may express its own suffering, or it may turn to a *you* that is simultaneously one and collective. A feminist in her poetic intentions, Pallarés has rightly been awarded such literary honors as the Poesía Nova "O Facho" (1979) and the Poesía Esquío (1984). Her poems appear in the journals *Nordés, Dorna, Grial, Coordenadas,* and *Festa da palabra silenciada* as well as in literary supplements of Galician newspapers, an important source of cultural information. Several of her poems can be found in the two-volume *De amor e desamor* (Of love and disaffection).

BOOKS
Entre lusco e fusco. Sada, Coruña: Castro, 1980.
Sétima soidade. Ferrol: Esquío, 1984.

WORKS IN BOOKS, PERIODICALS, NEWSPAPERS
Poems. *De amor e desamor.* Ed. Lino Braxe. 2 vols. Sada, Coruña: Castro, 1984–85. 1: 89–103.

TRANSLATIONS OF HER WORKS
"Hay una ciudad que me espera en el sur" ["Hai unha cidade que me agarda no sul"]. *Litoral femenino.* Ed. Lorenzo Saval and J. García Gallego. Granada: Litoral, 1986. 180–83.

SECONDARY SOURCES
Queizán, María José. "Sétima soidade: O amor, a dor e a morte." *Festa da palabra silenciada* 2 (1985): 44–45.

KATHLEEN MARCH

Palma, Felip; *see* Ventós i Cullell, Palmira

C   Palomar, Margarida
(20th c.) Journalist. No biographical information available.

BOOKS

La meva casa es diu somni i cançó d'algues. Barcelona: n.p., 1982.

KATHLEEN MCNERNEY

C   Pàmies i Bertran, Teresa
(B. 1919, Balaguer, Lleida– .) Novelist and journalist.

Born into a family of poor peasants, Teresa Pàmies became militant at a young age, when her father was a local leader in the Communist Party. She left school at age eleven to work in a garment factory. When the Civil War broke out, she moved to Barcelona and took an active part in war-related events, organizing and delivering political speeches and traveling to the front to encourage the troops. In 1937 she was named director of the JSUC (Joventuts Socialistes Unificades de Catalunya) and soon began to write for the revolutionary press. In the same year she edited and wrote for the JSUC weekly *Juliol*. She was also one of the founders of the Aliança Nacional de la Dona Jove in 1937. She represented the JSUC in 1938 at the World Congress of Youth for Peace, celebrated at Vassar College in New York State, and toured the United States to help raise money for the Spanish Republican government.

When the war ended, Pàmies went into exile, first to France and then, when the Second World War began, to the Dominican Republic. She moved to Cuba in 1940 where she worked in a restaurant and in a seamstress shop. She never abandoned her militant activities during these years, always following both Spanish and international political events and maintaining contact with other exiled leaders of the Franco opposition. After living a few years in Cuba, she went to Mexico City and enrolled in the Universidad Femenina, which was directed by Adela Formoso de Obregón. There she studied with Alfonso Reyes in the School of Journalism. She collaborated on film chronicles for the short-lived journal *Tricolor*. When a census on illiteracy was done, she volunteered and came to know the social conditions, poverty, and exploitation of the poorest Mexican class. Pàmies returned to Europe after the war in 1946, settling in Belgrade, where she worked in the Spanish language department of Radio Belgrade. As a result of the tensions between Tito and Stalin and finally the rupture between the two parties and countries, she was obliged for political reasons to leave for Czechoslovakia. From 1948 to 1959 she worked as editor of programs in Castilian and Catalan at Radio Prague. She arrived in Paris in 1959 with a stateless passport; after initial difficulties, she received permission to reside there and remained for twelve years. While working as a clerk in a sports shop and later in a knitting factory to support herself and her children, she continued to write militant articles and published work in *Serra d'or* and *Oriflama*.

In 1971 Pàmies returned to Catalonia and published her first novel, *Testament a Praga* (Prague testament). Written in collaboration with her father, Tomas, who had died in Prague, the story alternates between personal and political memoirs of their lives in Catalonia and abroad. In addition to her assiduous journalistic work, she has written several partly autobiographical books. This novelized journalism is most interesting for its firsthand accounts of political and social events related to the Spanish Civil War, the Second World War, clandestine militancy, and exile. Pàmies presents an ensemble of memoirs, chronicles, letters, reports from the period, personal diaries, and critical observations about literary events, as well as commentaries about her numerous trips and portraits of both humble and important people. Her attitude is characterized by an openness that never hides her Marxist affiliation and by an affable readiness to understand and pardon the failings of her fellows, whether friends, party comrades, or enemies. Straightforward and sincere, she presents the facts objectively and expresses optimism and confidence in the future.

Va ploure tot el dia (It rained all day) relates her observations of Spain after her thirty years' absence. At the same time she questions the wisdom of her return. The sequel, *Quan érem refugiats* (When we were refugees), recounts the Spanish diaspora throughout Europe and America following the defeat of the Republic. *Crònica de la vetlla* (Chronicle of the prelude) explains the local political events during two years of her childhood in Balaguer, from the fall of Primo de Rivera's dictatorship, with the ensuing tensions between parties on the right and left, to the outbreak of the Civil War. *Gent del meu exili* (Companions in exile) and *Records de guerra i d'exili* (Memoirs of war and exile) contain accounts of political and personal events and wartime anecdotes. *Dona de pres* (Prisoner's wife) is a novel about the wives of political prisoners and their work during the Franco dictatorship. *Si vas a París papà . . .* (If you go to Paris, Daddy . . .) is a diary of the events of May 1968, which she experienced firsthand. *Amor clandestí* (Clandestine love) is a novelized account of the persecutions and separations Pàmies and her husband, Gregorio López, secretary general of the PSUC (Partit Socialista Unificada de Catalunya), endured. *Maig de les dones* (Women's May) chronicles the first women's congress, celebrated at the auditorium of the University of Barcelona in 1976. *Cròniques de nàufregs* (Shipwreck chronicle) is a collection of the letters and personal testimonies of twenty-five women and fifteen men, through whom Pàmies creates a cohesive picture of life in postwar Spain; the forty civilians are not militant or even politically active people but simply survivors of the great collective shipwreck of the Spanish Civil War. *Aquell vellet gentil i pulcre* (Such a nice old gentleman) is a fictional account of war criminals who took refuge under Franco's regime.

Vacances aragoneses (Holiday in Aragon), *Busqueu-me a Granada* (Look for me in Granada), and *Matins de l'Aran* (Mornings in Aran) are travel books. *Memòria dels morts* (Memories of the dead) is a eulogy to her mother, who died in Balaguer while Pàmies was in exile; within a hazy framework, she imagines meeting her dead mother. *Rosalía no hi era* (Rosalia wasn't there), a travel book about Galicia, focuses on Rosalía de Castro. *Opinió de dona* (A woman's opinion) collects the articles Pàmies wrote for the daily paper *Avui* from the date of its founding, particularly pieces about feminism and politics during the period of transition after Franco's death (1972–82). *Cartes al fill recluta* (Letters to a drafted son) contains letters to her son, who was doing his military service during the 1981 attempted coup in parliament in Madrid. *Massa tard per a Cèlia* (Too late for Cèlia), written in the form of a travelogue, tells of the love between a Catalan girl and a Slovene volunteer in the International Brigades of the Civil War. *Segrest amb filipina* (Filipino abduction) is a story of intrigue involving a Filipino maid in Barcelona in the mid-1980s, a period of political upheaval and social transformation in the Philippines. The essay *Mascles no masclistes* (Nonsexist men) discusses men throughout history who have worked for feminist causes.

BOOKS

Amor clandestí. Barcelona: Galba, 1976.
Aquell vellet gentil i pulcre. Palma: Moll, 1978.
Aventura mexicana del noi Pau Rispa. Barcelona: Pòrtic, 1986.
Busqueu-me a Granada. Barcelona: Destino, 1981.
Cartes al fill recluta. Barcelona: Pòrtic, 1984.
Crònica de la vetlla. Barcelona: Selecta, 1975.
Cròniques de nàufregs. Barcelona: Destino, 1977.
Dona de pres. Barcelona: Proa, 1975.
Una española llamada Dolores Ibarruri. Barcelona: Martínez Roca, 1976.
Gent del meu exili. Barcelona: Sagitario, 1975.
Los que se fueron. Barcelona: Martínez Roca, 1976.
Maig de les dones: Crònica d'unes jornades. Barcelona: Laia, 1976.
Mascles no masclistes. Barcelona: Plaza & Janès, 1987.
Massa tard per a Cèlia. Barcelona: Destino, 1984.
Matins de l'Aran. Barcelona: Pòrtic, 1982.
Memòria dels morts. Barcelona: Planeta, 1981.
Opinió de dona. Barcelona: Edicions 62, 1983.

La primavera de l'àvia. Barcelona: Destino, 1989.
Quan érem capitans: Memòries d'aquella guerra. Barcelona: Dopesa, 1974.
Quan érem refugiats. Barcelona: Dopesa, 1975.
Rebelión de viejas. Barcelona: LaSal, 1989.
Records de guerra i d'exili. Barcelona: Dopesa, 1976.
La reraguarda republicana. Barcelona: Edicions 62, 1977.
Romanticisme militante. Barcelona: Sagitario, 1976.
Rosalia no hi era. Barcelona: Destino, 1982.
Segrest amb filipina. Barcelona: Destino, 1986.
Si vas a París papà . . . (Diari de maig 1968). Barcelona: Nova Terra, 1975.
Testament a Praga. Barcelona: Destino, 1971.
Vacances aragoneses. Barcelona: Destino, 1980.
Va ploure tot el dia. Barcelona: Edicions 62, 1974.

TRANSLATIONS OF HER WORKS
Cuando éramos capitanes (Memorias de aquella guerra) [*Quan érem capitans: Memòries d'aquella guerra*]. Barcelona: Dopesa, 1974.
Memoria de los muertos [*Memòria dels morts*]. Barcelona: Planeta, 1981.
Mujer de preso [*Dona de pres*]. Trans. Anna Murià. Barcelona: Aymà, 1977.
Vacaciones aragonesas [*Vacances aragoneses*]. Zaragoza: Heraldo de Aragón, 1981.

SECONDARY SOURCES
McNerney, Kathleen. "Stages and Struggles: Listening to the Wise Women." *Monographic Review / Revista Monográfica* 8 (1992): 50–56.
Möller Soler, Maria Lourdes. "El impacto de la guerra civil en la vida y obra de tres autoras catalanas: Aurora Bertrana, Teresa Pàmies y Mercè Rodoreda." *Letras femeninas* 12 (1986): 32–34.
Pérez, Genaro J. "Patria, madre y destierro en *Memoria de los muertos* de Teresa Pàmies." *Revista canadiense de estudios hispánicos* 14.3 (1990): 579–88.
Riera Llorca, Viçens. "La crònica novel.lesca de Teresa Pàmies." *Serra d'or* (May 1977): 325–27.
Servià, Josep Maria. *Catalunya: Tres generacions.* Barcelona: Martínez Roca, 1975.

MARIA-LOURDES SOLER I MARCET

C Papiol i Mora, Maria Angels

(20th c.) Novelist. No biographical information available.

Amor amb majúscula (Love with a capital L) won the Viola Prize in the Jocs Florals of the Ginesta d'Or in Perpignan. With a prologue by Joan Pelegrí i Partegès and a dedicatory poem by Maria Dolors Oliu, it is an idealized story of spiritual love in a small coastal town overrun by tourists. There is a typical love triangle, sentimentality, and a pervasive background of benevolent nature.

BOOKS
Amor amb majúscula. Prol. Joan Pelegrí i Partegès. Barcelona: Tallers de Coch, 1977.
Entre mimoses. Barcelona: n.p., 1979.

KATHLEEN MCNERNEY

C Paquim Garriga, Cecília
(20th c.) Poet. No biographical information available.

BOOKS
Memòria, buit. Barcelona: Nova Terra, 1980.

KATHLEEN MCNERNEY

C Paretas i Goterris de Pagès, Raimonda
(B. 1910, Barcelona– .) Poet.

Raimonda Paretas worked in a notions shop for many years, embroidering, knitting, and teaching these skills to others. She started writing when she was quite young, contributing poetry to various local magazines and articles to the women's section of the Barcelona newspaper *Las noticias*. Paretas has won a number of prizes in local contests over the years. Something of a personage in her neighborhood of Gràcia, she still runs the notions shop. She has two daughters and was widowed in 1986.

The publication of her book *Poesia menuda* (Minor poetry) resulted from her association with the group Poesia Viva, directed by Josep Colet i Giralt, who wrote the prologue for her collection. As the title suggests, hers is a simple and humble poetry, focusing on everyday items and events: a balcony on her street, the doves in her plaza, the mimosa and lemon trees. Her rhyme and meter are traditional.

BOOKS
Poesia menuda. Prol. Josep Colet i Giralt. Barcelona: Poesia Viva, 1981.

KATHLEEN MCNERNEY

C Pascual, Teresa
(B. 1952, Grau de Gandia, La Safor, Valencia– .) Poet.

A philosophy teacher, Teresa Pascual won the Senyoriu d'Ausiàs March prize in 1987 for *Flexo*. She has written two other books: "Els dies de pedra" (The days of stone) and *Les hores* (The hours), the last one the

284

winner of the 1988 Vicent Andrés Estellés prize. A principal characteristic of her poetry is the tendency toward the concise and schematic, the search for essence in the small, seemingly insignificant occurrences of daily life. Upon this she overlays the force of time, solitude, nostalgia, love, or death.

BOOKS
Arena. Valencia: Alfons el Magnànim, 1992.
Flexo. Valencia: Gregal, 1988.
Les hores. Valencia: Eliseu Climent, 1988.

WORKS IN BOOKS, PERIODICALS, NEWSPAPERS
"Poems." *Camp de mines. Poesia catalana del Pais Valencià 1980–1990*. Ed. Francesc Calafat. Valencia: Guerra, 1991. 173–78.

ISABEL ROBLES GOMEZ

G Pato Díaz, María Xesús
(B. 1955, Ourense– .) Poet.

With a degree in modern history from the University of Santiago, María Xesús Pato Díaz did historical research on the workers' movement in the province of Ourense from its inception to 1936. Her work is contained in an unpublished volume, "O movemento obreiro na provincia de Ourense" (The workers' movement in the province of Ourense). She stayed in Lisbon for some time and wrote a series of poems there.

Some of the poems in *Urania* originally appeared in the literary journal *Escrita*, published by the Association of Writers in Galician. A selection of her early work is included in *Escolma da poesia galega (1976–1984)* (Anthology of Galician poetry). Pato's poetry is composed of short verses based on themes ranging from intimate, personal motifs to modern topics (drugs and alcohol) to recurring subjects in Galician poetry, such as Rosalía de Castro.

BOOKS
Eloïsa. Vigo: Calpurnia, forthcoming.
Urania. Vigo: Calpurnia, 1991.

WORKS IN BOOKS, PERIODICALS, NEWSPAPERS
Poems, untitled. *Escolma da poesia galega (1976–1984)*. Ed. Xosé L. García. Barcelona: Sotelo Branco, 1984. 162–68.
Poems, untitled. *Escrita* 3 (Spring 1984).

SECONDARY SOURCES
Noia Campos, Camino. *Palabra de muller*. Vigo: Xerais, 1992. 43–46, 104–05.

MARIA CAMINO NOIA CAMPOS

C   Pazos i Noguera, Maria Lluïsa
(20th c.) Poet. No biographical information available.

Ausiàs March i l'amor (Ausiàs March and love) is a collection of poems and essays.

BOOKS
Ausiàs March i l'amor. Barcelona: Nova Terra, 1986.
Devastació—Gresol de nit. Barcelona: n.p., 1980.
El joc dels jocs . . . raons. Barcelona: n.p., 1978.

KATHLEEN MCNERNEY

C   Peña, Agna Maria Paulina de la
(19th c., València.) Baronesa de Corts. Short story writer.

Agna Maria Paulina de la Peña signed her work as Maria de la Peña. Constantí Llombart included the Baroness of Corts in his dictionary of Valencian writers, *Los fills de la morta-viva.* The only composition that she appears to have written in Catalan won the Jocs Florals of 1882. She contributed short stories in Castilian to *La ilustración popular económica de Valencia* between 1882 and 1889. She also wrote an essay on the cotton industry. She was made queen of the Jocs Florals del Rat Penat in Valencia in 1881.

BOOKS
Mes de mayo consagrado a la Santísima Virgen María. Madrid: V. Sáiz, 1879.
Pensamientos de Santa Teresa de Jesús. Madrid: Asilo de Huérfanos, 1882.
La Reina del Cielo. Madrid, 1885.
Santo Rosario dedicado a Nuestra Señora de los Desamparados de Valencia. Valencia, 1887.

WORKS IN BOOKS, PERIODICALS, NEWSPAPERS
"Juan Fuerte." *La ilustracion popular económica de Valencia* 1889: 337.
"Un viaje de la Virgen." *La ilustración popular económica de Valencia* 1882: 143–47.
"La visita de la vieja." *La ilustración popular económica de Valencia* 1883: 230.

SECONDARY SOURCES
Llombart, *Los fills de la morta-viva.*

CRISTINA ENRIQUEZ DE SALAMANCA

G   Penas García, Anxeles
(B. 1948, Teixeiro, Coruña– .) Poet and playwright.

A graduate in philosophy and arts from the University of Santiago de Compostela in 1970, Anxeles Penas now works as a teacher of language and literature in a secondary school in Coruña. Her creative activity includes both literature and art. Besides being a poet, Penas is a painter who depicts her surroundings: the sea, sailors, tavern owners, and boats. Although mainly devoted to poetry, she has also written for the theater and has contributed numerous articles on art and literature to the daily press. Her poems, in both Castilian and Galician, have appeared in several journals since her student days. In 1965, she won her first literary prize: the Flor Natural for Castilian poetry in the Juegos Florales of the Minerva School in Santiago. Since then, she has won many others. Her first book of poems in Castilian, *Con los pies en la frontera* (Standing on the border), was published in 1976. It was followed by a second volume, *Ya soy para tu muerte* (I'm already for your death). Her first volume in Galician, *Galicia, fondo val* (Galician valley), did not appear until 1982. At present, she has three new books of poems in Galician ready for publication: "Galicia, meu señor" (Galicia, my lord), a continuation of *Galicia, fondo val*; "Os anales do vento" (Annals of the wind); and "O santuario intocable" (Untouchable sanctuary). She has also written two plays: "A volta de Edipo" (On Oedipus), winner of the Abrente prize, and "Algún deus está a soñar" (Some god dreaming).

Penas's poetry expresses the beauty of contrasts, both structural and semantic; she creates images that are often visionary and experiments with overlapping rhythms. Penas tries to unite the elements of the cosmos with those of daily life, where love is a constant feature. Her metaphysical verses deal with the universal themes of love and death and the impossibility of achieving happiness in day-to-day life. In her angry verses, the poet attacks pretentious love, the intrusion of city planning on the individual, and social falseness.

BOOKS
Con los pies en la frontera. Coruña: Nordés, 1976.
Galicia, fondo val. Sada, Coruña: Castro, 1982.
O santuario intocable. Barcelona: Sotelo Blanco, 1992.
Ya soy para tu muerte. Madrid: Molinos de Agua, 1980.

WORKS IN BOOKS, PERIODICALS, NEWSPAPERS
"Catorce poemas." *Grial* 32 (1971).
"Espejo cóncavo." *Albaida* 1–2 (1977).
"Montaña rusa." *Nordés* 2–3 (1975).
"Oda a la espiral trialéctica." *Nordés* 1 (1975).
"O pobo no recordo." *Revolatura* 1 (1976).

SECONDARY SOURCES
Alfaya, J. "Ya soy para tu muerte." *La calle* 150 (1981).
Barros, Tomás. "A capacidade de expresión plástica e poética de Anxeles Penas." *La voz de Galicia* (29 Dec. 1984).

Cacheiro, *Poetisas galegas do século XX.*
Domínguez Rei, Antonio. "Anxeles Penas: 'Con los pies en la frontera.' " *La estafeta literaria* 618–19 (1977).
————. " 'A volta de Edipo': Una nueva visión del mito clásico." *El ideal gallego* 19 May 1974.
Noia Campos, Camino. *Palabra de muller.* Vigo: Xerais, 1992. 47–50, 106–07.
Pozo Garza, Luz. " 'Con los pies en la frontera': Poesía de Anxeles Penas." *La voz de Galicia* 8 Jan. 1978.
Sáez, Julia. "La poetisa Anxeles Penas, ganadora del 'Jorge Manrique.' " *Arriba* 8 Apr. 1977.
Vázquez de Gey, Elisa. *Queimar as meigas.* Madrid: Torremozas, 1988. 133–38.

MARIA CAMINO NOIA CAMPOS

C   Penya de Barcelosa, Calamanda
(19th c.) Poet. No biographical information available.

Calamanda Penya is cited by Juan P. Criado y Domínguez in his *Literatas españolas del siglo XIX* as a poet who contributed to *La veu de Monserrat* of Vic.

SECONDARY SOURCES
Criado y Domínguez 136.

CRISTINA ENRIQUEZ DE SALAMANCA

C   Penya i Nicolau, Victòria
(B. 1823/27, Palma de Mallorca; d. 1898, Barcelona.) Also Peña de Amer, Victòria. Poet.

Victòria Penya was known in her own time as one of the main figures of the Catalan *Renaixença*, as Francesc Matheu asserts in the introduction to the posthumous anthology *Poesies de Victòria Penya d'Amer* (The poetry of Victoria Penya d'Amer). Like the majority of *Renaixença* women writers, Penya started by composing in Castilian. In 1855 she published the collection "Poesías de Victòria Penya y Nicolau" (Poems by Victòria Penya y Nicolau) in the newspaper *El balear* in Palma, Majorca. She married Miquel Victorià Amer in 1860 and from then on lived in Barcelona. Penya was part of the social circle that launched the linguistic rebirth of the Catalan language and the renewal of Catalan culture in both Barcelona and Majorca. Her brother, known as Pere d'Alcàntara, was also a poet and a popular author of plays in Majorca. Miquel Victorià Amer, a poet as well, was one of the organizers of the first Jocs Florals in Barcelona in 1859, and he received awards in these competitions in 1865 and 1867.

Victòria Penya published in many journals in the Catalan area. In

288

Barcelona, she wrote mainly for *Lo Gay Saber, Calendari català, La re-naixença,* and *La ilustració catalana*; in Majorca, for *Museo balear de historia y literatura, ciencias y artes, Revista balear de ciencias y artes,* and *El balear.* In these journals she also collaborated, as author or editor, with Josefa Massanés, Maria de Bell-Lloch, Margarida Caimarí, Manuela de los Herreros, Agnès Armengol, and Agna de Valldaura, some of whom were her friends. Penya received numerous awards in poetry contests: the silver medal of the Ateneu Català for "Amor de mare" (Mother's love), in 1865; second prize of the Flor Natural for "Anyorança" (Yearning), in 1859; and first prize in the Flor Natural for "Una visita a mi patria" (A visit to my country), in 1873. She received awards in the poetry contests of the Academia Bibliográfica Mariana de Lérida in 1869, 1871, 1873, 1874, 1875, 1876, 1877, 1879, 1891, and 1897 and also in the poetry contest of the Valencian *Lo rat penat* in 1881 for "Catalina Sandoval." Penya took part in the Catalan linguistic controversy between the defenders of classic endings and the defenders of modern endings. The former position, launched by Marià Aguiló, was supported by writers close to him, including Penya. Penya's use of Majorcan forms in her writing, for example, generated some bitter comments from committee members awarding the Jocs Florals prizes in 1867; they considered her language careless.

Penya's poetry can be divided into three categories: religious, mater-nal, and popular. All her works express an unquestioning faith that is tied to the Church's commands. Her most characteristic devotion, to the Virgin Mary, inspired poems celebrating Castilian or Catalan dogmas and legends of the Virgin Mary, and Penya establishes an intimate identification be-tween the Virgin, as Mater Dolorosa, and her personal experience. In her marriage, Penya had several children who died, and her poetry reflects the agony of these losses. She dedicated many poems to dead friends and relatives. Her acceptance of the divine will and the hope of a later reencoun-ter with the departed are psychological devices that are not always convinc-ing and that sometimes seem forced: "No me sembla del tot mare / qui forsa d'amor no tinga / d'oferir sos fills a Deu / quan a la Gloria los crida" (I don't think a mother is / one who doesn't have the strength of love / to offer her children to God / when He calls them) (*Poesies* 2: 61).

Age, the approach of death, and nostalgia for lost youth are themes Penya develops through Marian symbolism. In poems such as "La casa de Nazaret" (Nazareth house) and "Floretes" (Little flowers), the Virgin weaves "de tela molt fina / tan fina que sembla qu'al Cel l'han teixida / Si m'en feya un vel, oh, quina reliquia" (very fine fabric / so fine that it seems Heaven has woven it. / If I made a veil, oh, what a relic) (*Poesies* 2: 140). In "La juventut perdida" (Lost youth), youth, like a transparent veil, transforms old age into a "camp plè de fruyts tots granats / y la mort, sobre roses estessa / una verge de tota puresa" (field full of ripe fruits /

and death, lying on roses / a pure Virgin). Youth takes away the veil of comfort, and thus "la vellesa es un erm cap al Nort / . . . y la verge que suau s'adormía / ara s'alsa feresta . . . ¡es la mort!" (old age is a hermit going north / . . . and the virgin who slept peacefully / gets up furiously now . . . she's death!) (*Poesies* 2: 112). In her poetry, Penya also creates a loving dialogue with Jesus in an intensely personal and emotional language that reaches mystical effusiveness. She combines symbolism of the Holy Family and the desire for union in a confidential tone that sometimes contains guilt: "¡Quina abrasada'm donares / Amor de la mía amor / fugires y te quedares / lo més adintre del cor" (What an embrace you gave me / love of my love / you fled and stayed / in the deepest of my heart!) (*Poesies* 2: 190). Other poems are reactions to contemporary issues: revolutionary events, antireligious feelings, and the power of science to deny religious mysteries and nullify blasphemy. In these poems, the certainty of divine vengeance is the dominant motif.

Penya's "Santa Teresa" (Saint Teresa), "San Francesch" (Saint Francis), "Mort i passió" (Death and passion), "La casa de Nazaret," "Floretes," "Cançó del naxement de Jesus" (Song of nativity), and "Idili" (Idyll) belong to the style of Verdaguer's *Idilios y cantos místicos* (Idylls and mystical chants). Francisco Blanco García said that "A la Verge Maria" (To the Virgin Mary), by its tone and novelty, "parece un preludio de las arrobadoras miniaturas de Verdaguer" (seems a prelude to the entrancing miniatures of Verdaguer) (57–58).

In her popular poetry Victòria Penya uses traditional forms and themes and frequently creates dialogues between female personae. Among her legends, ballads, and songs, she sometimes presents morbid ideas and cruel scenes.

BOOKS
Poesías de Victòria Penya y Nicolau. Palma: Balear, 1855.
Poesies de Victòria Penya d'Amer. Introd. Francesc Matheu. 2 vols. Barcelona: Ilustració Catalana, 1909.

WORKS IN BOOKS, PERIODICALS, NEWSPAPERS
"A Francisca Miró." *Calendari català* (1881): 71–73.
"A la Mare de Deu." *Academia bibliográfica Mariana de Lérida.* 1873. 133–35.
"A la Mare de Deu." *Academia bibliográfica Mariana de Lérida.* 1874. 172–73.
"A la Mare de Deu." *Calendari català* (1867): 79–81.
"A la Mare de Deu. Refugi dels pecadors." *Academia bibliográfica Mariana de Lérida.* 1877. 45–48.
"A la poesia." *Revista balear de literatura, ciencias y artes* 3 (1873): 36–37.
"A la Santísima Virgen de las Mercedes. En desagravio de las ofensas inferidas a su pureza." *Academia bibliográfica Mariana de Lérida.* 1869. 169–72.
"A la Verge María." *Academia bibliográfica Mariana de Lérida.* 1879. 255–58.

"A la Verge María." *Lo Gay Saber* 4 (1868): 26.
"A la Verge Maria." *Poetas baleares del s. XIX.* 268–71.
"Al meu fill." *Calendari català* (1871): 49–51.
"Al meu fill." *Lo Gay Saber* 18 (1879): 232–33.
"A ma filla." *Calendari català* (1869): 20–21.
"A ma filla." *Calendari català* (1880): 33–34.
"A ma germana Calamanda. En la mort de sa filla." *Calendari català* (1899): 39–41.
"A ma germana Calinise. Morta lo 8 de maig de 1865." *Calendari català* (1872): 98–99.
"A Maria en sa gloriosa Assumpció." *La renaixença* (1892): 574–76.
"A María Santísima en su soledad." *Academia bibliográfica Mariana de Lérida.* 1891. 117–18.
"A mes filles." *La renaixença* Year 10, 2.3 (31 July 1880): 87–89.
"A mi amada madre." *Revista balear de literatura, ciencias y artes* 2 (1872): 21–22.
"A mon fill. En lo dia de sa primera comunió." *Lo Gay Saber* 20 (1879): 271.
"A mon germà. En la mort soptada de sa aymada esposa." *Lo Gay Saber* 13 (1881): 139.
"Amor de mare." *Jochs Florals de Barcelona en 1865.* Barcelona: A. Verdaguer, 1865. 203–06.
"Amor de mare." *Poetas baleares del s. XIX.* 260–66.
"A mos germans Pere d'Alcantara Peña y Antonia Gelabert." *Lo Gay Saber* 9 (1881): 90–91.
"A Nostra Señora de la Academia." *Revista balear de literatura, ciencias y artes* 13 (1873): 197.
"A Nostra Señora de l'Academia. Balada." *Academia bibliográfica Mariana de Lérida.* 1871. 71–74.
"Anyorança." *Poetas baleares del s. XIX* 250–54.
"Anyoransa." *Calendari català* (1866): 26–27.
"Anyoransa." *Jochs Florals de Barcelona en 1859.* Barcelona: Salvador Maner, 1859. 81–84.
"A un jilguero." *Revista balear de literatura, ciencias y artes* 21 (1872): 325–27.
"A un ninet de Guix. Regalat per D. Jaume Lluis Garau." *Revista balear de literatura, ciencias y artes* 18 (1872): 277.
"Lo bon Jesuset." *La renaixença* (1892): 80.
"Lo breçolet." *Calendari català* (1900): 75–77.
"Cant de amor." *Calendari català* (1868): 41–43.
"La casa de Nazaret." *Lo Gay Saber* 15 (1879): 193–95.
"Despedida a mes estimades nebodes, Catalina Barceló y Joana Mir." *Calendari català* (1882): 49–50.
"En Josepet." *Poetas baleares del s. XIX* 256–58.
"En Jusepet." *Calendari català* (1873): 75–76.
"En Jusepet." *Revista balear de literatura, ciencias y artes* 1 (1873): 14.
"En l'album de don Ramón Picó y Campanar." *Lo Gay Saber* 3 (1881): 27.
"En l'album de D. Ramón Picó." *La renaixença* (1875): 221.
"En l'album de D. Ramón Picó y Campanar." *Calendari català* (1875): 95–96.
"En la mort de ma germana Nisseta." *Lo Gay Saber* 23 (1879): 296–97.

"L'home devant Deu." *Calendari català* (1870): 73–76.
"Idili." *Calendari català* (1902): 38.
"La iglesia de Port-Bou. Poesia dedicada al Senyor D. Claudi Planas." *La renaixença* (1882): 102–03.
"Ma granjeta." *Calendari català* (1901): 34–36.
"Mater Divinae Gratiae." *Academia bibliográfica Mariana de Lérida.* 1876. 136–39.
"Lo meu niu." *Llibre de la renaixensa.* Barcelona: La Renaixensa, 1888. 276–78.
"Mort y passió." *Academia bibliográfica Mariana de Lérida.* 1897. 57–58.
"La Nit de Reys." *Calendari català* (1874): 88–89.
"Plant per ma bona amiga la Señora Doña Dolores Vicat de Vicens." *Revista balear de literatura, ciencias y artes* 11 (1874): 181–82.
"Poesies." *Lectura popular* 7: 2–7.
"La primera tempesta." *La renaixença* (1890): 755–59.
"¿Qui com Deu?" *Calendari català* (1876): 29.
"La santedat del amor maternal." *Academia bibliográfica Mariana de Lérida.* 1875. 125–31.
"Sempre amb tu." *Jochs Florals de Barcelona. Any XXVIII de llur restauració.* Barcelona: La Renaixença, 1886. 67–72.
"Sia lo vostre cor sens macula." *Lo Gay Saber* 8 (1868): 58.
"Traducció." *La renaixença* (1896): 214–16.
"Una visita a mi patria." *Jochs Florals de Barcelona en l'any XV de llur restauració.* Barcelona: Catalana de Llogari Obrador y Pau Sulé, 1873. 49–59.

TRANSLATIONS OF HER WORKS

"Meinem Töchterchen" ["A mes filles"]. Fastenrath 294–96.

SECONDARY SOURCES

Blanco García, Francisco 1: 57–58.
Matheu, Francesc. "Nota editorial." *Poesies de Victòria Penya d'Amer.* 2 vols. Barcelona: Ilustració Catalana, 1909. 1: 5–7.
Segarra, Mila. *Història de l'ortografia catalana.* Barcelona: Empuries, 1985. 181, 185, 193.
Simón Palmer, *Escritoras españolas del siglo XIX* 524–26.

CRISTINA ENRIQUEZ DE SALAMANCA

C Peris Lozano, Carme

(B. 1941, Barcelona– .) Illustrator and writer of children's books.

Carme Peris Lozano studied drawing and painting at the Escola Massana and at the Escola d'Arts i Oficis Artístics de Barcelona. She has worked as a publicity illustrator and with various Catalan publishers in textbook illustration. A finalist for the Apel.les Mestres prize for text and illustration, she has written and illustrated books for children.

BOOKS

L'espardenyeta. Montserrat: L'Abadia, 1983.
Ivan i el llop gris. Montserrat: L'Abadia, 1987.
La tanca màgica. Montserrat: L'Abadia, 1985.

ANNA GASOL I TRULLOLS

C Perpinyà i Sais, Maria
(B. 1901, Verges, Girona– .) Poet, journalist, and translator.

Autodidactic, Maria Perpinyà worked on the daily paper *El matí* (Barcelona), where she was in charge of the section "La dona i la literatura" (Women and literature) and contributed articles on women and children. In addition to writing poetry, she translated French works and wrote literature for children. She was active in politics before the Civil War and militant in Acció Democràtica.

Her first book, *Poemes* (Poems), concentrates on love themes and features a lyrical tone and lively, precise language. *Terra de vent* (Land of wind) contains the same themes, adding a sense of nostalgia for the Empordà and a profound religious sentiment. Despite its simple appearance, Perpinyà's poetry is formally correct and characterized by a fluid musicality. The countryside is evoked with pictorial richness.

BOOKS

Poemes. Barcelona: La Revista, 1931.
Terra de vent. Barcelona: La Revista, 1936.

WORKS IN BOOKS, PERIODICALS, NEWSPAPERS

"Algunes consideracions sobre l'amor." *El matí* 16 May 1930.
"La bella almoina." *El matí* 21 Feb. 1930.
"El cavaller de Falkenstein." *El matí* 26 May 1929.
"Comentari al llibre de Mme Louise Paulleron sobre els hostals antics." *El matí* 29 Aug. 1929.
"Comentari sobre la poesia 'La rose efeuille' de la Santa de Lisieux." *El matí* 3 Oct. 1929.
"Comentaris sobre l'obra 'Lou Roubatori,' de l'escriptor provençal Teodor Aubanet." *El matí* 15 July 1929.
"Conversa amb un dependent." *El matí* 17 Oct. 1934.
"Cultura i pedanteria." *El matí* 27 Dec. 1930.
"Les disperses energies." *El matí* 10 Oct. 1934.
"Una doble tasca." *El matí* 21 Mar. 1930.
"Dones modernes." *El matí* 28 Nov. 1930.
"L'eficàcia del dolor." *El matí* 2 May 1930.
"L'elegància del dolor." *El matí* 9 May 1930.
"L'estil de Nadal." *El matí* 25 Dec. 1930.

"L'estrella perduda." *El matí* 31 July 1929.
"Estudi crític sobre poemes de Maria Teresa Vernet." *El matí* 12 May 1929.
"El gall de la cresta d'or." *El matí* 16 June 1929.
"La ginesta nadalenca." *El matí* 25 Dec. 1929.
"Gra de mill." *El matí* 6 June 1929.
"L'home que robà el vent." *El matí* 10 July 1930.
"La joia del retorn." *El matí* 13 July 1930.
"El jurament del llop." *El matí* 22 May 1929.
"Lectures." *El matí* 27 June 1930.
"La missió de la dona." *El matí* 31 Oct. 1930.
"Modes i temps inestables." *El matí* 13 Sept. 1930.
"Mudances." *El matí* 20 June 1930.
"Nord Amèrica i nosaltres." *El matí* 12 Dec. 1930.
"Petita bonica." *El matí* 18 Feb. 1930.
"El príncep de la mar." *El matí* 20 Feb. 1930.
"Reflexions sobre la moda." *El matí* 9 July 1929.
"El renec de la innocència." *El matí* 20 Dec. 1929.
"Sentiment i paraules." *El matí* 15 Aug. 1930.
"El tapís Xinès." *El matí* 28 June 1930.
"Les tardorals ventades," "Fidelitat," "El ponent i el rec," "Sinfonia de tardor," "Si ara ens prengués la mort," "Jardí nocturn," "Elogi de la joia," "Enyorança de la mar," "Fugacitat," "Retrobança," "El cor inquiet," and "Lliri." *La revista: Quaderns de mil nou cents trenta sis*. Spec. issue of *La revista*. Jan.-June 1936. 130–37.
"Un tòpic a rectificar." *El matí* 14 Mar. 1930.
"Els tres dons." *El matí* 17 July 1929.
"La vaca cega." *El matí* 6 June 1930.

ALBINA FRANSITORRA ALENA

C Pessarrodona i Artigués, Marta
(B. 1941, Terrassa, Barcelona– .) Poet and literary critic.

Marta Pessarrodona started writing poetry at the age of twelve. She studied history and Romance languages at the University of Barcelona and adopted Catalan as her literary language in 1964, though some titles and verses of her poems are in English or German. Her first published work, *Les possibilitats somnolentes* (Drowsy possibilities), appeared in 1965; it is a limited edition of poems that includes illustrations by some of her hometown friends. In the epilogue to *Poemes 1969–1981* Pessarrodona explains that she excluded these early poems from her 1984 collection because she felt they were unimportant.

Setembre 30 (September 30), the first book of poetry that the author acknowledges, contains a prologue by the well-known poet Gabriel Ferrater. The predominant topics of these twenty-seven poems are love and death, life and faith. In the epilogue Pessarrodona provides biographical information, revealing herself in a direct and sincere way.

In 1972 Pessarrodona went to England for two years as a lecturer of Spanish at the University of Nottingham. This visit was very significant: many of her experiences in the British Isles are reflected in later works, such as *Vida privada* (Private life) and *Memòria i . . .* (Memory and . . .), where the poet becomes nostalgic and evokes the beautiful English winter. She creates an intimate tone through her use of colloquial language, even though she maintains a high degree of lyricism.

In 1981 Pessarrodona published one of her most personal works, *A favor meu, nostre* (In my favor and ours), which contains her strongest expression of feminism. *Berlin suite* resulted from Pessarrodona's visit to Berlin, where she made many friends and grew more understanding of the contemporary European situation. A collection of her poems written prior to 1981 was published under the title *Poemes 1969–1981*. In this book she omitted epilogues from her earlier works, including the one to *Setembre 30*, and added a previously unpublished poem, "Eros més que Thànatos" (Eros more than Thanatos). Throughout her poetry, the vivid and realistic depiction of her experiences places Pessarrodona among the foremost poets in the Catalan language. Her work as a literary critic is also important: she publishes articles regularly in *La vanguardia* (Barcelona), *El país* (Madrid/Barcelona), *Avui* (Barcelona), and *Dones en lluita* (Barcelona).

BOOKS
A favor meu, nostre. Barcelona: LaSal, 1981.
Berlin suite. Barcelona: Mall, 1985.
Homenatge a Walter Benjamin. Barcelona: Columna, 1988.
Memòria i . . . . Barcelona: Lumen, 1979.
Nessa: Narracions. Barcelona: Plaza & Janès, 1988.
Poemes 1969–1981. Barcelona: Mall, 1984.
Les possibilitats somnolentes. Barcelona: n.p., 1965.
Les senyores-senyores ens els triem calbs. Barcelona: Abitat, 1988.
Setembre 30. Prol. Gabriel Ferrater. Barcelona: Ariel, 1969.
Vida privada. Barcelona: Lumen, 1973.

WORKS IN BOOKS, PERIODICALS, NEWSPAPERS
Poems. *La nova poesia catalana.* Ed. Joaquim Marco and J. Pont. Barcelona: Edicions 62, 1980. 172–79.

TRANSLATIONS OF HER WORKS
"The A.B.C. of Things" ["Lliçó de coses"], "Landscape with Obese Figure" ["Paisatge amb figura obesa"], and "Sad St. John's Eve" ["Nit trista de Sant Joan"]. *Modern Catalan Poetry: An Anthology.* Ed. and trans. David Rosenthal. St. Paul: New Rivers Press, 1979: 176–80.
"Berlín: Enero 1929" ["Berlin: Gener 1929"], "Schöneberg," and "Hallesches Tor."

Trans. Ana Maria Moix. *Litoral femenino.* Ed. Lorenzo Saval and J. García Gallego. Granada: Litoral, 1986. 191–98.

"The Cruelty of the Months" ["La crueltat dels mesos"]. Trans. David Rosenthal. *The Humanist* 34.6 (1974): 20.

"For Maria-Antònia, Caterina, and Clementina and Some—Not Many—Others: A Poem in Dedication to Forgotten Women Writers" ["Per Maria Antònia, Caterina i Clementina i tantes—no moltes—d'altres"]. Trans. H. Patsy Boyer. *On Our Own Behalf.* Ed. Kathleen McNerney. Lincoln and London: U of Nebraska Press, 1988. Frontispiece.

"In Memoriam," "Song like a Prayer" ["Cançó com una oració"], "Aiming at Sarah Bernhardt" ["Amb vocació de Sarah Bernhardt"], "Belle Dame Connue" ["Bella dama coneguda"], "Berlin: January 1929" ["Berlin: Gener 1929"], and "Springtime." *Five Poets.* Selected and trans. D. Sam Abrams. Barcelona: Inst. d'Estudis Nord-Americans, 1988. 30–41.

"Lesson about Things" ["Lliçó de coses"], "In the Manner of Mrs. Hughes," "This Year Nobody Will Send Me a Cattleya" ["Aquest any ningú no m'enviarà cap cadleia"], "Dove at a Barcelona Window" ["Colom a una finestra de Barcelona"], "Bergasse 19, Vienna—20 Mansfield Gardens, London" ["Berggasse 19, Viena—20 Mansfield Gardens, Londres"], "Homage to H. D.," and "Anna Gorenko." *Survivors.* Selected and trans. D. Sam Abrams. Barcelona: Inst. d'Estudis Nord-Americans, 1991. 75–91.

SECONDARY SOURCES

Marco, Joaquim. "Memòria i Marta Pessarrodona." *Destino* 11 July 1969.

Parcerisas, Francesc. "In the way of Mrs Hughes i la moral de Marta Pessarrodona." *Camp de l'arpa* Mar.-Apr. 1973.

Pi de Cabanyes, Oriol. "Marta Pessarrodona, entrevista." *La generació literària dels 70.* Barcelona: Pòrtic, 1971. 101–12.

MARIA LUISA GUARDIOLA-ELLIS

C   Pic de Aldawala, Roser
(19th c.) Playwright. No biographical information available.

Roser Pic de Aldawala presented two plays in Barcelona's Teatro del Liceo in 1877. The first, *Com sucsuheix moltes vegades* (As it happens many times), which premiered on 12 March, deals with the disappointments that appear after marriage: the wife feels that her husband's affection is disappearing and the husband is offended by his wife's refusal to remain at home. The distinguishing characteristic of the play is that it introduces the possibility of divorce, the regulation of which was being discussed in the National Congress at that time. The marital conflict is resolved conservatively: the couple's differences vanish when they discover a baby is coming.

Gent de barri (People of the neighborhood) premiered on 16 April. It is a sketch of Barcelona customs and manners that includes many references to Catalan and national politics and mentions the opposition between liberals and Carlists, the defenders of the most conservative branch of the Spanish monarchy. Some of the characters represent the early Andalusian emigrants to Catalonia, such as the city police officer whose language is a mixture of Catalan and Andalusian. The play also deals with the confrontation between the elderly, who still believe in an authoritarian tradition, and the young, who, adopting an ideal born of the French Revolution, regard the law as the highest standard. The magazine *Lo Gay Saber* (1 Feb. 1878) announced "Roser Pich" as the pseudonym of a dramatist who did an adaptation of one of Charles Dickens's novels for the Catalan stage.

BOOKS

Com sucsuheix moltes vegades. Joguina en un acte y en vers. Barcelona: Salvador Manero, 1877.
Gent de barri. Boceto de costums bosquejats en un cuadro. Barcelona: Salvador Manero, 1877.

CRISTINA ENRIQUEZ DE SALAMANCA

C   Pi de la Serra, Paulina
(20th c.) Short story writer. No biographical information available.

Quatre narracions (Four stories) includes "Història d'Emma" (The story of Emma), "El punt" (The point), and "El decapitat" (Beheaded), the story of a French official beheaded by his wife. Paulina Pi de la Serra also works on radio programs.

BOOKS

Quatre narracions. Terrassa: Amics de les Arts, 1982.

KATHLEEN MCNERNEY

C   Pinyol i Nolla, Maria Montserrat
(20th c.) Novelist.

Little is known about Maria Montserrat Pinyol i Nolla except that she went into exile in Mexico and returned to Catalonia. Her novel *La sang generosa: D'Orient a Occident* (Generous blood: From East to West) was first written in Castilian and published in Mexico; she later translated it into Catalan. The characters are fictional and the places deliberately

297

vague, but some historical facts are presented. It is a dramatic novel for young people about constancy, optimism in the face of hardship, and love for nature, life, study, travel, and culture. The ideology of pacifism pervades the story, as the author encourages young people to continue to resist wars started by their elders.

BOOKS

La sang generosa: D'Orient a Occident. Barcelona: El Tinter, 1982.

KATHLEEN MCNERNEY

C Pla, Walda
(B. 1913, El Masnou, Barcelona– .) Novelist.

Walda Pla is the author of two novels, *Salt d'euga* (The mare's jump) and *Amarga joia* (Bitter happiness). The first is a bildungsroman in which the protagonist, Rosana, becomes aware of her unhappy marriage and her subordination to her husband when a foreign woman spends the summer with them. The action takes place in a rural Catalan home, inherited by the husband's family from a widowed landowner. Rosana lives in an antagonistic relationship with her mother-in-law and sister-in-law and assumes the position of a Cinderella, as a result of her quiet character and her husband's unwillingness to defend her. The family life is disrupted by the visit of a beautiful African woman who has a professional life and a cosmopolitan air. The attraction felt by every man in the family toward her is the cue for Rosana to question her marriage and her value as a woman. The landscape descriptions and violent atmosphere within the family are reminiscent of Emily Brönte's *Wuthering Heights*. And the excitement generated by the African's presence is a metaphor for the social commotion brought to the Costa Brava by tourism in the early sixties.

Amarga joia is a less convincing novel. Set in Barcelona and in Italy, it describes the search of a young man in high society for pure, romantic love. His idealism is contrasted to the cynicism of his friends. Walda Pla rejects the frivolous life of the Catalan upper classes as well as feminism, revealing her belief that the women's liberation movement has created a type of woman who acts sexually like a man at his worst.

BOOKS

Amarga joia. Barcelona: Rafael Dalmau, 1968.
Salt d'euga. Barcelona: Rafael Dalmau, 1961.

SECONDARY SOURCES

Serrahima, Maurici. "Walda Pla: *Salt d'euga.*" *Serra d'or* 8–9 (1963): 46–72.

CRISTINA ENRIQUEZ DE SALAMANCA

C Planas Pardo d'Oroval, Pepita
(20th c.) Poet.

Pepita Planas Pardo d'Oroval is a member of the group Poesia Viva.

BOOKS
Abans i després del naufragi. Barcelona: Poesia Viva, 1986.
El meu racó. Barcelona: n.p., 1980.

KATHLEEN MCNERNEY

C Planelles i Planelles, Julia
(B. 1960, València– .) Poet.

The small sample of Julia Planelles's work in the anthology *Entranys per a l'augur* (Entrails for the augur) reveals a poetry that is direct in its representation of the poet's inner search for authenticity and her rejection of social idols.

WORKS IN BOOKS, PERIODICALS, NEWSPAPERS
"Poema pintar paraules," "Per tot el que més estime," "He cridat quan la nit s'embolicava," "De sobte evocàvem a nous déus," "La nit mossegava la claror del dia," "He visitat els llimbs," "La mare crida que vol morir," and "Els àngels endimoniats." *Entranys per a l'augur. Antologia de jove poesia catalana al Baix Vinalopó—1980.* Elx, Alacant: U Nacional d'Educació a Distància, 1980. 137–45.

ISABEL ROBLES GOMEZ

C Pomés, Angels
(B. 1935, Melilla– .) Poet.

After her mother's death, Angels Pomés moved to Casablanca, where she received her education in a convent run by French nuns. Pomés joined the civil administration in the Diputació de Barcelona. At first she wrote in French and Castilian, and in 1980 her work in Catalan received the Vallrina poetry prize in honor of Josep Maria López Picó. In 1982 Pomés published a selection of her poems in *Miscel.lània poètica*, a volume with work by two other poets, Assumpció Torras and Roser Matheu. Pomés delves into personal feelings in restrained poems that seek to solve the small mysteries of everyday life. Her vision emerges through images of dissolving elements, such as mud, tears, and shadows. Her sexual allusions can be striking: "la geometria verge d'uns fulls pàl.lids / per l'estilet puny-ent de la paraula / quedà prenyada de matisos càlids" (The virginal geome-try of pale pages / became pregnant with warm nuances by the sharp stylet of the word) ("Adveniment" [Arrival]). She also incorporates sexual images into human feelings, such as pain: "Nua m'has pres, Dolor . . . Nua i sor-presa / . . . I la carn m'has llaurat amb l'urpa fosca / . . . Vaig ser teva, Dolor" (Pain, you have overtaken me naked . . . Naked and shocked / . . . You have plowed my flesh with the dark claw / . . . You possessed me, Pain) ("Dolor" [Pain]). Her treatment of more topical subjects, such as in "L'ametller" (The almond tree), "Tardoral" (Autumn), or "Pas de dança" (Dance step), produces a gentler poetry, which can still have shocking images.

WORKS IN BOOKS, PERIODICALS, NEWSPAPERS
"Poemes." *Miscel.lània poética.* Barcelona: Fundació Salvador Vives Casajuana, 1982.

CRISTINA ENRIQUEZ DE SALAMANCA

Pompeia, Núria; *see* **Vilaplana i Buixons, Núria**

Pons, Simona; *see* **Gay, Simona**

C   Pons i Griera, Lídia
(20th c.) Writer of children's literature. No biographical information available.

BOOKS
No cal fer reverències. Montserrat: L'Abadia, 1981.

KATHLEEN MCNERNEY

C   Pons i Jaume, Margalida
(B. 1966, Palma de Mallorca– .) Poet.

Margalida Pons's first book of poems, *Sis bronzes grisos d'alba* (Six gray bronzes of dawn), won the 1985 Salvador Espriu prize for young poets, which was awarded by the Fundació Pere Vergès. This collection of twenty-four short lyrics explores the interiority of the self as it confronts the passage of time, the play of memory and desire, the pain of separation from the other, fear and confusion, and the struggle to gain clarity, certainty, and love. Rich in imagery, these poems portray intense moments of feeling and perception in which details of the natural world—the sea, sky, vegetation, mountains, seasons, dawn, and evening—are vividly delineated. *Les aus* (The birds) won the Premi Ciutat de Palma prize in 1987.

BOOKS
Les aus. Barcelona: Edicions 62, 1988.
Sis bronzes grisos d'alba. Barcelona: Edicions 62, 1986.

ANN ELLIOTT

C Portell, Carmina
(20th c.) Journalist. No biographical information available.

Carmina Portell has contributed to *Presència* and *Punt diari* of Girona.

BOOKS
El caval és meu. Girona: Aubert, 1973.

KATHLEEN MCNERNEY

C Portet, Renada-Laura
(B. 1927, St. Paul de Fenouillet, France– .) Also known as Vicent Valencià and previously known as Renada-Laura Calmón i Ullet. Critic of literature and art, translator, short story writer, novelist, and poet.

One of the few representatives of "Catalunya Nord," that part of southern France where Catalan is still spoken, Renada-Laura Portet is considered an expert on her region's toponymy, which she has shown to consist of an ancient substratum of Basque and a large component of Catalan that is sometimes rendered inaccurately into French. Her collection of stories, *Castell negre* (Black castle), was awarded the prestigious Víctor Català prize, which was revoked a few days later because of a misunderstanding about its imminent publication in French. The varied and moving stories often have women protagonists, some of them weak and passive, others strong and willful. This balance of personalities lends credence to the author's assertion that the writer's role is to witness rather than to judge. "La senyoreta Dorotea" (Miss Dorothy) features an independently wealthy older woman who takes a young lover; when he dies, she finds another. "Un estiueig" (A summer stay) also depicts an older woman and a younger man, but in this case the relationship is clearly off-balance and somewhat sinister. Set in rural southern France, the stories in this collection include accounts of greed, the life of a handicapped child in a small town, and a house haunted by strange music.

Portet's profession as a teacher in Perpignan is reflected in her novel *L'escletxa* (The crevice), an unusually detailed portrait of the world of work. The beliefs and idealism of Irene, a young female teacher, are constantly thwarted by the school administration as well as by ultra-right-wing teachers and students who harass her for her pro-Catalan attitudes. Basing much of the narrative on current conditions in the Roussillon, Portet describes the teacher's increasingly desperate reactions to the authorities' intransigence. In spite of the Llei Deixonne, which allows regional languages to be taught in French schools, the protagonist finds that teaching the course is almost impossible, since it would be considered extra for her and her students and could be offered only at lunchtime or after hours. This inconvenience has the desired effect of making some students drop the class, which is then in danger of being canceled for lack of interest. The novel also features a love relationship, which dissolves as Irene turns to literature as her real passion. Portet conveys the protagonist's feelings of fear and desire with a visceral directness that successfully involves the reader. Her prose is replete with irony: for example, a colleague in linguistics complains about Irene speaking a foreign language in the hallway; and the study of Japanese and Russian is encouraged in her school, but Catalan is unacceptable. Portet also employs enriching but nonpedantic references to Saint Teresa of Avila, Albert Camus, Pere Gimferrer, and other literary figures of her multicultural heritage.

Portet contributes to several literary and onomastic periodicals. She has won various prizes for her poetry and prose and has been a jury member in other contests.

BOOKS
Castell negre. Perpinyà: Chiendent, 1981.
L'escletxa. Barcelona: El Llamp, 1986.
Jocs de convit. Prol. Kathleen McNerney. Barcelona: Columna, 1990.
Lettera amorosa. Perpinyà: Trabucaire, 1990.
Memòries de la Viuda Reposada (published under the pseudonym Vicent Valencià). Barcelona: El Llamp, 1991.
Una ombra anomenada oblit. Barcelona: Columna, 1992.

TRANSLATIONS OF HER WORKS
"What If I Turn?" ["I si em regirés?"]. Trans. Kathleen McNerney. *Catalan Review* 3.2 (1989): 224–29.

KATHLEEN MCNERNEY

G   Pozo Garza, Luz

(B. 1922, Ribadeo, Lugo– .) Poet.

During Luz Pozo Garza's childhood her family moved to Viveiro, Lugo, where she stayed until the start of the Spanish Civil War. As a result of political persecution, her father was arrested by General Franco's government, and Luz Pozo went to Morocco with her family until 1940. During the postwar period, she completed her secondary school studies, received her diploma in piano studies, and later became a teacher. She graduated in Romance philology at the University of Oviedo and worked as a literature teacher in several secondary schools until she retired.

A bilingual poet, in Castilian and Galician, she has had her poems published in many journals and has also worked as a poetry critic, contributing numerous articles to the journal *Nordés*, which she cofounded and coedited in Coruña in 1975. This journal went through a second epoch, from 1980 to 1983, when it was edited by Luz Pozo and published by Ediciōs do Castro. She also wrote literary analyses for *Grial* and other Galician periodicals.

Her first book of poems in Castilian, *Anfora* (Amphora), was published in 1949 and reflects the poetry of youth. Passionate and vital, sensual and mythical, it features Danae, beloved of Zeus. In 1952 Pozo published *El vagabundo* (The tramp) and *O paxaro na boca* (The bird on the mouth). The first book, in Castilian, sings of freedom, life, and the beauty of nature. However, it also tries to express in elegiac form the author's feeling of incommunicability in love. The second book, in Galician, begins with love poems and is followed by songs to idealized forms in nature: the sea, people, and the land. A decade later, Pozo published *Cita en el viento* (Date in the wind), whose central theme is the sea. In the 1976 bilingual collection, *Ultimas palabras / Verbas derradeiras* (Last words), the theme of incommunicability between lovers reappears, together with the absence of the loved one.

In *Concerto de outoño* (Autumn concert) and her most recent book, *Códice calixtino* (Code of Calixt), Pozo uses Galician. In the first, she deals with love and existentialist concerns, her homeland ("Verbas a Rosalía"), the freedom of man, the scars of the Civil War, and artistic creation, poetry, and music. In the second work, the subject of love is united with an emotionally meaningful place, Santiago de Compostela. This city is doubly sacred for the poet: for its importance in Western history and as the place where she had romantic meetings with her lover. The lovers' relationship is idealized through their separation and made long-lasting by their vitality and constancy. Pozo's poems contain numerous sacred symbols: cathedrals, canopies, domes, chalices, and incense, together with all the symbols of Galician Romanesque art. Pozo evokes the past with mythical and real figures and pays homage to the beloved poets whose works live on. There is very little light in her poetry. Her images are generally represented by black and white; blue and violet sometimes appear in winter landscapes, in which violets, "camelias blancas" (white camellias), or "camelias enlutadas" (camellias in mourning) are mentioned. Hers is a landscape of shadows and constant rain, an appropriate setting for meditation. Luz Pozo's lyrical poetry explores deeply personal concerns and the different emotional states of love: nostalgia, plenitude, and worry.

BOOKS
Anfora. Vigo: n.p., 1949.
Cita en el viento. Viveiro, Lugo: n.p., 1962.
Códice calixtino. Barcelona: Sotelo Branco, 1986. 2nd ed. Vigo: Xerais, 1991.
Concerto de outoño. Prol. Antonio Pombar. Sada, Coruña: Castro, 1981.
O paxaro na boca. Lugo: Palacio, 1952.
Ultimas palabras / Verbas derradeiras. Prol. Tomás Barros. Coruña: Nordés-Poesía, 1976.
El vagabundo. Ribadeo, Lugo: n.p., 1952.

WORKS IN BOOKS, PERIODICALS, NEWSPAPERS
"Agora contemplamos a mar de Vigo." *La voz de Galicia* 8 Feb. 1986.
"A Paul Eluard." *Nordés* 12 (July 1983).
"Coma Dante chegando o Paradiso." *Nordés* 5 (Oct. 1981).
"Escuro designio." *Nordés* 10 (Jan. 1983).
"Homenaxe a Luís Seoane." *Nordés* 11 (Apr. 1983).
"Iba morrer un home." *Nordés* 1 (1975).
"Interpretación do sermón da flor." *Nordés* 2 (Jan. 1981).
"As maus dos cegos." *Nordés* 1 (1975).
"Morte en Compostela." *La voz de Galicia* 10 Mar. 1983.
"Na subita compaña." *Dorna* 6 May 1983.
"Poema en cinco lembranzas pra Rosalía." *Grial* 34 (1971).
"Poemas de Gernika." *Nordés* 6 (Jan. 1982).
"Pranto coral por Luís Seoane." *Grial* 64 (1979).
"Reminiscencia da nenez." *Nordés* 3 (Apr. 1981).
"Requiem por Romy Schneider." *Nordés* 8 (July 1982).
"A resposta." *Nordés* 4 (1976).
"Tocata e fuga." *Nordés* 1 (1980).
"Vemos fuxir." *Grial* 88 (1985).
"Vivir co pobo." *Nordés* 2–3 (1975).

SECONDARY SOURCES
Alvarez Cáccamo, X. M. "Música e cor no concerto de outono." *Faro de Vigo* 10 Mar. 1983.
González Garcés, M. "Códice calixtino de Luz Pozo Garza." *La voz de Galicia* 19 Mar. 1987.
———. "La poesía de Luz Pozo Garza." *La voz de Galicia* 8 Mar. 1970.
———. "*Verbas derradeiras* de Luz Pozo." *La voz de Galicia* 7 Nov. 1976.

Pamies, Teresa. "Luz Pozo." *Rosalia no hi era*. Barcelona: Destino, 1982.
Pombar, Antonio. "Concerto appassionato." *Grial* 75 (1982).

MARIA CAMINO NOIA CAMPOS

C Prat, Francesca
(20th c.) Poet. No biographical information available.

BOOKS
El soldat rosa. Valencia: Eliseu Climent, 1983.

KATHLEEN MCNERNEY

C Pratdesaba i Portabella, Pilar
(B. 1886, Vic, Barcelona; d. 1971, Sant Just Desvern, Barcelona.)
Poet.

According to *Les cinc branques* Pilar Pratdesaba published two volumes
of poetry: *Records de joventut* (Memories of youth), the first poems of which
are dedicated to the eight major planets she studied with her brother, and
Romeria als Santuaris de la Verge (Pilgrimage to the sanctuaries of the
Virgin).

BOOKS
Records de joventut. Vic: Biblioteca Vigatana, n.d.
Romeria als Santuaris de la Verge. N.p.: n.p., 1954.

WORKS IN BOOKS, PERIODICALS, NEWSPAPERS
"Mercuri a la seva germana la terra" and "Neptú." *Les cinc branques* 70.

NANCY L. BUNDY

C Prat i Batlle, Mercè de
(20th c.) Journalist and poet. No biographical information
available.

Mercè de Prat's collection forms the third volume of the series *Poemes i
dibuixos* (Poems and drawings) made for the Sala d'Art of the Picasso
workshop. The prologue to the poetry section is by Maria-Aurèlia Capmany,
who compares Prat's poetic voice to a recitative. The poet considers her
art a natural gift and strives for communication. Her poems deal with love
and sensuality, the birth of a child, the sea, and self-expression. She has
written for several newspapers.

305

BOOKS
Poemes i dibuixos. Vol. 3. Illus. Víctor Ramírez. Barcelona: Sala d'Art del Taller de Picasso, 1982.

KATHLEEN MCNERNEY

G Prieto Rouco, Carmen
(B. 1901, Vilalba, Lugo– .) Poet and playwright.

Carmen Prieto Rouco's first book of poems in Galician, *Horas de febre* (Hours of fever), came out in 1922. According to the Galician literary historian Ricardo Carballo Calero, *Horas de febre* contains descriptive, *costumbrismo* (local color) poetry, as well as poems of lyrical intimacy in which love occasionally appears. Prieto follows Rosalía de Castro and other nineteenth-century poets and criticizes herself for rhythmic defects in her poetry.

Prieto's other works include the librettos to the two-act operettas "Nubes de verano" (Summer clouds), which was composed by a friend and performed in Prieto's native village, and "Treidores celos" (Treacherous jealousy). Her plays—"A loita" (The fight), a monologue first staged in 1923; "O embargo" (The embargo), a tragedy in verse in four acts; "Madrastra" (Stepmother), a drama in one act; the monologue "Na boda do afillado" (The wedding of the godson); and the comic piece "O secreto da bruxa" (The secret of the witch)—are unpublished.

BOOKS
Horas de febre. Vilalba: n.p., 1926. 2nd ed. 1928.
Lluvia menuda. Ortigueira: n.p., 1956.
Violetas. Lugo: n.p., 1934.
A virxe viuda (Hestoria dun amor). Viveiro, Lugo: n.p., 1963.

WORKS IN BOOKS, PERIODICALS, NEWSPAPERS
"Lembranza." *A nosa terra* 216 (20 Aug. 1920).
"¡Nai Galicia!" *A nosa terra* 229 (1 Oct. 1926).

SECONDARY SOURCES
Carballo Calero, *Historia da literatura galega contemporánea* 562–65.
Couceiro Freijomil, *Diccionario bio-bibliográfico de escritores gallegos* vol 3.
Gran enciclopedia gallega vol. 25.

MARIA CAMINO NOIA CAMPOS

C Puig, Genoveva
(20th c., Tarragona.) Poet.

Genoveva Puig was exiled in Paris during the Spanish Civil War. *Claror d'alba* (Daybreak) features poems on love, religion, and exile. Some are free-flowing prose pieces. *Poema íntim: Paraules a Jesús* (Intimate poem: Words to Jesus) contains two parts: the first, glossed poems in a diary setting; the second, prayers. *Poesia* (Poetry) is made up of love poems and memoirs. *El gran manicomio* (The great nuthouse) is a novel in Castilian. Puig is also a composer and musician.

BOOKS
Claror d'alba. Barcelona: n.p., n.d.
El gran manicomio. Barcelona: n.p., 1971.
Poema íntim: Paraules a Jesús. N.p.: n.p., n.d.
Poesia. Barcelona: n.p., 1975.

NANCY L. BUNDY and KATHLEEN MCNERNEY

Puigmadrona, Aurora; pseudonym for **Ignasi Riera.**

C **Pujades i Botey, Mercè**
(B. 1880, Caldes d'Estrac, Barcelona; d. 1972, Caldes d'Estrac, Barcelona.) Poet.

Mercè Pujades lived in Switzerland during the Spanish Civil War but returned to Barcelona afterward. She directed the Col.legi Barcelonès de la Verge de la Mercè for sixty years. *Del meu camí* (About my path), which contains poems written between 1915 and 1954, was compiled and published by her former students. Many of the poems were written to be sung by children, and some are dedicated to specific individuals. She also dedicated a poem to Maria Montessori and wrote several Christmas poems.

BOOKS
Del meu camí. Barcelona: Dalmau, 1967.

NANCY L. BUNDY and KATHLEEN MCNERNEY

C **Pujal i Serra, Antònia**
(19th c., Barcelona.) Poet.

The sister of writer José Pujal i Serra, Antònia Pujal was a teacher who also studied in the business school in Barcelona and traveled extensively in Europe. The *Enciclopedia universal ilustrada europeo-americana* says that Pujal contributed Catalan and Castilian poems to several periodicals and that in 1901 she published *Poesías* (Poems), but this work is not available in major libraries. According to the same bibliographical source, she translated French, Italian, English, and German poets.

BOOKS
Poesías. Barcelona, 1901.

WORKS IN BOOKS, PERIODICALS, NEWSPAPERS
"Sin padre." *La ilustración de la mujer* 15 Apr. 1885.

SECONDARY SOURCES
Enciclopedia universal ilustrada europeo-americana. Vol. 48. Madrid: Espasa-Calpe, 1922. 455.

CRISTINA ENRIQUEZ DE SALAMANCA

C   Pujol de Canals, Montserrat
(B. 1897, Molins de Rei, Barcelona– .) Poet.

Montserrat Pujol contributed poetry to several regional journals. *Clixés de ruta (1919–1969)* (Vignettes of the road 1919–1969) is a long collection of traditional and religious poems, written on the occasion of her golden wedding anniversary. *Aforismes* (Aphorismes) is a collection of two-line bits of advice and philosophy written between 1974 and 1977; it also includes a poem dedicated to Jacint Verdaguer.

BOOKS
Aforismes. Molins de Rei: Puel.les, 1977.
Clixés de ruta (1919–1969). Illus. Carme Sala. Molins de Rei, Barcelona: n.p., 1969.

NANCY L. BUNDY and KATHLEEN MCNERNEY

C   Pujol i Maura, Maria Antònia
(20th c.) Poet. No biographical information available.

BOOKS
Observació i experimentació a parvulari. With Clementina Roig i Planas. Barcelona: Rosa Sensat, 1981.
Recull de poemes per a petits i grans. With Clementina Roig i Planas. Barcelona: Caixa de Pensions, 1976.

KATHLEEN MCNERNEY

C   Pujol i Russell, Sara
(B. 1957, Barcelona– .) Poet.

Sara Pujol teaches philosophy and literature in Tarragona and is active in the poetic group Espiadimonis in that city. She began writing poetry during her university years and won the Recull prize in Blanes in 1980. Her only published work, "Mar maduixa" (Strawberry sea) is in *Sis poetes 83* (Six poets of 1983). Her reflective poetry draws heavily on imagery from her personal visions of nature: "I si calia morir que fos / entre geranis fermentats als pous del mar" (And if death were to come, let it be / among geraniums fermented in wells of the sea) (59).

WORKS IN BOOKS, PERIODICALS, NEWSPAPERS
"Mar maduixa." *Sis poetes 83*. Barcelona: Mall, 1983. 53–69.

KATHLEEN MCNERNEY

G   Queizán Vilas, María Xosé
(B. 1939, Vigo, Pontevedra– .) Novelist, essayist, and scriptwriter.

María Xosé Queizán started writing articles for *El pueblo gallego* of Vigo when she was young. At the start of the 1960s, she spent time in France and became acquainted with the "nouveau roman français." A graduate in Galician philology, she teaches language and literature at a secondary school in Vigo and edits the feminist journal *Festa da palabra silenciada*, to which most contemporary Galician women writers contribute.

In 1965 she published her first novel, *A orella no buraco* (The ear in the hole), following the new French style, which in Galician literature was given the name "a nova narrativa galega." Queizán uses the techniques of interior monologue and the protagonism of objects that play an important role in an individual's life. The feminist ideology that would inspire Queizán's later work is not yet present. In *Amantia*, her second novel, the author contrasts female and male perspectives. The main character is Exeria, who lives in the fourth century BC and makes a series of trips around Europe to spread the "Priscilian" doctrine. The story describes the daily life of Priscilian women, their dreams, pastimes, and amusements. There are long dialogues among the women on issues that concern the author, including Galicia and the nature of femininity; but Quiezán also shows historical aspects of the period, such as rites, witchcraft, and religious doctrines. There are constant allusions to the world within the home, to crafts and clothing. During the same period, Quiezán also wrote several short stories for periodicals.

The fantasy *O segredo da pedra figueira* (The secret of the figtree stone) is situated in a prehistoric past. The lack of structural complications lends it the air of a book for young people. The story tells of the flight of the Amala tribe by ship after the invasion by the Lurpios. The text is constructed symbolically on a feminist theme. Intelligence, sensibility, memory of the past, and government are all identified with women, while passiveness and brutality are associated with men.

An active woman, Queizán has also worked in the theater, as scriptwriter, actor, and director. She is the author of an unpublished play, "Non convén chorar máis" (Don't cry any more). She works on video scripts; one of them, "Prisciliano," was awarded the Xunta de Galicia prize. As an essayist, she is mainly concerned with women's social problems and discrimination in Galicia and has written two books on these topics: *A muller en Galiza* (The woman in Galicia) and *Recuperemos as mans* (Recovering our hands).

Queizán's feminist point of view strongly influences all her work: "La herencia histórica que aceptamos, la cultura en general, es masculina. Las instituciones no funcionan para nosotras y estamos excluidas del sistema económico imperante. . . . Carecemos de cultura, de historia, de lengua. La lengua es la expresión de la realidad y como la sociedad, es patriarcal" (The historical heritage that we accept, and the culture in general, are masculine. Institutions don't work for us [women] and we are excluded from the prevailing economic system. . . . We don't have our own culture, history, or language. Language is the expression of reality, and like society, it's patriarchal) (*Recuperemos as mans* 98).

BOOKS
Amantia. Vigo: Xerais, 1984.
Amor de tango. Vigo: Xerais, 1992.
Antígona, a forza do sangue. Vigo: Xerais, 1989.
Evidencias. Vigo: Xerais, 1990.
Metáfora da metáfora. Coruña: Espiral Maior, 1990.
A muller en Galiza. Sada, Coruña: Castro, 1977.
A orella no buraco. Vigo: Galaxia, 1965; 2nd ed. 1984.
Recuperemos as mans. Santiago: Cerne, 1980.
O segredo da pedra figueira. Vigo: Tintimán, 1986. 2nd ed. Vigo: Xerais, 1989.
A semellanza. Barcelona: Sotelo Blanco, 1988.

WORKS IN BOOKS, PERIODICALS, NEWSPAPERS
"As botas." *Contos eróticos / Elas*. Vigo: Xerais, 1990. 49–62.
"Eros e Tánatos." *Grial* 56 (1977).
"María Xosé Queizán en *Evidencias*" (interview). With F. Franco. *Faro de Vigo* 15 Jan. 1990.
"A nova narrativa ou a loita contra o sentimentalismo." *Grial* 65 (1979).
Poems, untitled. *Nordés* 15 (1982): 23 and 17 (1983): 39.
"Sen que as visagras," "O Sena nace de ti," and "No inverno." *Festa da palabra silenciada* 1 (1984): 21–22.
"O tapete de ganchillo." *Grial* 61 (1978).

SECONDARY SOURCES

Blanco, Carmen. "Galicia e a muller en *Amantia*." *Festa da palabra silenciada* 3 (1986).
———. "María Xosé Queizán e o feminismo materialista." *Literatura galega da muller*. Vigo: Xerais, 1991. 93–102.
———. "*Recuperemos as mans* de María Xosé Queizán." *Grial* 76 (1982).
Carballo Calero, Ricardo. "*A orella no buraco* por María Xosé Queizán." *Grial* 10 (1965).
Ferrero, C. E. "*A muller en Galiza* de María Xosé Queizán." *La voz de Galicia* 2 Mar. 1979.
Hermida García, M. "Dende Thule polo mar." *Faro de Vigo* 30 Mar. 1986.
López Pereira, J. E. "Prisciliano: Del nacionalismo gallego a la narrativa gallega actual." *El correo gallego* 8 June 1986.
Mouriz Barja, Sabela. "A lucidez das *Evidencias*." *La voz de Galicia* 15 Feb. 1990.
Noia Campos, Maria Camino. "Elvira unha nova Antígona galega." *La voz de Galicia* 3 Aug. 1989.
———. *A nova narrativa galega (1954–1969)*. Vigo: Galaxia, 1991.
———. "Os novos narradores onte e hoxe." *La voz de Galicia* 13 May 1982.
"Una novela histórica: *Amantia*." *Boletín de la Biblioteca del Instituto Femenino de Bachillerato de Lugo* 17 (Feb. 1985).
Palau, J. M. "Literatura gallega: *Amantia*." *La vanguardia* 7 (Mar. 1986).
Panero Menor, Carmen. "*O segredo da pedra figueira* de María Xosé Queizán." *Nó* 1 (1986).
"*O segredo da pedra figueira* de María Xosé Queizán." *Luzes de Galiza* 3 (1986).
Xan Sucasas. "María Xosé Queizán na nova narrativa galega." *Vieiros* 3 (Oct. 1965).

MARIA CAMINO NOIA CAMPOS

C Rafart, Susagna
(B. 1962, Ripoll, Girona– .) Poet.

Susagna Rafart's only available work appears in *Fulls impermeables I*, a collection of the work of the Catalan Young Writers' Association. Her poetry celebrates love and nature; often written in sonnet form, it is somewhat reminiscent of her medieval and Golden Age predecessors.

WORKS IN BOOKS, PERIODICALS, NEWSPAPERS
"Poemes." *Fulls impermeables I*. Prol. Josep Maria Castellet. Barcelona: Mall, 1983. 163–75.

KATHLEEN MCNERNEY

C Ragué i Arias, Maria-Josep
(B. 1941, Barcelona– .) Short story writer, playwright, theater critic, and journalist.

Maria-Josep Ragué i Arias has a doctorate in philosophy and letters and also holds degrees in journalism and economics, all from the University of Barcelona. Active in the feminist movement, she is a member of the Associació Teatre-Dona and of the evaluating committee for dramatic readings for the Societat General d'Autors Espanyols. As a graduate student she taught from 1968 to 1970 in the department of Spanish and Portuguese at the University of California at Berkeley, and she is now a professor at the University of Barcelona. She has published numerous journalistic articles, theater criticism, and interviews with famous people. She has also contributed reports to scientific publications.

I tornarà a florir la mimosa (The mimosa will bloom again) is a collection of short stories, most of which have a feminist perspective. In them she denounces, among other things, the alienation and oppression of women within and outside the family and shows that suicide or madness is often the only form of liberation. *Clitemnestra* (Clytemnestra) is a version of the Orestes cycle from the point of view of Clytemnestra, who represents a matriarchy that predates the patriarchal tradition. Ragué i Arias co-authored a play with Isabel-Clara Simó and Armonía Rodríguez called "I Nora obrí la porta" (And Nora opened the door) for the Associació Teatre-Dona. It deals with what happens to Ibsen's Nora after she leaves home. The work has been performed but not published.

BOOKS

Clitemnestra. Barcelona: Millà, 1986.

Crits de gavina. Barcelona: Millà, 1988.

Els personatges femenins de la tragèdia grega en el teatre català del segle XX. Barcelona: AUSA, n.d.

I tornarà a florir la mimosa. Barcelona: Edicions 62, 1984.

SECONDARY SOURCES

McNerney, Kathleen. "Reinterpretations of the Classics: What's Old and What's New in Catalonia?" *Studies in the Humanities: International Drama and Feminism* 17.2 (1990): 172–78.

Pérez-Stansfield, María Pilar. "La desacralización del mito y de la historia: Texto y subtexto en dos nuevas dramaturgas españolas." *Gestos: Teoría y práctica del teatro hispánico* 2.4 (1987): 83–99.

MARIA-LOURDES SOLER I MARCET

C   Rahola, Pilar

(B. 1959, Barcelona– .) Novelist, journalist, and literary critic.

A member of the cultural staff for the Catalan TV station TV3, Pilar Rahola has degrees in Castilian and Catalan philology. Her first novel, *Aquell estiu color de vent* (That summer color of wind), has been translated into

Castilian and was a finalist for the Premi El Brot award in 1983. The novel features the personal reminiscences of nine characters about the summer of 1975. It is basically a bildungsroman, as eight of the young people entering adulthood experiment with politics, alternative lifestyles, relationships, and drugs. One of the youths commits suicide by throwing himself under a train; this act has a profound effect on the others, who begin to move from optimistic rebellion to doubt and disillusionment. Interspersed with the chapters of interior monologues are short reflections on the act of writing a novel. Similarly, *Aperitiu nocturn* (Nocturnal aperitive) comprises the interior monologues of its four protagonists—mother, father, son, and daughter—who steadily draw away from one another: the parents into the irrecoverable world of their pasts, the son and daughter into cynicism and nihilism. This postmodern novel explores the displacement of realistic narrative, the disintegration of the personality into incoherence, and the radical disorders of language.

BOOKS
Aperitiu nocturn. Barcelona: Pòrtic, 1985.
Aquell estiu color de vent. Barcelona: Pòrtic, 1983.

ANN ELLIOTT

C Raichs i Padullés, Carme
(20th c., Agramunt, Lleida.) Poet.

Recull de pensaments (Collection of thoughts) contains poems to Sant Boi, the suburb of Barcelona where Carme Raichs now lives, and also to Montserrat, Catalonia, and Pau Casals. Raichs repeats the image of the individual's smallness before nature. One of the most interesting pieces in the collection is "Jo vinc del silenci" (I come from silence), in which she speaks to her daughter, who is very different from herself. In the poem Raichs expresses fear for her rebellious daughter's future in a patriarchal culture, but as a mother she tries to be understanding and supportive and to explain her own development. *Poemes a tres temps* (Poems in three movements) ends with some interesting experimentation with calligrams.

BOOKS
Poemes a tres temps. Sant Boi del Llobregat: n.p., 1982.
Recull de pensaments. Barcelona: n.p., 1978.

KATHLEEN MCNERNEY

C Ramoneda i Soler, Maria Rosa
(20th c.) Poet. No biographical information available.

BOOKS
El meu reialme. Barcelona: Lluís Gassó, 1986.

KATHLEEN MCNERNEY

C Raspall i Juanola de Cauhé, Joana
(B. 1913, Barcelona– .) Writer of children's plays and poems.

Joana Raspall studied in the 1930s under Jordi Rubió i Balaguer, and her thesis showed an early interest in literature for children. A librarian, she has collaborated on several dictionary projects. While most of her literary production is dramatic, she has also contributed numerous stories to the journal *El pont* and has written some unpublished novels and stories.

BOOKS
L'ermita de Sant Miquel. Barcelona: Millà, 1964.
L'invent. Barcelona: Don Bosco, 1978.
Kònsum, S.A. Barcelona: Don Bosco, 1984.
Petits poemes per a nois i noies. Barcelona: Daimon, 1981.
El pou. Barcelona: Tremoleda, 1976.

KATHLEEN MCNERNEY

C Rausell i Soriano, Manuela
(B. 1839, València; d. ?) Journalist, poet, and playwright.

Manuela Rausell was educated by her parents and received lessons in arithmetic, grammar, and poetry. She contributed articles, folk tales, philosophical maxims, and poetry to several journals in Castilian: *Las provincias, Valencia ilustrada, La ilustración popular, La antorcha, La unión católica, El consultor, La lealtad, El zuayo, Valencia, La revista del Turia*, and *El comercio*. Some of her poetry was translated into Portuguese and printed in the Lisbon periodical *A nacao*. She also wrote for Constantí Llombart's Valencian calendar *Lo rat penat*. According to Llombart, she wrote two unpublished plays in Castilian verse—"Enemistad y amor" (Enmity and love) and "Los caprichos de la suerte" (Caprices of luck)—and was the first Valencian poet to write in Catalan and to become an honorary member of Lo Rat Penat. Llombart gives Rausell a hagiographic and sentimental biographical note in his dictionary, *Los fills de la morta-viva*.

 Manuela Rausell's Catalan poetry, published in *Lo rat penat* between

1880 and 1884, shares the characteristics of *Renaixença* poetry. These include the nationalist exaltation of particular places—in this case, the city of Valencia—historical romances based on local characters, and a conservative religious sentiment that combines devotion and patriotism. A collection of canticles, "Cent i un cantars" (A hundred and one canticles), received a prize in the Jocs Florals of Valencia in 1883. Rausell also published Catalan prose, the most important example being the story "Centelles y Solers o un amor entre dos odis (Llegenda del temps dels bandos)" (*Centelles* and *Solers* or a love between two hates—Legend of the times of rival bands), an updated version of the tragedy of Romeo and Juliet set in Valencia.

WORKS IN BOOKS, PERIODICALS, NEWSPAPERS
"El amor." *Las provincias. Diario de Valencia. Almanaque para el año 1892.* 117–20.
"Centelles y Solers o un amor entre dos odis (Llegenda del temps dels bandos)." *Lo rat penat* (1884): 25–37.
"Cent i un cantars." *Lo rat penat* (1884): 162–66.
"La flor del taronger" and "La mort d'en Ramon Boil, llegenda històrica." *Lo rat penat* (1883): 36–37, 135–44.
"La joya de Valencia" and "La plasa de la Mare de Deu." *Lo rat penat* (1880): 19–22, 67–69.
"La tradició d'Alacarch: Romans historich." *Lo rat penat* (1882): 95–99.

SECONDARY SOURCES
Llombart 574–79.

CRISTINA ENRIQUEZ DE SALAMANCA

C Rayó Ferrer, Eusèbia
(B. 1951, Palma de Mallorca– .) Novelist.

Eusèbia Rayó studied geography and history at the University of Palma but left before graduation to raise two daughters and to work for the government of the Balearic Islands. Her first novel, *L'alquímia del cor* (Alchemy of the heart), won the Guillem Cifre de Colonya prize in 1986. This tale for young people has magic and suspense, malevolent princes and kings, snake charmers, wise but unheeded alchemists, and, of course, a great adventure.

BOOKS
L'alquímia del cor. Barcelona: La Galera, 1987.

KATHLEEN MCNERNEY

Reina de Mallorca; *see* **Mallorca, Reina de**

C Requesens, Estefania de
(B. 1501/08, Barcelona; d. 1549.) Author of familial letters.

Estefania de Requesens belonged to a family of Catalan nobility that had great influence on the Castilian imperial court during the fifteenth, sixteenth, and seventeenth centuries. The correspondence between her and her mother, Hipòlita de Rois i Moncada, countess of Palamós, has been recently transcribed and published by LaSal in the volume *Cartes íntimes d'una dama catalana del s. XVI: Epistolari a la seva mare la comtessa de Palamós* (Intimate letters of a Catalan lady of the sixteenth century: Letters to her mother, the countess of Palamós). The introduction by Maite Guisado describes the characteristics of the epistolary form and provides a history of the Requesens family. Guisado stresses the importance of the letter as a linguistic document of the fifteenth century, explaining its medieval usage and its later, more elaborate form.

Estefania de Requesens married the Castilian noble Juan de Zúñiga, who became the tutor of Prince Philip, the future King Philip II of Spain. When Zúñiga was a member of the Consejo de Estado (State's Council), the couple moved to Madrid and lived in the royal court. Requesens gave birth to eleven children, of whom four sons and one daughter survived. She endured her children's deaths through her strong Christian faith, although sometimes her rationalizations reach pathetic tones. Her letters reveal a woman who considered herself a Catalan and a foreigner in the Castilian court, although she was not rejected there. But she was lonely, as a result of her husband's political duties. Requesens maintained a respectful but affectionate relationship with her mother and expressed typical maternal pride in her children, whom she regarded as being physically and morally superior to the other children of the nobility. Her correspondence records her double duties: as administrator of many family properties and as manager of her home. The exchange of gifts between mother and daughter, from cosmetics to homemade food, provides interesting details of women's daily life.

The references to political events in the court of Charles I reflect, as Maite Guisado points out, "una visió de la història des de dintre, viscuda als passadissos, a les cerimònies, als tornejos, en les audiències, en els trasllats de la cort, en l'espera de noves de guerra de l'emperador, en les malalties del príncep, al costat dels sofriments de l'emperadriu, de les tasques del preceptor" (a vision of history from the inside, lived in the corridors, in ceremonies, at tournaments, at hearings, at the changing of Courts, during the wait for war news from the emperor, and the prince's illnesses, at the side of the empress when she was suffering, through the chores of the tutor) (xxii). Requesens's letters provide the inside historical perspective of a woman. The British Museum holds the letters that Estefania de Requesens wrote to her son Luis shortly before her death.

BOOKS

Cartes íntimes d'una dama catalana del s. XVI: Epistolari a la seva mare la comtessa de Palamós. Prol., transcription, and notes by Maite Guisado. Barcelona: LaSal, 1987.

"Instrucciones a su hijo D. Luis." Ms. 16176, fol. 202. British Museum, London.

SECONDARY SOURCES

Torres Amat 532.

CRISTINA ENRIQUEZ DE SALAMANCA

C Rexach i Olivar, Agustina
(B. 1910, Girona– .) Poet and essayist.

Agustina Rexach studied to be a teacher but never practiced her profession. In 1957 she wrote for *Los sitios de Gerona,* now *Diari de Girona,* in which she published essays on religious and social themes. Rexach was awarded several prizes in competitions and Jocs Florals, including the Genet d'Or she won for seven consecutive years from the Acadèmia dels Jocs Florals del Rosselló Companyia Literària; she won the first medal in 1958. She also received awards in the Jocs Florals for the Aged and in those held in Cardona. In 1985 she was given the silver medal in the XV Certamen Literari de la Fraternitat Cristiana de Malalts i Minusvàlids for her essay "Montsenys."

Rexach wrote poetry for many years before actually beginning to publish pieces in *Vida catòlica* (Girona), in 1968, under her initials, ARO. She also contributed to *Presència, L'olotí, La comarca d'Olot, Butletí oficial de la Comunitat Turística de la Costa Brava,* and *Poetes de Nadal.* Her first book, *Els meus camins* (My paths), contains patriotic and love poems and shows great poetic sensibility and command of her art. In 1987 she published *El joc de la melodia* (The melody game). These poems on various subjects, are unified by their musicality and careful rhythmic structure. Agustina Rexach's poetry uses an intimate, romantic tone against a background of pure Franciscan ideology.

BOOKS

Itinerari personal: De Girona a La Garrotxa. Illus. Emília Xargay. Barcelona: Edimurtra, 1989.

El joc de la melodia. Introd. Josep Maria Ainaud de Lasarte. Prol. Narcís-Jordi Aragó. Illus. Emília Xargay. Girona: Edimurtra, 1987.

Els meus camins. Prol. Pere Ribot. Girona: Edimurtra, 1985.
Paisatge i llegendes del Montseny. Illus. Lluis Roura. Barcelona: Edimurtra, 1992.

ALBINA FRANSITORRA ALENA

C Ribas i Vives, Maria Assumpció
(B. 1953, Arenys de Munt, Barcelona– .) Writer of children's stories.

Maria Assumpció Ribas studied business and worked in an office while continuing her courses in philology. After living in several Catalan cities, she returned to her hometown, Arenys de Munt, where she teaches Catalan. She has contributed many stories to *Cavall fort, Tretzevents*, and *Avui* and has won two prizes: the Cavall Fort in 1985 and the Lola Anglada in 1987.

BOOKS
L'anell de l'aiguamarina. Montserrat: L'Abadia, 1988.
L'aventura de la vall del Corb. Montserrat: L'Abadia, 1983.
El canelobre màgic. Montserrat: L'Abadia, 1987.
L'Estel sent el temps. Terrassa: L'Ajuntament i la Caixa d'Estalvis, 1988.
El lladre del passat. Montserrat: L'Abadia, 1989.
Quan la Neus somiava truites. Barcelona: Magrana, 1988.
Salten bruixes per la finestra. Montserrat: L'Abadia, 1985.

KATHLEEN MCNERNEY

C Ribas Prat, Maria
(B. 1965, Sant Antoni, Eivissa– .) Journalist and poet.

Maria Ribas Prat won honorable mention for the Baladre prize with her collection of poetry *Clarejar* in 1980.

BOOKS
Cavalcada dalt Eivissa a l'hora dels silencis. Eivissa: n.p., 1981.
Clarejar. Eivissa: n.p., 1981.
Flors de Portmany. Eivissa: n.p., 1981.

KATHLEEN MCNERNEY

C Ribé i Ferré, Maria del Carme
(B. 1920, Reus, Tarragona– .) Short story writer and novelist.

In addition to her professional writings as a librarian, Maria del Carme Ribé has published stories in *Tele/Estel* and *El pont*. Her novel *Del dia a la nit* (From day to night), a realistic work with psychological themes, centers on the vicissitudes of a Barcelona family.

BOOKS
Del dia a la nit. Barcelona: Cadí, 1968.

GUILLEM-JORDI GRAELLS

C Riera Guilera, Carme
(B. 1948, Palma de Mallorca– .) Short story writer, novelist, and literary critic.

Carme Riera lived in Majorca as a child and moved to Barcelona to attend the University of Barcelona. She studied philosophy and letters, specializing in Spanish literature of the Golden Age. She is a professor of Spanish at the Universitat Autònoma of Barcelona and has also taught in a high school. Part of a narrative group of the 1970s that included several Majorcan writers, Riera is currently one of Catalònia's leading writers. Her fiction is lyrical, evocative, and carefully structured. Her first work, *Te deix, amor, la mar com a penyora* (I leave you, my love, the sea as a token), is divided into three parts. The characters act as free people who cannot be part of conventional society. Their stories deal with personal experiences, especially during the teen years, and one deals with an adolescent love affair set in Majorca.

Riera's works have a feminist point of view and present women in a realistic way. Her collection *Jo pos per testimoni les gavines* (I offer the seagulls as witnesses) focuses on women's relationships and portrays the equalization process of women in society. Riera wants women to speak up in a society where only the male voice has been heard. A Castilian translation of some of her stories has been published under the suggestive title *Palabra de mujer, bajo el signo de una memoria impenitente* (A woman's voice, under the symbol of an unrepentant memory).

In 1981 Riera published *Epitelis tendríssims* (Extremely tender epitheliums), a collection of erotic stories told from the female narrator's point of view. Riera turned to the novel the same year with *Una primavera per a Domenico Guarini* (A primavera for Domenico Guarini), which won the 1980 Prudenci Bertrana prize. This exceptional novel follows a biographical approach. Clara, a Catalan journalist, goes to Florence to report on Domenico Guarini's trial for his attack on Botticelli's *Primavera*. The hearing becomes part of her life: as details of the case come to light, she starts to solve some of her personal problems. Reflecting on the means of articulating her life and her account of the trial, she learns to look at contemporary as well as Renaissance ideologies and myths about women. Everything

319

takes her back to her childhood, and she finds the painting to be a mirror of her experiences. *Qüestió d'amor propi* (A question of self-esteem) recounts, in epistolary form, the intense but brief passion of a mature woman for a seductive but egotistical writer. Its background of pseudo-intellectual gatherings serves as a vehicle for the author's social criticism. *La escuela de Barcelona* (The Barcelona school) is a book of literary criticism on Carles Barral, Jaime Gil de Biedma, and José Agustín Goytisolo.

BOOKS
Contra l'amor en companyia i altres relats. Barcelona: Destino, 1991.
Epitelis tendríssims. Barcelona: Edicions 62, 1981.
La escuela de Barcelona. Barcelona: Anagrama, 1988.
Joc de miralls. Barcelona: Planeta, 1989.
Jo pos per testimoni les gavines. Barcelona: Laia, 1977.
Una primavera per a Domenico Guarini. Barcelona: Edicions 62, 1981.
Qüestió d'amor propi. Barcelona: Laia, 1987.
Te deix, amor, la mar com a penyora. Barcelona: Laia, 1975.

TRANSLATIONS OF HER WORKS
Cuestión de amor propio [*Qüestió d'amor propi*]. Barcelona: Tusquets, 1988.
"I Leave You, My Love, the Sea as a Token" ["Te deix, amor, la mar com a penyora"], "Some Flowers" ["Unes flors"], and "The Knot, the Void" ["Es nus es buit"], trans. Alberto Moreiras. "A Cool Breeze for Wanda" ["Una mica de fred per a Wanda"] and "Miss Angels Ruscadell Investigates the Horrible Death of Marianna Servera" ["La senyoreta Angels Ruscadell investiga la terrible mort de Marianna Servera"], trans. Eulàlia Benejam Cobb. *On Our Own Behalf: Women's Tales from Catalonia.* Ed. Kathleen McNerney. Lincoln: U of Nebraska P, 1988. 25–71.
Palabra de mujer, bajo el signo de una memoria impenitente [from *Te deix, amor, la mar com a penyora* and *Jo pos per testimoni les gavines*]. Barcelona: Laia, 1980.
Por persona interpuesta [*Joc de miralls*]. Barcelona: Planeta, 1989.
Una primavera para Domenico Guarini [*Una primavera per a Domenico Guarini*]. Trans. Luisa Cotoner. Barcelona: Norte, 1981.
Te dejo el mar [from *Te deix, amor, la mar com a penyora* and *Jo pos per testimoni les gavines*]. Madrid: Espasa-Calpe, 1991.

SECONDARY SOURCES
Ciplijauskaité, *La novela femenina contemporánea.*
Cotoner, Luisa. "Una primavera per a Domenico Guarini de Carme Riera." *Mirall de glaç: Quaderns de literatura* (Spring-Summer 1982): 52–57.
Nichols, Geraldine C. "Carme Riera." *Escribir, espacio propio: Laforet, Matute, Moix, Tusquets, Riera y Roig por sí mismas.* Minneapolis: Inst. for the Study of Ideologies and Literature, 1989. 187–227.
———. "Stranger than Fiction: Fantasy in Short Stories by Matute, Rodoreda, Riera." *Monographic Review / Revista monográfica* 4 (1988): 33–42.
Ordóñez, Elizabeth J. "Beginning to Speak: Carme Riera's *Una primavera para*

Domenico Guarini." La Chispa 85: Selected Proceedings. Ed. Gilbert Paolini.
New Orleans: Tulane UP, 1985. 285–93.

———. "Rewriting Myth and History: Three Recent Novels by Women." *Feminine
Concerns in Contemporary Spanish Fiction by Women.* Ed. Roberto Manteiga,
Carolyn Galerstein, and Kathleen McNerney. Potomac: Scripta Humanistica,
1988. 6–28.

Pont, Jaume. "Carme Riera y Guillém Frontera: Signos de la narrativa mallorquina." *Insula* 34.388 (1979): 3–4.

Tsuchiya, Akiko. "The Paradox of Narrative Seduction in Carmen Riera's *Cuestión
de amor propio." Hispania* 75.2 (1992): 281–86.

MARIA LUISA GUARDIOLA-ELLIS

C Riu, Maria Dolors

(20th c.) Poet. No biographical information available.

One of the poems in *Ventall de sentiments* (Fan of feelings) is called "Sóc
bergadana" (I'm from Berga), and several of them reflect Maria Dolors
Riu's love for the Berga region. The book is divided into two parts, "Esclat"
(Burst) and "Pensaments al vent" (Thoughts to the wind). The work is
patriotic and demonstrates a social consciousness. Some of the pieces are
dedicated to political figures in Catalonia, such as Jordi Pujol and Francesc
Macià; others deplore the poverty of the masses and contrast this destitution with military spending. Clearly a Catalanist, Riu nevertheless rejects
divisions and dedicates a poem to all Spaniards. She has a special sympathy
for the marginal, including the elderly, the poor, and prostitutes. Her
rhymes are traditional and she has composed a few sonnets.

BOOKS

Ventall de sentiments. Barcelona: IGOL, 1982.

KATHLEEN MCNERNEY

C Rius i Gil, Remei

(20th c.) Poet. No biographical information available.

Temps d'esplai: Intimitats (Leisure time: Intimacies), a collection of poems
inspired by the sea, contains children's songs and works praising the family.

BOOKS

Temps d'esplai: Intimitats. Illus. Enric Planas i Vilanova. Barcelona: n.p., 1982.

KATHLEEN MCNERNEY

C Roca i Perich, Maria Mercè
(B. 1958, Girona– .) Short story writer, novelist, and journalist.

Maria Mercè Roca has won prizes for both her short stories and for her journalism. She teaches Catalan and coordinates Catalan courses for adults offered by the city of Girona. *Sort que hi ha l'horitzó* (It's a good thing there's a horizon) is full of surprises, some delightful, others painful. Roca deals with many themes in these brief stories, which are unified by her keen observation and a fine sensibility that sometimes turns into a delicate sensuality. She ranges from traditional short stories to whimsical vignettes, which are provoked by the simplest everyday details—the address of a house expands into a portrait of its inhabitants and their particular traits; each ad in a newspaper conceals a tragicomedy; a wine list in a restaurant suggests multiple relationships. *Ben estret* (Real tight) follows this pattern and is populated with various characters in diverse situations. In "No escriuré cap novel.la" (I won't write a novel), a writer wins prizes for her short stories and people tell her she should write a novel. She tries to think of a theme important enough to write a novel about: death, love, war, dramas of passion? They all seem inadequate and she finally writes the title of the story on a piece of paper and goes to sleep tranquilly. Roca's fiction is distinguished by her original style and fresh insight.

In 1987, an outstanding year for Roca, she published three new books. *El col.leccionista de somnis* (The dream collector) again links brief vignettes, this time in the form of dreams told to a narrator-protagonist who cannot remember his own and consequently asks to hear those of others. The dreams are grouped loosely by the neighborhoods in which they are requested: in a plaza near a home for the elderly, the dreams reflect the concerns of old people; in a yard frequented by children, they show youthful imaginations and fears. Roca's first novel, *Els arbres vençuts* (The fallen trees), was a finalist for the Sant Jordi prize in 1986. It tells the chilling story of a woman's struggles to maintain her sanity while coping with unfulfillment and frustration. The tale is told after the woman's death by her daughter, Laura, who puts the information together from her mother's writings. The reader gets the benefit of three points of view: the woman's, Laura's, and that of the man she loved, whom Laura contacts after learning about him in her mother's papers. The novel evokes the passion and despair described in Charlotte Perkins Gilman's *The Yellow Wallpaper. El present que m'acull* (The present that welcomes me), winner of the Josep Pla prize, falls into the increasingly interesting subgenre of the family chronicle. The narrator, Miquel Planagumà, has a brief but pregnant conversation with his grandson Marc, which encourages the old man to gather all the family papers together and write a kind of history. The title refers to Planagumà's positive attitude at the end, in which he refuses to give in to nostalgia and returns to enjoying the present, in peace and joy. The title of *Perfum de nard* (Spikenard perfume) refers to the biblical incident in which a woman of ill repute bathed Christ's feet in an expensive aromatic essence and then dried them with her hair. The book is a triptych of three stories inspired by the evangelists but told here from very different points of view. Tamar, a Jewish prostitute who falls in love with a Roman soldier, seeks consolation from Christ but not forgiveness; the wife of Pontius Pilate is curiously attracted to the Jewish preacher and tries to save him; Mary Magdalene falls in love with him after he exorcises seven devils from her body. Roca's work is full of lyricism and is presented simply and casually, as if she were chatting with the reader over *a cafè amb llet* in her native Girona.

Roca has entered the field of young people's literature with *Com un miratge* (Like a mirage), the story of an adolescent's first love. *Temporada baixa* (Off-season) is a chilling psychological study of its neurotic male narrator. Among Roca's nonfiction work is *Capitells* (Capitals), a description of the cloister in Girona's medieval cathedral. Roca also works on Catalan television programs.

BOOKS

Els arbres vençuts. Barcelona: Proa, 1987.
Ben estret. Barcelona: El Llamp, 1986.
Cames de seda. Barcelona: Columna, 1993.
Capitells. Photographs by Josep Maria Oliveras. Girona: El Pont de Pedra, 1988.
La casa gran. Barcelona: L'Eixample, 1990.
El col.leccionista de somnis. Barcelona: Empúries, 1987.
Com un miratge. Barcelona: Barcanova, 1988.
Greuges infinites. Barcelona: Planeta, 1992.
Perfum de nard. Barcelona: Destino, 1988.
El present que m'acull. Barcelona: Destino, 1987.
Sort que hi ha l'horitzó. Barcelona: Selecta, 1986.
Temporada baixa. Barcelona: L'Eixample, 1990.

KATHLEEN MCNERNEY

C Rodés, Montserrat
(B. 1951, Barcelona– .) Poet.

In 1989, Montserrat Rodés earned an honorable mention in the Jocs Florals of Barcelona with "Ones trencades" (Broken waves). *Riu d'arena* (Sand river) includes this group of short poems as the final section, preceded by parts called "Silenci" (Silence) and "Fragments." Rodés contributed poems to various journals during the 1970s. She works in the publishing industry.

BOOKS
Riu d'arena. Valencia: Alfons el Magnànim, 1992.
La set de l'aigua. Barcelona: Edicions 62, 1991.

KATHLEEN MCNERNEY

C Rodoreda i Gurgui, Mercè
(B. 1908, Barcelona; d. 1983, Romanyà de la Selva, Girona.)
Novelist, short story writer, poet, and journalist.

Recognized in her lifetime as one of the greatest novelists and short story writers in Catalan, Mercè Rodoreda received important awards early in her career and in 1980 was awarded the highest distinction for a Catalan writer, the Premi d'Honor de les Lletres Catalanes, for her entire work. She is an acknowledged model for many Catalan women writers, for her creation of an authentic narrative voice to express women's inner struggles and for the connections she makes between exile and women's lives. Her works have reached an international audience.

The only daughter of a middle-class Catalan family, Rodoreda was withdrawn from school at the age of nine, but she remained an avid reader throughout her life. From her grandfather she learned the love of flowers that is reflected in her writing. Early in her career, the Club dels Novel.listes brought her into contact with the Sabadell Group of vanguardists, including Françesc Trabal, Joan Oliver, Armand Obiols (pseudonym for Joan Prat), and with other Catalan writers, specifically Pere Quart and C. A. Jordana. Rodoreda published stories in the Catalan journals *Meridià, Mirador, La Rambla de Catalunya, Publicitat,* and *Revista de Catalunya.* She also wrote four novels that she later repudiated: *Sóc una dona honrada?* (Am I an honest woman?), which anticipates her later use of interior monologue; *Del que hom no pot fugir* (What no one can escape); *Un dia en la vida d'un home* (A day in a man's life); and *Crim* (Crime), a parody of the detective novel.

Rodoreda established her literary reputation and won the Creixells prize in 1937 with the novel she considered her first, *Aloma* (1938). A stream-of-consciousness narrative of a young woman's brief love affair and abandonment at the outbreak of the Civil War, it portrays the heroine's quiet courage as she confronts the moral and social issues of her pregnancy.

A member of the Associació d'Escriptors Catalans, Rodoreda worked in the Institut de les Lletres Catalanes from 1936 until the fall of Barcelona in

1939, when she went into exile in France. From an arranged marriage in 1928 with her uncle Joan Gurgui, Rodoreda had a son, whom she left in the care of her mother when she fled Spain; she had already separated from her husband. During the Second World War Rodoreda worked as a seamstress in Limoges and Bordeaux. After the war she moved to Paris and, in 1954, to Geneva where she worked as a translator. Rodoreda shared her life in exile with the Catalan writer Armand Obiols until his death in 1971. Although she visited Barcelona after 1957, she did not reestablish residence there until 1979.

Rodoreda recalled the isolation and economic hardships of life during the postwar years as obstacles to her writing. After a long silence, she produced her best-known novel, *La plaça del Diamant* (The time of the doves), where her realism and artfully unadorned depiction of an ordinary woman's inner life in colloquial monologue reach their highest development. Written in exile, this work evokes pre–Civil War Barcelona as experienced by Natàlia, a young woman from the working-class neighborhood of Gràcia. Her survival of the war as a widow with two young children is intimately portrayed but also reflects the collective suffering of Catalans during this time. *La plaça del Diamant* has been translated into a dozen languages and made into a film for Spanish television. *El carrer de les Camèlies* (Camellia Street) describes without moralizing judgments the everyday physical and psychological struggles of a young woman who becomes a prostitute in postwar Barcelona.

Rodoreda's stories have been published in three collections, which demonstrate the changes in her art. The first, *Vint-i-dos contes* (Twenty-two stories), winner of the Víctor Català prize, includes stories that originally appeared in Catalan journals published outside of Spain. This series of bleakly realistic stories on the failure of male-female relationships shows the influence of Katherine Mansfield's stream-of-consciousness narratives. The second collection, *La meva Cristina* (*My Christina*), is in the mode of the fantastic and the uncanny that marks much of her later work. It concentrates on first-person narration, and metamorphosis and alienation are the recurrent themes. The third collection, *Semblava de seda* (It seemed like silk), includes stories published as early as 1938. The later stories are profoundly disturbing confrontations with death, solitude, and the imagination.

Mirall trencat (Broken mirror) combines realism and imagination in its detailed depiction of a family's rise and fall and in its focus on death and the presence of ghosts. Rodoreda's work moves from the realist mode of *La plaça del Diamant* and *El carrer de les Camèlies* toward the interior world of the fantastic, the hallucinatory, and the symbolic in *Quanta, quanta guerra* (So much war) and *Viatges i flors* (Journeys and flowers), winner of the City of Barcelona Prize and two Critic's Prizes.

The female narrator-protagonists in her novels of the 1960s are survivors, and the matriarch of the 1974 novel *Mirall trencat* forges her social and economic rise. These representations of the self yield to a visionary mode in the late 1970s and 1980s, as the details of everyday life take on hallucinatory aspects. The posthumous *La mort i la primavera* (Death and spring), a work written before 1961 and revised several times, reveals an even earlier presence of the symbolic and visionary and also a preoccupation with death.

Throughout her career, Rodoreda was a self-conscious artist. In her introduction to *Mirall trencat*, she lists the great nineteenth-century realists as her models, but in later introductions and interviews she mentions her admiration for Poe and Kafka. Her first-person narrators are often servants or elderly or isolated figures; and they are usually women, to whom she gives an intimate, authentic, and lyrical voice.

BOOKS

Aloma. Barcelona: Inst. de les Lletres Catalanes, 1938. Rev. ed. Barcelona: Edicions 62, 1969.

Una campana de vidre. Barcelona: Destino, 1984.

El carrer de les Camèlies. Barcelona: Club, 1966.

Cartes a l'Anna Murià, 1939–1956. Ed. Isabel Segura i Soriano. Barcelona: LaSal, 1985.

Crim. Barcelona: La Rosa dels Vents, 1936.

Del que hom no pot fugir. Badalona: Clarisme, 1934.

Un dia en la vida d'un home. Badalona: Proa, 1934.

Isabel i Maria. Valencia: Eliseu Climent, 1991.

Jardí vora el mar. Barcelona: Club, 1967.

La meva Cristina i altres contes. Barcelona: Club, 1967.

Mirall trencat. Barcelona: Club, 1974.

La mort i la primavera. Barcelona: Club, 1986.

Obres completes. 3 vols. Barcelona: Edicions 62, 1976–84.

La plaça del Diamant. Barcelona: Club, 1962.

Quanta, quanta guerra. Barcelona: Club, 1980.

Semblava de seda i altres contes. Barcelona: Edicions 62, 1978.

Sóc una dona honrada? Barcelona: Llibreria Catalònia, 1932.

Tots els contes. Barcelona: Edicions 62, 1979.

Viatges i flors. Barcelona: Edicions 62, 1980.

Vint-i-dos contes. Barcelona: Selecta, 1958.

WORKS IN BOOKS, PERIODICALS, NEWSPAPERS

"Aquella paret, aquella mimosa." *Joc d'asos*. Ed. Alex Broch. Barcelona: Magrana, 1981. 51–57.

"Camí de la guerra," "L'hora més silenciosa en el diari d'un soldat," and "Sònia." *Contes de guerra i revolució, I*. Ed. María Campillo. Barcelona: Laia, 1981.

"Obra poètica." *Els marges* 30 (1984): 55–71.

"Tres cartes," "Trossos de cartes," "Carta d'una promessa de guerra," "Els carrers blaus," and "Uns quants mots a una rosa." *Contes de guerra i revolució, II.* Ed. María Campillo. Barcelona: Laia, 1981.

TRANSLATIONS OF HER WORKS

Aloma [*Aloma*]. Trans. J. F. Vidal. Madrid: Al-Borak, 1971.

La calle de las Camelias [*El carrer de les Camèlies*]. Trans. José Batlló. Barcelona: Planeta, 1970.

Cuanta, cuanta guerra [*Quanta, quanta guerra*]. Trans. Ana Moix. Barcelona: Edhasa, 1982.

Espejo roto [*Mirall trencat*]. Trans. Pere Gimferrer. Barcelona: Seix Barral, 1978.

Jardín junto al mar [*Jardí vora el mar*]. Trans. J. F. Vidal. Barcelona: Edhasa, 1983.

Mi Cristina y otros cuentos [*La meva Cristina i altres contes*]. Trans. José Batlló. Madrid: Alianza, 1982.

My Christina, and Other Stories [*La meva Cristina i altres contes*]. Trans. David H. Rosenthal. Port Townsend: Graywolf, 1984.

La muerte y la primavera [*La mort i la primavera*]. Trans. Enrique Sordo. Barcelona: Seix Barral, 1986.

Parecía de seda y otras narraciones [*Semblava de seda i altres contes*]. Trans. Clara Janés. Barcelona: Edhasa, 1981.

The Pigeon Girl [*La plaça del Diamant*]. Trans. Eda O'Shield. London: Deutsch, 1967.

La plaza del Diamante [*La plaça del Diamant*]. Trans. Enrique Sordo. Madrid: Edhasa, 1982.

"Summer" ["Estiu"] and "That Wall, That Mimosa" ["Aquella paret, aquella mimosa"]. Trans. Josep Miquel Sobrer. *Catalonia: A Self-Portrait.* Bloomington and Indianapolis: Indiana UP, 1992: 71–80.

The Time of the Doves [*La plaça del Diamant*]. Trans. David H. Rosenthal. New York: Taplinger, 1980. Saint Paul: Graywolf, 1986.

Two Tales ("The Salamander" ["La salamandra"] and "The Nursemaid" ["La mainadera"]). Trans. David Rosenthal. New York: Red Ozier, 1983.

Veintidos cuentos [*Vint-i-dos contes*]. Trans. Ana Maria Moix. Madrid: Mondadori, 1988.

Viajes y flores [*Viatges i flors*]. Trans. Clara Janés. Barcelona: Edhasa, 1981.

SECONDARY SOURCES

Albrecht, Jane W., and Patricia V. Lunn. "*La plaça del Diamant* i la narració de la consciència." *Homenatge a Josep Roca Pons.* Ed. Albrecht et al. Barcelona: Indiana U Publications and the Abadia de Montserrat, 1991. 9–22.

Arnau, Carme. "L'àngel a les novel.les de Mercè Rodoreda." *Serra d'or* 25.290 (1983): 678–81.

———. *Introducció a la narrativa de Mercè Rodoreda: El mite de l'infantesa.* Barcelona: Edicions 62, 1979.

———. "Mercè Rodoreda o la força de l'escriptura." *Literatura de dones: Una visió del món.* Barcelona: LaSal, 1988. 81–96.

———. *Miralls màgics. Aproximació a l'última narrativa de Mercè Rodoreda.* Barcelona: Edicions 62, 1990.

————. "Mort et metamorphose: 'La meva Cristina i altres contes' de Mercè Rodoreda." *Revue des langues romanes* 93.1 (1989): 51–60.

————. "*La mort i la primavera*, de Mercè Rodoreda." *Insula* 42.485–486 (1987): 25.

————. "La obra de Mercè Rodoreda." *Cuadernos hispanoamericanos* 383 (May 1982): 239–57.

————. "Una segona edició en 'veu baixa': *Vint-i-dos contes*, de Mercè Rodoreda." *Els marges* 2 (1974): 105–14.

————. "El temps i el record a *Mirall trencat*." *Els marges* 6 (1976): 124–28.

————. "Vegetació i mort en la narrativa de Mercè Rodoreda." *Revista de Catalunya* 22 (Sept. 1988): 124–33.

Bergmann, Emilie. "Reshaping the Canon: Intertextuality in Spanish Novels of Female Development." *Anales de la literatura Española contemporánea* 12.1–2 (1987): 141–56.

Bieder, Maryellen. "Cataclysm and Rebirth: Journey to the Edge of the Maelstrom: Mercè Rodoreda's *Quanta, quanta guerra. . . .*" *Actes del Tercer Col.loqui d'Estudis Catalans a Nord Amèrica.* Ed. Patricia Boehne, Josep Massot i Muntaner, and Nathaniel B. Smith. Montserrat: L'Abadia, 1983. 227–37.

————. "The Woman in the Garden: The Problem of Identity in the Novels of Mercè Rodoreda." *Actes del Segon Col.loqui d'Estudis Catalans a Nord Amèrica.* Ed. Manuel Duran, Albert Porqueras-Mayo, and Josep Roca-Pons. Montserrat: L'Abadia, 1982. 353–64.

Busquets, Loreto. "El mito de la culpa a *La plaça del Diamant*." *Actes del Quart Col.loqui d'Estudis Catalans a Nord Amèrica.* Ed. Nathaniel B. Smith, Josep M. Solà-Solé, Mercè Vidal Tibbets, and Josep Massot i Muntaner. Montserrat: L'Abadia, 1985. 303–10. Also in *Cuadernos hispanoamericanos* 420 (June 1985): 117–40.

————. "*La mort i la primavera* de Mercè Rodoreda." *Cuadernos hispanoamericanos* 467 (May 1989): 117–22.

Busquets i Grabulosa, Lluís. "Mercè Rodoreda, passió eterna i fràgil." *Plomes catalanes contemporànies.* Barcelona: Mall, 1980. 57–64.

Cabré Monné, Rosa. "La dona en l'obra de Mercè Rodoreda." *Revista del centro de lectura* (Reus) 218 (Oct. 1970): 907–08.

Callejo, Alfonso. "Corporeidad i escaparates en *La plaça del Diamant* de Mercè Rodoreda." *Butlletí de la North American Catalan Society* 16 (Fall 1983): 14–17.

Campillo, María. "Mercè Rodoreda: La realitat i els miralls." *Els marges* 21 (1981): 129–30.

Campillo, Maria, and Marina Gustà. *Mirall trencat de Mercè Rodoreda.* Barcelona: Empúries, 1985.

Casals i Couturier, Montserrat. *Mercè Rodoreda: Contra la vida, la literatura. Biografia.* Barcelona: Edicions 62, 1991.

Castellet, J. M. "Mercè Rodoreda." *Els escenaris de la memòria.* Barcelona: Edicions 62, 1988. 29–52.

Ciplijauskaité, *La novela femenina contemporánea.*

Clarasó, Mercè. "The Angle of Vision in the Novels of Mercè Rodoreda." *Bulletin of Hispanic Studies* 57 (1980): 143–52.

Encinar, Angeles. "Mercè Rodoreda: Hacia una fantasía liberadora." *Revista canadiense de estudios hispánicos* 11.1 (1986): 1–10.

Forrest, Gene Steven. "El diálogo circunstancial en *La plaza del Diamante*." *Revista de estudios hispánicos* 12 (1978): 15–24.

García Márquez, Gabriel. "Recuerdo de una mujer invisible: Mercè Rodoreda." *Clarín* 30 June 1983: 6.

Glenn, Kathleen M. "*La plaza del Diamante*: The Other Side of the Story." *Letras femeninas* 12.1–2 (1989): 60–68.

Ibarz, Mercè. *Mercè Rodoreda*. Barcelona: Empúries, 1991.

Kulin, Katalin. "A diamant ter." *Filologiai Kozlony* 26.1 (1980): 78–84.

Lucarda, Mario. "Mercè Rodoreda y el buen salvaje." *Quimera* 62 (1987): 34–39.

Lucio, Francisco. "La soledad, tema central en los últimos relatos de Mercè Rodoreda." *Cuadernos hispanoamericanos* 242 (1970): 455–68.

Lunn, Patricia V., and Jane W. Albrecht. "*La plaça del Diamant*: Linguistic Cause and Literary Effect." *Hispania* 75.3 (1992): 492–99.

Martínez Rodríguez, María del Mar. "El lenguaje del auto descubrimiento en la narrativa de Mercè Rodoreda y Carmen Martín Gaite." *DAI* 49.5 (1988): 1162A.

Martí-Olivella, Jaume, ed. *Catalan Review* 2.2 (1988). Special issue devoted to Mercè Rodoreda.

———. "Estructuras joyceanas en la narrativa catalana y latinoamericana contemporánea." *DAI* 49.9 (1989): 2650A.

———. "Rodoreda o la força bruixològica." *Actes del Cinquè Col.loqui d'Estudis Catalans a Nord-Amèrica*. Ed. Philip D. Rasico and Curt J. Wittlin. Montserrat: L'Abadia, 1988. 283–300.

McNerney, Kathleen. "La identitat a *La plaça del Diamant*: Supressió i recerca." *Actes del Quart Col.loqui d'Estudis Catalans a Nord Amèrica*. Ed. Nathaniel B. Smith, Josep M. Solà-Solé, Mercè Vidal Tibbets, and Josep Massot i Muntaner. Montserrat: L'Abadia, 1985. 295–302.

Mees, Inge, and Uta Windsheimer. " 'Un Roman: C'est un miroir qu'on promène le long du chemin': Rodoredas *Mirall trencat* und die 'gebrochene Spiegal'—perspektive." *Zeitschrift für Katalanistik* 1 (1988): 662–72.

Möller-Soler, Maria-Lourdes. "El impacto de la guerra civil en la vida y obra de tres novelistas catalanas: Aurora Bertrana, Teresa Pàmies y Mercè Rodoreda." *Letras femeninas* 12.1–2 (1986): 34–44.

Nichols, Geraldine Cleary. "Exile, Gender, and Mercè Rodoreda." *Monographic Review / Revista monográfica* 2 (1986): 189–97. Also in *MLN* 101.2 (1986): 405–17.

———. "Sex, the Single Girl, and Other Mésalliances in Rodoreda and Laforet." *Anales de la literatura española contemporánea* 12.1–2 (1987): 123–40.

———. "Stranger than Fiction: Fantasy in Short Stories by Matute, Rodoreda, Riera." *Monographic Review / Revista monográfica* 4 (1988): 33–42.

Ortega, José. "Mujer, guerra y neurosis en dos novelas de Mercè Rodoreda (*La plaza del Diamante* y *La calle de las Camelias*)." *Novelistas femeninas de la postguerra española*. Ed. Janet W. Pérez. Madrid: Porrúa, 1983: 71–83.

Pérez, Janet. "Time and Symbol, Life and Death, Decay and Regeneration: Vital Cycles and the Round of Seasons in Mercè Rodoreda's *La mort i la primavera*." *Catalan Review* 5.1 (July 1991): 179–96.

Pessarodona, Marta. "Les dones a l'obra de Mercè Rodoreda." *Serra d'or* 25.290 (Nov. 1983): 675–77.

Poch, Joaquim, and Conxa Planas. *Psicoanàlisi i dona a l'obra de Mercè Rodoreda.* Barcelona: Promociones y Publicaciones Universitarias, 1987.

Pope, Randolph D. "Mercè Rodoreda's Subtle Greatness." *Women Writers of Contemporary Spain: Exiles in the Homeland.* Ed. Joan L. Brown. Newark: U of Delaware P, 1991.

Porcel, Balatasar. "Mercè Rodoreda o la força lírica." *Serra d'or* 3 (Mar. 1966): 231–35.

Roig, Montserrat. "El aliento poético de Mercè Rodoreda." *Triunfo* 22 Sept. 1973: 35–39.

Saludes, Anna. "Mercè Rodoreda, periodista." *Revista del centro de lectura de Reus.* 241 (Dec. 1972): 325–26.

Sobré, Josep M. "L'artifici de *La plaça del Diamant,* un estudi lingüístic." *In memoriam Carles Riba.* Esplugues de Llobregat: Ariel, 1973. 363–75.

Wyers, Frances. "A Woman's Voices: Mercè Rodoreda's *La plaça del Diamant.*" *Kentucky Romance Quarterly* 30.3 (1983): 301–09.

EMILIE L. BERGMANN

C Roig, Maria Carme
(20th c.) Poet. No biographical information available.

Maria Carme Roig's first work, a slim volume called *Records* (Memories), is dedicated to children, and the poems are simple evocations of everyday things: the train station, wood, the theater, a doll, the oak tree, a local festival. The descriptions are straightforward, revealing no surprises, and the rhythms and rhymes are clear and easy to remember. Most of the poems in *Trobades* (Encounters) deal with city life, sometimes nostalgically. The volume closes with several vignettes in prose.

BOOKS
Records. Córdoba: El Paisaje, 1985.
Trobades. Barcelona: Amarantos, 1988.

KATHLEEN MCNERNEY

C Roig de Nebot, Maria
(20th c.) Poet. No biographical information available.

Poemes Nadalencs (Christmas poems) is a collection of Christmas poems, written one or two a year between 1958 and 1981.

BOOKS
Poemes Nadalencs. Barcelona: n.p., 1981.

KATHLEEN MCNERNEY

C Roig i Fransitorra, Montserrat

(B. 1946, Barcelona; d. 1991, Barcelona.) Journalist, essayist, novelist, and short story writer.

A graduate of the University of Barcelona, Montserrat Roig has taught at universities in Spain, Great Britain, and the United States, but she devotes most of her time to journalism. She began her writing career at *Serra d'or* and since then has written for many other magazines and newspapers, including *El país, Triunfo, Vindicación feminista*, and *El món*. Her work in the print and electronic media has won her recognition and popularity throughout Spain. She has directed a number of television interview programs, which have kept her before the public eye and given her material for published anthologies. Her fact-finding studies of historical and current events have earned her a reputation as an investigative reporter. In 1978 she won the Crítica Serra d'Or prize for *Els catalans als camps nazi* (Catalans in Nazi concentration camps), the first thorough documentation on the subject. Her many travels—to Italy, England, Nicaragua, and Russia—provided her with rich resources for additional nonfictional writing. For example, her trip to Leningrad resulted in *L'agulla daurada* (The golden needle), an account of her visit interspersed with survivors' tales of death and deprivation during the city's siege in World War II. She wrote a daily column in *El periódico*, and these articles are collected in *Melindros* (Pastries). An objective yet sensitive observer of reality, Roig has taken a keen interest not only in the anonymous victims of war but also in women and their unwritten stories. In *¿Tiempo de mujer?* (Woman's time?), a collection of articles, interviews, and reflections, Roig reviews woman's image as portrayed by male society over the centuries and considers the dilemma of today's woman, who wants to discard the negative roles assigned her without losing her own unique identity.

Although an established journalist with many extraliterary preoccupations, Roig has also felt the need to develop her creative talents by writing fiction. Her imaginative works, written in Catalan and usually translated immediately into Castilian, focus on women and their struggle for freedom, self-definition, and love. Her first collection of short stories, *Molta roba i poc sabó* (Many clothes and not enough soap), received the Víctor Català prize for short novel in 1970. These stories about young people searching for meaning in life during the Franco regime introduced the milieu that would form the backdrop for her subsequent fiction: the stagnant, banal, middle-class society of Barcelona. Her first novel, *Ramona adéu* (Goodbye, Ramona), chronicles the lives of three women with the same name, who were born into three successive generations of the same family. Roig continues this family saga in her prizewinning *El temps de les cireres* (The time of the cherries) and in *L'hora violeta* (The violet hour). In the last two novels, her protagonists are middle-aged women facing many current feminist issues and still grappling with some of the problems that troubled their female ancestors. Roig's fourth novel, *L'òpera quotidiana* (The everyday opera), presents several characters who tell their life stories and divulge intimate feelings in arias, cavatinas, and duets. Roig changes direction in *La veu melodiosa* (The melodious voice) and creates a young male protagonist of exceptional ugliness. She continues nonetheless to explore the relationship between middle-class Barcelona society and one of its marginalized members and to expose a character's difficult confrontation with reality.

Whether following the format of musical compositions, diaries, or historical chronicles, Roig presents a melancholy group of unfulfilled or frustrated females caught within the restrictions of their environment. Rather than emphasize her characters' victimization, Roig is concerned with disclosing their suppressed struggle for freedom, tracing their steps toward liberation, and dealing with the issue of female identity. While successfully delving into the psychology of her characters, she documents the historical framework in which they move. Roig's novels primarily attempt to portray all Catalan women and to give fictional form to the questions she raises in her essays. Her journalistic training is often evident in her fiction: it can be seen in some of her characters, who either are journalists or work in the publishing world; in her strong grasp of current events; in her language and syntax; and in her rapid, disjointed presentation of materials. This blend of journalistic and fictional writing places Roig within one of the prominent trends in contemporary Spanish literature.

BOOKS

L'agulla daurada. Barcelona: Edicions 62, 1985.
Barcelona a vol d'ocell. With Xavier Miserachs. Barcelona: Edicions 62, 1987.
El cant de la joventut. Barcelona: Edicions 62, 1989.
Els catalans als camps nazis. Barcelona: Edicions 62, 1977.
100 pàgines triades per mi. Barcelona: La Campana, 1988.
Digues que m'estimes encara que sigui mentida. Barcelona: Edicions 62, 1991.
Los hechiceros de la palabra. Barcelona: Martínez Rosa, 1975.
L'hora violeta. Barcelona: Edicions 62, 1980.
Melindros. Barcelona: Ediciones B, 1990.
Molta roba i poc sabó. Barcelona: Selecta, 1971.
Mujeres hacia un nuevo humanismo. Barcelona: Salvat, 1982.
L'òpera quotidiana. Barcelona: Planeta, 1982.
Un pensament de sal, un pessic de pebre: Dietari obert 1990–1991. Barcelona: Edicions 62, 1992.
Personatges. Barcelona: Pòrtic, 1978.
Personatges. Segona Sèrie. Barcelona: Pòrtic, 1980.
Rafael Vidiella, aventura de la revolució. Barcelona: Laia, 1976.
Ramona adéu. Barcelona: Edicions 62, 1972.
Retrats paral.lels I. Montserrat: L'Abadia, 1975.
Retrats paral.lels II. Montserrat: L'Abadia, 1976.

Retrats paral.lels III. Montserrat: L'Abadia, 1979.
El temps de les cireres. Barcelona: Edicions 62, 1977.
¿Tiempo de mujer? Barcelona: Plaza & Janés, 1980.
La vaga obrera. Barcelona: Edicions 62, 1971.
La veu melodiosa. Barcelona: Edicions 62, 1987.
Un viaje al bloqueo. Moscow: Progreso, 1982.

TRANSLATIONS OF HER WORKS
La aguja dorada [*L'agulla daurada*]. Barcelona: Plaza & Janés, 1985.
"Amor y cenizas" ["Amor i cendres"]. Trans. Montserrat Roig. *Litoral femenino*. Ed. Lorenzo Saval and J. García Gallego. Granada: Litoral, 1986. 353–56.
Aprendizaje sentimental [*Molta roba i poc sabó*]. Trans. Mercedes Nogués. Barcelona: Argos Vergara, 1981.
El canto de la juventud [*El cant de la joventut*]. Barcelona: Península, 1989.
Dime que me quieres aunque sea mentira [*Digues que m'estimes encara que sigui mentida*]. Trans. Antonia Picazo. Barcelona: Península, 1992.
"The Everyday Opera" [selections from *L'òpera quotidiana*]. Trans. Josep Miquel Sobrer. *On Our Own Behalf*. Ed. Kathleen McNerney. Lincoln and London: U of Nebraska P, 1988. 207–34.
La hora violeta [*L'hora violeta*]. Trans. Enrique Sordo. Barcelona: Argos Vergara, 1980.
"How a Maid from the Eixample Tries to Sit Back and Relax in Our Beloved Barcelona" ["De com una criada de l'Eixample intenta d'escarxofar-se a la nostra estimada Barcelona"]. Trans. Deborah Bonner. *Catalan Writing* 7 (1991): 65–69.
La ópera cotidiana [*L'òpera quotidiana*]. Trans. Enrique Sordo. Barcelona: Planeta, 1983.
Ramona adiós [*Ramona adéu*]. Trans. Joaquim Sempere. Barcelona: Argos Vergara, 1980.
Tiempo de cerezas [*El temps de les cireres*]. Trans. Enrique Sordo. Barcelona: Argos Vergara, 1980.
La voz melodiosa [*La veu melodiosa*]. Trans. José Agustín Goytisolo. Barcelona: Plaza & Janés, 1987.

SECONDARY SOURCES
Alvarado Florian, Victor. "A propósito de 'Before the Civil War' de Montserrat Roig." *Ventanal* 14 (1988): 159–69.
Bellver, Catherine G. "A Feminine Perspective and a Journalistic Slant." *Feminine Concerns in Contemporary Spanish Fiction by Women*. Ed. Roberto Manteiga, Carolyn Galerstein, and Kathleen McNerney. Potomac: Scripta Humanistica, 1988. 152–68.
———. "Montserrat Roig and the Creation of a Gynocentric Reality." *Women Writers of Contemporary Spain: Exiles in the Homeland*. Ed. Joan L. Brown. Newark: U of Delaware P, 1991.
———. "Montserrat Roig and the Penelope Syndrome." *Anales de la literatura española contemporánea*. 12.1–2 (1987): 111–21.
Ciplijauskaité, *La novela femenina contemporánea*.

McNerney, Kathleen. "Contrasts in 'La Ciutat Condal': Visions of Barcelona in the Novel." *Ideas '92* 7 (Fall 1990): 103–08.

Nichols, Geraldine C. "Montserrat Roig." *Escribir, espacio propio: Laforet, Matute, Moix, Tusquets, Riera y Roig por sí mismas.* Minneapolis: Inst. for the Study of Ideologies and Literature, 1989. 147–85.

Rogers, Elizabeth S. "Montserrat Roig's *Ramona adiós*: A Novel of Suppression and Disclosure." *Revista de estudios hispánicos* 20.1 (1986): 103–21.

Zatlin, Phyllis. "Passivity and Immobility: Patterns of Inner Exile in Postwar Spanish Novels Written by Women." *Letras femeninas* 14.1–2 (1988): 3–9.

CATHERINE G. BELLVER

C   Roig i Planas, Clementina
(B. 1942, Barcelona– .) Textbook author.

Clementina Roig studied primary school education at the Escola Municipal del Parc del Guinardó and in 1966 obtained the title of monitor of cinema for children. In 1978 she received her degree in primary education along with the diploma for teaching Catalan from the Escola Universitària de Sant Cugat del Vallès. In 1981 she earned a degree in geography and history from the Universitat Autònoma de Barcelona. In 1980 she completed the Apple teachers' course How to Make a Curriculum at the University of Wisconsin. Roig has participated in conferences on educational reform in Madison (Wisconsin), Madrid, Barcelona, Brussels, London, Granada, Amsterdam, Budapest, and several cities in Italy. She has taught winter and summer courses at the Rosa Sensat school and at other schools in Spain. From 1981 to 1988, she was director of the former Escola de Mar of Barcelona. Her research includes studies on language and mathematics in kindergarten, reports on science museums in the school, and the work *Coneguem els nostres animals* (Knowing our animals), which was done for the Barcelona Zoo. She has been involved in creating textbooks for preschools. With Maria Antònia Pujol she edited *Recull de poemes per a petits i grans* (A collection of poems for young and old), an anthology of poems by Catalan authors that are comprehensible to children, and wrote *Observació i experimentació a parvulari* (Observation and experimentation in the preschool), a useful tool for teachers concentrating on preschool education. She has also written books on how to initiate discussions with children and stimulate their interest in new phenomena. She is the coauthor with Maria Teresa Codina i Mir and Montserrat Castanys i Jarque of *Visquem plegats i bé* (Let's live together in harmony), and she has written articles for *Cuadernos de pedagogía, Guix, IME, Infància,* and *Tele/Expres.*

BOOKS
Cerquem formes. Barcelona: Juventud, 1978.
Em faig gran. Barcelona: Juventud, 1982.

Equilibrem, compensem. Barcelona: Juventud, 1980.
Jo i les ombres. Barcelona: Juventud, 1980.
Observació i experimentació a parvulari. With Maria Antònia Pujol. Barcelona: Rosa Sensat, 1981.
On sóc? Barcelona: Juventud, 1978.
Què ens alimenta? Barcelona: Juventud, 1982.
Quin temps fa avui? Barcelona: Juventud, 1978.
Recull de poemes per a petits i grans. Ed. with Maria Antònia Pujol. Barcelona: Kairós, 1978.
Els signes ens parlen. Barcelona: Juventud, 1982.
Tot sona? Barcelona: Juventud, 1982.
Visquem plegats i bé. With Maria Teresa Codina i Mir and Montserrat Castanys i Jarque. Barcelona: Ajuntament, 1984.

ANNA GASOL I TRULLOLS

C   Romà, Maria Antònia
(20th c.) Poet. No biographical information available.

BOOKS
Aierols. Mataró, Barcelona: Agrupació Hispana de Escritores, 1981.

KATHLEEN MCNERNEY

G   Romaní, Ana
(B. 1963, Noia, Coruña– .) Poet.

A graduate in Romance philology from the University of Santiago, Ana Romaní started writing poems and taking part in readings with other poets of her generation when she was very young. Concerned with women's problems, she participated in cultural and literary activities with feminist groups. She began publishing poems in journals such as *Dorna* and *Festa da palabra silenciada*, the latter written exclusively by women.

Her first book of poems, *Palabra de mar* (Word of the sea), features the sea as a symbol of space and as witness to her feelings. Invoking an absent love, Romaní describes her loneliness, her troubles, her "embestida de amor en la muerte" (attack of love on death). This intimate poetry expresses eternal passion and premonitions of death and constantly refers to a symbolic, multidimensional love. In the words of Pilar Pallarés, who wrote the prologue, "el libro es la derrota del silencio porque es un viaje del silencio a la palabra. . . . Existe lo que tiene nombre; existe el amor porque lo inventamos en la palabra" (the book is the defeat of silence because it is a journey of silence to the word. . . . Everything that has a name exists; love exists because we invented the word).

BOOKS
Palabra de mar. Prol. Pilar Pallarés. Santiago de Compostela: Velograf, 1987.

WORKS IN BOOKS, PERIODICALS, NEWSPAPERS
"Naufraxio de amor." *Dorna* 7 May 1984.
"Ollando cara min." *Dorna* 2 Feb. 1982.
Poem, untitled. *Dorna* 3 May 1982.
Poem, untitled. *Dorna* 5 Jan. 1983.
Poem, untitled. *Dorna* 6 May 1983.
Poem, untitled. *Dorna* 8 May 1985.
Poem, untitled. *Dorna* 12 May 1987.
Poem, untitled. *Festa da palabra silenciada* 2 Mar. 1985.
Poem, untitled. *Festa da palabra silenciada* 3 Jan. 1986.
"Poema a Xohana Torres." *Festa da palabra silenciada* 4 Feb. 1987.
"Xa sei que me agardas." *Festa da palabra silenciada* 1 May 1983.

MARIA CAMINO NOIA CAMPOS

C   Roses d'Abad, Teresa
(B. 1924, Segrià, Lleida– .) Poet.

Teresa Roses d'Abad has published two books of poems, *Enllà del juny i les espigues* (Beyond June and the spikes) and *Les motllures* (The moldings). The first collection contains musical poems about children, nature, love, and time. The second includes poems about the family, memories of childhood during wartime, and an elegy. The title poem is about the passage of time—how to enjoy each day or to plan whatever time is left.

BOOKS
Enllà del juny i les espigues: Poemes. Prol. Jaume Agelet i Garriga. Illus. Coma Estadella. Balaguer: n.p., 1968.
Les motllures. Lleida: Inst. d'Estudis Ilerdenses, 1979.

NANCY L. BUNDY and KATHLEEN MCNERNEY

C   Ros i Vilanova, Roser
(B. 1950, Barcelona– .) Textbook author and writer of children's books.

Roser Ros has a BA in education from the University of Barcelona and an MS in education from the University of Vincennes. She has worked as a kindergarten and primary school teacher and is a member of the Associació de Mestres Rosa Sensat of Barcelona, where she has taught summer school courses since 1977. As a member of this group she has also participated

336

in discussions and conferences throughout Spain. In 1984 she collaborated on the exhibition of fairy-tale books and drawings, which was organized by the Caixa. Since 1987 she has edited the magazine *Infància*, a publication of the Associació de Mestres Rosa Sensat. Her short stories have appeared there and in the children's magazine *Cavall fort*. She has also prepared preschool textbooks and, with Rosa Boixaderas, published a collection of stories entitled *Nas de barraca* (Nose in the shack), written for children just learning to read. Her book reviews and articles on pedagogy have appeared in various specialized journals. In 1988 she helped create the video series *El camí de casa a l'escola* (The road from home to school), edited by the Generalitat de Catalunya.

BOOKS

Nas de barraca. With Rosa Boixaderas. Illus. Marta Balaguer. Barcelona: Onda, 1987.

Trenta-tres contes. Barcelona: Rosa Sensat, 1986.

ANNA GASOL I TRULLOLS

C Rosselló, Anna

(20th c.) Travel writer. No biographical information available.

Anna Rosselló's work falls into that hard-to-define genre between memoirs, fiction, and travelogue. Her husband, Josep Travesset, collaborated with her on all her works, which are based on their travels in Latin America.

Amèrica marginada (Marginal America) tells of their first trip to Latin America, in which they reflect, through an anti-imperialist prism, the past and the present of the "new" ancient continent. *No són 300 milions* (There are not 300 million), which refers to the alleged number of Spanish speakers in the world, is a study of the ethnic groups in Latin America that are struggling to preserve their native languages. In addition to gathering information about these groups, the authors record impressions of their personal experiences in Latin America. *O catalão: Un català a l'Amazònia* (A Catalan in the Amazon Basin) tells the story of a Catalan who marries a Tupi-Guaraní woman and devises a way to convey water from the Negro River to the high plateau. In thanks for his feat, the natives learn Catalan to make him feel more at home. *Després de la bel.licosa nit* (After the bellicose night) describes social and racial problems in the Brazilian provinces of Matto Grosso and Amazonas. *Illapa de Huancané* (Illapa of Huancané) is the story of an Aymara boy from Peru, adopted by a family of Catalan background, who grows up to be a lawyer and defends the rights of Aymara and Quechua Indians. *El més gran desert és una gran ciutat* (The greatest desert is a big city) portrays a Catalan family that goes into exile in Brazil after the Civil War in order to earn a living. It describes their troubles and disappointments and the courage with which they try to overcome their difficulties.

BOOKS

Amèrica marginada. With Josep Travesset. Barcelona: Pòrtic, 1971.
O catalâo: Un català a l'Amazònia. With Josep Travesset. Barcelona: El Llamp, 1984.
Després de la bel.licosa nit. With Josep Travesset. Barcelona: El Llamp, 1985.
Illapa de Huancané. With Josep Travesset. Barcelona: Servigraf, 1985.
El més gran desert és una gran ciutat. With Josep Travesset. Barcelona: El Llamp, 1986.
No són 300 milions. Barcelona: Pòrtic, 1983.

SILVIA AYMERICH LEMOS

C Rosselló i Miralles de Sans, Coloma
(B. 1871, Palma de Mallorca; d. 1955, Palma de Mallorca.)
Journalist and fiction writer.

Coloma Rosselló came from an upper-class Majorcan family of businessmen and landowners. She received a good education, learned French and English, and developed a broad literary understanding. A friend of Víctor Català and Carme Karr, she defended women's right to an education, but because of her literary activities she faced the antagonism of other women of her class, a situation reflected in her writings.

In 1892 she married Narcís Sans i Masferrer, a banker from Figueres, Girona, who was a member of the liberal party and became governor of Segovia, Avila, and Albacete. She had four children; one, Elvir, became a well-known writer and historian. Because of economic problems and her health, the family moved to the Carthusian monastery of Valldemosa. Her love for Valldemosa and the islands inspired her to become a correspondant for the Barcelona magazine *Feminal*, edited by Karr. In her articles Rosselló describes the beauty and interest of the "l'illa daurada" (the golden island). She also did some historical research and produced the Castilian book *Guía histórico-descriptiva de Valldemosa y Miramar* (Historical and descriptive guide to Valldemosa and Miramar), which was translated into French in 1915. In addition, she published *Valldemosines* (From Valldemosa), a collection of essays that contain popular themes and some scenic and historical descriptions of Majorca. In her writings she severely criticizes the superficiality of the upper class, especially the women, while idealizing the peasants and their way of life.

As Damià Ferré-Ponç says, the interest in Rosselló's work stems from the fact that she was one of the first writers to become aware of how

338

tourism would change the social life in Majorca. Rossello believed she owed her national and international recognition to her journalistic articles. She felt confident enough to debate Santiago Rusinyol about his description of the islands in *La isla de la calma* and, especially, about his sarcastic and condescending attitude toward women writers.

BOOKS
Guia histórico-descriptiva de Valldemosa y Miramar. Palma: J. Tous, 1910.
Guide historique et descriptif de Valldemosa et Miramar. Soller: La Sinceridad, 1915.
Valldemosines. Barcelona: L'Avenç, 1911.

WORKS IN BOOKS, PERIODICALS, NEWSPAPERS
"A la posta del sol." *Feminal* 64 (28 July 1912).
"La balada del vent." *Feminal* 100 (25 July 1915).
"Benhaja la neu." *Feminal* 94 (31 Jan. 1915).
"De la illa daurada." *Feminal* 40 (31 July 1910), 44 (27 Nov. 1910), 47 (26 Feb. 1911), 51 (26 June 1911), 55 (21 Oct. 1911), and 77 (21 Aug. 1913).
"Estudi sobre una obra femenina de literatura cultural italiana." *Feminal* 79 (26 Oct. 1913).
"Hosanna." *Feminal* 36 (27 Mar. 1910).
"Oli y olives." *Feminal* 37 (24 Apr. 1910).
"Valldemosines." *Lectura popular* 14: 481–512.

SECONDARY SOURCES
Ferré-Ponç, Damià. "Els escriptors i el turisme." *Lluch* June 1971: 28.

CRISTINA ENRIQUEZ DE SALAMANCA

C Rovira i Compte, Maria Carme
(B. 1925, Barcelona– .) Poet.

Maria Carme Rovira has studied ceramics, sculpture, history, archaeology, art history, and psychology. A member of the group Poesia Viva, she has published one book of poetry as well as other poems in anthologies.

BOOKS
Retalls de cada dia. Barcelona: Poesia Viva, 1982.

KATHLEEN MCNERNEY

C Rubiés i Monjonell, Anna
(B. 1881, El Port de la Selva, Girona; d. 1963, El Port de la Selva, Girona.) Writer of pedagogical materials and essays.

After earning a degree in pedagogy at sixteen, Anna Rubiés practiced her profession with enthusiasm and dedication. She taught in Lleida, Girona, and Barcelona before her appointment as director of the Mendizábal School in 1920, a job that allowed her to begin a series of reforms that she continued until her death. Rubiés became interested in the Decroly method of pedagogy after a trip to Brussels and promoted this system through conferences, courses, and publications. Her reform work reached its apogee during the Republic, when she initiated improved health care in the schools, such as obligatory showering, exercise classes, and regular visits by doctors. Most of her publications are in the field of teaching, and in this spirit she gathered and rewrote for children a number of classical stories. After the war, unable to implement some of her progressive ideas, she wrote descriptions of her homeland: *La comarca de l'Empordà* (The land of Empordà) and *Fragments de Tramuntana. Contalles de la casa vella* (Fragments from the Tramuntana. Fables from home). In 1961 at the Jocs Florals in L'Empordà she presented a work in the same local spirit, "De l'aplec de San Baldri" (From the gathering of Saint Baldri).

BOOKS

Aplicación del método Decroly a la enseñanza primaria. Madrid: Revista de Pedagogía, 1929.
Aplicación de los centros de interés en la Escuela Primaria. Madrid: Revista de Pedagogía, 1929. 3rd ed. 1932.
Biblioteca escolar Ramon Llull: Contes per infants de 6–7 anys. N.p.: n.p., 1933.
La comarca de l'Empordà. Barcelona: Selecta, 1960.
Contes de sempre. Barcelona: Elzevirana, 1933.
Cuatro años de experiencia en la lectura-escritura global. Barcelona: Bosch, 1938.
Experiencias didácticas. Madrid: Revista de Pedagogía, 1934.
Fragments de Tramuntana. Contalles de la casa vella. Barcelona: n.p., 1965.
Llibre de les besties. Barcelona: Elzevirana, 1933.
Llibre de les meravelles. Barcelona: Elzevirana, 1933.
Recull d'impressions en prosa i vers de les germanes Anna i Mercè Rubiés i Monjonell. N.p.: n.p., n.d.

SECONDARY SOURCES

Costa i Via, Montserrat. *Estudi de l'obra d'Anna Rubiés.* Barcelona: Fundació Salvador Vives Casajuana, 1971.

MARISA SIGUAN BOEHMER

C Rubiés i Monjonell, Mercè

(B. 1884, El Port de la Selva, Girona; d. 1971, El Port de la Selva, Girona.) Poet and educator.

Mercè Rubiés published two volumes of her own poetry, *Fullejant el llibre de la meva vida* (Leafing through the book of my life) and *Vint i quatre estampes de Comunió* (Twenty-four communion engravings), a collection of religious pieces written on the occasion of various first Communions between 1922 and 1959 in several places. *Recull d'impressions en prosa i vers* (Collection of impressions in prose and verse) is a joint effort with her sister Anna Rubiés and contains patriotic and family poems by Mercè.

BOOKS
Fullejant el llibre de la meva vida. 1947.
Recull d'impressions en prosa i vers de les germanes Anna i Mercè Rubiés i Monjonell. N.p.: n.p., n.d.
Vint i quatre estampes de Comunió: Poesies. Barcelona: n.p., 1959.

NANCY L. BUNDY and KATHLEEN MCNERNEY

C Rusinyol i Denis, Maria
(B. 1887, Barcelona; d. 195?, Barcelona.) Biographer, novelist, and poet.

The daughter of Lluïsa Denis de Rusinyol, a painter, composer, and writer, and Santiago Rusinyol, a painter and writer, Maria Rusinyol tried her hand at various arts but did not produce much in any medium. In the biography of her famous father *Santiago Rusinyol, vist per la seva filla* (Santiago Rusinyol as seen by his daughter), she spends much time trying to defend him, though she barely knew him when she was growing up. Her father abandoned the family when she was four months old and thereafter came home only sporadically, although the family traveled together occasionally. Rusinyol's only novel, *L'arna* (The moth), is didactic and full of clichés about a saintly woman and an evil one, set against a nostalgic background of wealthy, hardworking Catalan gentry who embody all the bourgeois virtues. The family's fortune is threatened by the appearance of a mysterious, sensual woman, whom the family takes in out of charity. The *Gran enciclopèdia catalana* mentions a *Llibre de versos* by Rusinyol, but it has not been located.

BOOKS
L'arna. Barcelona: Casa del Libro, 1953.
Llibre de versos. Barcelona: Catalònia, 1928.
Santiago Rusinyol, vist per la seva filla. Barcelona: Aedos, 1950.

SECONDARY SOURCES
Gran enciclopèdia catalana 20: 80.

KATHLEEN MCNERNEY

C Saavedra, Anna Maria de
(B. 1905, Vilafranca del Penedès, Barcelona; d. ?) Poet, critic, and translator.

Anna Maria de Saavedra published little poetry in Catalan journals; however, from the 1920s to the 1930s, her name appears as editor of or contributor to the most significant literary journals of the period: *Hèlix, L'amic de les arts, La revista,* and *Revista de poesia.* In the last, edited by Marià Manent, Saavedra was a member of the editorial staff, along with Tomàs Garcés, Jaume Bofill, and others. She translated poems by Rilke for this journal and published critical reviews on the Catalan poets Joaquim Folguera and Joan Sebastià Pons. However, the Spanish Civil War ended this activity.

Saavedra translated Ovid's *Metamorphoses*, in collaboration with Adela M. Trepat. She also translated Quintino Cataudella's *Historia de la literatura griega* and prepared a Castilian edition of *Libro del Consulado del Mar.* Between 1932 and 1939, she taught Latin and Catalan in the Institut Escola of Barcelona.

WORKS IN BOOKS, PERIODICALS, NEWSPAPERS
"Canta Perdiu, de J. S. Pons." *Revista de poesia* 2.7 (1926): 21–23.
"El Captaire." *Revista de poesia* 1.1 (1925): 4.
"Joaquim Folguera." *Revista de poesia* 1.5–6 (1925): 228–30.
"Migdiada." *La revista* Year 9 (June 1–16, 1923): 119.
"Poemes de Rilke: 'Font,' 'Soletat,' 'Cementeri.' " *Revista de poesia* 3.11 (1927): 6–7.
"Poètica d'Aristòtil. Introducció i traducció de J. Ferran i Mayoral." *Revista de poesia* 2.9 (1926): 172–73.
"Rosa." *Hèlix* June 1929: 3.
"El temps de tardor," "La finestra," "El cor espantadís," and "Salutació." *La revista* Year 12 (July–Dec. 1927): 98–100.

CRISTINA ENRIQUEZ DE SALAMANCA

C Sabaté i Puig de Delmas, Maria Dolors
(B. 1904, Cassà de la Selva, Barcelona; d. 1982, Barcelona.) Poet.

In *Poesies* (Poetry), a posthumous collection of lyrical and occasional poems, Maria Dolors Sabaté uses traditional verse forms to express her deeply felt sentiments about family, friendship, religion, death, and nature. She received a degree in music from Barcelona's Liceu conservatory in 1927.

BOOKS
Poesies. Prol. and illus. Maria Teresa Delmas i Sabaté. Barcelona: Claret, 1983.

NANCY L. BUNDY

C Sabi i Roges, Anna Maria
(B. 1914, Barcelona–) Poet.

Anna Maria Sabi read philosophy and arts at the University of Barcelona and specialized in Romance languages. She worked in schools in Poble Nou, Barcelona, and in Terrassa and was active in the theater group El Paraigües Groc of the Club de Amigos de la UNESCO in Barcelona. One of her poems, "I quan vegis que tot se t'escapa" (And when you see that everything is slipping away), is included in *Primera antologia 1965–1966–1967 del premi de poesia per a inèdits Mossèn Amadeu Oller.*

WORKS IN BOOKS, PERIODICALS, NEWSPAPERS
"I quan vegis que tot se t'escapa." *Primera antologia 1965–1966–1967.*

CRISTINA ENRIQUEZ DE SALAMANCA

C Sacrest i Casellas, Rosa
(B. 1907, Girona– .) Poet.

According to *Les cinc branques*, Rosa Sacrest i Casellas published two volumes of poetry, *Recull* (Collection) and *Intimes* (Intimacies), which are not available in major libraries in Catalonia.

WORKS IN BOOKS, PERIODICALS, NEWSPAPERS
"Boira." *Les cinc branques* 136.

NANCY L. BUNDY

C Sala i Prats, Eulàlia
(B. 1925, Terrassa, Barcelona– .) Poet.

Eulàlia Sala i Prats has published one volume of poetry, *De l'alba al crepuscle* (From dawn to dusk), consisting mainly of love poems and often presenting opposite viewpoints. For example, "Desengany" (Disillusion) is followed by "Esperança" (Hope). Several poems are dedicated to the art of poetry. Sala is also a painter and has written poems in homage to other painters.

BOOKS
De l'alba al crepuscle. Terrassa: n.p., 1966.

NANCY L. BUNDY and KATHLEEN MCNERNEY

C   Sales Folch de Bohigas, Núria
(B. 1933, Barcelona– .) Historian and poet.

Núria Sales's *Exili a Playamuertos* (Exile in Playamuertos) won the Marius Torres prize in 1960 in the Cantonigròs contest. The book has a drawing and prologue by the author, in which she claims to be against literary fads; and its content is, indeed, unusual. The first section is dedicated to suicides of various types. Sales condemns people who kill themselves to punish others, but in general she tries to understand rather than to judge and saves her criticism for those who are dead in life. As far as the custom of mourning is concerned, she feels that people should grieve for themselves rather than for others. The exile in the title refers to those who went to the Caribbean after the Civil War. Sales's work also has references to England and its history. In the long, closing poem, "Feministes" (Feminists), she praises the British suffragists who fought militantly for the rights of women. Condemning those who scorn the gains made by these women, she stresses that while they made progress the battle is far from over. Sales now resides in France.

BOOKS
Exili a Playamuertos. Barcelona: Ossa Menor, 1961.
Història dels mossos d'esquadra. Barcelona: n.p., 1962.
Senyors bandolers, miquelets i botiflers. Barcelona: Empúries, 1987.

TRANSLATIONS OF HER WORKS
"The Heroes" ["Els herois"]. Trans. Lillian Lowenfels and Nan Braymer. *The Literary Review* 7.4 (1964): 635. *Modern Poetry from Spain and Latin America.* Ed. Cesar Vallejo et al. New York: Corinth, 1964. 62.

KATHLEEN MCNERNEY

C   Salvà, Maria Antònia
(B. 1869, Llucmajor, Mallorca; d. 1958, Llucmajor, Mallorca.) Poet and translator.

Maria Antònia Salvà spent her life in Majorca, traveling on a few occasions to the Spanish mainland and once to the Holy Land. Her poetry is devoted to her Mediterranean environment and is deeply rooted in its traditions. She is considered a poet of the Escola Mallorquina, which flourished on the island as an independent counterpart of Catalan *Modernisme* and *Noucentisme* (cultural movement at the turn of the century). Like most poets of that school, Salvà was influenced by the Majorcan oral tradition of the *glosadors*, popular country poets. Her themes are mainly the island landscape and features of her immediate surroundings—farm work, country folk, and local customs and foods. For Salvà, nothing is too trivial to be turned into poetry.

She first became known for her translations of works by Francis Jammes, Alessandro Manzoni, Giovanni Pascoli, Saint Teresa, and Frederic Mistral. These writers all influenced her poetry, particularly Mistral. She also admired the Romantics and Jacint Verdaguer.

Salvà's first original composition was *Poesies* (Poems), and henceforth she devoted herself primarily to poetry. The quality of writing is consistent throughout her career. The poems are fresh and spontaneous and show an accomplished technique behind the simplicity of language and subject matter. She employs a great variety of rhyme and meter, and her lyrical descriptions of rural life and the Mediterranean scenery are colorful, lively, and appealing. In 1904 she won a prize in the Jocs Florals in Majorca.

Her three main collections of poems—*Poesies, Espigues en flor* (Blooming wheat), and *El retorn* (Returning)—contain her best work. They are written in standard Catalan and also feature words from the Majorcan vernacular. This combination enhances the natural imagery in her poems and creates a great lyrical effect by balancing sonority and lexical accuracy. *Entre el record i l'enyorança* (Between memories and nostalgia), her only prose work, is a retrospective view of her life and her art. Even in prose, her writing is lyrical and precise. *Antologia poètica* (Poetic anthology) and *Al cel sia!* (May she be in heaven!) both present good selections of her poems.

BOOKS
Al cel sia! Barcelona: Edhasa, 1981.
Antologia poètica. Barcelona: Selecta, 1957.
Cel d'horabaixa. Palma: Moll, 1948.
Entre el record i l'enyorança. Palma: Moll, 1955.
Espigues en flor. Barcelona: Altés, 1926.
Llepolies i joguines. Palma: Les Illes d'Or, 1946.
Lluneta del pagès. Palma: Moll, 1952.
Poesies. Palma: Joan Alcover, 1910.
El retorn. Barcelona: Lluïs Gili, 1934.

TRANSLATIONS OF HER WORKS
"Of a Cactus" ["D'un cactus"], "Four Are the Things" ["Quatre coses"], "Providence" ["Providència"], "To Rosebushes" ["Al roserar"], "Sickroom Diet" ["Règim"], and "Hope" ["Esperança"]. *Survivors.* Selected and trans. D. Sam Abrams. Barcelona: Inst. d'Estudis Nord-Americans, 1991. 11–23.

SECONDARY SOURCES
Alemany Vich, Luis. "Escritores baleares (Fichas bibliográficas)." *La estafeta literaria* 426–28 (1969): 104–19.
Carner, Josep. "La poesia de Maria Antònia Salvà." Salvà, *Antologia poètica* 7–18.
Sbert Garau, M. *M. Antònia Salvà i Ripoll: Apunts per a una cronologia mínima.* Llucmajor, Mallorca: Ajuntament, 1990.
Vidal i Alcover, J. *Poesia casolana de M. A. Salvà.* Llucmajor, Mallorca: Ajuntament, 1990.

ANNA MARIA SANCHEZ RUE

C Salvador, Sofia
(Early 20th c.) Poet. No biographical information available.

According to *Les cinc branques*, Sofia Salvador published one book of poetry, *Jardinet* (Little garden), which is not available in major libraries in Catalonia.

WORKS IN BOOKS, PERIODICALS, NEWSPAPERS
"Poema íntim." *Les cinc branques* 202.

NANCY L. BUNDY

C Samper i Baracco, Maria Carme
(B. 1950, Barcelona– .) Poet.

Maria Carme Samper studied languages and business and has contributed to various publications and radio programs. In *Onades de lluna* (Moon waves) she uses images from nature, often the sea, to express love: "Voldria ser sorra / de totes les platges, / voldria que tu fossis mar, / sentir el teu bes / cada instant. / i així, viure junts / capvespres de plata" (I'd like to be sand / on all the beaches, / I'd like you to be the sea, / and to feel your kiss / each moment, / and thus, live together / those silver sunsets) (91). Some of the poems in this collection are philosophical or psychological. Frequently time is a theme: "He escrit el meu millor poema / a les parets del temps / perquè resti inèdit per sempre" (I've written my best poem / on the walls of time / so it will remain unpublished always) (39). She works as a hairdresser in Barcelona.

BOOKS
Onades de lluna. Illus. Salvador Collell. Barcelona: Amurea, 1985.

KATHLEEN MCNERNEY

C Sanahuja i Bonfill, Isabel
(B. 1930, Caldes de Montbui– .) Short story writer.

As a child Isabel Sanahuja lived in Granollers, Barcelona, and Lleida, and at seventeen she moved back to Barcelona. She is active in the feminist movement and participates in the club Don.na, which sponsors lectures and various cultural events for women.

La dona que va perdre el cos (The woman who lost her body) is a collection of short stories published at the urging of poet Montserrat Abelló. The book is full of surprises, both happy and sad, all told with good humor and in a matter-of-fact tone that undercuts their fanciful nature. Female protagonists preponderate: from the woman who gets stuck in time and wonders if it is just a trick to make people take a break, to the feminist demonstrators who have a hilarious encounter with the "mossos d'esquadra" (local police). At times the lighthearted tone deceives the reader; "Bon Nadal per a tots" (Merry Christmas, everyone) tells of very polite bandits who choose Christmas Day to rob a family just as they are raising their champagne glasses, but the surprise conclusion suggests a novel way to end a marriage. Some of the stories deal with suicide, and several portray family relationships. They all share a fine sense of irony and a wild fantasy that make the reader take a new look at some old assumptions.

BOOKS
La dona que va perdre el cos. Barcelona: LaSal, 1985.

KATHLEEN MCNERNEY

C Sánchez Cutillas Martínez, Carmelina
(B. 1927, Madrid– .) Poet, novelist, and historian.

Granddaughter of the prestigious scholar and Cervantes bibliophile Francesc Martínez i Martínez, Carmelina Sánchez Cutillas began her writing activities with historical research work. Her book *Don Jaime el Conquistador en Alicante* received a prize in the Jocs Florals of Lo Rat Penat in 1957. She later became interested in the classic Valencian writers, publishing *Letres closes de Pere el Cerimoniós endreçades al Consell de València* (Last letters of Pere the Ceremonious addressed to the Council of Valencia) and reading her article "Jaume Gassull, poeta satíric valencià del segle XV" (Jaume Gassull, satiric poet of fifteenth-century Valencia) at the Ier Congrés d'Història del Pais Valencià in 1971.

Her more creative literary activity began with a book of poetry, *Un món rebel* (A rebel world), which was a finalist for the Valencia de Literatura prize in 1964. These fifty-five poems resound with the will to

347

protest, as the title suggests, and with anguish, the term Manuel Sanchis Guarner used in reference to the work of the poets born in the 1920s. These intimate, sincere poems about solitude, uncertainty, and dissatisfaction proceed from an incorruptible self within hostile and alienating circumstances. Perhaps for these reasons Sánchez Cutillas was also included in *Identity Magazine*'s anthology of realist poetry. These same characteristics are intensified in her second book of poetry, *Conjugació en primera persona* (Conjugation in first person), where the author reflects profoundly and directly on her world, daily reality, her country, and the condition of women. This last theme is particularly notable because Sánchez Cutillas is responsible for introducing a feminist consciousness into Valencian poetry.

Els jeroglífics i la pedra de Rosetta (Hieroglyphics and the Rosetta stone) presents a radical change in her poetry. The emotive quality and communicability of her first books here give way to a dense, almost hermetic poetry, characterized by the predominance of images and by constant cultural, historical, mythological, religious, and literary references. Verse is substituted with a rhythmical, tight, and concentrated prose that transports the reader to an original, literary world—a product, perhaps, of Sánchez Cutillas's extensive reading, which is not easily categorized. This disquieting book, unfortunately not well known, is for the moment a departure in the poetic work of the author. With *Llibre d'amic e amada* (Book of friend and beloved) she returns to the versification and language of her first books: images taken directly from daily life, memories, and popular expressions. These poems speak of love with exquisite sensitivity and delicacy. Her novel *Matèria de Bretanya* (i.e., Provençal poetry) won the Andròmina prize in 1975 and has been well received by the public.

BOOKS

Conjugació en primera persona. Valencia: Vives Mora, 1969.
Don Jaime el Conquistador en Alicante. Alicante: Inst. d'Estudis Alacantins, 1958.
Els jeroglífics i la pedra de Rosetta. Valencia: Eliseu Climent, 1976.
Letres closes de Pere el Cerimoniós endreçades al Consell de València. Barcelona: n.p., 1967.
Llibre d'amic e amada. Valencia: Ferrando Torres, 1980.
Matèria de Bretanya. Valencia: Eliseu Climent, 1976.
Un món rebel. Valencia: Vives Mora, 1964.

WORKS IN BOOKS, PERIODICALS, NEWSPAPERS

"A la reverent sor Francina de Bellpuig, monja professa al convent de la Puritat e cara cosina nostra." *Cairell* 7 (Feb. 1981): 5–7.

TRANSLATIONS OF HER WORKS

"As Rails of a Train" ["Com els rails d'un tren"], "The Futile Interment" ["L'inútil soterrar"], "Only Yesterday" ["Encara ahir, teniem"], "People, Anonymous Return" ["Gent, Anònim retorn"], and "The Time Has Come" ["Ha arribat l'hora"].

Trans. Ignacio M. Muñoz and Carl Keul. *Hasta morir tot és vida*. Valencia: Fermar, 1970. 36, 34, 32, 30, 38.

"This Imbalance" ["Aquest desequilibri"]. *Identity Magazine* 24 (1966): 46–47. (This issue, edited by Lluis Alpern, bears the subtitle *Anthology of Valencian Realist Poetry / Antologia de la poesia realista valenciana*.)

SECONDARY SOURCES
Pérez Montaner, Jaume. "Carmelina Sánchez-Cutillas: Una poètica de la qüotidianeitat." *Revista de Catalunya* (Oct. 1993).

ISABEL ROBLES GOMEZ

C   Sánchez Morales, Rosa
(20th c.) Poet. No biographical information available.

BOOKS
Mostra de poesia. Tortosa: n.p., 1981.

KATHLEEN MCNERNEY

C   Santamaria i Ventura de Fàbrigues, Joaquima
(B. 1854, Barcelona; d. 1930, Barcelona.) Poet, short story writer, and writer of religious prose.

Known by the pen name Agna de Valldaura, Joaquima Santamaria was a widely admired poet in her day, appearing alongside Dolors Monserdà de Macià in collections of verse. Today she is best remembered for her 1877 collection of Catalan religious traditions and legends, *Tradicions religioses de Catalunya* (Religious traditions of Catalonia), which saw several editions in both Catalan and Castilian over the next decades. The Joventut Catòlica literary competition awarded a prize in 1877 to these piously ingenuous, poetic renditions of historical and popular legends. Her poetry also won awards in the Jocs Florals of Barcelona and other cities. Santamaria published one collection of poems, *Ridolta* (Tender shoots), and a volume of poetry and short prose works, *Fullaraca* (Fallen leaves). She contributed to the Barcelona magazine *La bordadora* (The embroideress), a women's needlework magazine in Castilian, and *Lo Gay Saber*, a Catalan literary magazine. Her work also appeared abroad in the Catalan newspaper *L'auraneta* (Buenos Aires) and *La llumanera*. Several of her Catalan legends were published in *Lectura popular*, the literary supplement of the cultural review *Ilustració catalana*. Her contribution to the contemporary debate over the role and responsibilities of women is the volume *Breus consideracions sobre la dona* (Brief thoughts about women).

BOOKS
Breus consideracions sobre la dona. Barcelona: Tipografia Catòlica, 1866.
Fullaraca: Prosa i vers. Barcelona: Estampa Peninsular, 1879.
Ridolta: Aplech de poesias. Barcelona: Roca, 1882.
Tradicions religioses de Catalunya. Barcelona: Roca, 1877.
Tradicions religioses de Catalunya: Recullides i ara explicades de bell nou. Barcelona: Millà, 1948.

WORKS IN BOOKS, PERIODICALS, NEWSPAPERS
"L'ancell y l'atmetlles. Faula." *La llumanera de Nova York* 4.49 (1879).
"Tradicions." *Lectura popular* 20: 345.

TRANSLATIONS OF HER WORKS
Tradiciones religiosas de Cataluña [*Tradicions religioses de Catalunya*]. Barcelona: n.p., 1925.

MARYELLEN BIEDER

C   Sant-Celoni i Verger, Encarna
(B. 1959, Tavernes de la Valldigna, València– .) Novelist, short story writer, and poet.

With a degree in geography and history, Encarna Sant-Celoni now teaches Catalan for the Valencian Generalitat. Her fiction and poetry have been awarded various prizes, including the Joanot Martorell in 1985 for *Siamangorina*. This novel demonstrates her control of and inventiveness with the language, as well as her originality and gift for fantasy. The protagonist Eumàquia's inner voyage, her encounter with the self and the other, reflects the influence of Borges and Unamuno, but with a distinctly fresh voice.

The collection *Dotze contes i una nota necrològica* (Twelve stories and a necrological note) shows a fine irony and sense of humor. *La primera misiva* (First missive), written in Castilian, is an epistolary novel. Sant-Celoni has contributed to several journals and formed part of the collective of women who published the journal *Pandora* in the early 1980s.

BOOKS
Arran de pantomima. Valencia: Gregal, 1988.
Dotze contes i una nota necrològica. Valencia: El Cingle, 1985.
La primera misiva. Valencia: Ayuntamiento de Alaquas, 1984.
Siamangorina. Gandia: Ajuntament, 1986.

KATHLEEN MCNERNEY

Sant Jordi, Rosa de; *see* **Arquimbau, Rosa Maria**

C Sanz Masip, Maria Teresa
(20th c.) Poet. No biographical information available.

BOOKS
Vint i quatre poemes. Barcelona: n.p., 1973.

KATHLEEN MCNERNEY

C Sardà i Homs, Zeneida
(20th c.) Novelist. No biographical information available.

Dafnis i Maia (Dafnis and Maia) is a free and lyrical reworking of certain Greek myths. The simple but sensitive shepherd Dafnis falls in love with the beautiful but mysterious Maia, who turns out to be one of the Pleiades. Dafnis, through the friendship of an old man and his daughter, learns about true love and beauty. The old man's folkloric tales tie in with the ancient Greek stories to create a surreal world for which the boy decides to abandon his more earthly existence.

BOOKS
Adéu, Nereo! Montserrat: L'Abadia, 1982.
Dafnis i Maia. Barcelona: Laia, 1984.
Francesc Macià, vist per la seva filla Maria. Barcelona: Destino, 1989.

KATHLEEN MCNERNEY

C Sarduc, Imma
(B. 1960, Barcelona– .) Poet.

Imma Sarduc studied Catalan philology at the University of Barcelona. She has contributed to several literary publications, such as *Ampit* in 1984, *Territoris* in 1985, and *Reduccions*. She also helped organized the art exhibit Mont-Art 84 in Montornès del Vallès. *Hecatékali* is her first book of poetry. The title refers to two goddesses: Hecate, the Greek goddess with various powers who is especially associated with the infernal regions and known as the patroness of magicians and witches; and Kali, the Indian goddess of war and destruction. Sarduc begins each of the three sections of *Hecatékali* with a quotation of a writer: Antoine de Saint-Exupéry, Shichirô Fukazawa, and Henry Miller. Her use of fragmentations, collage, and entire lines in French leads to a rather hermetic and intellectual poetry. She is more accessible in her simpler pieces, such as the conclusion of poem IV in the middle section—"Visca l'amant etern / que es fa vitalista / davant la feredat estàtica / del moment!" (Long live the eternal lover / the one for life / in front of the static terror / of the moment!)—or the collection's brief, closing poem—"no sóc / sinó / una lleugera difusió / eterna / del possible / pateixo / massa" (I'm only / a light eternal diffusion / of the possible / I suffer too much).

BOOKS
Hecatékali. Prol. Josep Maria Sala-Valldaura. Barcelona: Les Edicions del Dies, 1986.
Pòrtic d'Aura-Mar. Valencia: Alfons el Magnànim, 1991.

KATHLEEN MCNERNEY

C Senye d'Aymà, Anna
(B. 1881, Manlleu, Barcelona; d. 1956, Barcelona.) Poet.

According to *Les cinc branques*, Anna Senyé d'Aymà published one collection of poetry under the title *Remolinada* (Whirlwind), which is not available in major libraries in Catalonia.

BOOKS
Remolinada. N.p.: n.p., 1922.

WORKS IN BOOKS, PERIODICALS, NEWSPAPERS
"Festa major." *Les cinc branques* 65.

NANCY L. BUNDY

C Serra, Isabel
(20th c.) Journalist and short story writer. No biographical information available.

In 1907, the women's journal *Feminal*, edited by Carme Karr, published two features by Isabel Serra, its reporter in Morocco. Under the title "Feminal al Marroch" (*Feminal* in Morocco), they described the customs of the country, with special emphasis on the situation of women. In the same journal, Isabel Serra published two short stories, "La menuda" (The little girl) and "El retorn" (The homecoming), as well as a play, "Sot a'ls vels" (Under the veils), although there is no record of the latter ever having been staged. "La menuda" is a criticism of orphanages and of the exploitation of orphans by the nuns who shelter them. In "El retorn," an emigrant's return to his place of origin provides the opportunity to reveal the social immobility in small Catalan rural communities. In "Sot a'ls vels" the author rejects the prospects that marriage offers a woman.

These stories were published in *Lectura popular* in 1917, and a review of the collection appeared in *Feminal*. The short bibliographical note in *Lectura popular*, possibly written by Francesc Matheu, mentions that Isabel Serra had been forced to give up writing and was, at that moment, one of the most famous dressmakers in Barcelona.

BOOKS
Narracions. Vol. 13 of *Lectura popular*.

WORKS IN BOOKS, PERIODICALS, NEWSPAPERS
"Feminal al Marroch." *Feminal* 6 (29 Sept. 1907).
"Feminal al Marroch." *Feminal* 7 (27 Oct. 1907).
"La menuda." *Feminal* 10 (26 Jan. 1908).
"El retorn." *Feminal* 17 (30 Aug. 1908).
"Sot a'ls vels." *Feminal* 70 (26 Jan. 1913).

CRISTINA ENRIQUEZ DE SALAMANCA

C Serra de Gayetà, Joana
(B. 1950, Pollença, Mallorca– .) Poet and novelist.

Joana Serra de Gayetà is a teacher whose work reflects with some melancholy the lost world of childhood and adolescence. *Taules de marbre* (Marble tables), winner of the Ciutat de Manacor prize, is a collection of short vignettes, or prose poems, that are descriptive portraits of everyday life and objects. Majorca is the background for pieces about summer and winter, tourists and rain; there are also lyrical descriptions of her student days and the difficulties of writing. The novel *Nosaltres esperàvem mister Marshall* (Waiting for Mr. Marshall), published in a single volume with Miquel Mas Ferra's "Massa temps amb els ulls tancats" (Too long with our eyes closed), won the Joan Ballester prize. It reflects the postwar years of the Marshall Plan, when children waited for powdered milk during recess while adoring Elvis Presley and other popular American stars. Serra de Gayetà has contributed poems to several journals.

BOOKS
Nosaltres esperàvem mister Marshall. Mallorca: Campos, 1976.
Taules de marbre. Mallorca: Mascaró Pasarius, 1974.

KATHLEEN MCNERNEY

353

C   Serrahima i Manén, Núria
(B. 1931, Barcelona– .) Novelist and scriptwriter.

Born to a conservative bourgeois family, Núria Serrahima received a traditional upbringing and primary education. She left her convent school at the age of fourteen for an intensive five-year study of painting, but she turned to literature shortly before her father's death in 1958.

Her semiautobiographical first novel, *Mala guilla* (Bad fox), depicts the historical, cultural, and social ambient of her adolescence as well as personal relationships, of which the one with her father emerges as the most significant. Serrahima emphasizes the school's repressive atmosphere, which aborts creativity and represses talent, especially that of female students.

L'olor dels nostres cossos (The odor of our bodies) comprises three novellas with common feminist themes, each with a first-person woman narrator. Thirty-six-year-old Gloria, the protagonist of the title novella, struggles with conflicting emotions during a wakeful night, while Rafael, her husband of fourteen years, sleeps soundly. Torn between love for her two children, the power of bourgeois norms and values, and the knowledge that her marriage is a sham, Gloria wavers between the desire for self-fulfillment, thoughts of marriage, and suicidal impulses, without coming to a firm decision. The protagonist of "Negres moments d'Emma" (Black moments for Emma) sorts through disordered recollections of significant moments. Brilliant, neurotic, insecure, alcoholic, suicidal, hysterical, promiscuous, and radically alone, Emma lives in a hallucinatory, fantastic world, alternating between homicidal urges and the desire to escape. "Amants" ("Lovers"), another collection of memories, is lighter in tone, as the sensual narrator recalls in alphabetical order the thirty lovers she has classified by initials. These lyrical, evocative fragments suggest prose poems.

Serrahima is also the author of a television drama entitled "Agressió" (Aggression), produced in Catalan by Manuel Lara. A feminist take-off on the "progressive" intellectual elitists of the post-Franco era, the story employs sex-role reversal to comic and telling effect, as three feminists meet in the home of a fourth. After a satiric dialogue, they raffle off one of their male acquaintances as a sex object, with the result that the man finds himself in the uncomfortable, traditionally female position of being pursued and seduced.

BOOKS
Diari sense dates. Barcelona: L'Eixample, 1990.
Mala guilla. Barcelona: Edicions 62, 1973.
L'olor dels nostres cossos. Barcelona: Edicions 62, 1982.

JANET PEREZ

C Serrano Llacer, Rosa Maria
(B. 1945, Paiporta, València– .) Writer of children's literature.

Rosa Maria Serrano taught at the Rosa Sensat School in Barcelona and returned to Valencia to help create the Gavina School, a cooperative of teachers self-defined as progressive and nationalist.

BOOKS
Adaptació de trenta sis rondalles valencianes d'Enric Valor. Valencia: Gregal, 1987.
Aplec: Llengua. Barcelona: Barcanova, 1984.
Ara va de caps. . . . Valencia: Federació d'Entitats Culturals de País Valencià, 1983.
David està malalt. Barcelona: Aliorna, 1988.
Hola i Adéu, Júlia. Valencia: Gregal, 1986.
Ma casa. Valencia: Conselleria d'Educació de la Generalitat de Valencia, 1985.
La paraula és una aventura. Valencia: Institució Alfons el Magnànim, 1981.
El quadern de Júlia. Valencia: Gregal, 1985.
Ui, ui, ui, quins ulls! Valencia: Federació d'Entitats Culturals del País Valencià, 1983.

ANNA MONTERO I BOSCH

C Simó i Monllor, Isabel-Clara
(B. 1943, Alcoi, Alacant– .) Novelist, short story writer, and journalist.

Isabel-Clara Simó received her degree in philosophy from the University of Valencia. From 1972 to 1983 she edited the Catalan magazine *Canigó*. She won the Víctor Català award for her collection of stories *Es quan miro que i veig clar* (It's when I look that I can see clearly) and was a finalist for the Ramon Llull award in 1982 for her novel *Júlia*. Her third book, *Idols*, won the Crítica del País Valencià prize. Other works include *Bresca* (Honeycomb), a collection of short stories; the novel *T'estimo Marta* (I love you, Marta); *El secret d'en Toni Trull* (The secret of Toni Trull), a book for young adults; and two detective novels, *La veïna* (The neighbor) and *Una ombra fosca com un núvol de tempesta* (A shadow dark as a storm cloud).

Simó's works are psychologically insightful. The author endeavors to draw out the peculiar characteristics of seemingly average personages in apparently normal situations. Whether the narrative is in the first person, the third, or a blend of the two, Simó immediately pulls the reader into the story. She writes in colloquial Catalan with some noticeable Valencianisms. Despite the simplicity of her language, she creates complex and often bizarre stories. Her work revolves around the following themes: the consequences of sexual taboos, traditional role-playing between men and women, the insensitivity of the wealthy bourgeoisie to the working class, and the isolation of intellectuals within a society. Although extremely critical she is not pessimistic and attempts to present a better vision of life. Her novels often have positive endings.

Bresca's ten short stories vary in style, but the prevailing theme is women's disillusionment with romantic relationships and marriage. The author emphasizes women's ignorance of their bodies and their limited knowledge of sex as causes of their unhappiness and neuroses. "De tant que et vull et truc un ull" (I love you so much I'll pluck out your eye) epitomizes the general mood of this collection. Two young people struggling with their own inconsistencies and insecurities move to a small town where they believe life will be quiet and dull. Slowly they discover that an intricate history of atrocities underlies the eventless routine of country living. Without being tragic or cynical, the author shows that no person or incident is truly simple. The irony of this story pervades the collection: women only free themselves from submissive roles when they are at a breaking point, and then an explosion of pain and destruction occurs. Simó's message is clear: women must assert their needs and desires, or their passivity will produce disastrous consequences for the individual and for society as a whole.

Testimo Marta encompasses all of Simó's major themes in an ingenious manner. The novel deals with incest and raises questions about feminism, marriage, the alienation of intellectuals, and the complexity of human perceptions. The protagonists, a young couple in Barcelona, recount their lives while focusing on their child, Marta. The primary narrator in the novel's first half is the husband, Ferran; in the second half, the voice switches to the wife, Lidia. Ferran and Lidia both had difficult childhoods. From the commencement of their courtship, their roles were clearly marked: his as the intellectual and the taker, hers as the more loving partner and, therefore, the giver. Throughout their relationship both sense a communication barrier, and their mutual distrust eventually causes their breakup. Ferran, a professor at an institute, also feels frustrated in his job. Lidia, restless to escape the boredom of the home, becomes a typist for a university professor who happens to be writing a book on social taboos. Through this professor and his work, Simó discusses some interesting theories on the alienation between men and women. Although both Ferran and Lidia have flaws, Ferran is the more difficult character with whom to identify. His arrogance and pettiness make Lidia's introspective nature a welcome contrast. Simó's female characters tend to be more resilient and sympathetic. Once again, she penetrates contemporary culture to reveal its hidden parts, believing that confronting society's negative aspects is an important step toward human progress.

El mossèn (The priest) is a novelized biography of the poet Jacint

356

Verdaguer; it has been serialized for radio by the author. *Alcoi–Nova York* (From Alcoi to New York) is a collection of stories; the title piece is a chilling exploration of life beyond death, identity changes, and additional possibilities for unusual existences. The other stories feature a satire on teachers, the portrait of a middle-class marriage in which the woman does all the work and yet is terribly grateful for her situation, a traveler who falls in love with a painting of the Virgin, and a child who kills his father for hitting his mother. Simó closes with a sensual story on female eroticism.

The culture, personality, and strength of the author are present in all her works. She despises hypocrisy and injustice but refuses to give in to Hobbesian philosophy. Her protagonists have the power of choice and can better their world.

Simó currently teaches philosophy at an institute in Barcelona. She is married and has three children.

BOOKS

Alcoi–Nova York. Barcelona: Edicions 62, 1987.

Bresca. Barcelona: Laia, 1985.

Dona i societat a la Catalunya actual. With Maria-Aurèlia Capmany, Magda Oranich, Anna Balletbó, and Maria Rosa Prats. Barcelona: Edicions 62, 1978.

Es quan miro que i veig clar. Barcelona: Selecta, 1979.

Històries perverses. Barcelona: Edicions 62, 1992.

Idols. Barcelona: Magrana, 1985.

Júlia. Barcelona: Magrana, 1983.

El Mas del Diable. Barcelona: Area, 1992.

El mossèn. Barcelona: Plaza & Janés, 1987.

La Nati. Barcelona: Area, 1991.

Núvols. Barcelona: Edicions 62, 1990.

Una ombra fosca com un núvol de tempesta. Barcelona: Area, 1991.

Raquel. Barcelona: Columna, 1992.

El secret d'en Toni Trull. Barcelona: Barcanova, 1986.

T'estimo Marta. Barcelona: Magrana, 1986.

Els ulls de Clídice. Barcelona: Edicions 62, 1990.

La veïna. Barcelona: Area, 1990.

TRANSLATIONS OF HER WORKS

"A Crumb of Nothing" ["Engruna de res"], trans. Spurgeon B. Baldwin, and "Melodrama in Alcoi" ["Melodrama alcoià"], trans. Charles Merrill. *On Our Own Behalf*. Ed. Kathleen McNerney. Lincoln and London: U of Nebraska P, 1988. 155–99.

Historias perversas [*Històries perverses*]. Trans. Marcelo Cohen and Maru Fernández de Villavicencio. Barcelona: Península, 1993.

"Womanpleasure" ["Plaer de dona"]. Trans. Kathleen McNerney. *Monographic Review / Revista monográfica* 7 (1991): 167–72.

TARA MCNALLY

C   Simó Oliver, Francina
(20th c., Mallorca.) Poet. No biographical information available.

BOOKS
Espires de cendra. Palma: n.p., 1959.

KATHLEEN MCNERNEY

C   Solà i Llopis, Maria Lluïsa
(B. 1918, Barcelona– .) Writer of short stories and books for children.

Maria Lluïsa Solà worked in several public libraries and finally in the Biblioteca de Catalunya until she retired in 1982. She has contributed stories to *Patufet* and *Cavall fort* and published a number of books for children.

BOOKS
Adéu, Serena. Barcelona: Cruïlla, 1986.
Anna. Barcelona: La Galera, 1973.
Aventures d'en Tau. Montserrat: L'Abadia, 1982.
En Jordi Pigat i la colla del gos. Montserrat: L'Abadia, 1979.
Un estiu a Rocagrossa. Montserrat: L'Abadia, 1975.
Jo més dues . . . fan cinc. Montserrat: L'Abadia, 1978.
Maraula blau-verd. Montserrat: L'Abadia, 1988.
Quan em deia Lala. Montserrat: L'Abadia, 1982.
Roda d'amics. Montserrat: L'Abadia, 1983.
Teresa i la seva colla. Montserrat: L'Abadia, 1976.

KATHLEEN MCNERNEY

C   Solà i Salvà, Natàlia
(B. 1934, Mallorca– .) Poet.

Natàlia Solà's first book of poetry, which she describes in the introduction as "un agradable col.loqui amb mi mateixa" (a pleasant chat with myself), is *Intensament blancs i grocs* (Intensely white and yellow), which won the Grandalla de Poesia prize in 1986. With an informative prologue by Esteve Albert and simple, elegant drawings by Fèlix Vicente i Solà, the collection is divided into four thematic sections: dreams and memories, a desire to communicate, friendships, and writing itself. The title refers to childhood memories of Majorca. Solà studied in Valencia and then moved to Andorra, where she devotes most of her time to teaching and composing music. The rhythms in her poetry vary, but they all have a musicality and sometimes evoke popular songs. A fine lyricism pervades her work, but in one poem she rails against politicians with a staccato series of words to describe their activities: "Esverats, . . . enganyant, . . . estúpidament, . . . exposen, . . . hermètics, . . ." (Scared, . . . deceiving, . . . stupidly, . . . they expose, . . . airtight, . . .) (25).

BOOKS
Intensament blancs i grocs. Prol. Esteve Albert. Illus. Fèlix Vicente i Solà. Andorra: Pirene, 1987.

KATHLEEN MCNERNEY

C Solé i Vendrell, Carme
(B. 1944, Barcelona– .) Illustrator and writer.

Carme Solé studied at the Escola d'Arts i Oficis Massana in Barcelona and illustrated her first book in 1968. In the last several years she has published books as both author and illustrator. She has participated in numerous group exhibits, among them the 1983 BIB (Bologna and Bratislava), and has been awarded various illustration prizes, including the National Illustration prize and the Janusz Korczak prize of Poland in 1979, the Lazarillo in 1981, and the illustration prize from the Generalitat de Catalunya in 1983. Among her important exhibitions abroad are those shown in Bologna, Tokyo, Paris, and London. She has collaborated in the illustration of several Catalan textbooks, and in 1980 and 1981 she illustrated the children's animation series *Victor i Maria* for King Rollo Films. Her books have also been published in other languages.

BOOKS
Bon dia escola: Fitxes de treball. With Maria Martínez i Vendrell. 3 vols. Col. Pensament i Llenguatge. Barcelona: Casals, 1986–87.
Llivia: Petita història d'un gos d'atura. Barcelona: Hymsa, 1982.
La lluna d'en Joan. Barcelona: Hymsa, 1982.
El nen del paraigua. Barcelona: Hymsa, 1984.

TRANSLATIONS OF HER WORKS
The Boy with the Umbrella [*El nen del paraigua*]. London: Blakie, 1985.

ANNA GASOL I TRULLOLS

C Soler i Guasch, Sílvia
(B. 1961, Figueres, Girona– .) Journalist and short story writer.

Sílvia Soler has lived in various Catalan cities: Olot, Calella, Terrassa, and, currently, Badalona. She studied journalism in Barcelona and now works for Ràdio Ciutat de Badalona. She has done other work related to her training, including collaboration with Pedro J. Blasco on the book *Angel Casas Show: Anecdotari secret*.

Arriben els ocells de nit (The night birds come) is a collection of lyrical stories. The themes vary, but all the protagonists are women. The strongest of the six stories is "Semblava de vidre" (She seemed of glass), which won the Recull prize in 1984. The subject is a piano teacher who has a collection of glass figures and who sometimes seems to be one of them. The story is told by a student, who once tactlessly mentions this resemblance and provokes a vehement, if somewhat predictable, glacial reaction. Imagery is Soler's strong point: in the title story the usual comparison of autumn with nostalgia, aging, and death is transformed by the quality of the light; the incessant rain in "De vegades encara plou sobre el meu teulat" (Sometimes it still rains on my roof) dins into the reader the mental state of the protagonist; the flashing beacon of the lighthouse in "Cileta far" (Lighthouse) punctuates the brightness and darkness in the life of Cileta; "La lluna, la pruna" (The moon, the prune) is a phrase taken from a children's song, and the protagonist, Clàudia, herself becomes a prune when her dream vanishes.

BOOKS

Angel Casas Show: Anecdotari secret. With Pedro J. Blasco. Barcelona: Pòrtic, 1985.
Arriben els ocells de nit. Barcelona: Pòrtic, 1985.

KATHLEEN MCNERNEY

C Soler i Marcet, Maria-Lourdes

(B. 1944, Manresa– .) Formerly Maria-Lourdes Möller Soler. Poet.

Maria-Lourdes Soler i Marcet is a librarian for the university library at Trier, Germany, and well versed in classical mythology as well as the history and culture of Catalonia. Her *Minorisa aeterna* (Eternal Minorisa) is a collection of poetry published on the occasion of the 1,100th anniversary of the city of Manresa. The twenty poems it contains are long, documentary pieces that are evocative and suggestive enough to be universal, in spite of their local and specific inspirations. She creates a feeling of timelessness with details of the town and its rhythms in "Les cadires del Passeig" (Chairs on Sidewalk Street); her strong feminist approach comes out in "Les pageses de la plaça" (Country women on the square); and her sense of history is apparent in "Mesopotàmia gentil" (Gentle Mesopotamia), a piece in which she also experiments with the configurations of words on the page. Perhaps her strongest poem is "Minorisa aeterna," in which she divides the history of her country into six epochs. The poetry is complemented by drawings of village and country scenes by Josep Vila i Closes.

BOOKS

Les bases: Pinacoteca poètica d'estampes d'una època. Barcelona: Columna, 1992.
Del jardí estant: Calidoscopi impressionista d'Alemanya. Montserrat: L'Abadia, 1991.
Minorisa aeterna. Illus. Josep Vila i Closes. Manresa: Ajuntament, 1990.

KATHLEEN MCNERNEY

C Soler i Puig, Helena
(B. 1967, Barcelona– .) Writer of children's stories.

Helena Soler i Puig is currently a student of Catalan philology. Her first book, *Carlemany a Girona* (Charlemagne in Girona), is a novelized account of a historic episode in the life of Charlemagne, whose adventures in Girona are disputed by historians.

BOOKS

Carlemany a Girona. Barcelona: Ambit Serveis Editorials (ASESA), 1988.

KATHLEEN MCNERNEY

C Soler Ribes, Magda
(20th c.) Poet. No biographical information available.

BOOKS

Sempre hi ha una escletxa de llum. Barcelona: n.p., 1979.

KATHLEEN MCNERNEY

C Solsona i Duran, Isabel
(20th c., Cervera, Lleida.) Poet.

According to Josep M. Razguín's prologue to Isabel Solsona's *Poemes de tardor* (Autumn poems), the author was a member of the rural landowning class and had illustrious ancestors. She married a physician, Dr. Josep Riu, and moved to Barcelona. The collection is divided chronologically into three sections: the poems written between 1959 and 1961 are intimate, spiritual, and full of household details; those from 1978 to 1982 are decidedly more intellectual; and the poems dated after 1982 have a nostalgic tone. Razguín sees the influence of Solsona's friend Palmíra Jaquetti in

her work. The book concludes with a conversation between the writer
Ramon Turull and Solsona.

BOOKS

Poemes de tardor. Prol. Josep M. Razguín. Cervera: Biblioteca de Cervera, 1985.

KATHLEEN MCNERNEY

C Solsona i Querol, Josefina
(B. 1907, Barcelona; d. 1960, Barcelona.) Also known as Cecília
Beltrán. Playwright, novelist, short story writer, and translator.

Josefina Solsona wrote articles and stories for many different publications.
Between 1922 and 1927 she contributed to the section "Cuentos propios"
in the newspaper *Las noticias*. One of her stories, "El jorobadito y la princesa" (The hunchback and the princess), won a prize in the women's supplement of the paper. She occasionally contributed to other publications, such
as the Mexican magazine *Abside*. From 1931 she wrote regularly for *Patufet*
(Barcelona, 1904–38) and was the only female contributor to that children's
weekly. From 1941 to 1948 she contributed weekly to *L'Atalaya* (Barcelona), a magazine that published work by many of *Patufet*'s former writers.
She also wrote stories for *L'Atalaya*'s "Pàginas de la vida," a section that
imitated *Patufet*'s "Pàgines viscudes."

Solsona's novels are written mainly for young readers. *L'encís blau*
(Blue enchantment) and *L'hora d'en Lluís* (Luis's hour) are two romantic
novels set in the daily life of Catalonia in the early 1930s. After the war
she wrote other children's novels in Castilian: *Los alegres cacharreros* (The
happy potters), *Alberto, Los caballeros de Santa Clara* (The knights of
Santa Clara), *Las vacaciones de Agustín* (Agustin's vacation), *Cuando
Agustín se llamó Pedro Claver* (When Agustín was called Pedro Claver),
and *Eulalia*. In 1943 she published the children's story *La dulce Julieta*
(Sweet Julieta).

During the 1950s two of Solsona's plays were staged for the first time.
"El misteri de ca l'encantat" (The mystery of the haunted house) opened
in 1950 on the morning program of the Teatre Romea and turned out to
be one of the most noteworthy productions of the morning sessions, a series
developed to introduce new authors. In 1952 "Maritza" opened at the Club
Diagonal theater. Many of her other plays have remained unpublished,
among which two texts, preserved in the Theater Institute Library, deserve
mention: "El cisne de Lohengrin" (Lohengrin's swan) and "A mitja llum"
(Low light).

Solsona translated three Italian works into Castilian, including Augusto de Angelis's *Il misterio di Cinecittà*. On 22 November 1956 she gave

362

a speech to the Astronomy Society of Spain and America entitled "From the Living into the Past," and on 16 February 1958 she gave the talk "Figures from Literary History" to the Sociedad Cultural y Recreativa Asteria. During the last five years of her life she helped the sculptor Joan Matamala i Flotats write a study on Antoni Gaudí and organize his documents on the architect.

BOOKS
Alberto. Barcelona: Balmes, 1943.
Los alegres cacharreros. Illus. Junceda. Barcelona: Balmes, 1943.
Los caballeros de Santa Clara. Barcelona: Balmes, 1943.
Cuando Agustín se llamó Pedro Claver. Barcelona: Balmes, 1946.
La dulce Julieta. Barcelona: Molino, 1943.
L'encís blau. Barcelona: Baguñà, 1933.
Eulalia. Illus. A. Batllori. Barcelona: Balmes, 1950.
L'hora d'en Lluís. Barcelona: Baguñà, 1933.
Las vacaciones de Agustín. Barcelona: Balmes, 1944.

WORKS IN BOOKS, PERIODICALS, NEWSPAPERS
"Al volver de la guerra" and "Solo." *Las noticias* 1927.
"El destino." *Las noticias* 1922.
"El jorobadito i la princesa." *Las noticias* 1926.
"El milagro." *Las noticias* 1925.

SECONDARY SOURCES
Curet 62.
Larreula, Enric. *Les revistes infantils catalanes de 1939 ençà.* Barcelona: Edicions 62, 1985. 27–28.

NURIA PI I VENDRELL

Sor Anna Maria del Santissim Sagrament; *see* Mas Pujol, Margalida Baneta

C Sorribas, Fernanda
(19th c.) Poet. No biographical information available.

Fernanda Sorribas is listed as a "poetisa catalana" (Catalan poetess) by Juan P. Criado y Domínguez in his *Literatas españolas del siglo XIX.* She contributed the poem "A un aucellet" (For a little bird) to a special issue of *La Llumanera de Nova York*, which was devoted to Catalan women writers and featured work by Josefa Massanés, Dolors Monserdà, Victòria Penya d'Amer, Maria de Bell-Lloch, Agna de Valldaura, Manuela de los Herreros, Margarida Caymarí, and Emilia Palau. Francisco Tubino, in his

Historia del renacimiento literario contemporáneo en Cataluña, Baleares y Valencia, groups her among the "poetisas catalano-mallorquinas."

WORKS IN BOOKS, PERIODICALS, NEWSPAPERS
"A un ancellet." *La llumanera de Nova York* May 1879.

SECONDARY SOURCES
Criado y Domínguez 156.
Tubino, *Historia del renacimiento literario contemporáneo*.

CRISTINA ENRIQUEZ DE SALAMANCA

C Suaris, Isabel
(15th c., València.) Writer of letters.

According to Martí de Riquer's *Història de la literatura catalana*, the poet Simon Palmer said that Isabel Suaris was an intelligent writer. The copy of a poetic letter she wrote to Bernat Fenollar is in a manuscript in Valencia but has not been published. Jaume Massó i Torrents also describes the literary correspondence between Suaris and Fenollar, as well as Palmer's praise of Suaris, in "Poetesses i dames intel.lectuals."

WORKS IN BOOKS, PERIODICALS, NEWSPAPERS
Letter to Bernat Fenollar. Ms. Municipal Library, Valencia.

SECONDARY SOURCES
Massó i Torrents, "Poetesses i dames intel.lectuals" 414–17.
Riquer et al. 3: 73, 364.

LOLA BADIA

C Suau, Núria
(B. 1920, Barcelona– .) Prose writer.

Núria Suau's only published work, the slim volume *Agredolç* (Bittersweet), is a collection of brief observations on life. Some are quite poetic and philosophical, some popular or humorous. The themes vary considerably, but she tends to dwell on domestic relationships and the foibles of her fellow human beings.

BOOKS
Agredolç. Barcelona: Adarme, 1976.

KATHLEEN MCNERNEY

C Sunyol, Cèlia

(B. 1899, Barcelona; d. ?) Also Suñol. Short story writer and novelist.

Born to a well-to-do Catalan family, Cèlia Sunyol was educated in the liberal style of the prewar bourgeoisie, which included learning languages and literatures such as English and French and, for women, becoming acquainted with feminist viewpoints that disappeared after the Spanish Civil War. Her description of this early period is of special interest because of its contrast with women's position in postwar Spain.

Sunyol's novel *Primera part* (First part) contains some autobiographical elements. The title refers to a particular period in the protagonist's life: from her early years to a first marriage that ends in widowhood. In memoir form, the narrator describes her childhood, spent in a typical prosperous family, and her authoritarian father, whose demands for his daughter's submission are frightening. Her relationship with her sisters, her first experiences of love, and an illness, tuberculosis, prompt her sojourns in Switzerland, Germany, and France. During one of these journeys, she meets her future husband, a man suffering from terminal tuberculosis. Presented by the author as an example of love, the experience of this relationship is harrowing, nearly driving the protagonist to madness. With verbal precision and an agile narrative technique, Sunyol creates two contradictory voices that seem to meet: that of the woman who bows to traditional dictates and the feminist voice of present-day Catalan women writers. Some isolated fragments contain veiled allusions to the Civil War. The mood of this novel, which was written before the author's full maturity, was succinctly expressed by Sunyol herself: "La meva infantesa morí aquell dia amb la mare. Dintre meu s'apagà alguna cosa feta de confiança i d'ingenuitat. Havia après que el mal pot venir a ferir-nos sense raó, obscurament, traïdorament" (My childhood died that day with my mother. Something went out inside me, something made up of confidence and naïveté. I learnt that evil comes to wound us for no reason, darkly, treacherously) (*Primera part* 29).

L'home de les fires i altres contes (The man of the fair and other stories) is a collection of unequal tone and quality, but two stories stand out: the title piece and "El bon mariner" (The good sailor). In "L'home de les fires" a female protagonist trying to write a story serves as the pretext for reflecting on the material conditions in which women create literature. The never-ending cycle of chores and their collision with an evanescent literary inspiration recall Virginia Woolf's *A Room of One's Own* and some essays by Pilar Sinués. In "El bon mariner," the author describes the world of a sailor's wife: the months of loneliness followed by the husband's arrival, which interrupts her regular routine. A sailor's wife is regarded as living a widow's life.

Cèlia Sunyol's stories appeared during a precarious period for Catalan

365

writing: right after the Civil War. They came out into a kind of literary vacuum but were so well accepted that Biblioteca Selecta collected them in a single volume and added Sunyol to its list of well-known writers, which included Josep Maria Sagarra, Jacint Verdaguer, Santiago Rusinyol, and Carles Riba.

Cèlia Sunyol translated Claude Houghton's *Passport to Paradise* and A. A. Thomson's *A Delightful Village* into Castilian.

BOOKS
L'home de les fires i altres contes. Barcelona: Selecta, 1950.
Primera part. Barcelona: Aymà, 1948.

WORKS IN BOOKS, PERIODICALS, NEWSPAPERS
"El 'meu' doctor Reventòs." *Recordant el doctor Reventòs: Homenatge dels seus amics.* Barcelona: Gustavo Gili, 1969. 105–09.

SECONDARY SOURCES
Enríquez de Salamanca, Cristina. "Cotidianeidad y creación literaria en 'L'home de les fires' de Cèlia Sunyol." *Monographic Review / Revista monográfica* 4 (1988): 242–56.

CRISTINA ENRIQUEZ DE SALAMANCA

C Suqué i d'Espona de Llimona, Carme
(B. 1904, Barcelona– .) Writer of plays and stories for children.

After a youth spent abroad, Carme Suqué returned to Catalonia and alternated between stays in Barcelona and Vic, the birthplace of her mother. She studied social work but soon became interested in writing and adapting works for children. Her sources are varied, from fables such as that of King Midas to stories by Oscar Wilde. She has also written puppet shows and has won various prizes. Her work has been successfully presented in the Teatre Romea and the Palau de la Música in Barcelona. She regularly contributes stories to the children's magazine *Cavall fort* and has written three novels for children: *Un conte del mar* (A story of the sea), *En Francesc, en Daniel i els quissos* (Francesc, Daniel, and the puppies), and *La cabanya del gorg* (The hut by the river).

BOOKS
La cabanya del gorg. Montserrat: L'Abadia, 1977.
La casa del mariner. Barcelona: La Galera, 1977.
Un conte del mar. Montserrat: L'Abadia, 1978.
Copare llop comare guineu. Barcelona: La Galera, 1979.
De la mar i del bosc. Barcelona: La Galera, 1980.
El fantasma del castell. Barcelona: La Galera, 1971.

El ferrer i el rei. Barcelona: La Galera, 1980.
En Francesc, en Daniel i els quissos. Montserrat: L'Abadia, 1979.
La lluna, la pruna. Barcelona: La Galera, 1987.
El pont del diable. Barcelona: Don Bosco, 1986.
El rei Midas. Barcelona: Don Bosco, 1979.

KATHLEEN MCNERNEY

C Sureda, Emília
(B. 1865, Mallorca; d. 1904, Mallorca.) Poet.

Emília Sureda wrote in nonstandard Catalan, using the Majorcan vernacular. She lived on Majorca all her life and wrote within the tradition of the Escola Mallorquina, which drew inspiration from the island's landscapes and its peasants, their customs, and their "gloses," a form of traditional, popular poetry. A slight influence of the Romantics can also be seen in Sureda's work. Her main themes, ephemeral happiness and the disappointment and sadness of unrequited love, are presented in the bucolic setting of Majorca. Her poetic images are natural and harmonic and show the author's great sensitivity to her surroundings. Her only volume of poems was published posthumously by Manuel Obrador. Unedited, these poems display freshness and candor and appeal to the reader's senses and feelings rather than to the intellect.

Sureda won prizes in the Barcelona Jocs Florals of 1899 for her poem "Vida pagesa" (Country life) and in the Majorca Jocs Florals of 1904 for "La lluna és morta" (The moon is dead), her most accomplished poem.

BOOKS
Poesies mallorquines. Palma: Obrador, 1905.

SECONDARY SOURCES
Benet i Torner, Josep Maria. "Poesies mallorquines de N'Emília Sureda." *Mitjorn* 1 (1906): 690.

ANNA MARIA SANCHEZ RUE

C Teixidó, Laura V.
(B. 1958, Barcelona– .) Writer of children's literature. No biographical information available.

BOOKS
Marraqueix enllà. Barcelona: La Galera, 1987.

KATHLEEN MCNERNEY

C   Tello Garcia, Alícia
(20th c.) Poet. No biographical information available.

BOOKS
Gemmes de la nostra terra. Barcelona: n.p., 1985.
Poemes papallones. Barcelona: n.p., 1980.
Triangle de llum i d'ombra. Barcelona: Columna, 1988.

KATHLEEN MCNERNEY

Tene; *see* **Mújica, Robustiana**

C   Tobella, Mercè
(B. 1896, Barcelona; d. 1972, Castelldefels, Barcelona.) Poet.

Mercè Tobella published two volumes of poetry: *Florida 1914–1919* (Flowering 1914–1919) and *Vida amorosa d'una dona* (A woman's amorous life). *Florida*, dedicated to her parents on their twenty-sixth wedding anniversary, includes poems set to music by the author and by her teachers. Several poems reflect Tobella's interest in music; others are dedicated to family and nature.

BOOKS
Florida: 1914–1919. Prol. E. Guanyabéns. Barcelona: n.p., 1919.
Vida amorosa d'una dona. N.p.: n.p., 1964.

WORKS IN BOOKS, PERIODICALS, NEWSPAPERS
"Adéu-Siau," "Hivernal," "A pomell gentil," "Quan contemples," "A la pluja," and
    "Cant de l'estimat." *La revista* 74 (Jan. 1919): 74.
"Florida." *La revista* 86 (Mar. 1919): 133.
"El primer pas." *Les cinc branques* 94.

NANCY L. BUNDY and KATHLEEN MCNERNEY

C   Toledo, Susanna
(B. 1944, Alcàsser, València– .) Poet.

Susanna Toledo's poems have appeared in various magazines, particularly *Llombriu* and *Reduccions. Les formes de la matèria* (The forms of matter), her first collection, contains thirteen intimate poems that skillfully describe landscapes and nature as analogies for feelings and emotions. These verses of apparent placidness and serenity nevertheless suggest a private drama and reveal the beauty of solitude.

BOOKS
Les formes de la matèria. Valencia: La Forest d'Arana, 1987.

WORKS IN BOOKS, PERIODICALS, NEWSPAPERS
"Cautelament les nafres." *Llombriu* 14 (Oct. 1985): 5.
"Gairebé un poema," "Espai tancat," "Fugacíssima visió," and "Floridura." *Reduccions* 31 (Oct. 1986): 18–21.

ISABEL ROBLES GOMEZ

Tolosa, Carlota.
Pseudonym for the collective of journalists headed by Ramon Barnils.

Carlota Tolosa wrote *La torna de la torna* (1985; Tit for tat), an investigative account of the execution of the revolutionary Salvador Puig Antich in 1974.

KATHLEEN MCNERNEY

C Torras i Calsina, Maria Assumpció
(B. 1915, Baix Llobregat, Barcelona– .) Poet and short story writer.

L'íntima estructura (The intimate structure) is a collection of Maria Torras's thoughts, presented as modern proverbs in long sentences or short paragraphs. They deal with time, nature, love, and morals. *Espigoleig* (Lavender), dedicated to Ausiàs March, consists mostly of religious poetry. Torras's imagery focuses on dualities—for example, opposing points of a quarter moon, a two-branched tree, echoes, and the dichotomy of good and evil. Her verse forms are varied and include a number of sonnets. She has also contributed to the literary journal *El pont.*

BOOKS
En la roda del temps i el desprendre-se'n. Barcelona: n.p., 1982.
Espigoleig. Illus. De Casas. Barcelona: Peñíscola, 1963.
L'íntima estructura. Prols. Manuel Bertran i Oriola and Pere Ribot. Barcelona: Peñíscola, 1970.

WORKS IN BOOKS, PERIODICALS, NEWSPAPERS
"La gran nevada." *El pont* 41 (1969): 31–32.
"Pinzellades": "Gravidesa: M'he anat afeixugant perquè el record," "Tresqueres amagades: Aquestes carreteres pacients," "Avui: Avui només tú," "Una mica: Una mica de brisa," and "El nom, La cosa: Joan, Joan." *El pont* 26–27 (1965): 42–45.
"Record humà d'Aurora Bertrana." *El pont* 72 (1976): 22–24.
"El Ton Canyaire." *El pont* 57 (1972): 13–20.

NANCY L. BUNDY and KATHLEEN MCNERNEY

C   Torrent Boschdemont de Figa, Francesca
(B. 1881, Agullana, Girona; d. 1958, Agullana, Girona.) Poet and novelist.

Francesca Torrent studied pedagogy but never practiced it. She published one novel, *Animes pariones* (Equal souls), and left one unpublished poetry collection, "D'aquell temps" (Of that time). The novel is a family history set in a "masia," a country house, in northern Catalonia. The prologue by Anton Busquets y Punset praises some of the Catalan feminists of his day—Josefa Massanés, Dolors Monserdà, and Víctor Català—and compares them favorably with George Sand, whom he calls a "monstruositat moral" (moral monstrosity).

BOOKS
Animes pariones. Prol. Anton Busquets y Punset. Girona: El Norte, 1910.

WORKS IN BOOKS, PERIODICALS, NEWSPAPERS
"Del juliol." *Les cinc branques* 64.

NANCY L. BUNDY and KATHLEEN MCNERNEY

C   Torrents, Mercè
(B. 1928, Folgueroles, Barcelona– .) Journalist and writer of children's literature. No biographical information available.

BOOKS
Aprendre a ensenyar. Vic: Eumo, 1988.
El gran joc de la Mercè. Barcelona: Lumen, 1984.
La Mercè boletaire. Barcelona: Lumen, 1984.
La Mercè de les oques. Barcelona: Lumen, 1981.
La Mercè fa dissabte. Barcelona: Lumen, 1984.
Els oficis de la Mercè. Barcelona: Lumen, 1981.
El primer llibre de la Mercè. Barcelona: Lumen, 1981.

TRANSLATIONS OF HER WORKS
Berta de las ocas [*La Mercè de les oques*]. Barcelona: Lumen, 1983.
Los oficios de Berta [*Els oficis de la Mercè*]. Barcelona: Lumen, 1983.
El primer libro de Berta [*El primer llibre de la Mercè*]. Barcelona: Lumen, 1983.

KATHLEEN MCNERNEY

C Torres, Narcisa
(18th c., València.) Also known as Rosa Trincares. Poet. No
biographical information available.

According to Carles Ros's *Práctica de ortografía para los idiomas castellano
y valenciano* (1732), there are only two extant sonnets by Narcisa Torres.

WORKS IN BOOKS, PERIODICALS, NEWSPAPERS
Sonnets. *Práctica de ortografía para los idiomas castellano y valenciano*. By Carles
  Ros. Valencia: Heredero de Vicente Cabrera, 1732.

SECONDARY SOURCES
Barberá, Faustino. *Conferencia sobre bio-bibliografía de Carles Ros*. Valencia: Fran-
  cisco Vives Mora, 1905.
Riquer et al. 4: 738.

KATHLEEN MCNERNEY

G Torres Fernández, Xohana
(B. 1931, Santiago de Compostela, Coruña– .) Poet, novelist, and
playwright.

Born in Santiago, Xohana Torres moved at an early age to Ferrol, Coruña,
where she lived until about the age of twenty and where her literary and
Galician education began under the direction of Ricardo Carballo Calero.
In 1957 she commenced her studies of philosophy and arts at the University
of Santiago, where she met other university students interested in Galician
literature. Together with these future Galician writers, she participated
in Justas Literarias and took a stand in favor of the Galician language,
which was to be her only literary language. In the same year, she published
her first book of poems, *Do sulco* (The furrow). She then gave up her
university studies and worked in radio for some years. She moved to Vigo,
married a merchant seaman, and directed a radio program in Galician. In
1956 she received the poetry prize from the Press Association of Vigo. She
published poems in several Galician journals; some poems appeared in the
original language in Mexican journals.

Torres has written two plays, *A outra banda do Iberr* (The other side of the Iberr) and *Un hotel de primeira sobre o río* (A first-class hotel on the river), which was awarded the Castelao prize for Galician theater. Her novel *Adiós María* (Good-bye Mary) won the Galicia prize from the Centro Gallego in Buenos Aires in 1970. She has also written two children's tales, *Polo mar van as sardiñas* (Sardine in the sea) and *Pericles e a balea* (Pericles and the whale), and translated many Catalan short stories and other well-known children's stories into Galician. In 1980 her second book of poems, *Estacións ao mar* (Seasons of the sea), appeared and received the Spanish Critics' prize in 1981. Another book of poems, *Tempo de ría* (Time of fiords), was published in 1992.

Although her two books of poems are twenty-three years apart, Torres continued to write poems, publishing them in journals and anthologies. Her constant work allows the reader to see her poetic evolution. The poems of her youth are characterized by freshness and naïveté and contain traditional Galician elements—Rosalía de Castro, the land, the rain, the river Miño, the Santiago cathedral—which are framed within a landscape that changes with the seasons. At the same time Torres sometimes shyly, sometimes daringly, denounces the poverty and oppression under which Galicia lives: "Negaron nosa voce nos camiños . . . / Pero eu non beberei na Xerra do silenzo" (They denied our voices along the way . . . / But I won't drink of the cup of silence) (*Do sulco* 15).

Two constant features in Torres's poetry are the repetition of themes and verse structures and her personal distancing from poetic fashions. Motifs in her first book reappear in the second, where feelings are expressed through the landscape and sea. The author associates the latter with memories of her childhood city, which she invokes in two poems entitled "Lorref" (Ferrol spelled backwards): "Lorref, ti compareces / desde un fondo dourado . . . / Lorref, quixera irme / Todo está feito xa, o peixe, as redes . . . / Lorref ultramarino, polo menos, / acompáñame ao sul, / anégame de acacias . . . / Todo o aprendin aquí, Lorref, na onda" (Lorref, you appear / from a golden depth . . . / Lorref, I want to go / All is done, the fish, the nets . . . / Lorref, across the sea, at least / come south with me / lure me with acacias . . . / All is learned here, Lorref, in the wave).

The most innovative element in *Estacións ao mar* lies in the poems memorializing her grandmother Lola, who symbolizes the Galician peasant: strong and resistant to suffering yet full of tenderness for her grandchildren, to whom she conveys an awareness of the oppression Galicians live under. Carmen Blanco, one of the people best acquainted with Xohana Torres's poetry, believes that "su poesía está cargada de originalidad e intimismo en cuanto al uso de un lenguaje nuevo en la expresión de los sentimientos, de las sensaciones, de los pensamientos más inefables" (her poems are full of originality and intimacy in that they use a new language in the expression of feelings, of sensations, of ineffable thoughts). The same critic highlights "la vivencia de la tierra, presente en cada uno de los poemas" (the experience of the earth, present in every poem) as the symbol of the woman-homeland, "fecundadora de vida" (fertilizer of life) (*Literatura* 133).

Her two plays deal with social issues, particularly problems in Galician society in the 1960s. *A outra banda do Iberr* is a symbolic story given existentialist treatment, while *Un hotel de primeira sobre o río* realistically deals with the expropriation of land for the construction of a hotel. In both plays, the female characters are the axle on which everything revolves and are portrayed as being superior to their male counterparts.

Her only published novel, *Adiós María*, combines social criticism and new narrative techniques. The story of a working-class family forced to emigrate, it is told by a fifteen-year-old girl who suffers the economic and social consequences of the move directly. The film-like narration reveals both the inner world of the teenager, with her personal problems, and the outside world, as seen through her experiences. A distinctive feature of the novel is the narrator's distortion of time.

BOOKS
Adiós María. Vigo: Castrelos, 1971; Galaxia, 1989.
Estacións ao mar. Vigo: Galaxia, 1980.
Un hotel de primeira sobre o río. Vigo: Galaxia, 1968.
A outra banda do Iberr. Vigo: Galaxia, 1965.
Pericles e a balea. Vigo: Galaxia, 1984.
Polo mar van as sardiñas. Vigo: Galaxia, 1968.
Do sulco. Vigo: Galaxia, 1957.
Tempo de ría. Coruña: Espiral Maior, 1992.

WORKS IN BOOKS, PERIODICALS, NEWSPAPERS
"Chámome imaxe á malva luz da hora." *Dorna* 10 (May 1986).
"A dura maxestá do silencio." *Vieiros* 2 (1962).
"O mar nin outra cousa quero." *Coordenadas* 1 (May 1981).
"Penelope," "As cousas non son o que parecen," and "Alas e ondas rendidas e nacendo." *Festa da palabra silenciada* 4 (1987).
"Ultimas illas." *Festa da palabra silenciada* 1 (1983).

TRANSLATIONS OF HER WORKS
Pericles y la ballena [*Pericles e a balea*]. Barcelona: Galaxia, 1984.

SECONDARY SOURCES
Blanco, Carmen. "A obra poética de Xohana Torres." *Literatura galega da muller*. Vigo: Xerais, 1991. 120–39.
———. "A poesia de Xohana Torres." *Festa da palabra silenciada* 4 (Feb. 1987): 11–16.
Cacheiro 83–91.

González Garcés, Miguel. *Poesia gallega de posguerra (1939–1975)*. Coruña: Castro, 1976.

Losada Castro, Basilio. *Poetas gallegos de posguerra*. Barcelona: Ocnos, 1971.

March, Kathleen N. "A patria de Xohana Torres." *Festa da palabra silenciada* 4 (Feb. 1987): 25–27.

Noia, Camino. *Palabra de muller*. Vigo: Xerais, 1992. 63–68, 104–05.

———. "Sobre a estructura de *Adiós, María*." *Festa da palabra silenciada* 4 (Feb. 1987): 7–10.

Rios Panisse, M. "A muller, eixe central no teatro de X. Torres." *Festa da palabra silenciada* 4 (Feb. 1987): 19–22.

Vázquez de Gey, Elisa. *Queimar as meigas*. Madrid: Torremozas, 1988. 106–14.

MARIA CAMINO NOIA CAMPOS

C Tous Forrellad, Pilar
(B. 1899, Sabadell, Barcelona; d. ?) Poet.

Showing a literary aptitude at a very young age, Pilar Tous began writing verses related to childhood games and situations; her earliest short poems were composed when she was nine. She contributed to several magazines, and much of her work appears in anthologies of Catalan poetry.

In 1921 she married the physician Ramon Cirera Voltà and moved to Barcelona, where her three children were born. An important part of her literary output developed during this stage of her life; in 1934, she published the collection *Vergeret d'Abril: Poesies* (Little April garden: Poems). The family took refuge in France in 1936 and returned to Spain in 1939. Tous took part in cultural and literary activities, attending dinners, plays, concerts, and poetry readings in private homes. The traditional nineteenth-century floral games were reinstated in 1943 with the celebration of the Fiesta de las Letras (Literary Festival) in Sabadell. Tous won the Flor Natural with *Figures i paisatge: Poesies* (Figures and landscape: Poems). Six bibliophile editions were handmade and illustrated by Ricard Marlet.

Tous, a collector of medals of the Virgin, won first prize in that category at the International Exposition of Stamps and Medals in Barcelona in 1958. Her third book, *Medalles* (Medals), was inspired by this activity; the compositions are mystical or devotional epigrams based on the various depictions of the Virgin that make up her collection. Since 1951, she has published only a biography of Agnès Armengol, another poet from Sabadell. The book won a prize in the Jocs Florals in 1952, which were held to commemorate the fiftieth anniversary of the death of Jacint Verdaguer.

Since her widowhood in 1958, Tous has written only occasional poetry, usually relating to family and home. She has an unpublished collection of poetry, "Glossa de messos" (Month by month), based on the months of the year, and a few other short poems, some of which are inspired by the past.

Pilar Tous is a visual poet, possibly influenced by her mother, a miniaturist painter. *Figures i paisatge: Poesies* best illustrates her talent for keen observation. She draws her subjects from human types and situations and from memories. Profound and sincere, often religious, autodidactic and spontaneous, Tous employs a rich vocabulary and easy metrics.

BOOKS
Agnès Armengol: Biografia. Sabadell: Joan Sallent, 1957.
Figures i paisatge: Poesies. Sabadell: Joan Sallent, 1943.
Medalles: Poesies. Barcelona: Torrell de Reus, 1951.
Vergeret d'Abril: Poesies. Sabadell: Biblioteca Sabadellenca, 1934.

MARIA INMACULADA PAUSAS

C Trepat, Marta
(20th c.) Short story writer. No biographical information available.

BOOKS
La fugida del pintor Notxa. Montserrat: L'Abadia, 1981.

KATHLEEN MCNERNEY

C Trian i Alfaro, Rosa
(B. 1924, Barcelona– .) Poet.

Rosa Trian i Alfaro studied humanities and belonged to the group Poesia Viva. The title of *Tardor* (Autumn) refers to her own rather late entry into poetry as well as to the season itself. The poems are simple, at times melancholic, and feature pleasant childhood memories. Her book *A l'entorn dels meus entorns* (The outlines of my environs) is more complex but still straightforward. The themes are patriotism, love, and solitude.

BOOKS
A l'entorn dels meus entorns. Barcelona: Poesia Viva, 1987.
Tardor. Barcelona: Claret, 1976.

KATHLEEN MCNERNEY

G Trillo, Xaquina
(B. 1916, Vilagarcía de Arousa, Pontevedra– .) Poet.

In delicate health as a child, Xaquina Trillo started secondary school late. There she studied French, music, and embroidery, as was customary for girls of upper-class families.

As a result of her father's pro-Galician activities during the Spanish Civil War, her family suffered extreme hardships. She made friends with several Galician writers, such as A. R. Castelao, Manuel Antonio, and Alvaro de las Casas. She also met Federico García Lorca while he was working in Vilagarcía with the Barraca Theater Group. She married very young and soon became a widowed mother with two daughters. She taught in primary schools throughout Galicia.

She has written many poems since her childhood, but she did not publish her first book, *Ceibos* (Free), until 1980. Several other collections quickly followed: *Xanela aberta* (Open window), *Tempos idos* (Times gone by), *Védelos aí van* (Look, there they go), and *Rosa dos ventos* (Compass rose).

Some of Trillo's poetry is very simple, both structurally and thematically. She often uses short verses with rhymes from popular songs to praise the objects of her everyday world: "meu dedaliño de prata" (my little silver thimble), "a ponte vella" (the old bridge), "a tuna" (the students' band), or "xanela" (a window). In longer poems, she celebrates some important figures of Galicia's history: "Castelao," "Bóveda," "D. Dinís," and "María Balteira."

Trillo's major theme is her country, which she portrays with objective, tangible realities. Many poems describe her favorite places: Santa María de Armenteira, San Andrés de Teixido, A Lanzada, Lugo, Fisterra. Of the Umia River, she writes: "Velaí vai ridente o río / soñando contos de amigo; vai de vagar amodiño / cara as terras de Albariño" (There goes the merry river / dreaming about friendly songs; it meanders along / facing the Albariño's lands) (*Xanela* 17). She uses different motifs to evoke the countryside: flowers, domestic animals, and birds that fly around vegetable gardens, granaries, or stone crosses. She also celebrates the bagpipe, the Galician cart, and the tradespeople typical of rural Galicia, such as shepherds, basketmakers, and lacemakers.

A few poems contain thoughts about old age or death and approach existentialist poetry.

BOOKS
Ceibos. Ponteareas, Pontevedra: n.p., 1980.
Rosa dos ventos. Vilagarcía, Pontevedra: n.p., 1989.
Tempos idos. Vilagarcía, Pontevedra: n.p., 1983.
Védelos aí van. Cambados, Pontevedra: n.p., 1985.
Xanela aberta. Ponteareas, Pontevedra: n.p., 1981.

WORKS IN BOOKS, PERIODICALS, NEWSPAPERS
"Bonaval." *El correo gallego* 28 June 1984.
"Ela." *Arosa poética* 4 (1988).
"Historia dunha frol do inverno." *La voz de Galicia* 3 Mar. 1988.
"In memoriam." *La voz de Galicia* 15 Jan. 1988.
"Na praza do Obradoiro." *El correo gallego* 24 July 1984.
"Pontevedra." *Diario de Pontevedra* 14 Sept. 1983.

"Quen será" and "O camiño." *Faro de Vigo* 15 Feb. 1983.
"Saudades." *La voz de Galicia* 11 Oct. 1988.

SECONDARY SOURCES
Noia Campos, Camino. *Palabra de muller.* Vigo: Xerais, 1992.
Vázquez de Gey, Elisa. *Queimar as meigas.* Madrid: Torremozas, 1988: 25–29.
Viana, Victor. "Una poetisa de Vilagarcía." *El correo gallego* 8 May 1983.
———. "Xaquina Trillo, poetisa." *La voz de Galicia* 30 Jan. 1988.

MARIA CAMINO NOIA CAMPOS

Trincares, Rosa; *see* **Torres, Narcisa**

Trolec, Isa; pseudonym for **Joan B. Mengual**

C Trulls, Maria
(B. 1861, Prats de Lluçanés, Barcelona; d. 1933, Igualada, Barcelona.) Poet.

Born to a very poor family, Maria Trulls suffered from poliomyelitis. Her illness and the family's social position prevented her from receiving any formal education. Her mother taught her to read, but she did not learn to write until she was thirteen. Her father espoused republican ideas and passed them on to her. As an adolescent she became interested in religion but later questioned the Catholic faith and adopted the belief in reincarnation. She began contributing poems to Barcelona's periodical *La conciencia libre*, where the work of other women writers, such as Rosario Acuña and Amalia Domingo Soler, also appeared. Her husband, Aurelio R. del Hoyo, published a posthumous collection of her Catalan and Castilian poetry, entitled *Obras poéticas de Maria Trulls. Escritora autodidacta igualadina. Desde mi encierro. Castellanas. Les meves filles catalanes* (Poetic work of Maria Trulls. Self-educated writer from Igualada. From my confinement. Castilians. My Catalan daughters).

Trulls devoted many poems to her companions in solitude—birds and neighbors—and to the description of the passing days as she saw them from her isolation. She had a sharp mind and commented ironically on the contradictions in human behavior. As a non-Catholic, she was critical of the common, unanalytical faith of those in her social milieu. She had rather conservative ideas about feminism but at the same time denounced traditional male authority that was exercised abusively. Condemning cruelty to animals, she took particular exception to bullfighting. She opposed traditional concepts of maternity and questioned whether mothers should love their children spontaneously. Some of her poems are political, calling for social justice and railing at dictatorial authorities.

Her Catalan poetry is similar to her Castilian work, although she uses only Catalan to describe Barcelona's popular celebrations, such as Christmas, Easter, and the Night of Saint John (June 21). She preferred assonant rhyme and long verses, usually octosyllables, and she used such strophes as "cantares," seguidillas, sonnets, and epigrams.

BOOKS
Obras poéticas de Maria Trulls. Escritora autodidacta igualadina. Desde mi encierro. Castellanas. Les meves filles catalanes. Igualada: Miranda, 1934.

CRISTINA ENRIQUEZ DE SALAMANCA

C Tubau i Jordi, Núria
(B. 1931, Barcelona– .) Playwright for children.

Núria Tubau has adapted a number of works for the stage and written a few poems as well. She taught drama to students for several years and traveled with theater groups to various places in Catalonia. Her *Princeses, deesses . . . foteses!* (Princesses, goddesses . . . trifles!) won the Ciutat de Barcelona prize in 1972. "Vi, fideus i fantasia" (Wine, noodles, and fantasy) was translated into Castilian and published as *Marco Polo el veneciano.* She now forms part of the group Teatre de la Parròquia de Sant Medir.

BOOKS
Any de neu any de Déu. Barcelona: La Galera, 1980.
Marco Polo el veneciano. Barcelona: Don Bosco, 1982.
El pais de les cent paraules. Barcelona: La Galera, 1982.
Princeses, deesses . . . foteses! Barcelona: Don Bosco, 1980.

KATHLEEN MCNERNEY

C Tudurí, Catalina
(Late 19th c., Menorca.) Poet.

Catalina Tudurí is described in Joaquim Maria Bover's *Biblioteca de escritores baleares* as a poet from Menorca who published in periodicals in Mahon and Majorca.

SECONDARY SOURCES
Bover de Rosselló, *Biblioteca de escritores baleares.*

CRISTINA ENRIQUEZ DE SALAMANCA

B Unzueta, Concepción
(B. 1900, Abando, Bizkaia– .) Poet.

Concepción Unzueta was a schoolteacher in several villages of Vizcaya, and her first articles in the magazine *Euskerea* concern teaching matters. Her first poems were published in Paris in the magazine *Eusko Deya*. Two of those poems, "Gomutakiak" (Memory) and "Gogo Ituna" (Sad soul), are included in *Mila euskal olerki eder* (One thousand beautiful Basque poems) under the pseudonym Utarsus. The first begins with the contemplation of nature and goes on to praise the love of people and country and, finally, the love of God; the second is an intimate poem that describes her loneliness.

WORKS IN BOOKS, PERIODICALS, NEWSPAPERS
"Gomutakiak" and "Gogo Ituna." Onaindia, *Mila euskal olerki eder* 701–02.
"Ikastoletan bi elez." *Euskerea* 22 (1930): 606.

MAITE GONZALEZ ESNAL

B Urretavizcaya, Arantxa
(B. 1947, Donostia– .) Novelist and poet.

Arantxa Urretavizcaya won the Escritores de Guipúzcoa prize for her poem "San Pedro bezperaren ondokoak." After working for the press for several years, she published an intimate work, *¿Zergatik Panpox?* (Why, Panpox?), about a disturbed woman who has been abandoned by her husband. Through a series of memories, the woman questions the past in a monologue about motherhood and her forsaken condition. In 1981 Urretavizcaya won the Ciudad Irún prize for her poem "Maitasunaren Magalean" (In love's bosom). *Aspaldian espero zaitudalako ez nago sekula bakarrik* (Since I've been waiting for you for a long time, I am never alone) contains three stories about three very different women. The first piece, "Carmen," is a first-person account of a friendship between two women; the second, in the third person, relates a nun's love for the figure of the infant Jesus in the crib; and the third is about an aged woman tracing the steps of a love lost in her youth. *Saturno* (Saturn), Urretavizcaya's first book with a male protagonist, was written in the minimalist style. Her work is characterized by an agile and simple narrative, since one of her concerns is to bring everyday language into literature.

BOOKS
Aspaldian espero zaitudalako ez nago sekula bakarrik. San Sebastián: Erein, 1983.
Maitasunaren Magalean. Gipuzkoa: Caja de Ahorros de Gipuzkoa, 1981.
Saturno. San Sebastián: Erein, 1987.
¿Zergatik Panpox? San Sebastián: Hordago, 1979.

TRANSLATIONS OF HER WORKS
Per què, menut? [¿*Zergatik Panpox?*]. Barcelona: Mall, 1982.
"Por que, Panpox" [¿*Zergatik Panpox?*]. *Antología de la narrativa vasca actual*. Ed.
Jesús M. Lasagabaster. Barcelona: Mall, 1986. 175–85.

MAITE GONZALEZ ESNAL

Valencià, Vicent; pseudonym for **Renada-Laura Portet**

C Valentí i Petit, Helena
(B. 1940, Barcelona; d. 1990, Barcelona.) Novelist and translator.

Born to a bourgeois family, Helena Valentí experienced the repression and restrictions of the Franco era in Spain during her formative years. After receiving a degree in Romance languages from the University of Barcelona, she escaped her culturally repressed milieu by going to England in 1962. She obtained a doctorate in literature from Cambridge University with a dissertation on Antonio Machado and served as a lecturer in Catalan at the universities of Durham and Cambridge. Her marriage to an Englishman ended in divorce, and, after several bohemian years in England, Valentí returned to Catalonia in 1974. She translated several works of the important contemporary feminist writers into Castilian and Catalan, including Virginia Woolf, Katherine Mansfield, and Doris Lessing.

Her first book, *L'amor adult* (Adult love), comprises eleven thematically related stories in which feminist motifs and autobiographical elements appear: the foreign woman in England, the enlightened and tolerant British husband, women's liberation posters, hostilities and lack of communication in marriage, unconventional sexuality and unwanted pregnancies, quantities of gin and the feminist movement per se, the "liberated" woman and the battle of the sexes. All the characters seem hypnotized by the mystique of their respective genders and thus are unable to mature.

La solitud d'Anna (The solitude of Anna) amplifies the existential concerns implicit in Valentí's earlier work, so that Anna almost incarnates female loneliness. Males, whose roles are secondary, are indifferent, insensitive, impotent, brutal, or infantile but always so self-centered that they are unaware of their lack of understanding and sensitivity. After three years of living with Lluís, Anna gets pregnant. She decides to have an abortion, and while she is in the clinic Lluís disappears. The general atmosphere of absurdity and despair holds little hope for marriage as an institution or for heterosexual love.

In *La dona errant* (The wandering woman) Valentí situates the action in the street, painting totally familiar figures from everyday reality whose private lives are nonetheless mysterious. The narrator likens the characters to pieces in a giant chess game that are moved by unknown forces. Valentí attempts to portray the younger generation's search for self and its place in the world, its struggle with inherited patterns of behavior, and the gap between these patterns and their own values.

Multiple tensions are at the core of Valentí's last novel, *D'esquena al mar* (With backs to the sea). Using a tightrope as metaphor, she explores layers of opposition between the two female protagonists, between the spheres of work and home, and between the worlds of technology and nature.

BOOKS
L'amor adult. Barcelona: Edicions 62, 1977.
D'esquena al mar. Introd. Maria Mercè Marçal. Barcelona: L'Eixample, 1991.
La dona errant. Barcelona: Laia, 1986.
La solitud d'Anna. Barcelona: Edicions 62, 1981.

TRANSLATIONS OF HER WORKS
"Children" and "The Other." Trans. Imma Minoves-Myers. *On Our Own Behalf.* Ed. Kathleen McNerney. Lincoln and London: U of Nebraska P, 1988. 75–104.

JANET PEREZ

C Valeri i Ferret, Maria Eulàlia
(B. 1936, Barcelona– .) Editor and writer of children's literature.

Maria Eulàlia Valeri has worked in the CEPEPC schools (Col.lectiu d'Escoles per l'Escola Pública Catalana) as a teacher and a librarian. She has collaborated on textbooks in Catalan and has also adapted fables and folktales, among which are some excellent versions of Hans Christian Andersen, the Grimm brothers, and Charles Perrault. A member of the Associació de Mestres Rosa Sensat, Valeri writes reviews of children's literature for *Faristol* and *Perspectiva escolar* (a publication of the Associació de Mestres) and coordinates, with Assumpció Lisson, the Seminar on Children's Bibliography. Valeri is the editor of two anthologies of children's songs, *Olles, olles de vi blanc* (Pots, pots of white wine) and *Cançons infantils populars catalanes* (Popular Catalan children's songs). She has published two collections of poetry, *Mites i somnis* (Myths and dreams) and *Les festes de tot l'any* (Holidays the year round). Her stories are written in simple language and speak to children of the things in their daily life: games, friends, birds. She has published articles on children's literature in various magazines and has participated in seminars, roundtable discussions, and conferences.

BOOKS
Aire, llum. Barcelona: Magrana, 1986.
Cada ocell al seu niu. Barcelona: La Galera, 1968.
Cançons infantils populars catalanes. Barcelona: Joventut, 1987.
La ciutat de les joguines. Barcelona: La Galera, 1966.
Danses i jocs populars catalans. Barcelona: Joventut, 1987.
Les festes de tot l'any. Barcelona: Magrana, 1987.
Hem perdut la pilota. Barcelona: La Galera, 1965.
Mites i somnis. Barcelona: Magrana, 1986.
Els ocells. Barcelona: Magrana, 1987.
Olles, olles de vi blanc. With Assumpció Lisson. Barcelona: La Galera, 1976.
Les quatre estacions. Barcelona: Magrana, 1986.
Si jo feia un parc. . . . Barcelona: Magrana, 1965.
Tots els nens del món serem amics. Barcelona: La Galera, 1971.
Veniu a buscar tresors. Barcelona: La Galera, 1966.

ANNA GASOL I TRULLOLS

C Valero i González d'Elies, Mercè
(B. 1916, Barcelona– .) Known as Martina d'Elies. Playwright, poet, and story writer for children.

Mercè Valero was born into a large family from Murcia and took care of younger brothers and sisters during her youth. She wrote feminist articles at the beginning of the Civil War. Her varied literary tastes include works by Rabindranath Tagore, Gustave Flaubert, Amado Nervo, Federico García Lorca, and Ramon Vinyes. Her interest in folklore and legends shows up in her work, which is mostly directed to children. *Teatre infantil* (Plays for children) contains four stories adapted for the stage, in which all the actors are children and the atmosphere is gentle and amiable, often with didactic overtones. Valero has also written stories for children and several occasional poems, which appear in other publications.

BOOKS
Teatre infantil. Barcelona: Dalmau, 1977.

WORKS IN BOOKS, PERIODICALS, NEWSPAPERS
"En Joanet, l'entremaliat," "Amor idealitzat," "Profecia," "Barcelona i Alguer," "La il.lusió del dia," and "Al dia de la mare." Colet i Giralt 89–95.

KATHLEEN MCNERNEY

G Valladares Núñez, Avelina
(B. 1825, Vilancosta, Pontevedra; d. 1902, Vilancosta, Pontevedra.) Poet.

According to the *Diccionario bio-bibliográfico de escritores gallegos*, Avelina Valladares Núñez was a humble person who underrated her own work, much of which has remained unpublished. The titles *Mi aldea* (My town), *A Ulla*, *A Galicia os que emigran* (Galician Emigration), *A probe orfiña* (Poor Orphan), and *Diálogo entre un peregrino que se dirige a Compostela y un labriego* (Dialogue between a pilgrim going to Compostela and a laborer) are cited in the article with no further information. She was awarded the Cruz de Beneficencia de Segunda Clase in 1894 by the Ministerio de Gobernación. She never married.

SECONDARY SOURCES
Couceiro Freijomil 3: 443–44.

KATHLEEN MCNERNEY

Valldaura, Agna de; *see* Santamaria i Ventura de Fàbrigues, Joaquima

C Vallhonrat i Costa, Josefina
(B. 1926, Vallès, Barcelona– .) Poet.

Josefina Vallhonrat i Costa's father was killed, along with other men in her village, in 1936. *Somnis i vivències* (Dreams and experiences) reflects the pain of that tragedy. Nature and faith are major themes.

BOOKS
Somnis i vivències. Prol. Paulina Pi de la Serra. Banyoles: n.p., 1983.

KATHLEEN MCNERNEY

C Vallors, Assumpta de
(Late 19th c.) Poet. No biographical information available.

WORKS IN BOOKS, PERIODICALS, NEWSPAPERS
"A . . . en sa Primera Comunió." *Lo teatre catòlic* 13 Aug. 1899: 1.
"A la montanya del Calvari. . . ." *Lo teatre catòlic* 3 Apr. 1900: 8.

CARMEN SIMON PALMER

C Vallribera i Fius, Maria Rosa
(B. 1941, Barcelona– .) Novelist and translator.

Maria Rosa Vallribera has done various work, from selling snacks to tourists on the Costa Brava and preparing insurance reports to translating for an Arab embassy, editing a dictionary, and teaching. *Un amor d'hivern, un amor d'estiu* (A winter love, a summer love) is a novel for and about adolescents. The protagonist, Bel, who works for her parents in a hostel in a beach town, suffers growing pains while she learns about love from two boys her own age.

BOOKS
Un amor d'hivern, un amor d'estiu. Barcelona: Empúries, 1988.

KATHLEEN MCNERNEY

C Valls i Riera, Consol
(Late 19th c.) Poet. No biographical information available.

WORKS IN BOOKS, PERIODICALS, NEWSPAPERS
"Miraula, ja s'axeca; dexa la mortalla. . . ." *Corona poética a Nostra Sra Santa Maria de Ripoll.* Vich, 1895. 152–54.

CARMEN SIMON PALMER

C Vallverdú i Torrents, Maria Dolors
(B. 1940, Reus, Tarragona– .) Poet.

Different parts of Maria Dolors Vallverdú's *Enllà de les paraules* (Beyond words) won prizes at the Jocs Florals in Perpignan from 1972 to 1975. The completed work is divided into three untitled sections: the first is composed entirely of sonnets; the second deals with interior spaces, dreams and secret thoughts, and the search for perfection; the third contains patriotic themes. Vallverdú refers to an earlier book, but it has not been found. She often writes of the passage of time and uses nature in her images.

BOOKS
Enllà de les paraules. Prol. Rafael Vilà i Barnils. Reus: Poblet, 1977.

KATHLEEN MCNERNEY

C Vayreda i Trullol, Maria dels Angels
(B. 1910, Lladó, Girona; d. 1977, Figueres, Girona.) Poet and novelist.

From the well-known Vayreda family of painters and intellectuals, Angels Vayreda wrote several books of poetry and two novels. She married Joan Xirau i Palau, and in 1939 they went into exile in Mexico. In 1950 they returned to Figueres. Her best-known work is the somewhat autobiographical novel *Encara no sé com sóc* (I still don't know how I am), in which she recounts the life of a young woman during the war who goes into exile in Mexico. She later returns to her homeland, leaving behind her young, newly married son. The point of view is the woman's, and she relates her feelings and reactions to her sometimes difficult, sometimes fortunate circumstances with candor and honesty. The most poignant moment in the novel is the death of her baby daughter in one of the bombardments; the most hopeful is the relationship between the protagonist and her little granddaughter, who comes from Mexico to spend summers with her in Catalonia. The novel won the Fastenrath prize for the best Catalan novel published between 1965 and 1971.

BOOKS
La boira als ulls. Figueres: Pradera, 1977.
Un color per cada amic. N.p.: n.p., 1977.
Els defraudats. Figueres: Empordà, 1980.
Encara no sé com sóc. Barcelona: Club, 1970. 4th ed. Barcelona: Club, 1985.
La meva masia. Figueres: Ingenieros, 1978.
El testament d'Amèlia. Barcelona: Altès, 1964.

KATHLEEN MCNERNEY

C Vayreda i Trullol, Montserrat
(B. 1924, Lladó, Girona– .) Art critic and poet.

A member of the well-known Vayreda family of Empordà, Montserrat Vayreda has written several collections of traditional poetry. *Ofrena de Nadal* (Christmas offering) contains religious poems pertaining to the Christmas season; it is illustrated with woodcuts of winter scenes, such as the feast of "Els reis" (The three kings). In the collection *Entre el temps i l'eternitat* (Between time and eternity), nature is a frequent topic, as are small, everyday things, such as the poet's study. Vayreda uses different verse forms, without straying from tradition. In his prologue to the volume, Miquel Saperas comments on the sentimentality and sincerity of the poems.

BOOKS
Afirmo l'esperança. Olot: Aubert, 1982.
Entre el temps i l'eternitat. Prol. Miquel Saperas. Barcelona: Altès, 1955.
Ofrena de Nadal. Barcelona: n.p., 1965.
Els pobles de l'Empordà. Figueres: Carles Vallès, 1984.

KATHLEEN MCNERNEY

G Vázquez Iglesias, Dora
(B. 1913, Ourense– .) Novelist, poet, playwright, and writer of children's literature.

A writer in both Galician and Castilian, Dora Vázquez studied to be a teacher and started publishing in *La noche*, a periodical in Santiago, in 1958. She later wrote for other publications, including *Vida gallega, El magisterio español, Escuela española, Vagalume,* and *Céltica.* She received many literary prizes, both for creative work and for critical studies, including recognition in 1963 for "Personalidade e obra de Pondal" (The personality and work of Pondal).

Vázquez has published a variety of works, including *Palma i corona* (Palm and crown), a reader for schools; *Tres cadros de teatro galego* (Three Galician plays); and *Campo e mar aberto* (Field and open sea), tales and Galician poems for children. She has written several other works for children, some in collaboration with her sister, Pura Vázquez, such as the plays *Monicreques* (Figures), *Fantasías infantiles* (Children's fantasies), in Castilian, and *Ronseles* (Wakes) and the book of poems *Oriolos neneiros* (Children's oriols). Dora Vázquez has published two works, *Bergantiñá* and "Augas soltas" (Loose waters), and, more recently, a collection of poetry, *Oración junto al camino* (Prayer along the road), and *Viaxe ó país dos contos e da poesía* (A trip to story and poetry land), a book of poems written with her sister.

There are two trends in her work, the didactic and the personal. As a writer for children, she emphasizes her didactic purpose, composing plays, stories, and poems that convey the Christian values that sustain her own faith in mankind. Children are shown examples of souls that strive to be virtuous through kindness and generosity. Dora Vázquez tends to give lessons in good behavior to both children and adults and often uses nature as a framework for her stories.

In her personal poetry, she sings of the Galician land, which, for her, is charged with goodness. With no particular attention to style, Vázquez expresses herself directly, often without any poetic rhythm in her verses. In *Irmá*, she cries over the absence of her beloved sister, who was living in Venezuela at the time, and evokes the loneliness she feels without her.

The novel *Bergantiñá* tells of a young peasant girl who manages to rise from extreme poverty and hardship to a comfortable position, not without great personal effort. The novel is told in the third person, with all the characters' psychological reactions expressed through extensive dialogue. The story is simple in structure and theme, giving prominence to the figure of the Galician woman, "o temple forte da verdadeira muller galega sofrinte e arranxadoira da vida" (the strong temple of the true Galician woman, suffering and arranging life). Through her own effort Bergantiñá raises her standard of living, brings up two children alone, and helps all those in need, while her husband, who has emigrated to Cuba, grows poorer and poorer. Emigration is regarded as a possible threat to the Galician sense of unity and as no solution to the province's rural poverty.

"Augas soltas" is narrated in the first person by the young son of wealthy farmers, who becomes a lawyer and undergoes a series of misfortunes that prevent him from living a happy family life. In the end, after a tragedy and the death of two characters who had hindered him, he finds the woman he loves. As in the previous novel, the Galician peasant woman is presented as the essence of virtue, in contrast to the inhuman and frivolous city woman.

BOOKS

Bergantiñá. Ourense: La Región, 1971. 2nd ed. 1972.
Caminos de plata y sol. Ourense: Comercial, 1966.
Campo e mar aberto. Lugo: Celta, 1975.
Fantasías infantiles. With Pura Vázquez. Ourense: La Región, 1980.
Irmá. Ourense: La Región, 1970.
Monicreques. With Pura Vázquez. Ourense: La Región, 1974.
Oración junto al camino. Barcelona: Rondas, 1985.
Oriolos neneiros. With Pura Vázquez. Ourense: La Región, 1975.
Palma y corona. Madrid: Escuela Española, 1964.
Un poema cada mes. Ourense: La Región, 1969.
Los poetas. With Pura Vázquez. Ourense: Ayuntamiento de Ourense, 1971.
Ronseles. With Pura Vázquez. Ourense: n.p., 1980.
Tres cadros de teatro galego. Ourense: La Región, 1973.
Viaxe ó país dos contos e da poesía. With Pura Vázquez. Ourense: Caixa Ourense, 1985.
A xeito de antoloxia: Poemas inéditos e publicados en galego e castelán. Ourense: n.p., 1992.

WORKS IN BOOKS, PERIODICALS, NEWSPAPERS

"Augas soltas." *Dúas novelas galegas*. Ourense: La Región, 1978.
"Bergantiñá." *Vieiros* 4 (1968).
"Estreliña do mar." *Contos infantis*. Vigo: Galaxia, 1970.
"Galicia na primaveira." *Coordenadas* 1 (1981).

SECONDARY SOURCES

Blanco, Carmen. *Literatura galega da muller.* Vigo: Xerais, 1991. 198–202.
March, Kathleen N. *Festa da palabra.*
————. "Vázquez Iglesias, Dora." In *Gran enciclopedia gallega,* vol. 29.
Noia Campos, Camino. *Palabra de muller.* Vigo: Xerais, 1992. 74–77.
Vázquez de Gey, Elisa. *Queimar as meigas.* Madrid: Torremozas, 1988. 19–24.

MARIA CAMINO NOIA CAMPOS

G Vázquez Iglesias, Pura [Purificación]

(B. 1918, Ourense– .) Poet, playwright, novelist, and writer of children's literature.

Pura Vázquez studied to be a teacher in Ourense and worked in a primary school from 1944 until her retirement in 1984, spending a number of years in Venezuela during this period. While she was in Caracas, she worked for the Ministry of Culture. From the age of fourteen, she published poems in journals and newspapers of her native town. She also wrote novels, short stories, and works for children's theater. She contributed to various publications, both Spanish and foreign: *La zarpa, La noche* (Santiago de Compostela), *La voz de Galicia, ABC* (Madrid), *Estafeta literaria, Poesía hispánica,* and others. She wrote extensively in both Castilian and Galician and received many literary prizes. Some of her books in Castilian include *Peregrino de amor* (Pilgrim of love), *Márgenes veladas* (Veiled margins), *En torno a la voz* (Around the voice), *Madrugada fronda* (Green dawn), *Tiempo mío* (Time of mine), *Desde la niebla* (Out of the mist), *Mañana de amor* (Morning of love), *Destinos* (Destinies), *Trece poemas a mi sombra* (Thirteen poems in my shadow), *Presencia de Venezuela* (Presence of Venezuela), *Los sueños desandados* (Retrospective dreams), and others in collaboration with her sister Dora Vázquez.

In Galician, she published *Intimas* (Intimacies), *Maturidade* (Maturity), *A saudade i outros poemas* (Health and other poems), and *O desacougo* (1971; Relief), all books of poetry. She also published books in Galician with her sister.

Pura Vázquez's work takes two directions: one comprises didactic poems, plays, and short stories for children, and the other features personal expressions of her deepest feelings for her country and the social problems affecting her people. Her work for children, possibly spurred by her pedagogical vocation, aims to teach children the need for good behavior, trust in others, and the capacity for forgiveness. She tenderly describes the beauty of life in nature, employing a childlike and religious tone. A figure in several of her poems is the child Jesus, who is addressed in Christmas carol rhythms.

Her intimate poetry is full of images of a benevolent nature in which birds, plants, and insects move in invigorating sunlight, in contrast to the opacity of rain and the darkness of night, when everything comes to a halt and remains silent. The rain, one of her recurrent themes, often accompanies memories of her beloved Galicia. Some poems express her identification with the sea and shipwrecks. In several poems Vázquez questions her own personal reality and the essence of time, and her poetry takes on nostalgic tones. Her reflections and doubts about her existence call to mind Christian existentialist philosophy, because Pura Vázquez is not an agnostic; she believes divinity is present in the whole cosmos. Serene and contemplative, her poetry imparts a religious feeling to the motifs from nature, which are presented as emanating from an elusive, incomprehensible deity.

Another theme in her poetry is the "saudade" (anxiety, sadness, and unrest caused by an absence), which she personally experienced during her stay in Caracas. This feeling, expressed in a veiled manner when she speaks of Galicia, its people, and its way of life, is especially evident in her books *Maturidade, A saudade i outros poemas*, and *O desacougo*. Her *saudade* is intimately identified with Galician rural life and memories of her childhood. In her last book of poems, *O desacougo*, the state of unrest in which the poet lives reaches a climax. She feels uprooted, with nowhere to settle, and begs the Virgin Mary to help her return to her land. Yet even in this state of existential anxiety, Pura Vázquez worries about Galicia's social problems and the poverty that forces many to emigrate.

Her only novel, *Segundo Pereira*, is a pessimistic story of family misunderstandings. The use of the second person as the narrator locks the protagonist into his reality and does not allow that of the other characters, who are full of defects, to be shown freely. An atmosphere of alienation, produced by a lack of communication within the family, pervades the story. The characters are simple, acting as mere representations of the virtues and defects that the author wishes to highlight.

In 1955, Pura Vázquez wrote that she never really knew how to say what poetry is, and that she hoped one day she would be lucky enough for someone to say she was able to write it (Fernández del Riego 304).

BOOKS

Antología 1944–1985. Ourense: n.p., 1990.
Antoloxia 1952–1971. Ourense: n.p., 1991.
Columpio de luna a sol. Madrid: Boris Bueva, 1950.
Contracto humano del recuerdo. Barcelona: Rondas, 1985.
O desacougo. Vigo: Galaxia, 1971.

Desde la niebla. Segovia: Amigos Antonio Machado, 1951.
Destinos. Caracas: Lírica Hispana, 1955.
En torno a la voz. Ourense: La Región, 1948.
Fantasías infantiles. With Dora Vázquez. Ourense: La Región, 1980.
Fuego de arcilla. Madrid: n.p., 1950.
Intimas. Lugo: Xistral, 1952.
Madrugada fronda. Madrid: Colección Palma, 1951.
Mañana de amor. Barcelona: Surco, 1956.
Márgenes veladas. Ourense: Diputación Provincial de Ourense, 1944.
Maturidade. Buenos Aires: Galicia, 1955.
Monicreques. With Dora Vázquez. Ourense: La Región, 1974.
Oriolos neneiros. With Dora Vázquez. Ourense: La Región, 1975.
Peregrino de amor. Larache, Mor.: n.p., n.d.
Los poetas. With Dora Vázquez. Ourense: Ayuntamiento de Ourense, 1971.
Presencia de Venezuela. Caracas: Lírica Hispana, 1966.
Rondas de norte a sur. Ourense: Caja de Ahorros Provincial de Ourense, 1968.
Ronseles. With Dora Vázquez. Ourense: n.p., 1980.
A saudade i outros poemas. Vigo: Galaxia, 1963.
Segundo Pereira. Ourense: La Región, 1978.
Los sueños desandados. Bilbao: n.p., 1974.
Tiempo mio. Segovia: Amigos Antonio Machado, 1951. 2nd ed. Madrid: Colección
    Palma, 1952.
Trece poemas a mi sombra. Caracas: Arte, 1959.
Verbas na edra do vento. Sada, Coruña: Castro, 1992.
Versos pra os nenos da aldea. Ourense: n.p., 1968.
Viaxe ó país dos contos e da poesía. With Dora Vázquez. Ourense: Caixa Ourense,
    1985.

SECONDARY SOURCES
Fernández del Riego, F. *Escolma da poesía galega.* Vol. 4. Vigo: Galaxia, 1955.
    304–09.

MARIA CAMINO NOIA CAMPOS

C   Ventós i Cullell, Palmira

(B. 1862, Barcelona; d. 1917, Barcelona.) Short story writer,
novelist, and playwright.

Writing as Felip Palma, Palmira Ventós i Cullell published her first short
story in the modernist literary magazine *Joventut* in 1901 and continued
publishing under her male pseudonym for the next ten years. Although
she lived in Barcelona, she set her works in rural Catalonia, portraying
the clash between individual desires, harsh natural forces, and traditional
social values. In the depiction of village life in both her stories and her
plays, she displays an especially effective use of colloquial dialogue. Her

early works are detailed representations of an implacable natural world, which, in later works, is tempered with lyrical descriptions and comical scenes reminiscent of the *costumista* (local color) tradition. Her longer works combine realistic portraits of the rural middle class with a sentimental treatment of human values. Conflict tends to resolve itself in either forced or voluntary solitude for the protagonist, whether male or female.

Ventós i Cullell wrote a collection of short stories, *Asprors de la vida* (Life's rough terrain), and a short novel, *La caiguda* (The fall). Her three-act play *Isolats* (Isolated people) was performed in the Teatre Català on 20 March 1909, and her one-act play *L'enrenou del poble* (Local uproar) followed in the same theater on 8 May 1909. She also published another three-act play, *La força del passat* (The power of the past). At her death she left an unpublished collection of rural sketches entitled "Visions d'un paratge" (1911; Local scenes) and several uncompleted manuscripts. Although she was not active in literary circles or the women's movement, she contributed occasionally to literary magazines and to *Feminal*, the early feminist cultural magazine. *Feminal* ran her picture (28 March 1909) when her first play was performed, and in 1916 published a tribute to her by Condesa de Castellà. The Arxiu Romea in Barcelona has several manuscripts of her plays.

BOOKS
Asprors de la vida. Biblioteca Popular de L'Avenç 28. Barcelona: L'Avenç, 1904.
La caiguda. Biblioteca Popular de L'Avenç 64. Barcelona: L'Avenç, 1907.
L'enrenou del poble: Quadro de costums en un acte. Barcelona: Bartomeu Baxarias, 1909.
La força del passat: Drama en tres actes. Barcelona: n.p., 1911.
Isolats: Drama de família en tres actes. Barcelona: L'Avenç, 1909.

WORKS IN BOOKS, PERIODICALS, NEWSPAPERS
"¡Abandonada!" and "¡Sola!" *Feminal* 8 (24 Nov. 1907).

SECONDARY SOURCES
Castellà, Condesa de. "Cronológica." *Feminal* 116 (26 Nov. 1916).
———. "Retrato." *La novela femenina* 1.14.

MARYELLEN BIEDER, with CRISTINA ENRIQUEZ DE SALAMANCA

C Verger i Ventallol, Maria
(B. 1905, Alcudia, Mallorca– .) Poet and journalist.

From a family of the Majorcan intellectual bourgeoisie, Maria Verger was educated on the island. In 1923 she obtained the post of librarian and file keeper at the Terrassa Town Hall. As a result of this professional activity, she wrote *Reseña histórica de los archivos y bibliotecas del Ayuntamiento de Tarrasa* (1924; Historical outline of the records and libraries of the Terrassa Town Hall), for which she received the Arxius prize in 1934 awarded by the Diputació de Barcelona.

Maria Verger's poetic works comprise three books: *Clarors matinals: Poesies* (Morning brightness: Poems), *Tendal d'estrellas: Poemes* (1924; Array of stars: Poems), and *L'estela d'or* (The golden wake). The first work has a prologue by Maria Antònia Salvà, who points out the descriptive quality of the poetry and its lack of variety. Verger's poetry is inspired by nature and frequently includes Majorcan motifs, such as the song to the almond flower, or Catalan motifs, such as those in praise of the country house. *Tendal d'estrellas* consists of twenty poems, some of which are dedicated to other writers, including Maria Antònia Salvà, Víctor Català, and the countess of Castellà. Verger's poetry grows more lyrical and personal as she develops, suggesting a confidential inspiration that does not exclude certain Becquerian reminiscences. *L'estela d'or*, her last collection of Catalan poetry, was published in 1934 as a homage from her Majorcan friends. Without losing her Romantic tone, the poet quivers joyfully in pantheistic song: "Soc un jardí en perfum ornat de sol . . ." (I'm a perfumed garden adorned with sun). The private dialogue with the Beloved acquires mystic tones: "Ales desplegades, com colom que es llença / ha vingut a mi / m'ha dit: Ara i sempre amb tu, lligada en fort nú a sobre el meu cor / com una llira blanca amb el calze d'or" (Unfolded wings, a dove taking off / came to me / and told me: Now and always with you, joined in a tight knot on my heart / like a white lily in a gold chalice) (21, 9).

In 1944, Manuel Ballester y Conde published a selection of critical articles on Maria Verger, *Maria Verger: Artículos y juicios críticos sobre su obra literaria* (Maria Verger: Articles and critical studies on her literary work). This book shows how Maria Verger came to be regarded as the representative of "la poesía femenina" (female poetry) (8). Almost all the critics praise this otherwise undefined characteristic of her poems: "alma exquisitamente femenina" (an exquisitely feminine soul) (8); "feminidad en las formas y en los procedimientos" (femininity in form and procedure) (11); "versos . . . femeninos, de esta feminidad moderna que exterioriza las sensaciones con gusto selecto de compañera de ensueño, no de esta feminidad *caballina* de ciertas clases de señoritas a la *dernier cri*" (feminine . . . verses, belonging to this modern femininity which conveys sensations with the careful taste of a dreamlike partner, not the *overpowering* femininity of certain types of young ladies who think they are the *dernier cri*) (16).

Verger's first book in Castilian was *Rutas maravillosas* (Marvelous routes), published with the subtitle *Poemas. (De mi viaje a América del Sur)* (Poems. [Of my journey to South America]). After evoking the sea voyage in the first two verses, she continues with poems about geographical places, dividing the book into the sections "Por tierras de Brasil" and "Por tierras argentinas." Visual and historical elements are important in the lyrical treatment, including numerous examples of outstanding regional scenery, topography, and etymology. Somewhat hackneyed and artificial, the work presents the American continent as a paradise for those fleeing an old, ruined Europe. All the poems are epic-heroic songs praising the New World, where the pure native and the awe-inspiring landscape exist as relics of an ideal place.

Her second collection of poems in Castilian, more lyrical and personal, is *Por la senda de las rosas* (Along the rose path). The author returns to clichés of love and nature to emphasize the beneficial power of life, identifying herself with a highly representative element of her hieratic and peaceful vision of the cosmos: the rose. Disturbing elements are immediately minimized or explained away: in a quartet, the author challenges Schopenhauer's pessimism with Leibniz's optimism. Night, in her previous book and in this one, is bright and pleasant, the countryside is welcoming and infinite, and a nightmare is transformed into the true happiness of the present. Thorns are unimportant compared to the scent and beauty of the rose. Verger evokes perfect love in nature's setting: the author-rose loves and is loved. The poet, conscious of her task as creator of beauty, perhaps goes too far in trying to show that everything is marvelous.

Several bibliographical sources mention that Verger was editor of *Gema*, a South American women's magazine founded in Barcelona in 1929. This magazine has proved unlocatable, and it is not included in the main catalogs of Catalan women's magazines of the period. Verger edited the women's section "La mujer, la moda y la casa" (Women, fashion, and the home) in the journal *Mundo católico*. The section's name indicates the type of issues covered: biographies of famous women; an article on woman's role as wife and mother in contemporary society. Columns were written and accompanied by poems by Maria Verger and famous women writers such as Rosalía de Castro or Gabriela Mistral. The finishing touch was usually a set of cooking, fashion, or decorating tips.

BOOKS

Clarors matinals: Poesies. Prol. Maria Antònia Salvà. Barcelona: Casa Provincial Caritat, 1924.

L'estela d'or. Palma: Alcover, 1934.

Por la senda de las rosas: Poema en vint i vuit cantos. Madrid: Artes Gráficas Iberoamericanas, 1970.

Reseña histórica de los archivos y bibliotecas del Ayuntamiento de Tarrasa. Barcelona: T. G. Hostench, 1942.

Rutas maravillosas: Poemas. (De mi viaje a América del Sur). Palma: Gràficas Miramar, 1966.

Tendal d'estrellas. Prol. Josep Maria Sagarra. Barcelona: n.p., 1931.

WORKS IN BOOKS, PERIODICALS, NEWSPAPERS

"Bajo el azul de un rincón de paz." *Mundo católico* 8 (15 Sept. 1935): 538.
"El centenario de Alfredo Nobel. La mujer es pacifista por naturaleza y por piedad." *Mundo católico* 6 (15 Aug. 1935): 398.
"Con los ojos claros y el alma limpia." *Mundo católico* 10 (15 Oct. 1935): 102.
"Una costumbre que ofende a la mujer." *Mundo católico* 3 (1 July 1935): 186.
"En el campo de la delincuencia. ¿Un aviso al futuro?" *Mundo católico* 11 (Nov. 1935): 172.
"Un grito de piedad de la mujer católica." *Mundo católico* 5 (1 Aug. 1935): 320.
"Haciendo un poco de historia femenina." *Mundo católico* 7 (1 Sept. 1935): 482.
"La influencia de la mujer en la sociedad y en el hogar." *Mundo católico* 1 (1 June 1935): 40.
"El jardín de la infancia en peligro. Lo que decían las madres modernas." *Mundo católico* 9 (1 Oct. 1935): 34.
"La mujer en la vida moderna." *Mundo católico* 2 (15 June 1935): 96.
"La mujer y la poesía." *Mundo católico* 4 (15 July 1935): 260.

SECONDARY SOURCES

Ballester y Conde, Manuel, ed. *Maria Verger. Artículos y juicios críticos sobre su obra literaria.* Barcelona: NAGSA, 1944.

INES CALVO
with the section on Catalan works by CRISTINA ENRIQUEZ DE SALAMANCA

C Vergés Bartés, Eulàlia

(20th c.) Poet. No biographical information available.

BOOKS

Dolça tardor. Barcelona: n.p., 1983.

KATHLEEN MCNERNEY

C Vernet i Real, Maria Teresa

(B. 1907, Barcelona; d. 1974, Barcelona.) Also known as Maria Teresa Barnet. Novelist, poet, and translator.

Maria Teresa Vernet wrote in both Catalan and Castilian. Her first novel, *Maria Dolors,* was published when she was nineteen years old. She is best known for this novel, although she later won the Creixelles prize for *Les algues roges* (Red seaweed). Despite her popularity before the Spanish Civil War, very little is known about her apart from her work and the occasional commentaries by fellow authors. She wrote steadily from 1926 until 1937, producing eleven works, including one collection of poems. Her verses are lyrical and optimistic, full of love and a tenderness she sees reflected in

394

nature. Her novels deal with female psychology and the conflicts arising from the family, love, sexuality, intellectual pursuits, and marriage.

Although Vernet grew up in Barcelona, she spent time in Paris, presumably for research purposes. Her father was a schoolteacher and her mother was very religious. Supported by her parents, she was able to devote all her time to studying, writing, and translating. She translated works of Louis Baudouin, Aldous Huxley, and James Joyce into either Catalan or Castilian. She also had a keen interest in music and played the piano. In 1930 she was elected president of the cultural section of the Club Femení i d'Esports (Women's Club for Sports) and collaborated with Anna Murià on the monthly bulletins. While it is not clear why Vernet discontinued her own writing, some believe it was because of the Spanish Civil War. She apparently never married.

Les algues roges, the most complete and complex of her novels, was republished in 1986 with an introduction by Maria Campillo. The central character, Isabel, is also the protagonist of the short story "El perill" (Danger) and is mentioned in the novel *Final i preludi* (Final and prelude). *Les algues roges* traces three years in the lives of Isabel and Marina, who become acquainted at a tennis club in Barcelona and meet again in Paris after Marina attempts suicide. Isabel takes her in, and thus begins an intense period of introspection and painful growth for each woman. Both learn to accept their independence and sexuality in a society that is slow to change. The traditional attitude that a woman must remain a virgin until marriage and thereafter stay in the home is challenged by emerging modern values that encourage women to assert their individuality. Although the novel ends in Barcelona at the original tennis club, the protagonists have developed a great deal. This novel treats subjects that are just as relevant now as when the work was first published.

BOOKS
Les algues roges. Badalona: Proa, 1934. Introd. Maria Campillo. Barcelona: LaSal, 1986.
Amor silenciosa. Barcelona: Central Catalana de Publicaciones, 1927.
El camí reprès. Badalona: Proa, 1930.
Elisenda. Barcelona: Quaderns Literaris 24, 1935.
Estampes de París. Barcelona: Quaderns Literaris 24, 1937.
Eulàlia. Badalona: Proa, 1928.
Final i preludi. Badalona: Proa, 1933.
Maria Dolors. Barcelona: L'Avenç, 1926.
El perill. Badalona: Proa, 1930.
Poemes. Barcelona: La Revista, 1929.
Presó oberta. Badalona: Proa, 1931.

WORKS IN BOOKS, PERIODICALS, NEWSPAPERS
"Desil.lusió." *La revista* (Jan.–June 1929): 5–16.
"Nit d'argent." *El pont* 1–5 (1956): 93–114.

"Notes al vol." *La revista* 7 (Mar. 1926): 44–46.
"Prop la llar encesa," "L'amor vindras amb mi . . . ," and "Dialeg." *La revista* (1927): 17–21.

SECONDARY SOURCES
"Maria Teresa Vernet, In Memoriam." *El pont* 67 (1974): 26–27.

TARA MCNALLY

C Via, Ramona
(B. 1923, Vilafranca del Penedès, Barcelona– .) Prose writer.

In his prologue to Ramona Via's *Nit de reis* (The epiphany), the publisher Joan Sales calls it a novel but explains that there is minimal fabrication. In fact, it is the diary of a fourteen-year-old girl who became a nurse during the Civil War. Written between September 1938 and June 1939 at the behest of a teacher who wanted Via to practice writing in Catalan, *Nit de reis* recounts the horrors of that period as seen through the eyes of a youngster who grew up quickly. Via had kept the yellowing papers for years when Sales discovered them and persuaded her to publish them. The author has also written a nonfiction book about the nursing profession, *Com neixen els catalans* (How Catalans are born).

BOOKS
Com neixen els catalans. Barcelona: Club, 1972.
Nit de reis. Prol. Joan Sales. Barcelona: Club, 1966.

WORKS IN BOOKS, PERIODICALS, NEWSPAPERS
"La Mútua." *El pont* 51 (1971): 32–38.
"La nostra època: I. Parla un jove." *El pont* 55 (1972): 12–17.
"La nostra època: II. Parla la mare del jove." *El pont* 56 (1972): 15–18.
"Poemes": "Goig de Viure: Per cantar el meu esperit lliure . . . ," "Maternal: El dia que vas fer els primers passos." *El pont* 37 (1969): 39–40.

KATHLEEN MCNERNEY

C Vicens i Picornell, Antònia
(B. 1942, Santanyí, Mallorca– .) Novelist.

In 1966 Antònia Vicens won the Vida Nova prize for the three stories published in *Banc de fusta* (Wooden bench), which comment on the changes in traditional life brought to Majorca by tourism. The same theme characterizes her first novel, *Trenta nou graus a l'ombra* (Thirty-nine degrees in the shade), winner of the Sant Jordi prize. Her second novel, *Material de fulletó* (Serial story), depicts women who are confused by a contradictory, violent, and hostile world.

As an author who has published with regularity, Vicens has progressively gained stylistic distinction, marked by a poetization of sordid or mediocre atmospheres and a subtlety of observation that burst into maturity in the novel *La festa de tots els morts* (All Souls' Day). The collection of stories *Primera communió* (First communion) and the novel *La santa* (The saint) ground her work in a more complex and magical dimension. *Quilòmetres de tul per a un petit cadàver* (Kilometers of tulle for a small cadaver), winner of the Ciutat de Palma prize, attempts a new narrative technique. In *Gelat de maduixa* (Strawberry ice cream), winner of the Ciutat de València for fiction, her usual themes are given a more diversified resolution and structure. Finally, *Terra seca* (Dry land), a finalist for the Ramon Llull prize, marks a step forward in this search for structure and widens the familiar referential world to include the new settings and personalities that reflect the transformations in Majorcan society. Antònia Vicens continues elaborating a personal and intricate chronicle with surprising critical vision.

BOOKS
Banc de fusta. Palma: Moll, 1968.
La festa de tots els morts. Barcelona: Nova Terra, 1974.
Gelat de maduixa. Valencia: Fernando Torres, 1984.
Material de fulletó. Palma: Moll, 1971.
Primera communió. Palma: Moll, 1980.
Quilòmetres de tul per a un petit cadàver. Barcelona: Laia, 1982.
La santa. Barcelona: Laia, 1980.
Terra seca. Barcelona: Planeta, 1987.
Trenta nou graus a l'ombra. Barcelona: Selecta, 1968.

TRANSLATIONS OF HER WORKS
Tierra seca [Terra seca]. Barcelona: Planeta, 1988.

GUILLEM-JORDI GRAELLS

C Vilaplana i Buixons, Núria
(B. 1931, Barcelona– .) Known as Núria Pompeia. Cartoonist, essayist, editor, humorist, short story writer, and novelist.

Born 2 May 1931 to an upper-middle-class family, Núria Pompeia experienced the Spanish Civil War as a child and later studied art in Barcelona's Escuela Massana, specializing in retables and altar pieces. In 1952, she married Salvador Pániker, a writer; the couple had five children. She worked first in publishing houses and then as editor in chief of the reviews

Por favor and *Saber.* Pompeia first became known for the ideological charge of her cartoons in prominent periodicals, including *Triunfo, Cuadernos para el diálogo, Sábado gráfico, Vindicación feminista, Dunia,* and *El món.* Her feminist drawings appeared in several foreign reviews: *Linus, Charlie Hebdo,* and *Brigitte.* She also contributed cultural articles to *La vanguardia* and directed the program *Quart Creixent* for Spanish television.

Her first book-length publication, *Maternasis,* combines cartoons and captions in a penetrating critique of the way the bourgeoisie reproduces itself from generation to generation; at the same time it presents a graphic history of the second sex, structured around pregnancy, motherhood, and the resulting changes in a woman's body and lifestyle. The first and only woman on the peninsula to become nationally known as a cartoonist, Pompeia owes her success above all to her creation of the brat Palmira, who is similar to Lucy in the "Peanuts" comic strip. An anthology of this strip, *La educació de Palmira* (The education of Palmira), displays a strong feminist bent, examining the ways traditional education deforms the female child's natural impulses and intellect and precipitates self-destructive tendencies. *Mujercitas* (Little women), a collection of Pompeia's earlier cartoons, is a satirical indictment of the social conditions that change the active, creative, and adventurous girl child into an inhibited, submissive conformist and a boring woman. Condemning puritanical morality, patriarchal justifications of male domination, and the emphasis on physical beauty, Pompeia undermines sexist role-typing and the "happily ever after" myth. *Cambios y recambios* (Changes and spares) is a more radically sarcastic exploration of the processes that produce contemporary female stereotypes.

Her first prose work is *Cinc cèntims* (Five pennies), a collection of twelve short stories with the same narrator. Written in vivid, precise, and colloquial Catalan, the stories exhibit a feminist viewpoint and Pompeia's characteristic, incisive humor. Common to all is her criticism of upperclass life and values, which are variously illustrated by a drunken dinner party, weekend rituals, pseudointellectual pursuits, family outings of the well-to-do, pseudoartistic collectors, and sexist education. The lack of any real or meaningful change beneath surface modernizations is underscored by such themes as politics within marriage, matrimony as paternalistic despotism, and women's frustrated hopes of liberation under first one political regime, then another.

Most recently, Pompeia published *Inventari de l'últim dia* (Inventory of the last day), a novel with many autobiographical elements. The work may be assigned by virtue of its title alone to the growing body of apocalyptic literature that has appeared in the second half of the twentieth century. A woman narrator returns to her family's abandoned ancestral home, which is about to be auctioned by the city government in an action similar to bankruptcy proceedings. Within the novel's single day, the woman re-calls her life in the house that is soon to be destroyed, examining, some-times humorously, her infancy, childhood, adolescence, and education and depicting the doubts and vicissitudes of her generation. No matter how personally the house is linked to her individual identity, it is symbolic of a class and a period. The novel simultaneously looks at what constitutes a worthy member of the bourgeoisie and reflects on the social and economic philosophy of Marxism and on the mechanics of power.

BOOKS
Cambios y recambios. Barcelona: Anagrama, 1983.
Cinc cèntims. Barcelona: Edicions 62, 1981.
La educació de Palmira. Barcelona: Andorra, 1972.
Inventari de l'últim dia. Barcelona: Edicions 62, 1986.
Maternasis. Paris: Pierre Tisné, 1966. Barcelona: Kairós, 1967.
Mujercitas. Barcelona: Kairós, 1975.
Pels segles dels segles. Barcelona: Edicions 62, 1971.
Y fueron felices comiendo perdices. . . . Barcelona: Kairós, 1970.

JANET PEREZ

C Vila Reventós, Mercè
(B. 1902– .) Poet. No biographical information available.

In 1917, Barcelona's magazine *Feminal* invited a group of young women to join the association Nostra Parla (Our Language), which was founded to promote the spiritual unification of the Catalan areas: Majorca, Roussil-lon, and Catalonia. In its 5 August issue, *Feminal* announced the names of the participants—among them, Mercè Vila, Clementina Arderiu, Carme Karr, Coloma Rosselló, Maria Antònia Salvà, and Dolors Monserdà.

Vila's first book, *Les hores* (The hours), anticipates the style and struc-ture of her later works, *Flor de l'amor. Magnolia perfumada* (Flower of love. Perfumed magnolia) and *Fugaç resplandor* (Brief brightness). A major source of her poetry is the contemplation of nature. She identifies trees with human beings: "són humans . . . aquells arbres fermats a la terra amb els braços alçats cap al cel" (They are human . . . those trees stuck to the ground with their arms raised toward the sky) (*Les hores* 31). Religious poems are infrequent in her first two books, and she prefers to avoid a search for consolation, presenting herself before the divinity as a defective human being: "amb l'engúnia del viure d'ahir i la taca damunt del meu rostre" (with the anxiety of my past behavior and a stigma in my face) ("L'ànima a Jesús," *Les hores* 58).

Love poems are rare. Like the earlier Catalan women poets Emilia

399

Quijano (who wrote only in Castilian), Victòria Penya, and Palmíra Jaquetti, Vila uses the image of the house; but for her, instead of being an intimate or mystical place, the house symbolizes an impossible love.

A more personal accent and a general feeling of a finished life characterize Vila's last book, *Fugaç resplandor*. Knowing that death is near, she imagines herself as a brief brightness: "pero aviat cobrirà la boirina amb el seu vel la fugaç resplandor" (and soon, the fog, with its veil, will cover the brief brightness) (9). Religious and mystical poems abound: "Papallona gentil . . . / jo, del calze fet d'or, beuré nectar d'amor" (Kind butterfly, I will drink nectar of love from the gold chalice) (18). The poem "In articulo mortis" is a prayer for clemency in a poetical style established by Josefa Massanés and Dolors Monserdà. Vila's feeling of coming death is apparent even in the way she approaches nature. She focuses on the chrysanthemum, the flower of death: "Ara només esguardo els crisantems blancs i daurats, i de color morada . . ." (Now I only watch the white and golden, and purple chrysanthemums . . .) (63).

BOOKS

Flor de l'amor. Magnolia perfumada. Poesies de Mercè Vila Reventós. Barcelona: Altès, 1921.
Fugaç resplandor: Poemes. Barcelona: Torrell de Reus, 1955.
Les hores. Barcelona: La Revista, 1918.

WORKS IN BOOKS, PERIODICALS, NEWSPAPERS

"Facis la vostra voluntat," "Mon amor," "Abril," "El meu prec," and "A ma germana Agnès." *La revista* 14 (Apr. 1916): 8–9.
"La finestra," "Allà en el llarg del caminal," and "Amb mon esguard." *La revista* 43 (1 July 1917): 250.
"L'herba ha crescut," "Cel de Febrer," and "He vist." *La revista* 103–06 (Jan.–Feb. 1920): 12–13.
"Otomnal." *La revista* 30 (1 Jan. 1917): 42.
"Proposit." *La revista* 7 (Jan. 1916): 9.

SECONDARY SOURCES

Guasch, Anton. "*Flor de l'amor. Magnolia perfumada*. Poesies de Mercè Vila i Reventós." *La revista* 136 (1921): 156.
J. Ll. "*Les hores*, de Mercè Vila." *La revista* 89 (1 June 1919): 89.

CRISTINA ENRIQUEZ DE SALAMANCA

C Vilar i Roca, Anna

(B. 1956, Barcelona– .) Writer of children's books.

Anna Vilar teaches in a public school in Barcelona and gives Catalan classes for the Generalitat. She has also collaborated on textbooks for schoolchildren.

Vet aquí que set reis una vegada (And so once there were seven kings) is a collection of stories about kings who have special characteristics. In *El saber perdut* (The lost wisdom) Vilar explores the use and abuse of science and technology in a medieval setting. *I un dia serà demà* (One day will be tomorrow) features a futuristic setting, where consumerism is rampant and obligatory and the female adolescent protagonist does not adapt to the situation.

BOOKS
I un dia serà demà. Barcelona: La Galera, 1985.
El saber perdut. Barcelona: La Galera, 1983.
Vet aquí que set reis una vegada. Barcelona: La Galera, 1982.

KATHLEEN MCNERNEY

C Villalonga, Maria Angels
(20th c.) Poet. No biographical information available.

BOOKS
Els arbres. Girona: Diputació, 1986.

KATHLEEN MCNERNEY

C Villalonga i Zaydin, Anna
(20th c.) Playwright. No biographical information available.

A writer from Majorca, Anna Villalonga always signed her work Aina Villalonga de Morey. The Catina-Estelrich theater company debuted her plays: "Celestina" (1934), about faith healing; "El Rebeinet" (1934), one of the first texts to consider the play of elements between Majorcan traditionalism and the impact of foreign customs; and "Cigala juliolera" (1937; July cicada), the last authorized work to be performed in Catalan before the Balearic islands fell under the Franco regime. In this same period she also wrote "Dos diàlegs" (1935; Two dialogues) and "Esperant el metge" (1936; Waiting for the doctor). In the postwar period the Agrupación de Teatro Regional performed "La corona comtal" (1947; The crown of the count), which was based on a historical theme. She was an assiduous contributor to the newspaper *La almudaina* and wrote "Coverbos de dones" (Women's projects) and "Maçoneries" (Masonries).

GUILLEM-JORDI GRAELLS

C Villamartín y Thomas, Isabel de
(B.?, Galicia?; d. 1877, La Garriga, Barcelona.) Poet.

A bilingual poet in Castilian and Catalan, Isabel de Villamartín was an early contributor to the Catalan cultural movement known as the *Renaixença*, which inspired the religious-patriotic feelings in her Catalan poetry. She won the first Jocs Florals in Barcelona in 1859 for her evocation of Clemencia Isaura, a medieval noble lady around whom a courtly love tradition had developed. Villamartín's unexpected success in this contest gave rise to the rumor that the poem's real author was her friend Víctor Balaguer. This assumption indicates the difficulties nineteenth-century women faced as producers of culture.

In 1861, Villamartín again participated in the Jocs Florals and won a secondary prize for "La creu de Cristo" (Christ's cross). Her poems were included in the first two nineteenth-century collections of Catalan poetry, *Los trovadors nous* and *Los trovadors moderns*. In 1865 the Catalan magazine *Calendari català*, edited by Pelai Briz, published her poem "La font de la riquesa" (The fount of wealth), and on 12 January 1862, the Ateneo de Mataró honored Villamartín with a reading of her poem "La desposada de Deu" (God's fiancée).

Villamartín's Castilian work includes *Pembé-Haré. Oriental*, a poem of oriental inspiration, and *Horas crepusculares* (Twilight hours), a collection of "cantares" and seguidillas. She also contributed to the magazine *La floresta* and published many poems in the *Correo de la moda*. The library in the Museo Víctor Balaguer in Vilanova i la Geltrú, Barcelona, contains her correspondence with Víctor Balaguer and some unpublished poems.

BOOKS
La desposada de Deu: Poesia. Mataró: Joseph Abadal, 1862.
Horas crepusculares: Colección de cantares y seguidillas por Doña Isabel de Villamartín. Madrid: C. González, 1865.
Pembé-Haré. Oriental. Gerona: Paciano Torres, 1856.
Poesía leída por Doña Isabel de Villamartín en el Ateneo Mataronés. Barcelona: Narciso Ramírez, 1872.

WORKS IN BOOKS, PERIODICALS, NEWSPAPERS
"A Catalunya." *Los trovadors moderns* 63–65.
"¡Adiós!" *El correo de la moda* 25 (1875): 235.
"A Doña Angela Grassi." *La floresta* (1857): 50–51.
"A Granada." *El correo de la moda* 23 (1873): 254.
"A la agonía de Nuestro Señor Jesucristo." *El correo de la moda* 23 (1873): 109–10.
"A la luna." *El correo de la moda* 23 (1873): 155.
"A la simpática niña Rosa Boullenger." *El correo de la moda* 23 (1873): 46.

"Als estels" and "La veu profética." *Los trovadors nous* 85, 204–06.
"A mi distinguido amigo Marcelo Planas y Casals." *El correo de la moda* 23 (1873): 10.
"Cantares." *El correo de la moda* 22 (1872): 35.
"Desencanto." *El correo de la moda* 22 (1872): 174.
"La esperansa es amor." *Calendari català* (1865): 85–87.
"Esperanza e ilusión." *La floresta* (1857): 74–75.
"La flor del jazmín." *La floresta* (1857): 42–43.
"La font de la riquesa." *Calendari català* (1866): 96–99.
"La mancha de la mora." *El correo de la moda* 25 (1875): 134.
"Más allá." *El correo de la moda* 24 (1874): 91.
"Mentiras dulces." *El correo de la moda* 22 (1872): 211.
"La niña afligida." *La floresta* (1857): 18–19.
"No te olvido." *El correo de la moda* 22 (1872): 50.
"Recuerdos de Argentina." *El correo de la moda* 22 (1872): 19.
"¡Siempre!" *El correo de la moda* 22 (1872): 131.
"Visiones de la noche." *El correo de la moda* 23 (1873): 78.

SECONDARY SOURCES

Cossío, José María de. *Cincuenta años de poesía española (1850–1900)*. 2 vols. Madrid: Espasa Calpe, 1960. 1: 477–78.
Simón Palmer, *Escritoras españolas del siglo XIX* 715–17.

CRISTINA ENRIQUEZ DE SALAMANCA

G Villar Janeiro, Helena

(B. 1940, Becerreá, Lugo– .) Poet, novelist, and writer of children's literature.

With a degree in pedagogy from the University of Madrid, Helena Villar teaches Galician language and literature in Santiago de Compostela, where she now lives. Her first book of poems, *Alalás* (Alalás), appeared in 1972, and beginning in 1975 Villar collaborated with her husband, Xesús Rábade Paredes, on the following works: *Símbolos de Galicia* (Symbols of Galicia), about the use of the flag, the coat of arms, and the anthem; *O sangue na paisaxe* (Blood on the landscape), and *No aló de nós* (Beyond us), two books of poems; and *O libro de María* (Mary's book), children's songs. They also wrote a novel, *Morrer en Vilaquinte* (1980; To die in Vilaquinte). Both the poetic and the narrative works have been awarded several literary prizes.

No aló de nós and *O sangue na paisaxe* contain intimate poems in which the poetic self reveals nationalist feelings, a close union with a wild landscape of sea and mountainside, and a spiritual communion with the deepest roots of the Galician spirit. Galicia is represented by the name

Matria. Galician children, the terrain, love, the sea, and autumn are the principal motifs.

Rosalía no espello (Rosalía in the mirror) appeared in 1985 as the individual work of Helena Villar. In the *Gran enciclopedia gallega*, Kathleen March has written: "Es un libro intimista de propósito autoanalítico cuyo punto de partida es la figura y obra de Rosalía Castro" (It is an intimate book, self-analytical in purpose, whose starting point is the figure and work of Rosalía Castro) (134). The book contains an epigraph by the great poet, which serves as a device to hold a dialogue with her, to share one's suffering, or to feel oneself in her verbal presence.

Villar has also written the children's novel *Patapau* (Wooden leg) and contributes to many periodicals. Her unpublished play "Furís e o rei don Duarte" (Furis and King Duarte) forms part of her activity in theater for schools.

BOOKS
Alalás. Lugo: n.p., 1972.
Lección conmemorativa sobre Rosalía. With Xesús Rábade Paredes. Santiago de Compostela, Coruña: n.p., 1980.
O libro de María. With Xesús Rábade Paredes. Santiago: Consellería de Cultura, 1984.
Morrer en Vilaquinte. With Xesús Rábade Paredes. Santiago de Compostela, Coruña: Universidad de Santiago, 1981.
No aló de nós. With Xesús Rábade Paredes. Santiago de Compostela, Coruña: Universidad de Santiago, 1981.
Patapau. Vigo: Galaxia, 1984.
Rosalía no espello. Santiago de Compostela, Coruña: Patronato Rosalía Castro, 1985.
O sangue na paisaxe. With Xesús Rábade Paredes. Santiago de Compostela, Coruña: Cerne, 1980.
Símbolos de Galicia. With Xesús Rábade Paredes. Santiago de Compostela, Coruña: Patronato Rosalía Castro, 1979.
Viaxe a Illa Redonda. Vigo: Galaxia, 1987.

WORKS IN BOOKS, PERIODICALS, NEWSPAPERS
"Abel Alba." *Andoriña* 2 (July 1985).
"Agallopa, meu neno, nun cabalo de vento." *Dorna* 4 (May 1982).
"Cambiáronlleme o Deus a María." *Encrucillada* 38 (1984).
"A cidade do abredo." *A nosa terra* 17 May 1984.
"Debaixo das acacias." *Festa da palabra silenciada* 3 (1986).
"Dramatizando a Rosalía." *Andoriña* 1 (Apr. 1985).
"Fillos en Compostela." *El correo gallego* 21 July 1984.
"A flauta de don Rubén." *Festa da palabra silenciada* 2 (1985).
"No recordo de mendiño." *Faro de Vigo* 4 June 1982.
"Pensamento." *Encrucillada* 50 (1986).
"Sángrame a dor. . . ." *Coordenadas* 1 (1981).
"Teño un amigo eu." *Encrucillada* 38 (1984).

SECONDARY SOURCES
March, Kathleen. "Villar Janeiro, Helena." In *Gran enciclopedia gallega* 30: 134–35.

MARIA CAMINO NOIA CAMPOS

C Villena, Isabel de
(B. 1430, València; d. 1490, València.) Religious writer.

Isabel de Villena was the illegitimate daughter of the writer Enrique de Villena. She changed her birthname, Elionor Manuel, to Isabel when she became a Franciscan nun at the age of fifteen. Abbess of the Trinity convent of Valencia in the best economic period of this city, she wrote *Vita Christi* (1487; The life of Christ) in Catalan for the nuns of her convent. Her only known work, it was printed in Valencia by her successor, Aldonça de Montsoriu, at the request of Queen Isabella I.

Villena was influenced by the emotive Franciscan style of the Devotio Moderna, the religious movement of interior devotion that inspired such works as *Imitatio Christi*, by Thomas à Kempis, and *Vita Christi*, by the Carthusian Ludolf of Saxony, the latter a book that Villena knew. Although the abbess follows in outline the tradition of the early Franciscan *Vita Christi*, such as *Meditationes Vitae Christi* of Pseudo-Bonaventura and the Catalan *Vita Christi* of Francesc Eiximenis, her work presents many special features. Its central characters are all women: the Virgin Mary, Mary Magdalene, Saint Anne, and other women who appear in the Gospels. Villena addresses a female audience and emphasizes such tasks as washing, sewing, child care, cooking, and aspects of courtly life like dancing, music, protocol, fashion, and jewels. Diminutives abound, giving an affectionate style to the text. The love story between Jesus and Magdalene is narrated with passion; in fact, the entire work is pervaded with love.

Villena's *Vita Christi* takes part in the early medieval debate on the good or bad nature of women. The abbess challenges misogynistic arguments that the female paradigm is Eve (who in any case was not perverse but poor, ignorant, and sorry for her sin) rather than Mary. For Villena, female nature is virtuous, not depraved, and women feel love more deeply than men. She also notes that Jesus preferred women to men and treated them with special kindness in his early life.

Isabel de Villena is the only known woman, besides Christine de Pisan, who entered the medieval literary debate on female good and evil, and her *Vita Christi* has been regarded as a reply to the misogynistic *Espill*, a long narrative poem by Jaume Roig, who also lived in Valencia and knew the abbess personally.

BOOKS

Vita Christi. Ed. Ramon Miquel i Planas. 3 vols. Barcelona: Biblioteca Catalana, 1916.

Vita Christi. Facsimile from the first edition. Valencia: Del Cénia al Segura, 1980.

Vita Christi. Ed. Lluïsa Parra. Valencia: Alfons el Magnànim, 1986.

Vita Christi. Ed. Lluïsa Parra. Introd. Rosanna Cantavella. Barcelona: LaSal, 1987.

SECONDARY SOURCES

Cantavella, Rosanna. "Isabel de Villena, la nostra Christine de Pisan." *Encontre d'escriptors del Mediterrani. València* 2 (Winter–Spring 1986): 79–86.

Fuster, Joan. "Jaume Roig i sor Isabel de Villena" and "El món literari de sor Isabel de Villena." *Obras completas.* Vol. 1. Barcelona: Edicion 62, 1968. 175–210. 153–74.

Hauf, Albert. *D'Eiximenis a sor Isabel de Villena: Aportació a l'estudi de la nostra cultura medieval.* Montserrat: L'Abadia, 1990.

———. "L'espiritualitat catalana medieval i la Devotio Moderna." *Actes del cinquè col.loqui internacional de llengua i literatura catalanes. Andorra 1979.* Ed. J. Burguera and J. Massó i Muntaner. Montserrat: L'Abadia, 1980. 85–121.

Sánchez Cutillas, Carmelina. "A la reverent sor Francina de Bellpuig, monja professa el convent de la Puritat e cara cosina nostra." *Cairell* 7 (Feb. 1981): 5–7.

ROSANNA CANTAVELLA

Vilorbina, Erinska; *see* **Vilorbina Galceràn, Maria-Mercè**

C Vilorbina Galceràn, Maria-Mercè
(B. 1914, Barcelona– .) Also Erinska Vilorbina. Novelist and short story writer.

Isolation and its consequences form the thematic thread running through Maria-Mercè Vilorbina's work. In *Equilibris* (Equilibrium), a collection of short stories, an individual's emotional balance is directly related to love and human contact, a need expressed mainly in the form of dreams. The characters are solitary people, and their dreams are a product of their own isolation. In "Nardula," the eponymous character is a man's dream: an ideal beauty. At the moment when the dream ends, the woman disappears. In "Assarona," the female character has a double life, living at night the life of an interesting woman—like the kind she sees in films—and during the day engaged in a monotonous routine. She finally realizes that this game distances her from her own self. Egotism and lack of commitment create the alienation felt by the protagonists in "Kukalakó" and in "Llunfineta Mabaduga." The stories' conclusions show how characters victimize themselves: Kukalakó finds a woman to whom he is attracted, but they remain strangers. Llufineta Mabaduga doesn't feel the need and responsibility to act until it is too late. The vision of perfect balance is accomplished in "Anímsor," in which the main character is fulfilled by loving not just one person but everyone. Giving oneself to others becomes the key to avoiding isolation.

The question of the gender of a narrator, or the implications of gender in the narrator's point of view, is resolved in *Klam* (Klam) through Klam's neutral voice. The story is not a new one since there are no new stories: everything is repeated. The narrator has lived through several time periods, accumulating wisdom and experience. The name Klam suggests an affinity with sounds—winds, voices, song. The characters Onà and On represent paradigms of the feminine and masculine worlds that live in proximity without reaching any real contact. While On is satisfied with his life—his work, the continuity of a family tradition—Onà feels isolated. She is an outsider, lacking any sense of lineage or of belonging. Taken as a child from her native land, the Greek island Karpusi, she ends up living in alien surroundings, including a house furnished by a male interior designer who presumably knows better than she how to fashion her own space. But Onà's discovery of the arts, especially painting and music, enables her to meet people she would not otherwise have known. While Klam as narrator remains outside the story, there is a certain affinity between the ungendered Klam and Onà: they both try to communicate. Klam completes the narration of the story, and Onà returns to Karpusi.

In *Aïllats* (Isolated), the voices are differentiated by color and by gender. The realm of the masculine voices includes clamorous ones indifferent to suffering (brown), those concerned only with material fulfillment (orange), and isolated voices (gray). But among them is also a sensitive male voice (green) that longs for communication and understanding. The female voices are also diverse: some live only by appearances, leading a frivolous life (ocher); others are always dreaming about love (mauve); and still others support the right to change an unjust male world (pale blue). Among this cacophonous chorus, the color white, of neutral gender, is the voice that will help the others overcome isolation.

BOOKS
Aïllats. Barcelona: Alta Fulla, 1984.
Divertiments. Barcelona: Alta Fulla, 1988.
Equilibris. Barcelona: Dalmau, 1970.
Klam. Barcelona: Pòrtic, 1980.

ELENA ELORRIAGA

C Vinyes Olivella, Cèlia
(B. 1915, Lleida; d. 1954, Almería.) Also Viñas Olivella. Poet.

Cèlia Vinyes spent her childhood and adolescence in Palma, Majorca, and received her degree from the Universidad Central in Barcelona. A bilingual poet, she taught Spanish literature at the Instituto Nacional de Enseñanza Media in Almería. In 1953 she married Arturo Medina, who served as her posthumous editor.

Vinyes decided to write upon returning to the university after the Spanish Civil War in 1939. On choosing Castilian as a literary language she was swayed by the Franco regime's active discouragement of Catalan. Vinyes's environment determined both her language and her discourse. Catholicism was then politically reinforced, and some poets responded to it as an existential and intellectual experience. She was a Roman Catholic, according to Medina, and in *Antología lírica* he claims that she became more intensely religious after 1944.

Her lyrical Castilian work, widely dispersed, began with *Trigo del corazón* (Wheat of the heart), a collection that contains poems from her early to middle stages, when she taught in Andalusia. *Canción tonta del sur* (Dull song of the south) is written in the style of children's jingles or "comptines," a genre later developed by Gloria Fuertes's pedagogical poetry. To Vinyes these songs provided a way to reenter the child's world, for she always saw children as direct objects of love and teaching. Both *Trigo del corazón* and *Canción tonta del sur* were published at her own expense.

On the publication of *Palabra sin voz* (Word without voice) at Alicante in 1953, Vinyes met the poets Vicente Ramos and Manuel Molina. According to Jacinto López-Gorgé, she then made a pilgrimage to Miguel Hernández's hometown, Orihuela, Murcia. In *Palabra sin voz*, her most well-rounded book according to Medina, she shows compassion for Almería and Almanzora, regions with scarce rainfall. She spoke so enthusiastically about the land she had freely chosen that Clementina Arderiu would call her "the Andalusian Majorcan."

In *Como el ciervo corre herido* (As the deer runs wounded), Medina collects his wife's Christian works. "El alma: Semana Santa" (1946; The soul: Holy Week) is a poem of happy offering to the deity. In "4 de abril" (1946), the iconic-religious aspect creates subtle images of feminine fortitude. Also reflecting the Christian existentialism of this period, "Lección" (1946; Lesson) depicts the lonely defenselessness of Christ. In "Canto alegre al Señor" (1952; Happy song to the Lord), the poet blesses God, who made her a worker. "Angeles son, que ya viene el alba" (1953; They're angels, dawn is breaking) has a brief but brilliant episode in which a mother incites her son to ideal courage: the child would like to go with the angel's army, but he cannot find his "abarcas," or hemp sandals. The formality and maturity the author had reached by the early 1950s is evident in her mixture of well-balanced sonnets and popular, neobaroque ballads. Guillermo Díaz Plaja finds remarkable the sonnet "El fondo negro del Cristo de Velázquez" (1944; The dark background of Velázquez's Christ) in *Antología lírica*. In this poem, which is dedicated to Valbuena Prat, the poet's faith enables her to see the paschal light of resurrection in the shadows of the cross.

Canto (Song), a posthumous collection of poems, includes "Azotea" (1951; Roof), a brief evocation of Almería's diaphanous landscapes, and "Muerte de Arquemoros" (1952; Death of Arquemoros), an elegy on a classical theme. Her other Castilian work consists of a novel, "Tierra del sur" (Land of the south); a play, *Plaza de la Virgen del Mar* (Plaza of the Virgin of the sea); and the children's stories *Cuento de la Paverita* (Paverita's story) and *El primer botón del mundo* (The first button of the world). Vinyes also left some didactic prose, including *Estampas de la vida de Cervantes* (Sketches of the life of Cervantes).

Vinyes's only Catalan book, the multifaceted *Del foc i de la cendra* (On fire and ashes), was published at the request of her poet friends Francesc B. Moll and Manuel Sanchis Guarner, who edited the book at Les Illes d'Or, in Palma, Majorca. Medina notes her use of the Majorcan dialect, as in "Lletra a l'estimat des d'un jardí de Mallorca" (Letter to my beloved from a garden in Majorca). In this remarkable poem Vinyes plunges into a stream of consciousness to describe the florid and radiant garden where she recalls time spent with her lover. "Les quatre ofrenes" (1935–36; The four offerings) is a fable of the literary vocation in battle with time and contingency; the passing of youth and life is symbolized by galleons and fishing boats.

In contributing to the renewal of postwar Majorcan poetry, Celia Viñas influenced Cèlia Vinyes, so that "quintillas," "romances," "décimas," and popular Castilian religious hymns shaped Vinyes's Catalan poetry. In both languages, the artist maintains musicality even at the metric ruptures. As for the stanza, she wants it to reflect her own serene being. This humane and versatile poet, a friend of the poets Carmen Conde, the Díaz Plaja brothers, and Eugeni d'Ors, was paid homage in a public gathering by a select group of Catalan poets one year after her death, when the Catalan language was timidly entering its second *Renaixença*.

BOOKS

Antología lírica. Prol. Guillermo Díaz Plaja. Ed. Arturo Medina. Madrid: Rialp, 1976.
Canción tonta del sur. Almería: Peláez, 1948.
Canto. Madrid: Agora, 1964.
Como el ciervo corre herido: Poemas sacros. Almería: Emilio Orihuela, 1955.
Cuento de la Paverita. Almería: Cajal, 1967.

Del foc i de la cendra. Ed. Francesc B. Moll and Manuel Sanchis Guarner. Palma de Mallorca: Moll, 1953.
Estampas de la vida de Cervantes. Madrid: Gredos, 1949.
Lecciones cervantinas. Almería: Cajal, 1976.
Palabra sin voz. Alicante: Ifach, 1953.
Plaza de la Virgen del Mar. Almería: Cajal, 1974.
El primer botón del mundo y trece cuentos más. Madrid: Everest, 1976. 2nd ed. 1980. 3rd ed. 1984.
Trigo del corazón. Almería: Independencia, 1946.

SECONDARY SOURCES
Casanova, Diego Antonio. *Vida y obra de Celia Viñas Olivella.* Prol. Gerardo Diego. 2nd ed. Madrid: Bachende, 1955.
Celia Viñas, in Memoriam. An Homage. Palma: Miramar, 1954.
Homenaje a Celia Viñas en el XX aniversario de su muerte. Almería: Cajal, 1974.
López-Gorgé, Jacinto. "Recuerdo de Celia Viñas en el XX aniversario de su muerte." *Estafeta literaria* 542 (1974): 14–15.
Salgueiro, Francisco. "La poesia de Celia Viñas." *La estafeta literaria* 605 (1977): 7–9.

MANUEL GARCIA CASTELLON

C Viusà i Galí, Núria
(B. 1945, Terrassa, Barcelona; d. 1982, Andorra.) Humorist.

Núria Viusà's family moved to France when she was very young, and she studied there and in England. She valued her own workshop experimentation more than further studies and soon began working as a graphic artist. She lived in Barcelona from 1972 to 1974 and during that period had her only exposition. Viusà was invited many times to show in Paris, but her private, almost reclusive personality ruled out such public exposure. She began a project in which the hero, Xumet-Man, played the role of Superman with the idealism of Don Quijote. She had finished only one section when she was swept away with her baby daughter in Andorra's disastrous floods in November 1982.

Her only book contains the unfinished "Xumet-Man" and the "Història d'Andorra." "Les aventures de Xumet-Man" (Xumet-Man's adventures) tells of a rather silly hero who derives his strength from sucking a pacifier. He sets out to investigate why everyone is constantly getting robbed, not by street criminals but by some mysterious force. The villain is Spain, represented by a beautiful woman who can eat only diamonds or pearls— or, when times are hard, bank bills. A delightfully ironic vision of past and present Spain charms the reader while harshly criticizing the ever-thirsty government institutions. The other piece is "Història d'Andorra"

(History of Andorra), in which she wittily explains how that country, where she moved shortly before her death, ended up with such a strange form of government.

BOOKS
Xumet-Man contre el monstre invisible. Història d'Andorra. Barcelona: Magrana, 1983.

KATHLEEN MCNERNEY

C Vives de Fàbregas, Elisa
(B. 1909, Barcelona– .) Poet and prose writer.

Elisa Vives has published the prose works *Vida femenina en el ochocientos* (Women's lives in the 1800s), the biography *Pau Casals*, and two books for children. Her poetry has not been published.

BOOKS
El globus de paper. Barcelona: La Galera, 1966.
Història de l'aquarel.la catalana. Barcelona: Centro de Acuarelistas, 1980.
Pau Casals. Barcelona: Dalmau, 1966.
Vida femenina en el ochocientos. Barcelona: Dalmau, 1945.

WORKS IN BOOKS, PERIODICALS, NEWSPAPERS
"El cardot" and "Enyor." *Les cinc branques* 138.

TRANSLATIONS OF HER WORKS
El globo de papel [*El globus de paper*]. Barcelona: La Galera, 1966.

NANCY L. BUNDY and KATHLEEN MCNERNEY

C Viza Vilà, Montserrat
(B. 1940, Mataró, Barcelona– .) Writer of children's literature.

A therapist for children with learning difficulties, Montserrat Viza Vilà has written a number of textbooks for young readers, all published by Parramón (Barcelona) and translated into English and French. She has also contributed to the magazines *Tretzevents, Cavall fort*, and *Avui*.

KATHLEEN MCNERNEY

Xènia; *see* **Karr i d'Alfonsetti, Carme**

C Xirinacs i Díaz, Olga
(B. 1936, Tarragona– .) Poet and novelist.

Olga Xirinacs began writing as a child but did not become known in literary circles until 1971. Since then she has won numerous prizes for both prose and poetry. Active in the cultural life of her native city, she believes that writers have an obligation to meet the public and broaden cultural understanding and that the money for military armament should be spent on cultural life.

Some of her favorite writers are Marcel Proust, Georges Simenon, Simone de Beauvoir, and Virginia Woolf, about whose suicide she wrote the novel *Al meu cap una llosa* (A gravestone at my head). In it she recreates wartime England, contrasting the suffering of ordinary people with the crisp, official version of the war's progress heard on the BBC. Woolf's presence is a shadow during the interval between her drowning and the recovery of her body, and her thoughts are interwoven with the reactions of the townspeople, whom she barely knew. The novel won the prestigious Crítica prize.

Much of Xirinac's poetry is love poetry. *Botons de tiges grises* (Gray stem buttons) is a lyrical, intimate account of an adolescent girl, set against the background violence of the 1940s. The author describes *Música de cambra* (Chamber music) as a book of memories into which are woven a series of strange adventures. *Llavis que dansen* (Dancing lips), winner of the Carles Riba prize of 1987, is a triptych. In the first and longest section, "La pell" (Skin), each poem begins with a line from Vergil's *Eclogues*; in the second, "Rive gauche: Inventari d'olors sobre la pell" (Left Bank: Inventory of scents on skin), each poem bears the title of a French perfume; the third, "Indicis de naufragi" (Signs of shipwreck), is inspired by the Italian poet Giuseppe Ungaretti's *Allegria di naufragi*.

In *Zona marítima* (Maritime zone) and *Mar de fons* (Troubled waters) the sea plays a central role. The first novel is set in the author's native Tarragona and focuses on a friendship between two women; the second explores philosophical questions of evil and creativity during a voyage between New York and England. *Tempesta d'hivern* (Winter storm) deals with the theme of the returning exile. In 1980 Xirinacs formed the group El Nus (The Knot) with several other writers and artists to collaborate on a work called "Tramada," which was supported by the Institut d'Estudis Tarraconenses.

BOOKS
Al meu cap una llosa. Barcelona: Proa, 1985.
Botons de tiges grises. Barcelona: Proa, 1977.

Clau de blau. Tarragona: Inst. d'Estudis Tarraconenses, 1978.
Interior amb difunts. Barcelona: Destino, 1983.
Llavis que dansen. Barcelona: Proa, 1987.
Llençol de noces. Barcelona: Proa, 1979.
Mar de fons. Barcelona: Planeta, 1988.
Marina. Barcelona: Empúries, 1986.
La mostela africana i altres contes. Barcelona: Destino, 1985.
La muralla. Barcelona: Columna, 1993.
Música de cambra. Barcelona: Destino, 1982.
La pluja sobre els palaus. Barcelona: Proa, 1990.
Preparo el té sota palmeres roges. Barcelona: Vosgos, 1981.
Relats de mort i altres matèries. Barcelona: Destino, 1989.
Tempesta d'hivern. Barcelona: Columna, 1990.
Zona marítima. Barcelona: Planeta, 1986.

WORKS IN BOOKS, PERIODICALS, NEWSPAPERS
"Art pobre," "Dels cinc poemes inspirats en la frase de Joan Llacuna: Estem sols sobre crits de profetes," and "Sols. Una paraula al nu, sense defensa." *El pont* 59 (1969): 11–13.

TRANSLATIONS OF HER WORKS
"If You Are Not There Anymore" ["Si tu no hi ets"], "Secret," and "The Day of the Dead" ["El dia dels morts"]. Trans. Montserrat Abelló. *Poetry Canada* 11.4 (1990): 23.
Zona marítima [*Zona marítima*]. Barcelona: Planeta, 1987.

KATHLEEN MCNERNEY

Appendix

BIRTHDATE

BEFORE 1800
C Mallorca, Reina de, first half of 14th c.
C Les Malmonjades, 14th c.
C Anonymous Catalan Medieval Woman Poet I, second half of 14th c.
C Anonymous Catalan Medieval Woman Poet II, second half of 15th c.
C Villena, Isabel de, 1430–90
C Borja, Tecla, 1435–59
C Suaris, Isabel, 15th c.
C Requesens, Estefania de, 1501/08–49
G Castro y Andrade, Isabel, 1520?–82?
C Boixadors, Jerònima de, ?–1562
C Llúria i de Margola, Maria de, 1630/32–1701
C Mas Pujol, Margalida Baneta, 1649–1700
C Esplugues, Margarita, 1738–?
C Giralt, Maria Angela, 18th c.
C Torres, Narcisa, 18th c.

NINETEENTH CENTURY
1800–49
C Massanés i Dalmau, Maria Josefa, 1811–87
C Jordà i Puigmoltó, Milagros, 1823–86
C Penya i Nicolau, Victòria, 1823/27–98

G Valladares Núñez, Avelina, 1825–1902
C Caparà i Busquets, Assumpció, 1829–1918
C Orberà i Carrión, Maria, 1829–?
G Castro, Rosalia de, 1837–85
C Caimarí de Bauló, Margarida, 1839–1921
C Rausell i Soriano, Manuela, 1839–?
C Maspons i Labrós, Maria del Pilar, 1841–1907
C Paler i Trullol, Enriqueta, 1842–1927
C Durán de León, Lluïsa, 1845–?
C Herreros i Solà de Bonet, Maria Manuela de los, 1845–1911
C Monserdà i Vidal de Macià, Dolors, 1845–1919
C Morlius i Balanzo, Remei, 1845/55–1930?
G Corral, Clara, 1847–1908
C Palau i González Quijano de Prats, Emília, ?–1883
C Villamartín y Thomas, Isabel de, ?–1877

1850–79
C Armengol i Altayó de Badia, Agnès, 1852–1934
C Santamaria i Ventura de Fàbrigues, Joaquima, 1854–1930
C Gili i Güell, Antònia, 1856–1909
C Trulls, Maria, 1861–1933
C Garcia Bravo, Magdalena, 1862–91

C Ventós i Cullell, Palmira, 1862–1917
C Aldrich i de Pagès, Trinitat, 1863–1939
C Karr i d'Alfonsetti de Lasarte, Carme, 1865–1943
C Sureda, Emília, 1865–1904
C Castellví i Gordon, Isabel Maria, 1867–1949
C Denis de Rusinyol, Lluïsa, 1867–1946
C Font i Codina, Mercè, 1867–1894/1900
C Anzizu i Güell, Mercè, 1868–1916
C Albert i Paradís, Caterina, 1869–1966
G Herrera Garrido, Francisca, 1869–1950
C Salvà, Maria Antònia, 1869–1958
C Rosselló i Miralles de Sans, Coloma, 1871–1955
C Cardet i Güell, Dolors, 1872–?
C Domènech i Escaté de Canyellas, Maria, 1877–1952
C Bardolet i Puig, Antònia, 1877/79–1956
C Furnó i Monsech, Maria Emília, 1878–1944

1880–99
C Pujades i Botey, Mercè, 1880–1972
C Bartre, Llúcia, 1881/91–?
C Ferré i Gomis, Adelaida, 1881?–1955
C Llorens i Carreres de Serra, Sara, 1881–1954
C Rubiés i Monjonell, Anna, 1881–1963
C Senye d'Aymà, Anna, 1881–1956
C Torrent Boschdemont de Figa, Francesca, 1881–1958
C Bassa de Llorens, Maria Gràcia, 1883–1961
C Rubiés i Monjonell, Mercè, 1884–1971
C Canalias, Anna, 1886–1934
C Pratdesaba i Portabella, Pilar, 1886–1971

C Rusinyol i Denis, Maria, 1887–195?
B Mújica, Robustiana, 1888–?
B Azpeitia Gómez, Julene, 1888–?
C Andreu, Francisca de Paula, 1889–?
C Anfruns de Gelabert, Maria, 1889–1965
C Arderiu i Voltas, Clementina, 1889–1976
B Artola, Rosario, 1889–?
B Eleizegi Maiz, Katalina, 1889–1963
C Milans, Mary de, 1890–?
C Anglada i Sarriera, Lola, 1892/96–1984
C Ibars i Ibars, Maria, 1892–1965
C Matheu i Sadó, Maria del Roser, 1892–1987
C Montoriol i Puig, Carme, 1893–1966
C Carreras i Pau, Concepció, 1894–1961
C Massot i Planas, Mercè, 1894–?
C Jaquetti i Isant, Palmíra, 1895–1963
C Tobella, Mercè, 1896–1972
C Masip i Biosca, Magdalena, 1897–1972
C Pujol de Canals, Montserrat, 1897–?
C Canyà i Martí, Llucieta, 1898?–
C Garriga i Martin, Maria dels Angels, 1898–1967
C Gay, Simona, 1898–1969
C Armangué, Josefa, 1899–?
C Bertrana i Salazar, Aurora, 1899–1974
B Bustinza y Ozerin, Rosa, 1899–1953
C Clavell d'Aranyó, Mercè, 1899–?
B Lizundia, Eustaquia, 1899–
C Sunyol, Cèlia, 1899–?
C Tous Forrellad, Pilar, 1899–?

NINETEENTH CENTURY SPECIFIC DATE UNKNOWN
C Alba, Sermena
C Arnillas de Font, Maria Amparo

C Cortés Wyghlen, Guadalupe
G Dato Muruáis, Filomena, ?–1926
C Farrès i Artigas, Josefina and Francesca
C Forner, Maria
C Mirallets i Piu, Rosa
C Palau de Vall-Llosera, Encarnación
C Peña, Agna Maria Paulina de la
C Penya de Barcelosa, Calamanda
C Pic de Aldawala, Roser
C Pujal i Serra, Antònia
C Sorribas, Fernanda
C Tudurí, Catalina
C Vallors, Assumpta de
C Valls i Riera, Consol

TWENTIETH CENTURY
1900–09
C Alcover Morell, Francisca, ?–1954
C Andreu, Angels, 1900?–?
B Unzueta, Concepción, 1900–
C Nicolau i Masó, Maria del Carme, 1901–
C Perpinyà i Sais, Maria, 1901–
G Prieto Rouco, Carmen, 1901–
C Maureso i Moragues, Joana, 1902–
C Vila Reventós, Mercè, 1902–
B Agirre Lasheras, María Dolores, 1903–
C Bayona i Codina, Mercè, 1903–72
G Fariña y Cobián, Herminia, 1904–66
C Murià i Romaní, Anna, 1904–
C Sabaté i Puig de Delmas, Maria Dolors, 1904–82
C Suqué i d'Espona de Llimona, Carme, 1904–
C Alonso i Bozzo, Cecília, 1905–74
C Dalí Domènech, Anna Maria, 1905–
C Montseny i Mañé, Federica, 1905–94
C Saavedra, Anna Maria de, 1905–?
C Verger i Ventallol, Maria, 1905–
C Casanova i Danés, Concepció, 1906–
C Sacrest i Casellas, Rosa, 1907–

C Solsona i Querol, Josefina, 1907–60
C Vernet i Real, Maria Teresa, 1907–74
C Rodoreda i Gurgui, Mercè, 1908–83
C Vives de Fàbregas, Elisa, 1909–

1910–19
C Arquimbau, Rosa Maria, 1910–
C Leveroni i Valls, Rosa, 1910–85
C Lewi, Elvira Augusta, 1910–
C Paretas i Goterris de Pagès, Raimonda, 1910–
C Rexach i Olivar, Agustina, 1910–
C Vayreda i Trullol, Maria dels Angels, 1910–77
C Grau i Puig, Roser, 1911–
C Masoliver, Liberata, 1911–
C Castanyer i Figueres, Maria, 1913–
C Díaz Plaja, Aurora, 1913–
C Pla, Walda, 1913–
C Raspall i Juanola de Cauhé Joana, 1913–
G Vázquez Iglesias, Dora, 1913–
B Albizu, Balendiñe, 1914–
C Benet Roque, Amèlia, 1914–
C Maffei Ginesu, Pinutxa, 1914–61
C Martínez Civera, Empar Beatriu, 1914–
C Mussons i Artigas, Montserrat, 1914–
C Novell i Picó, Maria, 1914–69
C Sabi i Roges, Anna Maria, 1914–
C Vilorbina Galceràn, Maria-Mercè, 1914–
C Alemany i Grau, Cecília, 1915–
C Cruzate i Lanzaco, Amàlia, 1915–
C Torras i Calsina, Maria Assumpció, 1915–
C Vinyes Olivella, Cèlia, 1915–54
G Morris, Anne Marie, 1916–
G Trillo, Xaquina, 1916–
C Valero i González d'Elies, Mercè, 1916–
C Gonzàlez i Cubertor, Assumpta, 1917–

C Montells i Vilar, Maria Angels, 1917–
C Abelló i Soler, Montserrat, 1918–
C Capmany i Farnès, Maria Aurèlia, 1918–91
C Cartañà Domenge de Sánchez de Ocaña, Elvira, 1918–
C Casanovas i Berenguer, Caterina, 1918–
C Maluquer i Gonzalez, Concepció, 1918–
G Mariño Carou, María, 1918–67
C Solà i Llopis, Maria Lluïsa, 1918–
G Vázquez Iglesias, Pura, 1918–
C Capellades Ballester, Enriqueta, 1919–
C Orriols i Monset, Maria Dolors, 1919–
C Pàmies i Bertran, Teresa, 1919–

1920–29
C Aragay i Queralto, Martina, 1920–
C Cardús i Malarriaga, Roser, 1920–74
C Fàbregas, Marta, 1920?–
C Massip, Laura, 1920?–
C Ribé i Ferré, Maria del Carme, 1920–
C Suau, Núria, 1920–
G Estévez Villaverde, Emilia, 1921–
C Fuster, Felícia, 1921–
G Pozo Garza, Luz, 1922–
C Cardona i Codina, Maria, 1923–72
C Via, Ramona, 1923–
C Mallarach Berga, Mercè, 1924–
C Roses d'Abad, Teresa, 1924–
C Trian i Alfaro, Rosa, 1924–
C Vayreda i Trullol, Montserrat, 1924–
G Amenedo, Cristina, 1925–
C Amorós i Solà, Maria Eulàlia, 1925–
C Beneyto Cunyat, Maria, 1925–
C Buigas, Maria Rosa, 1925–
C Coll Hevia, Concepció, 1925–
C Cugueró i Conchello, Maria Candelària, 1925–

C Rovira i Compte, Maria Carme, 1925–
C Sala i Prats, Eulàlia, 1925–
C Grau de Llinàs, Roser, 1926/28–
G Kruckenberg Sanjurjo, María del Carmen, 1926–
C Mata i Garriga, Marta, 1926–
B Minaberri, Marixan, 1926–
C Vallhonrat i Costa, Josefina, 1926–
C Bassas i Edo, Lliberta, 1927–
C Codina i Mir, Maria Teresa, 1927–
C Cortey, Maria Dolors, 1927–
C Mínguez i Negre de Panadès, Núria, 1927?–
C Portet, Renada-Laura, 1927–
C Sánchez Cutillas Martínez, Carmelina, 1927–
C Estrada, Lola, 1928–
C Guasch i Darné, Maria Carme, 1928–
C Mathieu Valette, Renée, 1928–
C Torrents, Mercè, 1928–
C Andreu i Rubió, Montserrat, 1929–74
C Crusells de Carol, Montserrat, 1929–
C Julió, Montserrat, 1929–
C Oleart i Font de Bel, Maria, 1929–

1930–39
C Albó i Corrons, Núria, 1930–
C Anglada d'Abadal, Maria Angels, 1930–
C Mulet, Maria, 1930–
C Sanahuja i Bonfill, Isabel, 1930–
C Serrahima i Manén, Núria, 1931–
G Torres Fernández, Xohana, 1931–
C Tubau i Jordi, Núria, 1931–
C Vilaplana i Buixons, Núria, 1931–
C Burgos i Matheu, Zoraida, 1933–
C Fabregat i Armengol, Rosa, 1933–
C Lisson Quiros, Assumpció, 1933–
C Oller i Torres, Maria Montserrat, 1933–
C Sales Folch de Bohigas, Núria, 1933–

C Cornet i Planells, Montserrat, 1934–
C Jaume i Carbó, Quima, 1934–93
C Solà i Salvà, Natàlia, 1934–
C Magraner, Margarita, 1935–
C Margarit i Tayà, Remei, 1935–
C Pomés, Angels, 1935–
C Valeri i Ferret, Maria Eulàlia, 1936–
C Xirinacs i Díaz, Olga, 1936–
C Ollé i Romeu, Maria Angels, 1937–
C Capdevila i Valls, Roser, 1939–
C Morera i Font, Glòria, 1939–
C Pallach i Estela, Maria, 1939–
G Queizán Vilas, María Xosé, 1939–

1940–49
C Contijoch Pratdesaba, Josefa, 1940–
C Manent Rodon, Montserrat, 1940–
C Martínez i Vendrell, Maria, 1940–
C Nyffenegger i Gerber, Beatrice, 1940–
C Valentí i Petit, Helena, 1940–90
C Vallverdú i Torrents, Maria Dolors, 1940–
G Villar Janeiro, Helena, 1940–
C Viza Vilà, Montserrat, 1940–
C Alibés i Riera, Maria Dolors, 1941–
G Heinze, Ursula, 1941–
C Peris Lozano, Carme, 1941–
C Pessarrodona i Artigués, Marta, 1941–
C Ragué i Arias, Maria-Josep, 1941–
C Vallribera i Fius, Maria Rosa, 1941–
C Ballester Figueras, Margarita, 1942–
C Canyelles, Antonina, 1942–
C Chordà i Requesens, Mari, 1942–
C Escobedo i Abraham, Joana, 1942–
G Mayoral Díaz, Marina, 1942–
C Roig i Planas, Clementina, 1942–
C Vicens i Picornell, Antònia, 1942–
C Cantalozella Mas, Assumpció, 1943–

C Oller i Giralt, Carme, 1943–
C Simó i Monllor, Isabel-Clara, 1943–
C Bosch i Verdaguer, Magda, 1944–
C Lleal Galceràn, Coloma, 1944–
C Solé i Vendrell, Carme, 1944–
C Soler i Marcet, Maria-Lourdes, 1944–
C Toledo, Susanna, 1944–
C Correig i Blanchar, Montserrat, 1945–
C Menero Ciutat, Maria Teresa, 1945–
C Miquel i Diego, Carme, 1945–
C Serrano Llacer, Rosa Maria, 1945–
C Viusà i Galí, Núria, 1945–82
C Guilló Fontanills, Magdalena, 1946–
C Oliver i Cabrer, Maria-Antònia, 1946–
C Roig i Fransitorra, Montserrat, 1946–91
C Bonet, Maria del Mar, 1947–
C Cistaré, Eulàlia, 1947–
C Company González, Mercè, 1947–
C Galícia i Gorritz, Montserrat, 1947–
B Urretavizcaya, Arantxa, 1947–
C Conca i Martínez, Maria, 1948–
C Lafontana i Prunera, Maite, 1948–
B Lasa, Amaia, 1948–
C Oliveras i Planas, Emília, 1948–
G Penas García, Anxeles, 1948–
C Riera Guilera, Carme, 1948–
C Barbal i Farré, Maria, 1949–
C Duran Armengol, Maria Teresa, 1949–
B Landa Etxebeste, Mariasun, 1949–
C Masllorens, Martha, 1949–

1950–59
C Lanuza i Hurtado, Empar de, 1950–
C Ros i Vilanova, Roser, 1950–
C Samper i Baracco, Maria Carme, 1950–

C Serra de Gayetà, Joana, 1950–
C Abeyà Lafontana, Elisabet, 1951–
G Ledo Andión, Margarita, 1951–
C Lienas i Massot, Gemma, 1951–
C Morell, Sussi, 1951–
C Rayó Ferrer, Eusèbia, 1951–
C Rodés, Montserrat, 1951–
C Arumí i Bracons, Anna, 1952–
C Bertran i Rossell, Maria Teresa, 1952–
C Cabanas-Duhalde, Josiana, 1952–
G Cibreiro Santalla, Pilar, 1952–
C Congost i Caubet, Maria Dolors, 1952–
C Ensenyat, Xesca, 1952–
C Ginesta, Montserrat, 1952–
C Marçal i Serra, Maria-Mercè, 1952–
C Pascual, Teresa, 1952–
C Aritzeta i Abad, Margarida, 1953–
C Balaguer Julià, Marta, 1953–
G Goldar, Xosefa, 1953–
C Malgrau i Plana, Fina 1953–
C Margenat, Assumpta, 1953–
C Ribas i Vives, Maria Assumpció, 1953–
C Amorós, Maria Lluïsa, 1954–
C Montero i Bosch, Anna, 1954–
C Aznar Rovira, Maria Teresa, 1955–
B Mintegi Lakarra, Laura, 1955–
C O'Callaghan i Duch, Elena, 1955–
G Pato Díaz, María Xesús, 1955–
C Bassas i Biarnés, Elisabet, 1956–
C Canela i Garayoa, Mercè, 1956–
C Garcia i Cornellà, Dolors, 1956–
C Garcia i Tudela, Maria Rosa, 1956–
C Jardí, Berta, 1956–
C Maresma Matas, Assumpció, 1956–
C Vilar i Roca, Anna, 1956–
C Aymerich i Lemos, Sílvia, 1957–
C Bes i Aubà, Maria Isabel, 1957–
C Cardona i Bosch, Fina, 1957–
C Coves Mora, Maite, 1957–
C Olesti, Isabel, 1957–
G Pallarés, Pilar, 1957–
C Pujol i Russell, Sara, 1957–

C Anfruns i Badia, Montserrat, 1958–
C Carranza, Maite, 1958–
C Fullana, Maria, 1958–
C Gardella Quer, Maria Angels, 1958–
C Masdeu i Abril, Josefina, 1958–
C Palau i Vergés, Montserrat, 1958–
C Roca i Perich, Maria Mercè, 1958–
C Teixidó, Laura V., 1958–
B Borda, Itxaro, 1959–
C Canela i Garayoa, Montserrat, 1959–
C Llauradó, Anna, 1959–
C Rahola, Pilar, 1959–
C Sant-Celoni i Verger, Encarna, 1959–

1960–69
C Mas, Hermínia, 1960–
C Mur, Mireia, 1960–
C Planelles i Planelles, Julia, 1960–
C Sarduc, Imma, 1960–
C Fernandez i Sempere, Susi, 1961–
B Irastorza Garmendia, Tere, 1961–
C Soler i Guasch, Sílvia, 1961–
G Arias Castaño, Xela, 1962–
C Jaén Calero, Maria José, 1962–
C López i García, Núria, 1962–
C Martí, Ferranda, 1962–
C Rafart, Susagna, 1962–
C Costa Mayans, Neus, 1963–
C Dodas i Noguer, Anna, 1963–86
G Romaní, Ana, 1963–
C Bel Oleart, Joana, 1965–
C Ribas Prat, Maria, 1965–
G Castro, Luisa, 1966–
C Janer, Maria de la Pau, 1966–
C Pons i Jaume, Margalida, 1966–
C Soler i Puig, Helena, 1967–

**TWENTIETH CENTURY
SPECIFIC DATE UNKNOWN**
C Abanté i Vilalta, Antònia
C Alzina i Camps, Margarida
C Antonés i Grau, Eulàlia
C Arnaiz Guillén, Maria Josep
C Arnavat, Maria Misericòrdia

C Avellaneda i Camins, Laura
C Balzola, Asun
C Barrera, Maria Rosa
C Bibiloni Pellicer, Mercè
C Bonaventura, Teresa
C Brossa Jané, Marina
C Busquets, Cristina
C Cabré de Calderó, Maria
C Castellà i Vals, Teresa
C Castellà Teixidor, Amanda
C Cobeña i Guàrdia, Judith
C Coll Domènech, Isabel
C Corderas, Núria
C Devesa Rosell, Mercedes
B Erramuzpe, Patxika
C Esteva de Vicens, Maria
C Fabra Carbó, Francesca
C Fàbregas Valentí, Elvira
C Ferran i Mora, Eulàlia
C Ferrer Royo, Consol
C Florera Serra, Núria
C Fontanet López, Encarna
C Font de Cabestany, Maria
C Forteza, Margarita
C Garriga de Cervelló, Maria
   Concepció
C Gasol i Llorach, Francesca
B Genua, Enkarni
C Ginestà, Marina
C Girona Serra, Marina
C Gisbert, Mireia
C Gispert, Maria
C Goberna, Maria Regina
C Grau Tarrafeta, Florència
C Igual, Maria Pilar
C Illa, Helena
B Iriondo, Lourdes
C Jové, Helena
C Kampistraus, Ana
B Lazkano, Maite
C Linyan, Mercè
C Llach i Tersol de Sospedra,
   Concepció
C Lorente, Angels
C Manzana, Sílvia
C Martínez i Pastor, Esther
C Martín i Martorell, Maria

C Masó Maristany, Angels
C Massana i Mola, Maria
C Mestre i Ferrando, Cassandra
C Mortes, Antònia
C Mulet i Salvà, Margalida
C Nadal i Baixeras, Maria dels
   Angels de
C Noguera Algué, Montserrat
C Obrador Torres, Margarida
C Oliu Carol, Maria Dolors
C Orfila i Cirach, Dolors
C Ormen, Elisabet d'
C Padró i Canals, Maria Rosa
C Palomar, Margarida
C Papiol i Mora, Maria Angels
C Paquim Garriga, Cecília
C Pazos i Noguera, Maria Lluïsa
C Pi de la Serra, Paulina
C Pinyol i Nolla, Maria Montserrat
C Planas Pardo d'Oroval, Pepita
C Pons i Griera, Lídia
C Portell, Carmina
C Prat, Francesca
C Prat i Batlle, Mercè de
C Puig, Genoveva
C Pujol i Maura, Maria Antònia
C Raichs i Padullés, Carme
C Ramoneda i Soler, Maria Rosa
C Riu, Maria Dolors
C Rius i Gil, Remei
C Roig, Maria Carme
C Roig de Nebot, Maria
C Romà, Maria Antònia
C Rosselló, Anna
C Salvador, Sofia
C Sánchez Morales, Rosa
C Sanz Massip, Maria Teresa
C Sardà i Homs, Zeneida
C Serra, Isabel
C Simó Oliver, Francina
C Soler Ribes, Magda
C Solsona i Duran, Isabel
C Tello Garcia, Alicia
C Trepat, Marta
C Vergés Bartés, Eulàlia
C Villalonga, Maria Angels
C Villalonga i Zaydin, Anna